THE SOCIAL MEDIA BIBLE

THE SOCIAL MEDIA BIBLE

LON SAFKO

DAVID K. BRAKE

TACTICS, TOOLS, AND STRATEGIES FOR BUSINESS SUCCESS

WILEY

John Wiley & Sons, Inc.

Library of Congress Cataloging-in-Publication Data:

Safko, Lon.
  The Social media bible : tactics, tools, and strategies for business success / by Lon Safko and David Brake.
      p. cm.
  Includes index.
  ISBN: 978-0-470-41155-1 (pbk.)
  1. Internet marketing. 2. Social media—Economic aspects. 3. Online social networks—Economic aspects. 4. Electronic commerce. I. Brake, David, 1966- II. Title.
    HF5415.1265.S24 2009
    658.8'72—dc22

                                                                    2009010838

Printed in the United States of America

10 9 8 7 6 5 4 3 2 1

CONTENTS

INTRODUCTION   ix

ACKNOWLEDGMENTS   xv

PART I
Background Basics and Tactics

CHAPTER 1	What Is Social Media?	3
CHAPTER 2	The Social Media Ecosystem	21
CHAPTER 3	Say Hello to Social Networking	43
CHAPTER 4	Everyone's a Publisher	69
CHAPTER 5	It's Not Your Father's E-Mail	95
CHAPTER 6	The World of Web Pages	117
CHAPTER 7	The Internet Forum	145
CHAPTER 8	The Ubiquitous Blog	161
CHAPTER 9	The Wisdom of the Wiki	181
CHAPTER 10	A Picture Is Worth a Thousand Words (Photo Sharing)	193
CHAPTER 11	Talking About the Podcast (Audio Create)	207
CHAPTER 12	Got Audio? (Audio Sharing)	223
CHAPTER 13	Watch Out for Vlogs (Video Create)	237
CHAPTER 14	Got Video (Video Sharing)	251
CHAPTER 15	Thumbs Up for Microblogging	263
CHAPTER 16	Live from Anywhere—It's Livecasting	287

theSocialMediaBible.com

CONTENTS

CHAPTER 17   Virtual Worlds—Real Impact   305

CHAPTER 18   Gaming the System: Virtual Gaming   325

CHAPTER 19   RSS—Really Simple Syndication Made Simple   343

CHAPTER 20   Spotlight on Search (Search Engine Optimization)   355

CHAPTER 21   Marketing Yourself (Search Engine Marketing)   373

CHAPTER 22   The Formidable Fourth Screen (Mobile)   391

CHAPTER 23   Let the Conversation Begin (Interpersonal)   417

PART II
Tools

CHAPTER 24   Social Networks   449

CHAPTER 25   Publish   473

CHAPTER 26   Photo   493

CHAPTER 27   Audio   509

CHAPTER 28   Video   519

CHAPTER 29   Microblogging   533

CHAPTER 30   Livecasting   539

CHAPTER 31   Virtual Worlds   551

CHAPTER 32   Gaming   561

CHAPTER 33   Productivity Applications   571

CHAPTER 34   Aggregators   599

CHAPTER 35   RSS   615

CHAPTER 36   Search   623

CHAPTER 37   Mobile   639

CHAPTER 38   Interpersonal   655

PART III
Strategy

CHAPTER 39	The Four Pillars of Social Media Strategy	673
CHAPTER 40	Your Social Media SWOT Analysis	699
CHAPTER 41	The ACCESS Model	717
CHAPTER 42	Evaluate and Organize Existing Resources	743
CHAPTER 43	Your Implementation Plan	757

| BIOGRAPHIES OF OUR EXPERTS | 775 |
| INDEX | 787 |

This book is a comprehensive guide to an important topic that is impacting your business, your customers, your coworkers, and everyone connected to them. That topic is *social media*, also referred to as *Web 2.0* at times. We hope you can use this book to accomplish three of the most important goals in business:

1. Increase your revenues.
2. Improve your profitability.
3. Ensure that you remain relevant, competitive, and alive in your industry.

If you own, manage, work for, or invest in a business of any kind—this book is for you. If you collaborate with coworkers to solve problems or create systems, services, or products that make your organization more competitive or more valuable to shareholders—this book is for you. If getting more customers or selling more to current customers is important to your business—this book is for you.

Using the systematic approach presented in this book you can learn how to:

- Increase your company and brand value by engaging people in new forms of communication, collaboration, education, and entertainment.
- Determine which social media tactics you should be using with your customers and employees.
- Evaluate and categorize the tools and applications that constitute the rapidly evolving *Social Media Ecosystem*.
- Make social media tools like Facebook, MySpace, YouTube, Twitter, blogging, podcasting, and hundreds of others a part of your business strategy.
- Do a social media **SWOT** analysis inside your company to improve internal operations and outside your company to create and monetize relationships with customers and prospects.

theSocialMediaBible.com

- Implement social media micro and macro strategies to give your business the competitive edge it needs to survive and thrive.

Experts and Authorities

Anyone claiming to be an authority on everything in the *Social Media Ecosystem* should be placed under a doctor's care. We can't imagine how anyone could be an absolute authority on "everything social media" given how fast new players and applications are appearing. However, we have assembled a group of people with special expertise and insights on particular aspects of social media. (A list of our experts, along with their brief bios, appears in the Biographies of Our Experts section in the back of this book.) In several chapters in this book you'll find Expert Insights in which our experts offer their perspective on the topic at hand. These selections have been edited and abridged from more extensive interviews that you can listen to in their entirety on this book's web site.

As authors, we think we're good at identifying what kinds of things you need to know about social media in order to make it work for you. In essence, we're facilitators who have a lot in common with our readers. Like you, we have people to manage, products to launch, payrolls to meet, and customers to wow.

When we began assembling this book, we asked ourselves what would make this book truly indispensable? The answer seemed clear. We needed to ensure that every chapter began with a compelling story or the best "What's In It for Me?" (WIIFM) we could summon. We decided we wouldn't include the chapter if we couldn't begin with a strong story or a compelling WIIFM. You're busy. Your time is valuable. You shouldn't have to wonder "What's in it for me?"

We are always looking for experts and authorities to contribute to the next revision of *The Social Media Bible*, new projects, and the web site, www .theSocialMediaBible.com. We invite you to go on the web site and apply to become a contributor.

The Audience for This Book

The audience for this book is fairly broad. You may be in sales, marketing, operations management, or human resources. You may be an entrepreneur or small business owner. Perhaps you're a senior executive at a major company (the C Suite). You could be an educator or in educational administration. (Social media, by the way, is changing the way we deliver and consume education, and this book can help you develop meaningful strategies for your institution.) You may be an investor or someone who researches particular companies or industries. It's entirely possible that you fall into more than one of these categories. We call these categories *audience personas,* and we've tried hard to make sure that the book keeps these personas in mind as we focus on those three crucial business goals.

Increasing Your Revenues via Social Media

The primary goal of any business is to make money. This generally means selling more goods or services to a growing customer base. Selling, advertising, and promoting what your business does is crucial to your success, and you'll find hundreds of helpful hints, tactical tidbits, and expert advice in these areas. Making money also depends on creating innovative products or offering compelling services that solve new problems or old problems in a new way. Developing, positioning, and perfecting products and services requires something different from sales and advertising; it requires good *marketing.* Too often people confuse marketing with advertising and sales. There's more to it than that.

Your Customer as a Collaborator—A New Way of Thinking

One of our heroes is Dr. Robert Lusch at the University of Arizona. Since the late 1990s, Dr. Lusch has advocated a new way of thinking in which you view your customers as "co-producers" of your products and services. Actually, Lusch doesn't say products and services as much as he says "offering." Your *offering* is the combination of product and service that constitutes the *complete customer experience.* By converting your customers (and potential customers) into collaborators, you are creating the optimal environment to increase your profits. Social media enables this new way of thinking.

Improving Profitability via Social Media

Compared to making money, saving money may not seem like fun. Saving money, however, is what successful businesses do when they employ strategies to maximize their profitability. If your business can implement ways to reduce your operating costs, you'll be able to keep more of every dollar that comes in the door.

Can social media help you save money? Absolutely yes! At one of our companies, we instituted a company *wiki* to help geographically dispersed teams share insights and best practices. The wiki has become a training tool for new employees and contractors, but it also has functioned as a virtual water cooler where people meet and share ideas. Has it saved the company money? You bet! We were able to take on more clients with fewer human resources; our initial training time has decreased by 50 percent; and our employees feel a collaborative spirit that has positively impacted moral. It's great to see talented people collaborate to identify and solve problems that, when left unsolved, cost time and money. Social media is impacting all of these *functional groups* and more within an organization.

Remaining Relevant, Competitive, and Alive

Social media is a relatively new phrase in our business vocabulary. It's probably at the same point in its evolution from jargon term to everyday word as the term *e-commerce* was in the mid-1990s.

Many of the world's best business schools changed their curriculum and even their school names to reflect the impact they thought e-commerce was having on the world of business. There was a scramble to understand how to harness the power of e-commerce. You could hear the heartbeats of entrepreneurs as they ran toward this new frontier. There was discernable fear among the established brick-and-mortar folks. There were sages and cynics. It was an exciting time to be sure. What did all of these people have in common? They wanted to make sure that their organizations remained relevant and competitive in a world where the rules were changing.

So here we are with social media, and the same thing is happening. There's a scramble to understand. But social media encompasses a much broader range of players, activities, and rules than e-commerce ever did. Arguably, e-commerce is a component of social media. In a 2008 survey conducted by Content Connections, 67 percent of the 664 people surveyed did not feel as though they could offer an exact and meaningful definition of social media. Yet, 99 percent of them felt that social media was going to impact their lives and the way we all do business.

It doesn't require an MBA or years of business experience to conclude that when people can't define something, but overwhelmingly believe it will impact their lives and the business environment around them, perspective becomes crucial to success.

So how do we aim to offer you perspective? By organizing this book and its companion web site in a way that will help you digest the basic facts, terminology, history, and applications of social media and then help you develop and implement a social media strategy that is customized for your organization.

The Organization of This Book

We hope you'll read all of this book, but the way you read it will depend on what you're looking for and how quickly you need to find it. The book is part *reference work,* part *how-to manual,* and part *business strategy* book. You can begin with any part of the book and then go to those chapters in other parts of the book that have a natural connection. If you're relatively new to social media, we suggest that you spend some time going through each part in order.

Part I introduces you to social media and gives you a helpful framework for understanding how various social media tools and applications are categorized. You'll also get some practical and tactical tips for using some of these tools. Part II introduces you to over 100 social media tools and applications in 15 different categories. You'll get a quick exposure to the features and functions of tools that can become part of your social media strategy. We include a handy *tool scorecard* for each group of tools to help you assess their value to your company. In Part III, you are provided with mini exercises and assessments to help you conduct a social media SWOT analysis on your company. You are then guided through a process of crafting and launching social media strategies that you have customized to the unique needs of your business.

The Web Site—An Interactive and Evolving Extension of the Book

This book and its web site, www.theSocialMediaBible.com, have been designed to work together to *organize* and *present* useful information that extends the material in the book. More importantly, the web site is an effective way to *experience* and *share* information among our community of readers. Here's what you'll find there:

- Examples of *best practices* from people and organizations who are already living in the social media ecosystem. What could be more valuable than first-hand reports highlighting successes and failures with different social media applications and strategies? Some of these take the form of case studies, and some are more casual, random even.

- *Links* to blogs, podcasts, and other resources that make it easier for you to capture and employ new strategies and tactics.

- *Interviews with people mentioned in the chapter:* We recorded many of our research interviews via digital audio or video. We edited them and posted them for relevant chapters. Some of these will have appeared already in a podcast, but we archived them for your use. We'll do the same with our user-generated content whenever possible. That is, we'll welcome, vet, and post interviews done by members of *The Social Media Bible* community.

- *Downloadable forms and templates:* If you're involving other people from your organization in any of the activities in this book, you'll find the downloadable exercises, forms, and templates from key chapters helpful.

Explore and Experiment

You need to explore and experiment with social media. We encourage you to proceed with a creative and collaborative spirit. Let us know what you think. Share your experiences with others. We encourage you to participate in the exploration of this new and evolving world.

Finally, we recognize that this book is not perfect. In writing a comprehensive guide to a topic that is as rapidly evolving as social media, we expect, unfortunately, that there will be errors and omissions. We may also offer a perspective in some chapters that is different from what others in this space might have already said. Heck, as authors we didn't always agree with each other. (Lon was the more passionate promoter of "everything social media" and David was the occasional skeptic, looking for the second and third order consequences of using a specific social media application or employing a particular tactic or strategy.) If our words should invite debate among readers and experts, we welcome the dialogue. Social media is about conversation. Social media also creates an atmosphere of self-correction. The wisdom of the many really is greater than the wisdom of the few. Although many people have reviewed and commented on the content in this book, we especially welcome your comments. We have set up a special online review for this book at www.theSocialMediaBible.com.

Thank you for joining us on this exciting journey into the new world of social media.

Lon Safko
www.innovativethinking.com
www.lonsafko.com

David K. Brake
www.contentconnections.com
www.davidkbrake.com

ACKNOWLEDGMENTS

This project was the largest and most passionate undertaking of my career and using social media to create a book on social media was by far the most enlightening.

When I first created the plan to write a book on social media, I thought it was going to be another typical business book; 250 pages, 20 plus chapters 50,000 words, the typical business book formula.

Then I realized that it was not only in my best interest to use social media, but also in a way I was required to use social media to create this book. I knew that if I asked the business community what they wanted in a book and wrote it that way, the book would be successful. What I didn't know at the time was the magnitude of the journey I was about to take.

We brought the initial concept of the book on social media to more than 1,000 people. They were mostly professionals with annual incomes over $100,000; most had college degrees, from Associates up to PhDs.

Of more than 1,000 surveyed, 66.4 percent said that they could not define what social media was, while 99.1 percent said that they knew social media would have a significant effect on them and their businesses. Let me restate this, two-thirds of these professionals didn't know what it was, but nearly 100 percent knew it was going to affect them. This is whom this book is dedicated to.

By using user-generated content and feedback, I also learned that the business community didn't want just another vertical business book; they wanted something much more comprehensive. They asked for a book that first explains, What are all of these things we keep hearing about? What's a blog, a vlog, a podcast? What is a "trusted network" and "wisdom of the crowds"? What is LinkedIn, MySpace, Flickr, and YouTube? So this became the blueprint for Part I, which in itself is a business book on the tactics of social media.

They then asked for a guide. They asked, Who are the players? Where do I post a video, or a podcast? What's the most used photograph-sharing site? So this became the second business book, or guide to the social media players. This section is Part II, the Tools.

theSocialMediaBible.com

Finally, they wanted a book that could pull all of this together answering the questions: "How do I use social media in my business? How can I incorporate this in my business plan? How do I make money using social media? Where's the ROI? How will this change the way I do business?" This became Part III of the book, Strategy.

We approached John Wiley & Sons, Inc. with a concept of three full-sized business books (two business books sandwiching a guide). They trusted the "wisdom of the crowds" and the result is *The Social Media Bible*.

The Social Media Bible is an aggregation of blogs, vlogs, podcasts, wikis, e-mails, and conversations. *The Social Media Bible* is a collection of other books and resources. It's a collection because I could never profess that I am an expert in all of the 15 social media categories identified including all of their nuances. I can't even profess that I am an expert in any one category. What I have done is pulled together information that many people have contributed.

Thank you to Jimmy Wales for creating Wikipedia and the Wikimedia Foundation and to all of the people from around the world who have contributed to Wikipedia providing such a valuable resource of cumulative human knowledge.

I want to personally thank all of the nearly 50 corporate partners who shared their expert insights both in the book and their executive conversations at www.theSocialMediaBible.com.

A heartfelt thank you goes out to my company partners and closest friends Geoff Clough and Linh Tang who picked up the slack at the company, allowing me to write and often to vent. Thank you also goes to Evo Terra for his *Podcasting For Dummies* book, bloggers like David Risley for his top 50 blog tips, and to my friends and colleagues: Steven Groves for all of his ideas; Francine Hardaway, Dan Nienhauser, Steve Zylstra, Joan Koerber-Walker, and Doug Bruhnke for their introductions; Amanda Vega for her help with PR and insights; Dan Willis for persevering through Microsoft red tape; Sean Tierney for inspiring me to do podcasts; Glenn Batuyong for helping with the web site and his technical edits; Cindy and Steve Bauer for their cabin hideaway in the mountains of Pinetop, Arizona, which prevented my writer's block from setting in; Joanne Zimakas for her incredible transcription skills and attention to detail of the more than 24 continuous hours of executive interviews; and to Nancy and Bill Lauterbach at Five Star Speakers who were willing to book me to speak about social media even when no one knew what I was talking about.

My personal gratitude also goes out to the staff of John Wiley & Sons, Inc. for all of the "wisdom" of that crowd, and especially to Peter Booth Wiley for his support and contributions, without which this book would have never been published. Also, thank you to Matt Holt for believing in and fighting for this unusual book; Kim Dayman for her marketing and design insights, which really put the polish on the design; Shannon Vargo for her incredible author wrangling skills, which allowed the book to be published; to Christine Moore for her insightful and meticulous editing talent, which made this book intelligible; Beth Zipko for pulling it all together to make the book complete; and Lauren Freestone for making this book look good!

And I want to mostly thank my wife Sherrie for working so hard both at work and around the house, for without her painting the deck, trimming the bushes, and taking care of business, I never would have been free from distraction and able to write. Forever and for always . . .

I hear the orchestra beginning to play, signaling that my time is up. So . . . THANK YOU!

—Lon Safko

On a warm Saturday morning in July of 2007 Lon Safko and I met at a bagel shop in Phoenix, Arizona, where we both live. We had never met before, but a mutual friend, Joan Koerber-Walker, had suggested that we get together. Lon wanted to write a book on social media; he could see the wave approaching and wanted "to be on the front end of it," as he told me. Joan knew that my company, Content Connections, specialized in helping publishers and authors use social media to develop, hone, and promote their content. From Joan's perspective it seemed like a perfect match.

What began as a favor for a friend turned into a pro-bono research project and then a co-authoring opportunity that has been one of the more interesting experiences of my life. (I will never look at a bagel quite the same way.)

This book is the result of a lot of hard work by a lot of people, and Lon has already thanked many of them. As for me, let me first thank Lon for his passion about social media. As an experienced book publisher it was a rewarding challenge for me to harness that passion. As a coauthor it was an educational though sometimes bemusing experience to get two different world views and working styles to mesh. As Kurt Vonnegut refrained in his masterpiece, *Slaughterhouse-Five*, "so it goes."

I'd like to thank several people without whom this book would not have been possible. First, there are several people at Content Connections who worked behind the scenes to get this book completed. On a daily basis Content Connections helps publishers create and engage a community around content. The folks at "CC" certainly helped me on a daily basis, and I appreciate their efforts. They include Holly McAllister, who runs the AuthorBound program. (AuthorBound is a division of Content Connections and specializes in working with individual authors to help them realize their dream of successfully publishing a book. The AuthorBound program has helped several authors secure publishing contracts with major publishing houses as well as navigate their way through a social media ecosystem that is changing the publishing world. You can learn more about how the Author-Bound program works by visiting them at www.authorbound.com. Holly is always ready to do whatever needs to be done to make a project successful. I would like to thank the senior management team at CC, Craig Beytien and Roland Elgey, professional colleagues yes, but experienced publishers and good friends who took on extra assignments (that would have gone to me) so I could have the time to work on this book. Holly, Craig, and Roland also gave me a lot of input and numerous timely articles and tidbits from the media on the topic of social media.

Scott Lunt and Margaret Thompson provided insight, support, and contributions to the book for which I am grateful. A small team of researchers and writers helped me compile the profiles in Part II of the book. They include Miachelle DePiano, Dawn Davis, Sarah Wray, Brandon Billings, Katie McAllister, Haley McAllister-Birkeland. Many thanks guys.

Finally, I'd like to thank my family for their ongoing support. Thank you Kristy, Aisling, Sydney, Adam, and Matthew. A lot happened in their lives as I worked on this book, yet their love and encouragement was always there. Writing a book is a process with a beginning and an end, but families are forever. Indeed.

—David K. Brake

PART I

BACKGROUND BASICS
AND TACTICS

CHAPTER 1

What Is Social Media?

Social media is one of those phrases that many people think they should know because it combines two familiar words. You know what *social* means. After all, people are social beings, relying upon one's abilities to interact with and influence others in order to survive. As a kid, your mother may have told you to "go outside and be social." To be social is a desirable thing. The word connotes something good.

Now take the word *media*. In a traditional sense, media includes things such as newspapers, magazines, and television. You might think of the *New York Times, BusinessWeek,* or CNN, three media giants with a tremendous amount of influence in society. While the word *media* does conjure up images of news organizations, it also brings up impressions of how the news is delivered: via print, audio, video, and photographs. Each is an important medium used to engage an audience by telling a compelling story or sharing important news.

Since the focus of this book is business and not journalism, stop the train here for a moment, just long enough to point out that there has always been a powerful relationship between the traditional media and business. The media has always been particularly good at gathering people to read, watch, or listen to something of interest. Whether it is sports, finance, fashion, or international politics, traditional media has something to offer you. Enter the people who advertise their products and services via commercials and print ads that accompany your favorite source of news. These advertisers use print, audio, video, and photographs in an attempt to influence our behavior. They rely upon the traditional media to help them get closer to you and your money. It's a symbiotic relationship that is generally accepted without question. You expect to get a sales pitch on every page and half a dozen commercial breaks during a broadcast.

Words, pictures, video, and audio can inform and inspire, just as they can influence and incite. Humans like to know about the good, the bad, and the ugly side of people, places, and situations, as well as to share this information with others, often as quickly as possible.

In the past, neighbors would meet on the corner and coworkers would meet at the water cooler to talk about and share what they read in the morning paper, heard on the evening news, or learned from a friend of a friend at a party. Sometimes the conversation assumed life-and-death proportions, and sometimes it was simply about a sale at a local store. But whatever it was, people listened and often responded.

Modern technology hasn't obviated the need to meet on the corner or at the water cooler, but it has greatly increased the amount of information available to share. Most importantly, technology has allowed everyone to participate in creating and delivering information to family, friends, and colleagues. Everyone has the ability to function as citizen journalists or market mavens. That is, you can capture a robbery at a local auto dealer on your camera-phone and send it to your local TV station within seconds. Or you can snap a few shots of the sporty new hybrid on the showroom floor and send it to your brother who's trying to reduce his carbon footprint.

Thus, from a business perspective, *social media* is about enabling conversation. It is also about the ways that this conversation can be prompted, promoted, and monetized. Definitions of *social media* and its cousin *Web 2.0* appear later in this chapter, but first the chapter takes a look at the darker and brighter sides of social media.

The Two Sides of Social Media

Did you hear the story about the extremely paranoid guy who can no longer go to football games because he can't stand the thought of the players talking about *him* in the huddle? In the new world of social media, this kind of paranoia may not be as extreme as this old joke would have you believe. That's because people are talking about you. They're talking about your business, your brands, and your products, too. What's more, you can't stop them. In fact, there are thousands of social media tools—and more on the way—that enable conversation among the masses of humanity with Internet access who may want to talk about you.

So be careful of what you do, and of what you say, and whom you say it to. Learn to live with the idea that it's nearly impossible to hide from friends, employees, customers, and others who are motivated to talk about you. People are going to talk and gossip and complain. This behavior is human nature, and in the new world of social media, you have virtually no control.

Now let's consider the bright side of social media. If you've got a great product or service in search of more customers, you want people talking about you. There's nothing like word-of-mouth to take your business to the next level. If your company has won an industry award or enjoys a reputation as a great place to work, you want people talking about you. In other words, conversation about you, your business, or your brand is not inherently a bad thing.

You may not have control over these conversations, but if you have a social media strategy and can get comfortable with some basic tools and tactics, you can use social media to your advantage. Really. You won't have total control, but you can have considerable influence, and influence is the foundation of successful relationships with customers, employees, vendors, family, and friends.

You've just learned the first three rules of social media for business:

1. Social media is all about enabling conversations.
2. You cannot control conversations, but you can influence them.
3. Influence is the bedrock upon which all economically viable relationships are built.

To this list, you could perhaps add a fourth rule: paranoia has a purpose.

Lessons Learned at Starbucks

Few would consider Starbucks, the Seattle-based company that has forever changed the way people look at a cup of coffee, to be paranoid. But they are, thanks to their employees and a blog-based web site that enables conversations among employees and customers. A quick visit to www.starbuckgossip .typepad.com reveals brief missives, musings, and rants about company policies, practices, customer behavior, and just about anything else having to do with the unique brand of coffee culture that Starbucks made famous. You won't mistake this for a company newsletter.

You can read about the Starbucks barista from Minnesota who was fired for trying to unionize employees. Not to worry, though: he got his job back. Starbucks officials were quoted on the site as saying that the termination and reinstatement had nothing to do with the effort to unionize. It may, however, have had something to do with the coverage the event received on the Starbucks gossip blog.

This story demonstrates what employees and customers can do when they decide to huddle together for a little conversation about your company.

What did Starbucks learn from this experience? They received a fast lesson on the first three rules of social media for business.

Is this unique to Starbucks, or is it happening other places, too? It's happening everywhere. A quick click to Glassdoor.com or JobSchmob.com and you'll see restless, wild, or world-weary employees ranting about their bosses and the working conditions at their companies. What you say inside your company is never too far away from becoming a feature on someone's blog.

Social Media and Web 2.0 Defined

You're not alone if you're not able to define *social media* and *Web 2.0* quickly and with confidence. In a survey the authors conducted while writing this book, nearly 70 percent of 600-plus respondents were not especially familiar with the term *social media*. Again, many people think they should know what the term means, but most are not sure. About the same percentage were not completely confident in defining the term *Web 2.0*. To be sure, the terms are closely related but not exactly synonymous. The reluctance to offer quick and confident definitions of these terms reflects the cautious and often confused discourse that many businesspeople exhibit today when the topic of social media enters the conversation.

It seems as though people are living in a strange new ecosystem of innovative and highly disruptive applications. People tend to fear what they don't understand. There is a lot to learn about this complex and rapidly evolving ecosystem—the social media ecosystem.

So Exactly What Is Social Media?

Social media refers to activities, practices, and behaviors among communities of people who gather online to share information, knowledge, and opinions using conversational media. Conversational media are Web-based applications that make it possible to create and easily transmit content in the form of words, pictures, videos, and audios.

Most likely you belong to several communities, and if you've ever used your computer or cell phone to read a blog, watch a YouTube video, listen to a podcast, or send a text message to other members of your group or community, you've already ventured into the social media ecosystem.

What about Web 2.0?

Web 2.0 is somewhat of a misnomer. It does not refer to a new and improved version of the World Wide Web, the information superhighway that's become ubiquitous over the last decade or so. There really is no new physical version of the Internet. In other words, it's not as though the highway has been widened by four lanes. But, to continue the analogy, there are a lot more interesting vehicles traveling on the highway, and some incredible places to stop along that highway, thanks to Web 2.0 technologies and the inventive people behind them.

Social media and Web 2.0 come together whenever one of these new technologies has as its primary goal to enable communities to form and interact with one another—to converse. This book does not distinguish further between Web 2.0 and social media, because the terms are closely related and *social media* is the more important of the two terms. In fact, you'll probably hear talk of Web 3.0 and Web 4.0 in the not-too-distant future. As such, it's probably easier to think in terms of social media tools and applications.

It's All about Engagement

Before you start a conversation, and certainly to continue one, you have to engage your audience. If you're in business, the litmus test for a social media tool or application is simple: does it allow you to engage with customers, prospects, employees, and other stakeholders by facilitating one or more of the following:

- Communication
- Collaboration
- Education
- Entertainment

A Closer Look at Engagement Strategies

Let's take a quick look at these four categories of engagement and a sampling of some of the social media tools associated with each.

Communication: If you've sent an e-mail recently, you've communicated. If you've used a service like Constant Contact or Survey Monkey to invite a group of people (via e-mail) to view your newsletter or take a quick survey, you've taken your communication to the next level using a social media application. If you've used Twitter to blast a quick text message to a group of friends or colleagues, you've used a specific social medium to communicate. If you've used Jott to convert a voicemail message into an e-mail, welcome to the world of social media. If you haven't done anything beyond e-mail, that's okay, too. This book is designed to make you comfortable with taking your business to the next level, from a social media perspective.

Collaboration: One of the earliest uses of the Internet was as a collaboration tool. If you've participated in a Listserv, a chat room, or a discussion board, you've already experienced collaboration to some degree. There are, however, several social media tools designed to foster collaboration among work teams, buyers and sellers, companies and customers, even authors and readers. Wikipedia, eBay, and Gather.com are all examples of applications and companies that offer a means of collaboration.

Education: Educating your customers and training your employees can be important to the success of your business. Several social media tools make the educational process easier and more dynamic. If you've downloaded music from Apple's iTunes, did you know that you can also download college-level lectures on a wide range of topics? Some businesses are using podcasts and YouTube videos as a means of educating others. There are virtual seminars and classes being held in Second Life. Some savvy real estate brokers are using blogs to educate potential buyers about schools, churches, and restaurants in their community.

Entertainment: Historically, some of the best commercials on television have been very entertaining and quite effective at selling products and services. They've also been expensive to produce and broadcast. Not so in the new world of social media. A quick search on YouTube using the phrase "Blendtec iphone" will let you see how a CEO of a company that makes blenders (yes, the kitchen appliance) was able to dramatically increase sales by shooting a series of videos showing him feeding different objects into his powerful blender, objects that included an Apple iPhone.

Now let's take a look at how one nationally recognized company is using a combination of these engagement strategies to drive business.

How H&R Block Engages Prospective Customers

What can be more practical than filing your income taxes? For decades now, H&R Block has helped wary and harried people prepare their tax returns at thousands of storefront offices throughout the country. Business grew through word of mouth. If you liked what they did for you, chances are you would tell a friend or relative. This fairly traditional business model helped H&R Block become the largest tax preparation service in the United States, a position it has worked hard to maintain.

Concerned that new technologies enabling new forms of person-to-person communication could impact their business model, H&R Block decided to experiment with social media by trying new ways of reaching their valuable client demographic. Using applications such as Facebook, MySpace, Twitter, YouTube, and Second Life (where they opened a virtual tax preparation store), H&R Block tried several tactics that included text messages (Twitter "tweets") to customers, and the introduction of Truman Greene, an affable, singing character who serenaded YouTube viewers with the brand's key consumer benefits. The Truman character also appeared on H&R Block's MySpace and Facebook pages in an effort to integrate his brand-enhanced persona into as many lives as possible. H&R Block's strategic goals were to communicate with, educate, and entertain their prospective customers.

Were they successful? According to *Advertising Age* and research firm RocSearch, H&R Block saw a 171 percent increase in online ad awareness and an overall increase in brand awareness of 52 percent. The experiment cost the company about 5 percent of its allocated marketing budget, so it wasn't free. But it's hard not to like those metrics. Without a doubt, H&R Block bought themselves a lot of new customers with this strategy.

Madison Avenue Meets Social Media

In the summer of 2008, just prior to launching the second season of *Mad Men*, the A&E network's highly acclaimed cable television drama about life in the fast lane of a 1960s Madison Avenue advertising agency, the network sponsored a contest in which *Mad Men* fans were asked to submit self-produced videos re-creating their favorite moments from the first season. The top prize included a trip to the show's set and a cameo appearance on one of the episodes. In essence, A&E was asking loyal viewers to shoot, star in, and produce what would certainly be—given the premise of the show—racy, raucous content that could be shared with friends and other fans of the show via YouTube, MySpace, and other social media applications. The hope was to facilitate fan-generated content and comments that would help A&E expand its audience.

Were the show's producers concerned that some really bad acting and horrific videography might damage the Emmy Award–winning brand? Probably not, providing that the content was memorable. Indeed, other fans would not expect Hollywood production values to be the basis for winning the contest. More than likely, fans themselves would look forward to entries that invoked hooting, hollering, and bawdy laughter upon watching other fans' attempts to re-create scenes with the show's trademark heavy drinking, prolific smoking, and insatiable secretary-chasing, behaviors of a bygone era and the very glue that made the first season stick. If the goal was to generate buzz among this lucrative fan base and to extend that fan base via word-of-mouth promotion of *Mad Men*'s equivalent of amateur night, then it was a brilliant strategy.

So what were the results of this social media strategy to collaborate with and entertain the show's fan base for *Mad Men*? According to the show's producers, it worked nicely. There were 17 winning entries that can be viewed on the A&E web site, where you can also see how many fan votes each entry received. You can also read comments posted about each video. The net result for A&E was that second-season ratings for *Mad Men* increased by 89 percent. Not a bad use of twenty-first-century media to advertise a television program about the good old days in the advertising business.

When Engagement Strategies Backfire

In an attempt to engage customers, the makers of Heinz Ketchup and Pepto-Bismol both sponsored video contests that allowed amateurs to produce brief commercials for their flagship products. According to representatives from both companies, there were some "very good" amateur commercials produced, but there were also a number of entries that put these household brands in a position of being parodied and ridiculed. One of the more memorable Heinz entries showed an adolescent boy dealing foil packages of Heinz to an addicted customer desperate for his next ketchup fix. Heinz executives did not honor the entry with any recognition whatsoever, let alone an award. You won't find the entry on the Heinz site, but it has led an active life on YouTube. Pepto-Bismol had a similar experience when several participants, in an attempt to sing about diarrhea, turned the contest into a joke. Heinz and Pepto-Bismol may not have made social media work for them in these instances, but they do deserve credit for being brave enough to experiment.

But what happens when you become the victim of social media without attempting a strategy that backfires? Look no further than the Kryptonite U-Lock, a bicycle lock based upon a trusted 50-year-old design. In 2004, an industrious cyclist figured out how to pick the lock using a ballpoint pen and posted the information on a bicycling blog. The word spread quickly. A YouTube video followed. The design flaw invoked a recall that has cost Kryptonite's parent company, Ingersoll Rand, over $5 million.

Chances are that some companies in your industry encourage the use of blogs and wikis among employees and customers. These can be great collaboration tools for coworkers to share general knowledge, special expertise, and even best practices. Blogs and wikis are also effective means of educating your customers, or of letting customers sing the praises of your product or service to each other. It's nice to get special insights from the blog of a design engineer who helped create one of your favorite products, whether it's a sports car or a software application. As a customer, you feel closer to the product. As more organizations discover the power of employee- and customer-generated content via blogs, wikis, and other applications, you can imagine how productivity, performance, satisfaction indices, and sales might rise. You could even argue that the Kryptonite bicycle lock debacle was an excellent example of how social media ultimately improved the quality and reliability of a product.

The next point to consider is what happens when an employee posts something damaging to your brand or reputation on a company-sponsored blog or wiki? Worse still, what happens when current employees, former employees, and customers create an independent blog or wiki assailing your company's products or practices? You quickly learn the difference between control and influence. Inside your company, you can control what employees share, say, and do with social media by instituting regulations and enforcing behavioral standards, but these can only apply to what they do on company time using company-provided equipment. Remember, in the vast social media ecosystem that lies outside your company, beyond your reach, there are no set rules of behavior. You can be assailed, spoofed, and blasphemed, and you have no control. It's as simple as that. However, you do have the ability to influence the conversation if you understand how the social media ecosystem works.

But, again, even that can end up balancing itself out a little bit and try to get those genies back in the bottle through the ongoing conversation. But they require people to really be citizens; they require people to really participate within their communities of interest.

Social Media Is Disruptive

Social media is a disruptive factor for many organizations. It will remain a mystery to many until it becomes commonplace, in the same way a toaster and microwave are common to your kitchen. The fact that many people will find it hard to understand what it is and how it works creates an opportunity for those who move first. People felt the same way about railroads, the telephone, automobiles, and airplanes. They were disruptive technologies too. Most people tend to avoid and even fear what they don't understand. They're willing to let other folks go first, the ultimate risk mitigation strategy. Don't make this mistake. Social media is already redefining the way people live and do business. You don't have to be a technical wiz to take advantage of the business opportunities that social media creates. History has already shown us that.

For example, it wasn't necessary to understand how the engine of a steam-powered locomotive worked to see that railroads would change the way people live and do business. As a result, the people and institutions that built the railroads made a lot of money, but so did the companies that manufactured locomotive engines and those that built boxcars—as did the entrepreneurs and business owners who bought property and set up shop in the towns whose fortunes were forever changed when the railroad came through.

You didn't have to understand the physics of flight to see that airplanes were fundamentally going to change the world. Companies that manufactured airplanes made a lot of money, but so did those that made luggage, as did those that started travel agencies or wrote travel guides about exotic locations. And don't forget rental car companies like Hertz and overnight airfreight carriers like FedEx. These are examples of companies that took the time to understand the business implications and applications of a new technology and then either found, filled, or created a profitable niche associated with that technology.

Find and Exploit Your Niche

If you make it your goal to understand social media in the context of your current business, to experiment a little, to harness its awesome power, to make it work for you, your chances of achieving success will dramatically increase. You might, however, see an opportunity to use social media to create a new kind of business. The microwave oven was invented when scientists and technicians using microwave technology in a lab setting discovered that it would rapidly heat and cook things. It didn't take long for someone to notice that a changing social pattern among busy families and two-income households might create a market for the time-saving properties of a microwave oven. As use of microwaves became widespread, someone conjured up the concept of microwave popcorn. You get the idea. Chances are there's a niche for you somewhere in the social media ecosystem.

The Formula for Success: Experiment and Explore

Can anyone guarantee your success with social media? Of course not, but here's your alternative: take a wait-and-see approach and do nothing. Perhaps it's all just a fad, something as short-lived as the telegraph or the citizens band radio craze of the 1970s.

Every era in the history of business has provided great opportunity for the first wave of explorers, experimenters, and investors. Those in the second wave, having made strategic and tactical alterations based upon the experiences of the first-wavers, have often enjoyed great success as well. Sometimes those in the third wave are able to make additional adaptations or find small, untapped niches. But those in the fourth wave? They generally get left behind and wind up wondering what happened.

Self-Assessment: Social Media Inside Your Organization

If you are part of an organization that has more than two or three people who make the business run, take a minute and answer the following questions:

- Would people in your organization be more effective if they could communicate more quickly and precisely with one another?
- Would people in your organization be more productive if they were able to work in a more collaborative environment?
- Does entertainment play a role in the way your company operates? In other words, could the environment be improved by increasing the fun quotient?
- Could employee training and development be improved?
- Do people in your organization feel as though they are stakeholders? In other words, are they fully engaged in the business's mission?

Self-Assessment: Social Media Directed Outside of Your Organization

If your organization has customers, investors, or vendors, and most do, ask yourself the following questions:

- Do you have a strong relationship with them?
- Do you know their names, their preferences, and their needs as they relate to your company's product or service?
- Do you know their accepted beliefs about your company's product or service?
- Have you ever asked them to help you create or improve your company's product or service?
- Would they welcome an opportunity to help you improve your company's product or service?

- Does your product or service create an opportunity for them to be entertained or amused?
- Do you currently do anything to educate them about the use or value of your product or service?
- Would they react positively to an opportunity to be educated concerning the use of your product or service?
- If asked, would they strongly recommend your product or service to a friend?
- Do many of them already strongly recommend your product or service?

If you answered yes to any of these questions, you need to learn more about and experiment with social media tools. For your organization to be effective, you need to consider methods to communicate, collaborate, educate, and entertain within your organization. To maximize your impact with customers and prospects, you need to understand how to employ specific social media strategies in an effort to influence the conversation about your company.

Expert Insight

Peter Booth Wiley, chairman of the board, John Wiley & Sons, Inc. Publishing, www.wiley.com

Peter Booth Wiley

. . . I started out independently as an author and publisher. I am a member of the sixth generation of Wileys involved in the publishing business; we are 201 years old. There is a seventh generation: two of my sons, both of whom are aggressively working in social media. I've been the chairman at John Wiley & Sons, Inc. since 2002. Prior to joining our board of directors in 1984, I was a magazine publisher and a newspaper reporter, a writer of articles for magazines, and the author of five books. . . .

. . . Years ago, social media was writing a letter, which was then handed to somebody who got on a horse (or handed it to somebody who was getting on a stagecoach) in the good seasons when it was dry. It would take a while to get from, say, Virginia to New York; and in the bad season when it was muddy it probably went by ship. Now we've got information and creative ideas flying through the air at the speed of the electrons. . . .

. . . Going back when we talked earlier, I talked about how we began experimenting with introducing computers into the business in the 1950s. But we tried to understand and experiment with computers and networks really aggressively 25 years ago, and our ideas about what we should be doing as a business came from our authors. We listened very carefully to them about what they thought was going to happen.

So that's part of it, and the other is creating a culture internally to Wiley that can implement not only gathering information while listening to authors and experts, but also developing within the company (or with partners, as the case may be) the necessary social experiences (I'm not supposed to use "platforms" anymore) that are helpful to us and to our authors and to our customers. . . .

. . . I think one of the things that's interesting about what we do is that we use social networks (now we use them electronically, before we used them in an interpersonal way) to understand who you are and what you are capable of doing. So in our initial conversation when you told me of your history in the world of technology, I was very impressed. And so Step 1 is, "Okay, I recognize that this guy is somebody who has been right on the cutting edge himself." Step 2 is to use our social network to evaluate your capabilities and your proficiency in whether you are going to be able to deliver to us a manuscript that we'll be able to sell.

And so it's very interesting the way in which the whole author/publisher relationship is evolving using social media. . . .

. . . Yes, it is interesting because we have a bookstore in *Second Life*. And we've actually published a number of titles in that area, and it has led me to think more about marketing and how you market. Because what we know is that in the traditional method when we talk about authors we use the term "platform" . . . what's Lon's platform? By which we mean, "Does he speak regularly at conferences, how big are they, is he going to get on *Oprah*, is he going to get on *Good Morning America*, will his books be reviewed?"

And in some of the traditional print forms for marketing, and specifically book reviews, they are having a very difficult time right now because print newspapers are failing. Book reviews are being either downsized or completely eliminated. Television works to a degree. I think it's very effective at times. We've had experiences with authors going on very high-profile television programs and selling a lot of books (like *Oprah*).

We've had experiences with other authors going on high-profile television programs and not selling a lot of books. And now we are looking more at the social media networks that authors have, and trying to understand the way in which you created your own community, digitally, and how we can get to that community to explain to people what your book's all about.

But the interesting thing is the way that you're actually "authoring" the book is creating the platform. . . .

. . . Of course, as a commercial publisher we are interested in metrics. So we are interested in seeing the evolution of the effectiveness of marketing and the effectiveness of networks. And we are at an early stage with that, but I really look to the libraries and their interaction with publishers. They are able to

(continued)

(continued)

measure usage. So say that they license 100 journals from us; they can look at which of those journals are being used. They look at two things. Impact factor, which is the impact of the content on the audience that it is trying to reach—journals are rated according to their impact factor. The other is usage. So the librarians are saying, "Okay, I've got these 100 journals but only 98 of them are really being used. Let's look at these two that we might eliminate or replace with other journals, and maybe they should remain in the collection even though there is a low usage."

So there are metrics being developed and I assume over time (right now we go to Google and we look up Lon Safko, and we can get a rough metric there) we will be able to measure more accurately the impact of your work and of your particular social network. . . .

. . . But let's go back to what we were talking about earlier and the way you are creating this book because this tells you a lot about where publishing is now and what its future could be like.

I wrote my last book in 2000; in that instance, an editor asked me to write the book. I sent the manuscript to the publisher. The publisher reviewed it and edited it and sent it to production. Production designed it and laid it out. It went to the printer and then to marketing and sales. And then it ended up in the customer's lap.

It's a very traditional model of print-on-paper. Right now we are seeing this continuous process, and we have a favorite graphic that we use at a lot of meetings. It's out on Frommers.com. So we are one of the leading travel-publishers and we've created this circle called the Travel Cycle. And we have looked at what do we do in the Travel Cycle. So the first part of the cycle is to *dream* about what you are going to do.

And you would look at travel newspapers, magazines, online forums, blogs; so right now we are doing travel newsletters, online forums, and blogs about travel.

And then you *plan*; and we are doing guidebooks and travel web sites with text, photos, video, podcasts, recommendations, interactive maps, and custom PDF guides.

And then you *go,* and when you are going we continue to interact with you with audio walking tours, and now we are going to be launching (or just launched) maps that will go on your iPods with airport guides.

And then after you come *back,* we share with customers and with the traveler online trip journals and online photo albums, and reviews and ratings. So there is a continuous process of interaction here, rather than the linear process I described earlier. And when you add to that what you are doing, which is working with the community (your community) to develop content, and review and refine the content, you have a completely different publishing model. . . .

To listen to or read the entire Executive Conversation with Peter Booth Wiley, go to www.theSocialMediaBible.com.

Expert Insight

Chris Heuer, founder, the Social Media Club, www.theSocialMediaClub.org

Chris Heuer

. . . I got started in interactive in 1994. I read a book by Howard Rheingold who I am now, thankfully, able to call a friend, and who has done some amazing work since. It was called *Virtual Community* and I read that pretty much every day after work at the Barnes & Noble at the time, because they really didn't have a lot of Internet distribution for people like me.

And after that I ended up starting a company with a bunch of friends in South Florida called Guru Communications. Somewhere around then, I started getting involved in Interact. So from the beginning for me, it has been about community elements and we used to talk about it. In fact, Howard Rheingold, in the book *Virtual Community*, talked about it as the idea of social computing.

And until a few years ago when Chris Shipley, and a couple of others around the same time, started calling it *social media,* it really started this mind shift across the way, and as a result of those activities I got back into it.

I taught Interactive Marketing at Miami Ad School; I did web design and multimedia classes there as well. I also got a chance to learn some things for some people, like topography, and other important Photoshop skills I get to use every now and then. And I've been involved in a lot of different things . . . I was at the U.S. Mint for a little while. . . .

. . . It's very exciting. And there's an interesting debate, as you know, that's raged on between some people like Andrew Keane, and others, who say this is a very terrible thing for us because it's just going to get a lot more noncreative people, not eloquent people, creating media and talking and video and audio . . . about things that they don't know about, spreading more falsehoods and all these other problems.

But you know there is going to be a little bit of bad with the good. But in the end the great thing about the system is, as you know from blogging, that it's self-correcting. You know, if I write something and it turns out that I am incorrect, you can almost assuredly bet that somebody is going to go ahead and correct that information. That's one of Robert Scoble's famous strategies that he employed very early in terms of how he was able to be so prolific with his blogging activities and almost everything he was able to get done. It was about not being afraid of being wrong, knowing that it was going to get corrected.

Now I didn't always agree with that, because there are some times you are wrong and, you know, 50,000 people or 100,000 people might end up getting the wrong information before it gets corrected. So that's kind of a little

(continued)

(continued)

unfortunate thing as you get to a certain size, in terms of responsibility you have as a citizen of this online community and this social world we live in.

But, again, even that can end up balancing itself out a little bit. . . . But it requires people to really be citizens; requires people to really participate within their communities of interest.

There is also a lot of work going on in geography. I've met a couple of blogging mayors in the past years. It was very, very interesting in doing things by connecting directly with their constituents. So it's really a fascinating time on all elements in terms of an entertainment side and the ability of self-expression, as well as getting into the civic-responsibility areas . . . and, of course, the emergence of citizen journalism and many of the other elements . . . it served a social side, as well as the social/entertaining side. . . .

. . . But it's more interesting, of late I've seen a little bit of quick-ish stuff forming. And of course this is one of the reasons why we created *Social Media Club,* to ensure that we can really have people collaborating better together. But we are an emerging industry; social media, as you know, still has not matured yet. So there's actually going to be differences of opinions and values and things that are we are seeing over time, as people get together in different groups.

We just really want to see more people collaborating across the different groups. There is a scale, really, that's inside of here, of course. But at the same time, there are some really great ways we can share tactics and other ways of actually connecting across our systems and across our different corners of the social media worlds in order to be able to accomplish our goals and to meet people who we need to connect with. . . .

. . . I am going to first quote my friend Ian Kennedy for Yahoo!, who had one of the best answers I've ever received for the question of what social media is, which was, "It's not something; it's what you do with it." . . .

. . . It's not a noun, it's an adjective! You know, social media . . . it's what we're doing; it's what we're doing with media. And the way I really look at it . . . I come back to the social computing stuff, a little more technical I guess. But really it's just those two words put together, modified, as you might imagine. You know, there's this social element to it, which is involving connecting with others. And that's really, to me, what it's all about. And, of course, media does reference to a medium, which is something we connect through, or with, or whatever verb you want to apply to it. But the idea being this is something we connect with other people through. And that is the sharing of common stories, going back to cave paintings, and that was back to the beginning!

Cave paintings were the original social media. . . . It was sort of a story, it was visual, and it had so many different elements to it. But when we get down to the bottom of it, it's how we interact with one another. Some people like video, some people like audio, some people like, let's just say, fooling people, giving them a hard time. Some people are good people who like to help and it really just reflects our overall humanity.

And the interesting thing is the majority of the dialogue is about the positive dialogue, the aspirational elements of, "How can we do this better?" To your point earlier, about you not wanting that information out there; well that's interesting as an amateur because it means you're willing to admit you're wrong. And there are still a lot of people out there who think that admitting they're wrong is a weakness, as opposed to strength. So I think it is a very important attitudinal element that you're bringing to it, as you get that experience. That's what we were talking about before. . . .

. . . You can go into an Internet café with a dollar in your hand and put out a piece of citizen-advocacy by just logging onto the Internet computer there. You don't even need to have a video camera or specialty equipment. If you're looking to distribute it more widely, of course, you want to have some more professional stuff in that.

But the point is it's really the democratizing of the access of information and the ability to share that information and publishing, in essence. . . .

. . . They talk about the original opening of the doors of the Internet to a broader audience back in the early 1990s, I guess, as being the biggest step in retrospect. What's happening now is much more so because it's making it accessible to the average, everyday person. And in fact, there are arguments being made that the same thing happened with TV, the same thing happened with newspapers and print.

But what we really go back to, historically, in terms of the greater significance of this era that we're living in now and the access to these technologies, is back to Renaissance, where we're looking at . . . it used to be only a few hand-transcribed Bibles that were going around. But as soon as they were able to make books that were vastly available and inexpensive—a good book was $2.00 to $3.00. When you have all these different people interacting and sharing their ideas and correcting their wrong ones . . . and being able to express themselves in new ways and collaborate and now we're actually able to build technologies to do this! Some people would say we are approaching a singularity. But it's actually much simpler than that. It really is a matter of us finally being able to balance the system, the ecosystem that we're in. It's for our mental competence—even for our ability to control our world to one degree and, and to another to interact with it.

One of the great things is that the majority of the people involved in this are aspirational toward how we can use it for positive ends . . . to everyone's benefit at the end of the day.

An interesting thing I do when I talk to people about this (because it sounds a little California-ish, hippie-ish, people might want to rally around this) but it really is about the market. It's actually understandable that

(continued)

(*continued*)

information efficiency in a market allows people to make the correct purchasing decision. It allows people to "not" make the wrong decision with regards to hiring people.

So when we get this accessing near-perfect information, it's actually better for the overall market, and it will actually accelerate our ability to innovate and create new things and solve old problems we never thought we solvable, and in incredibly interesting ways. . . .

To listen to or read the entire Executive Conversation with Chris Heuer, go to www.theSocialMediaBible.com.

Prepare to Explore the Social Media Ecosystem

The debate about social media's impact on society and business will continue. Social media, like many tools and appliances in our lives, can be used for perpetrating both good and evil. However you choose to use these tools, we advocate on behalf of good, ethical behavior, but you can already find plenty of examples of "the good, the bad, and the ugly" within the social media ecosystem.

In this book, you'll learn more about the functions of social media and be able to explore applications associated with them in more detail. You're about to begin a fabulous journey. We begin with a closer look at that social media ecosystem and its component categories.

Credits

Expert Insights Were Provided By:

Peter Booth Wiley, chairman of the board, John Wiley & Sons, Inc. Publishing, www.wiley.com.

Chris Heuer, founder, the Social Media Club, www.theSocialMediaClub.org.

CHAPTER 2

The Social Media Ecosystem

In the previous chapter, you learned that people are going to talk about you and your business. In this chapter, you'll discover that thousands of social media tools are available to help people share information and broadcast their feelings, beliefs, and attitudes. Many of these tools have sprung to life in the blink of an eye. Some of them were born and went extinct during the short period of time it has taken to write this book. Others have been around for a few years. Many of them complement one another. Some of them compete with one another. It's a veritable jungle out there—a social media jungle—and this chapter is going to give you a framework for surviving in this jungle.

A jungle is nothing more than a defined area where things eat each other to survive. What a perfect metaphor for business. Biologists would call a jungle an *ecosystem,* a good term to use here. A biological ecosystem is a sophisticated association of living organisms interacting with one another. Each single organism and the collective populations of organisms in an ecosystem function as components of an integrated whole. Some organisms cooperate with or complement each other, while others compete for resources essential for survival. The same principles apply when considering the relationships and interdependencies of tools and applications that live, breed, and compete in the social media world. Some compete with each other, while others work together quite nicely.

In an effort to talk about ecosystems, biologists have developed a classification system to group and categorize the animals, plants, bacteria, fungi, and protista (one-celled organisms) that inhabit the ecosystem. Within each of these five categories, you find organisms that have been grouped according to shared characteristics and functions. (You may remember from your high school or college biology course these hierarchical terms used to classify all life on earth: kingdom, phylum, class, order, family, genus, and species.) Using this system makes it easier to talk about the living world, because biologists have agreed, after nearly 300 years of discourse and debate, that humans, birds, and insects are all part of the animal kingdom while an aspen, a fern, and a rosebush are part of the plant kingdom. Using this classification system, members of each kingdom can be subcategorized even further. You get the idea.

It's worth noting that prior to the invention of the printing press in the mid-fifteenth century, scholars were not able to have meaningful, collaborative conversations about classification systems. They lacked a common vocabulary. Printed documents that could be distributed and shared within this scholarly community inaugurated a dramatic change in the way people could communicate, collaborate, and educate one another. Once a common vocabulary was established, entrepreneurs were able to leverage the work of the biological community into business opportunities. The pharmaceutical industry, for example, owes much to the five-kingdom classification system as well as the printing press, arguably one of the earliest social media tools to be embraced by business.

Clearly, the social media ecosystem has not been a topic of debate and discussion for 300 years. At this time, there is no universally accepted classification system for social media tools and applications. Having considered some of the recent attempts to categorize social media, the authors have decided to present for this book a relatively simple 15-category classification system that will make it easier to talk about the social media ecosystem.

The Big Picture: 15 Categories at a Glance

Table 2.1 shows the 15 categories for quick reference. The chapter numbers next to each category indicate where in *The Social Media Bible* you will find more detailed information about the tactics and tools of each category. Later in this chapter, you will find a concise description of each category and representative tools within that category—not *all* the tools, mind you. Just a sampling of some the more common ones. It is not necessary to absorb any of the details at this point. Try to see the big picture. The details appear in subsequent chapters.

On the Way Toward a Common Vocabulary

Take a quick look at the five sentences that follow this paragraph and ask yourself these questions: Prior to picking up this book, how many of the underlined words would you have recognized and been able to use

| Table 2.1 Social Media Categories |||
Category Title	Tactics Chapters	Tools Chapters
Social networking	Chapter 3	Chapter 24
Publish	Chapters 4–9	Chapter 25
Photo	Chapter 10	Chapter 26
Audio	Chapters 11–12	Chapter 27
Video	Chapters 13–14	Chapter 28
Microblogging	Chapter 15	Chapter 29
Livecasting	Chapter 16	Chapter 30
Virtual Worlds	Chapter 17	Chapter 31
Gaming	Chapter 18	Chapter 32
Productivity applications	Various Chapters	Chapter 33
Aggregators	Chapter 19	Chapter 34
RSS	Chapter 19	Chapter 35
Search	Chapter 20	Chapter 36
Mobile	Chapter 22	Chapter 37
Interpersonal	Chapter 23	Chapter 38

comfortably in everyday conversation? How many of these 12 words might your employees, colleagues, or customers be comfortable using? Take a guess. The goal of this exercise is not to make you feel either good or bad about your current social media vocabulary but to help you see the social media ecosystem in action as well as the need for a classification system to talk about it.

1. I've been getting her newsletter through *Constant Contact,* so I decided to *Google* her company last night.
2. As a power user of *Twitter,* I've become convinced of the value of *tweets*.
3. She has over 2,000 *Facebook* friends. No wonder her *blog* is getting traction.
4. Nowadays we put most of our training materials on the company *wiki* and rely upon *user-generated content* to keep it fresh.
5. I used to subscribe to his *podcast,* but since he started posting his program on *YouTube* and *Hulu,* I catch it on my *iPhone* when I can.

Ten years ago, these 12 words or phrases did not exist or meant something else. They are now part of a common functional vocabulary of a generation of your employees and customers. How many of these terms can you use effectively in daily conversation? If you're under the age of 25, you probably know and can use all of these words. If you're under 35, it's likely that you know at least nine of them. If you're under 45, you probably know at least half of them. If you're 55 or older, it's hard to say how many of these words you might know. Now, consider that in another two years these words will be household names for anyone with a computer and a mobile phone, regardless of age. Whether or not you are a student of the history of business or have seen a lot of that history firsthand, do you recall a time when a dozen words became part of the daily vocabulary of Main Street so quickly?

Do These 12 Words Belong in Your Strategic Plan?

A goal of most businesses is to understand the needs, wants, and desires of a target audience and then deliver products or services that monetize a relationship between you and your customer. The more effective a business is in producing products or delivering services, the more profitable it becomes. Several organizations are currently using each of the 12 words and phrases selectively as part of a broader social media strategy to reach and influence their target audiences. The Obama administration, for example, is now posting the president's weekly address to the nation on YouTube. It's a more effective way to engage millions of people. Many businesses have created Facebook pages in an effort to get closer to their target customers.

No matter how much you are convinced that these 12 words and phrases will become common in everyday conversation, you cannot know whether they should be part of your strategic plan. Why not? Because these words represent tools and applications, and you need to understand more about how each can be used and how each is categorized. You may want to know what tools are similar. An understanding of what tools are complementary would be helpful as well.

Survival of the Fittest

In biological ecosystems, organisms adapt to their environment or run the risk of extinction. Sometimes one organism will out-compete another for food and other resources crucial to survival. The same is now true of the social media ecosystem. The law of survival of the fittest will prevail. Some experts predict that up to 80 percent of social media tools and applications now on the market will either go out of business, merge, or be purchased by larger entities. For this reason, it is important to see the social media ecosystem as rapidly evolving. Particular tools may come and go, but if you understand the categories that these tools fit into as well as the common features and functions of each category, you can have an active social media strategy that is not tool dependent.

Category Descriptions and Their Tools

This section presents a concise description of the 15 categories in Table 2.1. Remember that no classification system is perfect. Biologists still argue about their system. This section attempts to group tools and applications in a category based on their primary function. Often, however, features and functions can overlap, making a tool appropriate for more than one category. After some experience with these tools, you may decide that, for your use, some of them belong in different categories. For now, however, use these categories as a functional overview of the social media ecosystem.

In considering this classification system, keep in mind that social media is driven by text, photos, video, audio, and simulated environments. The goal of all social media in a business context is to engage people. Engagement leads toward a desired action or outcome. For an employee, the desired outcome may be a more efficient work process that reduces a product's time to market. For a customer, the desired outcome may be an additional purchase or a strong recommendation to a friend. As a reminder, the four primary ways to engage people with social media are as follows:

1. Communication
2. Collaboration
3. Education
4. Entertainment

You may want to complete the following exercise after reading about each category: Place a check in the box next to each tool with which you are familiar. If you have used one of these tools in your business or personal life, circle the tool. Then, if applicable, indicate whether you used the tool internally (with employees) or externally (with customers and prospects). To help you do this, code the tool by placing an "I" (internal) or "E" (external) next to the circle. Keep in mind that not all of these tools lend themselves to external use. Don't be concerned if you haven't used many or any of these tools. Most people haven't. The goal here is to have you focus on where you are currently positioned within the social media ecosystem. At the end of this chapter, you'll have a chance to see how your score compares to others. These scores will become more important in Part III of the book, when you begin developing a social media strategy for your business.

Category 1: Social Networking

Many people confuse the terms *social networking* and *social media,* often using them interchangeably. They do not mean the same thing. The former is a category of the latter. Social networking tools allow you to share information about yourself and your interests with friends, professional colleagues, and others. Most of these tools allow you to create a profile and then post content (text, video, audio, photos) or link to things that correspond to your areas of interest or expertise. Few people join an online social network because they want to be sold something by someone else in their social network. The motivation to join a social network is almost always social rather than commercial. That said, many successful businesspeople practice social networking in the offline world because they realize that relationships often lead to business transactions. If you are a skilled networker in the offline world, you're likely to be very comfortable with online social networking.

Exercise: Check those tools you are familiar with. Circle and code those you have used:

- ❑ Bebo
- ❑ Facebook
- ❑ Fast Pitch!
- ❑ Friendster
- ❑ Gather.com
- ❑ KickApps
- ❑ LinkedIn
- ❑ MOLI
- ❑ MySpace
- ❑ Ning
- ❑ Orkut
- ❑ Plaxo

Category 2: Publish

Regardless of the business you are in, if you use any Web-based application to engage your employees, customers, or prospects, then you are to some degree a publisher. You will quickly discover that the content you present to your target audience will impact how people perceive your company. Publishing is a fairly broad category that includes tools that facilitate e-mail

campaigns, blogging, and wikis. There are even tools that help you manage
your online content.

Exercise: Check those tools you are familiar with. Circle and code those
you have used:

- ❑ Blogger.com
- ❑ Constant Contact
- ❑ Joomla
- ❑ Knol
- ❑ SlideShare

- ❑ TypePad
- ❑ Wikia
- ❑ Wikipedia
- ❑ WordPress

Category 3: Photo Sharing

The ability to archive and share photos may be very valuable to your
business. In this category, you'll find tools that help you manage photos.
A collision repair shop in Omaha, Nebraska, uses one of these tools to send
and receive images of specific parts and jobs in progress to and from its
vendors and customers. They are also able to archive images of difficult
repair jobs for educational use with future customers and insurance adjust-
ers. The ability to use photos to communicate, collaborate, and educate has
helped the shop realize greater efficiencies and profits.

Exercise: Check those tools you are familiar with. Circle and code those
you have used.

- ❑ Flickr
- ❑ Photobucket
- ❑ Picasa
- ❑ Radar.net

- ❑ SmugMug
- ❑ Twitxr
- ❑ Zooomr

Category 4: Audio

The iPod has become ubiquitous in society. The ability to download and
carry thousands of hours of songs, podcasts, and other programs on a device
that slips into a shirt pocket is truly amazing. Many college students now get
recordings (podcasts) of their professors' lectures to play back later. Some
company CEOs send out monthly messages to their workers via a podcast.
Thanks to a group of dedicated podcasters, you can now take self-guided
tours of several museums by downloading an audio tour before you leave
home. Indeed, audio appeals to people on the go, and it has certain

advantages over text-based tools and even video. It's unlikely that you're going to read something or view video while you're jogging, but audio is the perfect companion.

Exercise: Check those tools you are familiar with. Circle and code those you have used:

❑ iTunes

❑ Podbean

❑ Podcast.net

❑ Rhapsody

Category 5: Video

If a picture is worth a thousand words, what is the value of video? This is an important category because most of us have been raised with at least one television in the home. News, sports, entertainment, even infomercials have entered our lives on the television screen. That same content can now be viewed on your computer or your mobile phone. What's more, with video capability on your mobile phone, you can capture and share moments and events with others.

Exercise: Check those tools you are familiar with. Circle and code those you have used.

❑ Brightcove   ❑ Metacafe

❑ Google Video   ❑ Viddler

❑ Hulu   ❑ YouTube

Category 6: Microblogging

If you can communicate something important or meaningful in less than 140 characters, microblogging is a category you'll want to explore.

Exercise: Check those tools you are familiar with. Circle and code those you have used.

❑ Plurk

❑ Twitter

❑ Twitxr

Category 7: Livecasting

This category encompasses Internet radio and other applications that allow you to stream a live broadcast to an audience or social network. Livecasting offers a flexible means of engaging your audience by educating or entertaining them.

Exercise: Check those tools you are familiar with. Circle and code those you have used:

- ❑ BlogTalkRadio
- ❑ Live 365
- ❑ Justin.tv
- ❑ SHOUTcast
- ❑ TalkShoe

Category 8: Virtual Worlds

If for whatever reason you've ever desired to become an incarnation of someone or something else, then a virtual world may be worth considering. You don't have to go to extremes, however, to assume a persona and become part of a computer-generated world where you can interact with others in a virtual community. As Chapter 1 showed, some businesses are now setting up virtual storefronts in an attempt to do commerce in a virtual world. Sun Microsystems uses a virtual campus where employees can meet to collaborate with one another or conduct training. It's not quite the holodeck experience you'll find aboard the fictional Starship Enterprise, but it's close.

Exercise: Check those tools you are familiar with. Circle and code those you have used:

- ❑ Active Worlds
- ❑ Kaneva
- ❑ Second Life
- ❑ There
- ❑ ViOS

Category 9: Gaming

Gaming and virtual worlds have some things in common, but what sets them apart is the notion of cooperation and competition that is the very basis of gaming. Gamers are part of a fiercely loyal kind of online community. They spend hours playing in environments where conversation and shared experiences with other players across time zones and even continents is common.

Not surprisingly, many game manufacturers now offer product placement and advertising opportunities in their games.

Exercise: Check those tools you are familiar with. Circle and code those you have used:

❑ Entropia Universe
❑ EverQuest
❑ Halo3
❑ World of Warcraft

Category 10: Productivity Applications

This is a bit of a catch-all category, but the common denominator to all of the tools that live here is that they enhance business productivity in one way or another. Unlike many tools in the social media ecosystem that were created for the millennial generation's propensity to share the intimate details of their lives with friends and cohorts, tools in this category are serious business applications.

Exercise: Check those tools you are familiar with. Circle and code those you have used:

❑ Acteva
❑ AOL
❑ BitTorrent
❑ Constant Contact
❑ Eventful
❑ Google Alerts
❑ Google Docs
❑ Google Gmail
❑ MSGTAG
❑ ReadNotify
❑ Survey Monkey
❑ Tiddlywiki
❑ Yahoo!
❑ Zoho
❑ Zoomerang

Category 11: Aggregators

Tools in this category help you gather, update, and store information for easy access. Additionally, some aggregators leverage the wisdom of the crowd and tell you what other people are saying about a particular product, service, or brand. These can be excellent tools for capturing market intelligence.

Exercise: Check those tools you are familiar with. Circle and code those you have used:

- ❑ Digg
- ❑ FriendFeed
- ❑ Google Reader
- ❑ iGoogle
- ❑ My Yahoo!
- ❑ Reddit
- ❑ Yelp

Category 12: RSS

RSS is an acronym for Rich Site Summary. A lot of web content changes. The tools in this category automatically feed you current content from the web sites that are most critical to your business needs. It could be an industry blog, statistics posted on a competitor's site, or information from a government agency's web site.

Exercise: Check those tools you are familiar with. Circle and code those you have used:

- ❑ Atom
- ❑ FeedBurner
- ❑ PingShot
- ❑ RSS 2.0

Category 13: Search

In just a few years, *Google* has become synonymous with doing an Internet search. If people are using tools like Google to find people, places, and things that are interesting, essential, or desirable and you have a relevant product or service, then you need to know something about the tools in this category.

Exercise: Check those tools you are familiar with. Circle and code those you have used:

- ❑ EveryZing
- ❑ Google Search
- ❑ IceRocket
- ❑ MetaTube
- ❑ Redlasso
- ❑ Technorati
- ❑ Yahoo! Search

Category 14: Mobile

Mobile phones are quickly becoming the most important appliance you can own. In fact, many of the tools from other categories in the social media ecosystem can be accessed via your mobile phone, and yet there are specific tools that make your mobile phone a more powerful business ally. This category focuses on these tools.

Exercise: Check those tools you are familiar with. Circle and code those you have used:

- ❑ airG
- ❑ AOL Mobile
- ❑ Brightkite
- ❑ CallWave
- ❑ Jott
- ❑ Jumbuck
- ❑ SMS.ac

Category 15: Interpersonal

Tools in this category facilitate people-to-people communication and collaboration. To stalwart social media aficionados, many of these tools don't belong in the social media ecosystem, but if you're in the business of managing people, processes, or products, you need to be aware of these tools.

Exercise: Check those tools you are familiar with. Circle and code those you have used.

- ❑ Acrobat Connect
- ❑ AOL Instant Messenger
- ❑ Go To Meeting
- ❑ iChat
- ❑ Jott
- ❑ Meebo
- ❑ Skype
- ❑ WebEx

How Well Did You Do?

Did you complete the brief exercise that followed each category? If you're like many businesspeople, you're very competitive and you'd like to know how your score compares with others. Remember, this is not a test. At this point in the book, you're just trying to get comfortable with the categories in the social media ecosystem.

However, to satisfy your competitive tendencies, use the following chart to tally your scores:

How many tools did you place a check next to?   ——

How many tools did you circle?   ——

How many tools did you code with an "I"
for internal?   ——

How many tools did you code with an "E"
for external?   ——

Which category had the greatest number of checks
or circles?   ——

Your Social Media Awareness

If you placed a check next to 70 tools or more, your social media awareness score puts you in the top 1 percent of the class. Between 50 and 70 checks is impressive; clearly you've been watching what's happening in the ecosystem. Anything between 30 and 50 checks is still pretty good. If you had between 20 and 30 checks, your social media awareness is about average. Ten to 20 checks suggests that you could be a lot more aware of what's happening with social media. If you had fewer than 10 checks, you've got some catching up to do, and this book will help.

Your Social Media Experience

Being aware and being experienced are two different things. If you circled more than 25 tools, your social media experience is greater than 95 percent of the people surveyed as this book was being written. Anything between 15 and 25 is very impressive and suggests that you may already be experimenting with these tools and exploring new opportunities. If you circled between 10 and 15 tools, you're a little above average. Between 5 and 10 tools is about average.

Internal or External

These tallies are less important at this point and may reflect your primary function within your company. If you're in sales, you're probably more likely to be externally focused, and if you're in human resources, you're likely to be more internally focused. As you read the chapters in this book, keep in mind that your company's social media strategy can have both internal and external components, and just because you're in sales doesn't mean that you can't see some ways that operations could be improved via a strong internal social media strategy.

Which Categories Were Best Represented?

Chances are that your checks and circles are concentrated in fewer than three categories, which suggests that there's an opportunity for you and your company to explore and experiment. Fortunately, that's one of the goals of this book: to help you pick up a few of these tools and take them for a test drive before making them a part of your company strategy.

Expert Insight

Vint Cerf, father of the Internet and futurist,
www.google.com/corporate/execs.html

Vint Cerf

. . . Well, first of all labeling me the "Father of the Internet" is not fair to an awful lot of people, especially to Bob Kahn, because Bob started the program when he was in the Defense Department in 1972; and then he came to me when I was at Stanford in early 1973 and said, "You know, I have this problem. How do I hook all these different nets together?"

So the two of us did the basic Internet design, and it started the design of the TCP/IP protocols. But there are many, many people, both before and after that stage, that have contributed to make the 'Net what it is today.

So, I'm just happy that I participated in it because it has been a lot of fun. . . .

. . . It certainly has been something of a surprise to me that the users of the Internet, the consumers of information, have now become the producers of information on the network. It's very widespread. It shows up in a number of different forms. It shows up as blogs, it shows up as video uploads in YouTube and other similar services. It shows up at social game sites. Things like World-of-Work Map or Second Life. It's showing up as people with their own Web pages, e-mail, and distribution lists, and the like.

Some of those things have been around for a while. E-mail, of course, was invented in 1971, so it's an old media in some sense but still very heavily used as are distribution lists. There's chat and there are other kinds of more "real" time things, including video now.

So all of these different ways of interacting have been very rapidly absorbed by the public. Mobiles, which only recently have come on the scene, now account for some three billion users, not on the Internet but in the mobile world. But the Internet interfaces to many of the mobiles and so people are beginning to do texting in the mobile world, they are doing instant messaging;

they are doing e-mail exchanges, they are searching the Web from their mobiles.

What I'm seeing right now is a wide range of choices that people have in maintaining relationships and in interacting with people one-on-one, and in groups. I think this is likely to persist. Certainly, the sharing of information on the Internet has been dramatic. In the scientific world, equally so. Where scientists begin to build common databases that they can make reference to, like the human genome database or astronomical information, or the geophysical information, we are finding that scientific results occur faster because people have reference to virtually everything that is known about some particular phenomenon because it's been codified in these shared databases.

So now we're seeing an increasing amount of collaborative work in the online environment and something, which Google, of course, is intensely interested in.

. . . [I]n these mediums, it's possible to be abusive, and I am very concerned about the side effect of cyber-bullying and things of that sort. Others have expressed a discomfort with the fact that anything and everything can be expressed on the Internet, including negative information . . . whether it's accurate or not, it sometimes has an impact.

So we have a potential for both positive and constructive and also rather negative kinds of interactions in this online environment; and I think we're still trying to discipline ourselves in how to treat these different media in a way that protects us from some of the abusive behaviors.

I am thinking not merely of the social media, but more generally speaking; things like viruses and worms and things that are "Keyloggers" that are looking for user names and passwords, or identifiers of account numbers and things of that kind.

Those are all fairly pernicious abuses of this online medium, and I think we are still trying to learn how to cope with it socially and legally, as well as from the law enforcement point of view. . . .

. . . The FCC believes that it is responsible for all communications in the United States. It doesn't mean that it's responsible for communications outside the United States, but it has chosen to treat the "Internet" as a Title I Information Service.

There are some side effects of that, which I think are not relevant to this discussion, although they're of concern to me; having a lot to do with "Common Carriage" and things like that; but the FCC has chosen to forebear to regulate, except in cases it considers to be anti-competitive practices. And you'll note that there was a recent decision by the FCC with regards to Comcast and its attempt to manage network use in the presence of BitTorrent and other kinds of peer-to-peer file sharing applications.

(*continued*)

(continued)

The FCC censured Comcast for the way in which it undertook to do that management. There are other places in the world that are even more actively trying to control access to and use of the Internet. You're going to find that everywhere. The Internet is global in scope. It operates in virtually every country in varying degrees and countries have different views of what people should or shouldn't be able to do using this medium.

One of the biggest challenges, I think, is that no matter what position you take with regard to usage, you have the problem that if your position is different from some other countries' view, there is nothing that you can do to enforce your view, and vice versa.

And so then you get into this question of, "Under my rules my citizen was attacked by a person in another country and I'm looking for some kind of compensation."

You will not be able to deal with those problems unless there are more common agreements about what is or is not acceptable behavior on the Internet. And since the social views vary from one country to another, I think it is going to be hard for us to come to global agreements; but I think we will come to some agreements commonly.

For example, as far as I know every country in the world rejects child pornography as an unacceptable form of behavior, whether it's on the Internet or otherwise.

So, maybe there are other things that we can agree are commonly unacceptable and, therefore, should be either prevented or punished if they are detected. It's going to take a lot of international work to make that a reality. . . .

. . . And, by the way, I would like to say something about China. When you talk to Chinese people on the streets, you discover that some number of them actually appreciate the censorship. They like it; they believe they are being protected; now whether that's true is independent of how they feel about it, or how they, at least, say they feel about it. So we shouldn't make the assumption that the First Amendment notion, which is powerful in our Constitution, is necessarily universally accepted as preferable.

There are cultures where, in fact, the citizens want this kind of control. . . .

. . . This reminds me of an interesting phenomenon that happened in the last 1980s. I had asked permission from the U.S. federal government to connect MCI, which is a commercial e-mail service, up to the Internet. And they reluctantly allowed me to do that. The reluctance came from the concern that we would be carrying, or using, government-sponsored backbones to carry commercial e-mail traffic.

After I put the MCM mail system up on the Internet, immediately the other e-mail service providers said, "Well, you know, the MCI people shouldn't have an exclusive privilege." And so CompuServe came up and OnTime came up and some of the other commercial servers also came up on the 'Net.

And the side effects of this was that they could suddenly interchange e-mail with each other through the Internet, which before they could not do. So it's this standardization that creates the possibility of interoperability. And this is why our OpenSocial, I think, is an important effort . . . because it creates interoperability among those areas in social networks.

I think it will be very attractive for the users of those networks to be able to interact, regardless of which social networks systems you happen to be registered in. You know, we may see some interesting consequences of that interconnection as people begin to adopt it. There will be interactions that we might not have anticipated that are enabled by that standard. . . .

. . . I'm of course, perhaps understandably, excited and feel positive about a lot of these new developments. The Internet was designed to be fairly insensitive to specific media, so it does not know if it is carrying a digital image or voice or video or some other digitized object . . . you know, part of a program or a piece of Web page. It just does not know, and that's very deliberate. It was intended to be a general-purpose transport mechanism, and the consequences of that is . . . every device that produces digital output potentially can be interfaced to the Internet and this output transfers around and delivers to other places. I think that we are going to see a very significant increase in the number of devices that are able to connect to and interact with other devices on the Internet.

There had been some discussion about the earlier phases of Internet being "Internet for everyone" and now it is becoming "Internet for everything"! And I really do believe that. I think sensor networks, appliances, things at home, in the office, in the automobile, and that you carry around will all be "Internet enabled" and this allows us to manage them better. These devices can report their status to us; they can accept, command, and control from third parties. You can imagine entertainment systems being managed over the Internet by third-party entertainment managers; you simply "click" here if you want this movie or that song, and it takes care of the details of getting it to the CD player in the car or the hard disc that replaced the CD player, or your iPod or some other DVR or whatever you have. All of these are possible once these devices become part of the Internet.

And, of course, mobiles are contributing to that because as they become more and more prevalent with Internet capabilities, they too, will become remote controllers for many, many devices . . . .

To listen to or read the entire Executive Conversation with Vint Cerf, go to www.the SocialMediaBible.com.

Expert Insight

Michael Gerber, author, *The E-Myth* and Entrepreneur Advocate, www.intheDreamingRoom.com

Michael
Gerber

. . . E-Myth Worldwide, the company I founded in 1977, is the world's #1 business-development/redevelopment resource for small business, and now for the entrepreneur, as well. I am also the founder, chairman, and CEO of a new venture called The Dreaming World, as well as the founder of Capital Corporation whose purpose is to provide microfinancing for entrepreneurs and business owners.

I am the founding partner of Entrepreneurs Club Network, the purpose of which is to attract entrepreneurs to pursue conversations with each other and with people who have been inordinately successful at finding a venture and wrapping that venture up. And My Growth Resources, which is a venture that is in the works, in the making (at My Growth Partners, My Growth Managers, My Growth Coaches, My Growth Attorneys, My Growth Accountants, My Growth Capital, and on and on and on), to feed the resources of entrepreneurship to enable them to have turnkey capabilities and services that can help them to ratchet up their ventures, their ideas, and so forth and so on. . . .

. . . The entrepreneur is who I consider to be the creator of all things good and all things bad that happen in the commercial enterprise. The entrepreneur is critical to economic development, social development, and critical to breaking through into new places that we have never been before, critical in every industry; and every industry obviously is critical in the development of our social networks and our social awareness and our social capability. So great entrepreneurs create great things.

Dumb entrepreneurs create dumb things, but you cannot blame them because we are all pretty dumb and pretty great both at the same time.

But I cannot even imagine a world without entrepreneurship as its primary focus. The unfortunate thing is that we really haven't truly understood the true power of entrepreneurship as I have begun to communicate in my latest book, *Awakening the Entrepreneur Within*. And as I have communicated in all my ebooks, entrepreneurs are the inventers. They are, as Walt Disney calls it, "The Imagineers." They are the ones that conceive of a future that no one else could have imagined until some entrepreneur invented a venture to pursue it.

So entrepreneurs are constantly in pursuit of the impossible and that's truly the force, the economic force, the social force for every country, every market, and every human being on the face of the earth. . . .

. . . That's exactly what Steve Jobs still is. That's exactly what has created such huge mega-breakthroughs in our awareness of how to do things, how to get things done, what things to do, and why to do them that way.

If you look at the passion and the energy that drives that entrepreneurial imagination, you begin to see that as we become more socially involved, as we become more socially aware of all of the problems that we face in the world, you understand that it is going to be the entrepreneurs (in what I call this Age of the New Entrepreneur) who are going to break through all of the barriers that confront us. These barriers of energy, the barriers of water, the barriers of food, the barriers of income, the barriers of all the things that keep people where they are, as opposed to liberating them to do the things that we are capable of doing. . . .

. . . In fact [being an entrepreneur] is not a profession in my mind. It is a calling, not a profession. . . .

. . . I've been told that 67 percent of all companies in the United States are sole proprietorships. But understand those sole proprietors are not true entrepreneurs; they are what I have come to call technicians suffering from an entrepreneurial seizure. . . .

. . . They went out on their own, but they went out on their own to become their own boss, and that's not a worthy goal or a worthy ambition. Essentially it keeps everybody small. I get to be my own boss, but now I'm working for a lunatic who has never truly learned what in fact one needs to learn to build a truly stunning venture. The vast majority of companies in the world are not entrepreneurial at all. They're not interested in growth, they're not interested in breaking free of the past, and they're not interested in inventing a new modality and a new methodology, a new mindset. They are uninterested in transformation at all.

They are interested in simply replacing one job where I am working for someone else, to creating my own job where I am self-employed. So most small companies are really "frozen" at that place which is not where one expects them to go. They're frozen at a size, which is only the first step in the process of growing a company; it's called "small."

Obviously it has got to be small in order to begin, but it doesn't stay small if you're truly approaching it from an entrepreneurial perspective. . . .

. . . And if, in fact, you were able to start a small company knowing the "secret sauce" that's critical to transforming the situation that a customer (a very specific demographic) has, then you understand immediately that it is just begging to grow because there are all those many millions of people who are suffering from whatever inadequacy your company was invented to get rid of. . . .

. . . And if, in fact, you had examined how to get rid of it, how could you possibly stay small knowing that people are struggling without your solution all over the place. You could not possibly (stay small); you would have been compelled to grow. . . .

(*continued*)

(*continued*)

. . . The "secret sauce," in my mind, can be found in many, many places, but it is found in what I refer to as "hyper-speed" at McDonald's, or at Dell Computer, or at FedEx, or at Wal-Mart. It's the turnkey system. It's the operating system that enables those companies to differentiate themselves as preferentially unique from all other companies.

So there's the FedEx way, there's the McDonald's way, there's the Starbucks way, there's the Wal-Mart way. And their "way," in fact, is nothing more or less than a system; an organized methodology for producing their result in their way for their reason to satisfy a real problem with a real solution, that nobody else has figured out how to do just as well. And they've done that (each of those companies and many, many, many more) and I'm saying that every company can do that. Every person, who in fact, has an entrepreneur inside of him, inside of her, can see that as the template for building any company or selling any service or product to a world-class level. . . .

. . . When Ray Kroc started McDonald's he started it with the license that McDonald Brothers gave him. He started it to build the most successful small business in the world. McDonald's today (no matter what the shifts in the company have been) is the world's most successful small business. And in effect, even though it is a large company you understand the "secret of its success" resides in every single one of its stores.

And if it didn't, it would not be the brand that it is today. When you understand that, you understand what Tom Peters speaks to as "core excellence." How could you do it any other way? So excellence isn't even a question when you are driven (as Ray Kroc was and as Michael Dell still is) to build a stunningly successful company. Excellence is the critical component that is begging the question, "How do we do what we do, and how do we do it in such a way that we can deliver a promise, continuously, to our customer that we will never, ever, ever do any less than that in any other way?" . . .

. . . As the technology makes it available, more and more people need to learn about how to use that technology to reach the people they formerly could not reach because it was too expensive for them.

Social media is simply an identification of the technological resource that is available to everyone. They either take advantage of it, they either utilize it, or they fail to. And if they fail to, they cannot build a competitive advantage in their company. So we all have to be continually evolving as these forms, or exercises, are made available and as they begin to reveal themselves through technology, through innovation, through capabilities formerly not available to us. . . .

. . . Can you imagine when we did not have computers? Can you imagine any businesses doing business today without a computer? Can you imagine any business doing business today without Windows? Can you imagine any business doing business today without a fax? Can you imagine any business doing business today without a cell phone? Can anybody imagine doing business today without all of these tools, the vast majority (in fact, all of which I just mentioned) have only been available to us for a very short period of time. . . .

. . . Of course we have to take advantage of it! Of course that's the big problem in the big opportunity. The big problem is small-business owners are so "intense" in the servitude that they have obliged themselves toward; just doing it . . . doing it . . . doing it; busy . . . busy . . . busy; consumed with all the ordinary tasks that they are confronted with and have been confronted with for generations. They haven't the time to envelope these new capabilities that are just waiting for them to use them, and they pay that huge price. They pay the price of "no" innovation, "no" quantification, "no" orchestration which are the three essential disciplines of every managed company. And therefore they just end up working for a living. . . .

. . . I do not think the world of the entrepreneur has changed. I think that the ability to be an entrepreneur has increased almost exponentially, and that is primarily due to the Internet, due to technology, due to technological opportunities that continually reveal themselves daily. It is almost as though it is an infinite array of options available to us to invent.

I think that is also the bad news because in some way we believe that technology is critical to entrepreneurship. I do not believe that technology is critical to entrepreneurship; I believe creativity is. . . .

. . . And so we look today at the rate of startups of new businesses. We're told that half a million new companies are started in the United States every month. If you look at the failure rate of businesses that means that a significant number of those will not be here five years from now. And because of that, entrepreneurship is, we might say, on hyper-speed. That is, we get more and more and more people starting more and more and more ventures.

The failure rate is identically the same. And the failure rate is what I address in my *E-Myth* books. What I address is the awakening of the entrepreneur within. What I address in my new book, *The E-Myth Enterprise*, is that there are essential ingredients (I call them the *Seven Centers of Management-Intention*) that have never been altered, have never changed, and are absolutely essential if an entrepreneur is to truly become a leader of the enterprise. That leadership role, the seven essential disciplines of a world-class company that I describe in my *E-Myth Mastery* book are as important today as they were 100 years ago. . . .

To listen to or read the entire Executive Conversation with Michael Gerber, go to www.theSocialMediaBible.com.

A Look Ahead

The chapters that follow in Part I have been written to give you a closer look at the 15 categories of the social media ecosystem. Part I tries to give you a little history, some practical tips, and a strong sense of the what's-in-it-for-you factor for each chapter. Sprinkled throughout these chapters, you'll find insights from experts, interviews with some of the key people in the social media pantheon, and some clever commandments to give you a tactical feel for some of these tools.

Credits

Expert Insights Were Provided By:

Vint Cerf, vice president, Google, www.google.com/corporate/execs.html.

Michael Gerber, author, *E-Myth*, www.intheDreamingRoom.com.

CHAPTER 3

Say Hello to Social Networking

What's In It for You?

A *trusted network* is a group of like-minded people who have come together in a common place to share thoughts, ideas, and information about themselves. These groups sometimes include more than 100 million registered users that host more than 10 billion photographs—as with social networking site Facebook (www.facebook .com). A trusted network can also be as small as a single, influential person.

These social networks develop the trust that ultimately creates influence among your consumers. By developing and cultivating networks, your organization can create an opportunity to develop the trust that may result in more sales.

The desire to participate in conversation and influence prospects prompted the writing of a "Sales Manifesto" for a Fortune 500 client by James Burnes, vice president of development and strategy, Internet strategy, of creative services firm *MediaSauce*. The following excerpt showcases the need for embracing networks to drive business:

> Why do we sell the same way we always have? Because it's safe and reliable. Because it's what we know. Because we've become entrenched in thinking that what we have to say is what our customers want to hear. Because it has worked for the past (insert number) years!
>
> But the world is rapidly evolving. Advertising, messaging, and communication behaviors are changing more quickly than how we tell our story. Worse, our messaging is competing more and

more with the noise that overwhelms our target customers every day/hour/minute/second of their lives. Customers are tuning out our old messages while social media and the Internet connect them with information that bypasses our expensive marketing communications strategies.

The old tried-and-true tactics of the past (insert number again!) years like our flashy direct mail pieces, our witty trade media advertisements or those well written, but terribly expensive brochures, aren't setting us apart.

Worse, they aren't even being looked at. They're being ignored. And we're becoming irrelevant. We're becoming part of the noise.

Can we stop being noise and become relevant again? Yes! Absolutely we can. But we have to have a new way of speaking to our customers. We have to differentiate ourselves from the rest of the world and be fresh and exciting.

We need to transform the way we touch our clients, and integrate ourselves into the very fabric of what they do every day. We have to embrace social networks, digital connections, and the online experience and build an organization that embraces conversation and transparency.

We need to take advantage of a new approach to selling, where we are problem solvers and the "go to" team for our prospects whenever a project arises that we contribute to. Everyone sells [product]. We have to be bigger than our [product]. We have to solve our client's pain points.

We need to get digital. We need to take advantage of the tools digital and social media can provide us to open up new channels and speak to prospects on the business issues and problems they are trying to solve.

We need to tell our story in a way that doesn't just interrupt our clients, but engages them and gives them a reason to pass it along. We need to be viral, innovative, non-traditional, and aggressive in how we seek out new business.

How will we do it? By embracing the opportunities that social media offer us to become connected to our customers. We're going to build a culture where communicating, engaging and embracing the feedback, positive and negative, make us a better organization.

Burnes' manifesto showcases the need for transformation, and how social networks and those connections play a critical role in your business.

You will see a common theme throughout the chapters in *The Social Media Bible* that discusses people's tendency to congregate around Internet technology to exchange like information and grow into larger trusted networks. By definition, the Internet *itself* was the first electronic trusted network. When ARPAnet (see Chapter 20, Spotlight on Search (Search Engine Optimization) for more information about ARPAnet) connected its first group of computers together to share files, everyone assumed that their fellow users would follow a certain protocol, respect each other's files, and share the same interests.

Although Facebook recently beat out its fellow social networking site MySpace (www.myspace.com) for the first time in worldwide traffic—going from an under 14 percent market share to slightly over 20 percent in one year's time—MySpace is still getting 122 million unique visitors and owns 67.5 percent of the social networking market space in the United States, and is expanding beyond this country's borders. MySpace Latin America has been growing 10 percent each month to reach 6.8 million visitors—with 30 million additional visitors from Europe. Overall, international traffic for the site has grown from 53 million to more than 55 million unique visitors, with more than 40 million visitors from the United States alone in 2008.

Facebook is experiencing its own surge as well, and grew to 29.2 million unique visitors in the United States in 2008. Professional social networking site LinkedIn (www.linkedin.com) has been expanding by over 20 percent month-after-month to include more than 9.5 million unique visitors. These numbers represent a 77 percent growth for Facebook and 187 percent for LinkedIn. And social community Ning's (www.ning.com) platform exceeded 2.2 million unique visitors in 2008—which is up 326 percent from last year when it first began offering their create-your-own-social-network site. The third-, fourth-, and fifth-most popular social networks in the United States are MyYearbook.com, Tagged.com, and Bebo.com (owned by AOL)—each of which has 2 percent or less of the U.S. market share.

(To hear the Executive Conversation Interviews from Angela Courtin, senior vice president of marketing entertainment and content for MySpace; Krista Canfield, public relations manager for LinkedIn; Kyle Ford, the director of product marketing for Ning; and Bill Jula, founder of Fast Pitch!, go to www.theSocialMediaBible.com.)

The social networking site phenomenon has completely and rapidly changed the way that people interact—in terms of personal and professional relationships. And anytime there is a tool that millions of people in one place at one time all with common interests are clamoring to use, you, as a businessperson, need to understand and be a part of it.

Back to the Beginning

Social networks have been around as long as there have been humans to create them. When people were still living in caves and traveling in clans and tribes, those were the trusted social networks where people banded together to cooperatively work, live, and protect one another. The group was counted on for protection. The words *society, tribe, clan, team, group, pod, school, flock, colony, troop, drove, clash, caravan, mob, pounce, band, quiver, pack, congregation, litter, bevy, gaggle, herd, Americans, Europeans, Latinas, family, caucus, pro ball teams, New Yorkers, Catholics, Presbyterians*, and even a *business of ferrets* all refer to social networks with similar interests and a common bond—and most importantly, trust.

These are the groups that help people make life's most important—and not-so-important—decisions. Before you see a movie or go to a restaurant, don't you consult your trusted network of friends and now web sites? If you are looking for a job, who do you go to first? Most likely your trusted network of friends and colleagues. If you are buying a new car, you go to trusted networks of fellow drivers and informational web sites.

Anytime a group of people with similar interests and collaborative trust gather in one place, businesspeople need to be participating. In fact, businesspeople also need to provide and *be* that very trusted network for the product or service. Understanding social networks is actually a twofold process that requires participating in other networks as well as becoming one for customers and prospects. In fact, the best way to understand social networks is to first participate in one. There are literally thousands of different kinds available today that you can join for free both on and off line. But since the focus of social media is online, these are the groups upon which this chapter concentrates. The big two are the aforementioned sites MySpace and Facebook, with LinkedIn coming in as the largest professional network. These sites have amassed a great number of members all with one common interest and goal: to socialize. Since Facebook has declined to participate in *The Social Media Bible*, MySpace and LinkedIn serve as the main examples for this chapter. Another emerging site called Fast Pitch! is a great derivation on the professional social network theme, as a site designed for companies as opposed to individual businesspeople.

What You Need to Know

A social network, trusted network, virtual community, e-community, or online community is a group of people who interact through newsletters, blogs, comments, telephone, e-mail, and instant messages, and who use text, audio, photographs, and video for social, professional, and educational purposes. The social network's goal is to build trust in a given community.

Virtual communities that utilize Web 2.0 technologies to create and develop contacts have been described as *Community 2.0*. Social networking and strong bonds have been forged online since the early days of USENET (see Chapter 20, Spotlight on Search (Search Engine Optimization) for more information on USENET), and usually depend upon collective interaction and exchange between users. The ability to intermingle with like-minded individuals instantly—from anywhere on the globe—has considerable benefits.

Every social network has different levels of interaction and participation among members. This can range from adding comments or tags to a blog (see Chapter 8, The Ubiquitous Blog) or message board posts (see Chapter 7, The Internet Forum), to competing against other people in online video games such as MMORPG's (see Chapter 18, Gaming the System: Virtual Gaming).

Life Cycle

A membership life cycle for online social networks begins when members initiate their life in a community as visitors, lurkers, or trolls (see Chapter 7, The Internet Forum for more information). After becoming comfortable, people become novices and participate in the community dialogue. Once they've contributed for a period of time, they become regulars; and often-times, these regulars will break through a barrier and become leaders. Members who have been participating in the network for awhile and eventually depart are known as elders. The amount of time it takes to become an elder depends on the culture of the site. It can take only a few months or more than a year. This life cycle can be applied to many social networks such as bulletin boards, blogs, and wiki-based communities like Wikipedia.

The following examples of each of the phases in the membership life cycle uses the photo-sharing site Flickr:

- *Lurkers* observe the community and view photo content. They do not add to the community content or comments, and they occasionally visit the site to look at photos that someone has suggested.
- *Novices* are just beginning to engage in the community. They start to provide content and tentatively participate in a few threads. Such users make a few comments, become somewhat involved, and will even post some photos of their own.

- *Insiders* consistently add to the community discussion, comments, and content. They interact with other members and regularly post photos. They make a concerted effort to comment, rate, and participate with other members' material.

- *Leaders* are recognized as veteran participants. They connect with the regulars and are recognized as "contributors to watch." A leader would not consider viewing another member's photos without commenting on them, and he or she will often correct another member's behavior when the community considers it inappropriate. Leaders will reference other member's photos in their comments as a way to cross-link content.

- *Elders* leave the network for a variety of reasons. Maybe their interests have changed, or perhaps the community has moved in a direction that doesn't sit well with them. Their departure may be due to lack of time, lack of interest, or any number of other factors.

Contributing

There are many reasons that people want to contribute to social and knowledge-sharing networks like blogs and wikis (see Chapter 9, The Wisdom of the Wiki). In fact, the number of individuals who spend a great deal of time contributing to such web sites is pretty amazing. People usually become motivated to contribute valuable information to the group with the expectation that one will receive useful help or information and recognition in return. This kind of reciprocation is particularly important to many online contributors. Some individuals may also freely contribute valuable information because they get a sense of contribution and a feeling of having some influence over their environment. Social psychology dictates that people are social beings who are gratified by the fact that they receive direct responses to their input. Blogs are a good example of this kind of immediate acknowledgment, whereby readers can instantly comment on and participate in live content.

Dunbar's Number

In 1993, evolutionary psychologist Dr. Robin I. M. Dunbar of the Human Evolutionary Biology Research Group of the University College London anthropology department made an important discovery about the workings of social networks and human interaction. Dunbar proposed that the cognitive limit to the number of people with whom one person can maintain stable social relationships was 150. These are relationships where individuals know whom each person is, and how each person relates to every other person. The size of a typical social network is constrained to about 150 members due to possible limits in the capacity of the human communication channel.

However, through the use of social media tools and social networking, this number has grown to maybe many hundreds. And by linking your network to each of your contacts' networks, your effective number of usable contacts can be in the millions.

Remember, social networking isn't about allowing everyone who requests that you link to them do so. As author David Nour (*Relationship Economics,* John Wiley & Sons, Inc., 2008) puts it, it's not about the number of your contacts, but rather about the value that each one brings.

Social Network Examples

The best way to explain how a social network works is to describe a few specific social networks. Let's start with the largest social network, MySpace, and the largest professional network, LinkedIn.

MySpace: MySpace is currently the biggest and most popular social network on the Internet, and has more than 185 million members. Owned by Fox Interactive Media (News Corporation), it is an international interactive web site that allows its members to create a user-submitted network of friends, personal profiles, blogs, groups, photos, music, and videos (see Figure 3.1).

In August 2003, several employees of eUniverse—and members of the then-popular social networking site Friendster—saw the potential for this kind of site's popularity and launched MySpace. Not to be distracted by the usual start-up issues, this team's success was due in part to their complete infrastructure—including finance, human resources, technical expertise, bandwidth, and server capacity. Founder, chairman, and CEO of eUniverse Brad Greenspan oversaw the MySpace project, with help from MySpace team members Chris DeWolfe (its first CEO), Tom Anderson (MySpace president), and Josh Berman—as well as a team of programmers and other resources provided by eUniverse (including the key technical expert Toan Nguyen, who helped stabilize the MySpace platform).

Since the very first MySpace users were obviously eUniverse staff members, the company held contests to see who could recruit the most new members. Employees then used the company's resources to market MySpace to the masses. eUniverse utilized its own 20-million-member base of e-mail subscribers to quickly make MySpace the most successful social network today.

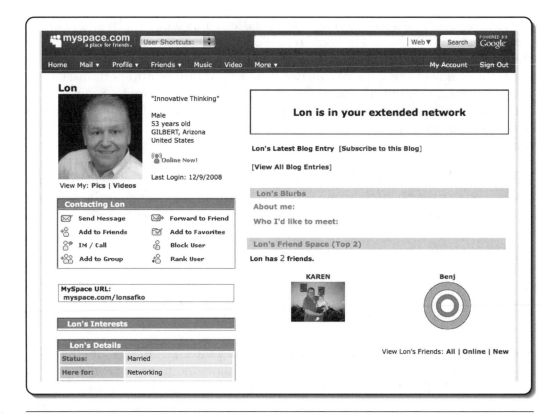

FIGURE 3.1 MySpace

In 2002, YourZ.com—designed to be a leading online data storage and sharing site and casualty of the dot-bomb era—owned the original MySpace .com domain. At that time, MySpace CEO Chris DeWolfe and a friend, while at YourZ.com, owned the MySpace URL and had intentions of creating a hosting site. DeWolfe believed that they should charge for MySpace membership, whereas eUniverse CEO Brad Greenspan felt that it was necessary to keep MySpace free and open in order to make it a large and successful community. It turned out that Brad was right.

DeWolfe and several other employees were later able to purchase equity in the new MySpace entity and its parent company eUniverse, which was renamed Intermix Media shortly before it was acquired in July 2005 by Rupert Murdoch's News Corporation—the parent company of Fox Broadcasting and other media enterprises. Fox acquired MySpace for $580 million, of which $327 million was directly attributed to the value of MySpace. Driven by tapping into the U.K. music scene, MySpace launched its U.K. version in January 2006, followed by a Chinese version shortly thereafter.

REVENUE MODEL. As can be seen with many of the other social networking sites and social media tools, the revenue models are fairly simple: paid subscription, free with advertising, and free with paid upgrades (aka "Freemium"). MySpace chose the free with advertising revenue model with no paid services. The site's overwhelming success through advertising revenue is due to its technique of mining the largest user database, second only to Yahoo!. This practice allows for highly targeted advertising that taps into their huge database of behavioral data, which serves up very specific and selected ads to each individual user.

On August 8, 2006, Google signed a $900 million deal with MySpace whereby Google would provide their Google Search and advertising tools to the site. MySpace has also provided opportunity and hundreds of thousands of dollars in revenue to other, smaller companies who created added functionality through accessories, plug-ins, and widgets—including Slide, Rock-You!, and YouTube.

MYSPACE FEATURES

Profile. MySpace profiles contain two standard text sections: "About Me" and "Who I'd Like to Meet." The members profile also contains "Interests" and "Details" sections. Within the "Details" section, "Status" and "Zodiac Sign" are always on display if the profile holder fills them out. Each profile also contains a blog with standard fields for content, comments, emoticons, and multimedia.

MySpace members may also upload images, one of which can be chosen as their default image—the one that is seen on the profile's main page, search page, and the image that will appear alongside the user's name on their comments, messages, and other personal input. The user can also embed Flash, music, and video. MySpace also provides a blogging capability that has been one of the site's most popular features since its inception.

Comments. Another popular feature of MySpace is the User's Friends Space comments section. This is where the "friends" or contacts of a given member can leave comments for all of the other viewers to see. As with most every blog, MySpace users can read and approve any comment and have the option to delete any comment before it is posted.

Customization. One of the most popular and powerful MySpace features is the user's ability to customize one's own profile page. This high-level interface allows a member with no programming experience whatsoever to simply drag, drop, and click one's way through creating a very unique web page with its own look and feel, fonts, colors, and rich media content. By utilizing MySpace Music and MySpace Videos, the user is just one click away from programming this multimedia content into her or his own web page.

Music. One of MySpace's unique hooks is that it provides profiles designed specifically for musicians and bands. These profiles differ from the average users', since they allow artists to upload as many as six MP3 songs of their own creation. MySpace has provided the very popular SNOCAP to unsigned musicians to post and even sell their music. And by using the trusted social networking environment that MySpace provides, many artists have created huge followings of fans and supporters. MySpace has even launched its own record label—MySpace Records—which is intended to assist and discover previously unknown talented artists. In fact, more than 8 million artists have already been discovered.

Bulletins. These types of posts are published on bulletin boards where everyone can read the content. They are useful for contacting your entire list of friends without sending individual messages to each. A bulletin can be about you posting new photos, an event like a party, a book or movie review, or just something new about you that you want all of your friends to know about (see Chapter 7, The Internet Forum).

Groups. The MySpace Groups feature allows a collection of users to share a common page and message board. Anyone can create a group, and a group's moderator can approve or deny anyone from joining. Some examples of MySpace groups are a special hobby such as surfing or scrapbooking, an illness support group, or the fans of a particular band.

MySpaceIM. In spring 2006, MySpace introduced the standalone software MySpaceIM—the company's own brand of instant messenger. MySpaceIM uses the member's account information to log in to its service. MySpaceIM USERS get instant notification of new MySpace messages, friend requests, and comments, which can be received on your computer, your PDA, or even your mobile telephone. This way you can stay in constant contact with all of your MySpace friends.

MySpaceTV. In the first quarter of 2007, MySpace introduced its version of YouTube, MySpaceTV. MySpace is also talking about providing this content on conventional television.

MySpace Mobile. MySpace fully understands the importance of the mobile telephone, and has created a variety of ways in which users can experience MySpace content on their cell phones. American cell phone provider Helio released a series of mobile telephones in 2006 whereby MySpace members can access and edit their own profiles as well as viewing others' in MySpace

Mobile. UIEvolution, a company that provides cross-platform access to data, and MySpace have also developed a mobile version of MySpace that works on a wider range of carriers, including AT&T, Vodafone, and Rogers Wireless. (For more information on mobile telephone marketing, see Chapter 22, The Formidable Fourth Screen (Mobile).)

MySpace News. In April 2007, MySpace launched a service called MySpace News that allows users to link to and display reports from their favorite RSS news feeds. MySpace News also lets members rank each news story by vote. As it is with Digg, a community-based news article popularity web site that combines social bookmarking, blogging, and syndication, the more votes a story gets, the higher up the page it moves. (For more information on RSS, see Chapter 19, RSS—Really Simple Syndication Made Simple.)

MySpace Classifieds. In August 2006, MySpace added full-service classified advertising that lets you buy and sell, find a job, and more—like you would see in any newspaper or online classified ads. MySpace Classifieds grew 33 percent in the first year alone.

MySpace Karaoke. On April 29, 2008, MySpace launched its MySpace Karaoke (ksolo.myspace.com), a feature that allows users to upload to their profile page their favorite audio recordings of themselves singing Karaoke. Friends of the user can then view and rate the performances. MySpace president Tom Anderson has stated that the video version will soon be available.

MySpace Polls. MySpace Polls is a feature that allows users to post polls on their profile and share them with other users. You can create your own unique polls such as for baby names, video of the week, favorite holiday, favorite Christmas movie, long hair or short hair, hottest guys, who is the best athlete, and so on.

MySpace Forum. MySpace also provides its users with the ability to create and participate in forums, such as automotive; business and entrepreneurs; campus life; career center; comedy; computers and technology; culture, arts, and literature; fashion; filmmakers; food and drink; games; and so on. (For more information on forums, see Chapter 7, The Internet Forum.)

Politics. Every 2008 presidential hopeful—from the most popular candidate to the lesser-known, minor-party participants—created a MySpace profile in the hopes of soliciting younger voters. Their profiles featured blogs, photos, and videos, and several involved and engaged their constituents in their campaigns through MySpace forums and features. Many people believe that Barack Obama's zeal for MySpace and social media had a significant impact on his voter turnout, which may have swayed the election in his favor.

Candidates aren't the only group that has utilized the power of MySpace connections. Political organizations such as Greenpeace, the ACLU, and Food Not Bombs have created MySpace profiles to keep in touch with and engage their membership base to keep in contact, to post events and information about proposed new legislation, and to inform, educate, and just build community.

Child Safety Issues. MySpace Senior Vice President Angela Courtin has made it very apparent that child safety is a matter of the utmost importance—and that MySpace takes every step possible to protect kids. For one thing, a user must be at least fourteen years old in order to create an account on MySpace, and age groups for fourteen- and fifteen-year olds are automatically set to private. Members who are sixteen years old and older have the option of setting their profiles to public or private, which means that no one can view or message a member under the age of sixteen. MySpace will also delete any profile and block the IP address of anyone suspected of inappropriate behavior.

LinkedIn: LinkedIn is an online professional contact database that was founded in December 2002 and launched in May 2007. The site allows its members to create a profile and network with the other 25 million LinkedIn members from over 150 industries. LinkedIn was established by former PayPal vice president Reid Hoffman, who is currently the company's president of product and chairman of the board. Dan Nye, previously executive vice president and general manager, investment management, of Advent Software, serves as its CEO (see Figure 3.2).

The typical LinkedIn member is forty-one years old with an average household income of $109,704. Sixty-four percent of members are male, and 80.1 percent are college graduates. Job title breakdowns are as follows: chairperson, 7.8 percent; executive/senior vice president, 6.5 percent; senior management 16 percent; middle management 18 percent; and 50 percent are decision makers.

FEATURES. The purpose of LinkedIn is to provide an online professional contact database of its members, and to allow them to link their profiles with those of people whom they know and trust—their connections. The LinkedIn user can invite anyone who is a LinkedIn member to connect with them. This list of connections then increases exponentially in value, due to the connections of your connections and their connections.

FIGURE 3.2 LinkedIn

The LinkedIn value proposition is often referred to as the Kevin Bacon effect. This makes reference to a popular trivia game called *Six Degrees of Kevin Bacon,* where a player names an actor in a movie, then an actor who has starred with that actor, then an actor who has starred with the second actor. This continues until you have named an actor who has also starred with Kevin Bacon within six contacts or degrees of separation. The concept for the game stemmed from a 1994 comment by Bacon that he had "worked with everybody in Hollywood or someone who's worked with them." The surprising part is that this always seems to work—not just with Kevin Bacon, but with anyone. This is based on the unproven, but amazingly effective idea that everyone on the planet can be connected through a chain of acquaintances by only four other people in between.

Primary or first connections on LinkedIn—people whom the user knows directly and to whom they are immediately linked—can be viewed and contacted at any time. Second-degree connections are contacts that the people you know, know; and third-degree connections are the contacts that *they* know, and so on. This continuous linking allows the LinkedIn member to see connections and be part of a trusted network that would otherwise be impossible to establish.

Members use LinkedIn to find jobs and business opportunities in response to recommendations from a contact in their network. Employers can list job opportunities and search for potential candidates, and job seekers can review the profiles of the person who is hiring to discover who in their first-, second-, or even third-connection contact list can introduce them. This design permits the member to see the relationships, but only contact someone they don't know through the chain of people they do know—a process that protects the privacy and integrity of the members from spamming and unwanted solicitation, and an approach that builds trust within the network.

If this is the first time you have heard of the LinkedIn six-degrees approach, it may seem confusing to you. A real-life example may help, from the content-creation stage for *The Social Media Bible.* When creating the list of Executive Conversations for *The Social Media Bible* web site, one of the authors researched and listed *New York Times* best-selling authors, CEOs, founders, and senior vice presidents of the largest companies in the world within the social media ecosphere. But how was a telephone call arranged with the CEO of a Fortune 500 company? How does one possibly walk in off the street, get past the gatekeepers, and begin a chat with a company founder or president? Typically it doesn't happen, but if you *know* people—or know people who know people—it could take place. (See James Burnes, MediaSauce for an example: blog www.blog.mediasauce .com/2009/01/09/linked-in-is-a-sales-secret-weapon/. Go to www.theSocial MediaBible.com for "clickable links.")

When writing Chapter 17, Virtual Worlds—Real Impact, Second Life was identified as the largest virtual world player in this space. The CEO of Second Life is Mark Kingdon—a natural subject for an interview. A LinkedIn search turned up Kingdon, and the site showed that he was three degrees separated from one of the authors. The chain of acquaintances revealed a direct contact named Doug Bruhnke, who was directly connected to someone named Steve, whom Bruhnke had worked with in the past. And Steve had gone to college with Mark Kingdon. Bingo!

Now, what do you think the odds were of getting in touch with Kingdon via a close friend and colleague? Very good, of course. And—given that there is good reason—what are the odds that his friend would pass an e-mail on to an old college roommate? Very good again. Sure enough, within 30 minutes of the initial contact with Doug, the author received a call from Mark Kingdon. That's the power of LinkedIn, and that's the power of belonging to one or more trusted networks.

Answers. LinkedIn has a feature called Answers (similar to Yahoo! and Google's Answers features), where users get to toss out a question to the entire community. This free feature is a very effective way of solving your most complex problems, and finding answers to questions like: who has a shopping-cart solution for a medium-sized online company, or where can one find an attorney who understands international copyright law, or does anyone know how to import products from China?

Groups. Like many other social and professional networks, LinkedIn has searchable Groups wherein a member can create a group about a particular topic—and other members can join the group to discuss a common interest or industry, hobby, college, religion, or political viewpoint. LinkedIn Groups are similar to forums (see Chapter 7, The Internet Forum for more on this topic).

Other. In addition to groups, forums, and personal connections, LinkedIn also offers its members the ability to conduct their own polls. Similar to the MySpace Polls, LinkedIn allows you to create and execute your own polls. Send them to your network, and it's free; send them outside your network, and you pay $50 minimum per response. In February 2008, the site launched a mobile version that gives access to LinkedIn over a mobile telephone and is available in six different languages: Chinese, English, French, German, Japanese, and Spanish.

BusinessWeek blogger Jon Fine wrote in his blog Coolfer: "What Do You Get for Two Million MySpace Friends and 26 Million Streams?"

Atlantic rapper T.I. has passed 2 million MySpace friends, his MySpace page has over 82.6 million views, and his hit single "Whatever You Like" has over 27 million streams at MySpace. Right now all of the songs at his MySpace page are collectively getting well over 1 million streams per day and to date have streamed over 138 million times.

How does all that translate into cash?

Contextual advertising on a MySpace page can bring in $15,000 per day if visitors listen to 1.5 million streams (which T.I. will easily exceed today). Those streams would generate even more revenue if the songs had an Amazon.com buy button (which they do not yet have). That's $105,000 in ad revenue for one week. Album sales, assuming a 15/85 digital/physical split, brought in (roughly) $5.42 million. First-week sales of "Whatever You Like" brought in $235,000 (ignoring here a la carte sales from other tracks on the album, as well as ringtones). The total of the three is $5.76 million. That's $3.75 per MySpace friend (again, not including ringtones). . . .

For the complete article, go to www.coolfer.com/blog/archives/2008/10/ what_do_you_get.php, or go to www.theSocialMediaBible.com to click the link.

Providers

There are a lot of different social network platforms, and a host of various social network providers. You can even create your own network with web sites like Ning, which allows you to create your own branded MySpace-type pages, or host your own social network with WordPress' BuddyPress (see Chapter 6, The World of Web Pages, and Chapter 8, The Ubiquitous Blog). The sheer volume and variation of providers are too numerous to list here, but some examples are Fast Pitch!, which is a professional network focused on your company instead of the individual (go to www.theSocialMediaBible.com to hear Bill Jula's (founder of Fast Pitch!) Executive Conversation). Then there are ACTORSandCREW, Adult FriendFinder, Advogato, ANobii, aSmallWorld, ASUIsTalking, Avatars United, Badoo, Bahu, Bebo, Biip, BlackPlanet, Boomj .com, Broadcaster.com, Buzznet, CafeMom, Cake Financial, Capazoo, Care2, Classmates.com, Cloob, College Tonight, DeviantART, DontStayIn, Elftown, Eons.com, Erotas Online, Espinthebottle, Experience Project, Facebook, Faceparty, Fetlife, Flixster, Flickr, Fotolog, Friends Reunited, Friendster, Frühstückstreff, Fubar, Gaia Online, Gather, Geni.com, Goodreads, Gossip report.com, Grono.net, GuildCafe, Habbo, hi5, Hospitality Club, Hyves, imeem, IRC-Galleria, itsmy, iWiW, Jaiku, Jammer Direct, kaioo, Last.fm, Library Thing, lifeknot, LinkedIn, LiveJournal, Livemocha, LunarStorm, MEETin, Meetup.com, MiGente.com, Mixi, mobikade, MocoSpace, MOG, Multiply, Muxlim, MyChurch, MyHeritage, MySpace, myYearbook, Nasza-klasa.pl, Net log, Nettby, Nexopia, Ning, Odnoklassniki.ru, OkCupid, Orkut, OneWorldTV, OUTeverywhere, Parlus, Passado, Passportstamp, Pingsta, Plaxo, Playahead, Playboy U, Plurk, ProfileHeaven, quarterlife, RateItAll, Ravelry, Reunion.com, Ryze, scispace.net, Shelfari, Skyrock, Sonico.com, Soundpedia, Stickam, Student.com, StudiVZ, Tagged.com, Taltopia, TravBuddy.com, Travellerspoint, tribe.net, Trombi.com, Tuenti.com, Twitter, V Kontakte, Vampirefreaks, Vox, WAYN, WebBiographies, Windows Live Spaces, Wis.dm, Xanga, XING, Xiao nei, Yelp, Inc., and Youmeo.

Top Social Media Sites (ranked by unique worldwide visitors November, 2008 comScore) blog.socialmedia.com/social-media-still-growing-a-lot/

1. Blogger (222 million)

2. Facebook (200 million)

3. MySpace (126 million)

4. WordPress (114 million)

5. Windows Live Spaces (87 million)

6. Yahoo! Geocities (69 million)

7. Flickr (64 million)

8. hi5 (58 million)
9. Orkut (46 million)
10. Six Apart (46 million)
11. Baidu Space (40 million)
12. Friendster (31 million)
13. 56.com (29 million)
14. Webs.com (24 million)
15. Bebo (24 million)
16. Scribd (23 million)
17. Lycos Tripod (23 million)
18. Tagged (22 million)
19. imeem (22 million)
20. Netlog (21 million)

Type in en.Wikipedia.org/wiki/List_of_social_networking_websites or go to www.theSocialMediaBible.com web site for all of the links.

Expert Insight

Angela Courtin, senior vice president of Marketing Entertainment and Content, MySpace, www.myspace.com

Angela Courtin

You know, I think the beautiful thing about MySpace is that it's different things to different people. We consider ourselves a Premier Lifestyle Portal that connects friends discovering popular culture, and making a positive impact on the world. We really look at it through a different lens. It really is about the experience . . . your personal experience on the space.

We also have a global community, so we are connecting people both domestically as well as internationally. We are in over 30 territories now; and again, I go back to the idea that it is about the fabric of what social media is: the profile of blogging, instant messaging, e-mailing. And then you also get to stream music and watch videos. You get to upload your own photos. At MySpace, you can go into classified listings. We've just created a new business for small businesses in order to advertise their own wares. You can check out events in your neighborhood, in the state, or in the country.

(continued)

(*continued*)

You can join groups. You can blog on forums and communities. You can search and befriend celebrities as well as bands, TV shows, your high-school and college friends, your fellow mommies—anyone in your network. So it really is what you want it to be and what you make it. . . .

There's really no typical demographic on our site. Our user base is expanding every month, and I think it's a misconception (as you say) that this is a young person's site. We're more than 85 percent over the age of 18, in terms of our user base. And there are 70 million users in the United States alone that have a profile. And if you think . . . one of my most favorite demographic nuggets to share with people is that 40 percent of all moms that are online are on MySpace. . . . That's a huge number, and they are not going there to spy on their kids; they are actually going there to engage in the tools that make social networking so powerful, as well as the discovery of content. . . .

I [always] go back to this: you can personalize it the way you want. If you want to have a very robust page, you can. If you want to keep it simple, you can do that as well. If you want to build a playlist of your favorite music that you like to listen to, or you just want to have a single track, there's that capability to expand and contract. It's really up to the user. . . . First and foremost, I think it's all about connecting and communicating—regardless of whether you are contacting your friends or community, or your favorite band or celebrity; but it also takes the next step. So it's *how* we communicate through e-mailing and instant messaging, connecting with people of similar interests, uploading photographs, commenting on photographs, sharing photographs. We make it very easy to stay in touch and maintain connection with your family or community of friends. And so this goes back to the analogy of scrapbooking. . . . It is a way to have a one-to-many conversation if you want to keep it that way . . . like, if you want to upload your baby's photos and send those to your friends and family, you can do that with the touch of a button.

So you can blog and you can share on a daily basis what your musings are on everything from politics to music, to your favorite cupcake joint in the neighborhood, or just whom you connected with. It may be an old high-school friend and you want to share that with your other high-school friends.

And then, of course, we're now creating a portable experience; and now you can take that online experience in MySpace and take it directly to your mobile phone. So you can connect whenever you want to, wherever you are, as long as you have your mobile phone . . . which is incredible for someone who is just an average user, connecting with their friends; but even extrapolating beyond that . . . for a band (whether you're signed or independent) the ability to be able to push out communication to 1,000, 14,000, 140,000, 1.4 million now became very acceptable.

To listen to or read the entire Executive Conversation with Angela Courtin, go to www .theSocialMediaBible.com.

Expert Insight

Krista Canfield, public relations manager, LinkedIn, www.linkedin.com

Krista Canfield

Basically what LinkedIn does is [to] help professionals accelerate their success. They can do that in any number of different ways, whether it be looking for employees and trying to get a bit more background information on them, and what they've done in the past and who they've worked with in the past. We've even had companies that have acquired other companies through the web site. Small business owners are using the answers portion of LinkedIn to get advice on building their business and taking it to the next level. So, it really depends on what success means to you, but LinkedIn can definitely help in a variety of different ways. . . .

One company actually got acquired by the Weather Channel, and LinkedIn helped facilitate that whole process. There was [someone who] knew that his company was going to be the perfect fit for the Weather Channel; he just wasn't sure how to get in front of the right person. So what he did was actually search for the person on LinkedIn that might be the right contact at the Weather Channel, sent him an e-mail and began an e-mail dialogue; and within a few months his company ended up getting acquired by the Weather Channel. So this is a demonstration of how LinkedIn can get you in touch with the right people and to make sure you are getting your business ideas, your own personal brand in front of the right people. . . .

It's very cool! And, you know, it's all about leveraging your relationships. I think the whole idea of creating LinkedIn in the first place was to keep in contact with all the different people that you've worked with in the past: friends, family members, coworkers, all those sorts of things. You know, a lot of times if you get someone's business card and you want to get in touch with them three years later down the line, and you do need that reference or you need that recommendation . . . a lot of times that person has switched roles and they're at a different company . . . and that e-mail address and phone number may no longer be of use to you. So, first and foremost, [the site] was meant to be a way to stay in touch with all of the people that you have worked with in the past, even if they have changed positions or switched companies. But the other thing that it really enables you to do is to find the right person who is going to be the right contact for you, no matter *what* company they may be at. If you're working on the relationship that you already have, you never know whom your best friend may know. . . . Chances are that one of your contacts

(continued)

(continued)

already works at a totally different company in a totally different world from what you do; so they have a whole different network of people that you could probably utilize that might help you accomplish your goals. It's all about working off of those relationships. It gets things done. . . .

We do offer premium accounts for those members that are looking to reach out to more people outside of their network; but for the most part, that free version can actually help you get a lot done. Some people either jump in there with both feet and try it out, without having to worry about something you need to pay on a monthly basis, until you are ready for that level of commitment. . . .

The average user is around 41 years old, and has a household income of just over $110,000. But we also have everybody—from like high-level CEOs . . . Bill Gates is on LinkedIn. We have professional athletes, like Yao Ming, who has a profile on LinkedIn. Both presidential candidates have profiles on LinkedIn. But we also have over 600,000 small business owners. So there's really a wide range of people that are on the web site, and certainly professionally from every single industry. Yes—over 25 million people across the world!

Well, yeah, we do actually have an API[1] that a number of different sites use. So, if you go to, say, *BusinessWeek*'s or the *New York Times* web site—or if you go to CXO Media (which owns cio.com)—there is another site called "Simply Hired" that's using our API. What's really cool about the API is it will show you—if you are reading an article in *BusinessWeek*—the first company that appears in the headline of the article. And if you give it permission to log into your account simultaneously while you are looking at that article, it will show you—if, say, the article is about Volkswagens—who you know in your network that knows someone who works at Volkswagen. So it is very powerful to a professional who may be looking at an article and saying, "Wow, my company's a great fit for Volkswagen." Or, "I think Volkswagen would be the perfect client for us." Or, "Wow, gee, I'd love to work at Volkswagen." To be able to sit there and say, "Oh, my friend, Joe, is connected to Susan who works at Volkswagen." So, it definitely makes the world a smaller place, and it really helps you get business done much more efficiently. . . .

To listen to or read the entire Executive Conversation with Krista Canfield, go to www .theSocialMediaBible.com.

Expert Insight

Gary Vaynerchuk, Wine Library Director of Operations, Host and Founder of *Wine Library TV*, www.WineLibrary.com

Gary Vaynerchuk

In October 2007 I decided to start video blogging under my name—GaryVaynerchuk.com—to kind of talk about the business behind *Wine Library TV* and just business in general—something I'm obviously very passionate about as well. I wanted a platform for that; and so that's been quite successful for me and has led to a lot of speaking engagements, consulting, and opportunities on that level.

So being very entrepreneurial, that's been fun; being artistic with the wine stuff, that's been fun. So I've been, kind of, scratching multiple itches. . . . I come from the lemonade-stand world, and the baseball-card world, and the snow-shoveling world . . . so I've been very, kind of, entrepreneurial my whole life. What's great about social media and where the world's at now is [that] you have the ability to build much bigger brands much quicker and at much lower price points; and that's a very big change in the way business is done in America.

The gatekeepers are [slightly] out of control . . . have *lost* control actually. No more editor/producer telling you what you can or cannot be, or deciding whether you can speak to the American people or the people of the world actually. We now have tools that allow us to communicate our message, whatever that may be, with zero cost; just the time and effort we put into the community. That is the fundamental shift of what we're living through right now. . . .

And commitment to our community. I think that's really . . . that's the real equalizer to money for somebody small, like myself, compared to the *Wine Spectator,* or a comedian compared to a top-notch comedian that's on Comedy Central. Whoever leverages their community and whoever builds a community better is in a position to win, whatever that may be. And so time, once again, continues to become important; time has become more valuable than ever, and I've already cited that people that care and give back are going to win. And I think that's a very powerful message, a very good message, and a very big opportunity for a lot of people. . . .

I think it's one step at a time. I think a lot of people ask me, "What was the tipping point; when you got on Conan, or you were on Leno, or *Nightline,* or *Wall Street Journal*?" And I think when you don't focus on tipping points and

(continued)

(*continued*)

just focus on pumping out good content—and you focus on hustling every day and answering your e-mail and caring about your community, putting out good content . . . I think you start realizing that you don't need a tipping point and that that's not really what fundamentally separates a victory from a loss. I think that for me it was just pumping out good shows every day and becoming part of the community; leaving comments and blogs and answering my e-mail and creating accounts in things like Facebook and Twitter; you know just working it. And I think that that is the way to success, it's always been; and the only difference is that now your fans and consumers and the people that care about you have the ability to build you quicker and easier and better because they have tools. Word of mouth has changed; not the way you build a brand. . . . Yeah, I mean I think the message is the whole game. I think the less polished it is sometimes, the better. I think that the lighting or the mic or the camera you use is so irrelevant and just such a stumbling block by many producers; many people that want to get into the game spend so much time on trying to figure that part out and that part has no value . . . none! I really think zero. Some of them, you know I mean . . . it's got to be watchable, you've got to be able to hear it, but outside of that, that's the threshold. . . . I think authenticity of the message is what really attaches people to the product, to the service, to the individual. And I think it's quality of message, not quality of the way we consume it, or the video or the sound. So I think it's very obvious what works.

You know, people like tradition, and commercials didn't need to get into million-dollar budgets; they just did because they had the money and people weren't making smart decisions, really! I really believe that. So I think that, you know, you've got to really take a step back and understand what people react to; and people react to things that are authentic, real, transparent, and deliver. And listen . . . some people really love watching something in HD; I get that! But I don't think that's going to be the differentiator from victory or defeat. I really don't! . . .

Building community is about giving a crap! That's where I separated myself from everybody else, or whoever else . . . I mean, those other people do a great job, but to me it's about really caring about your user base: listening to them, making them involved, letting them participate, caring about their thoughts, letting them have their say in molding the direction of what you do. And so to me it's just about caring. It's about taking the extra effort to read your e-mails, to respond to them, to meet them in person, to send them little gifts. To just care; I mean it's a very simple process. It's just one that's costly of time and money and that's something people aren't willing to invest.

To listen to or read the entire Executive Conversation with Gary Vaynerchuk, go to www .theSocialMediaBible.com.

For additional Expert Insights excerpts on this subject, go to www
.theSocialMediaBible.com:

- Chris Pirillo, geek and technology enthusiast
- Robert Scoble, famous blogger and author, Fast Company
- Chris Heuer, founder, the Social Media Club
- Kyle Ford, director, product marketing, Ning
- Stephanie Ichinose, director of communications for Yelp

Commandments

1. **Thou shalt create profiles and groups.**

    Go the most popular social networking sites—MySpace, LinkedIn, Facebook, Fast Pitch!—and create profiles and groups before someone else takes your names. Then create more profiles on lesser-known sites as well.

2. **Thou shalt use Open Social.**

    Google's Open Social/Open ID program will allow you to create a social networking profile and propagate it with just a click of the mouse. Just go to a new social networking web site, create a profile, and click Open Social ID and the profile is completely filled in. This will save you a lot of time typing in the same information over and over for each profile.

3. **Thou shalt participate.**

    Start out by reading the comments on a few selected sites and listen to where the conversation is headed. Once you have an idea about how to appropriately respond, then participate.

4. **Thou shalt build your own network.**

    Start building a following with your blog. Comment on other blogs and join in the conversation. Then consider building your own Group or social network by using Ning or WordPress Group Platform.

Conclusion

The key to networking—as with all of the social media tools—is to participate. Go to the sites mentioned in this chapter—LinkedIn, MySpace, Facebook, Flickr, YouTube—and any other social network platform you can think of and create your profile and groups. If you don't, someone else will take your name or industry group—and it will be lost forever. Use Google Open

Social or Open ID, which will allow you to fill in new profiles with the click of a button and will save you a great deal of time.

Chris Heuer, founder of the Social Media Clubs International, and Robert Scoble, famous Microsoft blogger, continuously say that to be successful in networking, first listen, then participate. It's like being at a social gathering.

So—join the party! You wouldn't walk into a party, step over to a group of people talking, interrupt, and immediately start telling them about yourself. (Well, maybe once.) But this is how people are currently marketing; and it's not really working that well. First, you have to actually be at the party. Then, you walk over, listen for a while, and then join in on the conversation with something valuable and appropriate to add. Social media marketing for businesses is exactly the same thing. To repeat, because it's important: you first have to be at the party, and then select a group, listen to them—and *then* join in with something valuable. That's how you build community, and that's how you build trust both off line and online.

To hear Kevin Marks, technology advocate for Google, talk about Open Social, and Chris Heuer and Robert Scoble talking about networking, go to www.theSocialMediaBible.com.

Readings and Resources

Baker, Wayne E. *Achieving Success through Social Capital: Tapping the Hidden Resources in Your Personal and Business Networks*. (Hoboken, NJ: John Wiley & Sons, Inc.)

Barney, Darin. *The Network Society*. (Hoboken, NJ: John Wiley & Sons, Inc.)

Basagni, Stefano, Marco Conti, Silvia Giordano, and Ivan Stojmenoviç, eds. *Mobile Ad Hoc Networking*. (Hoboken, NJ: John Wiley & Sons, Inc.)

Cross, Robert L., and Robert J. Thomas. *Driving Results through Social Networks: How Top Organizations Leverage Networks for Performance and Growth*. (Hoboken, NJ: John Wiley & Sons, Inc.)

Engelbrecht, Andries P. *Fundamentals of Computational Swarm Intelligence*. (Hoboken, NJ: John Wiley & Sons, Inc.)

Fraser, Matthew, and Soumitra Dutta. *Throwing Sheep in the Boardroom: How Online Social Networking Will Transform Your Life, Work and World*. (Hoboken, NJ: John Wiley & Sons, Inc.)

Grewe, Lynne. *Open Social Network Programming*. (Hoboken, NJ: John Wiley & Sons, Inc.)

Halpern, David. *Social Capital*. (Hoboken, NJ: John Wiley & Sons, Inc.)

Hart, Ted, James M. Greenfield, and Sheeraz D. Haji. *People-to-People Fund-Raising: Social Networking and Web 2.0 for Charities*. (Hoboken, NJ: John Wiley & Sons, Inc.)

Nour, David. *Relationship Economics: Transform Your Most Valuable Business Contacts Into Personal and Professional Success*. (Hoboken, NJ: John Wiley & Sons, Inc.)

Silver, David. *The Social Network Business Plan: 18 Strategies That Will Create Great Wealth*. (Hoboken, NJ: John Wiley & Sons, Inc.)

Turner, Bryan. *The New Blackwell Companion to Social Theory*. (Hoboken, NJ: John Wiley & Sons, Inc.)

Downloads

For your free downloads associated with *The Social Media Bible*, go to www.theSocialMediaBible.com, and enter your ISBN number located on the back of the book above the bar code. Be sure to enter the dashes.

Credits

Expert Insights Were Provided By:

Angela Courtin, SUP marketing, MySpace, www.myspace.com.

Krista Canfield, PR manager, LinkedIn, www.LinkedIn.com.

Gary Vanyerchuk, director of operations, Wine Library, www.winelibrary.com.

Technical Edits Were Provided By:

James Burnes, vice president, MediaSauce, www.MediaSauce.com.

Note

1. API (Application Programming Interface) is an organized method for communicating between different computer programs or between different modules of a single program.

CHAPTER 4

Everyone's a Publisher

The next six chapters look at the Publish category of the social media ecosystem. This broad category is a little misleading because technically you can publish all kinds of content, including video, audio, photos, and games. The Publish category has been organized to include the topics of e-mail, web pages, Internet forums, blogs, and wikis—tools that predominantly have been text based. That was yesterday, however. Today, nearly all of the tools in the Publish category can accommodate numerous applications from other categories. Your blog can have video. Your e-mails can include audio. Your wiki can have images, video, and audio. What's important to remember is that with social media, content is king. With the right content, you can attract an audience whose interests, activities, and needs can be monetized. Let's take a quick look at some social media publishing stories and see why (1) content is king, and (2) if you've got content, you are indeed a publisher.

Four Stories of Profitable Social Media Publishers

On his way to becoming a medical doctor, a funny thing happened to Arnold Kim; he became a publisher. Kim's blog site, MacRumors.com, attracts 4.4 million people a month and has emerged as one of the most popular technology destinations on the Web. What attracts that many people each month? A strong dose of speculation, gossip, rumor, user tips, and other information about Apple Computer and its products. What began as a hobby in 2000, before the term *blog* was a household word, has turned into an influential resource that experts estimate could be sold for $25 million or more. Dr. Kim, who recently left his medical practice and a six-figure income, has no immediate plans to sell his site, but he has easily

replaced his physician's salary with a six-figure income from MacRumors
.com, thanks to Google text advertising, banner ads, and sales commissions
from products promoted on the site. Though it's improbable that Apple will
ever become an advertiser on his site, companies such as Verizon, Audible
.com, and CDW have recognized the value of Kim's sizable audience.

Candy Is Dandy and E-Mail Is Swell

DailyCandy.com is a free daily e-mail whose national edition and 12 city-
specific editions sends a daily e-mail to its subscribers with information
about "hot new restaurants, designers, secret nooks, and charming diver-
sions in your city and beyond." The demographics of DailyCandy's audience
have attracted numerous advertisers eager to get closer to a group with
above-average household income and a penchant for the finer things in life.
The site features not only banner ads but a virtual window-shopping experience that showcases some of DailyCandy's favorite online shops. In August
2008, the cable company Comcast bought DailyCandy for approximately
$125 million.

Mommy Blogs

At Dooce.com, Heather Armstrong writes a mommy blog and has an audience of 850,000 readers who can't seem to get enough of her humorous
advice, insight, and perspective for modern-day mothers. Companies such as
Walgreens, JCPenney, Crate & Barrel, and W Hotels have paid handsomely
to engage the audience of Dooce, which has become a cash cow for Armstrong and her husband, both of whom quit their regular jobs to tend to the
site fulltime.

Breaking Up Is Hard to Do

At DivorcingDaze.com, you can hear two women from Manhattan, both
named Laurie, "share their adventures in divorce in this unique podcast,
always over a glass of wine. Or three." The site describes itself as "funny, sexy,
honest, and uncensored," and invites listeners to join their conversations on
"moms, marriage, breakups, sex, girlfriends, kids and parenting and city
life." The podcasts receive extremely high ratings—you can read them on
iTunes—and have an estimated 10,000 listeners. Advertisers on Divorcing
Daze.com include Avon, Hanes, and online lingerie retailer HerRoom.
Though the Lauries may be making some money via their podcasts, an
ex-husband decided to sue his former Laurie for producing content that was

"obnoxious, derogatory, or offensive," in violation of their divorce settlement, which prohibited Laurie from harassing or maligning him. The New York State Supreme Court ruled that her statements were covered by the First Amendment and consequently were not grounds for blocking the podcasts. The court did note, however, that some of the podcasts included statements that may be "ill-advised and do not promote co-parenting."

What's In It for You?

Before you start a new blog or master the particulars of podcasting, consider three compelling reasons to seriously think of your company as a potential publisher: (1) survival, (2) increased revenues, and (3) higher profit margins. Social media is changing the nature of the relationships with your employees, customers, and prospects. Information and opinions about your products and services will proliferate with or without any attempt on your part to control the source and flow of information. Consider Apple's position relative to MacRumors.com and the 4.4 million monthly visitors to that site. Apple cannot shut them down. Indeed, the court of public opinion (the blogosphere) would surely castigate them if they tried. Nor can Apple control what is said about their products and brand on Arnold Kim's site. But they can listen to what is being said about their products and attempt to leverage the wisdom of the crowd that Kim has gathered around him.

Social Media Judo

It may be counterintuitive to think of MacRumors.com as a massive, self-guided focus group, but imagine how much it would cost Apple to engage that many people to offer candid feedback about its offerings. You can bet on the fact that people inside Apple, whether officially or unofficially, are among the legions of visitors to MacRumors.com. And while they may have to sift through information they consider toxic to their brand, they may also discover ways to improve their products. In other words, the success of MacRumors.com as a respected publisher could actually be helping Apple increase revenues and profitability by aggregating valuable information for them. To see this as a viable tactic, you must be willing to believe in social media judo—using your opponent's mass, might, and energy to your advantage. If learning a little judo is what it takes to get your business to the next level, most businesspeople would be ready for the first lesson immediately.

Could social media judo help the ex-husband of one of the Lauries at DivorcingDaze.com? Suing for damages did not prove to be a winning strategy, but perhaps he could publish his own blog or podcast to counter the objectionable content on his ex-wife's site. There is, of course, an opportunity cost to be considered. The time Laurie's former spouse could spend publishing his reasoned counterpoints may have no financial benefit to him whatsoever. Were he a public figure whose very name had brand cachet, it might be wise for him to mount a publicity campaign via the blogosphere or through his own podcasts—as a form of damage control. Damage control is usually about survival, and it requires a defensive posture.

To really practice social media judo, however, Laurie's ex-husband would have to leverage the momentum of her audience for his benefit. How many of her 10,000-member audience might be interested in his perspective? How many men who have never heard of her site could become a member of his audience as a result of sympathizing with his efforts to counter the content offered by DivorcingDaze.com? How many companies have products or services that could be promoted to the audience that could be gathered by Laurie's ex-husband? Finally, what if Laurie and her ex-husband could develop a cooperative business strategy that would help them both? As the old saying goes, anything is possible in love and war.

Introducing Coopertition

Here's a word your spell checker won't recognize, though Laurie and her ex-husband might want to look it up for future reference: coopertition. The wiki-based Urban Dictionary (www.urbandictionary.com) defines coopertition as

> a hybrid of cooperation and competition . . . the term coined for the teaming up of two rival companies. The whole concept of "coopertition" is based on the idea of teams helping each other to compete. In simplistic terms, coopertition occurs when two or more vendors can go to market in one space, then be competitive in another space—partners and competitors.

This is a new concept for many businesspeople, but one that is gaining wider acceptance. If you view yourself as a social media publisher, not only will your content benefit from a plethora of links to and from other content sites, but your audience will expect it. Two travel services companies, TripAdvisor.com and Orbitz.com, exemplify the idea that your content can both compete and cooperate.

TripAdvisor.com has aggregated over 20 million reviews and opinions about hotels and destinations from real travelers. These ratings and traveler comments can be useful for anyone planning a trip but wanting to avoid the hype you might get from a hotel's own web site. Indeed, what could be better than having a few dozen or few hundred people rate the quality of the rooms, the service, the cleanliness, and the overall value of a hotel you might want to book for a few nights? In addition, when you're ready to book a room, TripAdvisor.com will help you shop for the best rate by linking you to several sites that specialize in online hotel reservations. Among these sites are Hotels.com and Expedia.com; both are sister companies of TripAdvisor.com and part of the Expedia Inc. family of companies. You'll also be linked to Orbitz.com, a competitor, and not part of the Expedia family.

What's the value of TripAdvisor.com sending someone away from its site, or those of a sister company, to Orbitz.com? It builds credibility for TripAdvisor.com because they appear to make the process of selecting and booking a hotel room more transparent for the consumer. They are not attempting to control their consumer's experience, and that also builds credibility. This credibility translates into consumer loyalty that manifests itself as 32 million monthly visitors and over 9 million registered users to TripAdvisor.com-branded sites. Orbitz.com offers ratings and reviews from travelers, and in this respect is a direct competitor to TripAdvisor.com, but somehow the coopertition has made both of these companies stronger.

Incidentally, TripAdvisor.com offers links from their home page to partner sites where you can book a cruise, find a cheap flight, read a travel guide, or create your own travel blog—once again, an example of proactively sending your customer somewhere else for content. Though this is a counterintuitive tactic, you are ultimately rewarded for this kind of cooperation.

Increasing Your Company or Brand Value

Let's return to Arnold Kim for a moment. The reason Dr. Kim might expect MacRumors.com to sell for $25 million is because of the size of his audience and the traffic patterns of that audience. A traffic pattern refers to how members of an audience behave and interact with your content. Kim's content is such that his readers return regularly for the latest news and rumors about Apple. What's more, many of them take an active role and actually contribute content, comment on content, or refer content to others. This type of audience activity makes MacRumors.com a sticky site, one that captures and holds visitors' attention. The site also has tremendous value to those who want to get close to Kim's audience. Furthermore, his content has high viral value in that a significant number of his visitors promote, share, or refer his content to others, some of whom then venture to the site for the first time. As this pattern is repeated, the audience grows, and so does its loyalty. The same principle is in play at TripAdvisor.com. The traffic patterns and the collaborative behavior of those who frequent the site make the brand a more valuable commodity.

Audience size and traffic patterns are not new concepts, however. Traditional media, newspapers, magazines, radio, and television have lived and died on their ability to present content that is sticky enough to get people to return regularly. Consequently, their advertising rates have been based upon audience size and traffic patterns. Yet, how many radio or television stations have made it a practice to send listeners or viewers to a competitive station? Historically, how many magazines or newspapers have enabled readers to help create content? Again, that was then. Today you'll find these traditional media welcoming both coopertition and user-generated content.

Monetize Your Expertise

One of the things the four publishers profiled at the beginning of the chapter have in common is that they were able to monetize their expertise. All of them had special knowledge or a unique perspective that they were able to convert into content that then attracted an audience. Another thing they had in common is that none of them exists in a bricks-and-mortar world. They are children of the Internet. This raises an interesting question for companies that transact business in the offline world. How do you create content and monetize your expertise, for example, if you are an auto repair shop, a bakery, or a wholesale lumber supply company? And what if it simply doesn't make sense for you to create content for the purpose of attracting advertising revenue from entities that may want to get close to your customers?

As the Web becomes more pervasive in everyday life, you need to determine how many of your customers or prospects are already online and how they behave online. Though this will be addressed in Part III of this book, it's important to figure out now what kind of content makes sense for you to publish, especially if you do business in the bricks-and-mortar world.

Would it be valuable to people who drive cars, for example, to learn something about how to get more miles out of a vehicle and avoid costly repairs? Probably. Ironically, the content that an auto repair shop might produce could have the effect of showing people how to eliminate or mitigate the need for repair shop services. Practically, however, the expertise demonstrated by the content and its publisher would engender a notion of credibility and trustworthiness that not all people in the auto repair business have attained. Now consider how that content could be enhanced with a combination of text, video, audio, and photos. Suddenly a virtual presence on the Web, where your expertise is translated into valuable content that is sticky and viral, can lead consumers to your real-world auto repair shop.

And what if those who become enamored with your content live 500 miles away? It's not likely that they'll drive that far to have their car repaired, but as your audience builds critical mass there are ways to focus locally. A supportive comment or quote from someone in the next state who finds your content very valuable could influence someone in your own area to visit your shop. Should your content make you a minor star on the Internet, you might take a page from brothers Tom and Ray Magliozzi, the stars of *Car Talk,* the most popular show on National Public Radio, and sell T-shirts, hats, and other branded merchandise. If you should become that popular, you might want to revisit the idea of selling access to your audience via advertising.

How would you develop content around your expertise if you owned a bakery or ran a lumber supply business? Better yet, how will you it do for your current business?

Back to the Beginning

The social media ecosystem requires you to think like a publisher; it is in the DNA of the human species to engage one another with things that inform, educate, and entertain. The gift of language itself has made everyone audience members. Listening, watching, and understanding enable people to function as part of a group. New technologies have enhanced the ability to engage one another. Social media may be the newest and arguably the most fascinating tools for engagement, but they are by no means the oldest.

From the time people lived in caves, content has been designed to engage one another. One of the earliest known cave paintings, located in southern France, depicts two people using straws to drink what is believed to be beer from a large, vaselike clay container. The straws were used to filter sediments. Beer, of course, was often safer than water. Why the cave painting was created is not known. It may have been designed to educate others in the tribal community, or it may also be the first known instance of a beer commercial.

Moving ahead to the fifteenth century, the invention of the printing press and moveable type revolutionized the creation and distribution of content. Suddenly people were able to communicate and share knowledge locally and across great distances. The printing press also ushered in a new form of education and entertainment—the book, which was initially owned by the wealthy or privileged classes and read to others by the literate. Advances in printing technology and distribution channels allowed the publishing industry to develop and thrive. Literacy rates climbed, and new forms of commerce were enabled. Over the years, consumer culture and behavior have been heavily influenced by Gutenberg's invention.

The telephone, radio, and television had similar impacts on society and business. Initially they were technologies used only by a few, but soon they became common household appliances. As they became more common, entrepreneurs, businesspeople, and bureaucrats found ways to leverage opportunities and create value using these tools. Content has been the common denominator of their success. Yes, even the telephone has relied upon content to achieve success and assimilation. Chat lines, 900 numbers, and offers from countless telemarketers testify to the importance—though not necessarily the value—of content. With the advent of mobile phone technology (discussed later in the book), a digital convergence is occurring where virtually all forms of media are now available via wireless phones.

It is now possible to watch an ESPN sportscast or download and listen to music and podcasts on your cell phone. Many mobile phones include photo and video functions that allow you to create, store, and share your own content. Recently LexCycle, the company that created an application called Stanza, a digital book reader for the Apple iPhone, announced that over 500,000 people have downloaded their e-book reader. The only thing that appears to be limiting its growth is the availability of content. Rest assured, more content is on the way.

What You Need to Know

You need to be familiar with some basic principles if you are going to become a successful social media publisher. Many of these are discussed in more detail in later chapters, but it's important to encounter and understand them now, in the context of the discussion about content.

Find a Voice That Can Fill a Need or Solve a Problem

The success of practically any business is dependent upon meeting consumer needs and solving problems with a well-positioned product or service. The same is true of content. What Heather Armstrong of Dooce.com discovered is that today's mothers have given themselves permission to be slightly ir-reverent, sarcastic, and even offbeat at times. She's positioned herself to be a voice for these women. Through her blogs, daily photos, and video mom-versations, her audience—all 850,000 of them—recognize a little bit of themselves in Heather. She's like one of those kids from high school who had the uncanny and enviable ability to say exactly what you wished you could have said first. A few hours later, you find yourself telling a friend something wickedly funny or wonderfully profound that she said.

So what need is Heather meeting? The need of her cohorts to be respected, relevant, and hopeful in a demanding, sometimes chaotic society. Heather has tapped into the common feelings, attitudes, and accepted beliefs of her audience. Can you do the same for your audience?

Establish Audience Archetypes or Personas

An audience is hardly a collection of carbon-copy beings waiting to be engaged. Your audience has some common needs and attitudes, but each person is unique. Because you cannot match your content to every audience member, it's necessary to create audience archetypes or personas by finding shared characteristics among the group segments. There are different ways to categorize people, but a good way to start creating these personas is to group your audience into four or five categories using particular demo-graphic or behavioral characteristics. Ask yourself the following kinds of questions about your audience:

- What are their age ranges?
- What kinds of towns and neighborhoods do they live in?
- What are their different education and household income levels?
- What do they like to do for fun and entertainment?
- What do they hope for?
- What do they worry about?
- What do they spend money on?

In many cases, your audience and your customers (or your employees) are one and the same, so the more you know about them already, the more prepared you'll be to begin creating personas. Don't be afraid to hone these personas or change them altogether if they don't seem to be working for you.

Recently the U.S. State Department has discovered the importance of audience archetypes on its DipNote blog (www.blogs.state.gov/). The site, created in 2007, now has an audience of more than 2 million. On the site, you'll find blogs and YouTube press conferences. According to a State

Department spokesperson, the blogs appeal more to older audience members while the YouTube press conferences attract a younger audience.

Create a Community

Your content should have the effect of drawing people together in the same way that a successful sports bar brings football fans together on a Sunday afternoon. People like to interact with one another and belong to groups with common goals and interests. That said, people do not like to be told what to do or forced to behave in ways that may seem contrary to their self-interests. Too much structure and too many rules will stifle your community. You must be willing to let the community evolve organically. Remember, you have influence but not control.

Creating a successful online community around your content means that you must help define the community's purpose. In keeping with our sports bar analogy, let's say your expertise happens to be beer—microbrews in particular. Is the purpose of your community to share information and tips about home brewing? Or is it to identify and rate the brewpubs of North America? These are two distinctly different purposes. Choosing the wrong purpose will impede your efforts to build a community.

Make It Free

There is a general expectation that things on the Web should be free. While there are some notable exceptions to this rule of thumb, you should be willing to make a lot of valuable content absolutely free and available to everyone. Things such as How-To reports, white papers, and other information that showcase your expertise should be highlighted as *free* and made easily accessible. Lest you think you cannot make any money by giving things away, recall the word "freemium," introduced earlier in this book.

Freemium is a word coined by Fred Wilson, a venture capitalist who in March 2006 was looking for a word to describe a new kind of business model in which online services were given away free in an effort to attract a lot of customers. The second part of the model involves presenting (or up-selling) an enhanced version of your product or service for a fee, or a premium. An interesting aside to this story is that Wilson didn't actually come up with the name himself. Instead he turned to his blog audience and asked them to suggest possible names for this business model. Jared Lukin, associated with Alcara, one of the companies Wilson had invested in, is credited with having come up with the name. The freemium concept applies here, though keep in mind that content is different than products or services.

Encourage User-Generated Content

Fred Wilson turned to his blog's audience to generate name ideas for a new business model. This is one example of User-Generated Content, or UGC. Arnold Kim welcomes comments and contributions on his site as well. In fact, contributions from his audience are an important part of Kim's success. The MacRumors.com community relies upon the intelligence-gathering, rumor-vetting abilities of the collective group.

Recently, National Geographic launched a UGC site called Everyday Explorers (www.everydayexplorers.nationalgeographic.com). Here is National Geographic's description of the site's purpose:

> There's an explorer in all of us.
>
> You've seen National Geographic's stunning videos capturing life in the wild and in exotic places around the world. Now it's your turn. Grab your camera and get shots of local wildlife and your pets, film your own environmental message, capture weather phenomena as they happen, or create a video travelogue about your favorite place. Post your video here, and check out other Everyday Explorers' clips. You can comment on each other's videos, rate your favorites, and much more.
>
> Shooting video is easy and inexpensive—most digital cameras and many cell phones have video capability—and uploading the clips takes just a few minutes. Your clip may be selected as a featured video, and you might even be contacted by National Geographic to include your film in our professional library.
>
> Become an Everyday Explorer and help us in our mission to inspire others to care about the planet.

In a few short months, people had submitted over 400 videos to the site, and National Geographic is well on its way to creating a loyal community built around common content interests.

The Five Ways that Content Engages People

Once you have created your content, there are only five behaviors that people will exhibit toward that content, and they may exhibit more than one of these at different times.

1. They will willingly become coproducers or content contributors. This is what UGC is all about. There really isn't a better way to engage people than to give them a stakeholder notion.
2. They will comment on content that you or someone else in the community has created. Their comments may serve to endorse or promote your content, or they may function as detractors.
3. They will refer your content to friends or colleagues. This behavior has viral value, but once again it may be done in a positive or negative tone.
4. They will simply read your content. Not a bad thing by any means.
5. They will ignore your content.

Your goal should be to motivate your audience to engage in behaviors one, two, and three as positively as possible. One of the best examples of engaging a community was the 2008 presidential campaign of Barack Obama. The campaign amassed an e-mail database in excess of 10 million names, all of whom he could address by their first name. To give some perspective on that, Obama's audience of supporters is greater than most cable news and interview programs. His supporters were encouraged to add comments, refer content to friends, and generally get involved. More than 3 million of them donated money to his campaign.

Get a Feel for Content Management Systems

Make a note of these tools that will be discussed in Part II:

- Blogger
- Joomla
- Typepad
- WordPress

Each tool is a content management system, sometimes referred to as CMS. These tools make it easier to create, update, and manage your content (including video, audio, photos, and blogs) and your community. As a publisher you will need a CMS. Check out the web sites for the *New York Times* (www.nytimes.com) or CNN (www.CNN.com), and you will see two stellar examples of a CMS in action.

Master the Social Media Press Release

The social media press release (SMPR) or social media release (SMR) functions like traditional press releases in that they present the who, what, where, when, why, and how embodied in a compelling story or angle designed to capture attention for your product, service, or company. But unlike the traditional press release, they can combine the use of video, audio, photos, and text to give the release added dimensions that have previously been too costly or technically difficult to produce.

Can You Really Make Money with Your Content and Your Community?

This chapter has provided some examples of people who are making money with their content and their online communities, but don't believe that it is easy. Here are some things to consider:

- Fourteen percent of male and 11 percent of female Internet users have blogs (according to the 2008 Pew Internet and American Life Project). The vast majority of these people do not make money. However, many of them never had the intention of making money.

- Google estimates that worldwide approximately 175,000 new blogs are born each day. That's a lot of channel noise.

- According to a July 16, 2008, Wall Street Journal Online article by Ben Worthen, most online communities created by businesses fail because "most businesses focus on the value the online community can provide themselves, not the community."

- The same article cites the research of Ed Moran, a Deloitte consultant who studied more than 100 businesses with online communities. Thirty-five percent of them had fewer than 100 members, and less than 25 percent had more than 1,000 members. A high percentage of them failed. Nearly all of them had difficulty gaining traction with their intended audience. Moran points out that many of these businesses become enamored with the various tools and technology when they should have been reaching out to potential community members.

You can make money with your content and you can help your business survive and thrive, but it's not accidental. You need to plan for success.

Expert Insight

John Blossom, founder and author, *Content Nation*, www.contentnation.com

. . . I've been a consultant in the publishing and technology industry for over 10 years and we help publishers and content technology companies with their marketing strategy, including social media as one of the things that they need to get their hands around.

I do a lot of analyses of the content industry. I'm always out there writing on my blog, Content Blogger, and now on Content Nation, www.contentnation.com, about what the trends are in the industry.

John Blossom

And a funny thing happened a couple of years back when Don Tapscott came out with his book, *Wikinomics,* which is a great book. I was reflecting on it and thinking about what the real scope of the influence of this social media trend might be, and I thought back to a Web post that I had done a couple of years earlier. And I noticed something; I started adding up things, if you will. And if you start looking at the current statistics, for example . . . if you add up all the people that are uploading videos in the world, roughly, looking at some stats from Universal Mccann International, a major ad firm, there are about 183 million people today uploading videos; 184 million people publishing Web blogs; 248 million people uploading photos; and 272 million people with social networking profiling services such as FaceBook and MySpace and what have you.

Needless to say, that's a heck of a lot of people. But then I looked at some other research from the Internet and they looked at, "How serious are these people? How many people are just playing around and how many people really want to do something?" And they came up with an interesting stat. They said that 27 percent of bloggers want to really influence other people's thinking. And that really began to carve into some interesting numbers.

For example, if you go out there and you put that number against bloggers, that means there are about 59 million serious bloggers out there in the world trying to influence people. . . .

. . . You add that up and that's the 24th largest nation in the world, about the size of South Korea. If you take it off the social networker population out there, that's about 74 million people. That would make it about the 16th largest nation in the world, about the size of Turkey.

So it began to dawn on me through these statistics that, really there are nation-sized groups of people out there publishing and wanting to influence other people's thinking. And this completely dwarfs what we're used to through traditional publishing media.

So I came up with a concept of *Content Nation.* And in this idea of the world as a nation of publishers, what is beginning to make us feel united and common, increasingly, is this idea of publishing. The idea is that anybody can publish anything to anyone in a highly scalable fashion and in a highly accessible fashion through the tools of social media. . . .

. . . It is staggering, and we're beginning to see how that begins to scale up in terms of its influence on marketing, its influence on enterprises, its influence on how people live their lives. And those that we begin to see, and what I outlined in the book, *Content Nation,* are some of the major trends that we're beginning to see in those sorts of things; that this is not just about people posting Web blogs and getting a little of influence; this is people whose influential publishing, either individually or on a mass scale, all of a sudden begins to change how the world happens and how the world begins to see itself.

One of the simplest examples I have in the very beginning of the book is the execution of Saddam Hussein. . . . A few years ago he was tried and was to be hung for the crimes he was found guilty of, and this was supposed to be a very highly controlled event, hush-hush. Well, what happened? Somebody at the execution has a cell phone with a video built in and was able to record this. And that found its way to the Internet and before long it was completely around the world. So here we had the most powerful nation in the world, the United States, and a sovereign nation in theory, the State of Iraq, unable to control what was one of the most tightly controlled acts by this those two nations, ever!

If you think about that balance of control, that really got me thinking about who's really in charge here. The good news about social media, I think, is not that we're looking at some sort of Marxist thing that's happening. There is room in social media for the powerful in the world and the everyday people. And the beautiful thing about social media is that *Content Nation* is about empowering everybody to work together to make everybody's lives better. . . .

. . . [It's also in the] hands of everyday people, and in the hands of marketers and other people who are trying to figure out, "Well, what is our relationship with people?" So both individuals are empowered, but also people in social systems and economic systems, are empowered to be able to work with one another more effectively. So we are creating more value for one another.

And for some companies, this can be a bit of a challenge, but others, including major companies out there, are learning to accept that this is the way that they need to talk to the marketplace, and learning how to get contact out there that engages people and begins to build their brand as a personal brand alongside other people's personal brands.

So, social media is a very powerful way to communicate with people, but it's also a powerful way for people to focus in, very rapidly and effectively, on what it is people really need and want and to be able to understand those needs rapidly and to deliver on them. . . .

. . . One of my favorite examples . . . is Dell. Dell Computer, a major company, had major problems in understanding the marketplace because it's

(*continued*)

(*continued*)

just so huge, moving so rapidly. How did they find out what it is that people really want and how did they get it into their products? Well, you can do market research and traditional things and the lifecycle of doing that is so long that you'll miss all your market opportunities.

They created an idea-collection web site called "Idea Storm," which is a social media site where people who are enthusiastic about Dell products, that use them, can pump in ideas and problems that they are having. People who are members of that site can click on individual things, vote on specific things that turn them on, and management and people who are working on the Dell-side of this portal can look at things that are happening and say, "Yeah, you're right! We should be able to change this, this, and this."

And then all of a sudden instead of waiting weeks, days, months, and years to get some of these changes in, all of a sudden on a regular basis you're getting blog posts out of "my view" forums. And you say, "I think these are the six or seven things that we're going to be putting effort into this month," or this week.

And so all of a sudden your ability to have conversations with markets and to understand what it is that people really want and need changes altogether. . . .

. . . And they "listened" on a conversational basis; not as in traditional market research where you have the interviewer talking to the marketplace. It's more of a conversational thing; it's peers talking to peers, and as such saying, "You know, that sounds like a good idea." And all of a sudden [it's] rapidly changing policies that might have taken "forever" or a long time, in any event, for a large company to change.

By the same token, I think that this empowers smaller economies and smaller businesses and smaller efforts at collaboration to come together very rapidly to create value in the marketplace. Because the technology is very affordable, or free oftentimes and highly scalable, all of a sudden people with good ideas can come into the marketplace, get visibility, be able to learn how to converse with the people in particular market segments that matter most to them, and be able to deliver to very niche markets, as well. So it's part of what I call "The Big Sombrero Economy." I'm sure you're probably familiar with Chris Anderson of *Wired* magazine's *Long Tales,* where he hypothesized that, "You're going to have a lot of hits, and then there are a lot of things that are manufactured that dwindle off into very small sales, but at a very high rate."

That's all well and good for mass-manufactured goods that have a long lifecycle, but what I see with social media is that we're getting into this curve that's three-dimensional, and it's curving up on the lip there; kind of like a big, fat sombrero that gets a little bit high-up on the ends there, and there's a big, shady part underneath that lip.

I think that through social media, we're creating in the long run, more net value out of small market opportunities that can scale rapidly to immediate and essential needs that may or may not ever scale into mass markets, but in the

. . . You begin to understand that it's not a matter of making more out of mass manufactured stuff but beginning to recognize that through social transactions you can define needs and wants more rapidly and respond to them more efficiently so that we're getting into more of a marketplace where you're talking either "mass-customization" or never going to "mass" in the first place, and meeting people's needs on a very particular basis more effectively.

So social media, for example, helps handmade goods. It helps people who are enthusiasts for sewing. It helps people in Third World economies that might be working on handmade goods and they are trying to raise financing for it and be a marketplace for it. So it helps capital transfer in and out of the marketplace efficiently on many different levels.

And of course, it changes the way that people just plain live. When you think of yourself as a publisher, the world changes. One of my favorite photos I have in the book (I've been compiling all sorts of illustrations in this and the online version of Content Nation.com which I hope get in the print version) is of a concert crowd at the end of a concert. And not so many years ago, the tradition was [that] to request an encore performance you held up your butane cigarette lighter, and now we have the tradition of people holding up their cell phones and they are taking pictures of what's happening there. As a matter of fact, Microsoft is now coming up with a product to try to capitalize on this idea of everybody sharing little clips of concerts, and what have you. They call it *Crowd Fire*. This idea the performer is up there and the audience is responding and saying, "Guess what? We're publishers, too!"

And so, in a way, it's the peers acknowledging . . . the peers saying, "You know what? Creativity is just a natural human thing." And we've been doing it for so long. Creativity and publishing doesn't have to come from the central source, but in fact, it can come from anywhere. . . .

To listen to or read the entire Executive Conversation with John Blossom, go to www.theSocialMediaBible.com.

Expert Insight

Tony Mamone, CEO and founder, Zimbio, www.zimbio.com

. . . We keep growing; it's just a fun thing to be a part of and definitely infectious here in the office just to watch our stats every month going up and up.

(*continued*)

(continued)

Tony Mamone

I think we did about 13 million unique visitors last month, so . . . I guess we need to change the tag line to "more than 10 million readers a month." . . .

. . . *Zimbio* is an interactive magazine. We focus on topics in popular culture, so we cover things like style and entertainment and sports and current events.

My background . . . I guess there's a long story and a short story; I'll go somewhere in the middle. I'm an engineer by training, but have now moved more into a business role. I have an interest and passion for Internet content and have been involved with it for quite a while now, starting off with a project that launched the site Find Articles.com, which was a poor man's version of Lexus Nexus, so it was way to search magazine archives and look up full text articles of popular journals and magazines.

I loved that project, really enjoyed working on it and the site was ultimately sold to C-net. And a few years ago, I decided I wanted to get my hands back into an entrepreneurial effort and create something from scratch, and as I thought about opportunities with my partner we saw real opportunities to do something interesting and innovative in the magazine publishing space.

So, hence, *Zimbio*. And a big part of what we do here at *Zimbio* is we are trying to create the most popular and influential magazine published in the world. We start with our flagship properties in [02:37.2].com. It's quite different from traditional print magazines. In a lot of ways from a reader's perspective, it's not too dissimilar from what you would find in a *People* or *Vogue,* or *Elle* or *Newsweek,* but the way we create it is fundamentally different.

We try to leverage technology to automate a lot of the publishing, and we tap into our members and our readers to actually write and create much of the content. . . .

. . . [I]t's hard to get specific stats, but our best guess is that we're one of the 10 most popular magazines on the Internet right now. There are definitely a few that are above us . . . *People* and *Time* and *Newsweek* still trump *Zimbio,* but we've passed a lot of great brands.

We are more popular than *Entertainment Weekly,* or *Sports Illustrated,* or *US Weekly Online*; and so we focus heavily on digital distribution. We don't have a print version right now. It's not necessarily something that we're going to want because as we look forward and look at what magazine publishing needs to be in 10 years, we believe that the core focus will be digital; and will . . . strip away the need for paper and ink and will sort of move toward the digital distribution model. And so we've just really focused our efforts there and we're doing quite well. . . .

. . . I think the Internet is the core focus and it will be the growth engine for the industry. At the same time, I think that print has a place, especially with magazines. There's just something fun about flipping through the glossy pages of *Rolling Stone* or checking out photos on the beach. I think there will be a place for print; I just believe the core focus of the industry and the growth engine for the industry will be digital. . . .

. . . When we started the demographic, it was a very, sort of Internet-savvy user. People that were surfing and finding these social media sites and, as we've grown, as you approach 10 million plus readers a month, you start to look a lot more like a mass media play; so at this point our readership is really a broad-spectrum of folks who tend to be in the 18- to 34-year-old range. That's where our core concentration is, but they are really evenly spread between males and females and they're also a worldwide audience.

About 50 percent of our audience is here in the United States, but we also have an awful lot of readers in Canada and the U.K. and India and Australia, and other English-speaking markets.

Our aspirations are that hopefully in the not-too-distant future we will start to offer other languages as well and we'll truly become a global brand. So it's a pretty big spectrum of folks that check out *Zimbio* and for different purposes. It's really a consumer magazine and consumer destination site. An awful lot of people are checking it out. . . .

. . . We've got lots of folks in Ireland and all over Europe. And it's kind of fun for me as an employee of the company. I get to come in every day and check out what the most popular stories were. And a lot of times it's a rugby player in Australia, or it's an actress who's quite famous in a different market that I haven't heard of. So it's sort of a neat way to stay up-to-date, not only on popular culture here in the United States but popular culture worldwide. . . .

. . . I think the magazine publishing industry, and really publishing in general is such a robust industry; there are so many publications out there and most readers tend to have many different magazines that they like to read. It's not a one-stop shop. It's not quite as cutthroat as other industries can be. There are plenty of people who read *Zimbio* and they also read a handful of other online magazines, and they subscribe to print; and so there's a little less of the, sort of, cutthroat nature that you might find if it were a conventional publication.

That said, you know I think many of the print magazines and the magazine publishers are starting to look at new media companies as a wave of growth that they're not seeing in their traditional business.

So as folks like the *New York Times* and *Time* start to evaluate their businesses and see that certain profit margins are going away and certain lines of their business aren't growing, you know they're a big company and they're looking for strategic areas of growth. Hopefully *Zimbio* boils up on their radar screen as an example of something that's working. . . .

. . . For my day-to-day job when I come into the office I don't think about what the exit strategy for *Zimbio* is. I think about what we're trying to build.

(continued)

(*continued*)

And that is a longer-term view; it's not this year, it's 5 to 10 years from now. What do we want the company to be and what do we want the brand to represent and how are we going to build an audience and how are we going to attract a readership and a contributor-base that's going to volunteer and continue to work on and improve the site and the content.

And that's just such a fun project that I'm not at all anxious and not in a rush to find an exit for the company. I'm really just having a great time building it. . . .

. . . If you walk up and down the magazine aisle at your supermarket and check out the headlines on the covers, it's a pretty good representation of what you'd find on *Zimbio*. We . . . actually cover a very broad spectrum of topics. You can find things on home décor, pets, and health topics and business topics. But our core focus is on four main categories: style, entertainment, current events, and sports.

And if you look into each of those categories on *Zimbio,* one thing that's unique about the way we cover this is that we tend to cover very specific and niche topics within those categories. So instead of covering celebrities, we cover very specific celebrities. Instead of covering sports, or even certain teams or leagues, we cover the actual athletes.

And what we try to do when you come to an athlete's section on *Zimbio,* is we try to show you a very diverse perspective, so you get a collection of photos and articles about a specific person or specific athlete, or a specific actress, a specific politician . . . and it allows you to deep drill and deep dive into one person who is making the news and making headlines, or that you're interested in. . . .

. . . There's a real craft to this and there's a history. If you look at the history of media, there are many different publications that have discovered that people like to read about other people. That's where it really gets interesting, and especially for a magazine where it's mostly [13:00.4] reading and you're sort of just browsing because you've got some time and you're interested in a topic. It's just great to get into the details of how people make decisions, and which people are involved in which stories. That's an angle that we like to take and it's really worked for us here at *Zimbio.* . . .

. . . Let me tell you a little story about the history of *Zimbio* and how we started, and sort of lead up to how we generate our content today.

When we first started, we really fully embraced user-submitted content. That was the core and 100 percent focus of the site as we launched. And we were encouraging people to submit articles and photos and write polls, and so forth. And for the first 6 to 12 months of the company's history, we continued to just focus on user-generated content.

It allowed us to grow and allowed us to get started and the nice thing about starting a company that's focused on user-generated content is you don't need a lot of front cash, or capital, in order to get started; and so you can begin to build a community and nurture that community . . . and it starts to take shape.

And as we started to grow, we really started to reach out to some of our readers and try and get a better sense for what value they were finding in the site. And as we talked to folks and as we watched them use *Zimbio,* we discovered that . . . they were indifferent to the source of the content. What they were interested in was high quality content and they wanted to see diverse perspectives on each story. So one thing that we offered that other folks didn't was that if they came to read the story about Obama street art and the graffiti artists that were drawing these amazing pieces of art about Barak Obama's candidacy, they saw three or four or five, or even more, different authors writing about it. And that was intriguing to them and was something that they liked. As we dug under the covers and peeled back what was going on there, we discovered that sometimes user-generated or user-submitted content was the best source. But other times there were traditional media sources out there, which we could license or find that would add to the mix.

And so where we have evolved to is we now offer a hybrid between citizen journalism and traditional media. So on *Zimbio* you'll find articles written by everyday people just like you, who want to share their opinion and have taken the time to write an article, or submit pieces of content that they feel are important and noteworthy. And you'll also find licensed articles from traditional sources, like *The Guardian,* or Associated Press, or Reuters, or *Business-Week.* And we try to mix the two, so that for each reader who comes to the site we can offer them the best of content that we have at our disposal. And that includes professional photography, it includes articles, news, and it includes opinion pieces by our membership. . . .

To listen to or read the entire Executive Conversation with Tony Mamone, go to www.theSocialMediaBible.com.

Expert Insight

Stephanie Ichinose, director of communications, Yelp, www.yelp.com

. . . I am the director of communications here so I manage a bunch of different functions. Primarily it is media relations, analysis relations, and the like. I work closely with our management team and I have been with the company since April 2006. Prior to that, I was managing a public relations team for Yahoo! that specifically sat right in the local space. . . .

Stephanie Ichinose

(continued)

(*continued*)

. . . It is a great company, and . . . what started to happen was I, personally, started looking at the competitive landscape. I noticed (this is back in late 2005–2006) that user-generated content was gaining traction in a way that it had not before; and so when I came across Yelp and was looking at them, it just seemed like a really interesting opportunity. . . .

. . . The interesting thing about Yelp and its approach to local search was that we recognized that there was this old model of "word-of-mouth" that existed. It is not even a model; it has just existed since the beginning of time, basically. Individuals would share a lot of interesting and valuable information between each other with these person-to-person conversations. And so it was like, "Where can I find a great doctor? Who's the best mechanic in town for my small, little car that needs some work on it?" And the question at that point is how do we capture these conversations and bring them online?

Initially, we set out to solve that problem and were surprised to find that by building a community of individuals within a particular city we were able to really incite and encourage these conversations. On the back-end, users were really passionate about sharing that information. Yelp started out specifically only in San Francisco. And we focused our first year of operations to building up the site, supporting the community that existed in the Bay area, and tried to figure out what worked/what didn't; that sort of thing.

And then in 2006–2007 it was really a focus more on, "Okay, can we replicate this and push it out to other markets, with the same sort of conversation-topics, in Chicago, in New York, in Boston?"

And we found, pretty quickly in 2006 that, in fact they do. We found that there was just something universal about people wanting to share all of their great hidden gems, or wanting to rave about specific businesses, the "Mom and Pops" that they want to support. And so there was a really interesting dynamic of community (and local community), that really resonated across the nation. . . .

. . . I think it is interesting that when we watch some of our most active Yelpers there is this notion that they are contributing right to the bloggers (or this community in San Francisco, or in their particular area, whether it's Dallas, Austin or Chicago, or wherever they may live); there's this notion of being able to support local businesses, help share that information so that others who are out there that might stumble across the information would find it helpful; and just sort of become a part of the local community of individuals who are passionate about sharing their experiences.

There is a network part of it, which is when you sign up on Yelp, you plug into a community of people who are like-minded, But then the broader effect is that information is then seen by so many more individuals. We have had 14 million unique visitors to the site in the past 30 days. And that number continues to grow and we are really excited about that. We currently have well north of 3.5 million reviews that have been written by Yelpers that contributed to the site.

Therefore, what that tells us is that there is a huge audience of people that are looking for this information and it is great that they are able to utilize this resource. In addition, we are then able to tap into the individual voices of the community, which is even better. . . .

. . . Actually, the co-founders really looked at the Craigslist model and figured out, "Okay, what did they do? What was part of their roll-out, and how did they achieve the success that they've achieved?" Therefore, there are some pages in this playbook; for instance, focusing and looking at individual markets and going deep, which is primarily what we did in 2005 . . .

. . . It has been interesting to watch the . . . part of that which is fueled by our growth in continuing markets. We currently have 21 actively managed communities in the major cities across the United States. But it has been fascinating to watch how each city ignites and how the communities are all very different and they all have their different cultural tones, and so on. But underneath it, all there is the same common thread; as in, "Wow, I am able to finally jump on my soapbox here and share all of my favorites." It is a little bit ego-driven, perhaps, but then the second part of that is about contributing back to the community in a meaningful way that is also heard by others. . . .

. . . I think what has been interesting to watch is that folks have made an analogy to Yelp as, "Oh, you are a social network?" And actually we see ourselves more as a local community site. And that's because when you log into a social network, you're effectively creating your account and inviting your social network to participate and engage, and finding folks who may already exist on that particular platform.

Whereas in Yelp, it's really more about joining a community of like-minded individuals who (guess what!) happen to live within the parameters of your geography, your city, and you all have a common interest. That is what Yelp is all about; that is, local businesses and services. And so, we are defining what that community discussion is about, and you plug into that and meet with others. And so there have been questions like, "Do Yelpers meet offline?" and that sort of thing. And they absolutely do.

It's probably because we all live within the same city; and very close people establish affinities, or interests. In particular are types of businesses, as in, say, Italian food or people who enjoy wines and a particular type of wine. And so often what we are finding is that Yelpers will organize groups and then meet offline and get together. So there is a really interesting social element there. All of these things speak very strongly to the notion of communities and we are designed to support that. . . .

. . . And that's what's illuminating. We've heard time and again that Yelpers are people who visit the site, perhaps more casually, just to find information. They may have lived in a particular city for all their life. Still

(continued)

(continued)

they're finding new businesses that they never knew existed. In addition, Yelp (and the reviews they are finding on Yelp) is inspiring them to go out and try something that is outside of their comfort zone and perhaps go a little bit further than they would have driven for, say, a pasta dinner. But they are exploring and they are discovering new businesses because they have a bit of a preview into that. The Yelp community is really saying, "Wow, this place is absolutely worth the 30-minute drive to (the next town over). You should check it out, it would be worth your while."

So we are finding that Yelpers write back in and say, "Wow, it's been extremely powerful in helping me find great businesses, and spending my money and dollars with locally owned operations is something I enjoy doing, and I now have the confidence to be able to extend myself beyond what I normally would, to the businesses I would normally support, and try new things."

So that's been an interesting phenomenon. . . .

. . . I mean, you hit on this notion that being able to identify what, in broad strokes, the Yelp community thinks about a business is helpful. What I think you'll find over time, though, is that being able to then dive down into the individual profiles of people who are talking about a business will even further refine those pick/sees.

Yelp is built entirely on this notion of community, and then individuals, as well, right? So my profile page has some general information about me, the light-hearted stuff (favorite movies, books, where I grew up, my interests in general). And so from there you immediately get a quick snapshot of what kind of person Stephanie is. And then you are able to look at all of my reviews, which serve in a way as lifestyle blogs. Like, as I go out to eat and that for the five or six restaurants that I may try this week, I'll write reviews of those and you get a sense of that. Everybody has different preferences and tastes, and so if you are following my blog and you decided at some point, "Hey, you know I have a lot in common with this type of person, and she's rating and reviewing things similar in nature to what I would." I would want to select what should be one of my favorites, and I could almost follow that individual over time.

So now, it's you building a small set of preferences on Yelp. And that way when you are doing searches, when you're logged in, you'll be able to refine enough to tell that these same voices are pointing you to the direction of the business that they've tried.

We believe that's important because understanding what a profile or a person is all about really helps instill an additional layer of trust and value in the information they are providing. . . .

. . . As for myself, for when I use the site in two different manners just for the purposes of keeping in touch with [15:37.3], but I will use my "logged-in" profile when I am doing searches personally. When I want to find something like a great seamstress, or whatever; and I have all of my favorites set so that the reviews of folks that I have been following for a while will pop up if these are business that they have rated and reviewed.

So it definitely helps out quite a bit. . . .

. . . And the interesting thing is that even when we take a look at Yelp overall, we look at all of the reviews and we look at our category breakdowns. What we are finding is that less than 34 percent of businesses reviewed on Yelp are restaurants. And 34 percent is a number that is a lot smaller than a lot of people would have guessed. . . .

. . . It is followed by the shopping category, which comprised about 23 percent of the reviewed businesses. Then there is beauty and fitness, which drops off at around 8 percent, entertainment at 7 percent, and local services at around 7 percent.

So the distribution of this type of review is really various and spans a lot of different categories. Where most people think we just judge restaurants, we actually have a lot more to offer. . . .

. . . So we find that Yelpers are truly passionate about showing everything that they consume locally, and so therein follows all of the other local services, spas, salons, manicures, and pedicures . . . that sort of thing. Those are the other categories that round-out nicely. . . .

. . . And that's our goal, really. It is all about connecting people with great local businesses. . . .

To listen to or read the entire Executive Conversation with Stephanie Ichinose, go to www.theSocialMediaBible.com.

Commandments

1. **Act like a publisher.**

    Think of your business as having content that can be valuable and relevant to your audience. Realize that content needs to be fresh and interesting and adjusted to the tastes of your audience.

2. **Know your audience.**

    Your audience can include customers but extends beyond them to include prospects, employees, vendors, and suppliers.

3. **Create content.**

    After reading this chapter, you should have a better idea of what your content really is. Develop it. Present it to your audience.

4. **Differentiate your concept.**

    Your content has a theme or conceptual basis. Make your content conceptually different from competitors in your space.

5. **Know your competition.**

    Determine where you can play together and where you can't. Remember that coopertition can be a ready and reliable tactic.

6. **Build a community.**

    When the viral power of a community is realized, your traffic patterns will significantly impact the value of your company.

7. **Seek influence but not control.**

    You simply cannot have control. Learn to live with this fact.

8. **Experiment.**

    There is no single formula for success with social media.

Conclusion

You may not want to be a publisher, but it's something you'll need to get good at—or delegate. Keep in mind that the four social media success stories at the beginning of the chapter didn't achieve their success by following a carefully prescribed formula. They began with a passion, found a voice, and then converted their expertise into a content-rich experience that gave rise to an active community. These successful pioneers have helped to create a set of ground rules and model tactics that everyone can learn from. The next few chapters take a closer look at some publishing tactics.

Credits

Expert Insights Were Provided By:

John Blossom, author, Content Nation, www.contentnation.com.

Tony Mamone, CEO, Zimbio, www.zimbio.com.

Stephanie Ichinose, director of communications, Yelp, www.yelp.com.

CHAPTER 5

It's Not Your Father's E-Mail

What's In It for You?

Do you think you know e-mail? Probably—since most people have been e-mailing for about a decade and a half now. Even before there was officially e-mail, companies were sending messages asking others in their trusted network to look at their web site or buy their products. And although spam (called by other names, such as "junk mail" or "rubbish") had existed in bulletin boards (see Chapter 7, The Internet Forum, and Chapter 6, The World of Web Pages), it—and other commercial marketing messages—came to fruition in an especially strong manner through the birth of e-mail. After all, there isn't any other form of advertising that has a more reliable return on investment (ROI) than e-mail. What other marketing medium allows you to reach 5,000 to 50,000 of your potential customers for (nearly) free (or very inexpensively priced with the help of an e-mail service)?

When e-mail is utilized correctly, its conversion rate—the rate at which it turns potential customers into actual customers—can be phenomenal. It has the power to exponentially exceed the results generated by conventional direct mail, newspaper, magazine, and cost-prohibitive radio and television advertising. The Internet is one of the very media that actually allows advertisers to count how many impressions, responses, conversations, and pass-alongs their ads produce, and thereby determine *exactly* how many sales can be attributed to each e-mail campaign.

E-mail is one of the oldest forms of digital social media, and is by far one of the most effective ways to stay in touch with your customers, transact with them, resolve their issues, recruit new customers, and develop your trusted network—and by the way, it's practically free.

That's the incredible value of the Internet. Everything can be measured. Companies can test and perfect which image works best, which headline is more effective, and which offer drives the most sales. This is why major corporations are moving the majority of their advertising budgets to online ventures. According to the *Silicon Valley Insider,* newspaper ad revenue has been declining at an alarming rate. The prediction is that newspaper ad revenue will continue to drop from $42 billion in 2007 to only $10 billion by 2017. That's a $32 billion loss in off-line advertising—and for good reason.

Back to the Beginning

The earliest form of e-mail goes back to the beginning of the 1960s. Single computer electronic mail—such as SNDMSG[1]—simply appended a file on an existing one on the same computer. Then, by opening that file, you could read what others had appended to it.

The first actual e-mail resembling present-day e-mails was sent around 7:00 PM in the autumn of 1971 as a test created by a programming engineer employed by Bolt, Beranek, and Newman named Ray Tomlinson, who had been chosen by the U.S. Defense Department to build the ARPAnet: the first major computer network, and the predecessor to today's Internet. Ray was working in Cambridge, Massachusetts, on Network Control Protocol (NCP) for a time-sharing system called TENEX and CPYNET when he sent his first e-mail between two side-by-side PDP-10 computers. He addressed it to himself, and he recalls the message most likely contained the text "QWERTYUIOP," from the row of keys on his computer.

By the end of 1972, Tomlinson's two e-mail software packages—called SNDMSG and READMAIL—had become an industry standard, right down to Tomlinson's first use of the "@" in e-mail addresses. When Ray was asked why he chose the "@" sign, he explained, "The 'at' sign just makes sense. The purpose of the 'at' sign indicated a unit price (e.g., 10 items @ $1.95). I used the 'at' sign to indicate that the user was 'at' some other host rather than being local." And when he was asked about spam—well, he said that he had never anticipated that.

What You Need to Know

As mentioned previously, the overwhelming reason for the popularity and widespread use of e-mail is its ROI and effectiveness, and, of course, the fact that it's nearly free. According to the Forrester DMA Gartner Group, e-mail marketing is significantly more effective than direct mail marketing. Some specific findings are in Table 5.1.

Table 5.1	Direct Mail versus E-Mail Marketing[a]	
Measurement	**Direct Mail**	**E-Mail**
Development Time	3–6 weeks	2 days
Cost Per Unit	$1.25	$0.10
Response Rate	0.1–2%[b]	5–15%[c]

[a] This doesn't mean that abandoning direct mail completely is the right choice for everyone. If you are selling RVs, for example, you had better keep sending direct mail pieces, since your typical buying demographic is older and not necessarily e-mail savvy. (However, an interesting note: the U.S. Census Bureau reports important changes for the coming years in the aging of the population. By 2050, one in five residents will be aged 65 or over, up from one in nine today. Refer to Part III of this book to determine which social media tool works best for your company, products, and demographics.)

[b] That's the same thing as taking 1,000 of your direct mail pieces, selecting one from the stack, and throwing the remaining 999 pieces into the trash.

[c] Some e-mail campaigns with which the authors are familiar have reached as high as 34 percent open rate.

Table 5.2 shows some additional statistics from an industry survey of 2,700 marketers that states their primary goals for using e-mail in their marketing programs.

These numbers are a surprise in that the highest usage of e-mail marketing isn't necessarily sales, but rather to build relationships with existing customers. The second-highest-rated use was to acquire new customers, and the primary use of e-mail for these marketers was to build and maintain their trusted network.

Table 5.2 Primary Goals for E-Mail Marketing Programs	
Build relationships with existing customers	60%
Acquire new customers	41
Sell products and services	32
Provide information	31
Build the brand	25
Drive traffic to a web site	21
Up-sell and cross-sell to existing customers	18

Source: www.MarketingProfs.com e-mail Marketing Benchmark Survey.

Inbox	E-mail
The Wall Street Journal Online	WSJ@listserv.punchline.net [on behalf of Wall Street Journal]
Sony Electronics	sonyelectronics@sony.m0.net
E-nnouncements from T. ...	noReply@rps-updates.troweprice.com
Hewlett-Packard	[Hewlett-Packard] us-specials@your.HP.com

FIGURE 5.1   From Line

E-Mail Terminology

Here are some important and often-used terms with which you should become familiar in order to maximize your e-mail marketing campaigns.

- *From line:* The sender of the e-mail is the first thing recipients look at. There are two components: what is displayed in the inbox and what is displayed when the e-mail is opened (see Figure 5.1).
- *Subject line:* The headline seen prior to opening the message gives a brief description of the subject of the e-mail. Recipients often decide whether to open an e-mail based on the subject line (see Figure 5.2).
- *Preview pane:* This element in many e-mail programs allows the recipient to view the first few lines of a message. This is also a big factor in getting the recipient to open the message (see Figure 5.3).
- *Open rate:* This statistic measures how many recipients opened the e-mail message, and either enabled the images or clicked on a link.

From	Subject Line
JCPenney	Home Sale: Redecorate with Savings
Quill.com	Look inside for sale offers selected just for you
Staples Newsletter	Regina, here's your July newsletter
Lands' End	DESIGN YOUR OWN JEANS

FIGURE 5.2   Subject Line

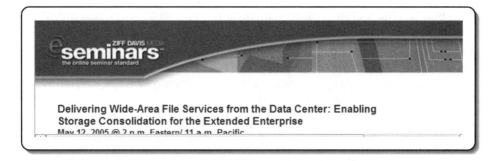

FIGURE 5.3 Preview Pane

This only works for HTML e-mails, because text-only messages have no images (unless, of course, you send a text-based message and ask your clients to click "receipt," which is not likely to happen). This is only the first of several necessary steps that you must take in order to convert readers of an e-mail message to visitors to your web site, and ultimately purchasers of your product.

- *Click-throughs:* These measure the recipients who clicked on a link or image within an e-mail, thereby opening the hyperlinked web page for additional content. Each link in an e-mail can usually be tracked separately.

- *Pass-alongs:* These are the number of recipients who forward your message along to a friend or colleague.

- *Bounces:* E-mails classified as *bounces* did not reach their destination and were bounced back to the sender.

- *Hard bounces:* These e-mails have been sent to a domain or e-mail address that no longer exists (or never did). You must have a system for deleting hard bounces immediately.

- *Soft bounces:* As opposed to hard bounces, soft bounces present a temporary condition that renders the e-mail undeliverable, the two main reasons for which are usually a full mailbox or a server down. You should resend soft bounces four times, and then delete them from your e-mail list.

- *Opt-outs* or *unsubscribes:* These events occur when a user requests not to be included on your e-mail list. This can be done after receiving your initial e-mail, or by having a permission box prechecked. The number of recipients who ask to have their e-mail address removed from your e-mail distribution list is the number of opt-outs.

- *Opt-ins:* These occur when a user actively elects to receive e-mails or promotional messages by checking an opt-in box, which can also be prechecked.

    Be aware that typically less than 5 percent will opt out, and less than 10 percent will opt in. An exception is the case of guest books, which typically have a 57 percent opt-in rate—and which can have a dramatic effect on responses to your e-mail.

- *Double opt-in or explicit permission:* Think of this as a double-dog-dare-ya. After the initial registration, a confirmation e-mail is sent to the user to which they must reply (either by hitting reply, or clicking on a URL contained within the e-mail) before you may add them to your e-mail list.

Spam with Your SPAM?

It has been estimated that e-mail users spend roughly 52 hours each year—that's about one hour per week!—sorting and deleting spam (junk e-mail) messages from our inbox. Cox Communication, the seventh-largest e-mail provider in the United States, estimated that almost 3.6 *billion* spam messages were delivered in 2007 alone. Statistics like these prompted the Can Spam Act.

The national Can Spam Act went into effect in the United States on January 1, 2004. This law preempts all state laws governing commercial e-mail, and applies to both business-to-business and business-to-consumer marketers. (State laws are still in effect as they relate to fraud.) The law applies most specifically to commercial e-mail messages (the category into which most marketing messages fall), and not to transactional or relationship messages, which are those that are sent to complete a transaction; provide warranty, product updates, upgrades, or recall information; and notify users of changes in terms of subscription or service or account balance information.

The term *SPAM* originally comes from the meat produced by the Hormel Meat Packing Company in Austin, Minnesota, in 1937. Then-president J. C. Hormel created an amazing little recipe: a spicy ham packaged in a handy 12-ounce can. He held

FIGURE 5.4 Spam

a contest to give the product a name as distinctive as its taste. The winner was SPAM, for SPiced hAM. During its very first year of production, SPAM grabbed 18 percent of the market. By 2002, more than 6 billion cans of SPAM have been sold with 44,000 cans per hour rolling out of Hormel. A can of SPAM is consumed in the U.S. every 3.1 seconds.

How does this translate to online clutter, though? Well, when it comes to the Internet, you've likely seen, heard, or even used the term "spam" and "spamming," which refer to the act of sending unsolicited commercial e-mail (UCE), which implies that someone has sent a message that has no value or substance inside.

How might a company feel about their product being likened to something without value or substance? Hormel's official position on the term *spam* is as follows: "We do not object to use of this slang term to describe UCE, although we do object to the use of the word 'spam' as a trademark and to the use of our product image in association with that term. Also, if the term is to be used, it should be used in all lower-case letters to distinguish it from our trademark SPAM, which should be used with all uppercase letters."

The essence of the Can Spam Act simply states that those sending e-mails have to be honest. It forbids the use of false header information, dictates that the "From" line must be real, demands that no use of deceptive or misleading subject lines occurs, mandates that all messages must give the recipient the ability to unsubscribe either through a link to a web site or a valid reply to an e-mail address, states that the opt-out links must be clear and conspicuous, and must work at the time the message is sent for 30 days thereafter. It orders that opt-outs must be processed within 10 business days, that each e-mail must include a valid physical postal address (while the original Can Spam Act said that a post office box does not suffice, the 2007 revisions of the Act said it was legal), that an ADV^2 warning label must be in the subject line only if a company does not have express permission (affirmative consent) from the recipient, and that one's mail servers must not have an open relay or allow others to send e-mail through their servers without their permission.

An important technicality to note: the law defines the sender as the party providing the e-mail's content—not the one renting the list, and not the list owner. Therefore, since any opt-outs are specific to the sender, you must obtain unsubscribe data from the list owner and add those names to your in-house suppression file. Remember: you only have 10 business days to process opt-outs.

The law also specifies that lists built with dictionary attacks, harvested e-mails, or randomly generated e-mail addresses are prohibited. A dictionary attack occurs when spammers connect to a server and ask to deliver mail to mailbox "A." If the server complies, then that address goes on their list. They then proceed to "AA," or "B," or any word or combination of letters that's in their automated dictionary. Randomly generated e-mails work the same way. Harvested e-mails require that someone search web sites—either manually or automatically—to collect all of the e-mails without the recipient's permission. Both of these techniques are illegal and can get you blacklisted.[3]

The Federal Trade Commission and states' attorneys general offices can enforce violations with civil action, which can include jail sentences along with fines ranging from $250 up to $2 million per message. Also, Internet Service Providers (ISPs) can enforce the law with a civil action for damages or for fines ranging from $250 to $1 million per message. In the case of fraud, there is no upper limit.

Spam Filters or Content Filters

Spam filters or content filters are online tools that are used to constantly survey and identify spam, and trigger spam blockers upon finding any.

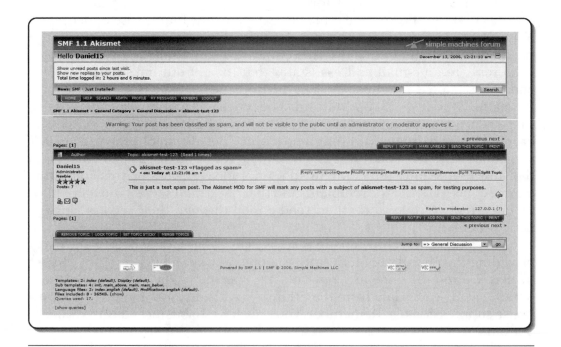

FIGURE 5.5 Spam Submit

Some phrases that often trigger these spam filters include: "Free _____," "$$$," "!!!," "Cash bonus," "ALL CAPS," "No Investment Necessary," "Satisfaction Guaranteed," "You Are a Winner," "No Purchase Necessary," "Social Security Number," and "No Strings Attached." How many times have you received an e-mail with one of these phrases in the subject line that actually offered any value? In fact, you're probably wondering why, if the laws in the United States are so tough, you still receive so much spam? Although the Can Spam Act went into effect on January 1, 2004, most (if not all) of the spammers had moved offshore, mostly to Asian countries, in December 2003.

However, there are resources on different web sites available to spam-check your e-mail subject lines before you send them, such as www.programmersheaven.com/webtools/Spam-Checker/spamchecker.aspx.

Content Really Is King

Just as it is in your web pages, your brochures, and your direct mailer, content is king—the most fundamental part of your e-mail. It therefore requires the most significant amount of attention. The most important rule in all marketing is the question of "WIIFM": "What's In It for Me?" If you don't clearly and quickly convey the WIIFM in every marketing message, e-mail, and communication you have with your customers, then your work will be ineffective.

Think about how your customers perceive your corporate communications. Every time you want your customer to look at an e-mail, visit your web site, or open a piece of direct mail, there is a transaction. It is very much like a sale, in that you are asking your customer to give you some amount of money (or attention) in exchange for you providing a service or product. The customer evaluates your offer and compares your product or service to the total cost of the transaction, which might include your customer going to a web site, driving to your location, sending something in the mail, reading and comprehending your offer, filling out a registration form, and completing credit card information before even getting to actually pay you for that item.

Your potential customer subconsciously calculates all of these costs of inconvenience and adds them to the product's dollar amount to determine the overall cost—and decides whether your product or service is a good value. In order to hook your prospects into investing their cost of inconvenience before they actually decide to purchase, you have to convince them of their WIIFM, or you've lost them—and the sale.

Enticing your customers isn't a one-time event. There could be as many as a dozen occasions during which you have to convince your customer that your product or service is worth the total cost of inconvenience and money.

It's this very concept—the idea that attracting customers is a one-time deal—that many companies too easily forget, and it therefore leads to poor conversion rates. This frame of mind leaves your e-mails unopened without ensuing click-throughs, pass-alongs, or visits beyond your home page, and usually results in shopping cart abandonment. Understanding the need to consistently woo your customers, however, will dramatically improve all of your marketing—in addition to what you do with e-mail.

Tips, Techniques, and Tactics

The 1.54-Second Rule/5.0-Second Rule

To understand WIIFM more clearly, take a more concentrated look at how people think, read, and evaluate these value propositions. Suppose, for some reason, that you really wanted to read the newspaper advertisements today. Your eyes are scanning over the page of many ads, one of which catches your eye. You decide to not turn the page, but to look at the heading for that ad. How long do you think you are willing to spend to determine if the WIIFM is worth your stopping to read further? A study showed that people are only willing to invest or spend 1.54 seconds of time to make that determination.

If that headline doesn't convince the reader—in those 1.54 seconds—that there is a significant WIIFM and convey that value, then the reader is likely to move on to another ad or another page. Think about it. Isn't that true for you? If you are reading ads or flipping pages in a magazine, do you spend any longer than a second or two before either stopping to read more or turning the page? How about when you listen to an ad on the radio or are watching television? Does 1.54 seconds sound about right? What about when you are scanning down a list of Google Search results? Is 1.54 seconds still accurate? This emphasizes the great importance of that opening sentence—whether it's on television, radio, magazine, newspaper, search results, web page, or your e-mail message.

In a newspaper, it's called the headline; in your web site, it's the header; and in your e-mail, it's the subject line. Your subject line has to convince your customer in roughly 1.5 seconds whether he or she should move on to the next stage of time investment. This is why the subject line is so important, and why segmenting is important, as discussed in the next section.

Only if you experience success in the first part of this transaction or value proposition of the WIIFM can you go to the next critical step—reading the newspaper ads. If a headline catches your eye and you subconsciously agree to spend or invest again in this next part of this transaction, how much time do you now give the ad before you determine whether to continue or turn the page? The answer is now 5 seconds. And while it may sound like a lot, by comparison, 5 seconds isn't much time to convey a second-level WIIFM. In fact, it's only about enough time to read one sentence.

The second part of this transaction in e-mail marketing is the opening line of your message. Within the first second of reading, your message has to convey a strong enough WIIFM message to keep your customer engaged—and has to do so in 5 seconds or less. If you are successful in these first two parts of the WIIFM transaction, your customer will continue to read your message to (1) fully understand your value proposition and (2) convert to purchasing your product.

The third step is conversion. If you have successfully convinced your customer that there really is something in it for them, then they will follow your e-mail message's call to action. In nearly every case, an e-mail's primary goal is to convert that message to a click-through to a web page. You might also define your conversion as a pass-along, a sign-up, picking up the phone, or only simply informing your customer. And your e-mail message is *always* about maintaining or building your trusted network by providing a WIIFM. Even if the definition of conversion for your message is only to inform, be sure that the value of that information is at least equal to the time your customer will need to spend to get it.

Segment to Maximize Conversion

By now, you should understand the importance of the 1.54-second and 5-second rules. The underlying message is that there isn't much time to hook your customers and show them your value proposition. So to help with this important step, the experts do something called *segmenting*.

Segmenting is no more than splitting your overall e-mail list into segments and testing the success of each of your e-mail components with your clients. One approach is to divide your total list into equal segments; you can also just pull a random sample from your list to test your message.

Splitting the total group into equal segments allows you to test your entire group in a more homogenous random sampling. Consider the following scenario. Suppose you have a total mailing list of 5,000 customers, a group that you split into five equal 1,000-e-mail segments. For each segment, you are going to craft five different subject lines. The word *craft* is important, because you will want to spend time and effort designing these subject lines and paying close attention to the nouns, verbs, and adjectives you use. Take your time. Create these five subject lines deliberately.

Now, send out all five segments. The important concept is to keep the rest of the entire e-mail the same. Make no other changes. By keeping all of the other e-mail message components identical, you are testing the effectiveness of only the five different subject lines. Give the e-mail a week or more, depending upon how your customers have reacted historically to your e-mails, and then look at the metrics. If the third subject line showed a significant rise in conversion, then look at what you did there and do it again. Look at which one of the subject lines converted the most poorly and stop doing that. It's that simple.

Your next e-mail should test your opening sentences while you keep the subject line consistent. Wait an appropriate amount of time, and then look at your statistics. The next steps are to segment and test your call to action and your use of images. You would be surprised to see that often a stock photo of a man instead of a woman—or vice versa—can make as much as a 20 percent increase in your e-mail conversion rates.

If you follow the steps above over a roughly six-month time frame, you will have tested and perfected your e-mail message WIIFMs, subject lines, opening sentences, calls to action, images, layout, color schemes, and even html versus text. You will be able to determine that your e-mail campaigns can have as high as a 30 percent conversion rate. How's that compared to a 0.1 percent conversion rate of conventional direct mail? And all the while you are building and reinforcing your trusted network.

Day Parting Will Get It Read

Another important component of e-mail marketing is a practice known as *day parting.* Most people have no idea of what that means, so if you don't either, don't feel bad.

The following example of day parting is one with which everybody is familiar. There is a time of day that is reserved for one particular type of television show on all the major networks. The time is Monday through Friday from 1:00 PM until 3:00 PM. What is it?

If you said "soap operas," then you answered correctly. Why do they call them *soap operas*? You never see too much soap (unless it was used during the gratuitous showering of a sexy star), and no one has ever sung opera. These aren't really called soap operas; they are called daytime dramas. What could have happened to get them their name?

You're right: laundry soap. For nearly a half century, stay-at-home moms—and now dads—have been watching these shows. So what's the importance of 1:00 PM to 3:00 PM? That's when little Johnny and little Sally go down for their naps—the first time during the workday that the stay-at-home parent can take her or his eye off their little darling to actually get some work done. And if you have ever had a child of your own, you quickly realize that laundry is a daily chore.

Can you think of any other hourly day parting on television—such as for news, prime time, and late night? Radio even has drive time, which is of course the time where the majority of radio listeners travel to and from work. These two time periods are traditionally from 6 to 10 AM and 2 to 6 PM, Monday through Friday, and represent the stations' highest listenership. Commercials cost significantly more during drive time.

Every media uses day parting for maximum marketing effect. Newspapers do it. What's Wednesday? Coupons and cooking (to sell more coupon products). This gives the reader Wednesday evening and Thursday to cut them out for Friday's shopping (most people get paid on Fridays, and therefore do their shopping that day). What about Thursday? Out on the town! Friday is too late to make plans, and Wednesday is too early. How about Saturday? Real estate and home repair. Sunday? Ads, ads, ads! This is the day during which the reader has the most time to read the advertising and to shop.

How about monthly day parting? Do you or your customers have more money in the beginning of the month or at the end? And what if you take day parting to the yearly interval, often called *seasonality*. Every company has seasonality. What do you think the slow time of year is for a construction company? It happens to be the same as the peak season for ski resorts.

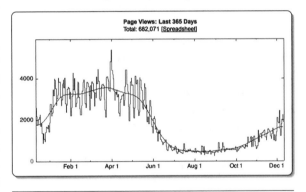

FIGURE 5.6 Seasonality

Understanding your customers' psychology, day parting and seasonality will dramatically increase your conversion rate. Let's look at when you send your e-mails. Is it at night? Over the weekend? What are your customers doing when your e-mail arrives? When does the highest amount of Internet (e-mail) traffic occur? It's Monday through Friday, 8:00 AM until 5:00 PM, then 8:30 PM until midnight, and all day Saturday and Sunday. No surprise there, right?

If you sent your e-mail at night, your customer is most likely to receive it first thing in the morning. Is this good? Isn't this the time the mailbox is filled from the night before with spam? Isn't this the time they just came into work and are getting yelled at from six different people, preparing for meetings, and running around? How careful do you think your customer will be in determining whether they hit "delete" on your e-mail? Wouldn't around, say, 11:00 AM be better? Wouldn't they have had time to go to those early-morning meetings and deleted all of their spam and other unwanted e-mails?

How about that weekend send-off? Is first thing on Monday morning really the best time for your customers to get your value proposition that they will only use 1.54 seconds or less to determine if they will read or delete?

Statistically speaking, Tuesday through Thursday from 11:00 AM until 3:00 PM is the best time to send your message, although it might be different for your particular customer. You need to test it. Now that you know about segmenting, try dividing and sending your e-mail message at different times of the day and different days of the week. See which one works best—and keep doing that!

A conference-goer once asked, "What if I sold canoes? What would be the best time to send an e-mail for that?" The answer for that year was, "Thursday, March twenty-first, at 9:00 PM." Why, you ask?

If you are selling canoes, you most likely have people's home e-mail addresses, as some companies are getting cranky about using the Internet at work for personal business. Customers for recreational items are often in front of their computers on a weeknight at around 8:30 PM. Allow 30 minutes to clean out their junk e-mails and have an empty inbox. So around 9:00 PM the canoe e-mail will arrive, and they will have plenty of time to look at it—and not simply dispose of it.

Thursday is the best day of the week, because a customer who is looking for a canoe is probably younger and possibly fit—and is therefore likely to be out of the house instead of in front of the computer on a Friday night. But the e-mail should arrive as close to the weekend as possible, so that the customer remembers to buy it on Saturday morning.

Considering seasonality, an e-mail for camping and other outdoor products should go out in the end of March. That's when people are thinking about spring and summer activities. In the fall, their thoughts go to, "Oh, man, how am I going to store all this stuff over the winter?"

See how a few rules and a little common sense can make e-mail marketing fun, challenging, and most important, rewarding? And by the way—it's almost completely free.

Providers

Deciding who is going to manage your e-mail list often leads to the decision, "Do I do it in-house or out-house?" This is a big decision. Do you have the resources to manage your own e-mail list? Can you be sure that every opt-out is removed within the 10-day period? Will you diligently keep a record of your opt-ins?

Outsourcing is usually less expensive than managing the human resources necessary to perform those duties in-house, and there's something to be said about an arm's-length relationship with a professional company whose only mission in life is to perform a given task to the best of their abilities.

While you can buy software packages and install them on your servers and PCs, and you can find several companies on the Internet, one good recommendation is Constant Contact. Located in Waltham, Massachusetts, Constant Contact has been managing corporate e-mail campaigns since 1998. (See Part II for more information on Constant Contact.)

This company has integrity, is respected in the industry, is whitelisted,[4] and even shut one of the authors down for a week before writing this chapter for too many bounces due to use of a seven- to eight-year-old mailing list.

Constant Contact and similar e-mail management companies automatically handles all of your requirements for you. They also have dozens of premade templates, spell checking, incredible statistics and analysis, and duplicate e-mail elimination, and they are very reasonably priced. Set up an account and get discounts by clicking the link at www.theSocialMediaBible.com.

Expert Insight

Eric Groves, senior vice president, Worldwide Strategy and Market Development, Constant Contact, www.ConstantContact.com

Eric Groves

We challenge our customers to be writing content that is so valuable that those who receive them will set up a folder in their e-mail box just for that company. When they provide content that is so valuable that customers want to hold on to it, then they have really changed and revolutionized the way e-mail marketing is used by businesses. It's no longer just a, "I'm going to blast it out and try to drive immediate business." It's all about asking, "How do I send out a communication that builds my reputation with my customers so that they want to come back?"

And everybody's getting so much e-mail these days that it's important to rise above . . . sort of . . . the chaff and everything that's out there. The way to do that is to write really good content, and to demonstrate your knowledge. And, let's face it: small business owners go into business because they are experts. Sharing the expertise that they have with their customers turns out to be one of the most powerful ways that you can actually market your business.

(continued)

(continued)

For example, if you ask a business owner, "What are the three most frequently asked questions that your customers ask you?" and they write them down and then I say, "Okay, that's content!" "Oh, okay, I can do that."

And that the funny thing is that somebody asks you an interesting question, and you write it down and you use it in your newsletter, and you give them attribution and say, "Hey, Joey, my new customer tried to stump me with this one, and here's the answer to the question that he had. And, oh, by the way, if you want to try and stump me, submit your questions to me at this e-mail address."

Now all of a sudden you've got your readers, who are not only invested in reading your campaign, but also in giving you content ideas. So there're all kinds of great ways to come up with content that's actually engaging and fun. . . .

And if you think about why people turn to a small business owner, it's because they have a relationship with them and they trust them. Trust, in any relationship, is built over time by sharing of valuable information; and that's all you're doing. I mean, if you were a restaurateur it could be as simple as sharing a couple of your recipes. . . .

On Spam

Well, the Can-the-Spam Act was enacted to really provide some peace to the folks in law enforcement to go after people who are sending fraudulent e-mail. And it does put forth a number of things that people, who are sending e-mail legitimately, need to be aware of.

A couple of those things are that you cannot falsify your sending address or use a bogus e-mail address to send from. And that's one of the reasons why, when you use Constant Contact, you have to verify the sending e-mail address you're sending from—just to make sure that you're in compliance of that.

Several other things that you have to do are to have your physical address embedded in the actual body of the message. And that's one other thing that we basically put on there for you. One of the other pieces is that you have to provide your recipient with the ability to un-subscribe. We have a tool called "Safe Un-subscribe" where with one click someone can remove themselves from the list.

Now, you have 10 days by law to remove these names from your list, but if you are using Constant Contact, you don't even have to worry about that. We take care of that for you. There are a couple other provisions within the Can-the-Spam Act, but those are the big ones.

On Granting Permission

Well, first of all, there are a couple of things you should know about permission. It certainly is perishable. If I say I would like to join your mailing list and I do not hear from you for six months, I'm going to forget that I gave you permission to join your list to mail to me. So it's really important that if you are going to be doing e-mail marketing, you are building a list of your customers that you do communicate with, at least on a quarterly basis.

To listen to or read the entire Executive Conversation with Eric Groves, go to www.theSocialMediaBible.com.

Expert Insight

John Arnold, author, *E-Mail Marketing For Dummies*, www.johnarnold.com

John Arnold

[E-mail] is really written for the small business owners who are in the trenches every day, just trying to get more customers and trying to live the life that they want to live. And if you're a small business owner, these days it's tough to find customers and it's tough to keep them coming back. You've got to be in front of them all the time. And e-mail marketing is such a low-cost tool. When you think about it, this is what's so powerful about that concept. . . .

You know when things are low-cost, that's great as a small business owner, but it can be a trap, too. You don't want to make sure that you're always just cutting your costs. What you want to do is grow your revenue. So if you find a low-cost tool out there and it's cheap and it doesn't work, you're really just wasting your money. But if you find a low-cost marketing tool that's cheap and it actually returns more than a dollar for every dollar that you spend, then it's a gold mine. And that's what e-mail marketing is. You spend a dollar and you get way more than a dollar back. In fact, the last time I checked this statistic, the Direct Marketing Association said that the average e-mail marketing ROI is over forty-five dollars for every dollar spent. . . .

Everybody uses e-mail. In fact, a recent study by AOL sort of indicates people read their e-mail at work, they read it at home, they read it in bed while in their pajamas, they read it in the middle of the night, they read it while they drive (don't do that!), they read it in church. . . . Twelve percent of respondents

(continued)

(*continued*)

said that! So you know, e-mail is getting delivered where your customers are looking. And if you want to say that that's passé and you want to pass up on that opportunity, well, then I guess maybe you have a better plan. But you should include e-mail marketing in your mix because everybody's there. And your message is getting delivered where people open it. . . .

Well, the first thing that you want to do is recognize that there is a key difference between e-mail programs that are designed for one-to-one e-mail communications, and those are programs like Outlook, where they are really only designed for one-to-one communications. You want to get a program that is going to work to deliver "one-to-many" e-mail communications. And those are called *e-mail service providers*. So Constant Contact is an e-mail service provider.

What they do is they just make it super easy for you to create an e-mail using one of their templates. So you don't need to know HTML programming, and you can still create a great-looking e-mail design. You can do a newsletter or promotion, anything that you can think of. You can create that and look professional and make it look like your business. And then they'll send it out for you so that you can get a high rate of deliverability and you can stay compliant with all the Can-the-Spam laws, and they will help you track your message. So as it goes out, you can tell who opened it, and when they have opened it, which links they click on in the e-mail. You can use that for your own marketing information.

So you really want to get started with somebody who knows what they are doing, and that is an e-mail service provider. And is it low cost? Of course it's low cost! Constant Contact's plans start at fifteen dollars a month. So you will waste fifteen dollars a month trying to do it with one-to-one e-mail programs. It is just so cost effective and so easy to use. That's really the first step. Just go with somebody who knows what they have been doing. . . .

You know, e-mail marketing is not as simple as just loading up all your e-mail addresses and clicking the send button. There are some things that you have to get over, some challenges. And if you think about it, e-mail marketing is both a challenge and an opportunity. Everybody faces those same challenges of collecting e-mail addresses the right way, with permission and the Can-Spam laws and those kinds of things, and deliverability.

So, if everybody faces those issues and you can overcome them, then you have a competitive advantage over your competition. So when you go with somebody like Constant Contact and they help you and they're with you every step of the way, then you're going to get over those challenges faster than somebody else who sits around and tries to figure that out on their own. So it's another reason to use the service and get that stuff done.

And Constant Contact's approach is, "We are there to help the small business owner grow." And when the small business owner's business grows, they reward us by using the product for a long time. So that's the core of the business model, and that's why we have learning resources on the web site, we have face-to-face seminars, we've got hints and tips newsletters, we've got frequently asked question files, we've got live support that's always free to our customers.

Need I say more? We are always there to give that helping hand and to make the business owners get the value that they think they should be getting, which is business growth. . . .

A lot of people like to use e-mail to drive traffic to their web site, but if your web site traffic spikes (and you are not going to have a company party because of that statistic because you really wanted sales), then you've got to back up and think, "Okay, how is my e-mail going to really drive sales, not just traffic to my web site?" So you might find out that that changes the way you're going to do your messaging. Maybe you want to create a special landing page on your web site and not just drive them to the homepage. Or maybe you're going to change your offer so that people click through straight to a shopping cart, so you can try to drive sales to the shopping cart in your web site.

So really, just having a plan and developing all your content around that plan is a super step.

To listen to or read the entire Executive Conversation with John Arnold, go to www.theSocialMediaBible.com.

Commandments

1. **Thou shall not spam.**

    You don't need to. As long as you're honest and understand the Can Spam Act, you're good! If you are using your e-mail list to build and maintain your trusted network and your trusted community, then give them reason to trust you. Ask yourself this question: are you informing your network that you really do have an offer that would benefit them if only they were aware of it? If the answer is yes, then send it.

2. **Thou shalt provide a significant WIIFM.**

    You always need to keep in mind that whether it's paper; electronic, e-mail, or web site text; or a brochure or cover letter, you have to convey a strong WIIFM to prove to your customer that there is a good rate of return on your value proposition.

3. **Thou shalt remember the 1.54-second and 5.0-second rules.**

    Remember, you only have 1.54 seconds to hook your customers and convince them in the subject line that they should invest their time and effort in reading and comprehending your proposition. Remember, also, that even if you convince your prospect to keep reading, you only have 5.0 seconds in the first sentence to get them to read the rest and not hit the delete button. Your messages have to be clear, concise, and understandable in these two allotted time frames.

4. **Thou shalt segment to maximize conversion.**

This is really about testing. You have to test your WIIFM, your 1.54, your 5, your images, and your layout to see what works for your customers and what doesn't. It's about understanding how your trusted network thinks, and figuring out what motivates them. Segmenting is about trial and error with a short cycle to find answers that only a few years ago marketers spent millions of their clients' dollars and years to understand.

5. **Thou shalt remember that day parting will get it read.**

By understanding how your customer thinks, and what they are doing during the course of their day, week, month, and year, you can send very effective e-mails. Appreciating your customer's larger monthly and annual cycles allows you to better allocate your e-mail and search engine marketing budgets. Day parting means getting your message to your customers when the timing is most right for them to receive it.

Conclusion

So what does e-mail marketing have to do with social media? *Everything.* Social media is about two-way communication between you and your customers. If you aren't communicating effectively—or at all because a spam filter is stopping your e-mail—then you're not marketing. Social media requires you to build trust in your network, listen to what your customers have to say, and provide value and a strong WIIFM.

The more you understand the most effective way to communicate through e-mail, the stronger your relationships will be with your customers. Remember, anytime you send an e-mail to your customer and they don't opt out, they decide to remain part of your network. If you can consistently provide value in the form of knowledge, information, resources, discounts, leads, examples, white papers, or even entertainment, your customers will continue to correspond with you. And like any relationship, the more they agree to converse with you, the stronger the relationship becomes. Remember the old adage, "The best compliment a customer can give you is a referral." Customers who trust you and buy from you will recommend that others do the same.

Readings and Resources

Arnold, John. *E-Mail Marketing For Dummies*. (Hoboken, NJ: John Wiley & Sons, Inc.)

Baggott, Chris, with Ali Sales. *E-Mail Marketing by the Numbers: How to Use the World's Greatest Marketing Tool to Take Any Organization to the Next Level*. (Hoboken, NJ: John Wiley & Sons, Inc.)

Bell, Arthur H., and Dayle M. Smith. *Management Communication*. 2nd ed. (Hoboken, NJ: John Wiley & Sons, Inc.)

Cavanagh, Christina. *Managing Your E-Mail: Thinking Outside the Inbox*. (Hoboken, NJ: John Wiley & Sons, Inc.)

Liew, Mun Leong. *Building People: Sunday E-Mails from a CEO*. (Hoboken, NJ: John Wiley & Sons, Inc.)

Mullen, Jeanniey and David J. Daniels. *E-Mail Marketing: An Hour a Day*. (Hoboken, NJ: John Wiley & Sons, Inc.)

Schneier, Bruce. *E-Mail Security: How to Keep Your Electronic Messages Private*. (Hoboken, NJ: John Wiley & Sons, Inc.)

Sterne, Jim, and Anthony Priore. *E-Mail Marketing: Using E-Mail to Reach Your Target Audience and Build Customer Relationships*. (Hoboken, NJ: John Wiley & Sons, Inc.)

Turner, Sean, and Russ Housley. *Implementing E-Mail and Security Tokens: Current Standards, Tools, and Practices*. (Hoboken, NJ: John Wiley & Sons, Inc.)

Downloads

For your free downloads associated with *The Social Media Bible,* go to www .TheSocialMediaBible.com, select Downloads, and enter your ISBN number located on the back of the book above the bar code. Be sure to enter the dashes.

Credits

Expert Insights Were Provided By:

Eric Groves, SVP, Constant Contact, www.constantcontact.com.

John Arnold, author, *E-mail Marketing For Dummies,* www.JohnArnold.com.

Technical Edits Were Provided By:

John Arnold, *E-Mail Marketing For Dummies,* www.JohnArnold.com.

Notes

1. The Send Message (SNDMSG) command was one instruction and function of Ray Tomlinson mail program that was first used in 1971 for TENEX. Another component as READMAIL. SNDMSG was used to send Electronic Mail from one user to another.
2. ADV is a label that tells the recipient that an e-mail is an unsolicited *advertisement*.
3. A blacklist or blocklist is a list of IP addresses or series of IP addresses that Internet Service Providers (ISPs) create to block or to prevent the sender of e-mail messages from a server that is suspected of transmitting spam. The term *blacklist* dates to 1619 and refers to a list of persons who are disapproved of or are to be punished or boycotted. More information regarding the Can Spam Act is available at www.ftc.gov/bcp/conline/pubs/buspubs/canspam.shtm.
4. Whitelisted is the opposite of the blacklisted definition above. ISPs will list a sender as a legitimate e-mail marketer and not block their e-mails.

CHAPTER 6

The World of Web Pages

What's In It for You?

According to Internet World Stats Miniwatts Marketing Group, there are an estimated 1,463,632,361 Internet users worldwide. This number breaks down as follows: Asia: 578,538,257; Europe: 384,633,765; North America: 248,241,969; Latin America/Caribbean: 139,009,209; Africa: 51,065,630; Middle East: 41,939,200; and Oceanic Australia: 20,204,331. This is the reason companies are all participating in the World Wide Web. These numbers show the staggering number of people who are participating in the World Wide Web.

The Web became mainstream in 1995. It all began in 1989 with 0 domain names (the name between the "www" and the ".com" for a web site), and has grown to more than 176.7 million in August 2008. Domain names—or web sites, as they're more commonly known—have been growing at a rate of 1.3 million per month, according to Netcraft, an Internet statistics reporting web site, each with an average of 239 pages per site. Even though no one knows for sure, or even can accurately guess, there were an estimated 29.7 billion web pages as of 2007 (see Figure 6.1).

The sheer magnitude of these numbers are the force that drives e-commerce, while also making competition difficult. If you have some basic understanding of how web pages work, then you have the ability to out-sell your competition—and thereby realize revenues and ROI that cannot be attained off-line.

Like any other process, once you realize some of the tactics, tools, and strategies, it's easier than you think to create highly visible, sticky web pages with a high conversion rate. *Sticky* refers to a web page that someone is willing to stay at for a higher-than-average amount of time before clicking "Back" or "Close." The tactics are easy to understand, the tools are easy to

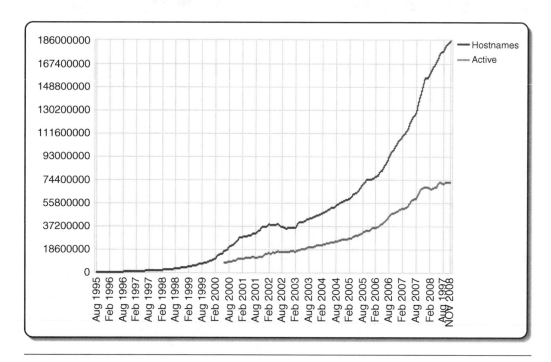

FIGURE 6.1   Total Sites across All Domains, August 1995, November 2008

Source: www.netcraft.com.

use, and the strategies are easy to implement. But before discussing these tools and strategies, consider a brief history of the Web.

Back to the Beginning

The very first web site, web page, and web server on the World Wide Web debuted in the latter part of 1990. The advent of global computer communication was physicist Sir Tim Berners-Lee's dream. During March 1989, while working at the European Organization for Nuclear Research (CERN) in Geneva, Switzerland, Berners-Lee wrote a proposal blueprinting how computers could be connected to easily share information across the globe through means of the Internet and the use of HTTP—or Hypertext Protocol based on Vannevar Bush's work in 1945 and TCP/IP, Transmission Control Protocol/Internet Protocol (previously created by Vint Cerf). Both HTTP TCP/IP are the systems used today to navigate across web sites and web pages.

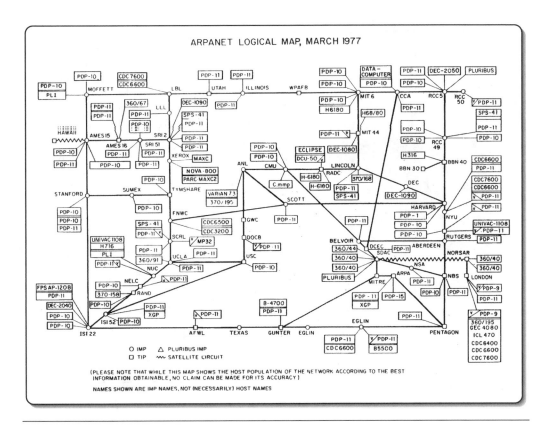

FIGURE 6.2 ARPAnet

For a complete explanation of HTTP, see Chapter 20, Spotlight on Search (Search Engine Optimization). For an interview between author Lon Safko and Vint Cerf, the inventor of TCP/IP, Transmission Control Protocol/Internet Protocol and co-designer of the Internet, go to www .theSocialMediaBible.com.

In 1990, Robert Cailliau[1] joined Berners-Lee and Cerf's team as a systems engineer. Soon, Cailliau became the staunchest supporter of connecting the Internet, HTTP, TCP/IP, Transmission Control Protocol/ Internet Protocol, and personal computers by means of creating the largest single information network on the planet. His goal was to help physicists share all of the information stored on each individual computer at the CERN laboratory, and hypertext would allow each user the opportunity to easily browse text on web pages using the HTTP links. The first examples of this were developed on Steve Jobs's NeXT personal computers (see *Sidebar* for details).

Next Computer

After leaving Apple Computers in 1985, Steve Jobs went on to form a company that he called NeXT Computers—with products that were designed with all the bells and whistles available for computers at the time. This first computer workstation was released in 1988, and had been developed specifically with the college student in mind (most likely due to Apple's early success in education—particularly in higher education). Jobs believed that if he could hook college students on his NeXT Computer during their college years, then they would want a similar model upon entering the workplace—and he would thereby be able to slowly push IBM and Windows out of the business market. However, the excessive amount of add-ons that were bundled in with the base model at that time drove the price far too high for college students who didn't have a surplus of cash to afford. NeXT was purchased by Apple in 1996. Much of the current Mac OS X was based on NeXT O.S. Operating System.

Berners-Lee developed a browser-editor with the intent of creating a tool that would allow its users to build spaces to share information. The world's first URL address, web site, and web server was info.cern.ch. It ran on a NeXT Computer workstation at CERN on Christmas of 1990. Many names were considered for this newly created sharing tool, and in May 1990, the creators settled upon the *World Wide Web* or *WWW*. At that moment, Robert Cailliau became the first person to ever surf the Web (*surf* having been derived from *Cerf*—a nod to co-creator Vint Cerf's contributions).

The world's very first web address was info.cern.ch/hypertext/WWW/TheProject.html.

This page was set up to explain how this new Internet worked, what Hypertext was, how to search the Internet, and even included technical data on how to create web pages. There is no record of how the very first pages looked, because they were being modified and updated daily.

The only available screen shot of the first web page/browser was taken three years later, in 1993. This image can be found at www.w3.org/People/Berners-Lee/WorldWideWeb.html. The primary difference between the 1990 screen and the 1993 screen was color; the first web page was displayed in gray scale.

The largest problem that the team had in expanding the Web beyond their own personal computers was the existing state-of-the-art computers. To make their new Web work, they needed to create browser software that could run on the then-popular DOS-based IBM, Compaq, and Tandy, which paled in comparison to the sophisticated NeXT Computer. In early 1991, the team began testing the DOS-style browser to work with any personal computer or terminal. To operate on DOS, they needed the browser to eliminate all graphics and the mouse in exchange for just plain text, as Microsoft's DOS could not recognize a graphic interface or the functions of a mouse.

By the end of 1991, Web servers began popping up in other institutions throughout Europe. The first Web server in the United States was at the Stanford Linear Accelerator Center (SLAC). Within one year of the web's inception, there were a total of 26 servers worldwide. By the following year, the number had grown to more than 200.

By 1993, PC and Macintosh users were able to access the Web through Mosaic, a program released by the National Center for Supercomputing Applications (NCSA) at the University of Illinois at Urbana-Champaign. Within only two years, the Internet went mainstream with dial-up connections to companies like CompuServe and America Online (AOL). And now, with an estimated 1,463,632,361 Internet users surfing 176,748,506 web sites containing more than 29,700,000,000 (est.) web pages, the World Wide Web has come a long way.

What You Need to Know

In order to understand how and why a web page is effective, it is important to first discuss a few basic marketing and psychological concepts. Although *The Social Media Bible* is not intended to replace a book such as *Marketing For Dummies*, some fundamental understanding of the psychology of a sale is necessary to fully understand how to develop an effective web page. The first concept to discuss is called the sales or buying funnel (see Figure 6.3).

The sales funnel is a metaphor that marketers use to imagine what prospects and customers are thinking as they move through their sales cycle—from the moment they realize they need your product or service to the time that they actually purchase. This cycle is especially critical with web pages, because it doesn't simply dictate the design of your home page. It

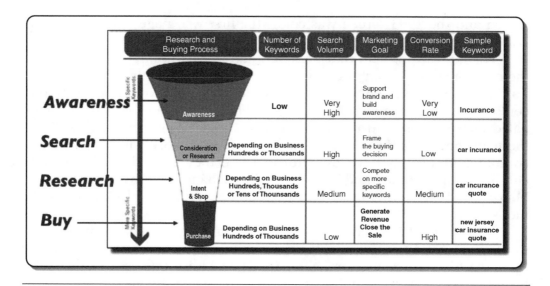

Research and Buying Process		Number of Keywords	Search Volume	Marketing Goal	Conversion Rate	Sample Keyword
Awareness	Awareness	Low	Very High	Support brand and build awareness	Very Low	Incurance
	Consideration or Research	Depending on Business Hundreds or Thousands	High	Frame the buying decision	Low	car incurance
	Intent & Shop	Depending on Business Hundreds, Thousands or Tens of Thousands	Medium	Compete on more specific keywords	Medium	car incurance quote
	Purchase	Depending on Business Hundreds of Thousands	Low	Generate Revenue Close the Sale	High	new jersey car insurance quote

FIGURE 6.3 Sales Funnel

requires that you have a specific web page designed specifically to accept and address the types of questions that your prospects have at any given moment during the buying cycle.

The stages that your prospects move through in their sales funnel are Awareness, Search, Research, and Buy. Let's take a look at these steps, using the example of an auto insurance salesperson in Phoenix, Arizona.

Awareness

Your (potential) client realizes that they are in need of car insurance. They begin to consider how they might get more information about auto insurance in their area, what they might ask about it, and what to type in the search engines to start their search.

Search

Your client will then begin to search the Web, looking for information on car insurance. They're conducting a very general search at this point, since they don't yet know what companies offer it or even what type they are looking for. Their search would likely only include terms like "auto insurance" or "car insurance." However, their frame of mind is less general than it was during the Awareness stage, as they have already begun to think about what they are looking for by choosing their key search terms.

Research

Once your client gets the chance to poke around and identify the companies that provide auto insurance, they then may drill down to searching with a term like "auto insurance quotes." Your prospects are now more knowledgeable, and their searches are much less general.

Buy

The last part of this cycle is the point at which your prospect is ready to purchase. They know what company they want to go with, they know the type of policy they are looking for, and their search becomes significantly different. Now they are searching for "Travelers auto insurance quote Phoenix." Makes sense, doesn't it? Don't all online consumers go through this process at one time or another—whether they're looking for insurance, shoes, or vacations?

The length of this particular buying cycle could last anywhere from one night to a year or more. If the buyer's insurance policy isn't due to be renewed until next year, then the client might begin looking now, wait to find out more details when he pays his next premium, and not complete his final research until the policy is due for renewal.

Now, let's put ourselves in the mindset of the prospect. If you were in the Search mode—looking only at this point for companies that provided auto insurance—and were taken to a page for Allstate where you were asked to enter your personal information for a quote and a phone call from a salesperson—what would you do? You would probably leave that page, because the information provided therein wasn't appropriate for what you desired during your "Search mode" of the cycle.

What if, on the other hand, you had completed all of the research necessary to choose an insurance company? You knew the type of policy you wanted, you studied the deductible, and you're ready to purchase. You search, you click, and you're taken to a specific insurance company's home page. Four clicks later, you still didn't find a place to get a quote; so what do you do? *You close the page.*

All that work the company did creating their site—optimizing their home page, paying for the pay-per-click just to get you there—and you leave. An ideal web page delivers the specific information your prospect is looking at during the appropriate time in their personal sales cycle. The lesson here: it's not about your home page; it's about everything that comes after.

Your Home Page Is Causing You Harm

However, most people erroneously believe that the home page is everything. They operate under the assumption that it's the only page that needs to be optimized and advertised, and the only place to which traffic should be driven. This is a misconception. Driving your prospects to your home page is causing you more harm than anything else you could be doing on the Web. Your home page is merely the cover of your book; it does not provide any of the information that your prospects are looking for.

Let's say a fellow worker who has read this book is holding it in her hand, and you ask her, "Where can I find the information in there about why home pages are bad?" Suppose that she responds by doing nothing but placing the book on the table in front of you, and pointing to the cover. How would you feel? Surprised? Confused? Angry? Wouldn't you expect her to open the book, find the chapter, turn to the page, and point to the paragraph? Well, that is akin to what your customers expect when they're looking for information on your web site. Don't simply point your prospects and customers to the cover. Your home page is meant for branding, because when you're advertising—whether online or off, and when all else fails—you still always need brand recognition.

However, you need to develop a plan that addresses your prospects' mindsets, and unearths what they are searching for through each step of their buying cycle. Each of the pages is easy to create, and must be simple to understand. The Awareness page could very well be your home page. If you have more than one product, however, you might need a top-level page that must be generic and have general terminology along with high-level information. The Search page needs to be a little more specific, and perhaps mention all of your products with a description and some what's-in-it-for-me for each. Your Research page needs to describe the distinct qualities of your products or services, so that your prospects can compare the value of your offering against all of the other competitors. And the last page—the Buy page—needs to only give your prospect the opportunity to review their order and, of course, to buy. Capture them when they are ready.

Designing a web page is unlike any other type of advertising you can do. Your web site captures your prospects and customers at the very moment in time when they actually desire that specific information. No other advertising can accomplish this. Another key difference is that your prospects are always asking for your specific help on a specific topic on a web page, and they are doing so voluntarily.

Your customers will engage with plenty of advertising involuntarily. For example, how do you feel when you open your mailbox and find it filled with junk, catalogs, and coupons? What is your reaction when telemarketers call you during dinner? Or survey people come up to you in the mall? Are you offended? Has your privacy been invaded? Are you annoyed? Now, compare that to how you feel when you seek out someone's advice on a question—and they are immediately happy to help you. Web pages provide the same kind of gratification—*if* you design them right.

Comparing web page design to direct mail advertising, a web page would be like a psychic mailman. The keywords that your prospect uses—based on where they are in the buying cycle—are like very precise mailing lists. The search engine result wording is like an envelope, and the exact web page you take your prospect to is the material inside. The web page contents have been designed specifically for what that prospect is looking for, and is delivered at the exact moment they ask for it. A well-designed array of web pages can convert your prospects into your customers.

This concept also applies directly and powerfully to your blog page, the photographs you share, video uploads, and podcasts as well. Be sure to have something for everyone at every stage or frame of mind.

There is one additional stage in this sales cycle funnel: Post-Sale. Your prospects may actually be in the Post-Sale stage of the customer life cycle and are seeking support, engaging in loyalty, participating in your blog, uploading videos about your product, and engaging in other related activities. Be sure that you have a mechanism to capture and retain your hard-earned customers, so that they will come back and, most important, refer their trusted network to you to become new customers. (Be sure to read the chapter on blogs, as this is the most effective way to keep your customers—and your company—in the loop.)

To broaden the appeal of your web pages, consider that your target audience's efforts may extend beyond the obvious. You need to consider your prospects, customers, resellers, distributors, the press, industry analysts, investors, and even employees who may use your web site as a resource or selling tool. Consider the needs and behaviors of all your important constituents. You may need to have specific web pages designed for each of them as they travel through their own sale (or thought) cycle.

Design Elements to Consider

The most basic concept to keep in mind when designing a web page is that this is where people tend to look *first* for information about your company or organization. Such design has essentially become a science. The *New York Times,* as well as many other major newspapers, are broken down into left and right pages, each of which contain six sections. The *Times* understands their customers' behavior so well that every story in their entire paper is specifically placed based on priority. The page split is designed to place important information where the eye looks first, and also takes into account how the newspaper will be folded by the reader when reading it on a train or other confined area.

(A great article about "How to Hold 'Em and How to Fold 'Em" can be found at query.nytimes.com/gst/fullpage.html?res=9F06E0D61738F935A 2575AC0A961958260.)

Madison Avenue advertisers never sleep (not a surprise, since Madison Avenue is in New York!). In their Landing Page Eyetracking Study of February 2005 (Figure 6.4), these advertisers showed that when bouncing low-wattage laser beams off the retinas of volunteers, people tend to look first at the *top left* of the page, time and time again. This comes as no surprise; after all, children are told to start at the top of the page on the left side. What does this say for web design? Put your most important message, image, or logo on the top left.

This study also showed that retailers who made their landing web page easy to read provided a strong what's-in-it-for-me, and favoring the top left section of the web page increased their conversion rate by as much as 64 percent.

Next, keep your message above the fold. While this term originated with newspapers, it refers to keeping your key message in the top window pane of your browsers; and don't expect your visitor to scroll down to find additional inspiration to stay on your page and hopefully convert.

Psychological Marketing

Another effective tool in marketing on the Internet is psychological marketing, which requires that you go way beyond the traditional techniques of studying the demographics of your customers and try to get into their heads. You need to ask yourself, "What are they thinking when they reach my web page? What are they doing *right now*? Which adjective should I use to describe my product on this page? Which words will cause more conversions?"

As this isn't a psychology or marketing book, there is no room here to discuss this subject at length. However, if you go to www.theSocialMedia Bible.com, you can use your password to download the "Psychological Hot Buttons" document (yours free as the owner of this book).

FIGURE 6.4 Eyetracking Study, February 2005

Source: Go to www.theSocialMediaBible.com for a "clickable link."
www.google.com/url?sa=t&source=web&ct=res&cd=1&url=httppercent3Apercent2 Fpercent2Fwww
.marketingsherpa.compercent2Ftelepercent2FLPET.pdf&ei=LqLBSN7wNKOmpATR4OjoBg&usg=AFQjC
NEAMuKbC7U7qwiRAOqRuP3FvQ8HVQ&sig2=oVF8QcXCIUe1PIbY0bIEZQ,   and   research.microsoft
.com/apps/pubs/default.aspx?id=77794

It's All about Conversion

What are you planning to do with all of the traffic you get to come to each of
your specific web pages? Don't let any of it go to waste. You've worked hard
to get every eye. The most important design element you can consider is your
conversion message. Now that you have your prospects' attention, what do

you want them to do next? You want them to convert. (And no, even though this is called *The Social Media Bible,* conversion does not refer to religion.)

The term *conversion* actually has a lot of different definitions in the context of web design. In fact, every different page you design—based on the rules from above—carries a different meaning of conversion. The most common and easiest to understand of these is "Click Here to Purchase." There are many others. Wikipedia defines "conversion" as: "In marketing, a conversion occurs when a prospective customer takes the marketer's intended action. If the prospect has visited a marketer's web site, the conversion action might be making an online purchase, or submitting a form to request additional information. The conversion rate is the percentage of visitors who take the conversion action."

If you have a pair of eyes on your home page, conversion means, "Read my message and click to another page." If your site visitor clicks to the next page that contains more detailed information and assists them through their sales funnel, you have a successful conversion. If you have someone land on a page that asks them to join your network and they sign up, you have a successful conversion. If they are asked to "pass this along to a friend" (referral) and they do, then your web page and call to action were effective and successful.

Accurately targeted traffic results in conversions—whether they are sales leads, large numbers of page views (visitors looking at pages), longer time on page or site (minutes spent interacting and reading: stickiness), brand awareness (due to immersion in the site and your marketing message), off-line contact (often consumers change to off-line contact through store visits or telephone calls), and pass-alongs (tell-a-friend referrals). Before you design the content of a web page, you must first consider its definition of conversion.

The most effective way to get someone to convert is to have a strong "What's In It for Me?" (WIIFM). Chapter 5, It's Not Your Father's E-Mail went into detail on WIIFM. The first WIIFM's 1.54-second rule and the second with its 5-second rule will make the difference between your prospect converting and leaving. Be sure you've read and comprehend the section on the importance of selecting the right image to help convey that WII-FM message.

Each page should have only one definition of conversion stated by your WIIFM message. Once your prospect has found your page, you need to provide that person with the exact information they are looking for and capture them with a strong WIIFM message that conveys that conversion. This is why a home page is harmful and ineffective: it has many conversions—probably every conversion your site has to offer. It's therefore somewhat confusing to your prospects.

Since Part I of this book is about tactics more than strategies (which are described in Part III), this section doesn't spend a lot of time on metrics.

However, whatever your definition of conversion is for each page, be sure to design the page in a way that allows you to measure it. If you don't gauge your conversions, then you can't manage them. If you don't set up Google Analytics or another way to assess your web site's traffic, then you won't know if all of your hard work was successful. Determining what to measure is easy: how many visitors came to that page, how many converted (clicked through), how many left.

If more people left your site than converted to the next step, then your conversion message was too weak, or it did not provide the call to action that your visitor was expecting. You need to constantly adjust and fine-tune your conversion message; test, measure, refine. Lather, rinse, repeat.

Here are a few other sample metrics to consider when quantifying your conversions:

- I want to increase the *number of orders* by 30 percent within one year.
- I want to increase the *click-throughs* on my page by 50 percent by next quarter.
- I want 25 percent more *visitors* who will look at *six pages* before leaving.
- I want the press to pick up our great *success stories,* resulting in *four trade articles* this year.
- I want to *reduce* the amount of tech *telephone support by 20 percent* this year by shifting it to *online support forums,* (YouTube how-to videos, tech support podcasts, and company blogs).

Some metrics will be difficult, and some even impossible to measure. There still is a great deal of benefit to gain from your efforts, however. An immediate order (e-commerce) is easy to track, but a lagged order (where your prospect comes back later to purchase) drives prospects to a retailer store (which applies to both business-to-business and business-to-consumer) or converts to a telephone order (Dell Computer has 5,000 separate 800 numbers for tracking). These are called "blended success metrics," and one way to measure these is by incorporating extras like coupons, unique and trackable special offers, cashier questions, unique telephone numbers or extensions, promo codes, and unique URLs.

B-to-B Success Metrics

Business-to-business (B-to-B) marketers have an even more challenging time measuring their metrics. Consider tracking data like immediate lead generation, immediate order via the phone, lead or other phone contact, lagged order long after the site visit (consider their buying cycle), faxed RFP/RFQ based on information learned on the site, catalog or brochure request, white paper download or request, newsletter, e-mail, or other registration and sales meeting request.

Testing Different Landing Pages

Keep in mind that you aren't limited to only one landing page per sales funnel category or conversion definition page; in fact, you can create many different pages that can each test different images, colors, backgrounds,

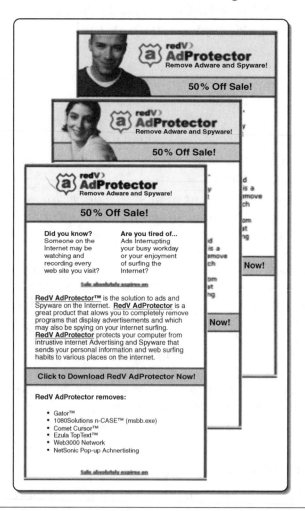

FIGURE 6.5 Landing Pages

fonts, headings, font sizes, layout, and WIIFMs (Figure 6.5). By testing multiple pages intended for the same conversion, you can directly compare the pages and determine which is converting most effectively. This is a lot like the practice of segmenting described in detail in Chapter 5, It's Not Your Father's E-Mail.

Conversions

- *Man:* 33 sales, $72,795
- *No picture:* 32 sales, $67,435
- *Woman:* 25 sales, $54,120

The "man" picture sold 8 percent more than "no" picture and 35 percent more than the "woman" picture.

The remaining design element you must always consider is the content. Search engines love good content—as do your prospects and customers. Above all, be sure that your web pages address your prospects' needs and desires, and always provide a strong call to action along with satisfactory value. Many experts interviewed for one of the author's podcasts—all of which can be found at www.theSocialMediaBible.com—had the same advice. To quote 2007 SEO World Champion Benj Arriola, "Content is king."

Techniques and Tactics

The purpose of this book is not to teach you all you need to know about how to design an effective web page. It is more focused upon helping you understand the big picture, and imparting some of the little-known—and better-known—tips and tricks picked up along the way. If you really want to get into the technical side of web page programming, get books such as *Creating Web Pages For Dummies* by Bud E. Smith and Arthur Bebak.

Even so, some techniques and tactics help avoid many of the common errors that most people make. The first and most damaging relates to fonts. Never use serifs.

A *serif* is a term for characters that have a line crossing the free end of a stroke, sometimes referred to as *feet and hats* (see Figure 6.6). This style of type face is thought to have been invented by the Romans. It is the most often used font and also one of the most legible styles in print, but *not* on the Web. The popularization of this font emerged in newspapers where the font size

FIGURE 6.6   Serif and Sans Serif Fonts

was nine points or smaller. Because this made large blocks of text difficult to read, adding the serifs—or the short line segments—created a sort of top and bottom line for the eye to follow when reading. Remember the faint blue lines that teachers taught writing with in first grade?

This aid became so helpful to the newspaper industry—particularly to the *New York Times*—that nearly all printed words are done with serifs. This is why the most common serif fonts have names like Times and Times New Roman. The only instances when a newspaper doesn't use a serif font is when the text is designed large enough to be easily read, such as a title of an article (in which case they often use Helvetica).

Here's an interesting test: take a page from the newspaper and look closely at the text. See how the serifs almost create a line across the top and bottom of the text? Now, slowly turn the newspaper page away from you so you are looking nearly on its edge, but can still see the text. The serifs almost join to create the definitive lines.

This effect is fine if talking about print, which usually has dpi (dots per inch) greater than 300. Newspapers can be printed at 600-plus dpi, and many magazines can be printed at up to nearly 3,000 dpi. That's a lot of dots for every inch. However, reading a computer monitor is a completely different story.

The Internet is, by definition, viewed through a computer monitor (or worse, a mobile screen). No matter how much you pay for your high-resolution flat-panel monitor, the highest Internet resolution you will ever see is . . . 72 dpi. This is a very poor quality compared to a printer. This is the case because the human eye can only see so many little bright lights—like those on your computer screen—per inch. At 72 dpi, serifs don't aid in reading; instead, they detract. The resolution of our monitors simply doesn't do justice to the fine detail of a serif. It just makes mud.

Web page and screen resolutions are rapidly getting better due to HD Video, ClearType fonts, and higher resolution monitors, but for now when designing a web page, be sure to always use nonserif or what they call sans serif fonts—such as Arial, Geneva, Monaco, and Tahoma.

"Trademark Sucks"

Another effective technique is to use trademarks in your copy. This section is called "Trademark Sucks" because trademarks are a very effective tool for sucking or hijacking your competitor's traffic away from competitors and onto your web site.

You can usually use another company's registered trademarks in your copy if comparing or contrasting different products or services. Comparative pages are generally considered fair use in the United States; however, Europe views this differently. Trademark sharing is frowned upon outside of the United States, where content, editorial, and blog sites frequently leverage brands in content. Be careful when you do this, and always check which rules apply where—since there have been cases where trademarks in hidden copy or meta tags have been litigated.

Keyword Placement

Question: Who shows up when you search for your brand? Is it you or your competition? Do a search, and find out.

As explained in more detail in Chapter 20, Spotlight on Search (Search Engine Optimization), the placement of your keywords can help with search engine rankings, and make it clearer to your prospects exactly what you're offering them. Start your content's paragraphs with keywords that make sense both to your prospects and search engines. Use nouns that describe the product or service accurately, and use them early. Use phrases that might be searched, and weave them into the copy. Make your copy unique to every page. You need to have a unique WIIFM.

Frames

Frames are programming techniques that create a grid of pigeonholes called *framesets*, wherein blocks of text from other web pages are inserted to create one visually pleasing page. Don't do this! Frames compile text from multiple web pages, and links to internally framed pages lead to dead ends—or pages with no text of their own. Frames will kill your site's search engine friendliness; even if you get the site indexed, the searcher's experience is very poor. Remember: no frames! For more information on Frames, go to www.useit

.com/alertbox/9612.html or visit www.theSocialMediaBible.com for click-able links.

Flash

Embedding Flash into your site is okay, as long as the navigation and content are also available elsewhere in the HTML code and on the page. Flash is an animated cartoon or film usually seen as a web site's home page introduction, created using Adobe Flash animation software as is a .swf file format. Full Flash sites are nearly unindexable (i.e., they are practically invisible to search engines) because Flash isn't code that a search engine can read; it's compiled movie code with no html code of its own. Even Google and FAST, both of which claim to index Flash files, don't seem to rank them too highly. Flash may seem cool for your designers and marketers, but Flash misuse can kill your search engine optimization and anger your prospects. How many times have you been caught in a home page Flash demo and ran for the mouse to click "Skip Intro"? Your prospects feel the same way, too. Use Flash sparingly—and correctly.

Page Titles

Pick a page, any page . . . and look at your page title. It's even odds that your programmer never gave your page a title and that it's still called "untitled"—or it has the same name as all of your other web pages. Perhaps it's even just your company's name. You must have unique, descriptive titles on each page of your site; primarily for the search engines, and secondarily for your prospects. Be sure to use explanatory titles. These are the essence of each page, the WIIFM. Use titles that are unique and compelling for the searcher. Be sure to include phrases a searcher is likely to type (do some keyword research). An accurate description of the page's content is much better than engaging in keyword stuffing—in other words, just adding random keywords. Your title can be as long as 90 to 100 characters, but it's best to lead with your strongest keyword differentiator, not your site or company's name. When titling your web pages, always consider plural and singular versions of a keyword.

Constructing Regional and Local Campaigns

It's important to understand the motivation behind the local searcher's query. If you are a local company, you must separate and differentiate your web pages by region or locale. Even if you are a national company, but sell and compete in different regions, localize your landing pages by using local state, town, city, county, and geographic names. This way, when your prospect is searching for a company in his area, your company will come up in his search—even if you are 1,000 miles away.

Off-Line Marketing Strategy

Before you had a web page, you likely had a conventional marketing strategy. What were the objectives of that strategy? And on an even more basic level, before you had this marketing strategy, what was the product or service that you wanted to sell? Your web page goals and objectives should align with your overall business goals and objectives. How close to your true goals and to your off-line strategy can you get in online advertising and web page content? More about strategy is discussed in Part III of this book.

Affiliate Marketing

Many marketers rely on affiliates—or partners in branding and marketing—to generate sales on a commissioned basis. However, affiliate-marketing problems can and do arise. When you use this kind of sales program, you are essentially supporting someone else to compete with you for web page traffic. You need to ask yourself how your brand is portrayed, how much traffic you're giving away to your affiliates, whether you're fighting with an affiliate for your own traffic, whether your affiliates are escalating prices and costing everyone more—and, essentially, whether using affiliates at all is a good strategy. Affiliate marketing can be very successful for some companies; but it's not for everyone. Refer to the Readings and Resources at the end of this chapter for more information on affiliate marketing.

Web Site Platforms

The purpose of this book is to explain concepts relating to the Web and social media. It isn't the intent of this book to be a detailed teaching guide. The different varieties of platforms upon which your web site can be constructed are becoming more plentiful every day. The most popular include HTML-based—the old standby that's been used for more than a decade; Joomla, an easier-to-use, open-source platform; Ning, an easy-to-use, community-building platform; and WordPress, which is also a very easy-to-use, open-source, robust platform. You will have to research your options further as new ones are coming online every day. Find a web site developer whom you can trust, and ask him or her to explain the pros and cons of each platform so you can find what's right for you.

Providers

This section tries to give you a starting point on companies that provide services to support the subject matter of the chapter. In the field of web page developers, the list is limitless. To find a good provider in this field, solicit help from your trusted network. Speak with someone you rely on before hiring a developer. Unfortunately, far more companies are out there that don't know what they are doing as opposed to those that do.

One of the most important decisions you will need to make once you do find a trusted developer is the base platform on which you will develop: HTML, Joomla, WordPress, Java, or another technology altogether? Many developers aren't skilled in building on all of these platforms. They usually prefer only one, and they stick to it. Do a little research on how each kind of platform works, and have your developer explain the pros and cons of each. Many web sites are actually combinations of platforms. Remember that when all else fails, HTML is usually the most reliable method.

Alexa (www.alexa.com) is a web traffic information company founded in April 1996. Alexa Internet grew out of a vision that web navigation should be intelligent and constantly improving by way of user participation. Along the way, Alexa developed an installed base of millions of toolbars, one of the largest web crawls, and an infrastructure to process and serve massive amounts of data. For Alexa's toolbar and web site users, this has resulted in products that have revolutionized web navigation and intelligence. Developers are able to use a set of tools that are unprecedented in scope and that allow entirely new services to be created on the Alexa data and platform, including a free ratings toolbar.

In-House/Out-House

Unless you want to learn how to program a web site yourself, you should leave the programming to the web developers. If you choose what's called a "high-level" platform such as Joomla or WordPress, you should at least learn how to create and modify web pages and blogs. It's easier than you think; it could save you the time and money that it takes to go back to the developer each time you need a small change; and it can be fun to do.

Expert Insights

David Cain, president and James Burnes, vice president,
MediaSauce, www.MediaSauce.com.

JB I think the biggest thing with citizen journalism and, earlier the higher level of user-generated content has always been the paradigm between trust and transparency with communication. I think that's the one thing that has kept the barrier there between traditional media and what we would call new media user-generated content media. I think that will be the ongoing opportunity for organizations to take advantage of to move forward . . .

JB I think the biggest thing about it is the realization that we've gone from a one-to-many broadcast message. We're publishing information that we want our consumers, prospects, and customers to be hear; to actually requiring ourselves to be prepared to actually have a real conversation with our customers. It's transforming the way we have to engage in sales and the prospecting process, the marketing process, customer relationships, customer support. The biggest opportunity that's bringing forth to us today is, "How do we create the use of conversations in a way that also allows us to promote our message and improve our product and services.

I think that the biggest challenge for organizations as this comes forward is the reality that people have the opportunity to nourish, they're not only going to be saying the things that you want them to say but the same context you have the opportunity to engage and really create transparency, as we mentioned before, by addressing both the good and the bad of how consumers are experiencing your product or your services or your brand, and then turning it into exciting consumers about your product if you properly engage in these tools.

(continued)

(*continued*)

So it's about transforming the way you communicate in the web site itself, as the platform, to answer your question, is the way that we're going to be able to do that more effectively, efficiently in the 24/7/365/50/50 world . . .

DC When I look at social media and I hear the term, and I think of how it changes the average web page of corporate America, I think that it's really a scarier word than it has to be for most people. Social media to me, if you just eliminate the term from what we are doing, nobody would have a problem if I sat down at a table and I said, "Tell me about your company; what it does and how it works?" Everybody has some level of comfort with that in a conversation in the off-line world. You have to or otherwise you wouldn't be able to make it in business. And really, what the online world does is it's taking that conversation to a URL . . . to any kind of social platform or any kind of platform, for that matter, where you can have this conversation in your own time and you can move from corporate messaging to the self-discovery of when I think of "online" I think that we're creating an experience here that's happens to max what's going on in the off-line world.

But they are fundamentally different than what you have when actually sitting across the table. And the difference is going to be that the audience is a lot more selfish, and the audience is a lot faster. So you have the time to engage like you would if you sat at the table and you've got to make it happen fast and you've got to make it relevant and interesting, and that's where all those buzz words of transparency and being authentic and all that come up. And to me, it's just what normal people do when they sit down and have conversation. You've got to be trustworthy, you've got to be honest, you've got to be real; otherwise people are going to look at you and say, "Whatever! Get out! I don't want to do business with you?" . . .

DC I would say that there are so many tools that when we meet people, a lot of times what's happened is they either become paralyzed with so many options . . . and then they make no progress . . . or worse yet they just go out and they just use the "Just Try Something" approach. So they amass a bunch of tools and they decide whatever's hot, or being used, or they heard about, or they've read about . . . and they just start saying, "Let's implement that; let's implement this." The reality is that we liken this to building a house. You know, when you make a decision that you're going to build a home, you wouldn't just send out a backhoe and start digging. You wouldn't start your home-building process by going to a furniture store (although my wife does), but regardless . . . I say that because it's true. Some people, I guess, would start at the furniture store, and pick out what they want a room to look like. But still, fundamentally, if you're starting at the furniture store, you've made a decision about what you want the house to do.

So the difference between what type of home you build if you're retired and have no kids versus what you have with a family of six. So how you look at your business, and fundamentally what you want to accomplish there, and how you want to live, is going to be how you decide what your web presence and that experience should look like; in the context of what you're going to do there and what kind of audience is going to be coming over.

So if I'm going to be a big entertainer, then I want a house built for entertainment. If I don't want anybody over and we're going to raise a family, then I might have a whole different layout. In any case I don't start with experimentation, I don't get caught up in the fact that there's so many choices. I have to step back and say, "What am I trying to accomplish, and what am I going to do here," and then build the right kind of experience that fits my audience . . . and that might not include all these tools and it might get it down to where there's a handful that are irrelevant.

JB I agree with that, David. In addition to that point, it's also the fact that there's a traditional mind-set that up to 2005/2006, that everything had to be in one location. The reality is that you have different audience members, different prospects, different customers who have different needs in different places on the web. And your initial issues online can have multiple presences. You can have micro sites for specific needs. You can have tools and applications set for different platforms. You can have your own site that has different integration of each of those pieces that serve your different audiences.

And so people try to be everything to everybody they want to serve on one site, but the reality of it is that the way people search to find information and the way social networks are influencing where people go, even to find information . . . you have to look at where your customers are going to be at in the moment in the process of a decision-making method . . . you know exactly where they're going to be at in that moment of making a decision . . . where you might become relevant . . .

JB The Vision Gap is sort of our CEO's brainchild, Bryan Gray. We have to give him credit because it's something that he brought to the table, and that's how we see organizations' opportunities to succeed in life.

You think about all organizations that are perfectly aligned to get results that they get. In other words, everything you're doing today, if you want to change them a year from now, two years from now, three years from now, you probably continue with the same kinds of results . . . whether it's for sales or marketing or product development, etc., etc.

We call that your "Present Past." In the context of what we see in organization and how we seek to pull off really big things, the organization should recognize, "If I were to change something today, if I want to aspire for something higher and greater than we have ever achieved doing the things we continue to do, what would that be?" We call it the "Highest Aspirations."

To get to the highest aspirations, think about big things . . . like your life depended on these things. If your business is a success or failure depended upon

(continued)

(*continued*)

big things, what would be the difference between the highest aspirations two to three years from now in your Present Past. What is the difference between those spaces? We call that your "Vision Gap."

Specifically we look at what it would take using these visual social media tools to help you pull off your biggest aspirations to succeed long-term . . .

DC Where I was going to comment there is . . . James does a better job of articulating that than I would, but I would say we live that model and when you live that model you're only good partners with people who are growing something as well. When we look at the marketplace we have to find people that are trying to pull off something that is . . . if you're getting what you want, we're a bad fit. And a lot of people, when you ask the question, "Are you getting what you want?" They always want more. But there is truly only a few organizations that really do . . . that really live that. Everybody would agree that you want more, but deep within, where the fundamental desire is that is driving that is not present, it will never happen.

An example I use that's simple but I knew two guys who were going to quit smoking. And one of them, at the New Year, five days into the New Year were smoking again. And I asked him when talking to both of them, they both seemed committed, but the underlying desire for why you wanted to quit smoking . . . one of them was thinking about having a family and raising kids; the other one, his girlfriend told him to. . . .

So the "girlfriend-told-you-to" only lasted five days before he was smoking again. The other guy that had the fundamental life change coming, quit smoking forever. So the whole idea here is that everybody can say they want something, but truly, your desires have to match it. And we look for it and it's a tough prospect to find organizations that really have the desire to do something different than they're dong now . . .

JB From a business perspective, that's how we recruit, too. And we're looking to hire people that will work in this organization who want things big every single day, and don't want to do boring, average, mediocre stuff.

You know, we are talking about prospecting for customers, or even building for us so we can align ourselves with the right business partners. It's all about people who have the highest aspirations and understand that achieving your highest aspirations requires risk. It's not the safe route. It's the road that requires recognizing that there's a massive difference between where you want to be and where you're going, and being willing to make a commitment, personally, mentally, culturally, as an organization . . . to align the resources and the initiative to get you to a place to achieve those highest aspirations.

And that's a good place to stay. I mean, fundamentally if you say all those things it's like, "Yeah, we're looking for people that really want it because they want to do something different, and they want to change; not because their girlfriend told them to . . ."

To listen to or read the complete Executive Conversations with David Cain and James Burnes, go to www.theSocialMediaBible.com.

Commandments

1. **Thou shalt understand your prospect/customer.**

   Have a firm grasp on what's important to them, what they are looking for, and what they expect to take away from your site. Only then will you understand how to create content that will really draw them in.

2. **Thou shalt understand the different sales funnel phases.**

   By recognizing the different phases that your prospect/client undergoes, you can develop specific web pages—and corresponding titles—that address their particular needs.

3. **Thou shalt implement metrics.**

   Really, if you can't measure it, you can't manage it. If you don't look at the numbers, you will never know if something you are doing is effective or a waste of your time. Once you have some analytics in place, test different ideas, layouts, taglines, headings, bullets, images, colors, and copy. Go with what works, and remember that this is a continuous process.

4. **Thou shalt understand the different conversion definitions.**

   Understand the different definitions of conversion you have for each and every page, and design each page specifically to attain that desired conversion.

5. **Thou shalt set specific measurable goals.**

   Set realistic and measurable goals for your web pages. This way, when you track these numbers, you will know when you are successful.

6. **Thou shalt remember that content is king.**

   Whether it's search engine optimization, stickiness of your page, or how well your page converts, it's all about content. If your content is valuable and meets the expectations of your prospects, then they will become engaged and most likely convert to purchasers.

7. **Thou shalt not use serif fonts.**

   Because of monitor resolution, fonts with serifs can become muddy and less appealing than a sans serif font.

8. **Thou shalt use frames and Flash cautiously.**

   Both frames and Flash make it difficult for search engines and hence your prospects to find you. Flash can also be annoying, so use it with caution.

Conclusion

Having a well-designed web page is probably the smartest thing you can do for your business. It certainly has the greatest return on investment. A cleverly designed site and page(s) will receive a high ranking on all of the search engines; be easy for your prospects and customers to find; provide valuable content for them; encourage them to stay longer on your site, thereby granting you a greater opportunity to convey your message; reduce customer service; expand your contact lists; build trust; and eventually convert them to a sale.

Readings and Resources

Carey, Patrick. *New Perspectives on Creating Web Pages with HTML, XHTML, and XML.* (Boston, MA: Mariner Books.)

Crowder, David A. *Building a Web Site For Dummies.* (Hoboken, NJ: John Wiley & Sons, Inc.)

Hiam, Alexander. *Marketing For Dummies.* (Hoboken, NJ: John Wiley & Sons, Inc.)

Kinkoph, Sherry Willard. *Creating Web Pages with HTML Simplified.* (Hoboken, NJ: John Wiley & Sons, Inc.)

MacDonald, Matthew. *Creating Web Sites: The Missing Manual.* (Sebastopol, CA: O'Reilly Media, Inc.)

McFedries, Paul. *The Complete Idiot's Guide to Creating a Web Page & Blog.* (Royersford, PA: Alpha Publishing, Inc.)

Prussakov, Evgenii. *A Practical Guide to Affiliate Marketing: Quick Reference for Affiliate Managers & Merchants.* (AM Navigator, LLC, 2007.)

Smith, Bud E., and Arthur Bebak. *Creating Web Pages For Dummies.* 6th ed. (Hoboken, NJ: John Wiley & Sons, Inc.)

Wagner, Richard, and Richard Mansfield. *Creating Web Pages All-in-One Desk Reference for Dummies.* (Hoboken, NJ: John Wiley & Sons, Inc.)

Downloads

For your free downloads associated with *The Social Media Bible,* go to www.theSocialMediaBible.com, and enter your ISBN number located on the back of the book above the bar code. Be sure to enter the dashes.

Credits

Expert Insights Were Provided By:

David Cain, president, MediaSauce, www.MediaSauce.com.

James Burnes, vice president, MediaSauce, www.MediaSauce.com.

Technical Edits Provided By:

James Archer, managing director, The Forty Agency, www.fortyagency.com.

Glenn Batuyong, Social Media Marketing Strategist, www.47ronin.com.

Note

1. Robert Cailliau, who worked at CERN, had independently proposed a project to develop a hypertext system, and partnered with Berners-Lee in hopes of getting the Web off the ground. He rewrote his project proposal, lobbied management for funding, recruited programmers, and collaborated with Berners-Lee on papers and presentations. Cailliau helped run the first WWW conference and became president of the International World Wide Web Conference Committee (IW3C2).

CHAPTER 7

The Internet Forum

What's In It for You?

The *forum* was the name for one of the first Internet-based networking and online communication tools—and still is a great way to engage people in an interactive ongoing conversation on a particular subject. If you want to start a debate, solicit advice, share an idea, run a poll, or just participate in a conversation on your favorite subject, this is where you go—to the forum (or chat room, as it's often called). A chat room differs slightly from a forum, however, because chat room participation requires the member to actively read and post to the conversation in real time, whereas in a forum, you can reply to responses days later. Either format allows you to log on, select a topic of interest, type your comments into a text file, and send them off so that others can see your thoughts—or *posts*—and have the opportunity to comment on your comment (which was a comment on the previous comment).

The forum builds strong community ties, loyalty, and really exemplifies the notion of a trusted network. You can easily apply this trend to your business and create a company forum, so that people from all around the world who care about your subject matter will read, participate, share ideas and concerns, and build a community of trust. By participating in other people's forums, you can develop your own credibility and strong ties with that community. As with all social media, it's about trust, participation, two-way communications, user-generated content—and it's free.

As an example, one forum web site—aptly named the Forum Site (www .theforumsite.com/), which was created in 2004,—put forth the following statistics as a snapshot of its activity: 3,210 Forums; 60,188 Members with 47 online, 96 new today; Topics 194,731; 2,971,801 Posts with 1,519 today; 37,748 Journals with 238,520 replies; 50,267 Pictures with 113,500 replies; and 97,272 Ratings, 565 Reviews, and 4,738 Polls.

theSocialMediaBible.com

Back to the Beginning

Forums—often referred to as chat rooms, message boards, and bulletin boards—go back to some of the very first uses of the private Usenet in the 1970s, and some of the early public Internet forums started at the beginning of the Web's first public uses in 1995.

The forum was the predecessor to the blog (see Chapter 8, The Ubiquitous Blog for more information). One of the author's own first experience participating in a forum was in 1986, when Apple announced eWorld—its own online service for communicating with their Value Added Resellers[1] (VARs; see Figure 7.1).

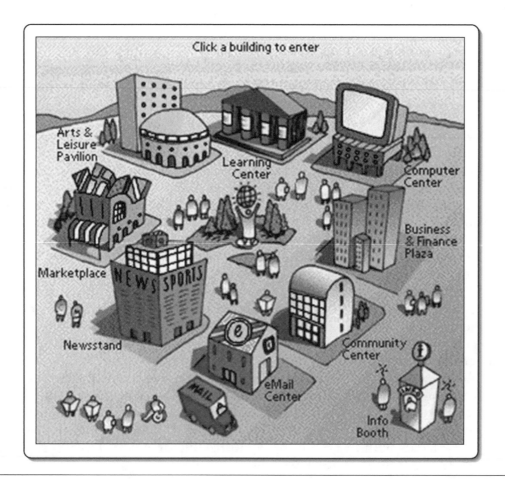

FIGURE 7.1 Apple eWorld Circa 1987

A VAR or Value-Added Reseller is a company that takes an existing product and adds its own value, usually in the form of a specific application for the product—for example, adding a special computer application and reselling it as a new product or package.

A strong sense of community or trusted network develops around forums, most of which have a theme or a conversation in which members share a common interest. Some of these include computers, cats, dogs, pets, sports, a particular team, religion, fashion, video games, politics, hobbies, cars, questions, comparisons, debates, polls of opinion—just about everything you can think of that people talk about. A forum is intended to promote an ongoing dialogue on a specific subject, which differs from the idea of a blog, since the owner of the blog is the one who posts a thought and allows comments—and then moves on to another thought.

What You Need to Know

A forum is a web site application that manages and provides a medium for ongoing online discussion on a particular subject (see Figure 7.2). The users

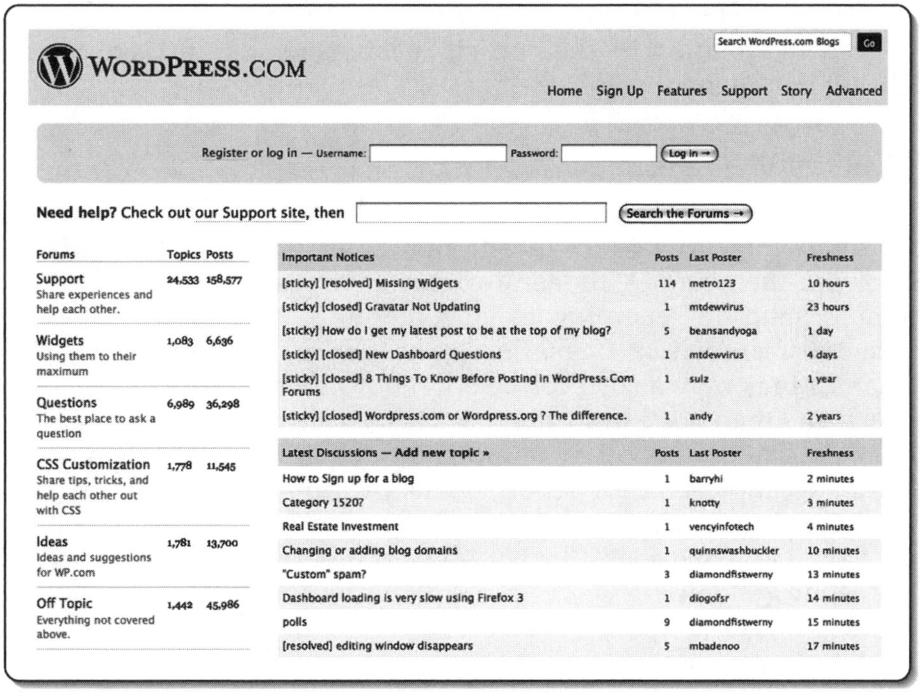

FIGURE 7.2 WordPress Forum Example

are a group of contributors or members, along with a moderator, who participate in the conversation. The moderator monitors the conversation to be sure that it adheres to rules and regulations set up by the forum owner(s). A member can begin a topic, which will allow others to comment on and add discussion to the previous posts or comments. This two-way communication is called a *thread*. In most forums, participants are required to register and sign in to take in a conversation or thread, whereas anyone is permitted to view them. However, anonymous visitors are usually prohibited from participating.

Forum Rules and Regulations

Forums are created, managed, and maintained by an individual or group of individuals who are referred to as *administrators*. Guidelines for all forums are created, and all participating members are required to follow them. These regulations are often found in the Frequently Asked Questions (FAQs) section of the forum, and the rules are usually basic and apply to common courtesy. Behavior that is prohibited includes insulting, swearing, harassing, inappropriate language, advertising, selling, spamming, personal information posting, sexual content, having more than one account, and warez or other copyright infringements. (*Warez* refers to works that are copyrighted and traded in violation of the copyright law, such as cracked or pirated versions of commercial software.)

Forum Moderator

Moderators—or mods—read and have editorial access to the posts/threads. Mods usually come to hold this position by being promoted from within the ranks of the members. A moderator can have control over banning and unbanning, splitting, renaming, closing, merging, and deleting threads. The Mods referee members' conversations to keep them free from rule violations and spam. Mods may also receive reports of guideline infringement from members, and then notify the offender when a rule has been broken in order to enforce the rules and, often, administer punishment. It is then up to the moderator to implement an action against, warning to, or banning of that member. First-time offenders are usually warned, whereas repeat offenders can be banned or banished for days—or even permanently. The offending content is always deleted.

Forum Administrator

An administrator (or admin) manages the technical requirements of the forum web site. Administrators are responsible for promoting and demoting

FIGURE 7.3 Captcha

members to and from their positions as moderators, keeping the site running properly, and sometimes acting as moderators themselves. These are usually the owners of the forum or are appointed by the owners and have the ultimate say in the operation of the forum.

Forum Registration

To be able to participate in a forum, you most likely will need to register. Once you do so, you become a member of the forum and can participate in a thread, or start your own group or topic of discussion. Most forums require that a member be at least thirteen years old; web sites that are collecting information from children under the age of thirteen are required to comply with the Federal Trade Commission's (FTC) Children's Online Privacy Protection Act (COPPA; see www.coppa.org). Most forums allow you to create a username and password, ask for a valid e-mail address, and ask the user to validate their registration through CAPTCHA Code (see Figure 7.3).[2]

You've seen these verification codes on many different logins and registration sites. Blogs have them to prevent the blogs from being automatically spammed.

Forum Post

A post is a text message or a comment that a member types out and submits. It is placed in a box that appears directly above the previous post box, and includes the member's username, icon, date and time submitted, and comment. In most forums, members can edit their own posts at any time after posting. This configuration of box upon box with more recent posts displayed in chronological order is called the *thread*. Once the original post has been made, subsequent posts will be placed on top of the previous one, continuing the conversation.

Most forum web sites limit both the minimum and maximum number of characters per post. These numbers are generally set at 10 characters for the minimum, and at either 10,000, 30,000, or 50,000 characters for the maximum, based on the administrator's decision.

Forum Member

Once you properly register to a forum, you become a member (or poster) and are recognized by the user name—or alias—that you choose. You can participate in posting threads to ongoing conversations, submit messages, and have access to all of the other features offered throughout the forum site. Members can use a signature (sig), photo, icon, avatar (see Chapter 17, Virtual Worlds—Real Impact), or other image that represents them and their posts (see Figure 7.4).

FIGURE 7.4 Avatars (left to right): Lon Safko, Robert Scoble's, Chris Heuer's, Club E's, and Chris Pirillo's

Forum Subscription

Members can subscribe to a forum, as they can with a blog. Subscription is an automated notification that alerts you when a new comment has been added to your favorite forum thread. This is done through RSS—Really Simple Syndication—or ATOM[3] feeds. (For more information on RSS, see Chapter 19, RSS—Really Simple Syndication Made Simple on how these feeds can be aggregated into one easy-to-read web page.) It's automatic, and every time there is a new post or comment, you see it without having to go to the forum web page to check.

Forum Troll

A member of a forum who repeatedly breaks etiquette—or *netiquette*—is referred to as a *troll*. This person deliberately posts inflammatory remarks in an attempt to incite irritated responses. When a troll posts a negative comment that engages other members to respond, it can create a flurry of angry comments, called a *flame war* or *flaming*. This activity happens often in forums, on Twitter (see Chapter 15, Thumbs Up for Microblogging), and even on social networking sites like MySpace and Facebook.

Flame wars take place when an ongoing dialogue becomes heated and its participants continue to post argumentative or inflammatory comments, which happens more often than you might think. It's especially frequent in forums that involve controversial groups and subjects like politics and religion. If a flame war breaks out, forum moderators will often warn the participants to stop the incendiary commenting. If this doesn't control the conversation and get it back on track, the moderator will then shut down the conversation thread—either for a finite period that is meant to give the participants ample time to cool off, or indefinitely. Excessive spamming can also cause flame wars and flaming.

Forum Spamming

Like flame wars, spamming is not appropriate or tolerated within the forum setting, and it's also considered a breach of netiquette. A spam message or post is defined as "any unsolicited communication that is not transactional, such as a message to complete a transaction, warranty, product updates, upgrades or recall information, change in terms of subscription or service, or account balance information" (see Chapter 5, It's Not Your Father's E-Mail, for a full history and explanation of spam). Forum spamming can also include any posting that is willful and malicious—such as repeating the same word or phase over and over to provoke a negative or aggressive response.

Someone on LinkedIn once sent out an obvious spam message to everyone on the network. The message read something to the effect of, "Hello, my name is . . . and I do consulting for . . . so call me for a free quote." The community went insane. Hundreds of backlash e-mails went to her and to other members reprimanding her for her inappropriate e-mail.

Forum User Groups

A *user group* is a group of forum members that grows out of a specific topic of discussion. The group keeps the conversation topic focused to what members of that group wish to discuss. By participating in this type of idea sharing and opinion sharing, the group members' passion on a specific subject forms a bond between them, and this bond is what makes the trusted network as effective and as loyal as it is.

For example, say you participate in an antique car collector's forum. After a while, the members will get to know you from the many posts and contributions you make to their forum. Then say someone wanted a recommendation on where to buy a hard-to-find part, and you suggested a resource; the members of that forum would trust you and your suggestion. You would have built their trust and friendship simply by participating. The same would hold true for a professional organization, a church group, or even a baseball league.

Forum Guest

A guest is an unregistered visitor to a forum site. Guests are generally allowed to access the entire site and read threads, but they are not permitted to participate and post comments in the discussions. To participate, they must be registered. A guest who visits a forum or group frequently without registering is referred to as a *lurker*. Lurking isn't necessarily bad; it's simply the way in which some people prefer to participate. It is somewhat like a blog; many people visit or subscribe to blogs and read them, but never comment on them.

Text Message Shortcuts

A lot of forum communication is done with text message slang or shortcuts. This is particularly popular in mobile text messaging, but is also used anytime you text in a manner that saves you keystrokes. (I'm no G9, but @TEOTD, ALCON, whether it's your BF or just K8T, BM&Y, there's always a BDN of people texting, but DQMOT.) For more about texting and text shortcuts—and to decipher this message—see Chapter 22, The Formidable

Fourth Screen (Mobile), and the downloads from that chapter for the complete Text Shortcuts Language Guide.

Emoticons

You've seen them. They're the little smiley faces that show up in your e-mail, on a web page, or in the text of a comment. *Emoticons* are "emotional icons"—a single symbol or combination of symbols that are used to convey emotions within the text message. Forums allow you to type a series of characters and symbols and have them automatically replaced and displayed as a small graphic or icon. A ":-)" will automatically convert into a " ," or a ":-(" will look like a " ." This also works in Microsoft Office programs like Word and Outlook. Microsoft's Messenger provides 70 different emoticons when you're messaging with friends to show them how you really feel. Emoticons are visual ways to express the way you feel when words alone just aren't enough. Try some emoticons in your next text message, e-mail, and Word document (see Figure 7.5).

Forum Social Networking

With the convergence of all things digital—photos, audio, music, and video—along with the popularity of social networking sites like LinkedIn and MySpace and photo-sharing sites like Flickr and Photobucket—forums have become much more social. Many of the forum platforms now allow its members to include personal photo galleries, personal pages, and real-time member-to-member chat.

Providers

While blogging is somewhat easier than participating in forums, and equally as effective for community-building, there are companies that provide software and Web-based solutions for setting up your own forum web site. You can create and manage the forum on your own server, setting it up on a provider's web site.

Create Your Own Forum Software

Ektron.com (www.ektron.com): Ektron CMS400.NET is a resource that provides a complete platform with all of the functionality necessary for developers and nontechnical business users alike to create, deploy, and manage your web site. Developers can take advantage of built-in Server

	Smile	:-) or :)		Open-mouthed	:-D or :d
	Surprised	:-O or :o		Tongue out	:-P or :p
	Wink	;-) or ;)		Sad	:-(or :(
	Confused	:-S or :s		Disappointed	:-I or :I
	Crying	:'(		Embarrassed	:-$ or :$
	Hot	(H) or (h)		Angry	:-@ or :@
	Angel	(A) or (a)		Devil	(6)
	Don't tell anyone	:-#		Baring teeth	8ol
	Nerd	8-I		Sarcastic	^o)
	Secret telling	:-*		Sick	+o(
	I don't know	:^)		Thinking	*-)
	Party	<:o)		Eye-rolling	8-)
	Sleepy	I-)		Coffee cup	(C) or (c)
	Thumbs up	(Y) or (y)		Thumbs down	(N) or (n)
	Beer mug	(B) or (b)		Martini glass	(D) or (d)
	Girl	(X) or (x)		Boy	(Z) or (z)
	Left hug	({)		Right hug	(})
	Vampire bat	:-[or :[		Birthday cake	(^)
	Red heart	(L) or (l)		Broken heart	(U) or (u)
	Red lips	(K) or (k)		Gift with a bow	(G) or (g)
	Red rose	(F) or (f)		Wilted rose	(W) or (w)
	Camera	(P) or (p)		Filmstrip	(~)
	Cat face	(@)		Dog face	(&)
	Telephone receiver	(T) or (t)		Light bulb	(I) or (i)
	Note	(8)		Sleeping half-moon	(S)
	Star	(*)		E-mail	(E) or (e)
	Clock	(O) or (o)		MSN Messenger icon	(M) or (m)
	Snail	(sn)		Black Sheep	(bah)
	Plate	(pl)		Bowl	(ll)
	Pizza	(pi)		Soccer ball	(so)
	Auto	(au)		Airplane	(ap)
	Umbrella	(um)		Island with a palm tree	(ip)
	Computer	(co)		Mobile Phone	(mp)
	Stormy cloud	(st)		Lightning	(li)
	Money	(mo)			

FIGURE 7.5 Emoticons

Controls to launch a site out of the box, or customize this initiation using CMS400.NET's well-documented API. Businesses benefit from an intuitive user interface that is extremely helpful in managing their site's content and messaging. A comprehensive SEO (search engine optimization) Toolkit ensures that potential visitors are able to find your site. Memberships, personalization, subscriptions, geomapping, and Web alerts keep your site visitors coming back; and social networking and Web 2.0 tools (including wikis, blogging, polls, and forums) grow your online communities.

Forum Web Site

Yuku.com (www.yuku.com): Yuku (Part of KickApps.com)[4] is a site that allows users to create and participate in profiles, image sharing, blogs, and discussion boards all in one place. Your Yuku account can have up to five different profiles, because although you don't always want to use the same profile, you *do* only want one account. Yuku's purpose is to help people connect and communicate online as easily and safely as possible. You don't need to download anything to use Yuku; all you need is an account, your profile, and your favorite Internet browser.

KickApps.com (www.kickapps.com): KickApps is a Web-based platform that makes it easy for you to add a wide array of social features to your web site. Whether you are a one-person shop or a global corporation, the Kickapps.com suite of applications are designed to integrate seamlessly with your web site and your brand.

Expert Insight

Amanda Vega, Amanda Vega & Associates,
www.amandavega.com

Amanda Vega

Personally, I've been on interactive space about 17 years now. I started out as the twenty-second employee of AOL, where I was a lowly chat moderator at the age of fifteen (laughter). So, I got a start in my career doing what all teenagers like to do; chatting online and then filling out reports about what people were chatting about. . . .

And it's interesting, too, because what we've discovered throughout the years is that while social media itself is kind of

(continued)

(*continued*)

global in nature, you know, it's the conversations through blogs and podcasts and people posting things on YouTube, and the bevy of conversations that happen from that, that the uses of social media across the world can be different, whereas . . . you know . . . U.S. bound and most of Europe, you see how the use of MySpace and Facebook by countries like Korea and Japan . . . they have their own little segmented versions of those two types of things. And, more importantly, when you start dealing with Korea and also Africa and some of your other southern European nations, they actually don't focus any of their social media through computers, because they just don't even have laptops at their disposal, especially in Africa. Everything is done through their mobile phone, and it's a way of life for them.

So they are actually way more active than the U.S. market, but just at a whole different level. So you have to start looking at what are the social networking spaces and then what are the needs and the ways that they use to do their blogging and their comment marketing and their communications just via the phone.

So you see a lot more use of short-messaging and a lot more snippets in conversations, with tiny links and things like that, so it is really interesting and fun. . . .

You know I can see on the global perspective, I think more of what truly is comment marketing and social media throughout those countries than you do, I think, in the U.S., for sure. Because that's how . . . much, like, we exchange simple text messages back and forth, and you see that as our society. . . . if you think it's frustrating here, it's like you said . . . it's a way of life. It's not the constant deluge of communication back and forth. And as quickly as we shoot text messages off to each other personally, they use their text-messaging to post across multiple social networks and to do commenting, and they're much quicker with their keystrokes and they can create tags much quicker than we do. And to them it is second nature, whereas to us, we are actually behind in that sort of communication. . . .

You know, I think in terms of the way that they're marketing, what you've seen is an influx of e-mail. Ten years ago you saw the first actual adoption of the corporate web site as a way of doing marketing, and that's not when it first started, right? I mean, we had web sites well before that, and e-mail almost 10 years before that as well.

But it was later in the mix where it was, "Okay, we have to have a web site," and people started thinking through why you were having it instead of just saying, "Well, of course we're going to have a web site; we're not sure what we're going to use it for, but we're going to have one because everyone else does."

You're inclined to see that now with social media. Ten years ago . . . social media, and the breadth of what it was defined as, was purely blogging and podcasting. It really didn't even have this meaning *social media* back then.

You had blogs and podcasts. And podcasts, at the beginning, were only voice and then you had video podcast for a while. So then, they are calling it *vlogging* and all this stuff, but now we kind of bucket it all.

So, for the clients what happens is they have to pay attention to e-mail as more conversation. So before it was just a customer base, back where you were just doing traditional brochures and handouts, and you know your investor-relations meetings and your press releases, and things like that. Well now, they have to adhere to a bigger group of standards; how each of the communications tools and sites out there have their own kind of nuances and blogs that are, kind of, run by the masses. You know they have to pay attention to that and they can't shy away from it. And what we've seen is, you know, there's still a struggle, I think, especially in larger companies. We see social media as an ad-campaign conduit instead of an ongoing way of doing business.

So you know, like you were saying, it's a business shift. It has to change at the company culture level and not be seen as just an advertising gig (laughter), and it's also made them more accountable for their opinions and gives companies their personalities. And sometimes that's uncovered some negative things for companies that have old ways of thinking and doing business. And we've seen it to where, you know, brands are kind of under a microscope now.

So you cannot run from it anymore. Although some think that they can, where it's the old, you know, early P.R. rules of thumb, where like if there are negative things going on, just ignore it they will go away. Like the bully in school where your parents told you that (laughter). In social media what we find is if you ignore it, it just gets worse because it just fires people up. . . .

Well, it goes back to . . . on the public-relations side of things, just like social media . . . (It's funny because our best case studies are those where . . . I guess it goes back and proves the point) . . . that it cannot be seen as advertising and you have to really be authentic in your conversations. We always say that, much like your examples in *Scientific America,* we obviously do a lot of PR and I'm quoted in *Brand Week* and *Ad Age* and I've been in the *Wall Street Journal* and all these great things. And I just thought, "the *Wall Street Journal;* wow, this is great, this is what every client wants, this must be amazing for us!" We have had all these quotes in all of our industry magazines, all over the Internet . . . you know, things like that. They really don't result, necessarily, in sales. However, an article written about the fact that I'm an avid surfer in *Surf Rider* magazine 10 years ago . . . and here's a girl who's surfing and talking about how boy shorts do not fit . . . ! So, I mean it's just no more than just a cute little article because it was a hobby of mine. We actually picked up three big clients from that article.

So it goes back to if you are authentic and you really participate and kind of produce yourself out there . . . that those are the things that result in

(continued)

(*continued*)

business. . . . Because, at the end of the day we always say . . . "When you get home from a busy day, you spent 12 hours in the office, your phone's ringing, you're trying to eat dinner . . . if you have a spouse or kids, you're trying to find five minutes to spend with them . . . if you're sitting down, finally, what do you pick up?"

Do you pick up your trade publication or do you pick up *People* magazine, or *Sports Illustrated,* or *Playboy,* or . . . whatever! What we all pick up is what interests us, right! For me, it's golf that grabs me, you know (laughter)!

My ad-agent mags sit there for four weeks and I have to read them all, once there, right? But you know when *Us Weekly* comes in the mail (laughter), that's what I'm reading on the treadmill! So the reality is, too, is that it goes back to what we're talking about. Those conversations cannot be just failed conversations, they show personality, right?

When CEOs of big companies want to put up a blog and just talk about, "Well, today at the company we did great things . . . because we always do great things and we wouldn't dare do anything that's not great! . . . and thanks for listening." And you are thinking, "Wow, that really . . . okay . . . revisits the brochure that I have. It's not interesting."

But if you show a little bit of personality, saying, "By the way, I'm the CEO of this major company. Did you know that this past weekend I just hosted a big dinner that was raising money for charity, and we raised $1 million for the National Arthritis Foundation . . . and here's some pictures linked to my Fotoblog area . . . showing some of that." Again, an authentic conversation that's passionate from the CEO, but the likelihood of them getting recognized by somebody else for the first time is pretty high; because you've actually related to a subject that's more appeasable to other people. And, again, it's just another valuable inbound link.

To listen to or read the entire Executive Conversation with Amanda Vega, go to www .theSocialMediaBible.com.

Commandments

1. **Thou shalt search and participate.**

   Pick a topic of your liking and search for a forum that has a group with an ongoing discussion on that topic. Begin as a guest, if it makes you more comfortable, and then register and participate for a while to see what you can learn from it. Think about the trusted network and loyalty that this forum is providing for you, and how you might be able to build that same kind of trust around your company or brand.

2. **Thou shalt set up your own forum.**

Once you've participated in a few forums and experienced what it is like to build these kinds of strong connections, you might want to next consider building this type of community around your company, product, or service. Give it a try. Using Yuku is a free and easy way to see if creating a forum is right for you.

Conclusion

While the forum is one of the oldest technologies on the Web, it still is a great way to easily create a trusted community around your company, product, brand, service, or subject matter. Try it! Set up your own forum, and invite a few friends, employees, customers, and prospects to engage in an ongoing conversation about your interests and what you do. It's free, and—as with many other social media tools—the ROI is unimaginable.

Downloads

For your free downloads associated with *The Social Media Bible*, go to www .theSocialMediaBible.com, and enter your ISBN number located on the back of the book above the bar code. Be sure to enter the dashes.

Credits

Expert Insight and Technical Edits Were Provided By:

Amanda Vega, CEO, Amanda Vega Consulting, www.amandavega.com.

Notes

1. Wikipedia defines a Value Added Reseller as: "A value-added reseller (VAR) is a company that adds some feature(s) to an existing product(s), then resells it (usually to end-users) as an integrated product or complete "turn-key" solution. This practice is common in the electronics industry, where, for example, a software application might be added to existing hardware."
2. CAPTCHA: Completely Automated Public Turing Test To Tell Computers and Humans Apart (see www.captcha.net) is a program that protects web sites against bots by generating and grading tests that humans can pass, but that current computer programs cannot. This term was coined in 2000 by Luis von Ahn, Manuel Blum, Nicholas Hopper, and John Langford of Carnegie Mellon

University. At the time, they developed the first CAPTCHA to be used by Yahoo!. For example, humans can read distorted text like that shown in Figure 7.3, but current computer technology can't.

3. Atom is an XML-based document format that describes attributes of a file known as feeds. Feeds are composed of a number of items known as entries. Atom is used to syndicate web content such as blogs, podcasts, and news to web sites and aggregation pages.

4. The KickApps-hosted, white-label platform puts social media and online video functionality directly into the hands of every web publisher who aspires to be a media mogul and turns every web designer and developer into a social media rockstar! With KickApps, it's now easier than ever for web publishers to leverage the power of social and rich media experiences on their web sites to drive audience growth and engagement.

CHAPTER 8

The Ubiquitous Blog

What's In It for You?

Scientists, psychiatrists, psychologists and counselors have known for a long time of the therapeutic benefits that accompany writing about personal experiences in a diary or journal. Blogs provide a convenient tool for writing about your individual thoughts and activities. Research shows that journaling improves your memory, sleep—and now, maybe even your bottom line.

In the twentieth century, professional reporters and publishers decided what the news was and determined how the public saw it. Though we might still have some professionals making these decisions in the twenty-first century, we now have personal reporters and publishers—more than 50 billion of them—who bring our news to us on a daily basis.

Although communication is—and always has been—a two-way process, the methods of communication to prospects and customers has changed dramatically over recent years. The use of social media digital tools have allowed for less reporting and more conversation. The web log, or blog, is the easiest and most effective way to provide a conduit for this type of communication. Blogs create communication, and communication builds trust—and blogs are completely free to build and access. In fact, in the year 2006, bloggers and other contributors to user-generated content were the reason that *Time* magazine named their "2006 Person of the Year" . . . "You."

theSocialMediaBible.com

FIGURE 8.1 Lon Safko Official CNN Reporter in Second Life.

Back to the Beginning

The term *blog* derives from *web log,* which is simply another word for an online journal. American blogger and author Jorn Barger was the first to coin the phase in December 1997, which prompted Peter Merholz to take the word *WeBLOG* and separate it into *We Blog* in a sidebar of his web page—www .Peterme.com—in May 1999. Entrepreneur Evan Williams first used the word *blog* as both a verb and a noun—in reference to posting to one's web log—and thus officially created the term *blogger.* Who better to do this than Williams—the developer for Pyra Labs' Blogger. com, the largest blogging platform in the world?

From 1983 through 1990—before HTTP was in common use—a service called Usenet was the primary medium for communicating over the World

FIGURE 8.2 EarthLink

Wide Web. Usenet featured a moderated newsgroup, which was either group- or individually controlled. In fact, these newsgroups were no more than simple forums (see Chapter 7, The Internet Forum). Around this same time, Brian E. Redman—generally known as the first individual blogger—began posting summaries of other interesting information he found on the Internet and thereby created his own blog called mod.ber (named for his initials, B.E.R.).

Back in the mid-1990s—before the personal blog became as popular as it is today—there were online communities such as GEnie, BiX, EarthLink, Prodigy, and CompuServe, all of which were the earliest ISPs (Internet Service Providers) and also provided bulletin board systems (BBS) and forums. Later, people would use this type of Internet software to create online diaries or journals to document daily activities of their personal lives. They called themselves *diarists, journalers,* and *journalists.* In 1994, a student at Swarthmore College named Justin Hall became recognized as one of the first bloggers. Science fiction writer Jerry Pournelle and software engineer Dave Winer are credited with establishing one of the oldest and longest-running weblogs: "Scripting News" (scripting.com/).

FIGURE 8.3   Prodigy

In 1994, an online diary called Wearable Wireless Webcam—which included text, photos, and video, broadcasting live using a wearable computer and EyeTap—was also credited with being one of the earliest blogs (see Chapter 16, Live from Anywhere—It's Livecasting). While this activity is referred to specifically as *livecasting* today, it was considered to be a form of the earliest semiautomated blogging of someone's personal life in the form of a video journal. This type of livecasting is also referred to as *sousveillance,* a term that describes the recording of an activity from the perspective of a participant experiencing that very event.

Other online journals began to pop up on the Internet in the mid-1990s. A computer programmer named John Carmack had his own widely read journal during this time on his "id Software" company web site. Video game developers Steve Gibson of Cary's video game Quakeholio (Shacknews), and Stephen Heaslip of Blue's News had been online since 1995. On February 8, 1997, Gibson was hired to blog full time for Ritual Entertainment—a turn of events that made him one of the—if not *the*—first paid bloggers.

Biologist and ecologist Dr. Glen Barry started his political blog back in January 1993, which became the oldest and largest political blog in history. Originally called Gaia's Forest Conservation Archives—and now operating under the name Forest Protection Blog (forests.org/blog/)—Barry began his blog as both an outlet for his passion to protect the forests and as his PhD project. Forests.org has evolved into one of the largest environmental web site portals in the world.

The earliest blogs were simply continuous updates of a standard HTML web site—a process that was difficult, and which required a certain level of technical knowledge to maintain the HTML code. However, more recent developments in browser-based blog platforms—enabling easy posting of articles in reverse chronological order and one-click editing features such as permalinks, blogrolls, and TrackBacks—made linking to other blogs and web pages easier (Figure 8.4). The ability to blog finally became accessible to the average nontechnical computer user.

FIGURE 8.4 TSMB Dashboard

Blogs can be used on a hosted service—such as Blogger.com or Going On.com—or can be hosted on your own server with software such as WordPress, Blogger, MovableType, or LiveJournal. (See Chapter 6, The World of Web Pages, for more information about WordPress. To hear the Executive Conversation interview with founder and developer of WordPress Matt Mullenweg, go to www.theSocialMediaBible.com.)

Nearly all web sites in the mid-1990s—personal and corporate—had a What's New or News section on them, which was usually sorted by date. This was essentially the earliest form of news-based blog. One such web page—the popular Drudge Report—was created by Matt Drudge and began simply enough: through Drudge's e-mails to his friends. In 1998, the Institute for Public Accuracy posted one-paragraph news releases a few times per week. The use of blogs grew slowly until 1999, and expanded especially rapidly during 2006–2008. As of the time of this writing, the number of blogs was approaching 200 million worldwide.

October 1998 brought the launch of Open Diary—a service that invented and introduced the reader comment, whereby readers could provide their own feedback to bloggers' posts. In August 1999, reporter Jonathan Dube of the *Charlotte Observer* published his own blog chronicling Hurricane Bonnie, which marked the creation of the first known use of a blog on a news site.

In March 1999, well-known blogger, programmer, and software author Brad Fitzpatrick began LiveJournal, a virtual community where users could go to blog or journal. In July of that same year, blogger Andrew Smales created Pitas.com—a version of the blog that was easier to maintain than a news page on a conventional web site. In August 1999, Evan Williams and Meg Hourihan of Pyra Labs launched blog publishing system Blogger.com, which was later purchased by Google in February 2003. In September 1999, a site called Diaryland—which focused more on the personal diary community—was started.

But people weren't just blogging about their personal lives and daily activities. In 2001, several popular political blogs emerged in the United States. British political commentator and speaker Andrew Sullivan created AndrewSullivan.com; attorney and journalist Ron Gunzburger launched his Politics1.com; political management essayist and author Taegan Goddard began Political Wire; University of Tennessee law professor and *Popular Mechanics* editor Glenn Reynold founded Instapundit; former jazz guitarist and software developer Charles Johnson established Little Green Footballs; and Democratic political strategist Jerome Armstrong started MyDD. Blogging was beginning to go mainstream, and was becoming so popular that there were how-to guides and established schools of journalism that began studying and comparing blogging to more conventional types of journalism.

In 2002, several comments made by U.S. Senate Majority Leader Trent Lott at a party honoring U.S. Senator Strom Thurmond proved to be appealing fodder for bloggers. Lott praised Thurmond by implying that the United States would have been better off had the longest-serving senator been elected president. Lott's critics interpreted these comments as approval of Thurmond's 1948 presidential campaign and his stand on racial segregation. This view was reinforced by documents and recorded interviews dug up by bloggers—such as Josh Marshall's Talking Points (www.talkingpointsmemo.com). The most interesting part about the event, however, is that even though Lott's comments were made at a public event attended by the media, no major media organizations reported on his controversial comments until *after* blogs broke the story. In essence, blogging helped to create a political crisis that forced Lott to step down as majority leader. The impact of this story gave greater credibility to blogs as a medium of news dissemination.

Blogging is often so timely that the mere term *blogging* has also come to mean *transcribed* or *editorialized,* as might occur during speeches or televised events. As an example, one could say, "I am blogging my reactions to speeches as they occur on television"—known as *liveblogging.* Many presentations are *tweeted* live using Twitter microblogging (see Chapter 15, Thumbs Up for Microblogging for more information on Twitter). These snippets of information can be tweeted to a presenter's followers or to the user's blog—using the freshest, most current information available.

In fact, during a recent presentation at a PodCamp weekend, a small giggle ran through the audience in the middle of a presentation about social media. The speaker stopped and asked what the chatter was about, and someone admitted that another audience member tweeted that there was a spelling error in the presentation. The speaker stopped the presentation, corrected the error, and thanked the blogging audience. How fresh is *this*?

The year 2004 saw blogs becoming increasingly widespread. News services, political consultants, and their candidates used blogs as outreach and opinion polls for their campaigns, and just to bond with their constituents. In the summer of 2004, blogs became a standard part of the publicity arsenal for the Democratic and Republican parties' conventions. Chris Matthews's MSNBC program *Hardball* and other mainstream television programs created their own blogs. And in that same year, *Merriam-Webster's Dictionary* declared *blog* as the word of the year.

Blogs were an especially important news source after the December 2004 tsunami. Sites such as Medecins Sans Frontieres used SMS text messaging to report from affected areas in Sri Lanka and southern India (for more on SMS, see Chapter 22, The Formidable Fourth Screen (Mobile)). And in August 2005, during Hurricane Katrina and its aftermath, a few bloggers located in New Orleans managed to maintain power and Internet connections, and blogged about the damage. Several blogs—including the Interdictor and Gulfsails—were able to disseminate information that the mainstream media did not cover.

In January 2005, *Fortune* magazine listed eight bloggers whom businesspeople "could not ignore": Peter Rojas (www.crunchbase.com/person/peter-rojas), Xeni Jardin (www.boingboing.net), Mena and Ben Trott (www.sixapart.com), Jonathan Schwartz (www.blogs.sun.com/jonathan), Jason Goldman (www.goldtoe.net), Robert Scoble (www.scobleizer.com), and Jason Calacanis (www.calacanis.com). Then, in September 2005, the British newspaper the *Guardian* launched a redesign that included a daily digest of blogs on page two. BBC News followed suit in June 2006 by instituting a blog for its editors.

In 2007, media mogul Tim O'Reilly proposed a Blogger's Code of Conduct to enforce civility on blogs by being calm and moderating comments. The code was proposed as a result of threats made to blogger Kathy Sierra. Tim O'Reilly stated, "I do think we need some code of conduct around what is acceptable behavior, I would hope that it doesn't come through any kind of regulation [but that] it would come through self-regulation" (www.radar.oreilly.com/archives/2007/04/draft-bloggers-1.html).

All of these clickable links can be accessed through www.theSocial MediaBible.com.

What You Need to Know

A *blog*—or *web log*—is a web site that is maintained by an individual with regular entries or posts that include commentary, thoughts, and ideas, and may contain photos, graphics, audio, or video. Posts are most often displayed in reverse chronological order. Most blogs provide news and content on a specific subject, while others operate as personal journals. Blogs usually have text, images, video, and links to other blogs and web sites that relate to the blog's subject matter. One of the most important features of a blog is the readers' ability to interact with the author through comments. While most blogs are made up of text, many bloggers prefer to add art (creating an artblog), photographs (a photoblog), sketches (for a sketchblog), music (or musicblog), audio (creating an audioblog—see Chapter 11, Talking About the Podcast (Audio Create)), or a podcast blog. And just like podcasting can mean either audio or video, blogging refers to anyone who writes an opinion about something.

A blog can be personal- or business-related. Business blogs can be used for internal communication to employees, or designed to be viewed by the public. Blogs used for sales, marketing, branding, PR, and communicating with customers and prospects are often referred to as *corporate blogs*.

Blogs can fall into a number of different categories. One kind provides a feature called a Question Blog—called *Qlogs*—where readers can submit a query through a comment, submission form, or e-mail. Blog writers and administrators are then responsible for answering these questions. A blog site that posts primarily video is called a *Vlog* (video blog web site); then there are blogs that only post links to other blogs, called *linklogs*. Blogs that post shorter posts and a lot of mixed rich media are referred to as *tumbleblogs*; and blogs about legal issues and information are called *blawgs*. And of course, the not-so-legitimate spamming blog is called a *Splog*. The entirety of all the blogs on the Internet is referred to as the *blogosphere*, while a collection of blogs located in the same geographical area is called a *bloghood*.

While most blogs are created and maintained just for fun, many are supported by advertising. Sites utilize resources such as automatic content-specific banners and other type of ad placements, like Google's AdSense. Most of the larger, more popular blogs that enjoy high monthly traffic are easily earning six figures in advertising income.

All of these different blogs spread out over the entire globe had to create the opportunity for blog-specific search engines. Besides the standard Google and Yahoo! search engines, other kinds each have a blog-specific option as well. There are online communities that help readers find the right blog for a particular topic or area of interest, such as BlogCatalog and MyBlogLog. In addition, there are blog-only search engines like Bloglines, BlogScope, and Technorati, which is the most popular blog search site at the time of this writing. Technorati (www.Technorati.com) actually provides lists of the most popular searches and tags used in posts (see Chapter 6, The World of Web Pages, for more information about tags).

A blog's popularity can be greatly enhanced by a high rating on Technorati, a site that was founded to help bloggers succeed by collecting, highlighting, and distributing information about the online global conversation. Technorati determines and assigns a ranking to each blog based on the number of incoming links (LinkLove), and Alexa user hits. As the leading blog search engine and most comprehensive source of information on the blogosphere, Technorati indexes more than 1.5 million new blog posts in real time and introduces millions of readers to blog and social media content. In August 2006, Technorati discovered that the most popular blog in the world was that of Chinese actress Xu Jinglei with a reported 50 million page views. They also cited the self-proclaimed "directory of wonderful things" blog Boing Boing, as the most-read group-written blog (www.boingboing.net).

Maintaining a blog requires work and a moderate amount of dedication and effort. (While working on writing *The Social Media Bible,* one of the authors only updated his blog a half dozen times and did not "Tweet" as frequently. One of his loyal readers scolded him.)

The Gartner Research Group expects that the novelty value of the blog will wear off eventually, since so many people who are interested in the phenomenon create a blog just to see what it's like. Gartner further expects that new bloggers will outnumber those bloggers who abandon their blogs out of boredom, and estimates that more than 200 million former bloggers have already ceased posting to their blogs, creating a huge rise in the amount of *dotsam and netsam* (a play on the term *flotsam and jetsam*), or unwanted objects on the Web.

There are currently more than 300 mainstream journalists who write their own blogs, according to CyberJournalist.net's J-blog list. Many conventional bloggers have now moved over to more conventional media, including liberal media scholar Duncan Black (known

FIGURE 8.5 Blooker Award

by his pseudonym, Atrios; www.eschatonblog.com), Instapundit's aforementioned blogger Glenn Reynolds (www.pajamasmedia.com/instapundit), political analyst and current events reporter Markos Moulitsas Zúniga of the Daily Kos (www.dailykos.com), American writer and futurist Alex Steffen of Worldchanging (www.worldchanging.com), and Time.com editor and author Ana Marie Cox of Wonkette (www.wonkette.com), who have all appeared on radio and television.

Many bloggers have actually published books based on their original blog posts; these types of blog-based books are called *blooks.* Authors include Salam Pax, *The Clandestine Diary of an Ordinary Iraqi* from The Baghdad Blog; Ellen Simonetti, *Diary of a Dysfunctional Flight Attendant: The Queen of Sky Blog*; Jessica Cutler, *The Washingtonienne: A Novel* (washingtoniennearchive.blogspot.com); Scott Ott's *ScrappleFace* (www.scrappleface.com). In 2005, the Lulu Blooker Prize was created for the best blog-based book. So far the only winner who has made it to the *New*

York Times bestseller list with his book was Tucker Max, who wrote *I Hope They Serve Beer in Hell*, or, as Max puts it, "My name is Tucker Max, and I am an asshole." It's difficult to believe that his book was on the New York Times bestsellers list for more than two weeks.

Providers

As with the other chapters' Providers section, there are far too many types and different companies to list here; but a few to get started with are as follows:

- Search for blogs on Google, Yahoo!, BlogSearch, and Technorati.com.
- Start your own blog on WordPress.com, Blogger.com, and GoingOn .com.

Expert Insight

Matt Mullenweg, cofounder of WordPress, www.WordPress.org

Matt Mullenweg

For me, it was always that I wanted to have the means of personal expression. I always enjoyed writing and, so, publishing. It was pretty exciting. And I would say that it was really the *interaction* from the readers. So, although blogging is great, I blog for the comments. Because I know if I say something that's wrong or anything like that, the readers will let me know. . . .

It [provides] access to people all over the world that you would never meet otherwise, so what's cool is that sense; because my blog's very personal. It's people who are interested in the same things that I am. Maybe it's jazz or economics or photography or WordPress. So the answer to why I started blogging is I find it very, very rewarding. . . .

We probably do super-well on the search engines, and actually [they don't] try too many tricks or anything specific to target us at Word-Press; [they] just create a really great user experience. Have the content well organized, have a permanent place for blogposts (which are often called a *permalink*). Just to use proper HTML headings, tags, or the titles to the heading tags for the titles, for the posts. Some of these things get a little bit geeky, but if you create semantic, well-structured, frequently updated content, I think search engines . . . are just trying to serve their use by being one of the better resources on the Web. . . .

The development is, you know, 95 percent user-different; so from release to release we have a time schedule that we plan on a year in advance. But in terms of features for release, it's really defined by what our users are asking for. So, for example, in the last release we had, sort of, a *wiki*-like tracking feature; so every version of every post is saved forever. So if you make a mistake or go off edit approach, you can go and see exactly what changed. Things like that. . . . Some of our users don't even know it's there. It's a really powerful tool that your competitors haven't thought about yet. So we were able to get it early because we listened very closely to our community. . . .

I think what you really have to do if you're a leader of an open-source process is something that inspires people, something that people can coalesce around and get them excited to work on, even though they are not getting paid. On the carrot stick, all you really have is the carrot! So, (laughter) you really have to make it fun and engaging, and I think people will come, especially since they will control it in such an amazing way that has impact.

To listen to or read the entire Executive Conversation with Matt Mullenweg, go to www .theSocialMediaBible.com.

Expert Insight

Robert Scoble, famous blogger, Scobleizer, and author, *Fast Company*, www.Socobleizer.com

Robert Scoble

I've been blogging since 2000. I used to plan conferences for health professionals, and for programmers and web developers; and that got me into blogging, which then got me into NEC, which in turn landed me into a job at Microsoft where I interviewed 600 employees. And *that* got me a job at Pod-Tech; and now I'm at Fast Company and I'm going around the world interviewing business and tech innovators. . . .

The company used to . . . really feel like they had to control the message; that meant they had control of their brand and they would be able to talk to

(*continued*)

(*continued*)

14 journalists and get their message across. And now a kid in Australia with 50 or 100 readers or friends can really change how you are perceived in the world. . . .

I would start by listening and participating rather than trying to talk, you know. Follow a bunch of friends on Twitter who really fill 100 blogs on Google Reader. You know, go over to Flickr to connect with that community. Go over to YouTube and understand that community. And listen and see what people are saying about your company and your products—stuff like that—and your industry, your job ability, your genre. And then—and *only* then—should you talk. You know, by then you're probably compelled to talk; because if somebody talked about you at a cocktail party, of course you're going to talk back, right? . . .

I don't know about a [favorite] title, but I read hundreds of blogs. . . . I have 700 feeds and my Google Reader and I read 3,000 people on FriendFeed and I follow 21,000 on Twitter . . . the thing is, it brings in, you know, . . . I surf that to see what people are talking about and then I use search engines; in fact, FriendFeed and Twitter have a search engine now. And you can see what everybody is saying about a certain topic, you know, like what everybody is saying about Barack Obama this morning. . . .

If you are feeling overwhelmed, [then] segment [your information]. Start putting it into folders or track fewer people. Back off on the number of people you are following or the number of blogs you're reading. I find I don't get overwhelmed. I just find that it's hard to find the real nuggets among the noise. . . .

Well, there was a group of us sitting around the lunch table at Microsoft and meeting with a developer, and we wanted a way to communicate with other people [that was] different than just text. I thought, why can't we just video this lunch conversation? Why do we have to write it up, because writing it up is just impersonal and it doesn't let us communicate the way I wanted to communicate—which is visually. And so I said, "Let's just buy a cheap video camera and film these kinds of conversations and see if we can change how people communicate. . . ."

[It was] a *Forrest Gump* kind of moment. . . . I've interviewed [people like] Rick Warren—who runs one of the largest churches in the world—to Bill Gates, to Mark Zeckerberg . . . all sorts of different people who've done interesting things in their lives. I focus mostly on the tech industry, but I'm rounding out to general business, people who are doing innovative stuff in business. I've been very fortunate to get them.

To listen to or read the entire Executive Conversation with Robert Scoble, go to www .theSocialMediaBible.com.

Commandments

While doing research for this chapter, the original intent was to take some items from David Risley's 50 Rapid Fire Tips for Power Blogging, paraphrase them, and turn them into "Commandments"—but David's list had just too much good information to choose from. So here are David Risley's 50 tips in their entirety. *(Thank you, David!)*

50 Rapid Fire Tips for Power Blogging

I have been blogging for a living for many years now. I've learned a lot and, today, I wanted to throw out a bunch of quick tips in rapid succession. The goals here are: (1) get lots of traffic to your blog, and (2) earn money with it. Okay, here we go (in no particular order):

1. **Use WordPress.** No other platform is as flexible with all the plug-ins, in my opinion.
2. **Post often.** I usually default to one post per day, when I'm asked. I try to do at least one per day on this blog, except for weekends.
3. **Use catchy blog post titles.** Put yourself in the shoes of a person who is casually surfing the Internet, seeing your post along with hundreds of others. Will your blog headline stand out? Copyblogger is an awesome source for information on writing.
4. **Ask open-ended questions.** One of the best ways to invite commentary on your posts is to ask for it. Ask your readers questions and tell them to answer in the form of a comment.
5. **Comment on other blogs—often.** I actually maintain a separate folder in Google Reader for relevant blogs I want to follow more closely than others. And, on those blogs, I comment regularly whenever I have something to say.
6. **Use Twitter.** You've GOT to be out there, being social. FriendFeed, too.
7. **Use Twitterfeed to pipe your latest posts into Twitter.** But, don't ONLY use Twitterfeed. You've got to be a real person on Twitter, first and foremost. Twitter should not replace RSS.
8. **Make your RSS feed obvious,** above the fold, and preferably use the orange RSS icon.
9. **Provide an RSS-to-E-mail option** so people can subscribe to your latest posts without being forced to use an RSS reader. Many people still don't use RSS. FeedBurner provides a free RSS-to-E-mail service.

10. **Use images in your posts.** Images communicate on aesthetic wavelengths words cannot.

11. **Use header tags** to separate sections in your blog posts, where applicable; H1, H2, and H3 tags. And use good search engine keywords wherever possible in those headers.

12. **Structure your blog posts for easy scanning.** Use header tags, lists, and so on. Avoid long sentences and long paragraphs.

13. **Avoid MySpace-style blog designs.** What I mean by this is super BUSY designs with too much on screen, animated graphics, and so on. These things make your blog truly suck and makes your content too hard to pay attention to.

14. **If possible, use a custom WordPress theme.** It is getting to the point where people can recognize cookie-cutter themes. It is okay to use one, but at least modify it so that you have a unique header design.

15. **Start your blog's mailing list as early as possible.** The sooner you start, the longer you have to grow your list and, trust me, that list can be used to make money later. Jeremy Shoemoney made this mistake. John Reese used to hound him about building a list. When he finally got around to it, he realized how important it was.

16. **Research and choose your mailing list option correctly the first time.** I recommend Aweber. What you choose is up to you; however, moving a mailing list later can be a huge pain. I know from experience.

17. **When choosing a topic** to focus your blog on, two things should be considered: (1) Your interest in the topic, (2) How marketable your topic is.

18. **Learn to SELL.** The way to a full-time income by blogging is to learn how to MARKET and sell things using your blog. Yaro Starak does a good job of selling via his blog, for example.

19. **Don't discount Facebook.** It is a powerful networking tool and you should take the time to build your network, just as you might on Twitter.

20. **Create a Facebook page.** On Facebook, create a page for your blog or yourself and invite your readers and Facebook friends to become fans. This page can be your blog's outpost on Facebook. Be sure to import your blog posts as notes.

21. **Don't be a me-too blogger.** You don't want to become a copycat news blog, where you type news-style posts about what is happening in a saturated market. In technology, this is common. Offer something unique that cannot be found everywhere else in your market.

22. **Learn to think about your blog as a business.** The blog is a promotional and delivery mechanism to your ultimate product or service.

23. **When writing your About Page, pay attention to what you write.** Don't just rattle off some dumb, cookie-cutter facts. Your About Page should tell a story of who you are and why your blog is worth reading.

24. **Do lots of videos.** Use TubeMogul to publish them in as many places as you can. And make sure your blog URL is not only in the video, but also in the text description that accompanies the video.

25. **When making videos, be REAL and be personable.** Your videos are an important component to your blog's brand. Don't waste the opportunity.

26. **Link to other, related blog posts regularly in your own posts.** Not only your OWN posts, but also the posts of others.

27. **Remember, blogging is a SOCIAL business.** Be accessible to your readers and proactively get out there and talk with other people in your niche.

28. **If you can afford it, travel to blogging conferences.** Not only can you learn a lot, but also socializing with successful people often breeds so much motivation and success in yourself that it is simply beyond words.

29. **Write an e-book, create some videos**—whatever—but the idea is to create something which is of value to your readers on your subject, and have it available to SELL to them on your blog.

30. **Get involved as an affiliate** and start linking to products relevant to your posts using your affiliate links. You are providing relevant links to your readers (valuable) while potentially making some money.

31. **Don't post low FeedBurner counts**. Do not show your RSS subscriber count unless you have a high enough number (at least a few hundred). A low number acts as social proof that your blog has no readers, and that's not good.

32. **Install Popularity Contest** or some similar plug-in which ranks your posts based on popularity. Whether you display this information in public on your blog or not, knowing which of your posts are most popular tells you that that particular subject material works and you should probably do more of it.

33. **Put relevant keywords into your blog's title.** Use All-In-One SEO to have more control over the titles across your blog.

34. **Use a photo gallery.** People dig photos, so a photo gallery can be a great component to your blog. If you use Flickr, check out the Flickr Photo Album plug-in for WordPress.

35. **Create an RSS widget** for your blog on WidgetBox and make it available for your readers to embed on their own blogs if they so choose.

36. **Spend some time creating some killer posts for your blog,** then link to them somewhere so that new arrivals can quickly see your best work. It is your best stuff, which is going to sell them into becoming a subscriber.

37. **Make sharing easy.** Put options on your blog for your readers to share your posts across social media. ShareThis is a great option for this.

38. **Share and share alike.** If you submit your own posts to sites like Digg or StumbleUpon, be sure to also submit other posts. I might even recommend a 10-to-1 ratio of other people's posts to your own posts. You do not want to develop a reputation on these sites as somebody who only submits to their own content.

39. **When you write a post for your blog, aim to be helpful.** You want your visitors to come away with a solution to the problem they arrived with. Chris Brogan does so well because his posts are truly helpful.

40. **Read other blogs often.** When starving for ideas to write about, go to your RSS reader and read related blogs. Often, your own post can be a response to a post on another blog. In fact, this is usually a good idea.

41. **Train your readers to do what you want, if needed.** If you're in a market where the people will not know how to use social media, RSS, and some of these other things that help promote your blog, TRAIN THEM. Write posts or do videos which show your visitors how to Digg a post, use StumbleUpon, how to use RSS, and so on. Perhaps you can educate them and they'll become part of your promotion army for your own blog.

42. **When starting a blog, decide on its mission.** Your posts should, for the most part, center around a specific theme if you want your blog to really take off. If you run a personal diary kind of blog, where you write about anything that comes to mind, your blog traffic will always be limited because your blog will never attract any particular segment of people. Stay on topic. If you have no specific topic, that's fine, but realize your blog is going to be more a hobby than a business at that point.

43. **Don't overload your blog with JavaScript widgets.** These things slow down the load speed of your site. In fact, just recently I had to get rid of the MyBlogLog widget on [my] blog because it was having some effects on page loading time.

44. **Use Analytics.** I personally use Google Analytics as well as the Word Press.com Stats plug-in on [my] blog.

45. **Use Windows Live Writer.** It is the best blogging client program out there. Even though it is a Microsoft product and a Windows-only product, it is also better than any Mac blogging client I have tried. And it's free.

46. **Be yourself.** I believe it is a good thing to show personality on your blog. Don't be a fake. People can see right through it. Chris Pirillo draws people to his blog and Ustream feed almost solely on personality alone.

47. **Don't write like you're writing for Britannica.** You want your spelling and grammar to be correct, but be colloquial. Talk to people like you would normally talk to people, not as if you're writing a PhD dissertation.

48. **Link to your social profiles on your blog.** Link your various social media profiles right on your blog so that your readers can connect with you outside the confines of your blog.

49. **Go where your readers are.** Every market is different. When I blog about blogging, I know most of my readers are pretty adept online and probably hang out in the social media space frequently. If your readers are young, they might be on MySpace. If they're Linux nerds, they may be in the Ubuntu forums. Regardless, you need to maintain a consistent presence in the spaces your readers congregate. Be an authority and be helpful, and traffic will be drawn over to your blog.

50. **[Spend] equal time reading and writing.** You should probably spend just as much time reading and learning as you do writing for your blog. This is how you expand your knowledge, become a better blogger, and get new ideas for your own site. Blogging isn't all about you. Remember that.

(Original list appears at www.davidrisley.com/2008/11/28/50-rapid-fire-tips-for-power-blogging/). Go to www.theSocialMediaBible.com for a clickable link.

Conclusion

Blogging is by far the easiest and most effective way to communicate with your customers and prospects. Starting your own blog is as simple as going to WordPress, creating an account, selecting the New Post button, typing your thoughts, and hitting Publish. That's really all there is to it. Please give blogging a try. It really only takes 15 to 20 minutes once a week, and is as easy as typing a half page in a standard word processor. By blogging, you create links by which your prospects can find you, you generate "Google Juice,"[1] you position yourself as an industry leader by providing the latest information in your field, you allow for a two-way conversation, and you build trust.

Once you have created a few posts, use all of your other forms of communication to promote your new source of information to your customers and prospects. Soon, the numbers will begin to grow, your LinkLove will increase—and the industry will be waiting to hear your next insights.

Readings and Resources

Banks, Michael A. *Blogging Heroes: Interviews with 30 of the World's Top Bloggers.* (Hoboken, NJ: John Wiley & Sons, Inc.)

Gardner, Susannah. *Buzz Marketing with Blogs For Dummies.* (Hoboken, NJ: John Wiley & Sons, Inc.)

Gardner, Susannah, and Shane Birley. *Blogging For Dummies.* (Hoboken, NJ: John Wiley & Sons, Inc.)

Gunelius, Susan. *Google Blogger For Dummies.* (Hoboken, NJ: John Wiley & Sons, Inc.)

Reeder, Joelle, and Katherine Scoleri. *The IT Girl's Guide to Blogging with Moxie.* (Hoboken, NJ: John Wiley & Sons, Inc.)

Rettbergl, Jill Walker. *Blogging.* (Cambridge, UK: Polity Books.)

Rowse, Darren, and Chris Garrett. *ProBlogger: Secrets for Blogging Your Way to a Six-Figure Income.* (Hoboken, NJ: John Wiley & Sons, Inc.)

Scoble, Robert, and Shel Israel. *Naked Conversations: How Blogs Are Changing the Way Businesses Talk with Customers.* (Hoboken, NJ: John Wiley & Sons, Inc.)

Scott, David Meerman. *The New Rules of Marketing and PR: How to Use News Releases, Blogs, Podcasting, Viral Marketing and Online Media to Reach Buyers Directly.* (Hoboken, NJ: John Wiley & Sons, Inc.)

Downloads

For your free downloads associated with *The Social Media Bible,* go to www.theSocialMediaBible.com, and enter your ISBN number located on the back of the book above the bar code. Be sure to enter the dashes.

Credits

Expert Insights Were Provided By:

Matt Mullen, cofounder, WordPress, www.WordPress.org.

Robert Scoble, author, *Fast Company*, www.Socobleizer.com.

Technical Edits Were Provided By:

James Burnes, vice president, MediaSauce, www.MediaSauce.com.

Note

1. Google Juice is the quality, power, and advantage that a web site has, which enables it to achieve a high ranking within the search results of Google.

CHAPTER 9

The Wisdom of the Wiki

What's In It for You?

The word *wiki* comes from the Hawaiian word for "fast" or "quick," and it alludes to the pace at which wiki content can be created. Wiki sites are also often referred to as "*What I Know Is*," which came after the original naming. Wikis are web sites that allow people to collect and edit their intelligence in one place at any time. It truly represents the social media foundation of user-generated content and the wisdom of the crowds.

A wiki is a browser-based web platform that lets volunteers contribute information based on their expertise and knowledge, and permits them to edit content within articles on specific subjects. Together, this material creates an encyclopedic-type knowledge base that is founded on the integrity of the contributor's additions. Wikis can either be open to the public or restricted to members or employees. Many companies today are utilizing the wiki to create knowledge management systems for retaining corporate information for collaboration and for training. By incorporating a company wiki, many firms can gather the collective knowledge of their employees on subjects such as policies and procedures, manufacturing and sales, company history, products—and even how to fix the fax machine's paper jams.

As wiki inventor and computer programmer Ward Cunningham puts it, "The wiki concept has become a study in what's now called 'social software.' With a wiki, I write the seed of the idea and I come back in a week and see how the idea has grown."

The wiki has become an extremely valuable, easy-to-use, free resource tool. It is as simple as Edit, Write, and Save.

Back to the Beginning

Ward Cunningham came up with the concept for the wiki in 1994 and installed it on the Internet (domain c2.com) on March 25, 1995. Cunningham

theSocialMediaBible.com

FIGURE 9.1 Wiki-Wiki Bus

wanted to create a unique online site for programmers involved in a type of software development known as object-oriented programming, which allowed the user to drag and drop, and just click to make easy edits. The first web site to be titled a *wiki* was Cunningham's own WikiWikiWeb (www.wikiwikiweb.com), originally described as "the simplest online database that could possibly work." Cunningham gave the site WikiWikiWeb this name upon recalling a Honolulu International Airport counter employee telling him to take the "Wiki-Wiki" shuttle bus in order to get from one airport terminal to another. Cunningham explained, "I chose wiki-wiki as an alliterative substitute for 'quick,' and thereby avoided naming this stuff quick-web."

Cunningham's initial design concept for his web site came from Apple's HyperCard, an easy-to-use programming language that the education industry had widely adopted for the Macintosh computer in the late 1980s and early 1990s. HyperCard was a graphic metaphor of a stack of index cards that contained links to other cards.

On March 15, 2007, the word *wiki* entered the online Oxford English Dictionary.

As Apple phased out HyperCard from its software library, software company Silicon Beach developed a programming alternative called the SuperCard. From the early to mid-1990s, Safko International Inc. was considered the largest SuperCard/HyperCard programming company in the country—with more than 150 programs and more than 1 million lines of code.

What You Need to Know

Cunningham and Bo Leuf—coauthors of *The Wiki Way: Quick Collaboration on the Web*—describe the wiki this way:

- A wiki invites all users to edit any page or to create new pages within the wiki web site, using a plain-vanilla Web browser without any extra add-ons.

- Wiki promotes meaningful topic associations between different pages by making page link creation almost intuitively easy, and showing whether an intended target page exists or not.
- A wiki is *not* a carefully crafted site for casual visitors. Instead, it seeks to involve the visitor in an ongoing process of creation and collaboration that constantly changes the web site landscape.

A wiki's ease of use lies in the fact that it allows documents to be collaboratively written using a web browser. While the wiki web site is called the *wiki*, a single page is called a *wiki page*—which consists of user-generated content and hyperlinks to other articles, wiki pages, and external web sites.

Editing and Creating

Wikis allow the users to easily generate pages with the click of a button from any web browser. The name of the wiki is condensed into a page title where spaces and some special characters are removed. This type of titling is called *Camel Case*. To see the Camel Case title of the wiki page called Matt Mullenweg—cofounder of WordPress on *The Social Media Bible* web site, go to the clickable link on www.thesocialmediabible.com/2008/08/29/matt-mullenweg-founder-ceo-of-wordpress/.

Simple Markup Language Tools

The system for creating and editing a wiki page is called SML (Simple Markup Language), or often simply called *wikitext*. If you have ever created a blog, then you know what this is. (If you haven't created a blog, you need to read Chapter 8, The Ubiquitous Blog, to find out why you should!) SMP is easy to use and has the "WYSIWYG" ("What You See Is What You Get") editing features of most common word processing software: bold, italic, underline, insert photo or video, center, right, left, and full justification, and so forth. Most wikis indicate who has made edits and when they've been made by keeping track of versions of the content, a feature that helps prevent mistakes and vandalism.

Security

Wikis are a very open set of documents, and are generally accessible to the public or an entire employee base—which only makes them all the more vulnerable to mistakes and vandalism. Wikis are designed to make it easy to correct errors, and they contain a useful Recent Changes page feature. This page lists all recent edits, when they were made, and by whom. In addition, wikis provide the previous unaltered version and what is called the "diff" feature—a tool that highlights the difference or changes between page revisions. This way, an editor can view the article before it was altered, compare it with the new page, and even restore the wiki page to its previous revision before the edit was made, if necessary.

While malicious vandalism can and does occur, a wiki's editors can easily catch it and revert to a previously stored edition to eliminate any unwelcome changes. Lars Erik Aronsson, a Swedish computer programmer, consultant, and founder of two Swedish web sites—the free electronic book archive Project Runeberg and the Swedish language wiki susning.nu—summarizes the controversy as follows:

> [When] most people . . . first learn about the wiki concept, [they] assume that a web site that can be edited by anybody would soon be rendered useless by destructive input. It sounds like offering free spray cans next to a gray concrete wall. The only likely outcome would be ugly graffiti and simple tagging, and many artistic efforts would not be long lived. Still, it seems to work very well.

Depending upon how openly a wiki is designed, it can be susceptible to intentional disruption. This is why most open wikis require that you become a registered member or user before you are allowed to edit the contents of an article. Any intentional disruption is known as *trolling*, or damage done by a troll. (For more information on trolls, see Chapter 7, The Internet Forum.)

Deciding whether to have an open or closed wiki presents one with pros and cons. While a closed wiki provides more security from vandalism, its content grows very slowly. An example of the difference would be Wikipedia versus Citizendium. Citizendium requires the user to provide a real name and even a biography before being allowed to make edits. While this makes this wiki nearly vandalism free, it also hinders wiki growth. On the other hand, Wikipedia's open forum allows anyone with Internet access to edit capabilities to the articles—therefore permitting the site to grow quite rapidly. In fact, Wikipedia's English language version (www.Wikipedia.org) has the largest user base among all wikis on the Internet, and ranks in the top-10 traffic of all web sites. (See below for more information on Wikipedia.) Other popular wiki web sites include WikiWikiWeb, Wikitravel, World66, Memory Alpha, and Erik Aronsson's Susning.nu, the Swedish-language knowledge base.

Wikis have gained such popularity that there are now two well-known annual wiki conferences: the International Symposium on Wikis (WikiSym) conference, which is dedicated to general wiki research, and the Wikimania conference, which focuses on research and practices of the Wikimedia Foundation's projects, such as Wikipedia.

Wikipedia

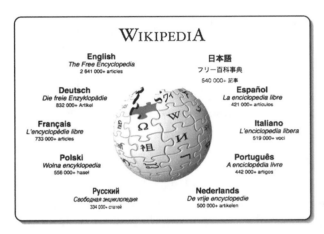

FIGURE 9.2 Wikipedia

Wikipedia is a nonprofit organization that provides a platform for the world's largest online user-generated content encyclopedia. The site contains more than 10 million articles, has been visited by 59,123,362 visitors (at the time of this writing), and is by far the largest and most successful wiki there is.

The following was copied directly from the Wikipedia entry on www.Wikipedia .org:

Wikipedia is a free, multilingual encyclopedia project supported by the nonprofit Wikimedia Foundation. Its name is a portmanteau of the words wiki (a technology for creating collaborative web sites) and encyclopedia. *Wikipedia*'s 10 million articles have been written collaboratively by volunteers around the world, and almost all of its articles can be edited by anyone who can access the *Wikipedia* web site. Launched in 2001 by Jimmy Wales and Larry Sanger, it is currently the largest and most popular general reference work on the Internet.

Critics of Wikipedia target its systemic bias and inconsistencies and its policy of favoring consensus over credentials in its editorial process. Wikipedia's reliability and accuracy are also an issue. Other criticisms center on its susceptibility to vandalism and the addition of spurious or unverified information. Scholarly work suggests that vandalism is generally short-lived.

In addition to being an encyclopedic reference, Wikipedia has received major media attention as an online source of breaking news as it is constantly updated. When *Time* magazine recognized "You" as its Person of the Year 2006, praising the accelerating success of online collaboration and

Table 9.1				
		Preceding Year		
Date	**Article Count**	**Increase**	**Average Increase/Day**	**Percentage Increase**
2002-01-01	19,700	19,700	—	54
2003-01-01	96,500	76,800	390	210
2004-01-01	188,800	92,300	96	253
2005-01-01	438,500	249,700	132	682
2006-01-01	895,000	456,500	104	1,251
2007-01-01	1,560,000	665,000	74	1,822
2008-01-01	2,153,000	593,000	38	1,625
2008-08-01	2,484,826	570,000	26	1,558

interaction by millions of users around the world, Wikipedia was the first particular Web 2.0 service mentioned. YouTube and MySpace were also mentioned as runners-up for successful user-generated content web sites.

Statistics in Table 9.1 show the phenomenal growth of wikis over the last six years.

Despite the criticism in regards to Wikipedia's potential bias and factual inaccuracies, many of the site's critics have agreed that the information contained within Wikipedia is actually quite accurate. Even though the Wikipedia Foundation repeatedly declined to participate directly in *The Social Media Bible*, the authors agree that web users should still be grateful for a resource like Wikipedia. This single site contains so much information on so many different aspects of the tools of social media. Wikipedia was an invaluable resource for the aggregation of information in this book.

MyGads

A great illustration of a very simple, easy-to-use, and free mini-wiki is a site called MyGads (www.MyGads.com). CommonCraft.com (www.commoncraft .com), a company that does great, simple, and easy-to-understand explanation videos, did one for MyGads on soccer team parents who need to keep track of which ones were responsible for bringing snacks to each game. The team coach created a page (mini-wiki) or a *Gad* on the MyGads web site, where team parents can add information to the page by just clicking and typing. The page contains information on all of the game dates, times, parents, and snacks. Because it is a MyGads page, the users can access the page through text message, instant message, or the MyGads web site. For example, soccer mom Sherrie is at the grocery store, and she needs to know if it's her turn to bring snacks. She sends a text message to MyGads that says, "June 26 Snacks." Within only a few seconds she receives a message back that says "Sherrie"; since she's in charge that week, she buys the snacks. It's as simple as that—and MyGads is secure, and always up to date.

Such a MyGads site would look like this:

Game Schedule		Snacks	
Date	Time	Date	Snacks
June 12	6:00 PM	June 12	Sheila
June 19	6:00 PM	June 19	Jenny
June 26	6:00 PM	June 26	Sherrie
July 3	6:00 PM	July 3	Vicki

MyGads is a useful resource for businesses as well; for example, let's say that you are a sales manager and need up-to-date inventory, price, and sales figures while on the road. MyGads works with most corporate databases, allowing you to keep the most up-to-date information on the MyGads page without any extra effort. You simply text message your MyGads page with "Medium Red Shirt," and instantly you get a message back: "247" in stock. And again, you can get all of this information through a text message or instant message, or from the web site. To watch the Common Craft demonstration video on YouTube, go to: www.youtube.com/watch?v=0S-WkhDygTA. Go to www.theSocialMediaBible.com for a clickable link.

Providers

While there are literally thousands of online wikis that contain millions of pages of information to choose from (the largest of which is Wikipedia), the easiest way to create your own wiki is to go to one of the following web sites that provide wiki platforms: www.PBWiki.com, www.WetPaint.com, or www.WikiSpaces.com. All of these wiki web sites allow you to create an account, then begin building your very own wiki.

Expert Insight

Jack Herrick, founder of WikiHow, www.WikiHow.com

Jack Herrick

It's pretty interesting, isn't it? It's amazing—the variety, type, and quality of information we get using the wiki method. It's been really eye-opening for me. Like when I started WikiHow, I wasn't exactly sure what was going to happen. I wanted to build this how-to manual, and all its different topics. But the wiki method is really amazing . . . seeing what type of information people are writing about. It's definitely veered away from the traditional how-to manuals at this point.

We have things about relationships, about . . . all the how-to topics you'd expect to find . . . how to fix your car, how to solve problems in your computer. But we've got just totally different types of topics; really wild things. It's really expanding the definition of what a how-to manual can be. . . .

Well, I've always really been interested in building a really big how-to manual; and I'll give you the long story here. I owned Psych-e How, which is sort of the Web 1.0 version of the how-to manual. And e-How got started in 1999 during the dot-com boom, and they raised a ton of money from venture capitalists. They had 200 employees, and they were writing this massive how-to manual; and at the time, I had nothing to do with that company. I was doing something totally different. [But] I knew the founder of e-How, and always admired the company. I thought it was a great idea. Unfortunately, when the first Internet downturn hit, [e-How] went into bankruptcy and had to lay off all 200 employees; and basically, the company went into a deep freeze. It was bought out by another venture capital–funded company, called IT-Exchange, and they tried to nurse the site along and find a business model that would work; [but] they also failed to do that. They just . . . it wasn't profitable, and they couldn't get it working. They were about to shut the site off, and it was a company I had heard about and I really liked their site. I didn't want to see it go down. [Even though] I was working at another company, I hated to see *How* die. So a friend of mine and I got together and bought the site. We were both working full-time jobs . . . but we sort of brought the site back to life.

We hired a couple of writers, and we started working [fixing] lots of bugs on the old site—and it started to work; and on a very, very small cost-basis we were able to get the site profitable and it was working quite well. We were pretty excited about it. But while I was doing that, I became a little disillusioned with

How. We hired writers; but . . . we found that you cannot hire writers to cover all the world's topics in all the world's languages. So, for example, I could hire someone to write about mutual funds, Viagra, you name any high keyword topic, and it was very profitable to have someone write about [topics like this]. But to write about some of the really obscure things—there is no business model for it; and it really wasn't my vision to have a how-to manual that was really only covering high-key TCP topics. I really wanted to have a how-to manual to cover every single imaginable how-to topic, and in multiple languages. And you just weren't going to get there with this professional writer model. At least you weren't going to get there in a high-quality method. You could take and put in a lot of junk, but that wasn't what I wanted to do either.

First, I was sort of puzzled about how we could accomplish this goal. In the process, [I was] taken around the Internet [and], like many people, stumbled upon Wikipedia and was just amazed at the quality [and] the breadth of information. . . . As I learned more and more about how it was written, I became even more impressed about what they were doing. So I started thinking, you know, if we could take the same wiki model and apply it to write a how-to manual. And so I tried that one. My engineer, Travis Daryl, and I sort of clevered away, and in late 2004, [we] tried to import the media wiki software and transform it to a how-to manual—something that would be better fitting for a how-to manual. And then we launched WikiHow on the anniversary of Wikipedia's birthday on January 15, 2005. . . .

Well, see, wikis are . . . there's nothing really specific out there as I herd the cats, to use that expression. I think there are a lot of people out there who want to do something, and a wiki allows you to put a certain [amount of information] together, and [give you] one place to do it. So, WikiHow attracts a group of people who are as passionate as [I am] about building a large, shared how-to manual; and it allows them to do that. So it works through its virtuous cycle. Where when I first started WikiHow, the very first month—we had it up in January 2005—we had over 2,000 people visit the site, and that was great.

And those 2,000 people may [only] be 5 or 10 people [who] actually wrote an article or edited something. And so there really wasn't much going on at the site in the very early days, but it works in a virtuous cycle where the next month you had these 5 articles, or 10 articles and those brought some people in from search engine traffic, and what have you. And some of the people read the articles and said, "Hey, this article is not very good. I can do a better job." And they pressed "edit" and they improved the content; and then the content got better, and maybe moved up in the search engine rankings, [which] brought more people in . . . who've also said, "Wow, I can do better than this!" And *they* pressed "edit" and improved the content and the cycle keeps going . . . and is still running today on WikiHow. Synergy! I think that it definitely happened in the case of WikiHow. It definitely happened in the case of Wikipedia, and I've

(continued)

(continued)

also talked to people who are working at Fortune 500 companies and hearing those same sorts of stories you heard. People within the enterprise are turning on wikis and finding that the knowledge in the organization is far more than people at the top would have assumed. Allowing this sort of bottom-up collaboration can happen on a wiki; [it] produces [impressive] knowledge, and . . . I think more organizations are going to try and figure this out and protect it.

One company that I've talked to is the U.S. State Department. They have a wiki internally called the Diplopedia which runs on Wikipedia software just like WikiHow and Wikipedia. So it's been a great resource for the State Department. . . .

In the wiki community there are thousands of people who contribute to WikiHow over any given month; and within that group there is a much smaller and tighter group of people that will number in the hundreds—people who I call the "Hard Core WikiHow Contributors"—and they are responsible for making sure the quality stays high. Every edit that goes to WikiHow is looked at by another human . . . a volunteer who looks at "edits" and says, "It is good" or "It is bad," or "I'm going to check this . . . am I going to send it out, or am I going to 'edit' this 'edit' to make it even better?" And so that's happening all the time, all day long in real time. Hundreds of people around the world are helping out. So that's our first line of defense. Then there's the reverse . . . if we miss something—or our volunteer editors (or "Hard Core Contributors") will often catch [it]; and if we make an error or let something slip in, readers will find it.

And . . . one of the things that is getting pretty exciting about wikis is [that] we are finding more and more ways to improve quality. You may notice at the bottom of every wiki page now there is a "Is this article accurate? [Yes/no button]" [that] people vote on; so it percolates pages that might have accuracy problems—and we work on them and improve them. This really allows situations where you would think there would be complete chaos—where we allow anyone to edit. We do not even require people to log in or tell us any information about themselves whatsoever; and yet [by] allowing anyone to edit, wiki creates a high quality.

To listen to or read the entire Executive Conversation with Jack Herrick, go to www .theSocialMediaBible.com.

Commandments

1. **Thou shalt visit wikis.**

Go look at the most popular wikis. Look at Wikipedia. Do some searching. Find a subject that you are passionate about. Read some of the articles . . . and comment on them. Add some facts. Correct some misnomers. Google other wikis, and check them out. Most importantly: participate and contribute.

2. **Thou shalt create a company wiki.**

Try to develop an internal company wiki. Go to one of the providers, sign up for an account, and create a wiki. Encourage other employees to participate; get them to create topic pages. Get others to contribute to the content. You will be surprised how fast your content and loyalty will grow within your trusted network.

Conclusion

Wikis are a great way to collect the wisdom of the crowd—whether it's a public wiki on a sport, hobby, or other area of interest, or a member-only company wiki that accumulates the collective knowledge of your employees. Wikis are a fun, easy, and free way to create your own information management system.

Without wikis like Wikipedia, the research and aggregation of the content in this book would have been significantly more difficult. Thank you to all of the contributors to Wikipedia, and the many blog sites on the Internet!

Readings and Resources

Blossom, John. *Content Nation: Surviving and Thriving as Social Media Technology Changes Our Lives and Our Future.* (Hoboken, NJ: John Wiley & Sons, Inc.)

Choate, Mark S. *Professional Wikis.* (Hoboken, NJ: John Wiley & Sons, Inc.)

Mader, Stewart. *Wikipatterns.* (Hoboken, NJ: John Wiley & Sons, Inc.)

Schwartz, Brendon, Matt Ranlett, and Stacy Draper. *Social Computing with Microsoft SharePoint 2007: Implementing Applications for SharePoint to Enable Collaboration and Interaction in the Enterprise.* (Hoboken, NJ: John Wiley & Sons, Inc.)

West, James A., and Margaret L. West. *Using Wikis for Online Collaboration: The Power of the Read-Write Web.* (Hoboken, NJ: John Wiley & Sons, Inc.)

White, Bruce A., and Andrew Pauxtis. *Web 2.0 for Business.* (Hoboken, NJ: John Wiley & Sons, Inc.)

Woods, Dan, and Peter Thoeny. *Wikis For Dummies.* (Hoboken, NJ: John Wiley & Sons, Inc.)

Downloads

For your free downloads associated with *The Social Media Bible,* go to www
.theSocialMediaBible.com, and enter your ISBN number located on the back
of the book above the bar code. Be sure to enter the dashes.

Credits

Expert Insight Was Provided By:

Jack Herrick, cofounder, WikiHow, www.WikiHow.com.

Technical Edits Were Provided By:

David Cain, president, MediaSauce, www.MediaSauce.com.

Jack Herrick, cofounder, WikiHow, www.WikiHow.com.

CHAPTER 10

A Picture Is Worth a Thousand Words (Photo Sharing)

What's In It for You?

The most important feature of photo sharing is that it's fun! Showing pictures to others is about sharing your memories with family members, friends, and colleagues. It's fun to display and remember your Christmas party guests, your coworkers at your promotion dinner, your child's school play, or the birth of your new son. It's also enjoyable to recall those moments with your friends and family—wherever they are in the world. There is also something to be said

FIGURE 10.1 Sedona, Arizona

about having all of your photographs organized into groups, sets, categories, events, and albums online where you can look at them anytime you wish—instead of having all of your memories stuffed in a shoebox in your closet or under your bed.

However, since this book focuses more heavily on utilizing social media for business than for fun, let's play "What if?" What if a prospect you were trying to land was doing some research on your product and went to Google Images, Flickr, or Photobucket and searched for either your trademarked name or a generic description of your product—and they found photo after photo? What if your prospect was preparing a budget presentation and needed photos of your type of product to secure funding, and their search consistently led them to your web site or photo-sharing site? Wouldn't you or your company be perceived as the best-in-class expert in the field?

Now, imagine that your prospect was only conducting a general search—as they might do during the research phase of their sales funnel—and your company's product photos continued to appear. (See Chapter 6, The World of Web Pages, for more information about the sales funnel.) What would your prospect think about your company and your product? And now ask yourself: What if this type of marketing opportunity was completely free?

This high-quality and low-cost exposure is exactly what photo sharing brings to your business marketing and communication plan. By simply uploading your company's product photos for free, you are participating in an area of Internet marketing that is highly targeted, competitively advantageous—and completely free of charge.

When you are uploading your company's product or service snapshots to your photo-sharing web site, be sure to remember the other items you have in your corporate shoebox. What if that same prospect also saw images of happy customers or your design or sales teams? How about some great shots of your company's headquarters, customer service installation, or repairs in progress? Take advantage of the resources that you already have, and use them frequently to provide visual proof of your business's dedication to its customers. After all, if only one prospect per quarter sees your photos and becomes a customer, isn't it worth the free posting?

Back to the Beginning

Photograph sharing dates back to the very first web page at CERN in early 1991. Whereas text was the most common information shared, photographs were easily second. The real rise of photo-sharing web sites grew with the popularization of the digital camera in the late 1990s. Before the advent of digital cameras, the process of going from print to Web was a tedious one that required a flatbed scanner and software. Digital cameras allow you to go directly from your camera to the Web with only one step, and without any additional hardware or software. It is as easy as plugging your camera into your USB port and uploading your images.

Of course, the next natural application of photo sharing that came about was via e-mail. Sending your brother the photographs of graduation, or Grandma pictures of the kids, became increasingly popular—and increasingly demanding on the user to create e-mails for every viewer. The desire for a one-stop personal photo gallery—with your own personal photographs available 24/7 forever—became an ever more appealing concept.

The other trend that quickly emerged—and added to the movement behind the photo-sharing craze—was the incarnation of web sites such as KodakGallery.com (and others like it) that allowed customers to order prints made from their digitally uploaded photographs. As these sites developed greater capacity to store and view higher-quality (larger file size) photographs, thumbnails, and slideshows, the ability to classify them into albums amplified their popularity. And to assist digital photo sharing, many photo-finishing stores—including local drugstores—could return photos in both print and digital CD formats.

With the advent of desktop photo-management applications such as iPhoto—containing photo-sharing features and integration that allow direct photo uploading, e-mail, and drag-and-drop through predesigned templates—the task of organizing, uploading, and sharing photographs was more simplified than ever. There are currently a plethora of online photo-sharing web sites that include online photo finishing, subscription-based sharing, peer-to-peer, peer-to-server-to-peer, peer-to-browser, and web photo album generators. Additionally, the process of sharing photographs has now grown beyond the digital camera and Internet to include camera cell phones, BlackBerrys, and PDAs (personal desktop assistants, such as the Palm Pilot). Today's standard camera phone allows you to take a picture, crop it, adjust the color, remove red eye, and e-mail it or immediately post that photograph to your web page or blog site—all with only a couple of simple clicks.

A Little about Digital Cameras

The cost of a good digital camera has dropped significantly over the past several years. You can actually buy a digital camera today for as little as $10 (for the Fisher Price Kid-Tough Digital Camera); however, a larger investment in a good digital camera would be worthwhile. You can get a high-quality brand-name digital camera for $100 to $150.

Besides the standard options that accompany most cameras—such as auto-focus, auto-aperture, and digital display—the most common way to determine the quality of the camera is—unsurprisingly—by the quality of the picture. This is measured in megapixels, or the total number of pixels—or dots—the camera records in a single image. The higher the number of pixels, the better quality the image. While most cameras start at about 3 megapixels, some run at around 5mp—and a few consumer cameras are available as high as 10mp.

A 5mp camera is a camera that can record 5 megapixels per image. A megapixel is 1 million pixels or dots per image. The total number of pixels is calculated by multiplying the total horizontal pixels by the total vertical pixels. Therefore, a 5mp camera will take a photo image with 5 million total pixels or dots.

The importance in the number of pixels or image quality of a digital camera doesn't really count much for online viewing of your pictures, since the best quality that your monitor can display is 72 pixels per inch both horizontally and vertically. This number becomes important when you enlarge your image to print it as, say, an 8″×10″ photo. A lower-quality photograph will appear grainy or fuzzy if not taken at a high enough picture quality. Anything above a 3mp camera should print your photographs at adequate quality, and a 5mp or better will do a *great* job.

What You Need to Know

The first step in this process is fairly obvious: to actually *take* a photograph. The most popular way to do so today is using a digital camera. Most are point-and-click with fully automatic features and take incredibly accurate photos. And, because digital cameras don't use film, you can take as many photographs as you wish at no cost whatsoever. So go out and click away, practice, try different ideas, and take a lot of pictures. It's free!

There are other alternatives to using a digital camera, like your camera-enabled cell phone. Many of the newer camera phones—such as Samsung's SCH-B600—can rival the quality of a good digital camera, and have as high as 10 megapixels. (At that point, it essentially becomes a digital camera that you can use to make telephone calls!) You also have the option of using your digital video camera set to "still" photography.

The next step is to transfer your photographs from your camera to your computer. The cable (usually USB) and software, if you need it, will have been provided to you by the camera manufacturer. If you are using a camera that takes its pictures on film, then you can have your photograph developer process your photos in a digital format or store them on a CD. If your photos are older and have already been printed on photo-paper, then you will need to digitize them through the use of a flatbed scanner and associated software. You can save time and effort if you still have the negatives for those photographs; then you can simply have your photo developer print them from the negative directly to a digital CD.

Once you've finished transferring, you can use a variety of software to crop, brighten/darken, sharpen, correct red eye, and otherwise enhance your photographs before uploading them to your photo-sharing web site. The most popular photo-editing application used today on both Windows and Macintosh computer platforms is Adobe's Photoshop. However, while Photoshop is one of the best and most versatile photo-editing applications you can buy, it does cost over $300.

That's why you should be sure to check the original CD that came with your digital camera, since most camera manufacturers ship their merchandise with photo-editing software. You can also download free photo-editing software from the Internet—like Google's Picasa, for example—that will allow you to restore old photos with marks, water stains, and scratches to excellent condition, and even let you add text and watermarks. And most photo-editing applications allow you to upload your photos directly to your web-based photo-sharing site with the click of a button.

Now that you have all of your photographs edited to perfection, the next step is simply to upload them to your favorite photo-sharing web site. Once you have created an account, just follow the directions on how to proceed. This usually is as simple as selecting Upload, then Browse, locating your image, and hitting OK. Many of these sites have their own uploader software applications that allow you to simply drag and drop your photos onto the application and automatically upload them to the web site. You can even transfer your photographs through your e-mail.

Once you've posted your images to a photo-sharing web site, you can organize them into sets and albums, and add captions, titles, descriptions, and meta tags (keywords). These keywords are the ones you would use if you were searching the site for a photograph like yours. (For more information on metatags and keywords, please see Chapter 20, Spotlight on Search (Search Engine Optimization).) You can also have friends, family, prospects, and customers comment on your photographs, and you can comment on others' as well. Most photo-sharing sites provide other services, like allowing you to order prints of your photographs, as well as create photo books or albums, and even custom calendars from your personal snapshots. And always remember to upload your photographs to Google Earth. By selecting the user photograph layer, you can upload your photos and view those of others as well, based on geographic location.

Privacy versus Piracy

While some people believe that you should be less fearful of piracy than obscurity, others just don't want their photographs taken and used by the Internet community at large—especially for commercial purposes. Online photo theft and fraud have become critical issues with photo-sharing web sites and their members. Nearly every one of these sites supports the Creative Commons License, which allows users to designate their photos by the level of copyright protection they wish to have. All the sites take theft seriously. (For more information on the Creative Commons License, see Chapter 11, Talking About the Podcast (Audio Create), or go to www.creativecommons .org.) The Creative Commons License allows many photo-sharing web sites to grant those with copyrighted photographs access to use the site to sell licenses to their photographs. So, in addition to helping to protect the photographer, they are providing a system for the photographer to make money through their photographs.

Techniques and Tactics

Although this chapter acknowledges the fact that uploading photos is largely focused on sharing with friends and family your images of birthday parties, bat mitzvahs, babies, and weddings, the purpose behind this book—and this chapter—is to show readers how to use photo-sharing web sites to create additional revenue. Businesses are using these techniques to share images of their products, tech support, employees, assembly lines, inventory, and happy customers.

You can help this process along by uploading as many photographs as you can, and entering the best meta tags as possible. Be sure that you use product names, applications, and serial/part numbers. In addition, make sure that your company names, geographic areas, and service description are part of the meta tags, captions, and even photo file names. Remember to approach this process from the mindset of a prospect or customer who is searching the site for you and your product or service. What words would you use if you were them? What kind of images would you want to see, or would you find helpful?

Most photo-sharing web sites allow you to create and participate in groups. Be sure to link your photos to the appropriate groups and communities on your photo-sharing site. For example, one of the authors presented with Matt Mullenweg, the Cofounder of WordPress, at the Arizona Entrepreneurship Conference. Twenty-one press photos of the event were taken. These pictures appear at www.flickr.com/photos/lonsafko/, with a group for these photos named #AZEC. The conference founders created a larger group named 2008 Arizona Entrepreneur Conference. This group pool combines 190 photographs from all of the other attendees. So you can look at just one smaller group of photos of the event or all 190.

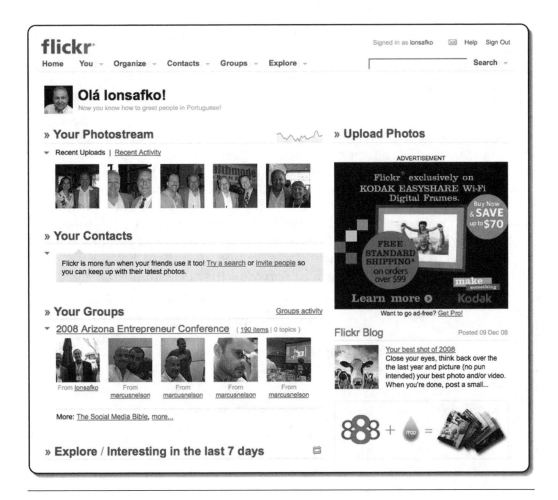

FIGURE 10.2   Flickr

Remember to install a free widget, gadget, or plug-in to your company web site or blogging site so that it will pull your photographs from your photo-sharing web site and place clickable thumbnail images on your web page. This step will introduce your prospects to the concept that you have photographs available for view on a photo-sharing web site and allow them to hyperlink directly to your photo site.

Providers

Choices are plentiful when it comes to selecting a photo-sharing web site. They include: Flickr, ShutterFly, KodakGallery, SnapFish, SmugMug,

PhanFare, DropShots, Fotolog, Multiply, MyPhotoAlbum, Panoramio, Pho-toBucket, Picasa, Pickle, PicMe, Pixamo, Slide, Tabblo, WebShots, Wink-Flash, Zenfolio, Zooomr, and Zoto. To determine which of these is right for you, take a look at a few of them in order to understand what features they offer in comparison to which are most important for you. It's also a good idea to maintain multiple photo-sharing web sites; after all, the more places you are on the Internet, the more exposure you have. As with all of the chapters in Part I of this book, don't get overwhelmed; just start off with one site, see if you like it, create an account, and start uploading your photographs.

For providers of digital cameras and camera cell phones, spend a little time online looking at reviews, prices, and blogs. The same holds true for photo-editing software. If you have Photoshop, then you have everything you need. If you don't, then check the box that your camera came in to see if the manufacturer provided software. If the answer is "no" to both, then do a search for free or reasonably priced software that best suits your needs.

Expert Insight

**Kakul Srivastava, general manager, Yahoo!'s Flickr,
www.flickr.com**

Kakul Srivastava

Flickr, at its core, is two things. First and foremost, it is a photo-sharing site, making it easier for people to share what is happening with their lives with their friends, their families, or potentially with the world. And it is really this last part—the second part of what Flickr is—that it really is a social media site.

When you think about traditional media businesses, you think about places where you find out about news and information; Flickr fundamentally is that. At the scale that we are today, we have 3 million photos uploaded on a daily basis, and you can only imagine the sound of 3 million shutters snapping across the world on any given day. We are really capturing what is happening in the world and in people's lives for a very, very personal perspective. So we see our vision as being the eyes of the world and really making that possible. . . .

It [is] actually really easy. I think, to start with, you have to take a photo; and luckily, for us today, you can take a photo with almost any device out there. Camera phones, which everyone has; there is an average of three camera phones for every human on the planet that are being used now. That's a really incredible number! And almost all of them have photo-sharing features in them, not to mention the huge adoption of digital cameras, as well, across the board.

So it is really easy to start taking photos, and then sharing them is the next step. That happens through the pervasiveness of Internet connections, not only through traditional devices like the PC, but again through phones and other devices as well. So it is actually pretty [simple] to get started. And then—[with] Flickr itself, for example—if you snap a shot with your camera phone, you just have to send it to an e-mail address here with Flickr, and it will be uploaded to your Flickr page. Then all of your friends and family can see what you are doing at that given moment. . . .

Yes, it is amazing and, of course, there is the mobile aspect of it, which is a really pervasive platform [wherein] you can just take it from any camera phone and share it immediately. Beyond that, we are integrated with almost all [of] the leading desktop photo applications, so you can go through any of the applications that people like to use and upload to Flickr from there. And, of course, the dominant way of sharing through Flickr is [probably] through our web site and our uploading application. You can just drag and drop a bunch of photos—or video for that matter—and share it with your friends and family. . . .

It starts with something very basic—which is that "this is something in my life and I want to share it." And if you think about what people were really trying to hold onto in the early days of photography—it was a memory. This is an important day; this is a birthday, for example, and I am going to take photos and share those with people.

With digital photos, the ease of sharing—as well as the ease of capturing these moments—has really expanded—from uses beyond just, "I want to hold onto this particular moment" to "I want to document everything that's mean-ingful to me in my life." That can be everything from, "Here is an interesting piece of graffiti I saw at the bus stop I was waiting in," or "Oh my God, there is a protest going on down the street from my office. I can capture it!" or "I'm in Galveston, Texas, right now and there is a hurricane, and I think the world might want to see this."

So it is really, *really* amazing how people are capturing and sharing what they are seeing. But what is interesting about a site like Flickr (which is not just about this content, but [also] the way that communities form around this content) is that people start interacting with the content in a very interesting way. So you almost have this second-order community effect starting to happen. For example, one of the biggest groups on Flickr is something called "Squared-Circle," and the premise of the group is really simple: people take a photograph of something circular and they crop it to a square and they upload it to this particular group. . . .

(*continued*)

(continued)

It has been just incredible to see how much meta-data and meaning our members have been able to find in some of this content. One of my favorites is [an] example of a photo of some dockworkers leaving the shipyard in the afternoon. One of the comments on the photo is by a Flickr member who says, "I remember as a kid; we lived down the street from this shipyard and at night we would see the light of the welding torches." And that's a really poignant moment that gives life to that photo in a way that it never would [just by] sitting in a library archive. So, again, the kind of things that people are starting to do with photo sharing is really tremendous; everything from the most banal thing of, "Here's what I had for my lunch today," to a deep and moving understanding of the world around us. It is very powerful!

One of the reasons that businesses come to Flickr is to actually engage with some of the customers who are using their product. If you search for pretty much any brand name on Flickr, you will find tens—if not hundreds—of groups where Flickr members are talking about the product or the brand and why it is interesting or helpful—or not helpful—to them. And that's an incredible way to have this two-way communication with your customers. . . .

The second aspect is advertising—also a known and loved model in traditional media—and [it] has very, very interesting implications with the social media side of the world with targeting, and with these rich two-way conversations that we were talking about.

The third here—and this is something more closely related to the photo sharing than the social media aspect of it—is that there are a lot of services that people want to have around their photos, whether it is standard prints or books or canvass prints of their photos, or canvass prints of other people's photos. There is a lot of incredible art that is being shared, so there is a rich business there.

And then the fourth—and probably the most recent, from a Flickr perspective—is a licensing business. You may have heard of the partnership that we recently announced with Getty Images that is going to allow Flickr members to actually monetize their images by licensing them. [There is also] the Commons Project—which we were talking about earlier—which is a way for institutions like the Library of Congress to show their images on Flickr. That is actually a completely separate initiative than Creative Common, which is a way to allow users to apply licenses to their images governing usage of how their content can be used. Our partnership with Getty Images lives right alongside our incredibly strong support for the Creative Commons. It is just another opportunity for people to choose how they want to license their image. . . .

You know, it is just a great, great field to be in. One of the things that we love about being here at Flickr, as part of Yahoo!, is we really are at the epicenter of some of the most interesting things that are happening. With social media on the Internet, Yahoo! has a deep commitment to the power of people and empowering people to do great things. You've probably heard a lot about

Yahoo!'s open strategy, and this is what social media is really a key part of. So we are very excited about that. We spent a lot of time talking about photo sharing, but from our perspective, video is a key part of that as well. We have launched video sharing on Flickr this year, and it is going really well.

So I think overall, we are just really excited to be one of the leaders in social media, and we are looking forward to being part of the innovation that this industry is really bringing about.

To listen to or read the entire Executive Conversation with Kakul Srivastava, general manager of Yahoo!'s Flickr, go to www.theSocialMediaBible.com or www.flickr.com.

Commandments

1. **Thou shalt take a lot of photographs.**

    Get a digital camera or camera phone and start taking pictures. Because they are digital, there are no associated development costs. If you don't like the way the picture came out, you can simply hit Delete. If you are satisfied with it, then save it to your hard drive. Like anything else, the more you practice, the better you become.

2. **Thou shalt edit your photographs.**

    While many photo-editing software applications have a one-click photo enhance feature, try using the manual adjustment sliders and effects. It's fun, and there's always an Undo function. To play it safe, always practice on a copy of the original photograph.

3. **Thou shalt upload.**

    Find as many photographs as possible that you already have. Combine them with the new photos you are taking, and upload them to the photo-sharing site of your choice. Creating an account on a photo-sharing site is easy, only takes about 10 minutes, and is free.

4. **Thou shalt use meta tags and descriptions.**

    Take a few minutes to think about the words that you will use to describe each photo, and the words that your prospects would use to search for your products and services.

5. **Thou shalt create and join groups.**

    Search your photo-sharing web site for groups that are similar and appropriate to the type of product or service you sell. Often, the best way to become part of a group or community is not to sell; a trusted network works *because* of the trust. Observe, participate—and *then* sell.

6. **Thou shalt comment.**

Participating means commenting. Comment on others' pictures, and encourage others to comment on yours. The more communication you have with one other, the more visibility your photographs will have.

Conclusion

Sharing your photographs with global communities, friends, family, co-workers, prospects, and customers and encouraging them to comment and communicate their feelings about your photos is the very essence of social media. Social media is all about two-way communication. Upload your photos, create communities, and start building credibility and trust with your clients and prospects.

Readings and Resources

Anderson, Todd. *Building a Photo Gallery with Adobe AIR.* (Hoboken, NJ: John Wiley & Sons, Inc.)

Busch, David D. *Digital Photography All-in-One Desk Reference For Dummies.* (Hoboken, NJ: John Wiley & Sons, Inc.)

Canfield, Jon, and Tim Grey. *Photo Finish: The Digital Photographer's Guide to Printing, Showing, and Selling Images.* (Hoboken, NJ: John Wiley & Sons, Inc.)

Chambers, Mark L., Tony Bove, David D. Busch, et al. *Digital Photos, Movies, & Music Gigabook for Dummies.* (Hoboken, NJ: John Wiley & Sons, Inc.)

Jamieson, Catherine. *Create Your Own Photo Blog.* (Hoboken, NJ: John Wiley & Sons, Inc.)

King, Julie Adair. *Shooting & Sharing Digital Photos For Dummies.* (Hoboken, NJ: John Wiley & Sons, Inc.)

Sahlin, Doug. *Digital Photography Workbook For Dummies.* (Hoboken, NJ: John Wiley & Sons, Inc.)

Downloads

For your free downloads associated with *The Social Media Bible,* go to www.theSocialMediaBible.com, and enter your ISBN number located on the back of the book above the bar code. Be sure to enter the dashes.

Credits

Expert Insight Was Provided By:

Kakul Srivastava, general manager, Yahoo!'s Flickr, www.flicker.com.

Technical Edits Were Provided By:

David Cain, president, MediaSauce, www.MediaSauce.com.

CHAPTER 11

Talking About the Podcast (Audio Create)

Why do you suppose some auto-makers are rushing to make their cars iPod-compatible? Because so many people who drive—especially those who spend a lot of time in their cars—like to listen to music, news, sports, weather, and other forms of audio information. Historically, this has been the exclusive domain of radio, an industry that was built upon finding ways to entertain, inform, and then sell stuff to a captive audience of drivers during the highly lucrative drive-time hours.[1] But that was then.

Automakers today know that the iPod has become such a ubiquitous and indispensable device that people want to bring them into their cars. And now you and your company can be there—and all of the other places people take their iPods—as well, provided you know why, when, and how to make podcasting part of your business strategy.

After one of the authors began podcasting, he received an e-mail from a listener requesting that the podcasts be saved and uploaded in an MP3 file format so he could more easily download the podcasts to his iPod. It turns out that every time a new podcast came out, the listener would transfer it to his iPod and listen to them at the gym. What an efficient way to use that time!

What's In It for You?

Podcasting is an effective way for you and your business to be heard—to capture the valuable mindshare of customers, prospects, and employees. And, like nearly all of the social media tools in the ecosystem, *it's free!* Podcasting is really easy and is much more psychologically desirable to your

theSocialMediaBible.com

customers and followers than just plain text. All kinds of anecdotal evidence supports this statement—such as one report which states that 75 percent of all journalists prefer rich media (see Chapter 6, The World of Web Pages), or the fact that school studies show that rich media is better for teaching. Almost all SEO (see Chapter 20, Spotlight on Search (Search Engine Optimization)) people have known this for more than a decade. Even Confucius (551–479 BCE) knew a picture was worth 1,000 words! A picture is worth a thousand words, an audio podcast is worth a thousand pictures, and a video is worth a thousand audios.

Back to the Begining

The word *podcast* comes from combining the terms "iPod" and "broadcast." The distribution of digitized audio recordings has been around—in one form or another—for as long as the Internet has existed. In the early days, it was just called audio. The first audio files commonly used on the Internet were *Waveform Audio (.wav)*—an audio file format for *DOS/Windows* computers. Later, the format moved to a highly compressed file called an *MP3 (Mpeg3)*. A standard audio recording runs about 1½ megabytes per minute, and MP3 could take a standard three-minute song or audio file at about 35 megabytes (mb), and compress it into as little as 3.5mb with nearly no quality loss. (Keep this in mind when creating your next Podcast—a twenty-minute session could run more than 30mb.) When surfing and downloading from the early Internet, file size mattered. A 30mb file could take more than an hour to download for those still using a dial-up modem.

The First Digital Audio Player

The term *podcast* actually applies to both audio and video recordings, yet most of the time refers only to audio broadcasting. And since the podcast was inspired by the Apple iPod digital music player, the word *iPod* itself is also a combination of words: "Internet" plus "pod"—or small, self-contained gadget. The term was first proposed by Vinnie Chieco, a freelance copywriter who was commissioned by Apple to introduce the new device to the public. When Chieco saw the prototype, he was reminded of the conversation between Dave and Hal in the movie *2001: A Space Odyssey* to "Open the pod bay door, Hal!" Dave's "pod" comment referenced the white EVA Pods of their spaceship, the Discovery One.

This portable music player designed by engineers at AT&T-Bell Labs in Murray Hill, New Jersey; Thomson-Brandt; and CCETT, at Fraunhofer IIS in Erlangen, Germany, was designed to play MP3 audio files. The MP3 format was approved as a standard format in 1991 by the ISO/IEC. The iPod would later be able to accommodate MP3, AAC/M4A, Protected AAC, AIFF, WAV, Audible audiobook, and Apple Lossless formats. iPod photo will display JPEG, BMP, GIF, TIFF, and PNG image file formats, and iPod video can play MPEG-4 (H.264/MPEG-4 AVC) and QuickTime video formats.

The Birth of the iPod

Former Philips Windows CE division executive Tony Fadell left the company in February 2001 to create his own firm, which he called "Fuse." He and his company developed a 5GB hard drive portable device that, as Tony would say, "Put 1000 songs in your pocket." After being turned down by RealNetworks, Tony went on to successfully cut a deal with Apple Computer. Apple announced the new Mac-compatible iPod on October 23, 2001, one month after Apple's launch of iTunes, their Internet music download site.

To this day, Apple's iTunes Store is the number-one digital music web site in the United States. According to Apple's CFO Peter Oppenheimer, iTunes is accounting for about 85 percent of all digital music sales nationwide. Apple has sold more than 3 billion songs (at about $1 each), via the iTunes Store and more than 100 million TV shows. In 2007, iTunes and the iPod were responsible for 36 percent of Apple's total revenue.

Podcasting is an equally accessible and entertaining application of the iPod. It's fun, and fairly simple—because everything you need to be able to podcast is either already built into your computer (hardware) or free to download from the Internet (software). There is really no excuse *not* to give it a try.

Podcasts are ordinary audio files and aren't limited to the iPod or the iTunes Store. You can listen to a podcast on any MP3 player or right from your browser from any web site that offers podcasts. Go to www.the SocialMediaBible.com for nearly 50 Executive Conversations podcasts with social media industry leaders. You can listen to an audio recording live by streaming it into an audio player, or you can download and save the file to your PC. Once you have the file stored on your PC, you can transfer it to an MP3 portable player, or just listen to it at any time from your MP3 player or from your browser.

Podcasts allow anyone, for the first time in history, to create their own talk show, interview, educational or training seminar, sermon, speech, presentation, or music file that can be distributed worldwide where literally tens, hundreds, or even thousands of people can play or download it and hear what you have to say . . . *for free.* You can create a following of colleagues, friends, and customers who care about what you have to say; and by podcasting, you've created a viral, entertaining, and informative medium through which you can be heard.

What You Need to Know

For the purpose of this chapter, *podcasts* are defined as audio files.

People prefer to call non-text files "rich media"; these include video, audio, and animation such as Flash. The more interesting you make your message, the more likely people are willing to hear it. Video is preferred over audio, and audio is preferred over text. However, video—while the most desirable form—does take the most effort and also requires the highest initial capital expenditure to create. You will need a computer, a digital video camera, and some video editing software at the very least.

On the other hand, podcasting is a great—and much simpler—expression of user-generated content, and all of the tools you need to create your own podcast are right there inside your computer. In order to create a podcast, all you need is your computer, the built-in microphone (or an external one, if your computer does not have a microphone built in), the free audio recording and editing software that came with the computer—and a little bit of creativity. You just hit Record, announce your message, hit Save, and upload it to a web site like PodBean.com for Internet distribution, and you are podcasting. So, for many, podcasting audio content is the easiest and most effective way to broadcast their personal message.

Podcast Components

A podcast can range from less than a minute to more than an hour in total length, depending upon its content. The podcast can sound slick, as though it was professionally produced, or have a rough-around-the-edges homemade flavor to it. It can start with an introduction to the content and speaker, and even have a musical intro. Many podcasts have more than one speaker, and sound like a radio interview or discussion. Whatever your choice of content, podcasts are effective, portable, and fun.

The Value of Podcasting

Creating successful podcasts on a given subject will allow you to build a loyal following, and convey to your audience that you are an expert in your industry or subject field. Your audience may be people who are interested in your subject area or in following what you do. Most importantly, they may be both existing and potential customers of your product or service.

As with all of the other chapters in this book, a strong "What's In It for Me?" is imperative. If your podcasts contain valuable takeaways, your listeners will continue to come back for more. They will also be able to provide user feedback—yet another benefit of podcasting. By allowing your listener the opportunity to give comments on your podcast, you can hear directly from your audience what you are doing right—and what you can do better.

Podcasts are like blogs in that they can be RSS-fed (see Chapter 19, RSS—Really Simple Syndication Made Simple, for more about RSS). Essentially your podcasts can be syndicated or distributed, and made available worldwide for free. People who like your podcasts and want to share them and be alerted when you've created more content can be informed every time you publish a new podcast.

Tips, Techniques, and Tactics

How to Create Your Own Podcast

Creating your own podcasts is easy, so don't be afraid if you've never created one. The process follows four steps; planning, recording, editing, and publishing.

A great resource for creating and distributing podcasts is *Podcasting For Dummies* by Tee Morris, Evo Terra, and Dawn Miceli. Go to www.theSocialMediaBible .com to download the Podcasting For Dummies primer e-book. It's free!

Planning

It's best if you plan your podcast out ahead of time—gathering and importing information, and then writing the script. Although the goal of podcast production is to make it sound professional, it doesn't have to be perfectly polished. It depends on your audience and your manner of producing the podcasts; many sound more relaxed and casual, while other producers go to great lengths to make their radio shows, audiobooks, and other recordings sound better

FIGURE 11.1 Podcasting For Dummies

than what is available from traditional media sources. Less than perfect is okay, but be sure the audio quality is good; your customers are more likely to listen to it all the way through. This less-than-perfect maxim holds true for all social media produced, and the reason is the audience's perception of the reasons for which the podcast was produced.

For the most part, when an audio or video has that polished, Madison Avenue, network production feel, it can safely be assumed that it cost a great deal to have it produced. It also stands to reason that if someone is writing a big check for the production, most likely there is an agenda for that media. And other than public service announcements (PSAs), that usually means that there is a commercial message behind all professionally produced media.

With social media, the content is by the people, for the people. It's ad hoc, fresh, spontaneous, unbiased, and noncommercial. Most commercial products and companies wouldn't want to be represented by anything less than professional quality. So, with less of a focus on production quality comes a perception of homemade, honest, truthful, and trustworthy.

Keeping this concept in mind, it's better *not* to strive for perfection—and to be very careful how self-promoting and commercial your social media message may sound. This holds true for your blogs, vlogs, podcasts, and any other form of media you might produce (excepting only your corporate web page). You can mention your product, or even have a quick introduction to it at the beginning of your vlogs for your sponsor, company, or yourself; just do it tastefully and keep it at a minimum. Otherwise, you will lose your listener's trust.

Introducing Your Podcast

The next step of planning is to sketch out the type of introduction that you want to have. It can include a verbal opening explaining who you are, what your subject matter is, and what you will be talking about in this episode. It can also be saved for future use as the introduction for your next podcast. Remember: your intro is your persona, your audio image, and your brand for you and your content.

Your introduction can also include a couple of riffs or a few bars of music. Get an idea ahead of time what you want the feel of your podcast to be; serious, businesslike, entertaining, educational, or other styles. Then pick about 5 seconds of music that conveys that feeling to your listener. Apple's GarageBand (assuming you own a Macintosh computer) is a great tool for this. In just a couple of minutes, you can select a few instrumental riffs (several seconds, or chords), and lay down a track (create a piece of music) that will really get your listener's attention. If you aren't lucky enough to own a Mac, then you can capture a few seconds of copyright-free music from any recording, or from the Internet.

The best part of working with GarageBand is that *anything* you create is copyright and royalty free. You always have to be sensitive about copyrights. Just because the music is on the Internet or a CD doesn't mean that it's free for you to use. Always keep in mind: *If someone else creates it, it belongs to someone else.* In order for you to use that music or sound, you will need written permission to do so. Otherwise, you could end up as Napster: The Sequel. And always keep in mind that if you (or anyone you know) play a musical instrument and can record it or play it directly into your PC via USB—you're good to go!

However—in terms of copyrighted music—there is the Creative Commons Project. Creative Commons (CC) is a nonprofit organization that has developed copyright licenses that grant certain rights to the public—rights that the owner of copyrighted material is willing to waive so that others may use his or her materials. The Creative Commons licenses vary, and can include dedication of copyrighted material to public domain or open content. For more information on the Creative Commons Project, please visit http://creativecommons.org/. And, for more information on U.S. copyrights, you can visit http://www.uspto .gov/ and select "Copyrights," or http://www.TheSocialMediaBible.com for clickable links.

Recording

When making your podcast, use a few bullet points or a slide show to convey your main ideas. You can then simply read a bullet and just speak spontaneously about that subject, without sounding too rehearsed or rigid. And if you don't want to plan out your podcast—then it's okay to just wing it!

Once you know what you want to say, it's time to record it. In order to begin, you will need to use your computer's built-in microphone or connect an external microphone for better quality. You will also need audio recording and editing software. Use Audacity, Sound Studio, GarageBand, or other inexpensive/free sound editing software, although you're welcome to use the more expensive and elaborate software list starting on page 215. (Some statistics suggest that nearly half of all of the creators of podcasts either are using or have used Audacity to record and edit their shows. It provides easy-to-use, high-quality tools—and it's free!) Another new open-source (free) recording and editing software is Koblo.com.

Some software editing programs can import sound files such as .wav, .aiff, .wma, and MP3s, and record from a microphone as well as from the computer's sound card and auxiliary devices. Some can even record VoIP (Voice over Internet Protocol) interviews, like telephone software such as Vonage and Skype. This is particularly handy if you want to have a talk-show format, and if you and your guest or cohost are working in different locations.

Signing Off

The last part of podcast planning involves writing or rehearsing your close or sign-off. During this part of the session, you should remind your audience of who you are and what your subject matter is, where they can find more of it, and perhaps mention your sponsor (if you have one).

Editing

You will need to edit your podcast somewhat. In most software packages—even the free ones that came with your computer or that you downloaded from the Internet—it's as easy as copying, cutting, pasting, and deleting. At the very minimum, you will need to delete the dead air at the beginning and end of your recording; and in most cases, you will want to paste together the sound and verbal intro and sign-off to your content.

Most audio editing programs include basic editing tools such as the ability to cut segments, mix tracks, convert formats, and split tracks (Figure 11.2). Some incorporate advanced tools like automatic gain controls and recording volume sliders. Many programs also feature a variety of effects and filters like the reverb (discussed in the following "Special Effects" section). This all might

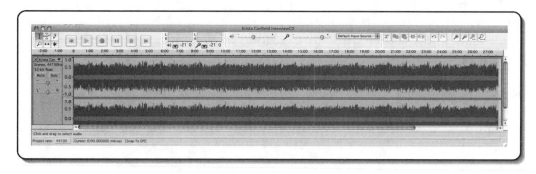

FIGURE 11.2 Audacity Sound Editing Software

sound a little scary, but after playing with the software for a mere 30 minutes, you might consider yourself an expert.

Publishing

The final step in podcasting is publishing. Because of podcasting's growing popularity, a lot of new software now has publishing podcast wizards built right into it. This software fully automates your podcast tags or keywords (see Chapter 20, Spotlight on Search (Search Engine Optimization) for more information on keywords), and RSS feed creation (see Chapter 19, RSS— Really Simple Syndication Made Simple). You simply click to publish, and you're immediately able to share your material. Podcasts are meant to be shared; the more people who share your podcasts, the more people who are sharing your thoughts and ideas—and the bigger the following you will have.

Liberated Syndication (www.Libsyn.com) is one of the largest media-hosting providers that podcasters use. For less than $10 a month, they'll give you all the bandwidth you need regardless of how popular your show becomes. Some people host their podcasts on their own server and have plug-ins to play the podcast directly from the web page, while most others upload it to podcast web sites—such as PodBean and iTunes (RSS)—where it is easily syndicated.

Special Effects

Special effects, properly used, can enhance your podcasts. By adding a little creativity and a special effect here and there, you can keep your content exciting and entertaining.

If your software has features that allow you to do so, you should first boost your volume and your bass. Most microphones—especially the inexpensive built-in types—can make your recording sound shallow and tinny. Boosting the volume and bass will add fullness and fidelity to your recording. Another (free!) piece of audio editing software called the Levelator does all that boosting for you (Figure 11.3).

Software

Podcast recording and editing software include: GarageBand, WordPress PodPress Widget, Sound Studio, Soundtrack Pro, Audacity, Evoca, ePodcast

FIGURE 11.3 Levelator

FIGURE 11.4 Digital Recorder

Creator, Gabcast, Hipcast, Odeo Studio, Phone Blogz, Podcast Station, Propagan, and WebPod Studio. This sounds like a lot to grasp, but remember, you only need one. Install a few editing applications, try them, and then stick with the one you like the best. It's that simple.

Hardware

Hardware can include your computer and accompanying microphone, desktop stand and lapel microphones, recording decks and mixers, telephone recorder interfaces (for recording directly off the telephone), headsets, and digital recorders. A $49 Overstock.com digital recorder was a great purchase. It is approximately $\frac{1}{2}'' \times \frac{1}{2}'' \times 4''$, fits in a breast pocket, works with a lavaliere or lapel microphone, and will record up to 12 hours of continuous stereo digital audio. Whenever making a new or unique presentation, on it goes—and a podcast is recorded without any effort. All that has to be done is add the intro and trailer, and it's ready to go!

Web Sites and Podcast Distributors

You can find a variety of different types of podcasts on the Internet today on a variety of topics that range from subject-specific, to informative and educational, to entertaining, to commercial, to the occasional rant.

Podcasts are everywhere. When the term *podcast* is Googled, about 162 million results are returned for sites like PodCast.com, Digg, MSNBC, CNN, Yahoo!, New York Times, PodcastAlley, NPR (National Public Radio), PodBean, Grid7, iTunes, iTunes University, Scientific American, NASA, and CBS News.

For some great examples of podcasts and amazing content from 50 of the social media industry's founders, CEO's, and vice presidents, go to www .SocialMediaBible.com, menu item Insights.

Providers

Most of the tools that will help you create killer podcasts are free, and many even came out of the box with your PC. The first thing to do is to check your computer to see what types of audio recording and editing software were included. If you're not satisfied with what you have, go to www.theSocialMediaBible.com to download the free software for Audacity.

This recording and editing software is great for adding your intro or music bumper at the start and finish—and it's free.

The Levelator (available from www.conversationsnetwork.org/levelator) is a drag-and-drop software application that levels the conversation in your audio tool. This application provides audio equalizing software that balances the volume of two people talking. This feature is useful to have, since one person is always a little closer to the microphone or on the recording side of the telephone. Other software applications include GarageBand, WordPress PodPress Widget, Sound Studio, Soundtrack Pro, Evoca, ePodcast Creator, Gabcast, Hipcast, Odeo Studio, Phone Blogz, Podcast Station, Propagan, and, WebPod Studio.

A store like Radio Shack is a great resource for inexpensive hardware that allows you to connect a digital recorder to your telephone. When recording podcasts, you can use a portable office telephone or a cell phone from anywhere in the world. Plug in a twenty-five-dollar interface, an eight-dollar earphone/mic, and a sixty-dollar digital recorder, and you're set to go with high-quality audio recording—everything you need to create professional podcasts for under a hundred dollars. In fact, while editing this chapter, one of the authors recorded an interview with Kyle Ford, the director of product marketing with Ning, while surrounded by pine trees in a cabin in the mountains of northern Arizona.

Expert Insight

Evo Terra, coauthor, *Podcasting For Dummies*,
www.podiobooks.com.

Era Terra

Well, there is a lot of information out there about starting a podcast, and the most common word that is given out is, "Just start, and figure it out as you go along." And that isn't bad advice for some hobbyist that just wants to play in the media. But for businesspeople—and for those who really want to get in to make a splash—I suggest they take a different route.

The very first thing I would suggest to people interested in podcasting is: do your homework. You know, find out if there are other people in the space that you are getting into. Most businesspeople are not going to say, "I want to open up an ice cream stand," without having some understanding of the ice cream market. You have to know what you are getting yourself into, even if you have no idea how to run an ice cream stand; you can, at least, know what the business is.

The same thing goes for podcasting. You can figure out what the competition is doing, if you want to think about it as competition. I don't. I use the word because we all understand it. But [you have to] at least understand what is competing with the topic of your podcast for people's time; and the other sorts of media that are doing the same thing, just not in a podcast form. Whether that's radio, or whether it's an audio book, you know, understand what your listeners are likely to want to listen to. Do your diligence. . . .

I could go on for days on what *not* to do. As I am often reminded myself, you know, there is no one right way to do things; but there are lots of wrong ways. There are lots of tip and advice books out there that will give you some suggestions; but one of the things I think I would caution people about is that, since we're talking about this user-generated content of podcasting, amateur people who have not had a lot of experience using the tools are getting into the space.

There are a lot of people out there advising that it's the content that's the most important, and I don't disagree with them. Content is *king*. You have to have something that is worth talking about and that is interesting to people. However, I think that oftentimes, this comes at the expense of quality. In fact, I have heard more than one person suggest that you ought to not worry about the quality of the show, because it's content that matters; and then discuss other reasons why quality does not matter. And I just . . . I have to disagree! And I have to disagree for one reason. I know how easy it is to make your podcast sound professional.

There are quite a few tools out there. I recommend that anyone starting out new in podcasting does not go out and spend crazy amounts of dollars. In fact, you should spend as little as possible. Download Audacity. It is a free software audio recording program. It works on both PCs and Macintosh systems, and it is, what I would estimate, 50 percent of the podcasters still use today. I still use Audacity. It's free and it's simple and it does just about everything you are going to want to do at your level.

Now, if you're an audio engineer—then that's a different situation. You will want a different tool set from that; but Audacity is wonderful.

Let's see . . . that's your number-one tool to do most of your work. There's another piece of equipment that I like to use called The Levelator. It is free software that you run your spoken-word audio through, and it magically (I don't mind using the word, because I have seen this tool work and I use it every day myself) brings up your audio level to a fantastic level. It is not a perfect tool; and there are plenty of engineers who don't like to use it. But my recommendation to all new people and all podcasters today is . . . if you are not using The Levelator and you don't have a good excuse why you're not using The Levelator . . . then you should be using The Levelator. It is amazing what it can do to your sound. . . .

Now there are some specialty tools which come into play if you want to record telephone conversations. Or maybe you want to buy a library of pre-licensed music, so that you don't sound like everybody else discovering the free stuff. There are those investments to make. But if it is your first time doing it . . . don't! Don't invest any additional money. Your computer most likely already has set up what you need to do to get started, even with a cheap, five-dollar microphone that it came with. I know many people that started out that way, but once they figured out what they wanted to do, [they] eventually graduate to bigger and better equipment. But start off with spending next to nothing. . . .

You know, quality has become very important—even though people don't recognize or realize it. I think one thing that's becoming easier to discern from the podcast listeners—as they have matured over the last four years—is the issue of authenticity. And I think you may be right [about sounding *too* good]. Early on in the process, if something sounded really slick and polished, you started wondering, "What's the underlying agenda? What corporate underwriting sponsorship is happening here?"

But I think consumers are becoming a lot more educated in that now. They're a little more sophisticated, and they are really able to get down to the message. If your goal is to try and sound like the guy who does the 10 o'clock news, then that's going to fail miserably. You know why? That's a terrible

(continued)

(continued)

delivery. They have to do that in a certain way because they have a certain amount of time to get to people before they get to bed, and they drag you along and put the weather at the end. . . .

To listen to or read the entire Executive Conversation with Evo Terra, to www.theSocial MediaBible.com or www.podiobooks.com.

Commandments

1. **Thou shalt podcast.**
   Go forth and podcast, often. Go and be creative! It's easy and free! Just try it. You will surprise yourself how good you are.

2. **Thou shalt not covet thy neighbor's copyrights.**
   Be careful not to take or use something that belongs to someone else. Creating a five-second song is really easy. There are even royalty-free sound bites and music you can use called "pod-safe" music.

3. **Thou shalt experience sound editing.**
   Sound editing sounds scary, but it is really easier than you think. Many good editing software packages either come free with your computer or can easily be downloaded from the Internet.

4. **Thou shalt not spend a lot of money.**
   Unless you really want to get into podcasting, don't spend a lot of money doing it. Remember in this one case that "good enough" might actually be *good enough*.

5. **Thou shalt RSS feed your podcasts.**
   By RSS feeding your podcasts, you are making them available to literally millions of potential listeners. You can learn more about RSS (Really Simple Syndication) in Chapter 19, RSS—Really Simple Syndication Made Simple.

6. **Thou shalt upload your podcasts to iTunes.**
   Be sure to upload your podcasts to iTunes. Tens of millions of people search iTunes every day looking for content that might be similar to yours. Be sure to follow their guidelines to ensure your podcast's success. And keep in mind that if your podcast falls under the "educational" category, you should upload it to iTunes' "iUniversity."

7. **Thou shalt keep your podcasts brief.**
   Most people only have about a 7-minute attention span for audio. Taking any more time than that will lose your listeners' interest. If you

have a 30-minute interview or a 45-minute panel discussion, leave it at length. If your audio file can be broken into 5- to 7-minute chapters, topics, or ideas, break it up.

8. **Thou shalt produce in the right file format.**

    Be sure that when you link or upload your podcasts, they are in a usable file format. While QuickTime is great for Macintosh users to play, Windows and PowerPoint users have difficulties with it. Most people want your content in an MP3 format that is compatible with their digital music players.

9. **Thou shalt be conscious of file size.**

    While you may have a lot to say, a 53mb file is just too large for most people to download and install on their digital players. Most music runs at about 3.5mb each, so try to keep your finished files in the single-digit mb range.

10. **Thou shalt be creative.**

    This, again, is the most important commandment. The more creative you are and the more "What's In It for Me?" you provide for your listener, the more people will download it, listen to it, pass it along to their friends, recommend it, and comment on it; and the more loyal listeners and followers/trusted network you will build. Remember to ask your customers to be collaborators of your content.

Conclusion

As long as your podcasts have a strong WIIFM, your listeners will keep coming back for more. The more you podcast, the more quality content and contributions you will provide to your followers, listeners, and customers. Keep podcasting, because it helps to build your trusted network; your customers/followers will perceive you as an industry/subject-matter expert; and when it's time to buy, you will be the one they think of first. It's free, it's easy, it fun—so do it!

Readings and Resources

Bove, Tony, and Cheryl Rhodes. *iPod & iTunes For Dummies.* 4th ed. (Hoboken, NJ: John Wiley & Sons, Inc.)

Cochrane, Todd. *Podcasting: Do-It-Yourself Guide.* (Hoboken, NJ: John Wiley & Sons, Inc.)

Frazer, J. D. *Money for Content and Your Clicks for Free: Turning Web Sites, Blogs, and Podcasts into Cash*. (Hoboken, NJ: John Wiley & Sons, Inc.)

Ihnatko, Andy. *iPod Fully Loaded: If You've Got It, You Can iPod It.* (Hoboken, NJ: John Wiley & Sons, Inc.)

Islam, Kaliym A. *Podcasting 101 for Training and Development: Challenges, Opportunities, and Solutions*. (Hoboken, NJ: John Wiley & Sons, Inc.)

Morris, Tee, Evo Terra, and Dawn Miceli. *Podcasting For Dummies*. (Hoboken, NJ: John Wiley & Sons, Inc.)

Morris, Tee, Evo Terra, and Ryan Williams. *Expert Podcasting Practices For Dummies*. (Hoboken, NJ: John Wiley & Sons, Inc.)

Ratcliffe, Mitch, and Steve Mack. *Podcasting Bible*. (Hoboken, NJ: John Wiley & Sons, Inc.)

Reeder, Joelle, and Katherine Scoleri. *The IT Girl's Guide to Blogging with Moxie*. (Hoboken, NJ: John Wiley & Sons, Inc.)

Scott, David Meerman. *The New Rules of Marketing and PR: How to Use News Releases, Blogs, Podcasting, Viral Marketing and Online Media to Reach Buyers Directly*. (Hoboken, NJ: John Wiley & Sons, Inc.)

Downloads

For your free downloads associated with *The Social Media Bible*, go to www.theSocialMediaBible.com, and enter your ISBN number located on the back of the book above the bar code. Be sure to enter the dashes.

Credits

Expert Insight and Technical Edits Were Provided By:

Evo Terra, author, *Podcasting For Dummies,* www.podiobooks.com.

Note

1. Drive time refers to 6 to 10 AM and 3 to 7 PM Monday through Friday when the majority of radio listeners travel to and from work and significantly more commercials are run.

CHAPTER 12

Got Audio? (Audio Sharing)

What's In It for You?

Today, more than 30 million people subscribe to podcasts, and that number is growing exponentially. Podcasts are essentially a vehicle for the many other types of media that individuals and businesses can use in the realm of social networking. You can add music, digital photos, animated company logos, colorful videos—anything that it takes to get your message across.

Creating and sharing audio is by far the easiest to create of all rich media. All of the tools that you need are in your computer already, and those that aren't are available for free from the Internet. You most likely already have a built-in microphone and the recording software (see Chapter 11, Talking About the Podcast (Audio Create)) in your PC. While audio isn't as appealing as video, it is a lot easier to record, edit, and share, so the trade-off between convenience and high-tech appearance is well worth it.

No one is an expert on everything, and when it comes to social media, it's hard to be an expert at all because the industry is simply changing faster than people can keep up with it. There are, however, a great number of people ahead of the pack, and hearing *their* insights is important. That's why this book and the associated web site present the collected wisdom of nearly fifty founders, CEOs, authors, and experts in the social media field. (See the many impressive and detailed Executive Conversations at www.theSocialMedia Bible.com.)

How does this apply to you and your business? You should be discussing with your customers and prospects what they would like to hear. The first step is to create some audio podcasts (see Chapter 11, Talking About the Podcast (Audio Create)) and then share them. While *The Social Media Bible* is not intended to be a how-to book, an important topic is the basics of sharing audio. This chapter discusses two prime examples: iTunes and Podbean.

Back to the Beginning

Many of the "Back to the Beginning" sections in these chapters—such as networking, blogging, photo sharing, and e-mail—begin the same way. File sharing, for example, goes back to the original ARPAnet and UseNet, and audio is the same. As soon as a network became established, people began sharing the many different kinds of files that they had—text, photos, images, video, and audio. Most of these "Back to the Beginning" sections are the longest ones in each chapter. But since there is little new material to report on audio sharing that hasn't already been covered in another chapter, the focus here is on some of the tools that have made audio sharing such an easy and successful business approach (see the previous chapter's "Back to the Beginning" for more information on the history of audio creation and sharing).

What You Need to Know

Every single day, your customers, prospects, and employees are inundated with information from e-mail, voicemails, junk mail, and memos. The important question for you to ask is: How do you get your important messages across to them in a way that doesn't get lost in all of that noise? The answer is podcasts.

As explained earlier in the book, a *podcast* is an audio or video recording that a person can subscribe to, receive, download, listen to, or watch using a personal computer, iPod, PDA, or mobile telephone. Your customers and prospects can therefore listen to or watch this information whenever and wherever they wish—in their cars, during lunch, in the evening, at the office, at the gym, while jogging, or even on their day off.

A podcast is similar to a television program or radio show, but easier to create and distribute, and it's free to do so. The process of audio sharing requires that you first create an audio file, and then make it known and available. Chapter 11, Talking About the Podcast (Audio Create) describes in detail how to create an audio file podcast, while this chapter focuses more heavily on the process of sharing it with others. A great book to help with this topic is Tee Morris and Evo Terra's *Podcasting For Dummies*. For extremely helpful step-by-step instructions on how to publish your podcast using iTunes, go to www.mvldesign.com/itunespodcast.html.

Let's begin by discussing iTunes, the most popular audio and video solution for downloading, playing, aggregating, and publishing your podcasts.

iTunes

Apple Computer developed iTunes for both the Macintosh and Windows operating platforms and released it on January 9, 2001, at the Macworld Expo in San Francisco. iTunes is used for playing, organizing, downloading, and publishing audio and video files through your desktop, laptop, mobile phone, and, of course, your iPod. iTunes allows users to connect to their store through the Internet, where they can purchase and download music, music videos, television shows, iPod games, audio books, various podcasts, feature-length films, movie rentals, and ringtones. iTunes is available as a free download for Mac OS X, Windows Vista, and Windows XP from Apple's web site (www.Apple.com). iTunes also comes bundled with all Macs, and some HP and Dell computers.

FIGURE 12.1 iTunes

On September 9, 2008, Apple CEO Steve Jobs reported the following iTunes downloads and product statistics. In July 2008, Apple's iPod had 73.4 percent of the U.S. MP3 player market share. SanDisk had 8.6 percent, Microsoft had 2.6 percent, and 15.4 percent was distributed between all other types of MP3 players. iTunes was the largest music distributor in the United States, topping big-name retail stores like Wal-Mart and Best Buy. iTunes has over 8.5 million songs, 125,000 podcasts, 30,000 TV show episodes, 2,600 Hollywood movies, and 3,000 applications for the iPhone and iPod. Apple's App Store had experienced 100 million app—or application—downloads in 60 days, with more than 3,000 applications listed. Ninety percent of the apps[1] are priced at less than ten dollars, and more than 600 apps are available for free.

Here's one example of an astonishing "app" that can be downloaded and installed on the Apple iPhone. One of the author's families was having dinner and listening to the stereo. A great song began to play that no one could identify. One member of the family stood up from the dinner table, held the iPhone up to the speaker for 10 seconds. The phone beeped, and the display showed the name of the song, the artist, and the album.

Jobs also announced that the iTunes Store had sold over 5 billion songs, and set a new single-day record of more than 20 million song downloads on December 25, 2007. He informed potential users that the iTunes Store's movies for rent included content from industry giants 20th Century Fox, Warner Bros., Walt Disney Pictures, Paramount Pictures, Universal Studios, and Sony Pictures Entertainment. Renting a standard-definition movie costs $2.99, while new releases cost $3.99. High-definition titles cost $1 more each, and these movies also work on all sixth-generation iPods.

The original media player software that was iTunes' predecessor was developed in 1999 by Casady & Greene, a software publisher of shareware products, created primarily for the Macintosh and called SoundJam MP. Original developers Jeff Robbin and Bill Kincaid sold SoundJam to Apple in 2000, where it was given a face lift and the ability to burn CDs, and rereleased in January 2001 with its new name: iTunes. iTunes was available only for the Macintosh line of computers until March 2007, when Apple released its Windows version. iTunes 64-bit versions for Windows became available on January 16, 2008.

FIGURE 12.2 QuickTime Audio

iTunes users can manage audio and video files on their personal PC, which is required for iPod operation and synchronization. Within the iTunes application, the user can engage in a variety of activities: create playlists, edit file information, record CDs, copy files to digital audio/video players, purchase audio and video files from the iTunes Store, download free music and audio podcasts, back up their music and video to CDs and DVDs, display a visualizer graphic effects screen, encode digital files in a myriad of formats, listen to any of a larger number of Internet radio stations, and publish audio files and podcasts to the iTunes Store. iTunes organizes music and video by creating virtual libraries wherein it stores and keeps track of each song's attributes—such as artist, genre, album, how often it's been played, the last time it was played, and the personal rating that users can give it. iTunes users can view their music libraries in one of four ways; as a list of songs by title; by the music's cover artwork; in an application called Cover Flow, which is an Apple-style slide scrolling catalog of artwork;

or a Grid View iTunes that can sort music by artist by album, and album by year.

iTunes can also rip or copy music from CDs, but not DVDs. Certain movie studios introduced iTunes Digital Copy in 2008—a bonus feature that is available on some DVDs, which provides an iTunes-compatible file for select films for otherwise copy-protected material.

iTunes can currently read, write, and convert between several types of files—including MP3, .aiff, .wav, MPEG-4, AAC, and Apple Lossless.

The application can also play any audio file and most

FIGURE 12.3 QuickTime Video

video formats that QuickTime can play. QuickTime is an application developed by Apple for both the Windows and Apple platform that allows the user to create and play videos in full screen, create movies for iPod, and download movies from the web. It includes audio processing features such as equalization, sound enhancement, cross fade, and Sound Check, which automatically adjusts the playback volume of all songs to the same level. iTunes can produce static, party, and new Smart[2] playlists that can be played randomly or sequentially.

iTunes 4.8 added a video application on May 9, 2005. Users can choose to view movies in a small frame in the main iTunes display, in a separate window, or in full screen mode. On October 12, 2005, iTunes offered the ability to purchase and view video content from the iTunes Music Store. Video podcasts—or Vodcasts—and other downloadable video files are in .mov, MP4, M4V, or .mpg formats.

On June 28, 2005, Apple announced that iTunes 4.9 would have built-in support for podcasting, which would allow its users to subscribe to podcasts for free in the iTunes Music Store or by entering the RSS feed URL. Once a user subscribes, any new podcasts would be automatically downloaded hourly, daily, or weekly, or manually. Users can listen to podcasts directly from the Podcast Directory, which is an index of user-generated content from commercial and independent podcasters. They can also browse podcasts based on their popularity, and even upload their own material to the iTunes Store. When this podcasting feature was added to such a mainstream and widely used application like iTunes, many podcasters reported that the number of downloads of their podcasts had tripled—and even quadrupled.

Because iTunes takes full advantage of podcasts' RSS features—in other words, its role as a podcatching client—iTunes is now considered to be one of the best in its class of any of the other web sites that provide downloadable audio and video. iTunes has been rated higher than the audio file multiplatform distribution software Juice and Windows Doppler, and is superior to other podcatching web sites Amarok, Winamp, and MediaMonkey. iTunes is also closely integrated with Apple's iWork and iLife software packages—applications that directly interface with the iTunes Library and access the user's songs stored within iTunes. iTunes allows music files to be embedded directly into Pages (Apple's web-page design software); iMovie, which allows you to create and mix movies from video, music, and photographs; iDVD, which allows you to take those movies and create your own; Keynote (Apple's version of PowerPoint); and any song created and exported from Garage-Band, Apple's music- and podcast-creating program. Any of these files are automatically added to the user's iTunes music library.

Ever since the first iTunes version—aptly titled 1.0—Apple gave its users Internet radio service access to the most popular streaming radio available. As of February 2008, iTunes Radio provided users with access to nearly 1,800 streaming MP3-format Internet radio stations. These stations make up every genre from music to sports to talk radio to more traditional radio stations as well. Unfortunately, Apple's newer version of iTunes no longer directly supports the Internet radio feature. However, users can enter their own stream feed to listen under the Radio tab by selecting the menu option Advanced, then Open Stream. QuickTime, on the other hand, does support Internet radio, and you can find iTunes plug-ins from iRadioMast (www .iradiomast.com).

Now that you've read about the largest music sharing, upload, and download web service in the world, let's discuss another web site called Podbean—one that hosts, syndicates, and distributes your uploaded audio files for free.

PodBean

Podbean (www.podbean.com, Figures 12.4 and 12.5) opened in July 2006, providing podcast publishing tools for users to begin creating professional-caliber podcasts. Podbean allows them to do so in a very short amount of time, with an easy point-and-click, bloglike environment—and requires no

FIGURE 12.4 PodBean

technical knowledge. The web site gives users the chance to manage, publish, and promote podcasts with just a few clicks. Podbean is applicable to a wide variety of podcasters—from education, religion, real estate, music, sports clubs, travel agents, government agencies, hobbyists, and entrepreneurs, to larger corporations.

Signing up for a Podbean account grants users a personalized podcast web site with one's own URL for banding. Users can even select themes or "skins" (see Figure 12.5) with different colors, fonts, and layout for their pages. Podbean also provides users with web-site traffic reporting and analysis tools, so that they are able to measure their podcasts' success and know exactly how they're performing. Podbean provides an in-depth,

FIGURE 12.5 PodBean Skin

multidimensional view of a site's visitors, subscribers, hits, and geographic location distribution, and even lets users download this data.

Most importantly, all of the Podbean pages have full RSS feed generation for RSS2, iTunes, and ATOM integrated right in. Podbean supports RSS 2.0 and ATOM feeds (see Chapter 19), as well as the extended Apple iTunes podcasting tags. Podbean also provides a Web 2.0–based podcast player that can be embedded directly into your web site, blog site, and other social networks. The more podcasts you create—and the more popular your podcasts become—the more regularly your files will be downloaded, the more storage and bandwidth you will require (see Chapter 13, Watch Out for Vlogs (Video Create), for more information on bandwidth). But no matter how popular your podcasts become, Podbean provides the storage and bandwidth you need for free. It also allows users to earn revenue through advertising, paid subscription, and merchandise sales. In fact, Podbean has a full-function online e-commerce tool provided to users for free.

Most of the social media tools covered in this book work on the freemium business model—meaning that most of the service that the providers give to users is done completely free of charge. Enterprises are awarded some additional services that do have a cost associated, which are usually very reasonably priced.

Providers

Here's a list of podcasting, podcatching, and audio and music distribution sites. iTunes is the largest for buying music and downloading audio podcasts, and PodBean is the web site. Visit the other web sites below to find specific content and services that are designed for the creation and distribution of audio podcasts.

www.iTunes.com
www.Podbean.com
www.digitalpodcast.com
www.podcasting.net
www.ipodderx.com
www.penguinradio.com/podcasting
www.feed-directory.com
www.podcast411.com
www.sportpodcasts.com
www.podcastalley.com
www.podcastpickle.co
www.podcastingnews.com
www.podcasting-station.com
www.podrazor.com
www.podcasthost.com
www.juicereceiver.sourceforge.net
www.dopplerradio.net
www.amarok.kde.org
www.winamp.com
www.mediamonkey.com

www.tdscripts.com/webmaster_utilities/podcast-generator.php (podcast RSS feed generator)
www.softwaregarden.com/products/listgarden/index.html (software list garden)

Expert Insight

Alan Levy, founder and CEO, BlogTalkRadio, www.blogtalkradio.com

Alan Levy

Well, we have two parts of the network. The main network is the network which we launched in October 2006, which we launched from scratch. I mean, we created this idea. . . . I came up with the name, *Blog-TalkRadio*. We had no content. We invented this technology which, essentially, incorporates using the phone, or any kind of phone, into the Web. And to date we've broadcasted about 110,000 segments . . . maybe about 115,000. Each day we broadcast 500 new live shows. You can see them all at BlogTalk Radio.com. They all appear here in our programming guides.

We have had everyone on the network, from John McCain, who has been on three times, to Yoko Ono, Brad Pitt, Brian DePalma, Salman Rushdie, famous authors, actors, and of course, thousands and thousands of bloggers. Anybody, really, who is looking to communicate a message and promote an idea or promote a book can come on *BlogTalkRadio* for free. All they have to do is create a profile, set up a show on when they would like to broadcast, and they can dial in and be "on air" in a matter of minutes. . . .

We found that . . . I'm either very crazy or very smart; I don't know which one yet, but we realized that a lot of people that had been coming on BlogTalkRadio were being asked to pay hundreds, if not thousands of dollars to have their own radio show. And we figured out a way to keep it at a very low-cost point by using the phone. That's my background, in phone technology. And by doing that we are able to provide the service for free. And I think that when you create a platform that is open and available, you look into democratizing the medium, much like blogging did for bloggers and tech space communication.

BlogTalkRadio is doing the same for audio and, soon-to-be, video. . . .

Yeah, we are very pleased with the quality. You know, when I first came up with the idea, the podcasting . . . and this is, you know, podcasting was something that I really did not know much about . . . I did not set out to create or become another podcasting company. I set up BlogTalkRadio because I created a blog for my dad, who was ill with lymphoma and cancer, and I wanted to . . . and I learned about blogs, and I realized that there were 75–80 million of them. And everyone's talking about "conversation," and I could not hear any. So I created it. We created a platform that allows live, interactive conversation using the phone, of course, as I mentioned . . . and we achieve it. That's the easy part of it.

So, for us, I do think we're more like a broadcast medium as an alternative. If you look at our audience, the guests that are on, [there is] such diversity. It is incredible the type of content, and then it's archived for the long run which we can then modify. . . .

We did build it from scratch, so we are . . . we have people looking at the site and our own internal customer service people and feature editors, and the like, and very often . . . you know . . . we'll get an e-mail from one of the hosts and it will say, "You know, we've got to call the FCC." And we say, "Fine, call the FCC."

I mean, they have no mandate here. This is a collection of conversations and it's all . . . it's monitored, it's run by us on our site. So there is no FCC. There is . . . but we do ensure that the quality is good, and we double up the best content, and the platform is not being used to facilitate hate or conversations like that, for example. . . .

Yeah, well, it is self-policing also, in a sense, because the hosts know that when they come on this network . . . they sign a form and they're responsible for content, and there's clearly terms and conditions; things they can and cannot do. And if they're in breach of those terms and conditions, I mean, they'll get a warning. But then, they'll be removed from the network. And there are no other places for them to go. . . .

So, you know, they're not going to go to Podcast, or they're not going to go to a podcasting platform because they don't even know how to create this podcast. We take care of everything from the broadcast, the live interaction, all the way through iTunes and the RSS feed. So, it is self-policing, and it's very exciting to see it grow and evolve. And many times the listeners become hosts. You know, they're getting involved and they say, "Why not! I could do one of these things."

To listen to or read the entire Executive Conversation with Alan Levy, go to www.theSocialMediaBible.com.

Commandments

1. **Thou shalt try iTunes.**

Go to www.Apple.com, and download iTunes for your Mac or Windows platform PC. Try it, even if you don't plan on buying and downloading music. See how the interface works. Refer to the previous chapter on podcasting, create a podcast, and try to upload your new podcast to iTunes. Get in the game. It really is here to stay, and the more you know, the more you can participate.

2. **Thou shalt try a podcast hosting site.**

Try using a podcast-hosting site such as Podbean. It really is easy to use; RSS syndication is just a one-click process, it's compatible with iTunes—and best of all—it's free! Just use your PC's built-in mic (or buy one for $8), open your sound edit software, and record your thoughts on your profession or other subject matter of interest to you. Think about the WIIFM (What's In It for Me?), from your customers' and prospects' point of view. What can you tell them in 10 minutes or less that is important to them? This way, they come away from listening to your podcast message with something of value. If you can give them that, then they will keep coming back, refer you to trusted colleagues, and perceive you as an industry expert. All this builds trust, loyalty, and revenue.

Conclusion

It's truly worth your effort to take some time to understand how easy and effective it is to download audio podcasts and music. You'll find that there is great ROI to uploading your podcasts, so that others are exposed to your professional thoughts, and can respond in kind.

Creating your new podcast is one thing, but making it available to your customers, prospects, and employees is quite another. It doesn't do you any good if you have captured your best ideas on audio but no one gets to hear them. So, share your ideas with the world. Upload your podcasts to iTunes and Podbean, and get your material out there. Embed your podcasts on your web site and blog site. Simply by creating a library of audio files with a great WIIFM content value will allow your customers and prospects to view you as an industry expert.

Consider your own reaction when you type an individual or company name into a search engine like Google, and see page after page of search results return. You immediately know that this person or firm has widespread presence on the Web. Seeing these dozens of pages of results—including web pages, blog pages, photographs, audio podcasts, and YouTube videos—prompts you to view this party as an industry expert. Now, isn't that how you want your customers and prospects to see *you*?

Readings and Resources

See Chapter 11, Talking About the Podcast (Audio Create), for readings and resources.

Downloads

For your free downloads associated with *The Social Media Bible,* go to www.theSocialMediaBible.com, and enter your ISBN number located on the back of the book above the bar code. Be sure to enter the dashes.

Credits

Expert Insight Was Provided By:

Alan Levy, founder and CEO, BlogTalkRadio, www.blogtalkradio.com.

Technical Edits Were Provided By:

James Burnes, vice president, MediaSauce, www.MediaSauce.com.

Notes

1. Applications or "apps" are small software applications that are designed to be installed in mobile telephones to increase the phones utility and for fun. Applications include: Multi-Touch interface, accelerometer, GPS, real-time 3D graphics, 3D positional audio, Google Mobile Search, Maps, Gmail, YouTube, and 100's more.
2. Smart playlists can be set to automatically filter your music library based on a customized list of selection criteria, similar to a database query. Apple recently introduced the Genius Feature as well, a tool that automatically generates a playlist of 25, 50, 75, or 100 songs from the user's library that are similar to a selected song.

CHAPTER 13

Watch Out for Vlogs
(Video Create)

The audio podcast chapter mentioned that a video recording can also be considered a podcast since the iPod and other digital playback devices display photographs, audio, and video. This book differentiates audio recordings as a *podcast* and video recordings as just *video* or a *vlog*. As the word *blog* stands for weB LOG, vlog, comes from Video web LOG.

What's In It for You?

Human psychology is such that the more robust or stimulating the experience, the more engaging it is, and the better we comprehend and retain that experience. An engaging video also ensures that your viewer will watch it to its conclusion. This is why people often prefer watching a good movie at the end of the day as opposed to reading or even listening to an audio book. The more senses that are involved in gathering information, the more engaging the process becomes. This accounts for the overwhelming popularity of YouTube. Creating video, vlogging, and video posting are all about utilizing this human trait to better educate and communicate with your network and with your customers.

The human being evolved to communicate first through facial expressions, and then through speech. Verbal communication is a relatively new human trait, and the written word is even more recent. Writing can be traced back only a half dozen millennia, while communication using facial expressions and voice tones is the oldest method that any living being has used. Nearly every species on earth that can share information does so in this way.

theSocialMediaBible.com

When two humans want to express an idea, thought, or concept, 55 percent of the communication comes from body language, 38 percent from voice, and only a mere 7 percent from the words. Letters and e-mails clearly don't contain inflection and body language, which is why writing can so easily be misinterpreted or misconstrued. Watching and listening to someone while they speak allows us to study facial expressions and tone in order to help build trust and make it easier to recognize when someone isn't being sincere. For this reason, vlogs can be the most effective way to communicate with your customers.

All it takes to create a vlog is a digital video camera, some free editing software, and—most importantly—*creativity*. Companies such as BMW, Quiznos, and Nabisco are using video to grab huge audiences and increase their market share (see Figure 13.1). Even a blender company can get over a million views of their product video in just 24 hours by using off-the-shelf technology and a little creativity (see the "Will It Blend" example at www .theSocialMediaBible.com).

FIGURE 13.1 | YouTube BMW

Back to the Beginning

Shortly after the introduction of the Internet, people were trying to push the limits of this new medium by providing more and more rich media: midi, music, audio, images, virtual reality images (QTVR), and video. The early restrictions were CPU speed and bandwidth.

What Is Video?

The technical measure of video content is *frames per second*, which means the number of still images every second. For standard film, the frame rate can be 32 frames (or images) per second, while video frame rates can range from 25 to 30 and even 50 to 60 frames per second for high-definition (HD) video, which means that for a standard video that is running at 25 frames per second, there are 1,500 separate images every minute. Based on the dimensions of the video screen, that can add up to a lot of data per frame (image), and a huge amount of information every minute. Getting all of that data through the earliest 300-baud modem (300 bits per second), or even today's 56K-baud modem (56,000 bits per second) is a monumental task. This is why the earlier videos (and even some today) were small in size, short in length, low resolution, and often ran choppy (less than 32 frames per second) as the Internet tried to serve that data to the user. And as all that data came in, the CPU tried to assemble it into a continuous-running, smooth video.

The *bit* is the most fundamental piece of data that a computer or any digital device uses to communicate, store, or display. A bit is a single 0 or 1; it's a charge or no charge. These digits of 0s and 1s are why today's electronics are called *digital*. Eight of these digits in a stream make up a single byte. Depending upon the computer, it takes as much as 4 bytes (32 bits) to represent a single pixel on your screen in a specific location—on, off, and color. So, if you have a 350k image, it would be 350,000 bytes (k stands for 1,000 in engineering, creating the term kb for kilobytes). That one image (frame) would consist of 350,000 bytes times 8 bits—or 2.8 million bits of information for a single image. Based on this, a 3-minute video would be 350k bits times 32 frames per second times 3 minutes (180 seconds), or more than 20 billion bits of information!

(continued)

(continued)

As the Internet grew, so did *bandwidth,* which is the size of the information conduit and the ability to push more bits through the wire or air—and, consequently, the amount of data that could be displayed. In the early days of the Internet, text was the first type of data because it could be transferred and displayed quickly due to the small amount of bits (32 bits per character). A full page of single-spaced text can be as small as 2k (2,000 bytes). A standard color image can be 350k, a 3-minute small-size video can be 20mb (million bytes), and a full-length movie can be more than 4.5gb (4.5 billion bytes)!

With present cable technology, a residential cable Internet connection can provide you with download speeds as high as 4 to 6 Mbps (million bits per second; M stands for million). High-speed cable Internet compared to a 56K dialup connection can run up to 70 times faster. For an additional fee—and assuming it is available in your area—most major cable providers, such as Cox Communication, Comcast, and Time Warner, also offer premium packages with speeds as high as 8 to 10 Mbps.

Yay for Apple QuickTime!

The first major breakthrough in video for the computer was Apple's release of QuickTime on December 2, 1991. For the first time, users were able to reasonably view good-quality, color videos on their computers. QuickTime was mostly about compression rate. The less information that needed to be sent out per frame, the more frames that could be transmitted, assembled, and played. Compression is about finding patterns in the data, creating a kind of shorthand for that pattern, and transmitting the shorthand data and rules, which represent much less overall information. Later versions of QuickTime maximized the video file size and allowed users to transmit very small videos through still-restricted bandwidth and play them on slow computers, but it worked!

With greater improvements in compression technology and increasingly faster

FIGURE 13.2 QuickTime

transfer rates for modems, the video that the Internet was delivering became better and better.

Microsoft also released Windows 3.0 in 1991, along with their own version of a video/audio player called Media Player. This eventually became Windows Media Player, which is now the Windows-based computer's standard file format for audio and video files.

The one other player that has had an influence on video players is RealVideo. The RealVideo Player was developed by RealNetworks and was first released in 1997 with its own proprietary video. Even though RealVideo is supported on many platforms—including Windows, Mac, Linux, Solaris, and several mobile phones—QuickTime and Windows Media Player still hold the largest market share.

With small-file-size compressed video available on the computer and distributed over the Internet, it was only a matter of time before people created web sites dedicated to sharing their thoughts through the use of video. On January 1, 2004, Steve Garfield launched his videoblog and announced that 2004 would be the "year of the video blog." In June of that year, Peter Van Dijck and Jay Dedman started the Yahoo! Videoblogging Group, which became the first—and to this day, most popular—community of vloggers.

The year 2004 also saw a growth in people interested in paying for vlogging. They had reached a critical mass and held their first conference the next year. Vloggercon was held in New York City in January 2005, and became the first videoblogger conference of its kind. On July 20, 2005, the Yahoo! Videoblogging Group expanded to more than 1,000 members. One year later, in July 2006, YouTube became the fifth-most-popular web destination, with over 100 million videos viewed, and more than 65,000 new video uploads every day. Today, YouTube's members are uploading 13 hours of video every minute and more than 1 billion video downloads per day!

Bandwidth and Storage

Up until the advent of web sites like YouTube, video distribution was still somewhat of a problem. The video files were larger and longer, and with more and more people watching them, the total amount of data transmitted from one's web site could be quite huge. Most Internet Service Providers (ISPs) charge by the amount of data served on your behalf from your web site if you exceed a maximum.

Also, downloading all of the data before you watch a video is time consuming and impractical. No one wanted to wait until a file was completely downloaded to start watching a video. As a result, video streaming was introduced. Streaming takes place when the ISP spoonfeeds the data to the computer at a slightly faster rate than is needed, so that the modem downloads the video without interruption while the user begins to watch it. This was an efficient solution for distribution. However, video storage then became a problem. Since videos can be very large in size—and people can have a lot of videos—the amount of disk storage became very expensive.

Along Comes YouTube

You can't discuss video creation without discussing video sharing; after all, it's what you do after you've created your video. (For additional information on sharing content, refer to Chapter 14, Got Video (Video Sharing).) With more people being connected to the Internet via broadband (high-speed transfer rate), such as DSL, Dish, and cable modems, the amount of data a person could download and view became less of an issue. CPUs became much faster, and the cost of disk storage plummeted. Then along came web sites such as Google's YouTube. YouTube, a video sharing web site allows users to upload, view, and share video clips. In February 2005, three former PayPal employees created YouTube. In November 2006, YouTube, LLC was purchased by Google Inc. for $1.65 billion USD, and now operates as a subsidiary of Google.

FIGURE 13.3 YouTube

In October 2006, the BBC launched its first official video blogging site for its children's television series *Blue Peter,* with a video asking children to name a new puppy character on the show.

Early employees of PayPal Chad Hurley, Steve Chen, and Jawed Karim activated the domain name YouTube.com on February 15, 2005. They developed their web site over the next several months, and YouTube was presented to the public in May 2005.

For more information on Video Sharing and Video Examples, please read Chapter 14, Got Video (Video Sharing); and be sure to visit www.the SocialMediaBible.com.

Lifecasting

Another extreme example of vlogs on steroids comes from Jody Gnant. She has created one of, if not the longest video documentaries ever. Jody

FIGURE 13.4   Jody Gnant

Gnant set up a web cam to her laptop and video streamed her life 24 hours per day for more than nine continuous months. For more information about Jody Gnant and on Lifecasting, see Chapter 16, Live from Anywhere—It's Livecasting.

Vlogging is so appealing because it removes geographic boundaries and truly creates a global community through personal interaction. People in the United States are also fortunate to live in a country where the government does not censor online videos. Because the FCC has opted to keep this information free of suppression (so far!), no restrictions have been placed on its content.

The U.S. Constitution's First Amendment—related to freedom of expression, speech, and press—applies to this last stronghold of personal expression. Ever since the printed word was created, some faction of society has attempted to censor it—whether it was the church, the government, or just the one paying for the printing. A censor has nearly always controlled views on society, politics, religion, and opinions in one form or another. Ever since the FCC was founded in 1934, it has censored everything related to radio and television content, leading up to the advent of cable TV in the 1970s. Nowadays, with the Internet's popularity, vloggers, bloggers, and podcasters can say what they want—and, of course, accept personal responsibility for the good and the not-so-good content that they are creating and distributing. Although the FCC is still responsible for the Internet, they have thus far chosen not to censor or regulate its content. (As Will Rogers once said, "Thank God we don't get all of the government we pay for.")

Josh Wolf (joshwolf.net), is a citizen journalist/vlogger in San Francisco who was jailed for longer than any other journalist because he refused to turn over his sources to the federal government.

A freelance journalist and independent videographer, Wolf was at the time of this writing in "coercive custody" at the Federal Detention Facility in Dublin, California. He was not charged with any crime and is being held under civil contempt charges. Wolf was incarcerated in July 2006 after resisting a subpoena to testify before a federal grand jury and for refusing to turn over his source material for video he shot of a San Francisco protest against the G8 Summit in 2005. His incarceration is virtually unprecedented. He is now the longest-imprisoned journalist in U.S. history for failure to comply with a subpoena.

What You Need to Know

Again, the most important thing to know is to *just do it!* The sooner you start vlogging, the sooner you will begin seeing results.

Uploading Your Videos

For more information on uploading video, please read Chapter 14, Got Video (Video Sharing), on video sharing.

Tips, Techniques, and Tactics

Creating Your Own Video

Vlogging can be as easy as using a cell phone with built-in video capabilities. However, while you can certainly use your cell phone, as famous blogger Robert Scoble does occasionally, starting with this level of quality is not recommended.

Buy or borrow a video camera, and just start shooting some video. While shooting a comprehensive video is more difficult than recording your voice in an audio podcast, getting something worth watching is not that hard, especially if there is good content—a valuable takeaway for your viewers.

Script Your Thoughts

It's always best to script your thoughts, or at least organize them as a list of bullet points. One suggestion for recording a video is to first create a Keynote presentation (PowerPoint, for non-Apple users). Position the monitor behind the camera or print the slides and tape them where you can speak to them while recording. Directly reading a script is the *worst* thing you can do.

Don't attempt to record too much at one time. If you can get through a slide, say "cut," take a deep breath, and start fresh with a new slide. If you are one of those people lucky enough to be able to just start talking, then by all means, do that. The bottom line is to do whatever you are the most comfortable with; you will come across as confident in the video.

Be sure to remember to record your introduction: who you are, your subject matter, and your web site address. Keep in mind that you must also record your conclusion, which will consist of a summary and a reiteration of who you are and your web site. The introduction and conclusion can also contain some music and even titles.

Editing Your Video

Once you have created some raw digital video, it's time to edit. Select a video editing application such as Apple's iMovie and import your video (see Figure 13.5). Pick out some theme music, still photos, and other additional video clips you might want to include. You can also do a voice-over by recording directly from the microphone over your still photos or video clips.

Your video editing software will allow you to create tracks, which will enable you to place your video in as the main track, insert your introduction in front of it, and even lay down a separate music track that will play

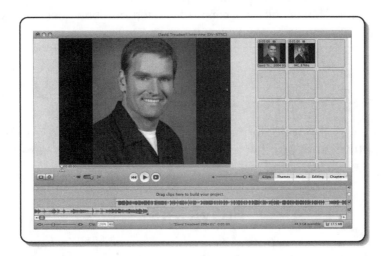

FIGURE 13.5 iMovie Screen

simultaneously. You can, of course, control the track volume, so that the background music remains in the background.

There are many choices for video editing software; the one you use will depend on your computer's operating platform, be it Apple or Windows. Macintosh aficionados use iMovie to create and edit videos, benefiting from the drag-and-drop features of Macintosh software. You could also use Adobe Premiere or Final Cut Pro on the Mac OS. If you are a Windows user, you can use Adobe Premiere or ArcSoft's ShowBiz.

Once you have your video ready for prime-time viewing, it's time to decide how to distribute and otherwise make available your motion picture work of art. The easiest and most effect web site is, of course, YouTube. The process is simple: you set up an account, select Upload Video, enter a description, answer a few other questions about your video, and hit Upload. Wait a few minutes, and your video is now available for viewing anywhere in the world, 24/7, for free!

Keep in mind that just because your video is on YouTube doesn't automatically mean that others will watch it and you will become an overnight success. It is now your responsibility to drive traffic to your video. You do this through RSS, blogging, e-mails, commenting, and the use of other social media tools, so read on. See the chapters on RSS, blogs, and e-mails for more information.

Many open-source content management systems, like WordPress, Joomla, or Drupal, have integrated widgets and capabilities that allow you to post your video content. This permits vloggers to host and distribute their own video blogging, right from their own web sites.

Note

The convergence of mobile phones with built-in digital video cameras allows users to capture and publish video content to the Web almost as it is recorded.

Providers

FreeVlog.org is a great resource created by *Secrets of Videoblogging* authors Ryanne Hodson and Michael Verdi. This site has launched a thousand videoblogs, and is really helpful to new vloggers.

Expert Insight

Stephanie Bryant, author, *Vlogging For Dummies*, www.mortaine.blogspot.com

Stephanie Bryant

The first video blog that I hosted was a video that I took of my cat. And it was really just, you know, 'cuz cat videos are just how people start doing video online. There are millions of cat videos out there, but it was just kind of a silly thing. I was just messing around with iMovie and I had my new digital camera with me and I was like, "Oh, look, it takes video." So I shot a little 30-second video of my cat attacking a toy. And then I edited it and posted it to my iJournal, and that was it. And then, about four days later I thought, "Well, I could turn this into a show. I could go around and video myself doing weird and stupid things and then post it to the Internet." And I thought this would be a really good idea! . . .

So I decided, "Okay, I'll do this and then I will videotape it. And then I will add it and post it to my video blog." And I called the video blog, *Hold My Beer and Watch This.* And I got involved in the video blogging group on Yahoo!, which is still one of the *very* best resources for video bloggers, and something I *strongly* recommend for anyone starting out . . . because you can ask all sorts of questions and every so often, you know, people are saying, "Oh, do we have to have this conversation again?" But most of the time somebody will give you a solid answer, which is kind of nice . . .

Yeah, "success stories"; I would say BMW is one of the biggest success stories, and they have been, consistently, from the very beginning in the video blogging movement. They have always had a BMW brand pod [or] video podcast available. And I think that shows a lot of savvy and forward thinking on BMW's part. I really give them strong props for that work. The quality and the consistency . . . they never pretend that it's not a BMW-branded thing. You know, they never try to make it a viral . . . something . . . except for this documentary, and even that is clearly made by BMW. So, I think that they really do a good job of blending the business part or just having their brand out there, as well as [establishing] the human connection. . . .

You can video blog with very simple equipment and still come up with a pretty decent video blog. There is a web site out there called http://www.freeblog.org which gets a lot of people started with video blogging, and it's a terrific resource; it's a real powerhouse in the video blogging community. They will tell you nuts and bolts, step-by-step . . . starting with, "I don't even have a blog" to "How to get a video blog up and running." . . .

(continued)

(continued)

When people talk about money and how much it costs to video blog and stuff, the thing that I suggest is that you look at your equipment, your time, and your personnel; how many people you have that can be part of the video blog, and how much video equipment and tripods, and so forth, that you currently have. Even if that's just your digital camera and a book that you prop it up on, and then how much time you personally have. And if you are lacking in any of those in a way that you feel will make your video blog less enjoyable for you, don't worry so much about audience, because at this point you don't have an audience. . . . It's just you. . . .

And if I were going to answer a question about what insights I have, I would say, "Keep the fun."

To listen to or read the entire Executive Conversation with Stephanie Bryant, go to www.theSocialMediaBible.com or www.mortaine.blogspot.com.

Commandments

1. **Thou shalt look at some of the most popular videos shared.**

    Go look at the most popular videos posted on YouTube and other video-sharing web sites. See what they have in common. Notice the strong entertainment value (entertainment is a very strong "What's In It for Me?").

2. **Thou shalt create a video.**

    Go out and create a video. Try it. Keep it light, and keep it short (three to five minutes). Try to have the highest WIIFM you can for your customers. Give them a takeaway in the form of information, such as an "I didn't know that," or a "You can use it that way"; or just plain have fun.

3. **Thou shalt not spend a lot of money.**

    If you have a digital video camera, start shooting. If you don't own one, borrow one first and try it to see if you like it. Download free software from the Internet, and have some fun editing.

4. **Thou shalt comment.**

    Start building a community around your videos, products, services, hobby, or other subject content (See Chapter 3, Say Hello to Social Networking, for more information on how to build networks and communities.)

Conclusion

Creating your own video is a lot of fun. It is a little more technically challenging than an audio podcast or a simple blog, but the rewards are well worth it. Video is almost always the best medium for communicating with your customers. Being able to share your expressions, inflections, and body language builds much greater trust and conveys sincerity to your viewers. Watching someone deliver her or his message is powerful. Just look at how television influences lives.

Don't be afraid of trying to create your own video. Don't spend a lot of money to start out. Use your existing camera or borrow one from a friend and start videotaping. The best way to experience vlogging—to borrow a sport shoe slogan—is to "Just Do It!"

Readings and Resources

Blake, Bonnie, and Doug Sahlin. *50 Fast Digital Video Techniques.* (Hoboken, NJ: John Wiley & Sons, Inc.)

Bryant, Stephanie Cottrell. *Videoblogging For Dummies.* (Hoboken, NJ: John Wiley & Sons, Inc.)

Dayley, Lisa DaNae. *Photoshop CS3 Extended Video and 3D Bible.* (Hoboken, NJ: John Wiley & Sons, Inc.)

Dedman, Jay, and Joshua Paul. *Videoblogging.* (Hoboken, NJ: John Wiley & Sons, Inc.)

Flash Video for Professionals: Expert Techniques for Integrating. (Hoboken, NJ: John Wiley & Sons, Inc.)

Hodson, Ryanne, and Michael Verdi. *Secrets of Videoblogging.* (Hoboken, NJ: John Wiley & Sons, Inc.)

Kennedy, Pete, and Maura Kennedy. *Make Your Own Music Videos with Adobe Premiere.* (Hoboken, NJ: John Wiley & Sons, Inc.)

Kobler, Helmut, and Chad Fahs. *Final Cut Pro4 for Dummies.* (Hoboken, NJ: John Wiley & Sons, Inc.)

Sadun, Erica. *Digital Video Essentials: Shoot, Transfer, Edit, Share.* (Hoboken, NJ: John Wiley & Sons, Inc.)

Underdahl, Keith. *Digital Video For Dummies.* (Hoboken, NJ: John Wiley & Sons, Inc.)

Downloads

For your free downloads associated with *The Social Media Bible*, go to www.theSocialMediaBible.com, and enter your ISBN number located on the back of the book above the bar code. Be sure to enter the dashes.

Credits

Expert Insight and Technical Edits Were Provided By:

Stephanie Bryant, author, *Vlogging For Dummies*, www.mortaine.blogspot.com.

CHAPTER 14

Got Video (Video Sharing)

If you can get 43 million views of your video because of its entertainment value—as did a twenty-three-year-old in Korea—or you can get 93 million views—as did one comedian who posted a six-minute segment of his comedy act—then wouldn't you? Especially if it was free?[1]

Read on for more information.

Video sharing is the easiest and fastest way to start building your social media portfolio. You and your company already have a box of VHS tapes or video on a hard drive somewhere. You need to locate that video, identify the best representation of your company, and start uploading it to video-sharing web sites. If you don't have good video, start making it. Uploading is free, it makes your message accessible to all of your prospects and customers, and it helps build your Google Juice!

As mentioned in the previous chapter, while video recordings can also be considered podcasts—since the iPod and other digital playback devices can display photographs, audio, and video—for the purpose of this book, audios are treated as *podcasts,* and videos are referred to as either *videos* or *vlogs.*

What's In It for You?

A blender company called Blendtec that is located in Orem, Utah, uploaded a funny in-house product demonstration video to YouTube. Within the first 24 hours, more than one million viewers watched their video; within the same 24-hour period, they sold out of their $600 Blendtec Blenders.

What would you pay to have your product or service's 1½-minute commercial viewed by over one million potential customers in 24 hours? You most likely couldn't afford this kind of media exposure. The Blendtec

FIGURE 14.1   Blend Tech

video has now been viewed more than 3.5 million times (see Figure 14.1). (To watch Blendtec president Tom Dickson blend a brand-new iPhone on the day they came out—and other video examples—go to www.theSocialMediaBible .com; or go to YouTube and search for "Will It Blend.")

Can anyone guarantee that the phenomenal success that Blendtec has enjoyed will happen for you? No, but when you already have the video or can produce it easily as did Blendtec —and it's free to upload—then what do you have to lose?

Back to the Beginning

As with several of the others chapters that have both a Sharing and a Creation chapter (such as this chapter and chapters 11 & 12 on Audio), the creation and sharing history of Video Sharing has been interwoven into the same story. And since Video Sharing's history is only a very small part of the larger video story, you can find this information later in this chapter.

What You Need to Know

The most important thing you need to know is to *just do it!* You have to start sometime, and the easiest way to do so is to gather all of the videos you currently have on hand and start uploading them to YouTube. It's actually simpler than you think. Set up your account (it's free), select Upload Video, follow the instructions, and there you have it. (For more information about creating your own video, see Chapter 13, Watch Out for Vlogs (Video Create).)

FIGURE 14.2   YouTube "The Guitar"

Go to YouTube and type in "The Guitar" or go to www.theSocialMediaBible.com to click on the link in the chapter section for a clickable link.

Examples are the best way to explain why uploading videos to a video-sharing web site can give you such a great rate of return on investment of your time. Three videos in particular discussed in this chapter have been extremely successful for their owners. One is a personal video, while the other two are business related. Remember, there's no guarantee that you will have the same success, but who knows?

The first example is one of the earlier and more popular videos on YouTube called "Guitar" (www.youtube.com/watch?v=QjA5faZF1A8; see Figure 14.2). This video of Pachelbel's *Canon* played on an electric guitar was created by a twenty-three-year-old from Korea named Jeong-Hyun Lim who recorded his video himself in his bedroom in his mirror. The video "Guitar" has had more than 54 million views to date—simply because it's entertaining.

Another example of how popular a self-made posted video can become comes from the comedian Judson Laipply, who posted a six-minute portion of his comedy act, which he called "The Evolution of Dance," on YouTube (www.youtube.com/watch?v=dMH0bHeiRNg; see Figure 14.3). To date, this video has had more than 109 million views—and has been the record holder for most-watched video on YouTube until recently, where a video for a music group has surpassed it.

FIGURE 14.3 YouTube "The Evolution of Dance"

Imagine having to invest nothing more than 10 minutes of your time uploading a video you already had in order to have 93 million people watch your six-minute commercial. While it doesn't happen often, there is an audience for a variety of works. How about that as an extraordinary ROI?

Go to YouTube and type in "The Evolution of Dance" or go to www .theSocialMediaBible.com to click on the link in the chapter section for a clickable link.

Uploading Your Videos

The only prerequisite for uploading videos is that they need to be in a digital format and not exceed the host's maximum file size. If you have made your videos relatively recently, they are probably already in a digital format. If your videos are still on VHS, then you will have to convert them.

You can buy some VHS-to-DVD recorders for under $100. Put the VHS video in, put in a blank DVD, hit Play, and when the video is at the end, you have a digital video on DVD. LG, Samsung, Sony, Toshiba, and Panasonic make some really good units. You can also find service providers that will convert your VHS videos inexpensively. Many services offer to accept your VHS tapes by mail and return them in a digital format recorded on a DVD. An example of this is Home Movie Depot, a company that charges anywhere from under $20 to more for damaged tapes.

You can also buy a VHS player made by Ion that connects directly to your computer via the USB port. Another alternative is to buy a converter box for about $250 that connects your VCR to your computer, such as the ADS PYRO A/V Link, Analog to Digital Video Converter that ships free with Adobe Premiere Elements 4.0 for around $160.

Once you have gathered all of your videos in a digital format, you can go to YouTube or another video-sharing web site and start uploading. That's all there is to it. Make sure you have your tags picked out ahead of time. (See meta tags in Chapter 20, Spotlight on Search (Search Engine Optimization).)

Once you have a list of your tags or keywords and a short description, then you're ready to upload. And, like the shampoo bottle says, lather, rinse, repeat: load, tag, repeat.

Keep in mind that simply uploading your content to a video-sharing web site doesn't create a post with an RSS feed. In order to allow your followers to subscribe to your chronological posts, the video has to be included as an enclosure in an RSS feed, similar to a podcast. This is a distinction that can be important if you are building a community and a following. By building your video into an RSS feed, it is easy for your video to become a viral one that is posted to the Web and passed around by word of mouth. Video posted to your blog is also video that isn't enclosed in the RSS Feed (see Chapter 19, RSS—Really Simple Syndication Made Simple).

Another advantage of posting a video to YouTube is the ability to comment back and forth and respond to comments the video posts have generated. In comment marketing, this kind of feedback is considered almost essential. Many videobloggers still feel that YouTube misses the main point, because their subscription model isn't RSS-based. So, although you can subscribe to favorite users in YouTube, that subscription can't be accessed in a video-enabled RSS reader such as FireAnt or iTunes. (For more information on RSS, see Chapter 19, RSS—Really Simple Syndication Made Simple. For more information on comment marketing, see the interview with Amanda Vega, from Amanda Vega Consultants.)

Peer-to-Peer

Another form of file sharing for music, video, e-books, movies, software, and other digital data is known as peer-to-peer (or P2P). P2P takes place when many computers on a network, connected via the Internet, all share digital data in the form of files. For example, if you want the latest music from your favorite band, you can download that copyrighted material by connecting to a peer-to-peer network, selecting the file, and downloading that file to your computer. All the while, your computer is being used to transfer digital bits of another file that someone else has requested. Once all of the bits have been downloaded to your computer, the file is put back together or assembled into the original working data file.

Napster

Peer-to-peer was made most famous—or perhaps infamous—when it was argued that 87 percent of all music available on Napster's download servers was copyrighted.

In June 1999, Shawn Fanning created an online music file-sharing service called Napster while he was attending Northeastern University in Boston. (Napster got its name from Fanning's nappy hair style. Napster allowed people to easily copy and distribute MP3 files between one another for free. This led the music industry to accuse Napster of huge copyright violations. Napster was shut down in July 2001 by a court order, but it paved the way for decentralized peer-to-peer file-distribution programs. Services and products such as Kazaa, Gnutella, CAN, FastTrack, LimeWire, Bit Torrent, and Freenet came later on.

Napster changed the way university students used the Internet. Any piece of music could be taken (or *ripped*) from a CD and stored on your hard drive. Then, simply by performing a search for that song title, all of the computers around the world with that file turned up in the listing. All you had to do was select the file and wait a few minutes for it to be transferred from that computer to yours. That's it!

Peer-to-peer and Napster technology allowed music fans to easily share with each other song files in any format. This led to the music industry's accusations of massive copyright violations—and a $5.3 million lawsuit against Napster and a fourteen-year-old girl.

BitTorrent

BitTorrent is a type of peer-to-peer file-sharing protocol used to distribute data such as movies, music, photos, software, audio, and other digital data files. One computer starts as the initial distributor of the complete file. Each peer-to-peer (or individually connected) PC that downloads data also uploads data to other peers. This provides a significant reduction in the original PC's hardware and bandwidth costs. It provides redundancy against system errors and reduces dependence on an original distributor. BitTorrent also reduces the liability of the original computer's distributed copyrighted materials, as the system actually passes around the data from machine to machine and compiles the completed files that have been transferred from many computers on the system.

Programmer Bram Cohen designed the BitTorrent protocol in April 2001, and it debuted on July 2 of that year. The original BitTorrent is now maintained by Cohen's company, BitTorrent Inc. This system is widely used to distribute copyrighted games, music, and movies that sometimes are still playing as first-run showings in theaters.

Providers

The following is a list of video-sharing web sites that are listed on Wikipedia: AniBOOM, AtomUploads (part of AtomFilms), BGVIP.TV, Big Think, Blinkx, Blip.tv, Break.com, Buzznet, Crackle, Dailymotion, EngageMedia, GameVideos .com, GoFish, Google Video, Hulu, iFilm, imeem, JibJab, Kewego, Liveleak, Metacafe, MSN Soapbox, MySpace, MyVideo, OneWorldTV, Ourmedia, pandora tv, Peekvid.com, Photobucket, Phpmotion, Rambler Vision, ReelTime.com, RuTube, Sapo Videos (only Portuguese), Sevenload, Stage6 (closed), Twango, Vbox7, Veoh, Viddler, Vimeo, Vuze, Yahoo! Video, YouAreTV, and YouTube.

Does this mean that you have to stay up all night uploading the same video to every one of these web sites? No! Just pick one or two, grab a video, and go for it. Look at some of the videos on only a few of these web sites. See which ones you like, and which are getting the highest number of hits. Then try to pick or create a video with the same kind of general content and upload it. Don't get overwhelmed; getting only whelmed is okay.

Expert Insight

George Strompolos, content partnerships manager, YouTube, www.youtube.com

George Strompolos

I am the content partnerships' manager here at YouTube, and that's really a fancy way of saying that I reach out to content creators and help them engage on YouTube and to distribute their content and to connect with audiences around the world. And so YouTube being an open platform, those content creators can take on many shapes and sizes. They can be someone as small as a video blogger producing videos in their bedroom, up to what we call a "broadband studio" or a "digital studio," which creates original content just for Internet distribution. And this goes all the way up to traditional media companies and premium content

(continued)

(continued)

providers that we are all familiar with: CBS and the National Basketball Association. . . .

So at its core YouTube is a web site where people can upload videos to share them with the world. It's also a great place to watch videos. It's actually an interesting fact that YouTube currently receives 13 hours of video uploaded to the site every minute! . . .

What you'll find is that people upload videos to YouTube for different reasons. Some of them just want to share pictures of their baby (or something like that), or videos of their baby, or their vacation footage. We certainly are happy to support that. However, it's becoming more and more common for amateur and professional content producers to produce content for YouTube and make a living out of it.

The way that they do this is they become a "partner" through my team, and they also have the ability to apply online at YouTube.com/partners, and basically tell us, "Hey, we're producing original content and not only do we want to share it with the world through YouTube, but we want to give you the ability to run ads against that content." . . .

And then we will share the majority of that ad revenue back to the content creator. So I call it a *performance-based* model. In other words, you can become a content partner, and if you upload video and it gets zero views, well there's clearly no ad revenue there, so nothing is being shared. But if you upload a video and it gets one million views, for instance, we put an ad on every single view. And so that ad revenue starts to accrue and, in many cases, can become significant for a lot of the Content Partners we have. . . .

The main format of advertising that you'll see on YouTube when you are watching a video (if you're watching a video from a partner) is what we call *in-video* advertising. And it is, essentially, a transparent overlay that shows up toward the bottom of the video window; and it's cool. It can be animated, and a cool example is when the Simpsons movie was premiering, the studio behind that movie ran an in-video overlay of Homer Simpson chasing a donut across the bottom of the screen. It goes pretty quick, you know, and it's usually relevant. I think they targeted that against comedy and animation content, so to that audience it was probably actually a nice surprise. And as a user, you can click on Homer Simpson and see, maybe, the movie trailer, or you can choose to close that overlay out, or just wait a few seconds and it will just disappear. . . .

So, you know, creating original content and sharing in ad revenues is one way to approach YouTube, and that's more from an entertainment perspective. But from more a marketing perspective, I've just been amazed at the way that companies actually think of clever ways to use YouTube. And "Will It Blend" is also one of my favorite examples.

I should defer to them, of course, but I did read an article at one point that their sales actually went up 300 percent as a result of their presence on YouTube. . . .

This is from a marketing effort that essentially cost them nothing: create a YouTube channel, no cost; set up a guy on camera with a blender (they make blenders so it cannot be that expensive for them), and blend a couple of cool things. And they were smart enough to blend things that are kind of hot and in the news. So the new iPhone comes out and they buy one on the first day and they blend it. And of course, people are searching for the iPhone video and things like that, and just the controversy of destroying something in a blender that is so sought-after is something that translates to a lot of video views. . . .

Here you have this tremendous marketing tool in YouTube, and for a company like Blendtec. What's interesting is that I read a blog post a few months ago from a well-known guy in Silicon Valley who said, "I see a future where your marketing can become a profit center." And if you look at "Will It Blend," that's a perfect example. So their marketing is clearly driving sales, but also they are providing original content.

So they are certainly welcome to join our partnership program, and if they are comfortable having other ads running against their videos, they can actually make money off those ads. So it's kind of an interesting situation there. . . .

You know, one of my favorite examples is a young guy named Lucas who has a character that he does on YouTube called "Fred." Lucas is about fifteen years old, I think, and he plays this character named "Fred" who is a six-year-old, and the shtick is that he is a six-year-old with anger management problems.

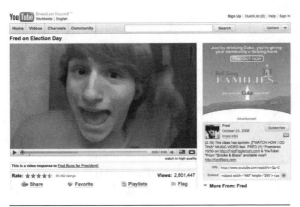

YouTube "Fred Frigglehorn"

It's kind of one of these things that are really made for kids—like a lot of Pixar Films, for instance—but it is also funny to adults. It's kind a bizarre thing, and you can see it at YouTube.com/Fred; and it's really just taken off like a rocket.

I think it's actually the fastest-growing channel in YouTube history.

And Fred is a partner, so we traffic ads against his videos and we share the majority of that ad revenue with him. He's at a point where he'll post a video, and within a matter of days, that video will have at least 3 million views, I guarantee. . . . Sometimes as high as 8 to 10 million! So that is about one video every week, sometimes more. There're cable programs, even network television producers that would die for those numbers. And I think it was the season finale of *American Idol* that did 35 million viewers. . . .

(continued)

(continued)

Absolutely an impressive feat, and if you look at someone like Fred who uploads a video and gets 3 million views at a minimum, all he has to do is post 10 videos and he's going to get that number of *American Idol* viewership. But don't forget that people are constantly watching these other videos, too. It's really a powerful thing, and I won't get into the details of this partnership, but he's making decent money off of YouTube, substantial . . . and he's, naturally, being approached by all kinds of brands, because he's (kind of) hitting that tween audience.

To listen to or read the entire Executive Conversation with George Strompolos, go to www.theSocialMediaBible.com.

Commandments

1. **Thou shalt convert any VHS videos to digital format.**

    Take all of your useful VHS tapes and either convert them or have them converted to digital format. Get your product videos, your service videos, your company party video (use discretion!), your happy customer videos, and get them ready for posting.

2. **Thou shalt upload.**

    The highest ROI comes in finding all of the videos you currently have and getting them uploaded to a site. Your customers can't see them if they aren't there. Get any existing video you have, figure out its keywords, and upload. It's free!

3. **Thou shalt post everywhere.**

    Once you are comfortable with one video-sharing site and have it loaded with all of your videos, consider posting your videos to a second or even a third video-sharing web site.

    Post them on YouTube, and on several of the other free video-sharing web sites. Don't forget to post to some of the lesser-known web sites such as Blip.tv, VideoEgg, and Daily Motion.

4. **Thou shalt comment.**

    Start building a community around your videos, products, services, hobby, or other subject content. (See Chapter 3, Say Hello to Social Networking, for more information on how to build networks and communities.)

5. **Thou shalt not post copyrighted material.**

    If you're going to post it, be sure you own the rights to it. Don't post something that belongs to someone else, *especially* if someone else owns the copyright.

6. **Thou shalt become familiar with the Creative Commons Act.**

> Go to www.theSocialMediaBible.com to find out more about the Creative Commons Act to find out what you can and cannot use when posting to the Internet.

7. **Thou shalt be sincere and have fun.**

> The most important step in this process is to be yourself, be sincere, and have fun. If you're not enjoying yourself when you are creating a video, it shows.

Conclusion

The common theme in this book is "Just Do It!" Video sharing is a great way to get your company and product names out there. The more "What's In It for Me?" value that the video has, the more it will be watched and passed along. Get your videos, pick out a few video-sharing web sites, and start posting. Be sure to mention the videos in your blogs and e-mails. Be sure that you have chosen the proper meta tags, so that when someone is looking for your content, they can find it. And be sure to use RSS feeds whenever possible. Look at other people's videos and descriptions, and plagiarize (just kidding!). Be inspired by their style and content.

Readings and Resources

Baig, Edward C., and Bob LeVitus. *iPhone For Dummies* (Hoboken, NJ: John Wiley & Sons, Inc).

Bove, Tony. *iPod & iTunes For Dummies* (Hoboken, NJ: John Wiley & Sons, Inc).

Larson, Lisa, and Renee Costantini. *Video on the Web* (Hoboken, NJ: John Wiley & Sons, Inc).

Shaw, Russell, and David Mercer. *Caution! Music & Video Downloading: Your Guide to Legal, Safe, and Trouble-Free Downloads* (Hoboken, NJ: John Wiley & Sons, Inc).

Zink, Michael. *Scalable Video on Demand: Adaptive Internet-Based Distribution* (Hoboken, NJ: John Wiley & Sons, Inc).

Downloads

For your free downloads associated with *The Social Media Bible,* go to www.theSocialMediaBible.com, and enter your ISBN number located on the back of the book above the bar code. Be sure to enter the dashes.

Credits

Expert Insight Was Provided By:

George Strompolos, content partnerships manager, YouTube, www.youtube.com.

Technical Edits Were Provided By:

David Cain, president, MediaSauce, www.MediaSauce.com.

Note

1. *Google Juice* is a term used to describe the results that follow when you search for your name, your company's name, and your product or service's name in Google or other search engines. The more listings and the more pages that a search engine returns to the searcher, the more Google Juice you have. The goal of this book is to squeeze as much Google Juice as possible out of your social media marketing and communications.

CHAPTER 15

Thumbs Up for Microblogging

What's In It for You?

American author Mark Twain once paraphrased French mathematician Blaise Pascal's famous comment by saying, "If I had more time, I would have written a shorter letter."[1] The character limitations on microblogging force us to communicate in a more succinct manner. The content of our text messages are written completely differently than our e-mails. This is why they are read.

If only Pascal or Twain had been writing during the dawn of microblogging. This increasingly prevalent trend's value lies in its portability, immediacy, and ease of use. It's simple to post a microblog for your friends, family, coworkers, clients, and prospects. Your complete thought must be conveyed in 140 characters or less!

Microblogging is text messaging and a little more. It can be as effortless as sending a text message from your cell phone to a select group of friends. Anyone can microblog as often as they like, and can promptly read posts from other like-minded bloggers. Microblogging includes the ability to send messages, audio, video, and even attached files; it empowers users to make friends; get directions; give and receive advice; review books, restaurants, and movies; obtain up-to-the-minute news; identify, research, and purchase products and services; update customers; inform clients; send calendar and event notices and news; and more. Or—in the particular case of *The Social Media Bible*—get advice on the book's chapters, the design, the content, interviews, and technical support.

Microblogging lets those who participate create small, intimate communities that are centered on topics such as politics, technology, or medical issues. You can read posts about cancer treatments and chemotherapy effects. You can send or read play-by-play updates from a conference happening at the moment you're reading. Microblogging lets your friends know where you are and what you are doing, and allows you to tell them things like, "I am at Twenty-fourth Street and Camelback Road. Anyone want to meet me for dinner?" With global, nearly real-time, mini-to-mini conversations; many-to-many IMs (Instant Messaging); two-way communication being sent and received on any computer, BlackBerry, PDA, or cell phone—microblogging is the epitome of social media two-way communication. For example, a recent conference featured musician, community marketer, and participant in the famed "One Red Paper Clip" story Jody Gnant (whose Executive Interview can be heard at www.theSocialMediaBible.com). Jody informed the audience that on the way to the presentation, she needed directions to find the venue. Within moments, she had 15 people microblogging her back with turn-by-turn directions. That's a powerful network, or, as Twitter puts it, "A global community of friends and strangers answering one simple question: What are you doing?"

Back to the Beginning

Microblogging began with the advent of the web log, or blog. After some time spent writing lengthy, detailed accounts, people began to post more condensed, convenient, portable, personal versions of their conventional blog posts into something that was termed a *microblog*. Microblogging was immediately hailed as conventional blogging's easier, faster, and more immediately accessible cousin. These benefits rapidly made microblogging an increasingly popular form of social interaction and communication, which people began using to seek and share information and daily activities.

One of the very first providers of the microblog was a company called Twitter, essentially providing technology that offered a simplified blogging service. Twitter was born in March 2006 as the result of an R&D project at the San Francisco–based start-up company Obvious. It was initially used by the company's own employees to communicate internally, and launched to the public seven months later in October 2006. On March 19, 2007, Twitter's official debut took place at the annual South by Southwest (SXSW) meeting in Austin, Texas—and it won the South by Southwest Web Award in the blog category. Jack Dorsey—Obvious CEO and the man behind the concept of Twitter—gave a humorous acceptance speech: "We'd like to thank you in 140 characters or less. And we just did!"

Twitter is a microblogging and social networking service that allows its users to send and receive brief (140 characters or less) text-based, micropost instant messages that are referred to as Tweets. These text messages are displayed on the user's technology of choice—be it a text-messaging cell phone, web site, PDA, Twitter web site, RSS (see Chapter 19, RSS—Really Simple Syndication Made Simple), SMS,[2] e-mail, or an application such as Facebook, Twitterrific, or a web page aggregator. These messages are also delivered to anyone who has signed up and been accepted to "Follow" your messages, and the same is true of any Tweets that you have requested and been approved to follow.

What You Need to Know

While Twitter is the most popular microblogging platform, it certainly isn't the only one. Other platforms gaining recognition are Jaiku—which started in Europe and has since been acquired by Google—Pownce (now defunct),[3] and PlaceShout. (For a more comprehensive list, please see the Providers section later in this chapter.) However, for the purpose of this chapter, microblogging is discussed primarily in the context of Twitter, since the company had the first-to-market advantage at the time of this writing—with 3,054,861 users and more than 2,000 new accounts being created every day.

To give you an idea of how aggressive some Twitterers (Twitter users) are, at the time of this writing, Twitterer and CEO of Stealmode Partners Francine Hardaway was following 1,757 other Twitters, and had 2,414 people following her. When asked about her network, Francine simply said, "Go where your friends are." (To listen to Francine's complete Executive Conversation, go to www.the SocialMediaBible.com.)

FIGURE 15.1 Would it kill you to update your twitter status if you're going to stay out so late?

Then there's the famous Microsoft Blogger, Robert Scoble—another Twitter fanatic. Robert is currently following 21,004 people and has 34,376 following his Tweets. And the winner of the largest Twitter network at the time of writing was Kevin Rose, founder of Digg, Revision3, and Pownce with 64,183 followers (while following only 104 Twitterers himself).

As your presence on Twitter or any microblogging service grows, people you don't know will begin to follow you. This is kind of like people reading your blog or visiting your web site. The number of people whom you follow will be significantly less because there are only so many messages you can read, just as there is a finite number of blogs you read or web pages you visit.

Tweeting and following constitute the two-way communication and trusted network that drive the microblogging community. Any time someone you are following ceases to deliver relevant "What's In It for Me?" content, you can simply decide to Un-Follow that person. This is the power of permission-based marketing, where you choose who is allowed to market and communicate to you. Opting not to follow someone is like having your own built-in, user-controlled spam filter.

While microblogging started with the early adopters, it is currently a primary way that thought leaders, technophiles, Millenniums, Gen Ys, and technologically savvy users keep in touch with each other. It has moved into the mainstream and is now widely used throughout the United States. For example, Democratic presidential candidates Barack Obama and John Edwards both microposted details of their runs for election while actually on the campaign trail. Additionally, the *New York Times*, the BBC, and several other traditional media organizations have begun using microblogging to post headlines and links.

While many give credit to Twitter for being the first microblogging platform, some believe that the micro-content trend has been around for a while—depending upon your definition of the term. In fact, many think that regular blogging should be considered micro-content, while others contend that posting a small note or bookmark on del.icio.us.com, or typing some text on a photo posted on Flickr or Facebook, or creating a review on Yelp is also considered microblogging. The purists of this movement still give Twitter credit for creating the first intentional interactive microblogging/micropost network.

The popularity of microblogging can be attributed in part to the ease of creating a micropost. While blogs are considered fairly simply to write and maintain, a two-sentence update is still easier. Microblogs are also significantly less complicated to digest than conventional blogs, especially when you are following several dozen or more Twitterers. This makes the Tweets more desirable, more current, and more likely to be read. Commenting on Tweets spurs an entertaining rapid-fire exchange of conversational Tweets from other Twitterers. And—like so many other social media technologies discussed in this book—Twitter and other microblogging platforms are free.

Since microblogging requires much less effort than conventional blogging, many people find it more entertaining. You simply send out a Tweet whenever you have a moment; there is much less pressure to regularly update your thoughts. Unlike your web page, blog page, MySpace, Facebook, and other networks you can post on, there is no blog-roll showing visitors how frequently (or infrequently) you blog. Many people are using microblogging to supplement their main blog by publishing short descriptions of their latest blog post—along with a corresponding link to create attention and drive traffic to the web or blog site.

Twitter and microblogging aren't just U.S. phenomena; microblogging is widely popular around the world. Twitter announced via blog on April 22, 2008, that it had created a version of Twitter for Japanese users. Japanese is now the second most frequently spoken (or typed) language on Twitter. Unlike the U.S. service, the Japanese Twitter service is advertising-supported (see micro-advertising below). And in China, by May 2007, there were 111 Twitter look-alike microblogging platforms. In spite of Twitter's efforts to populate the Chinese language with Twitter, the knockoffs have far surpassed Twitter's own progress.

The Micro-Sphere Is Not All Good

Trivial Pursuit

The most common criticism of microblogging is the trivial nature of most posts (see Figure 15.2). Most people perusing the Internet really don't care if someone is about to eat their dinner or is currently waiting for a plane. The ease of use and the lack of cost encourage people to become Tweeting maniacs, and people tend to lose a sense of responsibility by continuously Tweeting about the most mundane occurrences in their day-to-day lives. When you are following 500, 1,000, or 5,000 Twitterers—as well as receiving mobile telephone text messages, voice mails (home, office, and cell), news aggregators, snail mail, junk mail, and spam—it can create a social media overload. Some people who thrive on social media are so fanatical that they've essentially overloaded themselves with too much data. They are receiving information as a steady stream of noise that has made it nearly impossible to contact or communicate with them. Their e-mail is full and won't accept any more memos; their outgoing cell phone message asks that you "please don't leave me a voice mail, because I don't retrieve them anymore" (and the recording is full anyway); and they no longer respond to their Tweets.

On March 16, 2007, the *Wall Street Journal* claimed, "These social-networking services elicit mixed feelings in the technology-savvy people who have been their early adopters. Fans say they are a good way to keep in touch with busy friends. But some users are starting to feel 'too' connected, as they grapple with check-in messages at odd hours, higher cell phone bills

FIGURE 15.2 Twitter Tweets

and the need to tell acquaintances to stop announcing what they're having for dinner."

Micro-Spam

Fortunately—unlike the pattern that emerged when e-mail became a widely used communication medium—there have actually been very few spammers on microblogging networks. Microblogging is, for the most part, self-policing—much like other social media platforms. So anytime someone begins spamming, user outcry tends to react and keep it under control. However, this isn't to say that blog spam won't someday become as prolific as it is on e-mail today. As discussed in Chapter 7, in forums there is flaming or flame wars where other users will respond to a spammer with pretty nasty replies, which keeps spamming at a minimum. This reaction also happens in professional networks such as LinkedIn.

Micro-Advertising

We're also not seeing any type of corporate or sponsored advertising on microblogs—as of yet. Google's previously mentioned purchase of Jaiku may very well bring the kind of sponsored and contextual advertising that are ever-present in Google's Gmail. Twitter is using advertising to offset the costs of maintaining the site in Japan. After all, mobile telephone companies have been sending text messages that contain their—and others'—advertising for more than a decade. Can blogging be very far behind? Subsidized promotion seems to be the only way most social media technology providers can monetize their efforts. With all of the options available, it seems most people are reluctant to pay for a service either on a monthly basis or on a per-use basis. But as with Gmail, people seem better able to tolerate ads than invoices.

The Fail Whale

Only a year after Twitter was launched, it began experiencing outages with its user base. Because of its overwhelming popularity, the folks at Twitter still haven't been able to avoid server overload from the sheer volume of traffic to its site. The Twitter web site and service can sometimes be completely shut down for several hours. Although the company claimed that it had experienced approximately 98 percent uptime throughout 2007, that still translates into 2 percent downtime and a huge inconvenience for those who really count on this technology.

On the occasions during which the site is experiencing problems, Twitterers' attempts to Tweet or visit the web site are met with the all-too-familiar Fail Whale (see Figure 15.3). This character—an image of a happy cartoon whale being lifted by a multitude of small red birds using nets to hoist him from the ocean—has become somewhat of an industry icon for monumental failure. Due to their high-pitched twitter, the Beluga whale is known as the "canary of the sea." Not surprisingly, the message on the image reads, "Too many tweets! Please wait a moment and try again."

FIGURE 15.3 The Fail Whale

When people become dependent on a particular technology—like e-mail, BlackBerrys, or blogs—and that is taken away from them for even a short period, they become paralyzed. The social media industry as a whole has been too slow to sufficiently monetize its efforts. If this trend doesn't reverse, Fail Whales of all kinds will be appearing with more and more social media technology.

FIGURE 15.4 Leah Culver, cofounder, Pownce

A good example of this is Pownce. Pownce is similar to Twitter without a really distinct competitive advantage. People in the social media world knew it didn't have a sustainable business model either. Pownce didn't place unwanted advertising in your messages and didn't offer the industry fall-back revenue model of freemium products that could be purchased in addition to all of the free services Pownce offered. As a result, Pownce and its whale went belly up.

FIGURE 15.5

During the writing of this book, Leah Culver, the cofounder of Pownce, spoke with the authors of *The Social Media Bible* about her company, services, and business model. Then, without warning on December 15, 2008, came their e-mail that they were shutting down. Ironically, Leah Culver was on the cover of the July 2008 *MIT Technology Review,* where she was blowing a huge bubblegum bubble about to burst, accompanied by the headline, "The Next Bubble." The inside photo was her with the busted bubble.

To hear Leah Culver's interview, go to www.theSocialMediaBible.com. The interview remains on the web site to show how vulnerable this new industry is. More Pownce stories will occur as the industry matures.

How Safe Are Your Tweets?

On April 7, 2007, the well-known security researcher, author, and speaker Nitesh Dhanjani created the first Twitter security issue. Nitesh used SMS and

FakeMyText.com to send phony messages (posts) to people's cell phones. Luckily, the only cell phones to which he was able to send the counterfeit messages were ones for which he already knew the telephone numbers. To counter this weakness in their system, Twitter initiated a PIN system for authenticating SMS originating messages. Since then, both Twitter and Jott have taken measures to prevent this security lapse from happening again. You can read Dhanjani's article, "Twitter and Jott Vulnerable to SMS and Caller ID Spoofing," by going to www.oreillynet.com/onlamp/blog/ 2007/04/twitter_and_jott_vulnerable_to.html or go to www.theSocialMedia Bible.com to just click on the link.

On the Lighter Side of Microblogging

Some Twitter Jargon

Twitter is the most prevalent microblogging technology used today.

- A *Twitterer* is a person using Twitter to send out posts or *Tweets*.
- A *Tweet* is a post or text message sent from one Twitterer to another.
- The Tweeting community is called the *Twitosphere*.

Much like e-mail, once you hit Send, the Tweet is out there. A regretted Tweet is called a *MisTweet*. (Never Tweet after a bottle of Chardonnay.)

Google Maps has a mash-up called *Twittervision,* which shows users the geographic location of Twitterers.

Corporate Twitterers

Small, medium, and large companies alike are beginning to adopt social media tools into their marketing, public relations, communications, and customer service approaches. Like any early adopters, these companies will have a significant advantage over those who wait until social media becomes mainstream. Here are just a few of the many large companies that have incorporated microblogging into their corporate culture:

- Southwest Airlines regularly Tweets as one of its standard customer service tools. The following is an actual Tweet from Gary Kelly, CEO of Southwest Airlines: "CEO, Gary Kelly, appeared on CNN this am to address concerns regarding the safety and inspections of aircraft www .tinyurl.com/24ndxd 01:09 PM March 07, 2008" (a TinyURL is a clickable link to the Internet).

- The somewhat controversial Dave Winer—who calls himself the "original blogger" and inventor of RSS—Tweets his Followers on a regular basis about his River project at the *New York Times*. The project is what Dave calls a "river-of-news format," wherein a stream of short text messages about the latest breaking news from the *Times* is sent to followers via cell phone, PDA, or web page aggregator to create a news-roll of top stories. Dave explains, "I created the site because I wasn't getting enough news about products. It's that simple. I'm interested in the other stuff too, the finance, trends, parties, puppets—the River Project allows readers to prioritize and aggregate their news in one web site."

- Frank Eliason is a Comcast corporate manager and blogosphere liaison in Philadelphia's Center City region. Frank has the daunting assignment of monitoring blogs and Tweets for unfavorable posts aimed at Comcast. When Frank found a Tweet that said, "My Internet goes out every day at 3:30. Why would that be?" he answered right away, "That should not be. We should have that looked at. Send an e-mail with account info to We_Can_Help@cable.comcast.com"; signed: @ComcastCares. This type of immediate and personal customer service sets companies like Comcast apart from their competitors.

- Chief blogger at Dell Computer Lionel Menchaca was immediately on top of things when Dell's laptop computer batteries began exploding. Lionel got Tweets from customers and the media asking for information about the problem. He kept Tweeting and blogging, and continuously updating his customers with the latest updates he had. The industry—as well as Dell's customers—were shocked to see a company that big taking such personal care of its customers. This provided a huge public relations advantage at a time when Dell needed it most.

- Large businesses such as Cisco Systems and Whole Foods Market use Twitter to provide product or service information to their customers through Tweets.

- The Los Angeles Fire Department put the technology to use during the October 2007 California wildfires to get up-to-the-second information of where the fires were breaking out, where people were trapped, and where their help was needed most.

- NASA used Twitter to break the news of discovery of what appeared to be water ice on Mars by the Phoenix Mars Lander. Other NASA projects, such as Space Shuttle missions and the International Space Station, also provide updates via Twitter.

- News outlets such as the BBC have also started using Twitter to disseminate breaking news or provide information feeds for sporting events.
- Several 2008 U.S. presidential candidates—including Democratic Party nominee Barack Obama—used Twitter as a publicity mechanism. The Nader/Gonzalez campaign used Twitter and Google Maps to show real-time updates of their ballot access teams across the country.
- The University of Texas at San Antonio College of Engineering is using Twitter to relay information to students such as homework and reading assignments, last-minute schedule changes, and even when a professor is running late.
- Westwinds Church in Jackson, Michigan, uses Twitter as a part of its weekend worship services, and actually introduced the concept of Twitter Church. Westwinds runs training classes for Twitter and encourages members to bring laptops and mobile devices to church. On occasion, the Twitter feed will be shown live on the screens in the auditorium, and everyone is encouraged to give their input, make observations, and ask questions to encourage an interactive worship format.

Microblogging clearly has widespread global appeal, and it can play a vital role in keeping people safe during disasters and tragedies. During a recent earthquake, China's equivalent of Twitter technology was used to communicate the very first reports. Twitter has become the communication tool of choice by many emergency services around the world, and has been used by activists and journalists during other natural disasters.

A recent study conducted by the University of Colorado cited that during the California fires in October 2007, people were using Twitter to keep their friends, family, and neighbors informed of their whereabouts and of the location of the fires. This information was transmitted and received in nearly real time on a minute-by-minute basis by police, fire-fighters, and family members. Support organizations such as the American Red Cross (www.twitter.com/RedCross) were also using the site to co-ordinate their relief efforts and exchange minute-by-minute updates about the fires.

Twitter is also credited with doing a better job of getting information out during emergencies than the traditional news media or government emergency services, as was the case with the Virginia Tech shootings in April 2007. In the Virginia Tech case, the news media and family members were getting real-time updates via Twitter while it was actually happening.

Tweets in the News

The Wall Street Journal Digital Network Twittering the US Airways Plane Crash

Shira Ovide

Notch Another Win for Citizen Journalism

Janis Krums, a guy with a camera and a penchant for social media tools, posted one of the first and most remarkable photos today of US Airways Flight 1549 after it crash landed in the Hudson River.

"There's a plane in the Hudson," the Sarasota native wrote on the micro-blogging site Twitter just as reports began to break of the plane hitting the water off Manhattan's west side. "I'm on the ferry going to pick up the people. Crazy."

The photo, which Mr. Krums posted online using a Twitter photo-sharing site, has been viewed more than 43,000 times.

Social media tools like Twitter—which allows users to tap out 140-character status updates—have changed how breaking news events are recorded and covered. They made for on-the-ground reports from the Mumbai terror attacks in November, for example.

After he documented the Hudson River crash, Mr. Krums then became a minor celebrity in traditional media, too. He conducted an interview on MSNBC and says on his Twitter profile that he's preparing for even more interviews this evening.

Source: http://blogs.wsj.com/digits/2009/01/15/twittering-the-usairways-plane-crash/tab/comments/#comment-346
For a clickable link, go to www.theSocialMediaBible.com.

Providers

Entire ecosystems of web sites and technologies have been created around Twitter. Twhirl, for example, is an authoring tool (or software package) based on the Adobe AIR platform that connects users to Twitter as well as other sites. Tweet Scan and Summize, which Twitter purchased on July 15, 2008, are Tweet-specific search engines. Web site www.twitterholic.com tracks the most popular and active Twitterers, and provides a list of Top 100 Twitterholics Based on Followers. And sites like www.8zap.com support a live community bookmarking of news, video streams, and images.

There are also sites that tag with what are known as *hashtags* and *mashups,* such as www.Twittervision.com. Hashtags are a community-driven convention for adding additional context and metadata to your Tweets, so that they can be categorized and found easily by subject matter. Using a hashtag is similar to adding a tag to a Flickr photograph, or a meta-keyword to your web page. The main difference is that instead of adding the metadata behind the scenes—where the user doesn't see it—the hashtag is part of your Tweet. Hashtags allow you to create Groupings on Twitter, by simply prefixing a word or phrase with a hash symbol or pound sign (#)—like #hashtag, or #thesocialmediabible. Hashtags became popular during the San Diego brush fires in 2007, when California resident Nate Ritter used his hashtag *#sandiego-fire* to identify his personal Twitter updates related to the fires.

(For more information on hashtags, or to have your personal hashtags tracked in real time, go to www.hashtags.org.)

A mashup is a web application that combines data from more than one source into a single, integrated web site—as when real estate information is added to a Google Map. Another example is Travature (www.travature .com/), a site that has integrated airfare metasearch engines, wiki travel guides, and hotel reviews, as well as applications that allow travelers to share photos and stories. A mashup creates a new and distinct web page and service that has not been provided by either source. It also includes rich media or a combination of text, blog post, Tweets, images, audio, and video all in one place.

Microblogging beyond Twitter?

A number of services exist that have a similar concept to Twitter's, but that have country-specific versions of their services, such as www.frazr.com. Other sites—such as Jaiku—combine microblogging with other capabilities like file sharing and allow the Twitter user to attach a file to their posts.

Plurk is another microblogging platform that has been gaining in popularity. This service launched in May 2008 and gained considerable acceptance in Silicon Valley during its first 30 days. While the number of Twitter users are far greater than Plurk, Plurk's horizontal time line and group conversations create a more robust interface and adds a spatial dimension to microblogging that make it a good alternative to Twitter.

Other services include Yammer, which launched on September 8, 2008, at the TechCrunch50 Conference and is marketed as an enterprise version of Twitter. Yammer asks, "What's happening at your company? With Yammer you can share status updates with your coworkers."

Prologue is a microblogging tool created by Automatic—the makers of WordPress—that was released in January 2008 and allows its users to "post short messages about what they're doing" in a secured environment.

Then there's the Enterprise Social Messaging Experiment (ESME) created by Demo Jam at SAP Labs, which allows you to create new groups instantly by clicking on cloud tags or word frequency. For more information, see www.youtube.com/watch?v=y1dPAV8C0Tw or go to the www.theSocial MediaBible.com and click on the link.

SocialCast is a FriendFeed and Twitter tool for the enterprise, and Laconica is considered an Open Microblogging Tool—an open-source application (one where software source code is available to the general public, without a license that restricts or limits its use, modification, or redistribution) that can be installed on corporate servers and used behind the firewall.

And then there is OraTweet, created by Oracle—the world's largest enterprise software company—as a microblogging tool for internal employee and external client use. OraTweet allows companies, universities, and organizations to run their own in-house microblogs that keep their communications private and secure and that encourage the development of internal communities. OraTweet operates the same way as e-mail and instant messaging, but allows enterprises to broadcast messages safely within their own environments.

Some other sites include:

- *Status:* A lighter communication tool that displays an update of your team's progress on a single screen at one time.
- *Trillr:* A small group service intended for coworkers, partners, and customers to communicate. Trillr allows users to stay connected with quick, frequent exchange of data, and answers the question, "What's on your mind?"
- *I Did Work:* A task-based update tool that provides teams with the ability to leave short status messages. This site creates a work log that keeps a history of your progress and shares it with your team.

- *Joint Contact:* A collaboration tool that incorporates microblogging features and connects Twitter to your project status to inform your Followers of upcoming events. With JointContact, you can link your Tweets to your project management system.
- *BlueTwit-IBM:* Launched in 2007, an internal Twitter client that has been providing IBM employees with an alternative to e-mail.
- *Present.ly:* A micro-update communication tool that gives employees the ability to instantly communicate their current status, ask questions, post media, and more.
- *Mixin:* A service that spans both internal and external corporate communications and "lets you share your daily activities and intentions to get together more often with your friends."
- *Spoink:* A multimedia microblogging service that integrates blogging, podcasting, telephony, and **SMS** text messaging. Spoink supports all major mobile audio, video, and picture formats.

And then there's identi.ca, Jaiku, FriendFeed, Dodgeball, tumblr, and TWiT Army—and all of the most popular social networking web sites such as Facebook, MySpace, and LinkedIn, which have their own microblogging feature called a *status update*.

Expert Insight

Francine Hardaway, CEO, Stealthmode Partners, www.stealthmodepartners.com

Francine Hardaway

You know what blogs are; [they] started as web logs, [the] personal diaries of people who were on the Web, in which they put up their thoughts and shared them with their friends. Well, that of course has completely mushroomed into something much bigger. And so now there are—oh my goodness—there are like hundreds of millions of bloggers; although not all those blogs are populated all the time, but there are a great many blogs and regular bloggers. And most of mainstream journalism has gone to blogging.

So, that's blogging. Okay, microblogging is talking to people in 140 characters. And the great

(continued)

(*continued*)

thing about microblogging compared to blogging is that the platform (and it is called a "platform"—rather than somebody having to go to my blog or my blog being delivered to someone else's RSS feeder) [allows all of us to be] in the same place at the same time. And it's really a constant mini-to-mini conversation. . . .

[All of these different special-interest groups] are called micro-communities; and there are all kinds of them that come from Twitter. There are political micro-communities; there are technology micro-communities. There are some people that talk on Twitter only about things like HTML feeds and JavaScript, and there are other people who talk about cancer therapies and chemo side-effects. And each one of these is its own little micro-community, and you find them by getting on Twitter and following someone and finding out who that person follows. So it is basically like you go through a maze of your own followers or people that you follow, leading you to other people. And you can make so many new connections that way.

A great example [in my own experience] occurred when I bought a house in Half Moon Bay [in northern California], [after having] lived in Arizona for most of my career. And I though to myself, I've got to develop a network in Half Moon Bay, I only know two people . . . my daughters . . . and they'll get really tired of me *real* fast. So I just have been very active on Facebook, Twitter, and all the social media platforms; and I have developed an entire second network, up there in the bay area. . . .

I give highlights of what the speaker is saying [live while the speaker is speaking], so if you don't happen to be [at the event], you can join the conversation; and truthfully, the speakers take feedback from Twitter while they are presenting at a lot of conferences now; and they tune their presentation as they go. Sometimes there is a big screen in the front of the room and it has the Twitter feed on it for the conference. And if you post to the Twitter feed to the conference, it comes up on the big screen, and the presenter can answer your question, or give you the information. . . .

Well, what you have to watch out for is getting overwhelmed by information; and that's really a personal issue, you know. There are very few spammers on the microblogging social networks, because they're very easy to spot and they get self-policed. If some guy, you know, is following 3,000 people and does not have any followers (laughter) and he is just sending out messages all the time that say, "Buy my product, buy my products," the system is going to find him out very quickly and deal with him. . . . So right now it's pretty pure; and if you are overwhelmed by information, it is because *you* chose to follow a lot of people. It can be—well, let's see, what's the opposite of overwhelmed? You can be *under*whelmed pretty quickly by only following five people; then if each one of those five people posts three times a day, then you are only getting 15 Tweets a day. Whereas I get, you know, 6 to 7,000. . . .

There are too many microblogs and platforms out there, and some of them will get to a point where they cannot pay the bills; and so there will be a consolidation. I could never predict which ones; Google, for instance, now owns Jaiku. So it's probably not going anywhere. And Pownce is [was][3] probably not going anywhere either, because it has defined a little niche. If Pownce was to do something that Twitter does not (which is sending what is called—in technical jargon—a *payload,* meaning that you can attach a file) . . . If you want to send somebody a file and about 140 characters, Pownce is the way to do it. You can send pictures, you can share music. There is a lot of stuff you can do on Pownce that is not as easy to do on Twitter. . . .

They are finding their niches—that's right! I believe that social media platforms—and microblogging platforms especially—are going to all end up being interoperable . . . like e-mail. You know, like you are on Yahoo! e-mail and I am on Gmail and somebody else is on AOL; but we can all e-mail each other. Pretty soon, we will all be able to microblog each other. So you can be in your little community (which could be the people on Plurk, or . . . Twitter or . . . Jaiku), and still speak—when you want—to the other people in the other communities. And there's a lot of conversation going on around open source and the ability to do that. . . .

There are large numbers of users on these platforms that cannot really be moved; you know, they are not going to be moved. There's the certain point at which I stopped signing up for new services. I mean, I am probably the last person (because I am an imbedded early adopter), and I can stand a lot of noise in my signal; and I don't mind spending a lot of time figuring all this stuff out. But your average person who has a 9-to-5 job is going to pick a platform and stick to it. And so the job of the platform developer is going to be to make these platforms as close to real time and as interoperable as possible. . . .

To listen to or read the entire Executive Conversation with Francine Hardaway, go to www.the SocialMediaBible.com.

Expert Insight

Biz Stone, cofounder, Twitter, www.twitter.com

I'm the cofounder of Twitter, and before that I helped start a service called Vanga.com, which is a social journaling service that we started in 1999 in New York City. They are still there, but I left and I ended up working at Google. I was specifically on the Blogger team for a couple of years before I left there, and sort of got back into the start-up world with a project called Odeo. This is an audio on the

Biz Stone

(continued)

(*continued*)

Internet, a podcasting service, and it was actually when I was at Odeo that Twitter was actually a side project that we were working on that we fell in love with. This ultimately turned into its own company that just grew and grew and grew. That's where we're at today. . . .

Yeah, it's really just a short messaging service, at the simplest level, but a communication utility. What it becomes now that we have so many people using it, it really becomes the pulse of what's happening with the people and the organizations that you really care about most. So on the one hand, you use it to just communicate; on the other hand, you look through it to find out what's going on. . . .

Twitter is the name of the service, and it comes from the idea of the word that you can look up in the dictionary which is a "short trill, chirp, or burst of information," referencing a birdcall. People are tricked into calling it *individual updates*. Every time I give an individual update on Twitter, I actually get saved and achieved on Twitter. It becomes its own individual web page, and people have been referring to those individual updates as Tweets. This is the axis of Twittering, or sometimes I say "Tweeting," because they are fond of that word *Tweet*.

It is nothing that we officially stated. People starting using it, so it works out well for us. . . .

Yes, it's a short message, a short text message. . . . One of the key things about Twitter is that it's agnostic when it comes to what sort of device you prefer to use to interact with the system. So if you prefer to use SNS and mobile texting on a mobile phone, Twitter will work that way for you. But it also works over the Web and it also works with several thousand right now (more in the future), third-party independent pieces of software that you can either download for Mac or a PC, or use with Slash. Basically we opened up our infrastructure; we created an API so that smart developers around the world can create custom interactive software to interact with Twitter. . . .

I mean we did it early on just to, sort of, scratch an itch. One of our very early developers wanted to be able to interact with Twitter a certain way, so we created a very simple HI; in fact what happened was the service is simple and the API was so simple that even a beginner API developer could jump in and build something on Twitter that worked very quickly. So it became popular to build on top of Twitter, and what it did for us is that it created so much variety out there (of ways of interacting with Twitter) that it ended up just creating a lot of traffic and creating a lot of opportunities and options for people, which is great. . . .

Yeah, and it's really that mobile aspect that we were trying to get at early. Twitter was basically inspired by the away messages on IM, so if you ever used an IM tool, you see that your coworkers or your friends are in a meeting, out for coffee, or whatever. You can look at a group of 12 people and get a sense of what everyone's doing, what everyone's up to; but that's related to the computer and what they are doing on the computer. So when we took that idea and we just broke it out and we made it more mobile by adding the ability to interact with SMS, we made it more social by building in more features.

Then we created, basically, new kinds of communications—a kind of real-time group communications that really didn't exist before. And it's something that turned out that can be very useful for people. . . .

To listen to or read the entire Executive Conversation with Biz Stone, go to www.the SocialMediaBible.com.

Expert Insight

Dharmesh Mehta, director of product management, Windows Live Instant Messenger, www.get.live.com/messenger/overview/

Dharmesh Mehta

Windows Live Messenger has been around about nine and a half years now. We originally launched it back in 1999, and it was pretty much focused on just being an IM text solution. What you've seen over the years is, as we continue to grow, we've turned that from text chat and added voice and video. We then added photo sharing and games. We've added a ton of personal expressions so you can change your display pictures and record videos with your webcam. We allow you to have both those real-time conversations, but also a synchronous off-line instant message. And today Windows Live Messages is actually used by more than 325 million people worldwide. So it's come a long way over the last nine and a half years, and we hope to see that growth continue. . . .

So you have your contacts in your Messenger's main window, and you can start a chat with them—and it's not just about chat. You can share files, just drag them right into there.

Actually one of the latest things we've just added is a really rich photo sharing. If you drag photos in, you can look at a set of photos with one of your buddies; or you can, at the same time, change what photo you are looking at while you're commenting and chatting about them. You can save them to Cloud and have them permanently shared out where others can see them.

(continued)

(*continued*)

Again, you can share that just with your contacts or you can open it up to the whole Internet. . . .

That's actually . . . for a while people felt like, you know, you had to have a side-load photo-sharing application, or this side-load IM application, and their side-load e-mail application. But really, you're people and you have one set of people you want to interact with, some you might want to do some things with, and some another set of things; but whether you're in IM or you're up on the Web, or you're on your mobile phone, we want to make sure you can get your stuff. Whether that's photos or bios or being able to have real-time chat; we want to bring that context to you wherever you happen to be. . . .

So we offer a couple of different things on mobile phones. The first is for our PC users . . . when you're there chatting with someone and all of a sudden they go offline because they are no longer on their PC. The fact of the matter is many of those people are actually online on their phone and they can receive alerts. So we have connections from the PC and the web messaging experiences straight to your phone. And that's the first one.

But the one that I'm more excited about and continues to be growing really rapidly is about the fact that when you are on your mobile phone you now actually have far more phones that are data-capable. And so whether that's browse services for IM-ing or photo sharing; whether that's doing little micro-blogging and updating your status; or even on some of the higher-end phones, whether that's mobile or BlackBerry or Nokia and actually having rich client application.

Obviously you have to design those slightly differently; the context is different. There's different user experiences because of the fact that you're always reachable on your phone, but you may not always want to be reachable. But it's actually really exciting what's happening on the mobile phone, and it's really two things. It's (1) bringing the things that people have been doing on PC and the Web and extending them to the phone. But then in some countries you just come online on the phone and you may never, ever get on a PC. They may never get download apps onto a Windows PC, but you want to make sure that you have as great a mobile experience that's served from their phone. . . .

And it's interesting that the different scenarios that you encounter in some of these countries, where your phone not only becomes SMS . . . and SMS on your phone not only becomes just a way to have short chats with people, but it's also a great way of getting little bits of information.

If you find a short SMS text message and you get the weather, you get your latest calendar appointment, or you do a web search. These are all things that are done slightly differently depending on the type of phone you have and the type user you are. Mobile is actually a real exciting space for us, just for the amount of growth and the amount of different possibilities that are coming. . . .

On Windows Live Messenger today there are 325 million people who span the world, and so we are actually more of an international company than just being U.S. focused, like some of the other instant messaging companies, and in terms of demographic, it spans everyone. So it's all the way from young teens to even younger than that, all the way up to adults and seniors.

We recently did some reports looking specifically at a fast-growing demographic of the 70+ population that's starting to come online and wanting to chat with their grandkids and share photos and talk to them. And it's actually really interesting how IM, which once upon a time was really just restricted to, almost, college students and very young age ranges, really brought in all people on the planet. It transected. . .

And I say more than 85 percent of those are actually outside the U.S. It's an interesting trend that you talked about. You know, often sitting here in the U.S. we get very U.S. focused and we often think that a lot of technology starts here in the U.S. and spreads to other parts of the world. But going back to that discussion that we had on mobile, some of the most interesting things in mobile are actually happening in Asia; whether that's Japan and South Korea or in India and China, where users are coming online on mobile and may never use a PC.

Think of this from a global perspective. We're learning and discovering from other players, other competitors, and companies, just around the world. . . .

To listen to or read the entire Executive Conversation with Dharmesh Mehta, to go www .theSocialMediaBible.com.

Commandments

1. **Thou shalt begin microblogging.**

    Don't be afraid of microblogging. It's easy, it's free, and it's fun. It's a great way to stay in direct and immediate contact with whomever you choose—whether it's friends, family, club members, church groups, coworkers, prospects, or customers.

2. **Thou shalt Tweet.**

    Tweet! The technology isn't any good unless you use it. Tweets are only 140 characters, and are as easy to send as a text message. When you receive a relevant thought, text it out to your Followers. And remember to always have that "What's In It for Me?" content value.

3. **Thou shalt follow Twitterers.**

    Follow other Twitterers. Find people with similar interests, good ideas—or just people you care about—and see what thoughts they share on a daily basis. Remember, if you don't like what they have to say, Un-Follow them and go find others who provide you with that WIIFM content.

4. **Thou shalt invite others to follow you.**

Be sure to invite others to Follow you. They don't know that you are sharing so many pearls of wisdom unless you tell them. Send them your Twitter address, and Tweet them often.

5. **Thou shalt set up groups.**

Set up groups in Twitter (or platform of your choice) using hashtags. Set up one group for your existing customers, another for your prospects, and yet another for your coworkers. Send different and appropriate Tweets to each group.

6. **Thou shalt use news feed Tweets.**

Set up a Twitter News Feed, so that you can get all of the breaking news as it happens—and only that which interests you—whether it's business, lifestyles, finance, gossip, sports, international, health . . . and so on!

7. **Thou shalt use Tweets for internal communications.**

Try using Twitter for internal communications by setting up separate groups for your coworkers and employees. Send them status reports on the company's stock prices, new product developments, press releases, HR benefit updates, holiday information, or just an occasional atta-boy or pep talk.

Conclusion

Microblogging is a wonderful and interesting way to keep in touch with your family, friends, and coworkers. It's also an imaginative way to send quick updates on news, products, services, legislation, or any content that has a "What's In It for Me?" value to your customers and prospects. Keeping yourself and your company in the forefront of your prospects' minds—by giving them valuable information and updates—will likely convert prospects into customers.

Try it. Set up a free account, follow some like-minded Twitterers; invite other Twitterers to follow you. Monitor what they say. Evaluate the WIIFM value. Then begin Tweeting yourself. Monitor the responses from that. After a short while, you will begin to see the most effective content you can deliver to your followers.

As has been written in almost every chapter thus far, the most important thing to remember is not to get overwhelmed; in fact, whelmed is the state of mind you are looking to achieve. Try using a microblogging platform. Send some Tweets or posts. Read some Tweets or posts. And enjoy it. If it becomes overwhelming or loses its appeal, back off and Un-Follow. Like any technology, the key is moderation.

Readings and Resources

Banks, Michael A. *Blogging Heroes: Interviews with 30 of the World's Top Bloggers.* (Hoboken, NJ: John Wiley & Sons, Inc.)

Gardner, Susannah. *Buzz Marketing with Blogs For Dummies.* (Hoboken, NJ: John Wiley & Sons, Inc.)

Gardner, Susannah, and Shane Birley. *Blogging For Dummies.* (Hoboken, NJ: John Wiley & Sons, Inc.)

Gunelius, Susan. *Google Blogger For Dummies.* (Hoboken, NJ: John Wiley & Sons, Inc.)

Reeder, Joelle, and Katherine Scoleri. *The IT Girl's Guide to Blogging with Moxie.* (Hoboken, NJ: John Wiley & Sons, Inc.)

Rettbergl, Jill Walker. *Blogging.* (Hoboken, NJ: John Wiley & Sons, Inc.)

Rowse, Darren, and Chris Garrett. *ProBlogger: Secrets for Blogging Your Way to a Six-Figure Income.* (Hoboken, NJ: John Wiley & Sons, Inc.)

Scoble, Robert, and Shel Israel. *Naked Conversations: How Blogs Are Changing the Way Businesses Talk with Customers.* (Hoboken, NJ: John Wiley & Sons, Inc.)

Scott, David Meerman. *The New Rules of Marketing and PR: How to Use News Releases, Blogs, Podcasting, Viral Marketing and Online Media to Reach Buyers Directly.* (Hoboken, NJ: John Wiley & Sons, Inc.)

Downloads

For your free downloads associated with *The Social Media Bible,* go to www .theSocialMediaBible.com, and enter your ISBN number located on the back of the book above the bar code. Be sure to enter the dashes.

Credits

Expert Insights Were Provided By:

Francine Hardaway, CEO of Stealthmode Partners, www.stealthmodepartners.com.

Biz Stone, cofounder of Twitter, www.twitter.com.

Dharmesh Mehta, director of product management for Windows Live Instant Messenger.

Technical Edits Were Provided By:

Francine Hardaway, CEO of Stealthmode Partners, www.stealthmodepartners.com.

Notes

1. Thanks to Ed Nussbaum for this quote.
2. SMS is the abbreviation for Systems Management Server, which is a communications protocol that allows the exchange of short text messages between mobile telephone devices. In different parts of the world, the acronym SMS is used as a synonym for a text message or the act of sending a text message even if SMS isn't actually being used. With 2.4 billion active users, or 74 percent of all mobile phone subscribers sending and receiving text messages on their cell phones, SMS text messaging is the most widely used data application on the planet. In spite of its wide use, as a cost-cutting effort, on August 14, 2008, Twitter removed SMS access to their U.K. service.
3. Pownce is a good example of the changing landscape of social media. Leah Culver was interviewed just a few months before her company closed its doors on December 15, 2008. Her interview and insights are still as valid as ever, so we left them. Technology will change, some existing player will go extinct, and many new companies will take their place.

CHAPTER 16

Live from Anywhere—It's Livecasting

What's In It for You?

Whether you call it *web radio, net radio, streaming radio, e-radio, talk radio, Internet radio, livecasting, lifecasting, webcasting, web conferencing,* or *webinars,* broadcasting information online is all about creating live content that uses the Internet to distribute (or *stream*[1]) that content. All of these terms refer to the process of producing your own, current content, and then distributing that content live over the Internet. You can actually create your very own radio or television show that will only be as expensive as your production costs dictate. You are the host, the production manager, and the talent. You can speak about nearly anything you wish. You can broadcast your show each day, each week, or only when you feel like it. You can put on a live presentation, perform training, introduce or demonstrate a new product or service, create a preventative maintenance program for your customers, or just talk with a special guest about what's new in your industry. It's easy to do, it's a powerful medium, and there's no cost.

Think about that for a minute: for the very first time in history, you can actually produce your own radio or television show and distribute it to everyone around the world—live—for free!

Back to the Beginning

As with the other kinds of rich media creation discussed in this book, livecasting falls into two major categories: audio (radio) and video (television). This chapter discusses how you can create your own radio show and broadcast it to your prospects, customers, coworkers, and fan base. In the video/television category, the chapter discusses how you can create your very own television show and broadcast that content for free.

Internet Radio

Technologist and author of eight books—including *Exploring the Internet* and *A World's Fair*—Carl Malamud first pioneered web radio in 1993. Each week, Malamud would interview a different computer expert during what he called the "first computer radio talk show." The show wasn't really livecasted, as it was prerecorded and distributed one by one to his listeners—who then had to download and play each audio file (an early version of podcasting). Malamud broke important ground, however, by introducing the concept of Internet radio.

The first groups to actually broadcast audio live over the Internet were existing commercial radio stations that were already producing audio content. The crossover from existing terrestrial radio stations or networks was logical and natural; all that the stations needed to do was take the existing content that they were already broadcasting over AM/FM radio frequency and broadcast it over the Internet. WXYC—89.3 FM in Chapel Hill, North Carolina—became the first commercial radio station to begin broadcasting over the Internet (not transmitted through wireless means) on November 7, 1994. WXYC had actually begun testing their broadcasts three months earlier, in August of that year. On that very same day in November, WREK—91.1 FM in Atlanta—also streamed their first radio show over the Internet; unlike WXYC, though, WREK did not advertise what they were doing until later.

That same month, the very first rock and roll concert was broadcast live, with the Rolling Stones becoming the "first cyberspace streamed concert." Mick Jagger welcomed his concert's listeners with, "I wanna say a special welcome to everyone that's, uh, climbed into the Internet tonight and, uh, has got into the M-bone. And I hope it doesn't all collapse."

Commercial Internet-Only Radio Stations

The next step in Internet broadcasting was for individuals—rather than traditional radio broadcasters—to take advantage of this new, effective, and free technology. People began creating their own radio show content and transmitting it over the Internet—from everywhere. A new industry was born.

In November 1995, the Minneapolis, Minnesota–based NetRadio Company founded by Scott Bourne and radio veteran Scot Combs began using

The logic of invention has always been intriguing. So many of the creations in places like the Smithsonian Institution were conceived by people who were merely taking "the next logical step in the evolution of technology." Seldom does someone create something out of nothing, or make major leaps ahead. They simply "take the next step."

For example, Alexander Graham Bell's March 10, 1876, invention of the telephone is often considered as a major breakthrough in communication technology by a genius of a man. But when looking at it in context, the telephone was simply an extension of the already-in-use telegraph. And Alex wasn't the only one taking the next logical step; on the very same day that Bell filed a patent for his device that could transmit speech electronically, Elisha Gray also filed his patent within hours of Bell. Bell simply got there first, and received the patent—which started a legal battle over the invention of the telephone that Bell eventually won.

At the time, most people weren't aware of the fact that so many others around the globe were simultaneously working the "next logical step" in telecommunications. Nearly 16 years earlier, in 1860, Antonio Meucci invented *his* version of the telephone, which he called the *teletrofono,* or telectrophone. And twenty-two years prior to Bell in 1854, a French telegraphist named Charles Bourseul published in the magazine *L'Illustration* his plan for transmitting sound—and even speech—over an electrical wire.

RealAudio to stream music over the Internet. The company started with only four formats and had expanded to include more than a dozen formats within two years.

NetRadio became so popular that audio formatting company Real-Audio made it a preset on their RealMedia audio players. NetRadio also received the first trial ASCAP (American Society of Composers, Authors and Publishers) license, which became the prototype for all Internet radio network licenses. The company is credited with another first: broadcasting, in July 1996, the first Internet-only, live weekly concert series. NetRadio—which at its peak of popularity hosted more than 125 music and talk radio channels—built its listener audience to more than 50 million listeners every month.

Radio audience research company Arbitron (which collects listener data about radio audiences similar to the way that Nielsen Media Research collects information about TV audiences) began rating Internet-based radio stations in 1997. They found that NetRadio continuously held 8 of the top 10 rankings. The Navarre Corporation purchased NetRadio and merged the company into one of its subsidiaries later that year, and NetRadio closed its doors in 2001. NetRadio played an important role in the development of Internet audio streaming and paved the way for other providers.

Livecasting

Livecasting as it is known today was made possible by the evolution of smaller, lighter, more energy-efficient (battery) hardware, which included more portable laptop computers, longer-life batteries, a video camera, and wireless Internet connections. As these technologies became more effective and widely used, more and more people began sharing their lives with the world via the Internet.

The first person to continuously broadcast his life live, in real time—with a first-person video from a wearable camera—was University of Toronto professor Steve Mann. Mann experimented with wearable computers and video cameras, and was streaming video as early as the beginning of the 1980s. His work eventually led to the Wearable Wireless Webcam.

In 1994, Mann transmitted his daily activities 24 hours a day, 7 days a week in a continuous stream of video that was truly the first lifecast. While wearing a camera and display, Mann broadcasted, over the Internet for others to see, every event of his day-by-day goings-on, while inviting his viewers to communicate with him through text messaging in real time. Because of this early success and popularity, Mann grew his community of lifecasters to more than 20,000 members.

The next lifecasting phenomenon took place in 1996 with the emergence of the JenniCam—a video that followed the life of Jennifer Kaye Ringley until December 2003. This was followed by collegeboyslive.tv, a site that showed streaming live video of a group in their dorm room, and the University of Toronto's 1998 move to begin livecasting video streaming web sites. Then, in February 1999, the HereAndNow.net web site founded by Lisa Batey—or Nekomimi Lisa, as her fans knew her—began livecasting 24/7. Batey and her roommates began to share their college life experiences in live, unedited 24/7 Internet video streams. Unlike JenniCam and other lifecasting of their time, HereandNow.net broadcasted their video in higher quality and was the first to stream both full-motion video and audio. HereandNow.net stopped broadcasting in 2001, but Batey's community still exists in a chat room and Yahoo! Group.

In December 1999, Josh Harris (creator of the CBS television show *Big Brother*) introduced "We Live in Public," a formatted, conceptual art experiment where he placed telephones, microphones, and 32 robotic cameras in the home that he and girlfriend Tanya Corrin shared. Viewers were able to text Harris and Corrin through their web site's chat room. Josh Harris is currently founder and CEO of Operator 11 Exchange (www.operator11 .com), a Hollywood-based company that is an Internet-based television studio and online web site.

Then in 2000, Mitch Maddox, a former computing systems manager who called himself the "DotComGuy," hit the Web. Maddox's project was to live for one year starting on January 1, 2000, without leaving his Dallas, Texas, home. Maddox ordered all food and necessities off the Internet and had them delivered. His house was monitored 24/7, and several video feeds were streamed online. The DotComGuy project had a large number of sponsors, including United Parcel Service, 3Com, Network Solutions, Piper Jaffray, Travelocity, and Peapod. Maddox's project attracted a lot of attention from the media, but public interest gradually faded away.

In early 2001, "Pud" Kaplan claimed on his web site that due to the dot-com crash of 2000, Mitch's investors were not going to pay him the $100,000 cash bonus he had been promised for successfully living online for an entire year. Mitch later claimed that this was a mutual agreement and that the $100,000 was required to pay for keeping the project online for that year. The phenomenon of livecasting simply continued to grow.

Justin.tv: The first person to significantly popularize the concept of live-casting was Californian Justin Kan. While living in San Francisco in early

2007, Justin founded something he called "Justin.tv." While wearing a webcam attached to his baseball cap, Justin began streaming his life in a continuous, live video, beginning on March 19, 2007, at midnight. Justin is actually the person credited with giving this process the name *lifecasting*. He generated a lot of media attention when he announced he would wear his webcam twenty-four hours a day, seven days a week and broadcast his life—nonstop. Justin's interview with NBC *Today* show reporter Ann Curry vaulted him into national attention in April 2007.

The credit for Kan's computer hardware goes to Kyle Vogt, one of the four founders of Justin.tv. Vogt created the portable live video

FIGURE 16.1   Justin.tv

streaming computer system that Justin used to broadcast, and he recalls,

> I moved to San Francisco so I could be closer to the rest of the team. I mean *really* close. The four of us lived and worked out of a small two-bedroom apartment. I spent my time becoming an expert in Linux socket programming, cell phone data networks, and real-time data protocols. Four data modems in close proximity just don't work well together, so packet loss was as high as 50 percent. I fought with these modems for weeks but finally managed to wrestle them into a single 1.2 Mbit/s video uplink. The new camera emerged from the pile of Radio Shack parts, computer guts, and hacked-up cell phones that had accumulated on my messy desk. It uses thousands of lines of Python code, a custom real-time protocol, connection load balancing, and several other funky hacks.

FIGURE 16.2   Justin.tv

Enter Justine Ezarik: On May 29, 2007, designer Justine Ezarik became the second livecaster on Justin.tv with a livecast streaming from Pittsburgh, Pennsylvania, entitled iJustine.tv. Justine changed the format a bit by aiming the webcam at herself, rather than using the host's point-of-view approach that was used in

FIGURE 16.3   Justine.tv

the past. Another major difference between Justine and Justin is that Justine spent considerably more time interacting with her viewers. Where Justin was more "this is what I am seeing," Justine was "here I am, interact with me." Justine was more conversational through text chat, and watching the feed was almost like being with her and talking face to face.

In the spring of 2007, Justin announced that he was going to make his technology available to the public through something he called "the big rollout." Justin.tv created more than 60 different channels to accommodate the continual flow of applicants wanting to create their own livecasts. Soon there were a wide variety of participants—from college students to graphic designers, a Christian family radio station to a Subaru repair shop. By the summer of 2007, livecasting channels were being added to Justin.tv at an average rate of two per day. The site expanded to nearly 700 channels by the fall of 2007.

Justin.tv generated more than 1,650 hours of daily programming that depicted characters like Australian shark hunter AussieBloke; eighteen-year-old "I'm a Plastic Princess" Meagan; culinary expert Justopia; San Francisco model Krystyl Baldwin; twenty-two-year-old "Roxie," the San Luis Obispo, Silver Lining "Everyday Housewife"; and Jane, a twenty-year-old Texas musician. Justin.tv became an open network on October 2, 2007, a move that enabled anyone to register and begin broadcasting their lives. Within only 11 days, Justin.tv had registered 3,200 broadcasting users.

On October 14, 2007, Randall Stross reported in the *New York Times:*

> This month, after seven months of beta-phase broadcasting, Justin. tv formally declared that it was open for business to one and all. In its first five days, the company said, it created 18,500 hours of video and pulled in 500,000 unique visitors. What those statistics do not show is how long anyone stuck around. In a sampling I did last week during a weekday, only 44 viewers, on average, could be found at each of the eight most heavily visited channels.

While Justin.tv catapulted livecasting to the public media forefront, there had actually been webcams livecasting for several years; however, these sites were offering content that was decidedly more adult in nature. Because of the staggering amount of revenue that adult pornography sites generate, most web-streaming technologies were actually developed to support them. A major provider of adult content reported that "with web sites generating as much as $52 million a month, companies like Sun Microsystems, Cisco, and Microsoft will certainly continue to advance streaming technology."

What You Need to Know

Do-It-Yourself Radio

Do-It-Yourself Radio is another form of livecasting. You are broadcasting live to an audience via the Internet. While more do-it-yourself Internet radio shows are limited to 1 hour and not 24 hours, it's still about communicating with your followers, live.

BlogTalkRadio is an Internet-based audio/radio platform that allows users to host their own, live Internet broadcast radio shows—needing only a telephone, Internet access, and a browser. BlogTalkRadio has been referred to as "a populist force in cyberspace,"[2] and "the dominant player in the latest media trend, one that allows anyone with a web connection to host a talk show on any topic at any time of day. It is the newest form of new media; the audio version of the Internet blog."[3]

Telecommunications executive and former accountant Alan Levy founded BlogTalkRadio, and is now its CEO. After creating a blog to update family members about his ill father, Alan launched Blog TalkRadio in August 2006. He wanted to create a way for bloggers to communicate more directly—and in real time—with their audiences. (To listen to Alan Levy's incredible interview, go to www.theSocialMediaBible .com.)

Washington Post reporter Howard Kurtz has written many times about BlogTalkRadio in his "Media Notes" column, and claims, "The process is nearly idiot-proof. The host logs on to a Web page with a password, types in when he wants the show to air, and then—using a garden-variety phone— calls a special number. The computer screen lists the phone numbers of guests or listeners calling in, and the host can put as many as six on the air at once by clicking a mouse. Listeners can download a podcast version later."[4]

BlogTalkRadio allows up to five callers at any given time to participate in the Internet radio show itself, while the number of listeners is virtually unlimited. The user's radio shows are streamed directly from the host's web page during live broadcasts, and the shows are recorded, archived, and streamed as on-demand podcasts after the initial broadcasts. One can also subscribe to these shows through RSS feeds (see Chapter 19, RSS—Really Simple Syndication Made Simple, for more details on this process). You can post your BlogTalkRadio shows to your Facebook, MySpace, and other social networking web pages. And, since BlogTalkRadio is advertising supported, it's also free!

Conventional Radio Stations Weren't Happy

The ability to use inexpensive technology to webcast your own radio shows worldwide has allowed independent media to flourish. And as you might imagine, conventional radio broadcast stations weren't very happy with their new, free, global, Internet-based competition, which led to a series of controversial royalty legislation bills, congressional hearings, reforms, and appeals. As this book isn't intended to discuss historical legal aspects, you can learn more about this field by researching the following terms:

- The 2002 Copyright Arbitration Royalty Panel (CARP)
- The 2007 United States Copyright Royalty Board approval of a rate increase in the royalties payable to performers of recorded works broadcast on the Internet
- The 2007 Internet Radio Equality Act (HR 2060)

The good news is that even given the continuous controversy, in September 2008, the Copyright Royalty Board has decided to keep the royalty rate the music publishers must pay for each digital track they sell at 9 cents per song for companies like Apple and Amazon. However, faced with an industry in transition, with new rules being written constantly, the three-judge panel opted to keep the royalty rate the same for the next five years. Many argue that instead of the per-track fee, the Copyright Royalty Board should have set the rates as a percentage of digital music revenues.

Webinar, Web Conferencing, and Webcasting

As discussed at the beginning of the chapter, the earliest form of webcasting or broadcasting video live over the Internet was called "web conferencing." This particular method used conferencing software that connects two or more people or computers via the Internet, giving them the ability to speak and see one another simultaneously. People were able to conduct live meetings or presentations using this many-to-many two-way Internet video communication.

Webcast: A *webcast* takes place when a live broadcast or prerecorded media file is distributed over the Internet using streaming technology. It is broadcasted or distributed as a single-content source to many viewers simultaneously, or as a one-to-many one-way broadcast. Webcasting has many applications for commercial companies, including investor relations presentations, annual meetings, seminars, and e-learning. The largest web-casters today are existing radio and television stations that either simulcast their over-the-air (cable) broadcasts or provide their content in a pre-recorded on-demand-type viewing.

Webinar: The word *webinar*[5] comes from the combination or concatenation of the words *web* and *seminar,* and is another form of one-to-many webcasting. Much like a presenter and audience at a live, on-ground seminar, a webinar usually entails one-way (occasionally two-way) communication. Text chat is often part of web conferencing; it allows the audience to communicate, ask questions, and interact with the presenter in real time. The audio portion of the webinar can be technically achieved by a conference call, wherein the presenter addresses the audience over a speakerphone while presenting visual information via the Internet.

State-of-the-art webinar software uses VoIP, or Voice over Internet Protocol (like Vonage telephone service), that allows the two-way audio conversation to also be transmitted over the Internet. This eliminates the need for conference telephone calling, and allows the software to capture both of the activities that are taking place on the screen (the video as well as the audio conversation). The complete webinar capture is able to be distributed and played again at a future date.

Videoblog

The videoblog is the same as the conventional blog, except that it uses short, prerecorded video in addition to text to convey your messages. (See Chapter 8, The Ubiquitous Blog, for extensive detail and explanation on the origin and use of videoblogs.)

Ustream.tv

Ustream.tv is a public platform that grants anyone the opportunity to lifecast through live streaming video for free. It was founded in March 2007 and currently has more than 320,000 registered users who generate more than 350,000 hours of live video content per month. The Ustream site generates more than 10 million unique visitors per month and has received $11.1 million in funding for new product development.

Ustream also won some acclaim during our recent political campaigns for its usefulness in campaigning. While campaigning in the 2008 U.S. presidential election, former senator and presidential hopeful Mike Gravel became the first candidate ever to stream a debate using Ustream.tv. The site allowed Gravel to address a larger number of voters' political questions in real time.

Jody Gnant: Singer, Songwriter, Livecaster, and Community Marketer

Jody Gnant was walking down the sidewalk toward a coffee shop for an interview. She was carrying her laptop; but not the way others carry their laptops. She had it open, facing her, and she appeared to be typing on it. It turned out that she wasn't channeling some inner geekiness, but rather that she was a really clever marketer doing something called *lifecasting.*

FIGURE 16.4 Jody Gnant

Jody introduced herself, set the laptop on the café table, and explained exactly what she had been doing—that the meeting and conversation was streaming live across the Internet to everywhere in the world. People could just tune in and watch Jody's (and now the interviewer's) life unfold in front of them. The scene was reminiscent of the Jim Carrey movie *The Truman Show*, but this was real life! During the conversation, Jody paused to type a few keystrokes. When asked what she was doing, she replied to the interviewer, "Oh, one of my viewers wanted to know how you spelled your name."

Jody is a terrific musician, and through livecasting she's built a trusted loyal fan base that followed her continuously, 24/7, for more than nine months of live broadcasting. Jody explained that her fans would wait for her to wake up in the morning, watch her make and drink her coffee, and go about her life as a struggling musician. Jody says that her lifecasting strategy resulted in a dramatic increase in the awareness of her and her music, and that within a week after her starting her broadcast, her MySpace video garnered more than 186,000 views and hit the number-three position. Cinema advertising giant ScreenVision showcased Jody's music as preshow entertainment in 4,000 movie theaters nationwide. Her music is finding an audience, and she is receiving orders for her album *Pivot* from all over the world. "It's an exciting combination of interactive and noninteractive media," says Jody. "People can choose to tune in and just watch the events of my life unfold, or they can log on and have an immediate effect on my career."

Jody further explained that the process of lifecasting had given her the opportunity to change the lives of the countless people who counted on her to be there for them every day. She emphasizes that the experience changed her life for the better, and forever. She has since discontinued her lifecast after nine months of continuous broadcasting; as Jody puts it, it was really exhausting, and it cut into her personal life.

In addition to her roles as musician and lifecaster, Jody also happened to be the 15th participant in the "One Red Paper Clip" story that a creative college student in Saskatchewan, Canada, named Kyle MacDonald began on July 12, 2005, with a great idea—and one red paper clip. Kyle decided to offer his one red paper clip in exchange with anyone who was willing to trade up. He first traded his paper clip for an ugly fish pen. The pen then traded up for doorknob, and the doorknob for an old Coleman camping stove. He continuously traded up for an entire year, until July 12, 2006—when he traded up for his own home! Jody took part in the project by giving away one year's rent for her Phoenix, Arizona, duplex in exchange for studio time during which she could record her album. After recording this very album, Jody designed a cover wherein the "i" in *Pivot* is one red paper clip.

(To learn more about the One Red Paper Clip, and to listen to Jody Gnant's incredible interview, go to www.theSocialMediaBible.com.)

Providers

So what does all of this livecasting have to do with you and your business? Well, people like Josh Harris, Jennifer Ringley, the DotComGuy, Jody Gnant, and Justin Kan moved what was a new and unfamiliar technology into the mainstream, thereby turning it into yet another possible way to get in touch with your employees, colleagues, customers, and prospects.

If you want to get started with your own Internet radio show, the best place to start is with BlogTalkRadio. It's easy to set up and simple to use, and because it's advertising based, it's free. Other options for Internet radio and real-time audio communication are Skypecast.com, Waxxi.us, iChat, AOL AIM, and TalkShoe.com. Since the list is always changing, be sure to go to www.theSocialMediaBible.com for more up-to-date information on who's who in this space.

If you want to create your own television show or start your own livecast, be sure to check out Ustream.tv, blogtv, EveryScape, Fly on the Wall, Hasan M. Elahi, The Invention of More, Justin.tv, Social network service, Sophie Calle, Sousveillance, Stickam, and Tom Green Live. All of these web sites allow you to set up an account and begin your own livecast/radio show for free.

Expert Insight

Jody Gnant, singer, songwriter, and community marketer, www.jodygnant.com

Jody Gnant Laptop

Well, first and foremost I consider myself to be a singer/songwriter. That's what I've wanted to do since I was eleven years old; and I kind of always knew I was going to have to do it independently if I did not want to compromise who I wanted to be as an artist. Luckily, I was born and raised in a time when the Internet was being born and raised right around me, and so I kind of grew up with the Internet and the development of it.

I was chatting online at, you know, thirteen years old with the nickname of "Scooter," even before the Internet transitioned over to being more of a corporate arena for companies to put up these flashy web sites and wow the rest of us with their technical attributes. Now it is actually coming full-circle. The Internet has been brought back to the people, so to speak, with social media, and it is really an exciting time to be an independent artist and to be able to promote what I do independently. So that is what I do. I sing, I write songs, and I put them out there for the world to see on the Internet.

Like I said, it seemed as if, when I was a little kid sitting on my dad's lap with the modem, with the rotary phone . . . it would just sit. . . . I don't know the technical term for what modem that was, but it was actually at that point about the people too. We would sit there and we would chat and we had the monochrome screens; you really could not do anything else. You could play Zork, which was like a great game. Love that game. However, other than Zork and chatting online, the Internet did not do much yet.

Then the companies took it over and I now feel like it is . . . it is being handed back to the people. That is kind of what I am all about as a musician; the entire reason I have decided to be a songwriter and a singer in the first place was to effect positive change. And I think that is why I like the Internet so much and why I like these tools—like blogging, livecasting—is because it allows us to continue to make that positive change in our own special way. Each of us has our own voice, and the Internet gives us the distribution channel for it. . . .

Lifecasting is. . . . I think it is awesome! Wikipedia explains it as a continual broadcast of a person's life through the general media. And basically a lot of lifecasters actually wear a camera and give the first-person

(continued)

(continued)

perspective of what they see on a day-to-day basis, and so it's their lifecast. But I wanted it to be viewed as a promotional tool to launch the release of "Pivot," which was the album that I had recorded and released as part of my "One Red Paper Clip" trade. And so we decided that we would just start broadcasting. And we broadcast the recording, mixing, mastering, and printing of the record . . . the rehearsing of the band for the CD release party; and then we would broadcast the CD release party . . . "Live . . . On the Internet!" with all these multicam systems and then . . . actually I was only going to do it for the six-week feed after the CD release party. But it dawned on me once I had had the CD release party, that really this was becoming the world's longest documentary *The Life and Times of an Independent Singer/Songwriter* (and the struggles that they go through).

So it actually became more of a journalistic process for me, and capturing for posterity what I was trying to accomplish as an artist. And . . . at some point, [it] became less of a promotional tool and more of something that was a personal mission for me to capture. The fact that there were other people along for the ride was just so cool, because people could actually choose to get involved in the process in real time. You know, if they wanted to affect how my music career was going, there was a chat right there; and they could do something about the fact that I was lost in L.A. And they would get on and Google and they would figure out where I was and they would say, "Go left down Wilshire!" So here I am having my own personal GPS through the Internet. Or—they could just sit back and watch the show.

And [something else that] dawned on me was that—even though I started using it as a promotional tool—without even knowing it, in just in the way that we were handling the situation, we had started to create a community. And so all of a sudden there were hundreds of people that would just come by on a daily basis to get a smile. People have told me that they were in the hospital coming out of a coma and they genuinely didn't know how they were going to survive the next seven weeks of a car accident; and then stumbled upon my lifecast. And the community is what helps them get through that time; and then they show me their scars and, you know, it is really humbling to know that what started out as a promotional tool ended up being a home and a community that still exists even without me.

Right now I am not lifecasting on the Internet, but there are 36 people on the chat befriending each other and talking about what they are going to be doing in their [lives]. It is very humbling; and it is not just broadcasting if you do it right . . . [Then] it is actually community building, and probably the most enriching experience I've ever done for myself.

When you are doing a community marketing project, [you have to know] who you are focusing on, and which community you are trying to build. It is integral to know which [group] you are going after and how you want to affect them at the end of the day. What is interesting to me is that [there are] lives being affected. No longer am I just selling a product. You know when I was lifecasting, my response to every single thing that came across my plate was being broadcast and analyzed and, perhaps remixed and copied, or inspiring somebody else. And so as somebody who has—kind of—planned on being in the music business, the concept of living your life in the public eye was not completely foreign to me; but living it in such a way that every single thing you were doing could have an impact (whether it be negative or positive) on somebody's actual life all of a sudden became a huge responsibility . . . even above and beyond the content that I was putting out musically. . . .

Even if you think about trying a new product, you know . . . (laughter) and I was trying a new product live on the air, and somebody would see it either being really great or really bad. And I guarantee (and I'm not trying to jump around here) that what is really interesting is that . . . in, say, trying new coffeemakers in the lobby of my apartment complex, we would go out every morning and we would get this coffee. And because the lifecast also had a chat room attached to it, it was real-time feedback from people that were participating in the chat. And so you can actually count and monitor how many times a specific brand name is mentioned in the chat. And you can then monitor what types of questions are being asked about your brand. You can monitor every time somebody says, "Hey, I bought this specific product because you tried it in your lifecast and you said it was good." And so you become a brand ambassador of sorts, of every single brand that you pick up in your life. And the lifecasting, in that sense, is a really powerful brand-integration model in that sense . . . [something] you will see a lot more of in the coming years in terms of what's being put out there on the Internet.

And community marketing, in general—where the community is actually . . . I don't want to say "celebrities" . . . the community, the spokespeople, the brand ambassadors. And it becomes less about celebrities and more about trusted community members giving their thumbs up, too. We already see it now; but I think even more so as lifecasting and as citizen journalism become more of the valid form for the rest of the media world to pick up on and embrace, we will see a lot more of that kind of integration in the marketing in general. It's very powerful!

I think if your friend told you to go see a movie because it was the best movie he had ever seen, you would go see that movie over and above and beyond Tom Cruise getting on the television and then saying, "It's the best movie I've ever seen!" Because you have a bond with your friend. . . .

To listen to or read the entire Executive Conversation with Jody Gnant, go to www.the SocialMediaBible.com.

Commandments

1. **Thou shalt explore livecasting.**

   Go and explore some of the web sites mentioned within the chapter. Take a look at what Justin Kan has done with Justin.tv. Take a look at Alan Levy's BlogTalkRadio. Sign up for an account. Get to understand what options are out there for when you are ready to create your own radio/television show.

2. **Thou shalt get a webcam.**

   Go on, get a webcam and try it out. You can buy one for around $25. If nothing else, try a video chat with some friends or colleagues. Become comfortable with the technology. The next time you are on the road, try livecasting with your family, a friend, or a coworker. You will be surprised how different it is when you're able to see the person with whom you're speaking while away from your home or office.

3. **Thou shalt try a webinar or your own radio show.**

   Produce and perform a webinar. Create one for your prospects. Always keep the "What's In It for Me?" content in mind. Present your slides, have some real-time audio, and be sure to have some live text chat. You'll be surprised how differently your prospects will view you and your company.

4. **Thou shalt try a web conference.**

   Try setting up a web conference the next time you need to meet with colleagues—even if they are only on the other side of town. You can use iChat if you are a Macintosh aficionado, or AOL AIM on either platform. All you need is an inexpensive webcam and a free account. Again—like the sports shoe slogan says, "Just Do It!"

Conclusion

Whether you're someone like Justin, Justine, or Jody, or just someone who wants to build a community of trusted followers—or if you ever wished you had your own talk radio or television show—then you need to explore livecasting. A friend of one of the author's does a weekly show every Friday at noon, and over the past year, he has built a fan base of more than 5,000 people. While that number won't get the attention of the *New York Times*, it certainly is a great personal, loyal, trusted network of potential book buyers for his next novel.

What if you did a weekly radio show where you interviewed industry experts (like the Expert Insights on www.theSocialMediaBible.com)? How would your customers and prospects perceive you and your company—even if you only did it a few times?

Invite your prospects to a webinar where you talk about something important to them (always remember the WIIFM factor). Discuss new legislation, an innovative product or service, maintenance tips, installation, your development or manufacturing team, or a message from the president or CEO. This step will really humanize your company, and put a face on an otherwise faceless corporate entity. The best way to build trust is to talk with your customers and prospects.

And like the other social media tools, it only takes some time and creativity.

Readings and Resources

Novak, Jeannie, and Pete Markiewicz. *Web Developer.com Guide to Producing Live Webcasts.* (Hoboken, NJ: John Wiley & Sons, Inc.)

Purcell, Lee. *Web Developer.com Guide to Creating Web Channels.* (Hoboken, NJ: John Wiley & Sons, Inc.)

Downloads

For your free downloads associated with *The Social Media Bible,* go to www .theSocialMediaBible.com, and enter your ISBN number located on the back of the book above the bar code. Be sure to enter the dashes.

Credits

Expert Insight Was Provided By:

Jody Gnant, singer, songwriter, and community marketer, www.jodygnant.com.

Technical Edits Were Provided By:

David Cain, president, MediaSauce, www.mediasauce.com.

Notes

1. Stream/streaming/multicast occurs when Internet-rich audio or video content is continuously uploaded and fed into your computer as you listen to or watch it. It is the opposite of the typical on-demand file downloading, wherein you have to wait for the entire file to be downloaded to your computer before you can play it.

Streaming can deliver live, real-time content, or prerecorded podcast-type files (see Chapters 10 through 14 for more information on these topics). With live-casting, the audio/video content is broadcast live and is playing in real time; the listener has no control over the broadcast, as in traditional broadcast media.

2. Howard Kurtz, "With BlogTalkRadio, the Commentary Universe Expands," *Washington Post,* March 24, 2008; www.washingtonpost.com/wp-dyn/content/article/2008/03/23/AR2008032301719_pf.html.

3. David Levine, "All Talk?" Condé Nast's Portfolio.com, February 26, 2008; www.portfolio.com/culture-lifestyle/goods/gadgets/2008/02/26/Internet-Talk-Radio?page=0/.

4. Kurtz, "With BlogTalkRadio."

5. The term *webinar* was actually registered by Eric R. Korb in 1998 with the United States Patent and Trademark Office, but was too difficult to defend, so the term is in common use today.

CHAPTER 17

Virtual Worlds—Real Impact

What's In It for You?

Any time you can become part of a "trusted network with a million-plus people in it," don't you want to be part of that—especially if you have similar interests?

In an interview, the CEO of Linden Labs, Mark Kingdon, said that Second Life—the 3-D virtual world created by Linden Research Inc.—experiences more than 1.2 million log-ins every 30 days, with more than 2 billion user-created items stored on the Linden servers. That sounds like the ultimate in *trusted network* and *user-generated content*. Second Life is only one of many three-dimensional gamelike virtual worlds or environments, but it is the largest virtual world without a gaming foundation. And according to Mark, when Google and its many resources create Lively, their own virtual environment—they are "validating the virtual world market." When these types of huge companies are inventing in this type of a social environment, there must be a reason.

In addition to being a fun, entertaining way to pass the time, virtual worlds give you the opportunity to browse new and unexplored domains, visualize and participate in imaginary communities, and do business in a virtual marketplace with real customers and colleagues. With companies like IBM, Coldwell Banker, Dell, Armani, Ben & Jerry's, BMW, CISCO, Coca-Cola, and Domino's Pizza doing business in Second Life, there is most likely good reason for *you* to be there as well.

Back to the Beginning

Virtual worlds began with simulators, which were three-dimensional graphic representations of a virtual or simulated environment. Then in 1968, Internet pioneer Ivan Sutherland developed the first computer-based virtual reality. Almost two decades later, in 1984 a NASA grant brought three incredible minds together: Jaron Lanier, Dr. Thomas Furness, and Dr. Sam Wise. These three men made significant improvements to the virtual world and its sensory input, despite the fact that they were far apart geographically and working in highly demanding fields. Lanier, a researcher at Atari Labs, became the CEO of VPL Research (first multiperson virtual reality [VR] and first commercial virtual reality products) and vastly enhanced the then-bulky VR goggles; Furness created an elegant VR environment while working at the Wright-Patterson Air Force Base in Mansfield, Ohio. He and a team of 16 PhDs had developed a closed-cockpit feedback system where the inside of the F-15 fighter plane's cockpit was painted flat black and the pilots piloted their planes through television screens that showed a virtual representation of the actual world around them. Wise was the director of spinal cord injury for the Palo Alto Veterans Administration Hospital when he developed the sensory glove—which later became Mattel's data glove.

During the 1980s and 1990s, one of the authors, Lon Safko, worked independently on his own, commercially available virtual environmental system called SoftVoice (later renamed SenSei when ported from the Apple II to the Macintosh Platform in 1986). While Linier, Furness, and Wise's system was intended for F-15 fighter pilots and astronauts to perform complex repair without the need of dangerous space-walks, SenSei was developed to help the physically disabled access computer technology and their environment (see SoftVoice/SenSei discussed next).

While developing this VR platform, Safko was lucky enough to spend a day brainstorming with Dr. Furness and William Gates Sr. at the University of Washington; as Dr. Furness put it, he "had to see a system nearly as elegant as my own . . . especially when mine cost $5 million dollars, and yours can be purchased for $2,500." As a result of this meeting, Dr. Wise became a member of the corporate board of directors and advisors for Safko International Inc. in 1989 and provided a great deal of support and industry knowledge. He and John Williams, the author of the Americans with Disabilities Act, helped guide Safko International through the late 1980s and into the 1990s during the turbulent times of rights for the disabled and by advising on technology applications that helped the severely disabled.

The application of this three-dimensional virtual world was first implemented as an operating system for the Apple II, then Macintosh computers, and was intended to help the disabled and to teach individuals who had never used a computer before how to access its technology. It's hard to imagine today that during the early to mid-1980s most people had never used a computer before. And by definition, a disabled person had never used a computer due to physical disabilities.

The SenSei System (referred to in the sidebar) was designed so that a user with no computer experience could sit down at a computer, look at the screen, and intuitively know what to do next. If they wanted to type, they selected the typewriter; to place a telephone call, they selected the telephone; to turn on the lights, select the light; to turn off the television, select the television; and so on.

The SenSei System included a collection of world's firsts, such as the fully graphic virtual environment operating system, first voice recognition, environmental control, telephone control, nurse call, all-in-one IR media control, electronic hospital bed control, software version user guides, and even ToolTips, the little window that pops up when you place your cursor over a button and explains what that button does.

The SenSei System later became the archetype for the Apple Newton (first PDA ever) and Microsoft's "Bob" operating system. The original SenSei operating system code and hardware now reside in the Computer History Museum, in Mountainview, California; Apple Computer Inc., Cupertino, California; the U.S. Library of Congress and the Museum of American History, Smithsonian Institution, Washington, DC; and is credited as the first computer to save a human life.

Figures 17.1 through 17.3 are examples of the SenSei System and the work done with the first commercially available three-dimensional virtual environment operating system.

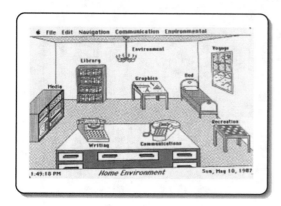

FIGURE 17.1 The SenSei Operating System, 1987

FIGURE 17.2 The SenSei Operating System, 1992

Figures 17.4 and 17.5 are examples of Microsoft's "Bob" OS and the Apple Newton OS.

The first three-dimensional MMOG or MMORG (the acronyms for Massively Multiplayer Online Game or Massively Multiplayer Online Role-playing Game, coined by developer of Ultimate Online Richard Garriott in 1997) virtual environment was created more than 35 years ago. In these MMOGs, participants would play the role of the main fictional character, and were challenged with obstacles that need to be overcome in order to advance their status in the game. This first game was called the Maze Game, Maze War—or simply "The Maze"

FIGURE 17.3 The SenSei Operating System, 1994

FIGURE 17.4 Microsoft's "Bob" Operating System, 1995

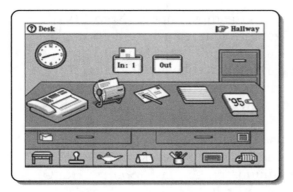

FIGURE 17.5 The Apple Newton
Operating System, 1993

(see Figure 17.6). The avatars or representations of the player were eyeballs, and the environment was a three-dimensional wire-frame maze. The Maze was played on the original Internet—a system called ARPAnet—and could only be played on an Imlac computer, which was the first networked graphics workstation, which debuted in 1970.

During an MMOG, a large number of players interact with one another in a virtual world meant to resemble the real world. This game-culture social interaction and competition motivates users to keep coming back. Most of the earlier games were similar to the more traditional Dungeons & Dragons, which remains the best-known and best-selling role-playing game, with an estimated 20 million people having played it and more than $1 billion in related book and equipment sales. The two most popular MMOGs today are Blizzard Entertainment's World of Warcraft and Microsoft's Halo 3 (designed by Bungie Studios).

On October 4, 2007, Microsoft announced that Halo 3 had officially become a global phenomenon, garnering more than $300 million in sales in the first week alone. The critically acclaimed Xbox 360 exclusive, which was released worldwide on September 25, 2004, was "the fastest selling video game ever—and one of the most successful entertainment properties in history." Microsoft went on to claim,

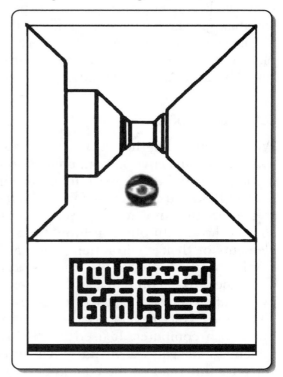

FIGURE 17.6 Maze War

Halo 3 is quickly staking its place as the most popular Xbox LIVE® game in history with members gathering in record numbers to play on the world's largest online gaming and entertainment network on TV. More than 2.7 million gamers have played Halo 3 on Xbox LIVE in the first week, representing nearly one-third of the seven million Xbox LIVE members worldwide. Within the first day of its launch, Halo 3 players racked up more than 3.6 million hours of online game play, which increased more than eleven-fold to more than 40 million hours by the end of the first week—representing more than 4,500 years of continuous game play. (*Source:* HuliQ News, "Halo 3 Records More Than $300 Million in First-Week Sales Worldwide"; www.huliq.com/36851/halo-3-records-more-than-300-million-in-first-week-sales-worldwide.)

(You can read more about gaming in the next chapter. Chapter 18, Gaming the System: Virtual Gaming.)

Other early virtual-world prototypes emerged over the next several years, including Fujitsu Software Corporation's WorldsAway, CompuServe's Dreamscape, and educator Zane in 1987, becoming the first-ever online virtual world game for the Commodore 64 personal computer. The game was played using a modem, a telephone line, and Quantum Link, which eventually became America Online.

SoftVoice/SenSei

While certainly not the first virtual world, SenSei was the first commercially available virtual environment created to give the severely disabled access to a computer and their environment around them. This project was created back in 1986 and called SoftVoice, which stood for Voice Activated Software. It later became known as the SenSei System, and it was originally designed so that those with physical limitations could access a computer and other elements of their environment, such as lamps, telephones, and even electronic hospital bed controls. The first system ran on the most sophisticated and widely used computer at the time: the Apple II.

SenSei allowed its users to access all of its functions through voice commands. Once developed, the system was quickly redesigned for the new Macintosh computer. It used its distinctively different graphic operating system to navigate a virtual environment, which allowed access to the software functions of the computer by selecting, for example, a typewriter for word processing, a telephone to make a call, or a lamp or radio to turn on and off electric appliances. The user could control the computer navigation by moving one's head to activate a head-mouse, or simply by speaking the task they wished to perform. This gave the physically disabled—as well as any computer novice—the capacity to use a computer with little or no knowledge of how one operated, which was important in 1985.

Many original technologies spun off of SenSei's decade-long development, including the first fully graphic operating system, the first PDA, the Apple Newton OS, the Microsoft operating system "Bob," voice-activated environmental control, electronic hospital bed control, infrared television and media control (voice-activated all-in-one controller),[1] the first-ever software user's guides, tool tips where you place your cursor over a button and a window pops up to tell you what that button does, and more.

The author personally had the pleasure of working with Steve Wozniac's post-Apple startup, Cloud Nine, the company that developed the first All-In-One-Controller for infrared devices such as TVs, radios, VCRs, and stereos. Because the device had an RS-232 connection inside its case, crossover into the virtual world of the computer operating system was possible, using the real-life control of media equipment.

As with the wheelchair ramp and other disabled accommodations, many of these inventions—and their significant contribution to society—became mainstream. Eighteen of them are now housed in the permanent collection of the Museum of American History, Smithsonian Institution, in Washington, DC, along with 14 more inventions maintained by the Computer History Museum in Mountainview, California.

Second Life

Philip Rosedale founded Linden Research Inc. in 1999 after conducting some early tests with virtual worlds while studying physics at the University of California San Diego. Many believe that Neal Stephenson's novel *Snow Crash* inspired Philip to create Second Life (even though Rosedale claims that he had imagined the concept before reading the book).

Rosedale set out to develop a VR system that would allow its users to become fully immersed in a 360-degree virtual world experience. He produced the Rig—a large, slow, expensive, and difficult to wear and use system. However, the Rig eventually evolved into the Internet software

FIGURE 17.7 Lon Safko in Second Life

Linden World, which was designed to allow its users to play games and socialize with other users in a 3D online environment. Linden World then grew into today's Second Life (SL) software experience.

The key to SL's success came as Rosedale observed participants at an investors' meeting gravitating toward the social, collaborative, and creative nature of Second Life. This caused Rosedale to see the importance of focusing more intently on the user-generated content and social networking aspects of his project—the very aspects that made Second Life such a success.

Second Life launched on June 23, 2003, and was closely followed by the unveiling of a 3-D virtual world intended for younger audiences, Teen Second Life. While Second Life caters to members over the age of eighteen, Teen Second Life is restricted to members between thirteen and eighteen. With child online security as important as it is, the age restrictions are closely monitored.

What You Need to Know

A virtual world, or virtual environment, is usually an Internet-based simulated environment inhabited by avatars or graphic representations of its interactive users. An avatar can be represented textually, by a photograph, logo, image, or a three-dimensional cartoonlike person, animal, or object.[2] While not all virtual worlds are three-dimensional, many began as forums, blogs, and chat rooms where communities and trusted networks were created.

Figure 17.8 shows examples of two avatars used in Second Life—those of Mark Kingdon, CEO of Linden Labs, creators of Second Life, and one of the authors. Mark's photo is on the left; his avatar is to the author's right.

Figure 17.9 shows examples of blog type avatars.

Virtual worlds are often mistaken for user-immersed games in which players navigate their way through a simulated environment, shooting, fighting, and interacting with other players' avatars (that are controlled either by humans or the game itself)

FIGURE 17.8 Kingdon Safko Avatars

with the goal of winning or overcoming a predetermined challenge. While virtual worlds may appear similar to and were inspired by these types of

FIGURE 17.9 CNN in Second Life

games, they are designed to serve a completely dissimilar purpose. There is no game-winning objective in a virtual world. Virtual worlds are designed for people from around the world—and their avatars—to enter into, navigate, and interrelate by engaging in personal, one-on-one communications. The intent of a virtual world is to encourage users to explore, learn, interact, do business, meet, and make friends with new, multicultural people from around the world that they otherwise might never have had the opportunity to encounter. Virtual worlds may appear to be simulated versions of the real world, an accurate re-creation of part of the real world, or even an Alice-in-Wonderland-type fantasyland where reality has no place. Immersing oneself in this virtual world—or *metaverse*—environment is referred to as having a *telepresence*.

Virtual Economy

Most of these worlds have even gone so far as to create and develop their own virtual economic systems. Second Life, for example, has a currency called the Linden Dollar (L$). While Lindens are fictitious and only negotiable within the confines of Second Life, the people at Linden Labs have made it possible to put real money into the virtual world and withdraw it as well; the Second

Life economy does translate into real-world money. Not all virtual worlds have the same capability. By setting up an account with a (real) credit card attached, the Second Life member can transact actual business. You can go to the mall and "buy" clothes, new hair, or even a car using Lindens (L$). Once the transactions have taken place, your credit card is charged (or credited), at the then going rate of Lindens per one U.S. dollar, and you don't need to be a vendor or own a shopping cart; you only need to be a resident with a credit card. Virtual products can include buildings, vehicles, animations, clothing, skin, hair, jewelry, plants, and furniture—almost anything that you can find in that environment. At the time of this writing, the exchange rate for buying Lindens was $L231.60 in real-world money and $L184 per dollar at the LindenX^{TM} Exchange on the Second Life web site. Selling Lindens at the LindenX^{TM} Exchange could be done at one dollar for $L283 pulled out of Second Life. Linden Labs has even gone to the extent of recording/complying with a value added tax (VAT) for many European countries.

While an exchange rate where you can purchase a suit for five dollars or new hair for seventy-five cents may seem small, many people have actually made money in this virtual world. In fact, at least one person became a millionaire. In November 2007, *BusinessWeek* ran an article by Rob Hof entitled "Second Life's First Millionaire," which told the story of Anshe Chung. Hof's article stated, "Anshe Chung's achievement is remarkable because the fortune was developed over a period of two and a half years from an initial investment of $9.95 for a Second Life. Chung (Ailin Graef, Second Life Persona) achieved her fortune by beginning with small-scale purchases of virtual real estate which she then subdivided and developed with landscaping and themed architecture for rental and resale. Her operations have since grown to include the development and sale of properties for large-scale real-world corporations, and have led to a real life 'spin off' corporation called Anshe Chung Studios, which develops immersive 3D environments for applications ranging from education to business conferencing and product prototyping." (To read the rest of this article, go to www.businessweek.com/the_thread/techbeat/archives/2006/11/second_lifes_fi.html.)

While stories like Chung's make for good press, few people have found this kind of fortune in a virtual world. However, it *is* possible. In Second Life Mainland, prices run about $11.50 per square meter (at the time of this writing), and more for island and waterfront property. Properties are around 640,000 square meters on average, 410,000 of which are bought and sold by Groups each day—which equals roughly 1,050,000m or 16 regions of

Mainland land that is bought and sold daily. Virtual Worlds Management—the leading virtual worlds trade media company—estimates that commercial investments in the virtual worlds were in excess of $425 million in Q4 2007, and $184 million in Q1 2008.

Enterprise in Second Life

Many enterprises now have a presence in Second Life. Most people still don't completely understand how businesses can make money in a virtual world, but three things are clear: some are doing it; some will figure it out; and merely having a presence in Second Life can give a company great brand recognition. As CEO of Linden Labs Mark Kingdon states, companies are using the Second Life platform for gauging customer reaction, receiving feedback, and testing prototypes; and—in the case of one of the author's own businesses—Paper Models Inc. has a storefront and 3D displays showing the models adjacent to the Social Media Bible Beach, www.slurl.com/secondlife/Pinastri/215/8/21, and selling some "first-life" products. This was an interesting transformation for Paper Models, which is now selling electron-based (PDF) items to real people via the Internet for real profits—versus selling virtual products in a virtual store to virtual avatars that simply represented real people. This kind of engagement in Second Life gives companies a significant competitive advantage. (To listen to the entire Mark Kingdon interview, go to www.theSocialMediaBible.com.)

FIGURE 17.10   ACS Memory Tree

Some businesses are also using the metaverse as a meeting place as well—for customers, prospects, and even employees. IBM has utilized Second Life on a regular basis as a forum for their engineers from around the globe to meet, exchange ideas, or see PowerPoint presentations—while never having to leave their respective offices. During a project in 2007, one of the authors used Second Life to meet with paper model developers from the Ukraine. In fact, the first time in scheduling a call with developers—to discuss the American Cancer Society's Kiosk Design—it came as such a surprise to the author to actually hear the voice of Roman Vasilev, a developer with whom the author been working for over two years via e-mail and the Internet. Up to that point, they had been able to "speak" with each other and exchange ideas and concepts in real time—and for free.

Sun Microsystems is another example of a company that has created its own island in Second Life dedicated solely to employee use. Their virtual island is a place where employees can go to seek help from colleagues, exchange new ideas, or advertise an innovative product. The American Cancer Society has its own in-world presence with its help island, which was established to raise awareness and provide support for this widespread, life-threatening illness. Paper Models was honored to sponsor and participate in ACS's Island Dedication in the fall of 2007 (www.slurl.com/second life/Pinastri/246/4/22, an event that accompanied the free distribution of a 3D model of its landmark in-world Memory Tree, a virtual tree that is surrounded by small flashes of light. Each flash of light represents the memory of someone who has passed away from cancer. While on the island, you can download a pdf, print it, and—with a little glue and scissors—re-create the virtual ACS Memory Tree in real life. (To download your free ACS Memory Tree, go to www.papermodelsonline.com/acstree.html.)

One of the authors was also given the chance to work with ACS member Steven Groves (Estaban Graves in Second Life) and ACS in sponsoring an International ACS Donation Kiosk Design Contest. Second Life developers from around the world competed in creating the most imaginative freestanding kiosk where residents within Second Life could pledge donations to help fight cancer. Dozens of entries were submitted; the winner was announced at the 2008 ACS's Second Life Relay For Life Launch Event. (Go to www.papermodelsonline.com/amcasodo kiin.html to download your free copy of the ACS Kiosk winner paper model.) Two monumental events took place at this event, in addition to presenting the winner of this contest. First, in anticipating a good turnout for the event, Linden Labs agreed to assign additional servers to accommodate the high level of computation and distribution of data needed to bring so many avatars together at one time. Even with this precaution, so many avatars (residents) participated in this event that Linden Labs' servers were

FIGURE 17.11 SL Kiosk Design Finalists

taken down and Second Life shut off until they were able to reboot. The second phenomenal occurrence was that the American Cancer Society raised more than $200,000 in real cash for its research at the 2008 Relay For Life in Second Life, up from $120,000 in 2007. (Be sure to visit the American Cancer Society's Island for this year's events.) Besides making some history and raising a significant amount in donations for a great cause, Paper Models had fun, garnered a great deal of publicity, and are now branded as having a presence in both first-life and Second Life.

At the time of this writing, other companies that are utilizing Second Life to conduct their business are 20th Century Fox, Armani, Avnet Inc., BBC Radio, Ben & Jerry's, Cisco, Coca-Cola, CNN, Coldwell Banker, Creative Commons, Dell, Disney, Domino's Pizza, IBM, ING Group, Mazda, MTV, Reuters, Starwood Hotels, Toyota, Wells Fargo, Paper Models Inc., and John Wiley & Sons, Inc. As an example, Wiley has a bookstore in Second Life where you can go, sit, and meet other book lovers. Many of the companies above pay someone to represent them 24/7/365 so when you walk into their building, an avatar (with a real person operating them) will greet you and answer any questions you have about their product or service.

The Social Media Bible In Second Life

You guessed it. *The Social Media Bible* has a Garden in Second Life. Pinastri,158/205/21—www.slurl.com/secondlife/Pinastri/158/205/21—is what is referred to as a Second Life URL, or "SLURL." It can be typed/pasted into a standard web browser, and if you have a Second Life account, it will take you/your avatar there right away. This makes it easier to connect a Second Life location to the 2D web browser. *The Social Media Bible* gives away a virtual device here that is called a HUD (Heads Up Display) at the back of the garden, where you can take it and listen to any of the Executive Conversation podcasts while continuing to explore the garden—or anywhere else in Second Life. *The Social Media Bible* will continue to build the content of the Social Media Garden so it becomes a virtual world resource for all things social media. Just go to the SL address above and select the SLurl; or go in-world in Second Life and look for the group "Social Media Bible Evangelists."

Your Own Second Life

Second Life appears as an example throughout this chapter since it is the most popular virtual world platform in use today. Many others are listed in

FIGURE 17.12 TSMB in SL

the Providers section of this chapter; even Google has decided to compete in this space, as mentioned earlier, with their newest virtual world, Lively. To understand how a virtual world works, Second Life will remain as an example. See The Social Media Bible in Second Life (Figure 17.12).

To participate in Second Life, you can simply visit www.Second Life.com and download a program that allows you to enter this virtual world. This program, client, or viewer is free. Once you create your account (also free), you become a resident of Second Life. Now you are able to explore, interact with other residents, participate, learn, create, buy, socialize, and network.

Second Lifers refer to their world as *the grid*, which is divided into 256 × 256-meter areas of land called *Regions* or *Sims* (short for Simulators). Each Region is created and housed on a single computer server and is assigned a unique name and content rating—either PG or Mature. While in SL or on the grid, your avatar can get around by walking, running, jumping, or riding in vehicles. Your avatar can also fly and quickly jump from one region of the grid or one place to another, or you can teleport—TP—directly to that location.

The ability to create virtual objects such as chairs, clothes, and even buildings from primitive shapes called *prims* is also built into Second Life. A scripting language called LSL (Linden Scripting Language) is similar to C++ programming language. LSL allows Second Lifers to add behaviors to these objects, like having avatars cross their legs when sitting on a chair. Other options to create more complex 3D virtual objects are sculpties, textures, and animations. A sculptie is short for *sculpted prim*, which is a prim whose shape is created by an array of x, y, and z coordinates. Sculpties are used to create more complex, organic shapes for virtual goods.

Figure 17.13 shows an example of cows and horses created using sculpties.

FIGURE 17.13 Sculpties

The Avatar

The Second Life avatar often has a cartoonlike, yet slightly human appearance and may be male, female, or androgynous—in the case of an avatar being a boat, mythical creature, or even a pile of rocks. Avatars may be casually dressed, in a tuxedo, or wearing wildly ornate costumes that users can change at any time. You can even pay a service to take your photograph and create a skin that looks exactly like you do in real life, but many residents just choose to display themselves as their alter ego. An avatar's real identity is anonymous; you cannot access any personal details about an avatar's identity (a precaution that was implemented to provide age verification and protect children).

Avatars can communicate through instant messaging (IM)–type text chat. They can alternately use a voice chat component that allows users to actually speak aloud to a computer's microphone using Voice over Internet Protocol (VoIP)[1] to transfer the two-way voice in real-time communications. Avatars are also able to send and receive e-mail, and their Instant Messages will roll over to an avatar's real-life e-mail when they log off if they choose to select this option. (See the Mark Kingdon Executive Conversation video at www.theSocialMediaBible.com.)

Expenses in Second Life

Even though this book continually touts the low- and no-cost benefits of social media, Linden Labs has adopted—as have most companies in the social media ecosphere—a freemium business model. (If you want to just browse and explore, however, your account is completely free.) Second Life offers a Premium Membership for $9.95 per month that entitles its users to own a small amount of land up to 512m without additional fees. It provides extra technical support and a salary or stipend of L$300 per week. If you own larger areas of land, you will incur additional rent or a Land Use Fee. Most members refer to this fee as *tier*, since this is the manner in which it is charged—tiers that range from $5 per month or more depending upon the amount of land you own. As a member, you can choose to purchase land from another member or resident directly.

You can also purchase a different type of land that is known as a Private Estate. This usually consists of one or more Private Islands or Regions, and has a completely separate set of regulations and pricing policies. A Private Region is 65,536m (about 16 acres), and costs $1,000 to purchase with a $295 per month maintenance fee. Included in the ownership of a Private Estate is the member's ability to alter the terrain of the land.

Second Life Stats

Second Life had a banner year in 2008. There were 16,785,531 registered Second Life residents spending more than $100 million USD on virtual goods and services, and participating in more than 397 million hours in world. The residents bought and sold more than 43,965,696 square meters of land with a total of 1.76 billion square meters of land owned by its residents, and as many as 76 thousand residents logged on at any one time.

       www.blog.secondlife.com/2009/01/15/q42008/
       www.secondlife.com/whatis/economy_stats.php
       Or go to www.theSocialMediaBible.com for "clickable links."

Providers

While Second Life is the most popular of the virtual worlds available, there are plenty of others to choose from, including:

- Active Worlds (a Second Life–like virtual world)
- Coke Studios (promotes music and bands)
- Cybertown (personal chat, inbox, message board, and free e-mail)
- Disney's Toontown (games, events, and contests to promote Disney)
- Dreamville (a virtual world that includes blogs, photo sharing, and customizable homepages)
- Dubit (online worlds and social networks for young people to engage, interact, communicate, and learn while having fun)
- Entropia (real people, real activities, and a real cash economy in a massive online universe)
- Habbo Hotel (a virtual world where you can meet and make friends)

Others are IMVU, Kaneva, Google's Lively, the Manor, Mokitown, Moove, Muse, the Palace, Playdo, the Sims Online, Sora City, There, TowerChat, Traveler, Universe, Virtual Ibiza, Virtual Magic Kingdom, Voodoo Chat, VPchat, VZones, whyrobbierocks, Whyville, Worlds.com, Yohoho! Puzzle Pirates, and the erotic-oriented Red Light Center.

Expert Insight

Mark Kingdon, chief executive officer, Linden Labs, creators of Second Life, www.SecondLife.com

Mark Kingdon

There's something like 2 billion items in the databases; you know, content and scripts that Second Life residents have created. It's really a powerful platform for co-creation, for collaboration, and just for [generating] amazing things. . . . We do a lot of our meetings *at* Linden Labs inside of Second Life. I would say that I spend anywhere from one to four hours a day in Second Life and—as you can imagine because folks at Linden Labs are so involved in the Second Life experience—we have an amazing array of creative avatars. You can have jellyfish, tugboats, beagles, piles of rocks; it's just an endless array of crazy avatars. It's a blast!

Second Life is a platform and a set of content-creation and collaboration tools that members use to populate this incredible three-dimensional environment—this virtual reality—with immersive experiences. So Second Life is a destination, but it's [one] that's really created by the residents using the platform tools that we provide. And we have had—over the last sixty days, I think—1.2 million log-ins, as people come to Second Life. So it's a really rich and vibrant community with members from literally every country in the world. . . .

Well, the amazing thing about Second Life is, kind of, the breadth of the use-cases, right? Just like the real world, [Second Life] is incredibly diverse; [and] the audience—or the user base—is incredibly diverse [as well]. So the use-cases are as broad in Second Life as the experiences would be in the real world. People use Second Life to go to a live-music venue and hear a concert in an intimate setting. They use it to go shopping with friends. They use it to create a personal space, like their own home, that they can enjoy in the virtual world. They use it to connect with other people around a common interest, a common concern, a common problem they share. Companies use it to work together to create products in a rapid-cycle product-development process, or for virtual meetings, for virtual learning. . . .

It's companies like the IBMs, Sun, Intel, Dell, Orange, British Telecom, Mattel, CIGNA; lots and lots of companies around the world are using Second Life in their business. I saw Mattel having a shareholders' meeting in SL. Whether it's CIGNA creating a help island where their customers can connect with health information in a unique way, [or] Cisco doing a developers

(continued)

(continued)

conference Q&A in Second Life—the use-cases are really, really broad. [And] it's an amazing way to experience a product before it's built. I think that we've only just started to scratch the surface on the "possible"—right? [Because] up until now I think that we were very much in [an] exploratory phase in the virtual world space. But what we're seeing now is companies who come back a second and third time, trying new ideas, and new approaches to doing business. . . .

One of the things that I can tell you is that we're really working hard to listen to our user base and to understand what our core customers are looking for in the platform. One of the really important customer segments that we want to develop further is the enterprise customer segment; so we've been listening to enterprise customers very closely to understand what their specific needs are. So, as we make adjustments and changes and improvements to the core Second Life platform, it's more supportive of enterprises and educational institutions. I think you should keep your eyes peeled, because as of next year [2009], there are going to be a lot of things that we do with and to the platform to enable business in a substantial way as we continue to support our core audience around the world.

To listen to or read the entire Executive Conversation with Mark Kingdon, go to www.theSocialMediaBible.com.

Commandments

1. **Thou shalt try out a virtual world.**

    Take a look at a few of the many available virtual world web sites, and become a member of one yourself. Sign up for a free membership and use it to explore. Don't be discouraged by the initial difficulty in navigating your way around. It isn't always intuitive, but you will become a pro in no time. The principal skills you need to focus on to have a satisfactory first experience is movement, communication, and how to find things to do that interest you.

2. **Thou shalt explore other company's successes.**

    Take a look around. Google some of the companies listed throughout this chapter and read about some of their successes. Get ideas about what has worked from them. After researching several companies, you will begin to formulate a plan about what will work for you and your company.

3. **Thou shalt explore selling.**

    Can you sell your products or services in a virtual world? Should you set up a virtual store? Can you partner with someone who already has a strong presence in a virtual world? Can you cross-promote between first-life and your virtual life? Think about how you might get started marketing and selling in a virtual world to see if it's right for you and your business.

4. **Thou shalt explore meetings and training.**

    Investigate the idea of holding your next design, sales, or marketing meeting in a virtual world. You must realize that there will be an initial learning curve for everyone, but once you bridge that curve, it's fairly easy from there on out. Maybe HR would like to present; maybe it's a new product or service you want your satellite offices to see. You can even do a PowerPoint-like slide presentation within the virtual world.

5. **Thou shalt join the community.**

    Take a look at the search menu options, and look for groups with whom you might have common interests within the virtual world of your choice. Find a group that shares a similar interest to yours and meet with them, share ideas, make friends.

Conclusion

The concept of doing business in a virtual world is still new. There is a tremendous opportunity for enterprises to participate in a huge trusted network of like-minded participants—in which many may be prospects. As with most technologies, it's the early adopters that get the home-team advantage. You won't know if marketing in a virtual world is right for you and your company until you explore the concept. Pick a virtual world, sign up for a membership, visit a few in-world businesses, talk to the business owners, talk with their customers, meet other avatars, follow and meet with groups within the community—and better understand how virtual worlds work.

Readings and Resources

Moore, Dana, Michael Thome, and Karen Haigh. *Scripting Your World: The Official Guide to Second Life Scripting.* (Hoboken, NJ: John Wiley & Sons, Inc.)

Perigo, Julie. *Winners in the Second Half: A Guide for Executives at the Top of their Game.* (Hoboken, NJ: John Wiley & Sons, Inc.)

Robbins, Sarah, and Mark Bell. *Second Life For Dummies.* (Hoboken, NJ: John Wiley & Sons, Inc.)

Rufer-Bach, Kimberly. *The Second Life Grid: The Official Guide to Communication, Collaboration, and Community Engagement.* (Hoboken, NJ: John Wiley & Sons, Inc.)

Rymaszewski, Michael, Wagner James Au, Mark Wallace, et al. *Second Life: The Official Guide.* (Hoboken, NJ: John Wiley & Sons, Inc.)

Terdiman, Daniel. *The Entrepreneur's Guide to Second Life: Making Money in the Metaverse.* (Hoboken, NJ: John Wiley & Sons, Inc.)

Weber, Aimee, Kimberly Rufer-Bach, and Richard Platel. *Creating Your World: The Official Guide to Advanced Content Creation for Second Life.* (Hoboken, NJ: John Wiley & Sons, Inc.)

Winder, Davey. *Being Virtual: Who You Really Are Online.* (Hoboken, NJ: John Wiley & Sons, Inc.)

Downloads

For your free downloads associated with *The Social Media Bible,* go to www .theSocialMediaBible.com, and enter your ISBN number located on the back of the book above the bar code. Be sure to enter the dashes.

Credits

Expert Insight Was Provided By:

Mark Kingdon, chief executive officer, Linden Labs, www.SecondLife.com.

Technical Edits Were Provided By:

Steven Groves, CEO, Executive Conversations, www.StevenGroves.com.

Note

1. VoIP or Voice Over Internet Protocol is the technology used to digitizing voice into discrete packets of digital information and transfer or transmit that conversation over the Internet. Vonage is an example of a VOIP long distance telephone service.

CHAPTER 18

Gaming the System:
Virtual Gaming

What's In It for You?

Online gaming is another one of those Internet phenomena that just keeps gaining popularity. The trusted networks of the MMORPG—or Massively Multiplayer Online Role Playing Game—community are in many cases, in the millions. In fact, Blizzard Entertainment, creators of World of Warcraft (WoW), announced recently that the MMORPG game World of Warcraft "as of October, 2008 is played by more than 11 million gamers around the world. World of Warcraft has also achieved new regional subscriber milestones, with more than 2 million players in North America, more than 1.5 million players in Europe, and more than 3.5 million players in China." The developer of Ultima Online (the company that created a great deal of MMORPGs) Richard Garriott first coined the term *MMORPG* in 1997. WoW: www .blizzard.com/us/press/081028.html.

As of January 2009, Xbox LIVE had more than 17 million subscribers: www .latimesblogs.latimes.com/technology/2009/01/microsoft-xbox.html, and even Barack Obama purchased advertising in the online racing game, Burnout Paradise during his campaign: www.gamepolitics.com/2008/10/09/report-obama-ads-burnout-paradise.

Many people tend to view online video games as an activity with no business value—a waste of time in which only teenagers participate. However, any time you have 50,000 to 8 million people in the same place with the same interests in a trusted network, a business opportunity exists. In fact, only 25 percent of online gamers are teenagers; the average MMORPG player is approximately 26 years old. Fifty percent are employed full-time, 36 percent are married, and 22 percent have children. They include high school and college students, professionals, homemakers, and retired individuals.

On average, they spend 22 hours per week playing these games, and there is no correlation between hours spent playing and age. Sixty percent of all players report that they have played for 10 continuous hours at one time or another. Eighty percent of MMORPG players also play on a regular basis with someone they know in real life such as a romantic partner, family member, or friend. In fact, MMORPGs provide highly social environments where new relationships are forged and existing relationships are reinforced. Many players report feeling strong emotions while playing, and a recent statistical study showed that 8.7 percent of male and 23.2 percent of female players have even had online weddings. The average MMORPG player is by no means average.

(For more information about online gaming, be sure to also read Chapter 17, Virtual Worlds—Real Impact.)

What You Need to Know

An MMORPG is a genre of computer/Internet games where a large number of players interact with one another in a virtual world via the Internet. In an MMORPG, players assume the role of a fictional character, often in a fantasy world. This first-person play allows the participant to control his or her character's actions in an ongoing virtual world—usually hosted by the game's publisher—that continues to exist and evolve. Worldwide revenues for these types of games exceeded a half billion dollars in 2005, with U.S. revenues exceeding $1 billion in 2006.

Features that are common to all MMORPGs are themes, progression, social interaction, culture, and customization of the player's character. Most MMORPG's themes are based on fantasy and science fiction, such as the genre's two most popular games: Dungeons & Dragons, and World of Warcraft. Another sub-genre of on-line games are called FPS or First Person Shooter such as Halo3.

All MMORPGs have some kind of progression

FIGURE 18.1 World of Warcraft

for the main character's player, or avatar. You can earn points or capabilities, gain inventory or wealth, or be challenged with more difficult levels. The reverse is true as well; if the main character fails at the challenge—such as combat with another player's character, or with the character generated by the game itself—points are taken away, inventory is lost, and the main character is often forced to go back to the beginning or simplest level. This play/challenge/replay cycle is called the *level treadmill* or *grinding*.

In an MMORPG, characters are encouraged to communicate with one another, and often team up. By doing so, individual players can offer their skills to other players, which results in many players becoming members—or even leaders—of that particular group. In many MMORPGs, a player's specialized abilities can be categorized as a *tank* (one who absorbs blows and protects members from the enemy), or a *healer* (who keeps the members of the team healthy). There's a *DPS—Damage per Second*—who inflicts damage; the *CC* or *Crowd Control* character, who temporarily controls the opponent; and there's the *NPC* (*Non-Player Character*) who makes the opponent lose control of her or his actions and abilities. There is also the *Buffer* or *Debuffer*, who use their abilities to affect opponents. Most players can have one, none, or many of these characteristics. Most MMORPGs have a *Game Master* or *Moderator (GM)*—who is either a paid employee of the publisher or a volunteer from the game. The GM's job is to supervise and manage the game world.

Much like Second Life, MMORPGs run on the publisher's server 24/7/365, which means you can access and play anytime day or night. In order to play, participants download client software that's able to run on their PCs. The player then connects to the game's world by using the software and the Internet. This software can be made free—as with Second Life—or for purchase, as with World of Warcraft and EverQuest. Some MMORPGs require a monthly subscription, while others are moving to what is called a *thin client*, where the game can be played without the use of client software, using only a web browser.

Back to the Beginning

As mentioned in the previous chapter on Virtual Worlds, a very fine line exists between participating in online gaming and a virtual environment (Figure 18.2). Nearly every successful MMORPG today is a role-playing, full-immersion, three-dimensional virtual world scenario. This type of game play dates back to the early 1990s, while the earliest online game—called Maze-War or the Maze—which was much like the later PacMan, where you maneuvered through a maze while being chased by objects that would

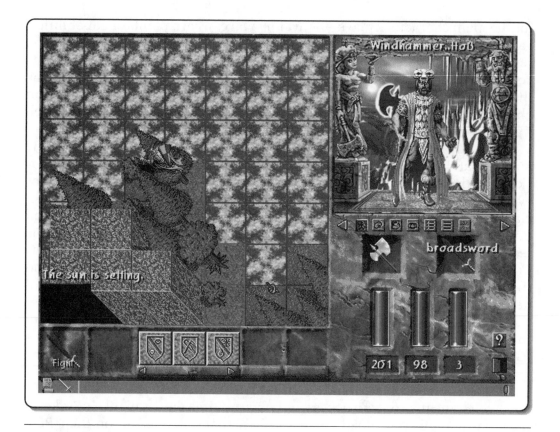

FIGURE 18.2   IOKesmai

harm you—began back in the 1970s (again, see Chapter 17, Virtual Worlds—
Real Impact for more information). In 1984, Islands of Kesmai was released:
"a semi-graphical, multiplayer, two-dimensional game interface that scrolled
with turn-based play, where players moved in tiles on a grid utilizing short
commands and key presses to find items on the floor of the dungeon."

The first fully graphical multiplayer game, Neverwinter Nights, a role-
playing game (RPG) set in a huge medieval fantasy world of Dungeons
and Dragons, hit the Internet in 1991 and received promotion from then-
president of America Online (AOL) Steve Chase (Figure 18.3). Then there
were MMORPGs from the Sierra Network—the first online multiplayer
gaming system—that became popular in the early 1990s, like The Shadow
of Yserbius (released in 1992), The Fates of Twinion (1993), and The Ruins of
Cawdor (1995).

FIGURE 18.3 NWNights

FIGURE 18.4 EverQuest

It took the National Science Foundation Network (NSFNET)—a major part of the early 1990s Internet backbone—until 1995 to remove their restrictions on the Internet. This relaxing of rules allowed developers to create more massively played titles such as Meridian 59—the typical three-dimensional, first-person game play. Then in 1996, the Korea-based company Origin Systems released

Nexux: The Kingdom of the Winds in a pay-to-play MMORPG. The following September, the company launched the Ultima Online (UO), a game similar to D&D where there are lands to explore, houses to design and build, quests to complete, rare treasures to hunt for, exotic creatures to tame, and an almost infinite array of characters for building an MMORPG fantasy game. UO is similar to many of the other previous Ultima games (too many to list), and to this day is still being played on both the Internet and private consoles.

While both of these games really helped to create the MMORPG genre, EverQuest brought MMORPGs into the mainstream in the United States. EverQuest was designed by Brad McQuaid, Steve Clover, and Bill Trost, developed by Sony's 989 Studios and its spin-off Verant Interactive, and was published by Sony Online Entertainment (SOE) in early 1999.

There are basically three MMORPG business revenue models: pay-to-play, free-to-play with in-game advertising and merchandising, and buy-to-play. Pay-to-play is where the player sets up an account and pays what is usually a monthly subscription to have access to the game. Free-to-play is where a player can log on and just play for free. And buy-to-play is where the player first buys the game, then can play online for free. Holding the largest pay-to-play MMORPG market share is Blizzard Entertainment's World of Warcraft, followed by Final Fantasy XI and Phantasy Star Online. Titles with large market shares in the free-to-play category are MapleStory, Rohan, and Blood Feud, with the most popular buy-to-play game being Guild Wars.

Social Impact

Nick Yee (www.nickyee.com), a research scientist at the Palo Alto Research Center, studies online games and immersive virtual reality. Yee has created something called the Daedalus Project, which he explains as "an ongoing study of MMORPG players. MMORPGs are a video game genre that allows thousands of people to interact, compete, and collaborate in an online virtual environment. Over the past 6 years, more than 40,000 MMORPG players have participated in the project."

Yee's Daedalus Project has generated some interesting articles, such as "Superstitions: Exploring Superstitions in MMOs and How They Develop" and "Social Architectures in Virtual Worlds: How Do the Rules in Virtual Worlds Encourage Certain Social Behaviors?" Yee makes the following statement in his "Social Architectures" article:

> We tend to think of altruism and gregariousness as personality traits. Some people are more helpful; other people are more chatty. One reason why I'm fascinated with MMOs is because it seems that

game mechanics also change how communities and individuals behave. For example, when people had to ask casters for "binds" (i.e., set their respawn point) in the original EQ, it seemed to help create a cultural norm of asking for help in general. In a way, altruism was not only an aspect of individual players; it was also partly fostered by the game mechanics. This "social architecture" of virtual environments is interesting because it hints at the possibility of shaping community and individual behavior via game mechanics.

Yee sees a potential for human behavior in the real world to change due to the types of behavior that are becoming more acceptable in virtual gaming worlds. By participating in an online world, players can more easily develop and embrace these particular traits and attributes once they've moved from their gaming interactions to those in their everyday lives.

British writer and game researcher Richard Bartle studied multiplayer RPG players and classified them into four primary psychological groups: explorer, socializer, killer, or achiever. Erwin Andreasen (www.andreasen .org) then expanded Bartle's classifications and developed this concept into the 30-question Bartle Test—which more than 521,112 gamers have taken and which is available on the their Gamer DNA web site at www.gamerdna .com/quizzes/bartle-test-of-gamer-psychology.

Bartle's and Andreasen's data includes over 200,000 of the original responses that Andreasen recorded between the years 1996 and 2006. Originally designed for MUD (multiuser dungeon) participants, it remains relevant to new virtual worlds and MMORPGs. Scoring is interesting and entertaining. The original wording of all questions has not been changed, except to modernize certain terms (such as replacing MUD with the more encompassing MMORPG).

The CDC in MMORPG WoW

Although MMORPG participants invent imaginary characters to play in what are usually considered make-believe games, one particular incident took place that proved to be great practice for a real-life disaster. On September 13, 2005, the Corrupted Blood epidemic hit (www.wowwiki .com/Corrupted_Blood; see Figure 18.5). "Upon engaging the demon, players were stricken by a 'Corrupted Blood' which would periodically sap their life. It inflicted 250 to 300 points of damage (compared to the average health of 4,000 to 5,000 for a player of the highest level at that time) every few seconds to the afflicted player. The disease would also be passed

FIGURE 18.5 Corrupted Blood

on to other players who were simply standing in close proximity to an infected person. Originally this malady was confined within the Zul'Gurub instance, but made its way into the outside world by way of hunter pets that contracted the disease. Within hours, Corrupted Blood had infected entire cities because of their high player concentrations. Low-level players were killed in seconds by the high-damage disease. For days carpets of skeletons riddled the highest populated towns and were rendered uninhabitable by the persistent plague."

This was a temporary programming error that created a virtual plague that infected and spread rapidly from character to character throughout Blizzard Entertainment's World of Warcraft—and resembled a real-life disease outbreak. This virtual plague attracted the attention of psychologists and epidemiologists across North America. The Center for Disease Control actually used this incident as a research model to study both the progression and transference of a disease and the potential human response to large-scale epidemic infection.

Virtual Economies

Like Second Life, MMORPGs also have thriving virtual economies. Virtual money can be earned through game play, items can be bought and sold, and wealth can be accumulated. And these virtual economies can have an impact on the economies of the real world, as demonstrated by Anshe Chung's ability to become the first real—or first first-life—millionaire generated from Second Life's virtual land. (See Chapter 17, Virtual Worlds—Real Impact, for Chung's full story.)

Edward Castronova (www.mypage.iu.edu/~castro/home.html)—one of the early researchers of MMORPGs—demonstrated that a supply-and-demand market that exists for virtual items often crosses over to the real world or first life. This crossover assumes that the players have the ability to sell or barter items to each other for virtual currency, and that the currency translates—and exchanges—into real-world currency.

This real/virtual world currency connection is having a profound effect on players, the gaming industry, and the courts. When Castronova first studied the trend in 2002, he found that a highly liquid—and often-illegal—currency market existed. At one point, the value of EverQuest's in-game currency exceeded that of the Japanese yen. Some players—referred to as *gold farmers*—make a living by using these virtual economies. A few of the game publishers prohibit the exchange of real-world money for virtual items, whereas virtual worlds such as Second Life and Entropia Universe support and profit from this system. This link between currencies is common in virtual worlds, but rare in MMORPGs, where it is generally accepted that this kind of exchange is detrimental to game play. When real-world wealth can influence greater rewards than skillful game play, the incentive for strategic role-play and real game involvement can become diminished.

This blurred boundary between the various currencies has also led to the proliferation of in-world gambling. Because gambling is illegal or controlled in so many areas of the world, Second Life was forced to remove and prohibit gambling within its virtual world.

Raids

A fast-growing segment of the **MMORPG** is the *Raid,* which is an adventure or part of the parent game designed for specific groups of players—often 20 or more. Raids are copied from the parent game and allow that particular segment to be separated from the rest of the game world. This reduces competition, provides for faster game play downloads, and lessens screen-refresh lag times.

Single Player

Even though the MMORPG is designed for multiple players and social interaction, many games allow the user to interact solely with the game itself. As a result, many of the most popular MMORPGs have now developed single-player play options. Even the older Dungeons & Dragons Online was retro-fitted to allow for single play. This change has increased the popularity of the MMORPG, because many of the gamers prefer to play while interacting with the computer only or off-line. One of the authors recently tested an MMORPG car race game called FlatOut 2. While the racing interaction and competition with others from around the world is exciting, sometimes just taking the car out for a spin or against the computer can be a lot of fun as well.

User-Generated Content

More and more MMORPGs are encouraging user-generated content. Ultima Online provided a 30-page book that instructs players on how to collect, trade personal libraries, and build houses. In fact, any noncombat-type MMORPG relies on user-generated content—including textures, architecture, buildings, objects, and animations—much like the 2 billion user-generated items on the Linden Labs server. (Listen to the interview with Mark Kingdon, CEO, Linden Labs—Second Life, at www.theSocialMediaBible.com.)

Console-Based MMORPGs

Again—although the MMORPG is intended to be played via the Internet by large numbers of players at any given time—two major video game manufacturers are releasing console-based MMORPGs, including The Age of Conan for the Xbox 360, which will allow the user to play these online games on their Xbox consoles or their PC while online.

The Largest MMORPG: World of Warcraft

World of Warcraft—commonly known as WoW—was designed by Rob Pardo, Jeff Kaplan, and Tom Chilton, developed by Blizzard Entertainment, published by Vivendi Universal, and released on November 23, 2004. WoW is

FIGURE 18.6 WoW

considered a fantasy MMORPG, and is the fourth game released by Blizzard (the first was Warcraft: Orcs & Humans in 1994). World of Warcraft differs from other MMORPGs in many ways. Players complete quests and experience the world at their own pace, whether it be a few hours here and there or entire weeks at a time. Additionally, their quest system provides an enormous variety of captivating quests with story elements, dynamic events, and flexible reward systems. World of Warcraft also features a faster style of play, with less downtime and an emphasis on combat and tactics against multiple opponents. World of Warcraft is currently the world's largest MMORPG, with more than 11 million monthly subscribers, and holds the Guinness World Record for the most popular MMORPG ever with an estimated 62 percent of the MMORPG market in April 2008. While most online MMORPGs have peaked or flattened, WoW is really still "wow!"

The management of Blizzard Entertainment "didn't see the connection between WoW and social media's 'trusted networks'" and declined to participate in *The Social Media Bible*. To read their response, visit www.theSocialMediaBible.com.

FIGURE 18.7 Halo3

Halo3

Halo3 is a first-person shooter or FPS video game. It was developed by Bungie software exclusively for the Xbox 360 video gaming console. Halo3 is the third edition in the Halo series, and concludes the trilogy story that began in the original Halo game. The game's themes are based on an interstellar war between twenty-sixth-century humanity—led by the United Nations Space Command—and a collection of alien races known as the Covenant. The MMORPG player assumes the role of the Master Chief, a cybernetically enhanced super-soldier, as he wages war in defense of humanity assisted by human Marines as well as an allied alien race called Elites, which is led by the Arbiter.

On September 25, 2007, Halo3 was released in Australia, Brazil, India, New Zealand, North America, and Singapore; in Europe one day later; and on the following day in Japan. There were 4.2 million copies of Halo3 in retail outlets on the day before its debut, and the game grossed more than $300 million during the first week following its release. Within the first 24 hours, more than one million people played Halo3 on Xbox Live. As of January 3, 2008, Halo3 has sold more than 8.1 million copies and was the best-selling video game of 2007 in the United States.

FIGURE 18.8 Halo3

At the time this paragraph was being written, there were 68,064 Halo3 players online, with 604,821 unique players and 1,342,417 battles logged in the last 24 hours, and a UNSC Campaign Kill Count of 6,737,856,503.[1]

In-Game Advertising

As discussed in Chapter 17, Virtual Worlds—Real Impact, in-game advertising is growing in popularity. The following article from TechCrunch shows the level of interest of many of the Fortune 500 companies regarding in-game advertising.

FIGURE 18.9 In Game Ads

Google to Buy Adscape for $23 Million

Nick Gonzalez, February 16, 2007

After some rumors of a deal earlier this month, Google has expanded it's advertising reach by moving into video game advertising with their $23 million acquisition of Adscape. Adscape is a video game advertising company whose AdverPlay product lets developers place dynamic ads right inside the game and Real Virtual Gateway product enables two-way text, audio and video communication via SMS Text or e-mail.

May 2006, Microsoft had acquired a similar in-game advertiser Massive to run advertising across its Xbox Live and MSN gaming platform. The WSJ (subscription) placed the deal in the $200 to $400 million range. Massive claims they "can provide publishers and developers $1–$2 profit per unit shipped for their titles." AdverPlay and RVG are the product of 5 years of development and consist of 1 issued and 30 pending patents.

Source: www.techcrunch.com/2007/02/16/google-to-buy-adscape-for-23-million or go to www.theSocialMediaBible.com for "clickable Links."

Providers

There are currently over 225 different major MMORPGs available today—far too many to list here. The following is a link to MMORPG.com, which lists all of the current MMORPG games, genres, developers, fees, and a whole lot more: www.mmorpg.com/gamelist.cfm?bhcp=1.

Expert Insight

Scott Clough, Avid Online Gamer, www.myspace.com/brandrath

Scott Clough

Actually, I was playing a tabletop role-playing game, since probably the early 1980s. I started with games like Dungeons & Dragons, and honestly as a teenager I probably spent all of my free time doing so.

I then moved into playing computer games, especially ones that had elements of role-playing games in them. . . . Zork was a very early one; very simplistic. Then I moved up to playing games such as Ultima, Might & Magic, Art's

(continued)

(*continued*)

Tale . . . and then they started making some of the Dungeons & Dragons into computer games.

I got involved in the online role-playing at about 1996 when I went through a divorce and had suddenly lots of time, and in 1997 Ultima Online (the first of the genre) came out. And it gave me something to fill up my time.

I played Ultima Online until EverQuest was released, and that was probably an online game that probably really made the whole genre successful, because the numbers became staggering . . . how many people were playing.

It had graphics that were just amazing; it had a world that was in full realistic, and I think all the current big games owe a lot to EverQuest.

I used to play games with almost all my free time, but in later years I've learned to limit my playing. I also try to make sure it doesn't dominate my life, and I stopped playing particular ones when I realized I'm not being entertained. But I always look for something else to move onto.

So I've tried a lot of the games over the years. I wish I had tried the FlatOut one; I'll have to look that one up. . . .

It was interesting; I got really interested in fixing up computers for myself and then I was building bigger and badder machines for friends and family, even. One day I was online all over the games and I was looking for another job, and a guy who I was gaming with, never met, I had said to him I was seeking a new job. And he said, "Would you be willing to relocate?" And I said, "Yeah, sure, as long as it was Arizona."

The next day I had an interview set up, and since then I have been working in computer support and eventually ending up here at Hewlett Packard. . . .

Well, [MMORPG] was a term coined by Richard Garrett, creator of Ultima Online. It means, "Massively multiplayer online role playing game." Yeah . . . a mouthful! . . .

Well, yeah, it gives an explanation of it. The term was kind of coined to differentiate the different kinds of games that were out there at the time. You've got to realize, this kind of game was an evolution, and it's still in process. What had happened is back in the day, people were playing the very games I spoke of, such as Ultima, some of the Dungeons & Dragons games, and they were very active. The thing they kept saying they wanted to do was to be able to have a friend come over, like you with our brother, and play head-on-head or in the same world with it. And it was just a natural interest to say, "Hey, if we can make it so you can play with two, four friends, why not do it over the new medium called the Internet," back at that time. And as you know, Richard Garrett's Alarm . . . was the first one. And actually it was interesting because they had eight different versions of their stand-alone game before they came out with Ultima Online; and amazingly enough it's still out there! . . .

Yes, but it also has some drawbacks, because where as a bot is going to react in a set mode based on the programming (and that has been developed more each year), some players that you get out there can be unethical. And they use cheats, hacks, exploits (as it's called out there) to get the edge on you rather than by skill. . . .

Well, it's really interesting. It's people in all the demographics, I would say. This is a hobby that has no separation by race, sex, religion. . . . You know a lot of the people out there try to classify the online player as a teenage boy, you know! But I've run into family groups that play, moms, dads, and the kids. I have met professionals who play everything, from computer engineers to lawyers to police officers, to soldiers sitting over in Iraq. . . .

You know the biggest appeal is the ability to be another person, or another entity. You can be a hero or a villain, just depending on how you want to play or the aspects of the game. There are some people out there who are dedicated to the role-playing aspects, and it's interesting because the games have started to have to modify to have to get there.

So they have dedicated role-playing servers, where everything you say or do is supposed to be in character. There are other servers who are dedicated to player versus player, and that's a real big growth area currently. And I would say most of the arguments in the games are about character balance in player versus player. In case you weren't aware, but that's where other players kill/defeat real players in the game, and usually you get some type of reward.

But I think the real attachment in the games is the community aspect. Usually most of the games allow you to form up a group, usually called a guild. And the guild . . . you get to display your name over the name of the character; you get to solve a harder quest, kill the toughest monsters while working with people. And they do things such as raids where they get 50+ people to go after a single creature.

And while you're doing this you chat and you develop friendships. I've even known people to get married and divorced as a result of playing this game. . . .

It's something to watch because it's a new and developing technology, and games such as World of Warcraft have shown the worldwide appeal of such games. But you know, it's not just the game itself that is being sold. There's now a thriving industry on the items that are in the game . . . virtual items.

There's a third-party market on games guides, there's help web sites. There's even companies out there that are selling online money gold and characters for real-world cash. Now most of the games are like, trying to shut this down, this behavior. And most players do not like it. And also some of the games are based on the current entertainment industry. There's a Matrix game, Pirates of the Caribbean, Star Wars, and there's even a Star Trek game in preproduction right now. . . .

Yeah, there's online money. Actually, since most of the games are fantasy, it's gold, but there's also items in the game that people desire. Say for instance, a really powerful sword that's a very rare find. There's an organization out

(continued)

(*continued*)

there that goes and they—do what's called "camping." They sit there and wait for the avatar that has it, they take it and then when they get it, rather than using it for that character they turn it over to their company that sells it online. And I've seen back on some of the eBay-equivalent sites [they] are selling some of this stuff. I've seen items sell for hundreds of dollars. . . .

Actually if you're interested in statistics there's a great site, www.mmorg .chart.com, and they actually chart how many people are playing in certain games, the basic activities. And you can actually look at how the games have gone up and down in their numbers . . . fascinating numbers . . . and the runner of the site tries to put it all in scientific methods, and he tells you where his data comes from so you can make your own evaluations on the reliability.

If you're more casual and you just want to know what your kids are getting involved in, you can go on the web and look for sites like www.alakazimes.com; you can go to the manufacturer of World of Warcraft and get information off of those. You can also buy magazines such as *PC Gamer,* which is one example. And you can always tell them apart because they will have screen shots of the various games on their cover usually.

But really, if you just want to know about the games, just go to any place that sells the software, such as Best Buy Electronics, and you'll see they have their own sections, their own shelves, and you can look at the game boxes and read what they're claiming that their world gives to you. You can actually buy even game guides that tell you how the game is played.

To listen to or read the entire Executive Conversation with Scott Clough, avid online gamer, go to www.theSocialMediaBible.com.

Commandments

1. **Thou shalt visit the occasional MMORPG site.**

   Go look at the most popular MMORPGs, and choose one to play. This is the perfect opportunity to buy an Xbox and Halo3 as a tax deduction under market research (see your tax professional for advice about this first, of course!). Experience it firsthand. Look for in-game advertising. See how it's used. Understand its application. Maybe it isn't right for you, your product, or your service, but what if it is?

2. **Thou shalt read MMORPG articles.**

   Read some articles about MMORPGs. MMORPGs are popular and have a very strong fan base, but the size and influence of the market can be staggering if you are unfamiliar with it. Study a few MMORPGs so that when the Fortune 500 companies have figured out how to effectively monetize in-game advertising to its huge loyal user base, you will be there.

3. **Thou shalt understand in-game advertising.**

Read a few articles about in-game advertising. If all of the major online advertisers are buying and building companies that provide in-game advertising, maybe there is a reason. Encourage others to follow along until everyone understands the application and potential of this powerful new media.

Conclusion

The moral of the story is to remain open to all of what's going on around you in the world of social media and advertising. MMORPGs provide a huge base of trusted networks. When you have people with the same interest who participate in trusted social networks that are more than 600,000 members strong in any given 24-hour period—and 8 million participants in one game alone—you might want to be aware of this as a businessperson. As you can see by the number of existing games, numbers of participants, and the rate at which this marketing opportunity is growing, companies like Microsoft and Google will figure out how to effectively monetize it. You need to be aware, informed, and there when it happens.

Readings and Resources

Armitage, Grenville, Mark Claypool, and Philip Branch. *Networking and Online Games: Understanding and Engineering Multiplayer Internet Games.* (Hoboken, NJ: John Wiley & Sons, Inc.)

Jennings, Scott, and Alexander Macris. *Massively Multiplayer Games For Dummies.* (Hoboken, NJ: John Wiley & Sons, Inc.)

Johnson, Brian, and Duncan Mackenzie. *Xbox 360 For Dummies.* (Hoboken, NJ: John Wiley & Sons, Inc.)

Mileham, Rebecca. *Powering Up: Are Computer Games Changing Our Lives?* (Hoboken, NJ: John Wiley & Sons, Inc.)

Downloads

For your free downloads associated with *The Social Media Bible,* go to www .theSocialMediaBible.com, and enter your ISBN number located on the back of the book above the bar code. Be sure to enter the dashes.

Credits

Expert Insight Was Provided By:

Scott Clough, avid online gamer, www.myspace.com/brandrath.

Technical Edits Were Provided By:

David Cain, president, MediaSauce, www.MediaSauce.com.

Justin Lacey, senior interactive developer, MediaSauce, www.MediaSauce.com.

Note

1. UNSC Campaign is the Brute Infantry Specialist Kill Count within the Halo3 game. At the time of writing, according to the UNSC Campaign Report, the total number of Enemies KIA (Killed In Action) was 6,737,856,503. This in-game "killed" number is now higher than the world's estimated population at 6,704,845,726.

   Bungie, the developers of Halo3, monitors and reports statistics on the their game's usage. Bungie's servers record all manner of statistics when you play, all of which are used to track players across all of their Halo3 games, multiplayer and campaign alike.

CHAPTER 19

RSS—Really Simple Syndication Made Simple

What's In It for You?

For the first time in Internet history, you can syndicate or distribute your fresh web-site content worldwide for free. That's right. No longer do you have to subscribe to a news service or be part of a large media organization in order to send your news or receive news from any other web site from all over the globe.

RSS—or Really Simple Syndication—is a one-click solution that allows all of your content to be sent to your followers the moment you publish it. The reverse is also the case; you can have each of your preferred blogs and news stories sent to you automatically without having to take the time to search all of your favorite web sites every day for new content and updates. Simply adding a syndication button to your blog site lets your followers click your Subscribe button and instantly receive your latest breaking blog.

But what exactly does RSS have to do with building an online following for your business? Let's start with some basic information, so that you can see how this really simple concept can be easily applied to your own company.

Back to the Beginning

The early RSS formats date back to 1995, when computer scientist Ramanathan V. Guha and several of his colleagues developed the Meta Content Framework (MCF)[1] at Apple Computer's Advanced Technology Group between 1995 and 1997. In July 1999, Guha developed the first version of RSS (0.9) for My.Netscape.com. Guha's Netscape colleague Dan Libby is responsible for improving the first RSS by incorporating Dave Winer's "ScriptingNews" format, which he dubbed "Rich Site Summary" (see more on Winer next). Winer is

FIGURE 19.1   RSS Icon

a pioneer of RSS as Really Simple Syndication, and his Scripting News is one of the oldest blogs on the Internet, having been established in 1997.

Dan Libby and Netscape abandoned the development of RSS for more than eight years when, in April 2001, new owner AOL restructured the company and eliminated that particular project. This allowed two new developers to pick up where Netscape left off—the first being the RSS-DEV Group, and the second being UserLand Software owner Dave Winer. Winer created software that could read and write in a modified version of RSS 0.91, which he made available on his UserLand web site. In December 2001, Winer applied for a U.S. trademark, but failed to respond to the United States Patent and Trademark Office, and his trademark application was rejected.

Winer continued to develop and release improvements to his RSS project, the most significant of which came in 2000 when he introduced a version that could enclose audio files. This technology made the still-new process of podcasting (see Chapter 11, Talking About the Podcast (Audio Create)) much easier and more user-friendly. Then, in December 2001, RSS-DEV Working Group—which by now included Guha and O'Reilly Media—developed RSS 1.0. Winer released his newest major revision of his RSS—2.0—in 2002, which then took on the name Really Simple Syndication.

With both developers working on the same technology at the same time—yet each on their own—there has always been controversy as to who should get credit for the development of RSS. Atom was born out of this controversy in June 2003. Atom was a ground-up redesign of the RSS delivery system that was adopted by the IETF or Internet Engineering Task Force, Proposed Standard RFC 4287 (see the following for more details about Atom's creation and development). The Atom Syndication Format is similar to the RSS format and uses the XML language employed for web feeds. The Atom Publishing Protocol (AtomPub or APP) is a simple HTTP-based protocol for creating and updating web resources. Web feeds allow software programs to check for updates published on a web site.

In July 2003—the month following Atom's inception—Winer assigned his copyright for RSS 2.0 to the Berkman Center for the Internet & Society while starting a term as a visiting fellow at Harvard. Winer, Jon Udell, and Brent Simmins launched their group—which they titled the RSS Advisory Board—to provide support to RSS 2.0. Mozilla Firefox was the first browser to adopt the familiar orange RSS subscribe (feed) icon with its radio broadcast waves, and within a few months, Opera Software, Microsoft Outlook, and Microsoft Explorer all recognized RSS as an industry standard. Computer book author and web publisher Rogers Cadenhead took over as head of the RSS Advisory Board in January 2006 upon Winer's departure. The RSS format was revised again in June 2007.

Atom

In June 2003, IBM software developer Sam Ruby created a wiki to discuss the deficiencies of RSS and to solicit ideas about syndication. Ruby wanted to come up with a better system than Blogger API or LiveJournal—the ones that were currently being used. More than 150 developers and prominent members of the online community came out to support the development of Atom, including Jeremy Zawodny of Yahoo!, Brad Fitzpatrick of LiveJournal, Glenn Otis Brown of Creative Commons, Timothy Appnel of O'Reilly Network, Mena Trott of Six Apart, David Sifry of Technorati, Jason Shellen of Blogger, and others. Even RSS originator Dave Winer gave Atom his full support. By July 2003, the project code names "Necho," "Pie," and "Echo" had become known as Atom 0.2. Google added Atom to its Google News and Google Blogger in December 2003—an event that marked the full support of the syndication community.

In June 2004, the Atompub Group was formed by Paul Hoffman and Tim Bray (codeveloper of the XML specification), which moved the Atom project to the Internet Engineering Task Force or IETF. In December 2005, the IETF accepted the Atom Syndication Format as the industry standard. Thanks to coeditors Robert Sayre and Mark Nottingham, the Atom Publishing Protocol was declared the standard in October 2007 in their IETF RFC 5023 (Internet Engineering Task Force Request for Comments #5023).

Even though Atom 1.0 is an IETF standard and widely supported by many podcasting applications such as iTunes and Google, RSS 2.0 still remains the most widely used and accepted format. Many web sites, such as those of the New York Times, CNN, and the BBC, will only publish their feeds in the RSS 2.0 format.

What You Need to Know

RSS is a way to feed (or web feed) your web pages, blogs, audio, video, and photographs automatically to people who subscribe to your feeds. In other words, every time you create something new on the Internet and hit Publish, a feed goes out to everyone who has asked for an update. Your followers are automatically notified through e-mail, mobile texting, or Tweets (see Chapter 15, Thumbs Up for Microblogging), and your content is automatically added to their reader or aggregator page. You can also subscribe to this kind of material from others, and have news headlines, stock quotes, blogs, and other frequently updated information automatically sent to your reader page or feed reader—which can be either PC- or browser-based.

The only requirement for you to subscribe to a feed is to go to your favorite web site, blog, or news site, locate the Subscribe button or the familiar orange RSS Subscribe button, and select your feed reader (or paste the link into your Add Subscription box). That's it! Now each time that web or blog page publishes new content, your reader page will be notified and provided with a copy of that new content.

Reader or Aggregator

A reader, or aggregator, is a program or web site that will check and continuously search all of the blogs, news sites, or other web sites to which you have subscribed for new content (see Figure 19.2). If fresh material is identified, the reader page will show a summary of that information with a link to that page. This way—instead of having to visit all of your favorite web sites, news sites, and blogs—the newest content comes to you, and is

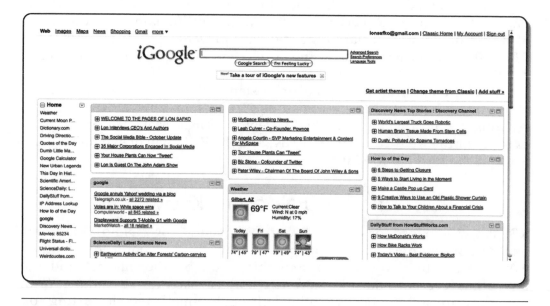

FIGURE 19.2 iGoogle Reader

aggregated—or summarized—in one reader page. Some web pages allow you to subscribe in RSS, Atom, or both formats.

iGoogle Reader (Aggregator): These reader pages or aggregators are designed as a stand-alone software program or as a web page (browser-based), such as iGoogle. Web-based or browser-based feed readers allow the user to access aggregated content from any Internet browser.

Social Bookmarks

FIGURE 19.3   Social Bookmarks

Social bookmarks are small icons found on nearly all blogs, web sites, news sites, sports sites, or any pages that provide fresh, updated content on a regular basis. By selecting your feed reader or aggregator icon, the content feed is automatically added to your specific reader page. Most of these social bookmarks are a one-click addition. Some feed readers might require you to copy and paste the URL of your favorite news or blog page into an Add Subscription text box. It's easy, and only requires one step.

Providers

Page readers or aggregators are free; below is a list of the many readers you can choose from:

Aggregators

- Akregator
- AOL Explorer
- Avant Browser
- Blam!
- BlogBridge
- Bloglines
- BottomFeeder
- Camino
- Claws Mail
- Cooliris
- Epiphany
- FeedBeast
- FeedDemon
- FeedGhost

- Feedreader
- Feedview, a Firefox extension
- Flock
- FreeRange WebReader
- Gnus
- Google.com/Reader
- Hubdog
- IBM Lotus Notes
- iCab
- iGoogle
- Internet Explorer
- K-Meleon
- Liferea
- Mail
- Maxthon
- mDigger
- Mercury Messenger
- Microsoft Office Outlook
- Mindity
- Mozilla Firefox
- Mozilla Thunderbird
- MyYahoo!
- NetNewsWire
- Netscape Browser
- Netscape Navigator 9
- NewsAccess
- NewsBreak
- Newsbeuter
- NewsFire
- NewsFox, a Firefox extension
- Newsgator
- Omea
- OmniWeb
- Opera Mail
- Opera web browser
- Pegasus Mail
- RSS Bandit
- RSSOwl
- Safari
- Sage, a Firefox extension
- SeaMonkey Mail and Newsgroups
- Shiira
- Sleipnir
- Snarfer
- Tencent Traveler
- The Bat!
- Thinfeeder
- Vienna
- Windows Live Mail
- Windows Mail
- Zimbra

Web-Based Software

- aideRSS
- AmphetaDesk
- Bloglines
- Daylife
- Drupal Aggregator Module
- Fastladder
- Google News
- Google Reader

- Imooty.eu
- Live.com
- mDigger
- Netvibes
- Newsknowledge
- Pageflakes

- Planet
- Rojo.com
- Seeking Alpha
- Spokeo
- Yahoo!

Media Aggregators

- Akregator
- Amarok
- Canola
- Flock
- iTunes
- Juice
- Mediafly SyncClient

- MediaMonkey
- Miro
- Rhythmbox (GNOME)
- Songbird
- Winamp
- Zune

Expert Insight

Pete Cashmore, founder and CEO, Mashable,
www.mashable.com

Pete Cashmore

So I'm the founder and CEO of Mashable.com, and Mashable is one of the leading social media blogs. We cover social networks and social media sites, like Twitter and Facebook and MySpace and Digg and YouShoot; and we essentially provide the latest news on their services, we review new companies that are launching Internet space. We give our opinion on those companies so to provide a resource list.

So say if you're a band, where are the top 20 sites you should be using to promote your band? So we have three pieces. We do resource lists of the best companies in the space. We do opinion on what's happening in a kind of social networking

(*continued*)

(continued)

space, and we also do straight reviews of new social media, social networking sites. . . .

Sure, well, I mean we have a number of different user-types on this site. We have visitors who are looking for information. There'll be companies who are thinking about launching a company, and they are looking for information about the market and what a competitor might be doing.

So it's that kind of developer/executive kind of role. We also have just general web users—people who are passionate about the space. So people who are on, for instance, these social media sites already, people who use Facebook, people who use Twitter. So there's that demographic, as well, where they just want to use new services and find interesting new sites to try out.

There's also some degree that can be investor groups—where people who are looking to get invested in new companies or are looking for what's the hot new thing, what's happening, what are the trends to look out for. And also, you know, just to spot something new before it goes big.

So I guess that would be the basic demographics. There is also, to some extent, bloggers and journalists, and eventually anyone who has [been] following this whole social networking/social media trend. . . .

Yeah, that's right. . . . We feature social media, which is fairly broad anyway. We started off being social networking news, but what happened over the span in which we were around, which was three years so far, is that social networking essentially became the Web; and social networking became ingrained as a feature in virtually every web site. It became something that was expected rather than something that was remarkable and unusual. So as a result, obviously, coverage has broadened a little bit.

If it's social, we cover it. A lot of stuff on the web these days is social. . . .

Yeah, I mean our basis is always "add value." You know, what's the value of this story or this article? You know, what you can take from it. And where we try to add value in every piece, even when we cover news, we don't cover it in a straight way, we cover it in a way that's also, and again, "What does this mean for the market? What does this mean for you if you're a developer? What does this mean for you if you're a web user?"

So even in the news items we are showing some "value add," and always there is a load of "value add" in things like . . . so I'm looking at the front page and we have a list of tools for family travel, so . . . we also build these lists which are by their formats incredibly useful, where you say, "What are the top sites in this category, in this particular niche?"

So even use-end lists and, of course, we do how-to posts as well. All of these are really about building value. I'm always focused on what's the value of beyond just straight news. . . .

I think it's kind of a weakness of the blog format we are trying to increasingly overcome is that we have this huge archive of content that is incredibly useful, and that we do let people know that exists and that it's available to them, because a lot of the time with blogs you see the first 10 posts on the front page and you don't realize that this blog might have 15,000 posts, of which 100s of them might be on this topic. So, yeah, we also try and direct people to what's useful from our archives and what's kind of an interesting resource on that topic. . . .

Yes, and we also go beyond the blog format to some degree, and we have a job section, and we also have a beta invite-sharing section where some of these new sites go into private base, which is to say you cannot get access unless you've been invited by someone who is already in . . . so we have this patron-invite section. You'll see that on the network on the site, where you can exchange invites to new sites, where you can say, "I have an invite for this site, does anyone else have?" It's kind of a sharing thing where if you go and share invites with someone else, you're more likely to get an invite to a site that you want to access, too.

We've gone a little bit beyond the blog format. We have a number of features for which we do events. Which, for instance, in somewhere of 2008 we did a U.S. tour where we went to seven cities and events for the tech community. I mean, that's a whole other part of the business, and that's an interesting part that has certainly grown for us this year.

So we certainly go beyond simply writing content and creating content, and we're more about community, more about, "Can we offer job listings, can we offer this exchange of patron-invites, and can we bring these communities together in real life with Mashable's events?". . . .

Well, especially right now . . . jobs can be . . . jobs are on the "jobs" tab at Mashable. You can post a job for $100 for 30 days, and right now in the current economic climate that's obviously something that's an essential resource for anyone in the industry. If you do, unfortunately, happen to get laid off, there are good resources for that. And Mashable Jobs is one of those. . . .

So we have a cool team of writers, and they've been writing for, like, three years, so we have a huge archive of posts. I don't actually know the number right now, but it will be, I think, somewhere in the range of definitely over 10,000, I think possibly around 20,000 articles. We have this cool team of writers who put out news every day, who put out resources every day. We also have guest writers who join us and occasionally give some expertise on a certain topic. So we might not have the expertise to cover, say, a PR topic, but we have someone who's an expert in that field who can write with expertise and add value. So it's a combination of our cool team and guest authors who can come on board.

Essentially anyone can write to us and say they're interested and this is their expertise area, and we'll determine if we think that would be interesting to our audience.

To listen to or read the entire Executive Conversation with Pete Cashmore, founder and CEO of Mashable, go to www.theSocialMediaBible.com.

Commandments

1. **Thou shalt sign up for a feed reader.**

    Go to one of the many web sites that provide a feed reader, such as iGoogle. This way, every time you open that page, all of the freshest content from the entire Web to which you subscribed will be there waiting for you.

2. **Thou shalt go forth and subscribe.**

    Go to your favorite web sites, blog sites, and news sites and hit the Subscribe button. Follow the directions, copy and paste the URL in the Add Subscription text box—and you're ready to go.

3. **Thou shalt be sure your site has social bookmarking.**

    Make sure that your company's web and blog pages have Subscribe and social bookmarking buttons, so that your customers and prospects can be easily, instantly, and automatically updated on all of your business's news.

Conclusion

The two most important items you need to know about RSS are as follows: (1) You can provide a one-click solution to any friend, family member, associate, customer, or prospect that will allow them to automatically view any new content the moment you hit your Publish button. You don't have to e-mail, call, or text message them; simply by hitting your Subscribe button, they are part of your syndication. (2) Be sure to subscribe to all of your favorite web, blog, and news sites. This way, all of the updates that you care about will be instantly sent to your reader page, and you'll never have to search the Web, site after site, to see if new content and updates have been published. It all comes to you!

Readings and Resources

RSS, or Really Simple Syndication, is a one-click process. If you wish to learn how to actually program RSS or Atom, you probably don't need to read the books suggested below. *Do*, however, read books such as *Social Media Marketing: An Hour a Day*, by Dave Evans and Susan Bratton. If you want to learn the programming aspect of RSS, here's a comprehensive list of resources.

Amiano, Mitch, Conrad D'Cruz, Kay Ethier, et al. *XML: Problem—Design—Solution.* (Hoboken, NJ: John Wiley & Sons, Inc.)

Ayers, Danny, and Andrew Watt. *Beginning RSS and Atom Programming.* (Hoboken, NJ: John Wiley & Sons, Inc.)

Crowder, Phillip, and David A. Crowder. *Creating Web Sites Bible.* 3rd ed. (Hoboken, NJ: John Wiley & Sons, Inc.)

Evans, Dave, and Susan Bratton. *Social Media Marketing: An Hour a Day.* (Hoboken, NJ: John Wiley & Sons, Inc.)

Evjen, Bill, Kent Sharkey, Thiru Thangarathinam, et al. *Professional XML.* (Hoboken, NJ: John Wiley & Sons, Inc.)

Finkelstein, Ellen. *Syndicating Web Sites with RSS Feeds For Dummies.* (Hoboken, NJ: John Wiley & Sons, Inc.)

Heaton, Jeff. *Programming Spiders, Bots, and Aggregators in Java.* (Hoboken, NJ: John Wiley & Sons, Inc.)

Holzner, Steve, and Nancy Conner. *Joomla! For Dummies.* (Hoboken, NJ: John Wiley & Sons, Inc.)

Huddleston, Rob. *HTML, XHTML, and CSS: Your Visual Blueprint for Designing Effective Web Pages.* (Hoboken, NJ: John Wiley & Sons, Inc.)

Hunter, David, Andrew Watt, Jeff Rafter, et al. *Beginning XML.* 3rd ed. (Hoboken, NJ: John Wiley & Sons, Inc.)

Myer, Thomas. *Dashboard Widgets for iPhone.* (Hoboken, NJ: John Wiley & Sons, Inc.)

Orchard, Leslie M. *Hacking RSS and Atom.* (Hoboken, NJ: John Wiley & Sons, Inc.)

Reinheimer, Paul. *Professional Web APIs with PHP: eBay, Google, PayPal, Amazon, FedEx plus Web Feeds.* (Hoboken, NJ: John Wiley & Sons, Inc.)

Sabin-Wilson, Lisa. *WordPress For Dummies.* 2nd ed. (Hoboken, NJ: John Wiley & Sons, Inc.)

Downloads

For your free downloads associated with *The Social Media Bible*, go to www.theSocialMediaBible.com, and enter your ISBN number located on the back of the book above the bar code. Be sure to enter the dashes.

Credits

Expert Insight Was Provided By:

Pete Cashmore, founder and CEO, Mashable, www.mashable.com.

Technical Edits Were Provided By:

James Burnes, vice president, Media Sauce, www.MediaSauce.com.

Note

1. Meta Content Framework (MCF) is a specific format for structuring metadata (behind-the-scenes information that the web browsers and search engines look at) about web sites and their data.

Spotlight on Search (Search Engine Optimization)

To some experienced members of the social networking community, Search Engine Optimization (SEO) may seem like an old-school process. However, it is still the very foundation of how search engines index all of your web site's pages—and therefore, how your customers eventually find you. SEO is incredibly important and relevant to any business. In fact, some people have only two pieces of information on their business cards: their name and their web address. At least one person has gone one step further: only the image of the Google Search Bar with his name in it printed on the face of the business card.

FIGURE 20.1 Google Search Bar

Web sites have become such an important marketing tool nowadays that they essentially serve as the foundation for everything that's done in business. The processes of SEO and Search Engine Marketing (SEM, the focus of the next chapter) are all about being sure that when people are trying to find you, your company, your product, or your service—they can.

What's In It for You

Search Engine Optimization (SEO) and Search Engine Marketing (SEM) are techniques by which you optimize your web pages, photos, and even videos to maximize search engine rankings. They are practices that almost everyone

theSocialMediaBible.com

has heard of, but that few people understand. Search Engine Marketing requires implementing the optimization of your web pages and a Keyword Sponsored Link Advertising Program or SEM. While SEO and SEM are two completely different functions, they are equally important; both refer to your web site's ability to be recognized by the major search engines. This chapter discusses Search Engine Optimization.

When people are conducting an online search for the type of product or service you provide, they will use their favorite search engine—Google, Yahoo, MSN, Ask, or some of the many others available today. They will type in one, two, or three words that they think best describe what you do, and hit Enter. How well you have completed your SEO will determine your position on the search engine results pages. If you did a good job, you will rank high—if not in the first position, then at least on the first page of results. Ensuring that your page appears on this first page is referred to as an *organic listing* or *organic search,* and in terms of SEO, it simply means that you are optimizing your web page(s) so you have the best ranking possible as determined by the search engines.

A plethora of books can teach you the specifics of all of the SEO techniques you can perform to guarantee you always have the highest ranking in the organic listings, but that's not what this chapter is about. Rather, this chapter explains the dozen or so techniques that anyone can perform that will probably attain 95 percent of everything you need to do to get your company's web pages or personal web pages listed in the top-10 search engine results for any given keywords.

Back to the Beginning

SEO has been around ever since the first search engine searched for the first computer file. Surprisingly, Google and Yahoo were not the first search engines; Gerard Salton, a professor of computer science at Cornell University, beat them by nearly a half-century. His search engine, and the use of Hypertext (see below), were actually developed in 1965 to locate and retrieve files from the earliest computers.

Salton worked in the field of information retrieval. He and his group developed the SMART (System for the Mechanical Analysis and Retrieval of Text) Information Retrieval System. As a result, Salton authored a 56-page book titled *A Theory of Indexing,* which explained his search theories—many of which are still used today.

Hypertext and the 1960s

In 1960, Ted Nelson developed Project Xanadu.[1] He coined the term *hypertext* in 1963 from *hyper* (meaning motion) and *text* meaning . . . well, text. This moving text then led to the development of the term *HTTP* (Hyper Text Transfer Protocol)—which are the first four characters of every web page address; and *HTML* (Hyper Text Markup Language), which is the language used today to create web pages. And of course, *WWW* stands for "World Wide Web."

Here's an example of how a typical web address would read if spelled out completely:

- *Original:* www.theSocialMediaBible.com/Index.html
- *Spelled out:* World Wide Web.theSocialMediaBible.Commercial/Index Page.Hyper Text Markup Language

(For a live interview with the inventor of the Hyper Text Protocol, Vint Cerf, go to www.theSocialMediaBible.com.)

Enter the Military and ARPAnet

Salton's and Nelson's work eventually led to the 1972 creation of ARPAnet (Advanced Research Projects Agency Network; see Figure 20.2), the predecessor to today's Internet. The very first official search engine emerged in 1990. It was called Archie—from the word *ARCHIvE*—and was created by McGill University student Alan Emtage in Montreal, Canada. By 1993, there were only a few hundred web sites to index, most of which were owned by colleges and universities.

Search capabilities allowed early Internet users to access a file; however, they didn't come with the ability to share files back and forth. For this application, Tim Burners-Lee developed FTP (File Transfer Protocol), a program used in place of HTTP for uploading and downloading files directly from a server.

The Internet has come a long way since the inception of HTTP, HTML, FTP, and Archie. SEO is an incredibly important element of Internet marketing that requires you to create a web page in the most efficient manner possible to facilitate its retrieval by a modern-day search engine.

What You Need to Know

A typical Internet search has three components to it. The first is a huge database that contains every word from every page from every web site in the

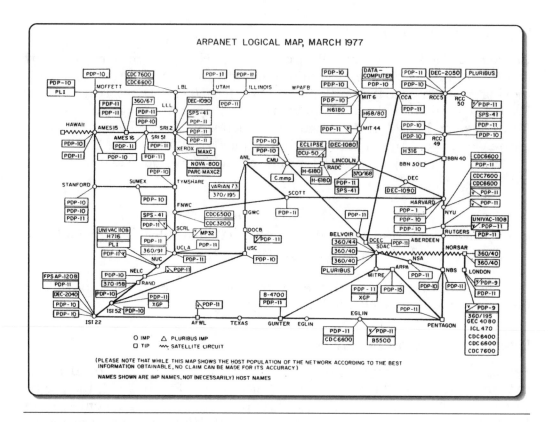

FIGURE 20.2 ARPAnet

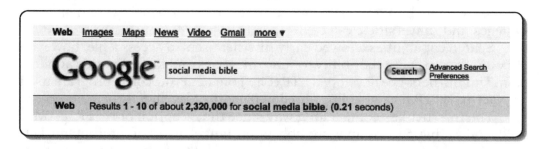

FIGURE 20.3 Google "Social Media Bible" Search

world. This database can be searched and matched very quickly against any word(s) that you enter into a search engine. For example, at the time this chapter was written, a query of the term "social media" in Google (see Figure 20.3) returned "Results 1–10 of about 95,600,000 for Social Media. (0.27 seconds)."

Thus, Google was showing the first 10 results—or matches—of 95.6 million possible matches; and it found all 95.6 million records in less than 0.27 seconds (see Figure 20.4). Pretty impressive!

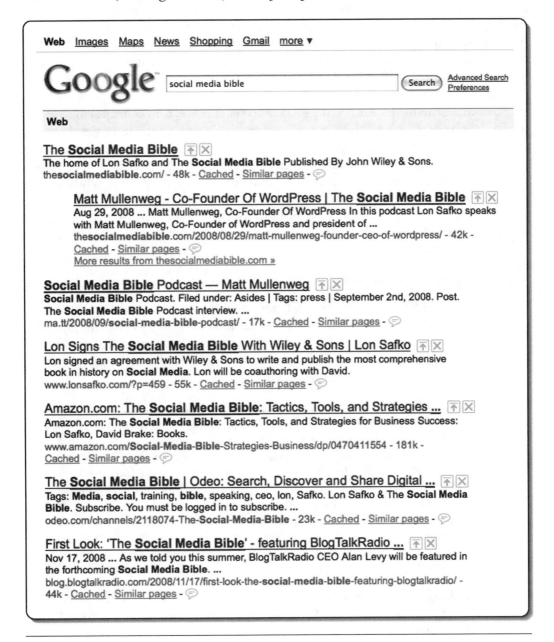

FIGURE 20.4 TSMB Search

The second component of a search engine is its spiders, robots, or just bots. These terms are metaphors for automated computer programs that go out and creep around on the Internet—find a web site, and crawl from page to page indexing and cataloging each page's content. Sound creepy? In reality, the search engine's computer simply opens a home page, captures the content, and goes onto the next page, and does the same thing. And the reason that activity usually takes place at night is that Internet traffic is at its lowest.

James Burnes of MediaSauce describes it this way: "Because search engines are constantly indexing sites across the web, it is imperative that business' content be updated as soon as possible online to increase the relevancy and likelihood that your content will appear the next time someone searches for content. The reality is that bots/spiders run 24/7/365. The sooner you add content relevant to a user's search terms, the quicker you have a chance to be in front of them."

The third part of the process is your typical search interface, which is what you see when you go to Google or Yahoo! when you enter your query and see the results.

Search Engine Optimization

Let's first look at SEO, or organic listings. You can do many different things to your web site to achieve a high SEO ranking. While many are ethical, some are not. Most of them are fairly simple to execute, however, once you know how they work; nearly all of them are time-consuming. Everything you do in

---

The truth be told: Al Gore never actually meant to say that he invented the Internet. The joke was somewhat misleading and out of context, related to a statement Gore made during an interview with Wolf Blitzer on CNN's *Late Edition* in 1999. When asked to describe what distinguished him from his challenger for the Democratic presidential nomination, Senator Bill Bradley of New Jersey, Gore replied, "During my service in the United States Congress, I took the initiative in creating the Internet. I took the initiative in moving forward a whole range of initiatives that have proven to be important to our country's economic growth and environmental protection, improvements in our educational system."

Source: www.snopes.com/quotes/Internet.asp; CNN's transcript of that interview: www.cnn.com/ALLPOLITICS/stories/1999/03/09/president.2000/transcript .gore/index.html.

---

terms of SEO is meant to satisfy the search engine's algorithm (pronounced "Al-Gore-Rhythm"; you can insert the joke of your choice here).

The Infamous Algorithm

An algorithm is just a mathematical formula that each search engine uses to determine how well your page matches against the user's query. Remember, Google or Yahoo!'s only real purpose is to return the most relevant match. The more sophisticated the algorithm, the more relevant the match is; the better the match, the more you will use that search engine. The incentive for a Google or Yahoo! is that a search engine will make more revenue from their advertisers every time it's used. When you consider Google's 2007 revenues were $17.91 billion, a lot is riding on the quality of its algorithm.

If you want to see how your web site is listed in the search engines, go to either Google or Yahoo! and type "site: www.yourdomain.com" (no spaces) into the search box. This will pull up all of the pages that have been indexed by that search engine. If an important page of yours isn't listed, it's not indexed—and you need to find out why.

Everyone—including the authors of this book—wants to know exactly how each of the search engines work. But the fact is that no one knows. As you can imagine, anything that helps generate $18 billion in revenues is a closely guarded secret. So how do you find out what you can do to get that competitive edge? You test, test, test, and add a little common sense. The good news is that certain techniques will get your web page ranked top in the search engines. Don Schindler, Digital Strategist at MediaSauce, www .MediaSauce.com said:

> "The search engine algorithms are based on "trust" and search engine language. They want to trust your web site, they want to trust that what you say you are is what you really are. They want to trust your relevance on the subject the searcher cares about. The search engine language is keywords, tags and text. Right now, it is all a search engine can read. If your web site is relevant but can't be properly understood then it can't be ranked properly. When it comes to trust—the age of your site is important as well. If the URL is new to search engines, it is not trusted as much. If it is older and has had content on it for a long time, then the search engines trust the site more than new. This doesn't mean that site is put up and forgotten. Old content does not help drive SEO unless it is very meaningful to the audience."

The Key to Keywords

The most important criteria that a search engine examines are your keywords. These are the words that you (or your web programmer) have told the search engine are the best possible words to describe the content on your web page. These terms are placed into something called *meta tags,* which are the first thing you will see when you look at the code for your web page. Here is some of the HTML code text for The Social Media Bible web site:

<!DOCTYPE html PUBLIC "-//W3C//DTD XHTML 1.0 Transitional// EN" "www.w3.org/TR/xhtml1/DTD/xhtml1-transitional.dtd"> . . .

<title>The Social Media Bible</title>

<meta name="generator" content="WordPress 2.6.5"/> <!-- leave this for stats--> . . .

. . . <link rel="alternate" type="application/rss+xml" title="The Social Media Bible RSS Feed" href="theSocialMediaBible.com/ feed/"/> . . .

. . . <meta name="description" content="The home of The Social Media Bible Published By John Wiley & Sons, Inc."/>

<meta name="keywords" content="social media, social media bible, lon safko, marketing, pr, sales, innovation"/>.

Take a thorough look at your meta tags. There is a chance that your web page is missing an important component in terms of your keywords, and this is where you look to find out. The missing components may have happened because the technical person programming your page didn't know what the meta tags should be and didn't bother to ask, whereas your marketing person knows your keywords, but might not be quite sure what a meta tag is. That's why you need to find out!

Content Is King

This industry has a saying: "Content Is King." The content of each of your web pages is critical. Evaluating that content—and choosing the most appropriate words to describe it—are an important part of SEO. You can read the page several times, or go to www.theSocialMediaBible .com and find the downloads for this chapter. A fun little macro there will help you. Copy the text from the page that you want to analyze, and paste it into a Word document. Run the Key Word macro, and it will tell you every word you used in that text and the exact number of times you used them. Look at the list, and disregard words like *at, is, a,* and *the.* Look at the main words, and determine which are the most important. This will help generate a list of keywords.

Once you've created your list, either place those words in your Meta Data line using a web page programming tool such as DreamWeaver, or give it to your technical person to do. It will literally take less than five minutes, so don't pay an exorbitant fee.

One of the most important pieces to SEO is the URL. Having proper keyword terms within the URL can really help your SERP position because of algorithm. Search engines put much emphasis on the URL. Not only is it good to have keywords in the main URL but also in the sub-domains like www.businessnamekeyword.com/keyword-keyword-keyword.html and make sure you use dashes and not underscores as some search engines have problems reading underscores as separations.

Next is the Title Tags. Title tags should be your keywords but they should also match the content. If the Title Tags are not matched for the content or they are duplicated for multiple pages, the search engines will downgrade the Title Tag emphasis in indexing. Using less than 70 characters in the Title tags helps the search engines to focus on what the page means to the site.

Meta-Descriptions are important not for keywords but for users to understand what the page is. If you do not have a description for each page, the search engine may not know what to use for the description of the site and will either pull content from the page or pull a description from their database which can be written by a directory web editor. The main thing you should take from here is that it is important if you want users to hear your message. This shouldn't be longer than 150 characters.

Finally, you can add Meta-Keywords. Only use 7 to 10 keywords in this section. Any more are wasted and considered unnecessary by most SEO experts.

"MediaSauce frequently uses the free tools from Webconfs.com to analyze the keywords. We like them because it automatically disregards words that the search engines don't see and it picks up the title tags, keywords, navigation and alt tags on the page," recommends Don Schindler, digital strategist for MediaSauce, www.webconfs.com/keyword-density-checker.php.

The Fresher, the Better

The next most important criteria is the notion of *content freshness.* Think about it. Many of our company's web pages haven't been changed since the year of the flood! If your job was to return only the most relevant results from a search, and two pages came up—one from 2003, and one that was updated yesterday—which page would you return to the customer?

The search engine assumes that the fresher the content, the more relevant the web page will be, which is where common sense comes in. You need to keep your content current. This is why all search engines put such a high priority on blogs, because blogs (see Chapter 8, The Ubiquitous Blog) by definition are new and fresh.

Don't ever try to fool the search engines into thinking that your content is fresh by changing a word or two and resaving. They know, and they penalize. Search engines actually compare, page for page, the difference between your new page and the one they last indexed. If it isn't considerably different, then you don't get the index points.

External Reputable Links

This crucial topic applies to web pages and blogs. An external reputable link is the place where another web site links back to yours. The more external web sites that link back to your web site, the better. Think about the logic behind this. Let's use two hypothetical web sites again—yours and your competitor's. Say that the search engine sees that 25 other web sites are linking to your competitor as a resource, and no one is linking to yours. Which one of you gets the higher ranking?

Of course, people have attempted to figure out how to try to beat the system. One group sold placement on a web site that consisted solely of web page links to other web sites. Sites like these are called *link farms*—don't use them! (This is where the word *reputable* comes in.) Search engines look at the content of the referring web sites to see if there is any similarity. If another web site is linking to yours, there is probably a reason; and there should be some similar words. If the referring web site is only a bunch of links . . . you get penalized. Again, think about the search engines' responsibility and interest in returning the best possible matches.

A very simple test can show you how many other web sites are linking back to yours. Go to Google and type "link:www.yourdomain.com," or go to Yahoo! and enter "linkdomain:www.yourdomain.com." You will immediately see how well you are doing. If you don't have at least 20 or so links to your site, you will need to consider setting up a link exchange campaign. This is where you search the Internet for complementing but not competing web sites, contact them, and pitch them on the notion that if they link to your site from their site, you will do the same for them. This tends to take a lot of time and follow-up, but it's worth it in the end.

One more tip: always check to be sure that each of your web pages has a unique page title, as discussed earlier in the chapter. All too often, web sites contain many untitled pages. This is a foolish oversight, and it's easily corrected. Name your pages, and ask your technical person to simply type the name in and save the page. That's all there is to it! It's a little bit of effort that can have a significant effect.

Last, read (or reread) Chapter 5, It's Not Your Father's E-Mail, and understand the importance of WIIFM (What's In It for Me?), because no matter how high your page ranking is—or how many potential customers you get to visit your web site—if they don't find something of value, they are out of there!

Don Schindler, digital strategist at MediaSauce, www.MediaSauce.com said:

> "This is actually a very, very important. External links mean more than almost all other pieces. This is also why black hat **SEO** guys can be successful quickly. They use unethical linking strategies to build networks and link sites together to push a site up to the top of a **SERP** for a specific keyword. But these sites quickly fail because search engines are getting better at discovering these sites and blacklist them.
>
> Every site has 'voting' capability for any other site. If site A is linking to site B, then site A is passing along some of its PageRank to site B. If site A links to a lot of sites on the same page, then it's voting relevance or link juice is degraded. If site A and site B are just linking back and forth to each other then both sites might be degraded.
>
> The higher the site's PageRank the more voting power it has. You want quality links from sites with high PageRank but that are also relevant to your content. If the search engines see that the two sites do not have anything in common, then the link juice will be degraded.
>
> Some of the highest ranking sites are sites where links cannot be purchased like .edu or .gov sites. There are many ways to link your site to other sites especially through social media. Blog commenting is one of the most popular."

Practices to Avoid

Keyword Density: There is also an aspect of **SEO** known as *keyword density.* Search engine spiders check this by analyzing your list of important keywords and checking the number of times those words are actually used on your web page. This helps to prevent a process called *hijacking,* which occurs when someone lists important words such as "presidential election" for a web site that sells shoes in order to garner traffic for the site. Think about how much traffic you might generate with keywords that aren't true. It's actually *none*, because search engines check and penalize for this kind of dishonest keyword stuffing. Four to seven percent density is good for any given keyword. Go to the download section of www.theSocialMediaBible .com for your free Word Density Analyzer Macro.

A quick word of caution on web sites that have Flash web pages: because they don't have text content and keywords, getting a high ranking on such pages has been impossible in the past with a standard Flash design. Flash sites can now be optimized via web objects to showcase content. URL, title tags, description, and keywords are all available to use. Building an alternative HTML site specifically for the search engines is not only possible but is widely used and effective.

You Can't Hide Cloaking: A practice called *cloaking* is also worth mentioning. No, it doesn't have anything to do with *Star Trek*'s Klingons' ability to go invisible. It's about trying to hide your stuffing keywords—the ones that really have nothing to do with your content, and are only there to hijack web traffic—in plain sight. How might one do this? By loading your page's content with those unrelated words in a text color that is the same as the background. What would you see? Nothing!

However, the search engines are wise to this, and can spot it quickly— and if you get caught trying to cheat a search engine, you will be banned from that search engine for up to five years. Imagine learning that your web page will never be listed in a search again for the following half a decade. Try explaining that to your supervisor or to your board of directors.

Tips, Techniques, and Tactics

Here is a quick list of some of the techniques mentioned in this chapter, and some that weren't addressed:

- Don't flood or stuff keywords with words not found in your pages' content.
- Don't bury or cloak text with the same color as the background or in margins.
- Don't participate in link farms.
- Don't use redirects, URLs, or web addresses that don't have pages, but only redirect the browser to another page unless you use a 301 redirect

to permanently direct traffic to another site. Also you need to make sure you redirect your www.domain.com to domain.com—search engines see www and your domain.com as two separate sites. A permanent redirect on the www is a must.

- Do have at least 25 reputable external links back to your site from other reputable sites—it's a good start. Much more are required today to get significant SERP ranking movement. Remember, they must link from other high-traffic or high-impact sites within your industry.
- Do use vortals or Vertical Web Portal, directories (hubs), and blogs for link backs. See Chapter 6, The World of Web Pages, or search Google for more information.
- Do rearrange your keywords to create keyword phrases.
- Do be sure that the keywords in your metas match your page content.
- Do create unique titles containing your most important keywords.
- Do include your keywords in your meta description.
- Do create good content (which contain your keywords).
- Do have at least eight keyword hyperlinks (internal, external, anchor).
- Do have at least eight keyword alt tags.
- Do place your keywords in your anchor code (see your programmer for this).
- Do place your keywords in your file names: .jpg, .gif, .asp, .php.
- Do link PDFs and text documents with keywords in actual content of those documents.
- Do create comprehensive sitemaps. There should be two sitemaps. One for users, which can be a straight HTML page and one for Google which should be XML. This is very helpful for search engines.
- Do place your keywords in captions and headings. H1 headings have the most emphasis followed by H2, H3, then bold.
- Do use bullets, bold, and underlined (hyperlinked) text, for emphasis for both your viewers and the search engine spiders.
- Do keep your pages fresh with at least 15–25 percent change. While there is no "time" limit on freshness, the fresher the better!
- Do use subdirectories: www.yourdomain.com/aligator/yourpage.html. The best solution is to use www.yourdomain.com/aligator/your-page and eliminate the ".html". Also, never go over four slashes total, and never use variables or "?" in the html.

- Do use subdomains: www.aligator.yourdomain.com, where you create a folder with a keyword name. See your IT person to learn if and how you can do this.
- Never use FRAMES to build a web site. Search engines cannot read web sites that are inside frames.
- Keep navigation out of javascript with dropdowns. This is also harder for search engines to read.

Dozens and dozens of search engine criteria are used nowadays. Every time you score in a particular area, your web page gets points. Once the search engine's algorithm has tested everything and has awarded all of the possible points for each category, the algorithm then computes an overall *page rank*. You can see every page's ranking in the Google menu bar as a progressive green bar. The greener your page gets, the higher it's ranked. (Side note: the term *page rank* was first used by one of the founders of Google, Larry Page. Perhaps it's more than a coincidence that it's called "page *rank*.")

Providers

SEO is a skill set that requires some technical understanding of HTML and how web pages function. The purpose of this chapter is to make you aware of the importance of SEO, to give you some tools that will allow you to check your existing web pages to see if they have been properly designed, and to begin setting up your SEM keyword campaign. The biggest question that you likely have at this juncture is whether you wish to take on these additional projects yourself, assign them to someone else internally, or hire a consultant to accomplish these tasks for you. It always comes down to in-house or out-house.

Literally thousands of companies can perform SEO (Search Engine Optimization), but there are few especially good ones. Now that you have read this chapter, you can much better determine which are superior. A simple question to ask a potential SEO contractor is how they feel about cloaking. If they support these practices, just ask them to leave. The best way to win at SEO is to be honest. If you do the right things, you will be listed highly on the search engines. If you try to trick them, it may work for a while; but you're likely to be caught eventually, and you'll suffer the consequences.

Expert Insight

Benj Arriola, 2007 SEO world champion, www.benjarriola.com.

Benj Arriola

I was really fascinated [when I first heard about] SEO; I'm pretty much a competitive person. I like to challenge myself and see how far my skills will reach in comparison with the rest of the people in the world. So that was my main interest. It was not really to win; it was really to test out the skills that I have. And I believe, in any SEO contest, it's a learning process where you discover new things. So when I tried it out—and I've done several contests also in the past—I was fortunate enough to win both the contest and a brand-new car in 2007.

So, what it is. Search Engine Optimization, from the word itself . . . often might be a web site, to perform well, a search engine, as we all know in the Internet today existing in many of the web sites. Google is almost like a verb today. People will say, "You Googled it."

People get to web sites today through these search engines. They search for what they're looking for. It could be a product, it could be a service; and in Search Engine Optimization this [means] making sure that web sites perform well, and search engines give these web sites top rankings. Top rankings are the first position in the search engine results—trying to be there in the top number-one spot, or at least to be in the first three pages. Because, as research shows, most people don't go beyond the first page. . . .

Comparing [SEO] to traditional media; you know, compare it to a TV, print, and radio. With Search Engine Optimization, at least you know that your target market is really searching for *you*; unlike TV ad spots, where you are relying on demographic data, hoping that the watching audience is your target market, even if they're not really looking for your product or service. . . .

First, there are really some credible Search Engine Optimization companies out there, and there are also some that aren't. . . . They think they know what they are doing, but they don't "really" know what they are doing; or some purposely do not know what they are doing, but they are still selling the service. So, pitfalls. First is guaranteed rankings: any company that guarantees rankings or ranking. That is already a red flag. You cannot really guarantee an organic spot; what you could guarantee, probably, is a sponsored result, or using Pay for Click advertising. But that is also not guaranteed, depending on the budget a client is willing to spend.

There are so many companies that are focused on ranking today. And SEO today is slowly moving into the direction of looking into conversions,

(continued)

(continued)

where a conversion is either a sale or a lead or having someone . . . having a visitor download the software . . . the trial software, an e-book, a white paper. That is what you want. You want someone to use your site, because sometimes you can concentrate so much on ranking that even though you get the number-one spot for your targeted keyword, if they visit your site and they are not pleased, they hit the Back button, they go to the number-two one and they *are* pleased, you lost your market right there. . . .

I believe that SEO works hand in hand with everything else in the whole Internet marketing business. SEO teams and your web-development team should have no conflicts at all. I believe usability and SEO also go well hand in hand. And I believe every other form of Internet marketing should work well with SEO, from e-mail marketing to social media marketing. All of this should merge together in one big pen. . . .

So, basically that contest was . . . the keywords were about global warming. So what I wanted to make is, really, a good-content site; because a web site with really good content could be viral . . . and add that twist of controversy, add something that would push people to really . . . when someone reads it they should have a feeling that they really want to pass it on to someone they know. It could be in any medium; by word-of-mouth, by phone, by e-mail, by IM, in forums, in blogs . . . and that's the viral . . . that's the whole viral content.

Now, if your site isn't virally working already, imagine just putting in social media within it, from social bookmarking to social networking, each person is connected to another person. It makes the spread even go faster. And when that spreads, that's the ultimate link maker right there.

To listen to or read the entire Executive Conversation with Benj Arriola, go to www.the SocialMediaBible.com.

Commandments

1. **Thou shalt understand your keywords for every page.**

   Be sure that every individual page is analyzed for its own keywords. You want to bring your customer to the exact page at the exact time they are ready to convert. (See Chapter 6, The World of Web Pages, for more on this.)

2. **Thou shalt check your page titles.**

   It's an easy thing to do, and to overlook. Open your pages and look in the Title Bar. Come up with a title that includes your most important keywords, and remember to do so for every page.

3. **Thou shalt check your meta keywords.**

Open your page, select View, then Page View, and look for your meta keywords. If they don't reflect your content, then you won't get ranked highly.

4. **Thou shalt build your external reputable links.**

Type "Site: www.YourDomain.com" into Google, and see how good you are doing. If you don't have 20 external reputable links, then go get some.

5. **Thou shalt never try to trick a spider.**

Never, ever try to trick a search engine spider. It might work for a while, but they always will catch you. If they do, you could be banned from search engines for up to five years.

6. **Thou shalt always have a strong WIIFM.**

This is always the most important commandment. Whether it's SEO, SEM, e-mail, web pages, or a hard copy brochure, your marketing message *always* has to have a strong "What's In It for Me?" (See Chapter 5, It's Not Your Father's E-Mail, for more information on this.)

Conclusion

What does SEO have to do with social media? A lot! It's all about having a presence on the Web. It's about being found exactly when your customers are looking for you. It's about being found before your customers find your competition. It's about always showing up in a listing no matter what your customer types in when they're trying to find your product or service—despite where they are in the buying cycle, or whatever keyword they think is relevant. And it's about being part of the World Wide Web with integrity.

Readings and Resources

Darie, Cristian, and Jaimie Sirovich. *Professional Search Engine Optimization with ASP.NET: A Developer's Guide to SEO.* (Hoboken, NJ: John Wiley & Sons, Inc.)

———. *Professional Search Engine Optimization with PHP: A Developer's Guide to SEO.* (Hoboken, NJ: John Wiley & Sons, Inc.)

Grappone, Jennifer, and Gradiva Couzin. *Search Engine Optimization: An Hour a Day.* 2nd ed. (Hoboken, NJ: John Wiley & Sons, Inc.)

Jones, Kristopher B. *Search Engine Optimization: Your Visual Blueprint for Effective Internet Marketing.* (Hoboken, NJ: John Wiley & Sons, Inc.)

Kent, Peter. *Search Engine Optimization For Dummies*. 3rd ed. (Hoboken, NJ: John Wiley & Sons, Inc.)

Ledford, Jerri L. *SEO: Search Engine Optimization Bible*. (Hoboken, NJ: John Wiley & Sons, Inc.)

Downloads

For your free downloads associated with *The Social Media Bible,* go to www.theSocialMediaBible.com, and enter your ISBN number located on the back of the book above the bar code. Be sure to enter the dashes.

Credits

Expert Insight Was Provided By:

Benj Arriola, 2007 SEO world champion, www.benjarriola.com.

Technical Edits Were Provided By:

James Burnes, vice president, MediaSauce, www.MediaSauce.com.

Don Schindler, digital strategist, MediaSauce, www.MediaSauce.com.

Note

1. Project Xanadu was the very first hypertext project, founded in 1960 by Ted Nelson. "Today's popular software simulates paper. The World Wide Web (another imitation of paper) trivializes our original hypertext model with one-way ever-breaking links and no management of version or contents."

CHAPTER 21

Marketing Yourself (Search Engine Marketing)

Search Engine Marketing (SEM) is one of the most effective ways you can market and advertise your web site on the Internet. There is nearly no financial risk; the costs are incredibly low when compared to any type of conventional advertising; and, unlike any other advertising, it's based on performance. There is, however, a great deal of risk involved if you don't understand that everything you say and do is part of your online brand.

People forget that you can't separate one from the other and it gets them in trouble. When was the last time you've heard a newspaper, radio, television, or magazine tell you that if your ad doesn't generate calls, you don't have to pay for it? Never.

Although it's possible for this chapter to be read and implemented without reading Chapter 20, Spotlight on Search (Search Engine Optimization), you are strongly recommended to also read that chapter. The two are complementary; one is the yin to the other's yang. And although either can be executed without the other, the synergy of doing both well can put you in the top of the rankings.

What's In It for You?

As discussed in Chapter 20, Spotlight on Search (Search Engine Optimization), when you take the time and follow the simple guidelines to making your web page appealing to the search engine spiders, you will rank the highest on the organic or nonpaid listings. When you add a well-thought-out SEM keyword advertising campaign, you will own the sponsored listings. When SEO and SEM are combined on one web page, the rankings are unstoppable.

theSocialMediaBible.com

SEM Stands for Search Engine Marketing

When someone is looking for the type of product or service you provide, they will use their favorite search engine—be it Google, Yahoo!, MSN, Ask, or one of the countless others available today. They will type in one to several words that they think best describe what you do or offer, and they will hit Enter.

SEM in part means marketing your web page(s) through a paid CPC (Cost-Per-Click) or PPC (Pay-Per-Click) marketing plan. You still have to consider your blog (see Chapter 8, The Ubiquitous Blog). If you are running an SEM campaign and are paying for PPC, the extent to which you manage your keyword campaigns will determine where you show up on the Sponsored Links section of the search page, how much you are paying per click, and what you are spending each month for that campaign. This is referred to as a *paid listing*. When you use Yahoo!, Google, or other search engines to perform a search, you will usually see the organic listings in the left column, and the paid listings on the right column (or sometimes in the top several rows on the left above the organic listings).

Back to the Beginning

SEM Is Named and Introduced

The SEM advertising system first appeared in February 1998, when Jeffrey Brewer presented the Pay-Per-Click concept at the TED8 conference in California. Goto.com founder Bill Gross is given credit for conceiving of PPC while working at IdeaLab in Pasadena, California. Gross's 25-employee start-up became Yahoo!'s Overture, which is Yahoo!'s Search Engines' Pay-Per-Click system.

Google offered its own, impression-based form of search engine advertising in December 1999, based on CPM or Cost-Per-1,000 impressions (or views). They introduced AdWords in October 2000, which allowed their users to create their own ads for placement on the Google Search Engine result pages. In 2002, Google switched to PPC, the then-successful Yahoo! advertising model.

What You Need to Know

Assuming that you have read Chapter 8, The Ubiquitous Blog, and began blogging, and read Chapter 20, Spotlight on Search (Search Engine Optimization), and have performed your SEO, your pages are gradually being ranked higher in the organic listings. It's now time to work on your SEM—or simply, your Pay-Per-Click advertising.

PPC advertising requires that you decide which keywords or keyword phrases you used in your SEO campaign are most important—the ones that best match those that your customer will type into a search engine when trying to find your site. It's also the words and phrases that come directly from your web site's content—the words you will be able to pay for when a potential customer clicks on your link.

The definition of SEM used in this chapter is relatively generic, as the best way to experience the ease and excitement of creating and managing an SEM campaign is by actually *doing* it. Also, each search engine is a little different in terms of how you go about creating an account, adding funds to your budget, and reporting on its success.

While there are many providers of PPC, banner advertising, and other pay-for-performance advertisers, Google is by far the largest. According to VentureBeat Digital Media, the top five search engines in market share at the time of this writing were as follows: Google 61.6 percent; Yahoo! 20.4 percent; Microsoft 9.1 percent; AOL 4.6 percent; and Ask 4.3 percent. There is still a several-year trend of Google gaining market share (mostly from Yahoo!). What does this mean? That it's probably best to start your SEM campaigns with Google AdWords, as it already owns almost two-thirds of the market share or two-thirds of your potential customers.

Start Your SEM Campaign

To launch your SEM keyword campaign, you should begin with a three word keyword phrase. Three words are significantly more specific than a single word and will have a higher keyword—the one you like best. Go to the SEM provider for your search engine of choice, such as Google AdWords, Yahoo! Search Engine Marketing (formerly Overture), or Microsoft's AdCenter, and sign up for an account; you can do this with a credit card or a PayPal account (Figure 21.1). Then follow the easy steps to complete your registration and set up a keyword campaign.

After you select your keyword, you'll want to see what others are willing to pay each time someone clicks on the word from the sponsored links section of that search engine. The more generic the word, the more expensive the CPC (Cost-Per-Click) is. Often, the keyword you like best is one that other advertisers desire most as well. This can drive the CPC up to a point where you may want to consider using a less effective—but less expensive—keyword.

While most keywords can cost under one dollar, many are as high as five dollars per click, and they can even go as high as eighty dollars for terms like

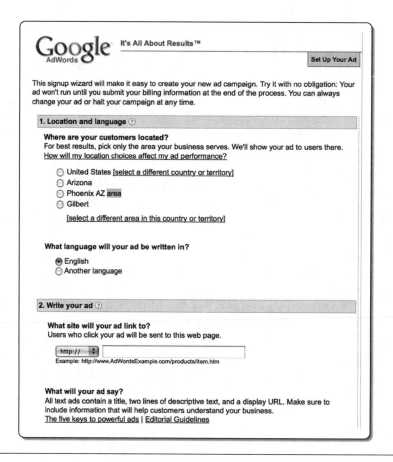

FIGURE 21.1   AdWords Wizard

"Austin DUI," for example. Once you've done several keyword campaigns, you will find the *sweet spot*—the word that generates the most traffic at the lowest CPC.

What Are You Willing to Pay?

The next step is to indicate how much you are willing to spend on each click. It's a bidding system, and even though the last CPC was fifty cents, you may want to raise the stakes and claim that you're willing to pay one dollar for that same click. By bidding higher, you have the opportunity to be placed higher on the search engine's list of paid sponsors. Remember: the reason and purpose in life for a search engine is the theory of relativity—that is, they must always return the most relative search results. The same is true for paid sponsors; the victory doesn't always go to the highest bidder. Your organic page rank—and how often your sponsored click has been used in the past—all determine your position.

Now that you have selected a keyword and know how much it will cost you each time someone clicks on it, the search engines will ask for your monthly budget: how much you are willing to spend each month on clicks for that keyword. Start with a small amount—say, $100—and watch the keyword's progress over the next 30 days. That's all there is to it!

The next time you go to that search engine and type in your keyword or keyword phrase, you will be listed in the sponsored link section. If someone is listed above you, it means that they are willing to pay more than your maximum bid, or that they historically had a good click-through rate (which means that people clicked on them more often than the competing sponsors).

How the Search Engines Charge You

The good thing about the search engine's bids is that you don't have to pay your full bid Price-Per-Click if someone picks you over the competition. You only have to pay two cents more than the next higher bidder. This continues 24 hours a day, so at the end of the month, you may have a surplus of funds in your budget. If your funds become exhausted, you will receive a notice from your search engine partner that your money is about to run out, and you will be asked if you would like to add more money. If you do, everything continues normally. If you choose not to, you simply no longer appear in the sponsored listing.

Just as there is always someone trying to beat the SEO system with techniques like link farms, cloaking, and keyword stuffing, people try to beat the SEM system as well. Suppose, for example, that your competitor hires someone at minimum wage to sit and click on your sponsored link all day. Within a short amount of time, they would have spent your entire SEM budget!

Things like this really did happen for a while. Then the search engines got wind of it and stopped it from happening. Now search engines track your Internet Protocol, or IP Address, which is a number assigned to your computer that looks like this: 74.213.164.71. An IP Address is unique and identifies each computer on a network. It can be for private use on a Local Area Network (LAN, like at work or your wireless network at home), or for public use on the Internet or other Wide Area Network (WAN, a network that interconnects geographically distributed computers, LANs, or the Internet). The search engine checks the IP Address of the clicker, and if there are multiple clicks from the same user, it credits your account—and even bans that user from clicking in the future. (Don't you just love this stuff?)

Once you see the Return on Investment (ROI) on your SEM keyword campaign, you will want to go back to the search engine and create additional campaigns for new keywords and phrases. While teaching at a conference in Portland, Oregon, one of the authors met someone who manages 165 keyword campaigns every month! He said that he spends a lot of money on them, but that they usually return 350 percent of what he spends in sales—and generates new customers. This alone is worth the cost of customer acquisition.

Tips, Techniques, and Tactics

To get started on your own SEM campaign, take the following steps:

1. Go to www.theSocialMediaBible.com and download your Key Word macro.
2. Use the macro to determine your most important key words.
3. Use the keyword finder in Google or Yahoo! to gauge what others are paying for the keywords that you have selected.
4. Determine how much of an initial budget you are willing to spend on each of your keyword campaigns.
5. Consider two- and three-word keyword phrases, as they are often less expensive and significantly more specific—and can return more effective results.

Providers

SEO and SEM both represent skill sets that require some technical understanding of HTML and how web pages function. The purpose of this chapter is to make you aware of the importance of both of these processes; to give you some tools that will allow you to check your existing web pages to see if they have been properly designed; and to begin setting up your SEM key word campaign.

The biggest question you probably have at this juncture is whether you wish to take on the SEM projects yourself, assign them to someone else internally, or hire a consultant to accomplish these tasks for you. As with SEO, the next decision you have to make is whether to complete these projects in- or out-of-house. Many companies can manage your SEM campaigns, but always keep in mind that someone else won't watch your money as carefully as you would watch it. Unless you have a dedicated person who can manage your campaigns, managing a consultant might be easier.

Considering the information presented earlier on the top five search engines by market share at the time of this writing, you'll probably want to start with Google, and then look at Yahoo!. Remember that even though Google and Yahoo! account for 82 percent of the total market, your particular customers might prefer using the Ask search engine. Experiment, and try different search engines to determine the most effective way to reach your customers.

Expert Insight

Gretchen Howard, director of online sales and operations, Google AdWords, www.google.com/corporate/execs.html

Gretchen Howard

. . . I'm a director at Google and I work on online sales and operations and I've been at Google for about two and a half years. I had a varied path before I landed at Google. I worked in financial services and also in consulting before that. . . .

. . . Sure, let's start with an acronym that you mentioned from the start, Search Engine Marketing, or SEM. Search Engine Marketing is really not intermixed with online advertising. It refers to programs that enable advertisers to run relevant ads alongside search results. So when users perform queries on a search engine, such as Google, online advertisement will also come up. . . .

. . . These onlines are featured advertisements that you're talking about; this is what we call AdWords. So AdWords is just Google's online advertising program. And we really like to describe AdWords as, it may sound a little corny but I like to explain it as a match-making service that can match businesses and customers. They're really the tools that connect businesses to a product and services that sell and customers who are looking for those specific products and services, and online. And it's really done by matching relevant products and services to customers' search queries and the thing that excites me most about AdWords is that it's highly targeted and cost-effective. So it's a measurable system that helps advertisers, both large and small, find their customers online. . . .

. . . It's all about relevance, and so it's really easy to set up. One thing, just to take you quickly through how it works: When you go to http://www.google.com/adwords you selected "daily budget" you create an ad. And you target your ad by choosing key words and a geographic location, and then you let it

(continued)

(continued)

run. So it's a cost-per-click model, which means advertisers only pay when users click on their ads. And then they are delivered to the advertisers' web site.

So a click can be as low as one cent and you can modify your daily budget at any time. So you're not trapped into a large fee at any time. . . .

. . . It's a pay-per-click model, and that's why our philosophy is that all advertising should be relevant, targetable, and cost effective. And that's why the pay-per-click model comes in because it holds us accountable and not the advertisers with customers. . . .

. . . The other thing that it does is it really levels the playing field. And so it offers this powerful, measurable solution to the needs of both small and niche businesses, as well as large brand advertisers. So in some ways it really democratizes the Web, which is just ground-breaking. . . .

. . . And it doesn't matter how specific. I mean the more specifically someone's looking for something, the easier they're going to find exactly what they're looking for. And so the user-experience and the customer-experience are both important to their business, and it helps both Google and the online advertisers, as well. So it's really a win-win situation. . . .

. . . So we have an ad-traffic-quality team and they're constantly at EQ. We have a three-stage system for detecting invalid clicks. The three features are (1) Proactive real-time filters, (2) Proactive off-line analysis, and (3) Reactive investigation. And this combined approach is really the essence of click-fraud management. The goal is to cap the net of invalid click's efficiently, live, in order to have a high degree of competence so that actual malicious behavior is effectively filtered out.

So by proactively filtering these clicks, potentially worth hundreds of millions of dollars every year, we're able to provide a very effective protection against attempted click-fraud, and we take it very seriously. . . .

. . . Google has devoted significant resources and expertise to developing proactive and technically sophisticated measures to filter invalid clicks before advertisers are ever charged for them. We recognize that advertiser satisfaction, from an advertiser's point of view is extremely important. So we investigate every click-fraud claim that comes into us and we really try to respond to those advertisers' requests as appropriately and timely as possible. . . .

. . . And if we don't catch it proactively (and we do catch most of them proactively) we will absolutely credit advertisers retroactively because the last thing we want is for advertisers to be negatively effected by click-fraud in any way. . . .

. . . But I think this integrity is so key to the essence of our business that it's extremely important for our customer-experience and our advertiser-experience to be top notch. . . .

. . . AdWord actually is very easy to get started. I like to break it down into three main steps. First: As in any time you're creating an advertising campaign, especially an online marketing campaign, I think the first step and advice that I always give people is, "Know your audience; identify your goals." Precision is the key to search advertising. You want to reach the right advertisers at the right time.

Take a good look at the products or services you are selling and the customers who are buying them. You'd be amazed at how many people don't know who their target audience is and this is an essential first step. Then once you have a clear sense of your business, you need to focus on how to reach those customers and you'll need to understand and define what your ultimate goal is, so you can actually measure success.

Then you can look to target specific languages or geographic locations that your business serves, and that could be your region or that could be global. . . .

. . . That's one of the beauties of online advertising. You can change your geographic targeting at any time. So you can expand or contract or actually make seasonal changes based on geographic trends as well. . . .

. . . I think, you know, if you are someone in northern California and you're selling a snowboard, you can have a huge presence in the winter in northern California, but in the summer it's a slow time. So why not market those snowboards to folks in New Zealand where it's winter in your summer? So it's a great way to discount the seasonality of your business. . . .

. . . And that leads me to point #2 and how to get started. It's the second tip that I tell people: "You really have to create effective campaigns." So the first step in that is choosing powerful keywords. Really start brainstorming and expand your list as broadly as possible, and then narrow your focus. Try to think like your customers do and use two- to four-word combinations instead of general words so you really target the audience that you're going after.

The other piece is that advertisers need to write what I call, "Got-to-Click" ads. So those are ads that users feel *compelled* to click on and learn more. Get to the point quickly, convey key product benefits, like free shipping or promotion; and then use "strong-calls-to-action" such as "buy now" or "sign-up today" and really direct users to the landing piece on your site that most relates to your ad. And not just to the general landing page, but make it as specific as possible so people get to the information that they are looking after and so they don't have to navigate further once they reach your web site. . . .

. . . Keep the complexity out of the interaction and you will have many more sales than you ever dreamed possible. And I think that's a great point.

The third step is, "Track, test, adopt, and thrive." You really need to adopt an attitude where you're continually looking at the data that the online advertising provides you, and you continue to experiment. The online advertising environment is really dynamic and you can look at your marketing results and keep a close eye on statistics. And again, this is different from any other form of advertising.

(continued)

(continued)

You can leverage conversion-tracking software. Lots of people provide free software and at Google it's the Google Analytic product, but there's lots of tools like Google Analytic that provide data that will allow you to glean insight into your web site and how to improve it and make changes so you can achieve your goals. . . .

. . . I think using two- to four-word combinations instead of general words is . . . helps you become more targeted to reach that very specific audience, and it is usually much cheaper than a general keyword. . . .

. . . There are lots of other kinds of advertising we do. You can do print campaigns and you can do TV campaigns. . . .

. . . You can do audio campaigns, but I think that will take another whole session when there's time. But we're always looking at ways we can be innovative and, again, bring that targeted, measurable approach to general advertising. . . .

. . . AdSense is (and this is not my area of expertise) the team that manages our relationships with publishers. So they manage something called the "Content Network." The best example of this is to think about the *New York Times*. They have an online presence and they run AdSense advertisements on that page from various publishers that are relevant to the content in their stories.

So if you're online on the New York Times.com and you're reading a story about dogs, there might be advertisement shown from different pet food providers. And that's why we call these publishers, such as the *New York Times*, our AdSense publishers. . . .

. . . Anyone can put AdWords or AdSense ads on their blog and basically anytime someone clicks through an ad from your published site, such as a blog, part of that revenue that's derived from clicking through that ad is shared with the publisher. . . .

. . . It's great for blogs and any type of publishers to actually have that relationship with Google, and it also provides valuable advertisements to their users based on the subject that they're writing about. . . .

. . . You can start at Google.com/Adword, you select a daily budget. That's how much you want to spend per day. You actually create an ad, you write a text ad, and then you choose your key words and geographic location, and that's it! You let it run. So it's really quite easy to set up. You don't have to be tech-savvy to do it. There is a wizard that will take you through step-by-step. But there are some common mistakes that people do do when setting up an account that I'd be happy to walk-through if that's an interest. . . .

To listen to or read the entire Executive Conversation with Gretchen Howard, go to www.theSocialMediaBible.com.

Expert Insight

Linh Tang, coauthor, *Launching Your Yahoo! Business* and *Succeeding at Your Yahoo! Business*, www.LinhTang.com

Linh Tang

Yeah, virtual-electronic-retailing—or V-E-Tailing—is about selling products that are digital. And what I mean by that is you could have [any kind of product]. Ours is paper models; and our Paper Model Inc. is three-dimensional advertising, creating corporate specialty products and school projects. We specialize in replicas of buildings and monuments and even . . . cars. Our main customer is the education market; one model that made our site popular is "California Missions." We've had a lot of fourth-graders who have to come in and build that for their school projects; they come to our web site, download it, print it out on a computer, and within 30 minutes to an hour they have a replica of that particular model. . . .

That's the beauty of electronic retailing. Once you create the product, it's there! People continuously come and purchase your product—unlike eBay, [where] you continuously have to take pictures, upload to your store, and—once you've sold that particular item—go find new products.

Well, SEM marketing first started with optimizing your web site and doing link building. But with social media, it has taken . . . I believe it has taken the corner. What I mean by that is now it incorporates blogs, videos, RSS, social networks, alerts. Now, with the limited time people have, they don't want to come visit your site every day. But what you can do is feed out your information to all these other networks. I call it "The Mall." Why do you want to be at "The Mall"? Because everyone else is there. . . .

Now everybody can get traffic to their web site. You can do a little bit of Search Engine Marketing, but what happens when they're there? Now social media tools, such as video and blogs, give your potential customers added value, added information. For example, one of the web sites I'm working on is Office Chairs Outlet. We did a product demo of one of the chairs, just as if you were walking into the showroom and getting a demo from a salesperson. Now, all the other web sites out there have a little description, which they all get from the manufacturers anyway. But here, we are actually doing a demo for you. So you don't even have to sit and read the page of descriptions; you could actually just sit there and watch a 30-second video of how that chair works, how that chair operates, how it's ergonomic and why it's the best. . . .

You can now put your link, your URL, your web site information on YouTube. So, if anybody went to YouTube, [they could be sent] back to your site for further information. The beauty of YouTube is you can often imbed that

(continued)

(*continued*)

video onto your web site or blog. So you don't have any expensive streaming or hosting fees. . . .

The social media ecosphere is huge. There's a lot of tools out there, and what you should really do is sit down with a social media strategist to see, "What's your first step?" Is it doing video, or just doing a blog? We've seen success by just doing that. You can blog about anything. It doesn't have to be just about your product only—and that's what was going on with Search Engine Optimization, was that you were just "optimizing" using your web site for your information, your keywords.

To listen to or read the entire Executive Conversation with Linh Tang, go to www .theSocialMediaBible.com.

Expert Insight

Patrizio Spagnoletto, senior director of marketing, Yahoo! Search Marketing, www.searchmarketing.yahoo.com

Patrizio Spagnoletto

. . . I have been with Yahoo! for about seven and a half years, and in my current role I manage the marketing team for the search-marketing product, which is basically the product where small and medium-sized businesses (or businesses of all sizes) can be listed in Yahoo! Search results. . . .

. . . To be more specific, it's the marketing part. So our team focuses on the awareness of the product, customer acquisition/retention, and just making sure that our customers, overall, are getting the most out of their investment with us once they start participating in this "sponsored-search world," and that happens through education, communication, and innovation of products that we provide for their products or features of the current search product. . . .

. . . When somebody goes to a search engine on Yahoo.com and searches for, let us say, cars (more specifically a used Honda), what the user has just done is show an explicit intent that he is looking for and willing to purchase that specific product. Now if you flip that and put your advertiser hat on, that is probably the single most qualified lead that you will ever be able to receive. And that is because unlike other marketing media in Sponsored Search, it is the user that tells us that they are interested in buying our products and services. And this all happened because of the search engine results page. . . .

. . . And in fact when you think about it in context of direct response (meaning what a business wants to increase their sales), I really do not think there is any other marketing medium out there that is as affective as Sponsored Search. And we are doing a lot of research to justify a statement like that.

Having said that, marketers have multiple objectives. You know, whether it is "response" (and Sponsored Search does a great job there), or if it's "awareness" (or other mediums like television and the offline world; or graphical ad display which I was a major player in), it is really the combination of the two that makes a business be really successful. Where the sum of the two is much greater than the individual parts.

Yahoo is really in a unique position in that it is truly the only business that can offer the two products on an own-it/operate-it site. On the Yahoo! site you can buy banners and you can buy sponsor search; and therefore, really create what we call a 360 Campaign where you can surround the user with both graphical and sponsor search. . . .

. . . Banner advertising is what most of us see when we go on pretty much any site. It is those graphical advertisements, sometimes they are video, or what we call "rich media," or sometimes they are just static images. But it is a graphical way, for an advertiser to convey their message. And Yahoo!'s invention is a leader in this and has been since the inception of Yahoo!. And we are very good at targeting users through some of our own proprietary data on the back end. This is done in the way that we are able to target (whether it be demographic, behavioral, or graphic), or just some of the ways that we are able to match graphical advertisements with the users. Because online search is where you have the benefit of the user actually telling you what it is that they are looking for. With "graphical," it is really about the more general persona of a person that is visiting the site. . . .

. . . What we typically ask our small-business customer is, first and foremost, what is your objective? If their objective is really that they want *direct response,* that is a clear signal that they should really be investing at least their first trunk of money to Yahoo! Sponsor Search. And that is because it is by far the most effective medium to garner more sales. And for Sponsor Search is very easy to sign up for it on Yahoo!. You can do so online through a simple process, or you can, literally, just call in. We have reps that can help you go through this final process, the latter honestly being very unique to Yahoo!.

One of the things that we pride ourselves on is really helping our prospective customers by being, literally, just a phone call away from them. . . .

. . . And when you phone in for the sign-up process, what they will do is walk you through the actually online sign-up form, but with the advantage of just giving some of the "best practices" of thinking through. For example, what key words to choose or how to write an effective description. So that is available right now. . . .

(continued)

(*continued*)

. . . We think it is extremely valuable because, as you probably know, small businesses are experts at what they do, but they are not necessarily experts at advertising, let alone Sponsored Search advertising. And so we feel it is almost *our* responsibility (and to be honest with you, it is in our best interest) to make sure that these customers get set up correctly the first time around so that they can start receiving the best results right off the bat. . . .

. . . Actually, you can trace it all the way back to a company that was called Go To.com, which started in the late 1990s. That company that we branded to Overture which subsequently was purchased by Yahoo!, and then rebranded to Yahoo! Search Market. So we are, quite honestly, the pioneers of paid search. We are the ones who invented the category that represents more than half of online spending. So it is something that is a good thing for us to think back on. . . .

. . . So our model is what we call a "pay-per-click model" frequently referred to as PPC. So the first comparison is to all other mediums, so let's say you are buying a newspaper ad or anything that is offline. There is a fixed cost to those purchases, which you may or may not recuperate, depending on how many people actually purchase your products. So in a newspaper, you will buy a half-page for, say $1,000 (I'm making up these numbers, of course), that is a stock cost, and you are going to try to make it up.

Where as with Yahoo! Search Marketing, in a PPC model, you only pay when somebody actually clicks on your listing on the Yahoo! Search results. And the price is not set by us; it is actually set by the advertiser. And this is what you are referring to as a "bidding mall." If you think of every *keyword market-place* as exactly that (a marketplace), advertisers will bid to be listed in those search results. It is important to know that it is not just how much you bid that determines your position. There are other factors in there, including the quality of the listing, and that is because we want to make sure that the experience for the users is optimal. So "quality of the listing" means we want to make sure that it creates a "relevant result" for our user. And we reward or we penalize if the listing is not good. . . .

. . . If all listings are created equal, meaning that the quality of each of the listings is exactly the same, then the amount you bid is really what will determine who shows off first, if you will, and second and so on and so forth. But I put that caveat of the listing quality because it is a really poignant one. So let me give an extreme example.

Let's go back to our used Honda car. If I was an advertiser and my listing says, "Buy the best car ever, at my site now" and by contract your listing said, "Quality used Honda cars at reasonable prices," my guess is that your listing is of a much higher quality than mine is because it speaks specifically to what the user was looking for. . . .

. . . And as a result, even if I am bidding, say 60 cents per click and you are bidding 20 cents per click, you may actually show up higher than I may because of the quality of your listing. And, again, all the numbers are completely fictitious. . . .

. . . It becomes even more important when you combine it with our display advertising because the user sees multiple impressions. So if you imagine a banner that talks about your used Honda car sale, and then actually apply it finally to a search query, and then a searcher sees your listing and recognizes the name of your company because they have seen it on a banner. That's what I was referencing, the two pieces really working hand-in-hand to increase not only the awareness of the brand, but ultimately in a product like that, the click-through rate and, obviously, the sales that follow. . . .

. . . Sure, so if you go to Yahoo.com there are a couple of links that will take you to a sign-up process. The easiest one is at the bottom of the page. It is Search Marketing, so very descriptive. And at this place you will go through a couple of pages that will help you understand what the product is about, as I have done for you now. There are, at the core, really four steps.

The first one is *targeting*. So it is understandable whether you want your listing to appear to the entire nation or a specific geographical component, or area.

The second one is *choosing your keywords*. The used Honda is a perfect example of what we mean as a keyword.

The third is determining *how much you want to bid*. So back to your example of your pay-per-click, and we refer to that from the advertiser perspective "as your bid."

And then last but not least, obviously, is the usable budget, the marketing budget.

In addition, with Yahoo Search Marketing, you can start your campaign for as little as $30. Although I will be honest with you, we encourage advertisers *not* to pay down at that limit, not because we want them to spend more, but quite honestly, it is because in many categories today they have become fairly competitive. So we want our advertisers to make sure that they have enough money in their accounts so that their listings appear and getting enough "click-through"-ing so that they start to get the returns that they are looking for.

So it is one of those models where you have a little bit of efficiency of scale, and if you spend a little bit more you actually see a lot more return. And by the way, when I say a little bit more I do not mean in the thousands of dollars. For most advertisers, a couple hundred dollars is more than enough to get the feel of how this process works and then start deciding if they want to invest more in it. . . .

(continued)

(continued)

   . . . So let us go back to our example. If somebody types in the keyword "car" that is an extremely broad word; and if I am selling used Honda cars where if I put my listing under the keyword "car," I am going to get all sorts of people and not necessarily all of them will be looking for what I have to sell.

   However, if I choose as the keywords "used Honda cars" then almost by default I am limiting the queries (or the users) to the ones who are looking for exactly what I have to sell. Now there are two benefits in doing so.

   The first is (what I just mentioned) a much more qualified prospect for you. And the second is, from the planning perspective, terms that have two or more words in a keyword phrase are, generally speaking, a little bit less expensive than what we call "head-turns to our cart."

   Therefore, if you combine the two, you are getting better-qualified leads at a lower cost and that is really the best of both worlds for advertisers. . . .

   . . . So if an advertiser knows what they are doing (and I really emphasize that) because there are a lot of advertisers who come in with the expectations that they can set up an account in 10 minutes, and then all of a sudden see sales fly. That is not going to happen, I will tell you that right now.

   But if you know what you are doing (and by that I mean really taking the time to learn the account and the interfaces, and the teachers are there at your disposal) and take the time to manage it, then you will see the returns that you are designing. We have countless advertisers who see those on a daily basis, which is, quite honestly, why they stay with us.

   And going back to the objectives of our team, this is to make sure our advertisers really do, clearly and simply, understand how to optimize their account. . . .

To listen to or read the entire Executive Conversation with Patrizio Spagnoletto, go to www.theSocialMediaBible.com.

Commandments

1. **Thou shalt perform SEO.**

   The most effective way to win at SEM is to perform your SEO first. Even though you are paying to be placed in the sponsored links section, your position will depend on your page ranking (see Chapter 20, Spotlight on Search (Search Engine Optimization)), and how many times your link is clicked. If no one clicks your link, you will move lower and lower in the sponsored links until you disappear. You will be dropped, even if you are willing to pay the most.

2. **Thou shalt understand your keywords for every page.**

Be sure that every individual page is analyzed for its own keywords. You want to bring your customer to the exact page at the exact time they are ready to convert. (See Chapter 6, The World of Web Pages, for more on this.)

3. **Thou shalt check your meta keywords.**

Open your page, select View, then Page View, and look for your Meta Keywords. If they don't reflect your content, then you won't get ranked highly.

4. **Thou shalt always create good content.**

Never, *ever* try to trick a search engine. It might work for a while, but they always will catch you, and possibly ban you from their sites for up to five years.

5. **Thou shalt focus on the WIIFM.**

This is always the most important commandment. Whether it's SEO, SEM, e-mail, web pages, or a hard copy brochure, your marketing message *always* has to have a strong "What's In It for Me?" (See Chapter 5 for more information.) Even with paid or sponsored links, you have to have a strong WIIFM to hook your searcher to first read the subject line, and then to read your description. If each of these is written well, the searchers will click on you—and not your competition.

6. **Thou shalt search engine market through Pay-Per-Click.**

Try it; it's fun. And while it's nearly the only place you need to spend any money while marketing on the Internet, it has the potential to return more than 300 percent of what you spend.

Conclusion

What does SEM have to do with social media? As much as SEO does—in other words, a good amount. Again, it's all about having a presence on the Web, building community, and generating revenue. It's about being there when your prospect is in the buying phase of his or her cycle, ready to click on the Purchase button. You have to be found when someone is looking for you—whether it's on your web pages, in your photos and videos, on your podcasts, or on your blog. The combination of SEO and SEM is the most cost-effective way to achieve this goal.

Readings and Resources

Jones, Kristopher B. *Internet Marketing*. (Hoboken, NJ: John Wiley & Sons, Inc.)

Kent, Peter. *Pay Per Click Search Engine Marketing For Dummies*. (Hoboken, NJ: John Wiley & Sons, Inc.)

Miller, Michael. *Online Marketing Heroes: Interviews with 25 Successful Online Marketing Gurus*. (Hoboken, NJ: John Wiley & Sons, Inc.)

Tang, Linh. *Launching Your Yahoo! Business*. (London, England: Que Publishing), 2006.

Tang, Linh. *Succeding at Your Yahoo! Business*. (London, England: Que Publishing), 2006.

Zimmerman, Jan. *Web Marketing For Dummies*. 2nd ed. (Hoboken, NJ: John Wiley & Sons, Inc.)

Downloads

For your free downloads associated with *The Social Media Bible*, go to www.theSocialMediaBible.com, and enter your ISBN number located on the back of the book above the bar code. Be sure to enter the dashes.

Credits

Expert Insights Were Provided By:

Gretchen Howard, director of online sales and operations, Google Adwords, www.google.com/corporate/execs.html.

Linh Tang, coauthor, *Launching Your Yahoo! Business* and *Succeeding at Your Yahoo! Business*, www.LinhTang.com.

Patrizio Spagnoletto, senior director of marketing, Yahoo! Search Marketing, www.searchmarketing.yahoo.com.

Technical Edits Were Provided By:

James Burnes, vice president, MediaSauce, www.MediaSauce.com.

CHAPTER 22

The Formidable Fourth Screen (Mobile)

What's In It for You?

Mobile telephones are the epitome of both digital convergence and social media, and have probably done more to advance social media than any other single digital device. One of the first major breakthroughs after the Internet was created was cellular technology. Today's cell phones allow people to download music; read a blog; surf the Web; receive their e-mails; take and share photos and video; Jott speech-to-text messages to themselves and others; Tweet to groups in excess of 6,000 followers; capture a photo of a billboard with an embedded link that takes the user to a product web site; have a five-star rating of all Italian restaurants within walking distance of your cell phone; get step-by-step directions on how to get from here to there; access maps, art, and encyclopedic information; watch a movie; take a high-quality photograph; post that photograph to a social, web, or blog site; text message; blog; update your web site; listen to a podcast; organize your address book and calendar; record your notes . . . and oh yeah—you can even make a telephone call.

According to a press release from the research firm IDC's Digital Marketplace Model and Forecast (www.idc.com/home.jhtml):

FIGURE 22.1 MobileWeather

- Nearly a quarter of the world's population—roughly 1.4 billion people—was using the Internet regularly in 2008. This number is expected to surpass 1.9 billion unique users—or 30 percent of the world's population—in 2012.

theSocialMediaBible.com

- China passed the United States in 2007 to become the country with the largest number of Internet users, and the country's online population is predicted to grow from 275 million users in 2008 to 375 million users in 2012.

- Nearly half of all Internet users will make online purchases in 2008. By 2012, there will be more than 1 billion online buyers worldwide making business-to-consumer (B2C) transactions worth $1.2 trillion. Business-to-business (B2B) eCommerce will increase tenfold, totaling $12.4 trillion worldwide in 2012.

- Global spending on Internet advertising will total $65.2 billion—nearly 10 percent of all ad spending across all media—in 2008. This share is expected to reach 13.6 percent by 2011, as Internet ad spending grows to $106.6 billion worldwide.

- Roughly 40 percent of all Internet users worldwide currently have mobile Internet access. The number of mobile Internet users reached 546 million in 2008, nearly twice as many as in 2006, and is forecast to surpass 1.5 billion worldwide in 2012.

- The most popular online activities today are searching the Web, finding information for personal use, using Internet e-mail, accessing news and sports information, and accessing financial or credit information. In addition to these activities, more than 50 percent of online users worldwide are using instant messaging and playing online games. The fastest-growing online activities include accessing business applications, creating blogs, online gambling, accessing work-related e-mail, and participating in online communities.

- The most popular online activities among mobile Internet users include searching the Web; accessing news and sports information; downloading music, videos, and ringtones; using instant messaging; and using Internet e-mail. By 2012, downloading music, videos, and ringtones will become the number-one activity among mobile Internet users worldwide.

According to John Gantz, chief research officer at IDC,

The Internet will have added its second billion users over a span of about eight years, a testament to both its universal appeal and its availability. In this time, the Internet has also become more deeply integrated into the fabric of many users' personal and professional lives, enabling them to work, play, and socialize anytime from anywhere. These trends will accelerate as the number of mobile users continues to soar and the Internet becomes truly ubiquitous.

Given the recent advances in mobile technology, the one tool that you must have to access this wealth of social media is a good cell phone. As Kakaul Srivastava of Yahoo!'s Flickr said "There are three cell phones for every human being on the planet. Get one, learn how to use it, and participate!"

Back to the Beginning

A mobile telephone, wireless phone, or cell phone is a mobile, battery-operated electronic device used for voice or data communication over a network of cell sites, which is interconnected to the public switched telephone network (PSTN). Between 1880 and 1900, Nathan B. Stubblefield of Murray, Kentucky invented the first "wireless telephone." Stubblefield's "Cave Radio," which later became known as his "Cave Phone," was the first U.S. patent for a wireless telephone and was issued in 1908 (#887,357). Stubblefield's phone was able to communicate without the use of wires using a radio signal similar to what we have today. The concept of creating a mobile telephone goes back to 1915, when an internal memo from American Telephone & Telegraph discussed the development of a wireless telephone as it is known today.

However, it wasn't until 1947 that AT&T's Bell Labs developed the first base stations (cells), upon which they continued to expand through the 1960s. Canadian inventor and electrical engineering professor Reginald Fessenden is credited with the development of the first Radiophones and shore-to-ship communications during World War II. Later, during the 1950s, the military used radiotelephone links, which were radio-based wireless portable communication devices. By 1973, hand-held cellular radios had become available.

The wireless phone with which people are familiar today was first patented in the United States (#3,449,750) on June 10, 1969, by George Sweigert of Euclid, Ohio. The first official mobile telephone call was placed on April 3, 1973, by Motorola executive and researcher Martin Cooper, from what has been accepted as the first practical mobile phone. His handset was portable and modern, but awkward and heavy.

Japanese company NTT launched the first commercial citywide cellular network—called 0 Generation, or 0G—for mobile telephone service in 1978. The first fully automatic cellular networks—1G or 1st Generation—were introduced in the 1980s. And in 1981, the Nordic Mobile Telephone (NMT) system went online in Denmark, Finland, Norway, and Sweden. NMT first enabled the mobile phone for use internationally by creating "roaming" on other networks in other countries, a process that accelerated mobile phone use throughout northern Europe.

Motorola DynaTAC was the first mobile phone that the FCC approved in 1983; during the following year, Bell Labs developed modern cellular technology based on multiple base stations—or *cell sites*—each of which provided service to a small area or cell which partially overlapped and handed over the data transmission from cell to cell. This allowed a conversation to continue as the mobile phone traveled between cell sites.

The first modern digital cellular technology or 2G (2nd Generation) was launched in 1991 in Finland by Radiolinja, a company that is now part of Elisa Group.[1] Mobile data services on mobile telephones first appeared in Finland in 1993, beginning with SMS,[2] person-to-person text messaging. The first commercial payment system for credit cards was launched in the Philippines by Mimick Banks in 1999 and by mobile operators Globe and Smart simultaneously.

The very first mobile phone content that was ever sold was ringtones in Finland in 1998. In 1999, the first mobile telephone designed to give wireless access to Internet e-mail was the Nokia Communicator. The new multiuse electronic devices created a new category of cellular telephone technology called the *smartphone*. In 1999, Japanese company NTT DoCoMo joined the conversation again by launching i-Mode, the first mobile Internet service—which is the world's largest mobile Internet service today and makes roughly the same amount as Google in annual revenues. NTT created the first commercial launch of the 3G (3rd Generation) mobile phone on the W-CDMA[3] standard in 2001. Today, more than 800 million people are accessing the Internet with their mobile phones.

It wasn't until the 1990s that the mobile phone truly became mobile. Prior to that time, mobile phones were large, heavy, bulky, and not easily carried in a jacket pocket or purse. Most mobile telephones had been installed as car phones until that time, but with the development of smaller digital components and better battery technology, mobile phones became small enough for us to carry.

By the end of 2007, the number of mobile telephones had surpassed 3.3 billion subscriptions worldwide—which represents more than half of the world's human population, and makes the mobile telephone the most common electronic device and most widely used technology in the world.

The Handset

Nokia currently holds approximately 40 percent of market share, making it the world's largest manufacturer of mobile phones. The remaining market share for the other major mobile phone manufacturers is approximately Samsung at 14 percent, Motorola at 14 percent, Sony Ericsson at 9 percent, and LG at 7 percent. These five manufacturers account for more than 80 percent of all mobile phones produced worldwide.

The remainder is divided among companies like Apple Inc., Audiovox (now UTStarcom), Benefon, BenQ-Siemens, CECT, High Tech Computer Corporation (HTC), Fujitsu, Kyocera, Mitsubishi Elec-

FIGURE 22.2   Nokia Mobile Phone

tric, NEC, Neonode, Panasonic (Matsushita Electric), Pantech Curitel, Philips, Research In Motion, Sagem, Sanyo, Sharp, Siemens, Sendo, Sierra Wireless, SK Teletech, Sonim Technologies, T&A Alcatel, Huawei, Trium, and Toshiba.

Mobile telephone technology nowadays includes everything from the very basic mobile phone to the full-featured telephones with web access and multimedia capabilities—such as musicphones (SonyEricsson Walkman), cameraphones (Cybershot), videophones, the RIM BlackBerry, smartphones, LG Dare, PDA (Personal Desktop Assistants),[4] Nokia N-Series of multimedia phones, and the most recent addition to the bunch: the Apple iPhone and Google Android.

Phone Features

Today's mobile phones boast features beyond making a simple telephone call. Cell phones can now send text messages; perform Internet browsing; playback MP3 music; record memos; organize personal information, contacts, and calendars; send and receive e-mail and instant messages; record, send, receive, and watch images and videos using built-in cameras and camcorders; play different ringtones, games, and radio; perform push-to-talk (PTT); utilize infrared and Bluetooth connectivity; perform video calling; and serve as a wireless modem for a PC. Nokia and the University of Cambridge have even introduced a bendable cell phone called "The Morph."[5]

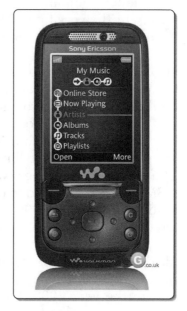

FIGURE 22.3   MobileMusic Download

To read Nokia's entire press release on "The Morph" go to www.nokia
.com/A4136001?newsid=1194251, or visit www.theSocialMediaBible.com
for all of the clickable links.

The mobile phone data services are most widely used for text messaging,
music and picture downloads, video gaming, adult entertainment, gambling,
and video/TV. Total revenues for paid mobile data services now exceed the
revenues of paid services on the Internet—and is expected to grow to more
than $300 billion by 2012 worldwide.

Mobile Applications

The most common data service used on
mobile phones today is SMS text messaging. More than 74 percent of all mobile
phone users—over 2.4 billion out of the 3.3
billion—are actively using text messaging
on a regular basis. Mobile telephone service providers earned revenues of more
than $100 billion for SMS text messaging
alone in 2007.

FIGURE 22.4 Morph

Many companies have claimed to
have sent the very first SMS text message.
According to a former employee of NASA,
Edward Lantz, the first message was sent
via one simple Motorola beeper in 1989 by Raina Fortini from New York
City to Melbourne Beach, Florida. Fortini used upside down numbers that
could be read as words and sounds. The first commercial SMS message
was sent over the Vodafone GSM network in the United Kingdom on
December 3, 1992, from Neil Papworth of Sema Group using a personal
computer, to Richard Jarvis of Vodafone using an Orbitel 901 handset.
The text of the message was "Merry Christmas." The first SMS typed on a
GSM phone is claimed to have been sent by Riku Pihkonen, an engineering
student at Nokia, in 1993 (www.wapedia.mobi/en/Text_Messaging). Go to
www.theSocialMediaBible.com for clickable links.

The next most common use of mobile data services is for music. Music
file downloads generated more than $31 billion in revenue last year, with the
next in line being ringtone downloads.

In the year 2000, Finnish telephone company Radiolinja (now Elisa)
introduced the first mobile news service, delivered via SMS text messaging.
After that came videogames, jokes, horoscopes, TV content, advertising, and

FIGURE 22.5 Text Message

other content downloads. Mobile products sales for ringtones, games, and graphics are displacing the money that is spent on traditional youth products such as music, clothing, and movies.

Other mobile data services range from conducting a job search or seeking career advice from Monster.com; to transferring up to $1 million in cash from one mobile account in one country to another overseas; to paying your utility bills in one city and a parking ticket in another. Mobile devices and applications are seen as remote controls for the web, or, as director of strategy for Crayon Marketing Adam Broitman puts it, "The mobile phone is our remote control for our lives!" (See Broitman's Expert Insight later in this chapter, or listen to Adam Broitman's Executive Conversation by going to www.theSocialMediaBible.com.)

Rich Media

More and more content is being developed for the mobile telephone, as it has quickly become a mass media device—and even commonly called "the Fourth Screen" (with the other three being movie, television, and the PC). With the advent of the iPhone, Android, and other similar smartphones, movie distribution companies are taking new rich media distribution seriously and making it possible to download full-length movies from your PC and transfer them to your phone (in addition to downloading them directly from your mobile device).

Mobile technology is becoming so prevalent, in fact, that it has elicited the creation and inclusion of new words to our everyday vocabulary, one of which is the term *mobisodes*. A mobisode is a short episode of a popular television show that is specifically intended for mobile device viewing. Radio, television, and satellite TV broadcast media all require us to tune in at a very specific time (same time, same channel) in order to catch a given program or breaking news, unless you record it using DVR or TiVo. If you aren't able to get to your TV set in time to view or record it, you either miss the program altogether, or you have to wait for the next broadcast time. Subscribing to a mobile news feed, however, enables you to receive this information anywhere, at any time.

What You Need to Know

Over the past several years, the mobile telephone has become increasingly more important to one's participation in social media. With popular net-
working sites such as MySpace, LinkedIn, and Facebook; photo-sharing sites like Flickr, Smug-Mug, and Photobucket; video-sharing web sites such as YouTube; and information sites like Wiki-pedia, mobile telephone web access is more im-portant than ever. Even personal publishing platform WordPress (see Chapter 6, The World of Web Pages) has plug-ins now that give mobile phone users the ability to view their blog sites. (See Downloads at the end of this chapter.)

FIGURE 22.6 MySpace Mobile

According to Brandon Lucas, senior director of mobile business develop-ment for social networking site myspace.com, MySpace Mobile United States had more than 1.4 billion impressions in one month. In fact, Lucas stated, "It wasn't until we rolled out m.myspace.com, a version of MySpace that displays on your mobile phone, that we got a sense of how powerful demand was for MySpace on cell phones." CEO of mobile community Mocospace Justin Siegel cites 1 billion visits to his site since its inception, and Facebook Mobile has surpassed both groups, claiming 4 million unique registrations.

Technology research group ABI Research conducted an online survey which found that nearly half (46 percent) of those who use social networks have visited these sites through their mobile phone. Of these, nearly 70 percent have visited MySpace, with another 67 percent also visiting Facebook.

Twitter

Twitter has also made a huge impact on texting, microblogging, and com-municating through the use of a mobile phone. Please read Chapter 15, Thumbs Up for Microblogging, for a more in-depth description of Twitter and "Tweets."

Real-Time Social Engagement

The portability of the mobile telephone promotes real-time, living in the moment, or life presence for its user. The device allows users to participate in an event and share their reactions and ideas with others instantly.

In 2000, this interaction might have been as simple as holding up a cell phone toward the stage at a concert and letting the person on the other end of the connection hear a song. Today, from a mobile telephone one could photograph the concert, videotape it, blog about it, and share it with friends, family, and colleagues even before the show ends! Being able to share these important experiences in real time creates strong social bonds.

In one case, a stolen mobile phone was even returned to its owner based on photographs that its camera took automatically and uploaded to the Web. And as far as sharing your experiences through text messaging, Twitter is a great way to post instant, up-to-the-minute news about what you are doing and thinking. (See Chapter 15, Thumbs Up for Microblogging, for more information on microblogging and Twitter.)

Reviews

Mobile user-generated content creates a powerful trusted network, whose recommendations can have a significant impact on your decision making. If a restaurant review comes from someone whom you know has a relationship with—whether it's a friend or just someone from your hometown—you're likely to receive their review with much more trust than one from a paid critic.

A great enterprise example of this is Yelp.com, a web site that you can access through your computer or through your mobile phone. Connecting to Yelp allows you to check out reviews for any kind of business just by typing in your zip code, or simply allowing your GPS-enabled mobile phone to tell Yelp where you are located. So, for example, if you are looking for a great pasta restaurant near the corner of Main and Broadway, Yelp will show you a half dozen or more restaurant reviews from people who live in that area and who have actually eaten at those restaurants. (To hear or read the Executive Conversation interview with Stephanie Ichinose, the director of communications for Yelp, go to www.theSocialMediaBible.com.)

Mobile Marketing

The popularity of marketing to mobile phone users has grown steadily since the rise of SMS in Europe and Asia in the early 2000s. During this time, businesses began collecting mobile phone numbers to send both wanted and unwanted (spam) advertising messages to their users. Due to global government regulations, SMS has become a legitimate form of advertising. Unlike the public domain in which the World Wide Web exists, mobile carriers control their own networks and have set guidelines and best practices for the entire mobile media industry.

The Mobile Marketing Association and the Interactive Advertising Bureau (IAB) have established strict guidelines and are evangelizing the use of mobile phones for advertisers. This initiative has been very successful in North America, Western Europe, and several other regions.

Another issue with which some countries are dealing is mobile spam advertising messages that are sent to mobile subscribers without an explicit opt-in (see Chapter 5, It's Not Your Father's E-Mail, for more information on opt-ins). This is due to mobile carriers' sales of subscribers' telephone numbers to third parties. Legislation often requires permission or an opt-in from the mobile subscriber to advertise to them, which has seriously delayed the growth of mobile advertising and marketing. The mobile carriers require a double opt-in from the subscriber and the ability for the consumer to opt out at any time by sending the word *STOP* via SMS or text messaging. These guidelines are very similar to the 2004 U.S. Can Spam Act and are established in the MMA Consumer Best Practices Guidelines (see below). All mobile carriers in the United States voluntarily follow these guidelines. (For more information on the Can Spam Act, see Chapter 5, It's Not Your Father's E-Mail.)

In 2002, Labatt Brewing Company ran the first successful cross-carrier SMS advertising campaign. Since then, mobile SMS advertising has gained recognition as a new advertising channel and a way to communicate to the mobile consumer. Large consumer brands have accepted SMS advertising, and have created mobile domain names that allow their consumer to text message their brand name while in a store or at an event. Motorola's ongoing campaign at the House of Blues venues is another example of well-designed mobile advertising. The House of Blues allows their patrons to send their mobile photos to the LED display board and their online blog in real-time.[6]

Mobile Web Marketing

For online mobile advertisers, the Mobile Marketing Association (MMA) provides a set of guidelines and standards that specify recommended formats for ads and mobile presentations. Google, Yahoo!, and other major mobile content providers are selling mobile advertising placement as part of their advertising services.

Bluetooth Connection

Bluetooth began in 2003 as a wireless radio protocol technology called *frequency hopping* or *spread spectrum* that chops up the data being sent and transmits chunks of it on up to 75 different frequencies. This allows data transmission utilizing short-range communications from fixed or mobile devices, creating a wireless personal area network or PAN. Bluetooth provides access and secure information exchange between devices such as mobile phones, digital cameras, telephones, personal computers, microphones and headsets, printers, GPS receivers, and video game consoles. Since Bluetooth provides secure high-speed transmission of data, it is an appropriate technology for mobile advertising and marketing. Companies like ProxiBlaster.com, bluetoothmagnet.com, and bluecasting.com are providing Bluetooth marketing solutions. Using Bluetooth, companies can automatically send media files to all Bluetooth-enabled devices, such as mobile phones, PDAs, and laptops within a range of around 100 meters. This is commonly referred to as bluecasting, bluetooth broadcasting, or proximity marketing.

Location-Based Services

Location-based services (LBS) are a great way to send geographically specific advertising and SMS messages to a mobile phone subscriber based on their GPS—or radiolocation—or trilateration location for those not GPS equipped. Radiolocation and trilateration are methods by which a cell phone's location is determined based on its signal strength to the closest cell-phone towers. People have heard of the woman stuck in her car in a blizzard at night who was saved by rescuers who used radiolocation and trilateration to find her car in the snow bank. LBS can even be used to locate a stolen phone or kidnapped person.

Day-to-day uses for LBS might include locating the nearest type of business or service that a customer is looking for—such as an ATM, restaurant, or doctor; determining meeting room schedules; executing turn-by-turn navigation to a specific address; locating friends on a map displayed on your mobile phone; receiving personal alerts, such as notification of a sale on gas and traffic updates that can include warnings of traffic jams and bad weather; finding taxis, people, employee, or rental equipment location; fleet scheduling, identifying passive sensors or RF (Radio Frequency) tags for packages and railroad train boxcars; or using an EZ Pass, toll watch, or other geographically targeted mobile advertising.

Mobile LBS marketing has also been used for mobile coupons or discounts that are sent automatically to mobile subscribers who are near advertising retailers, restaurants, cafes, or movie theatres. In 2007, Singapore mobile carrier MobileOne initiated an LBS advertising campaign that involved many local marketers, which was widely accepted by its subscribers. Companies offering location-based, geo-targeted advertising or geo-messaging include Loopt.com, Dodgeball.com, and GeoMe.com (in Spain).

Mobile Gaming

Mobile gaming takes place when a video game is played on a mobile phone, smartphone, PDA, or handheld computer. The first game that was factory-installed on a mobile phone was called Snake, which came equipped on certain Nokia models in 1997. Snake has actually become the most popular mobile video game on the planet, and is regularly played by more than one billion people worldwide.

FIGURE 22.7 Mobile Gaming

Mobile games can be factory installed, installed via memory card or Bluetooth, or—in most cases—downloaded from the carrier for a fee. They can include both stand-alone and networked multi-player games. (See Chapter 17, Virtual Worlds—Real Impact and Chapter 18, Gaming the System: Virtual Gaming, for more information on virtual worlds and gaming.)

One of the most popular gaming applications for mobile technology today is online mobile gambling. In 2005, PokerRoom, a poker software application, was developed by Ongame where the player can play poker in a single player or multiplayer mode for real or play money.

MMORPG

In addition to ordinary mobile gaming, MMORPG—or Massively Multi-player Online Role Playing Games—have become very popular with mobile phone users. (See Chapter 18, Gaming the System: Virtual Gaming, for a complete explanation of MMORPG.) The first of these for the mobile audi-ence were called TibiaME and were developed by CipSoft SmartCell Tech-nology. The company is also working on a gaming application for the first cross-platform MMORPG called Shadow of Legend, which is designed to be played on both PCs and mobile devices.

Location-Based Games

There are even games that one can play on mobile phones that use geo-graphic location technology such as GPS. These are called location-based games, and they integrate the player's position into the game play, making the player's coordinates and movement the main elements.

The most well-known example of a location-based game is a high-tech treasure hunt game called Geocaching, which is played throughout the world by adventure seekers equipped with GPS devices. The basic idea is to locate hidden containers—called geocaches—outdoors, exchange a hidden gift, and then share your experiences online. Geocaching has become popular with all age groups—especially for people who have a strong sense of community and support for the environment. (You can learn more at www .geocaching.com.)

Mobile In-Game Marketing

There are five popular categories of mobile gaming: interactive real-time, 3D games, massive multiplayer, social networking, and casual games (the most popular kind). Casual games are single-player and very easy to play. In addition to many old favorite video games such as Space Invaders, Tetris, and Solitaire many of the big video game companies have scaled down their computer and console games and have created mobile divisions such as PlayStation Portable and Nintendo DS. Many companies have developed their games directly for mobile phone play.

Large brands are now delivering advertising messages within those mobile games, and often even sponsoring an entire game to drive brand, sales, and consumer engagement. This type of advertising is known as mobile *advergaming* or *Ad-funded mobile gaming*. Puma running shoe brand developed a comprehensive engagement marketing campaign by creating a racing game that coincided with the Shanghai F1 race. Their Advergame was called F-Wan, which sounds like F1 for Formula One racing and means "play" in Chinese. The racetrack was designed in the shape of their Puma logo, a jumping wild cat with its tail extended. F-Wan was a multiplayer game, allowing up to four gamers to race against each other. The top three best scores each week would win Puma merchandise.

Mobile Viral Marketing

Mobile viral marketing is similar to the e-mail and Internet variety. Its distribution and communication rely on customers to transmit a particular company's content—known as *mobile viral content*—via mobile SMS to other potential customers in their trusted network, and encourage these contacts to pass the content along themselves. To begin a viral marketing campaign, the enterprise *seeds* (or sends) content to first-generation key customers—also called *mavens* and *influencers*—who become *infected* with this information. These individuals, or *communicators*, then forward the message to recipients, who are encouraged to do the same and keep the message moving. The better the "What's In It for Me?" content, the more effective the viral spread of this message will be. In one case, the Italian Passa Parola (Spread of Mouth) campaign reached 800,000 users solely by using viral marketing.

Mobile Marketing Future

A recent survey stated that approximately 89 percent of major brands are planning to market their products through SMS text and multimedia mobile messaging. One-third of those brands are planning to spend about 10 percent of their total annual marketing budgets on mobile marketing. Within five years, more than half of all major brands are expected to spend between 5 percent and 25 percent of their total annual marketing budgets on mobile marketing. Of the companies that responded to this survey, 40 percent of them have stated that they have already begun mobile marketing to their audiences because of their ability to reach a specific target audience, in a specific geographical location, with a very specific marketing message. For more information go to www.airwidesolutions .com/press2006/feb2106.html.

Messaging Convergence

Multifunctional services are becoming more popular with mobile phone users because of the ability of these services to integrate SMS text messaging with voice—such as *voice SMS*, where voice replaces text. One such company is called Jott.

To sign up for the Jott service you simply create a free account with you name, group names, and telephone numbers. Once this is complete, you call an 800 number and talk to the answering machine, which asks, "Who do you want to Jott?" You could give your own first name, and Jott replies with your full name. After a confirmation and a tone, the user leaves a standard voice message. Within moments, that message is transcribed from voice to text, and sent to both the user's cell phone as a text message and to a designated e-mail account.

Jott is a great service when you get an idea, remember something, or need to be reminded of something. You can simply "Jott" yourself. This is particularly good when you're driving 60 miles per hour on the freeway, walking down the street, eating at a restaurant—any place where finding paper and a pencil is inconvenient. It's also great to be able to Jott people to tell them you are running 10 minutes late while driving in the car.

To listen to the Executive Conversation with John Pollard, the founder of Jott, please go to www.theSocialMediaBible.com.

The Mobile Marketing Association

The Mobile Marketing Association (MMA; www.mmaglobal.com) is a global nonprofit association that strives to stimulate the growth of mobile marketing and its associated technology. The MMA has more than 600 global member companies that include agencies, advertisers, hand-held device manufacturers, carriers and wireless operators, retailers, software and service providers, aggregators, technology enablers, market research firms—as well as any company focused on the potential of marketing via mobile phone.

Mobile Phone Technology

FIGURE 22.8 iPhone

The Apple iPhone: As a certified developer for Apple from the mid-1980s to the mid-1990s, one of the authors had a front-row seat to the advent of the many innovations that paved the way in the world of technology. Twenty years later, Steve Jobs is still at it. This chapter would be incomplete without mentioning Apple's iPhone due to the impact this single product has had on social mobile.

On January 9, 2007, Apple announced their version of the smartphone: the iPhone. The iPhone connects to the Internet, plays multimedia, and of course, is a fully functioning mobile phone with text messaging and voice mail capabilities. The iPhone has a touch-screen that replaces a mobile phone's conventional keyboard. It includes both still and video cameras, plays MP3 music and audio files, and proudly represents the fourth-screen category with a fully functioning video player similar to the Apple's iPod. The iPhone allows its users to create, upload, share, and view audio, photographs, and video.

With the iPhone's ability to connect to the Internet, you can browse a web site, read a blog, access traffic reports, view your stock portfolio, or do anything that you can do with a standard PC and an Internet connection.

After repeated attempts to encourage Apple to participate in *The Social Media Bible,* they unfortunately declined.

Google Android: The Android is Google's answer to Apple's iPhone. It's a smartphone mobile device built on an open-system platform in cooperation with the Open Handset Alliance (OHA), which is a business alliance of 34 firms including Google, HTC, Intel, Motorola, Qualcomm, Samsung, LG, T-Mobile, Nvidia, and Wind River Systems, which have joined together to develop open standards for mobile devices. The Android can function with any mobile carrier and features Google Search, Google Apps, Gmail (Google's e-mail system), and GTalk (Google's Instant Messaging application). Google's entry into the mobile advertising market is both welcomed and viewed as the company's intention to dominate the mobile-based advertising market as it did with the desktop.

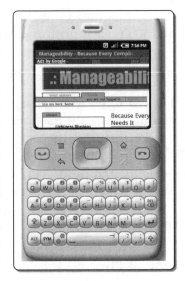

FIGURE 22.9 Android

As with all open platforms, a rush of high-quality developers are currently building the very best and most advanced applications possible. Similar to the advance in market share that computer technology has enjoyed over the past three decades, this open platform will create more applications, features, and benefits, and will dramatically increase Android's market share. With Google's dominance in Web-based advertising combined with the relatively untapped mobile advertising market, the company's revenue potential for dominating mobile marketing is huge.

Providers

Mobile social networks and communities are one of the fast-growing sectors in social media. Founder and CEO of Amanda Vega Consulting and active blogger Amanda Vega points out that even in third-world countries where the average person cannot afford to own a computer or have access to high-speed broadband Internet, they usually can afford a cell phone. This is why there are currently more cell phones on the planet than there are people. (To listen to Amanda Vega's Executive Conversation, go to www.the SocialMediaBible.com.)

The following is a list of mobile social networking web sites that provide a type of mobile data service. As with the Providers sections of other chapters, don't get overwhelmed. Just pick out one or two, visit their sites, read their benefits, and try it for yourself:

- 3jam.com introduces SMS 2.0, which allows you to text message with your friends in a new way, and provides 3jam SuperText—your free text message inbox on the Web. You can send and receive text messages for free when you're online, achieve reliable message delivery to anyone with a mobile phone, and—unlike IM—reply to-all group texting and other new tricks for your phone.

- Aki-aki.com is a Germany-based mobile social network web site.

- AirG.com is a mobile community with more than 20 million unique users worldwide, interconnected to more than 100 mobile operators in over 40 countries.

- BrightKite.com allows you to see where your friends are and what they're up to in real time.

- Broadtexter.com is a mobile social community that lets you communicate with your audience, members, supporters, or patrons.

- Buddyping will manage all of your online social networks, locate friends who are nearby, manage your calendar, arrange a meeting, browse places in your area, and group message friends using your mobile.

- CallWave is another example of digital messaging crossover. This system allows you to forward your mobile phone voice mail messaging to transfer all of your recorded voice mails to your e-mail or the CallWave web site. With CallWave, you never have to retrieve your mobile phone messages again, since they've all been sent to your e-mail.

- Dodgeball.com alerts all of your friends to where you are at that moment so you can meet.

- Facebook Mobile is Facebook on your cell phone.

- Flagr.com shares cool places from online or right from your mobile phone.

- Friendstribe.com is a mobile social network specifically designed to be accessed through your mobile phone through text messaging.

- Funkysexycool.com is a fun, free, fast way to flirt and date with over 250,000 members from around the world using your mobile phone.

- Groovr.com helps users stay connected both online and off-line by allowing them to move seamlessly from laptop to mobile phone to meet new friends in new places.

- Hobnobster is a web and mobile relationship service for singles to search and communicate with other quality singles online and through their mobile phone.

- Imity.com is a free application for your mobile phone that uses Blue-tooth to sense other phones around and form a social network—online, off-line, and all the other lines.
- Jaiku.com (now part of Google) users can create a microblog and connect with friends posting from the Web or by mobile SMS, or from desktop computers.
- JuiceCaster.com lets you instantly share your photos and videos with friends or directly to your MySpace, Facebook, or other social networking web sites from your mobile phone.
- Kiboze.com delivers interactive product information—such as print advertisements and billboards—to a user's cell phone on demand.
- Loopnote.com lets you create alerts that you can receive via e-mail, IM, text, or RSS.
- MeetMoi.com is a safe and easy-to-use dating service that uses ground-breaking technology to find people around your location and lets you browse pictures, send messages, and connect with members, all from your mobile phone.
- Mig33.com connects you to people from around the world through IM, chat rooms, e-mail, shared photos, SMS—and, of course, you can make cheap calls.
- Mobiluck.com lets you tell your friends where you are, receive alerts when they are nearby, and chat 24/7 for free.
- Moblabber is a group text messaging service, similar to a personalized message—only mass-produced and treated as if it's an ongoing conversation.
- Mocospace.com is a mobile-based social networking web site.
- myGamma.com is a phone and web community where you can interact with people and showcase yourself by creating a private community with only invited friends with whom you can chat and share your blogs and photos.
- MySpace Mobile is MySpace on your cell phone.
- NowThen.com is a new way to capture the pulse of your life in mobile photos. Just snap, share, and store your moments for free.
- Placestodo.com helps you remember, share, and find new places and things to do.
- Rabble.com is a location-based social networking application you download to your mobile phone that allows you to combine all the things you love doing on the Web on your phone.

- Rader.net is an instant picture and video-sharing site.
- ShoZu connects your mobile phone to the Internet and allows you to interact with a huge list of web sites and communities including Flickr, Facebook, YouTube, Blogger, and more.
- Socialight.com lets you create, share, and discover virtual sticky notes stuck to actual places all around you.
- The3gdatingagency.com is a mobile phone access dating web site that is a great way to find new friends or partners for fun, dating, and long-term relationships.
- Treemo.com is an online and mobile community for sharing digital media, empowering self-expression, and transforming creativity into action by offering an ever-evolving gallery of video, audio, photography, words, and visual art, which inspires visitors to create their own digital expressions—and to share those creations with the world.
- Twitter.com is a service for friends, family, and coworkers to communicate and stay connected through the exchange of quick and frequent answers to one simple question: What are you doing? (See Chapter 15, Thumbs Up for Microblogging, for more information on Twitter. Be sure to also listen to the Executive Conversation with Biz Stone, the founder of Twitter, at www.theSocialMediaBible.com.)
- Veeker.com is video and picture messaging service for your mobile phone and the Web.
- Wadja.com is a mobile web, media, and social messaging service that manages your communication and interaction from your friends, family, and address book contacts.
- Yelp.com is a geographically based review web site that is accessible through your mobile phone. Just open your phone, access Yelp, and see what others have said about that restaurant, movie, or mechanic in your area. (See information earlier in the chapter, and listen to the Executive Conversation with Stephanie Ichinose, director of communications for Yelp, at www.theSocialMediaBible.com.)
- Zannel.com is a way for you to instantly share what you're doing, feeling, and seeing with your friends as it happens by allowing you to create your own mobile page where you can post videos, pictures, and text updates with your mobile phone.
- Zemble.com allows you to text message large groups of friends from your mobile phone by sending just one text message.

- Zinadoo.com allows you to set up your own voting, subscription, text in–text out SMS services, to promote your mobile web site, and to keep in touch with your community through SMS.

- Zingku.com is supercharged mobile text and picture messaging for you and your friends.

- Zyb.com is a mobile-based web site that lets you organize all of your personal information such as contacts, pictures, text messages, and calendar events online.

With a list like this, there's bound to something that everyone can use!

Expert Insight

Adam Broitman, director of strategy and ringleader, Crayon Marketing, www.amediacirc.us

Adam Broitman

Since I have been hearing about mobile, at large, I have been hearing people talk about mobile advertising. People are saying that 2005 was the year of mobile; 2006 was the year of mobile; 2007 was the year of mobile; and we keep hearing this from people in reference to mobile advertising. When I think of mobile advertising, I largely think of putting banners on a WAP [Wireless Application Protocol] page or just a mobile phone; and I do not think that that is necessarily where it's at. . . .

I think mobile marketing (using the mobile phone, which is central to all our mediated experience) is much more palatable and much more likely to become the next big thing. When I refer to "mobile marketing," I [mean] using a mobile phone for social networking and using QR codes [Quick Response Codes]—which is very big in Asia right now. This is where users can see a print ad and actually take a picture of it; and the optics of their camera gives them feedback from that ad and it continues the experience (which would otherwise be a very two-dimensional marketing experience). . . . [It's] the same way that a barcode works. A lot of what the carriers and mobile manufacturers are looking to do now is (and this is actually very big as of . . . the announcement of the G1, the new Google Android phone) have the optics of your camera actually *read* a two-dimensional (2D) barcode with information embedded in it; so, for example, a URL. So I take my camera and let's say, I am looking at an ad for Kraft and I see a little code at the bottom and it says, "Take a picture with your camera for more information"; so I snap that picture. It can bring me to a coupon [on] a mobile web page, or any number of destinations that were laid out by the brand.

It is a really cool way to engage consumers. And I do not really consider it the push advertising of years past; it's more of that pull advertising, where users can actually gain more information, when and how they want to gain that information. . . .

I think there has also been a lot that has been going on with the carriers, because [they] have not be able to adapt quickly to this new environment and . . . monetize mobile marketing as quickly as they would have liked. So they're putting limitations on the types of things that you can do. The famous deck—the "Verizon" deck when you power up your Verizon phone—has hand-selected content that limits what users can get on a mobile phone.

So with the inception of Android and open-source mobile content development and platforms, everyone can now create to these platforms. Therefore, I think we are just at the beginning of the realization of mobile content, mobile marketing, and that space is large. . . .

Fourth Screen. . . . it's funny that a couple of years ago people were referring to it as the "third screen." Actually, one of the first mobile marketing companies was Third Screen Media, which was then bought by AOL. Now they are calling it the "fourth screen." I personally feel that we are going to have five, six, seven, eight, nine, ten screens; all different screens, but it is ultimately going to be the same content, just accessed in different ways. . . .

When AOL came on the scene a number of years back, at the inception of the Internet, it was a walled garden; similar to the way that Facebook and MySpace [are]. That model simply doesn't work. People want to own their own data; they want to bring it wherever they want, which is a total beta-portability movement. In addition, the walled-garden model simply does not work. Therefore, I think that this movement toward open standards is inevitable. The fact that Google is pioneering it and some people are not happy with that (because they feel like Google is trying to control information) is preposterous, in my opinion. This is because it really is an open system; and Google is not controlling anything. They just happen to have the largest "reach" in terms of the ability to monetize all of this content and all of this activity online. . . .

Open platform . . . which speaks purposely to the point whereas OS 10 is so successful. You just mentioned Steve Jobs; he did a 180 when he came back to hassle and he opened up the platform that now everyone is developing. Now you have an operating system that is enjoying, I think it is 7 to 8 percent market share in the U.S., I'm not sure. . . .

The Google Android. . . . Well, from what Google has said, the platform is completely separate from any hardware or carrier. So the Open Handset Alliance aims to create this platform, much like Linux or Unix, where it is not dependent on any specific type of hardware, and in the mobile arena, any

(*continued*)

(continued)

carriers. So I do not think that they could actually go back on that, because Google does not actually own it. It is a product of the Open Handset Alliance, which is pretty interesting. And I think the play there is that Google knows the more access they have to putting their ads next to relevant content, the better off they are. Since they have such penetration online now, they'll be able to parlay that into many different arenas; which is why they were bidding on the 700 MHz spectrum a few months back, because they didn't want someone else to purchase that block and own those airwaves.

So the more open the world is, the more that Google can monetize the world of content; and this is because their technology is so far superior than anyone else's, which we see in the fact that Microsoft and MSN only have such a small percent of search share, and Yahoo also has a very small percent. They think we do not have the targeting capabilities that offer that advertising solution that Google does.

To listen to or read the entire Executive Conversation with Adam Broitman, go to www .theSocialMediaBible.com.

Commandments

1. **Thou shalt learn more about mobile marketing.**

   Read some mobile marketing blogs. Watch how some of the big players are branding, selling, and interacting with their customers and prospects through mobile marketing. Give this commandment 15 minutes, two or three times a month. Follow mobile marketing to see when it's the right time for you to jump in.

2. **Thou shalt understand the technology.**

   Understand the technology's capabilities. No need to go totally geek, but just understand the main features and benefits of the major players. Before reading this chapter, did you know you could do that much with a simple smartphone? Spend a few minutes to see how the iPhone and Android work. The more you understand about how the technology functions, the better you will understand how to apply it to your own marketing and advertising concepts and campaigns.

3. **Thou shalt set Google Alerts.**

   Set some Google Alerts for the terms "mobile marketing," "mobile advertising," "mobile marketing [fill in your industry terms]." See what others are doing in your industry with mobile marketing. Most important, remember to keep an eye out for the competition by including their company, product, and services names in your alerts.

4. **Thou shalt try mobile applications.**

Set up a Jott account and see how you quickly cannot live without it. Get a few of your customers and prospects to opt-in on receiving your company updates in their e-mails and their mobile phones. Try Twitter for communicating with your employees. Capture a photo or, better yet, a two-minute video at your next conference and send it to a few key prospects who could benefit from that "What's-In-It-for-Me?" content.

5. **Thou shalt try the mobile Web.**

Try accessing your favorite sites with your mobile phone. Go to Yelp the next time you're out and want a good restaurant recommendation in your area. If you are GPS enhanced, try getting directions the next time you're lost (especially you guys out there). Important: See what it takes to get your web site mobile ready. If it's WordPress, you need only a plug-in (see the following Downloads).

Conclusion

Wow! Mobile phone technology is advancing at breakneck speeds while new features are being added every day. The mobile telephone is truly social media in a box that includes nearly every social media tool in one device. Today's smartphone lets you take pictures; upload them to your blog or photo-sharing site; send them to friends, colleagues, and customers; or view others' photographs. And you can do the same with audio, music, and video.

You can surf a web site, get Tweets, and send and receive text messages. You can receive up-to-the-minute news and stock quotes, traffic reports, and weather. You can listen to music, watch a full-length video, have it wake you on time in the morning, give you turn-by-turn directions, let you know the best pasta restaurant closest to you . . . and even make a call.

As the smartphone continues to develop and become part of everyone's "remote controls for life," more and more companies will understand how to better serve you with demographically specific, geo-targeted, trusted network, permission-based information and advertising.

Mobile marketing is expensive, and companies and providers have only begun to understand how to best serve information to trusted customers using this technology. While mobile marketing might not be a viable solution for every business right now, it likely will be soon. You owe it to yourself and your company to monitor this industry. Watch the technology, and follow the players in this field so that when it is the right time for you to begin to mobile market, you will recognize the opportunity.

Readings and Resources

Ahonen, Tomi T., Timo Kasper, and Sara Melkko. *3G Marketing: Communities and Strategic Partnerships.* (Hoboken, NJ: John Wiley & Sons, Inc.)

Andersson, Christoffer, Daniel Freeman, Ian James, et al. *Mobile Media and Applications, From Concept to Cash: Successful Service Creation and Launch.* (Hoboken, NJ: John Wiley & Sons, Inc.)

Ballard, Barbara. *Designing the Mobile User Experience.* (Hoboken, NJ: John Wiley & Sons, Inc.)

Brenner, Michael, and Musa Unmehopa. *The Open Mobile Alliance: Delivering Service Enablers for Next-Generation Applications.* (Hoboken, NJ: John Wiley & Sons, Inc.)

Chehimi, Fadi, Leon Clarke, Michael Coffey, et al. *Games on Symbian OS: A Handbook for Mobile Development.* (Hoboken, NJ: John Wiley & Sons, Inc.)

Eylert, Bernd. *The Mobile Multimedia Business: Requirements and Solutions.* (Hoboken, NJ: John Wiley & Sons, Inc.)

Hirsch, Frederick, John Kemp, and Jani Ilkka. *Mobile Web Services: Architecture and Implementation.* (Hoboken, NJ: John Wiley & Sons, Inc.)

Iwacz, Grzegorz, Andrzej Jajszczyk, and Michal Zajaczkowski. *Multimedia Broadcasting and Multicasting in Mobile Networks.* (Hoboken, NJ: John Wiley & Sons, Inc.)

Karlson, Bo, Aurelian Bria, Jonas Lind, et al. *Wireless Foresight: Scenarios of the Mobile World in 2015.* (Hoboken, NJ: John Wiley & Sons, Inc.)

Klemettinen, Mika. *Enabling Technologies for Mobile Services: The MobiLife Book.* (Hoboken, NJ: John Wiley & Sons, Inc.)

Niebert, Norbert, Andreas Schieder, Jens Zander, and Robert Hancock, eds. *Ambient Networks: Co-Operative Mobile Networking for the Wireless World.* (Hoboken, NJ: John Wiley & Sons, Inc.)

O'Farrell, Michael J., John R. Levine, Jostein Algroy, James Pearce, and Daniel Appelquist. *Mobile Internet For Dummies.* (Hoboken, NJ: John Wiley & Sons, Inc.)

Sauter, Martin. *Communication Systems for the Mobile Information Society.* (Hoboken, NJ: John Wiley & Sons, Inc.)

Sharma, Chetan, Joe Herzog, and Victor Melfi. *Mobile Advertising: Supercharge Your Brand in the Exploding Wireless Market.* (Hoboken, NJ: John Wiley & Sons, Inc.)

Shorey, Rajeev, A. Ananda, Mun Choon Chan, and Wei Tsang Ooi. *Mobile, Wireless, and Sensor Networks: Technology, Applications, and Future Directions.* (Hoboken, NJ: John Wiley & Sons, Inc.)

Downloads

For your free downloads associated with *The Social Media Bible,* go to www.theSocialMediaBible.com, and enter your ISBN number located on the back of the book above the bar code. Be sure to enter the dashes.

Credits

Expert Insight and Technical Edits Were Provided By:

Adam Broitman, director of strategy and ringleader, Crayon Marketing, www.amediacirc.us.

Notes

1. Today the Elisa Corporation is a leading Nordic communications services provider and a publicly listed Eurotop-500 company, with operations in the Nordic countries, the Baltics and Russia. They serve some 2 million consumers regionally and around 15,000 enterprises internationally, offering a wide range of subscriptions with services. Their revenues for 2007 were EUR 1.57 billion and they employ nearly 2,900 people. Elisa's global alliance partners are Vodafone and Telenor.

2. SMS—or Short Message Service—is a communications protocol that allows for the interchange of short text messages between mobile telephone devices. SMS text messaging is the most widely used data application on the planet, and in many parts of the world the term "SMS" has become synonymous for a text message or for sending a text message.

3. W-CDMA or Wideband Code Division Multiple Access is a type of 3G cellular network. W-CDMA is a higher-speed transmission protocol used in the Japanese FOMA and UMTS system, a third generation to the 2G GSM networks deployed worldwide.

4. The Apple Newton was the first PDA released in 1992 and sold until 1998. During the 1980s, while president and CEO of Safko International Inc., one of the authors collaborated with the Advanced Technology Group at Apple. After demonstrating the fully graphic human interface (GHI) of the SenSei Operating System to Apple and General Magic, it quickly became the archetype for the Apple Newton Operating System.

5. Morph is a concept that demonstrates how future mobile devices might be stretchable and flexible, allowing the user to transform their mobile device into

radically different shapes. It demonstrates the ultimate functionality that nano-technology might be capable of delivering: flexible materials, transparent electronics, and self-cleaning surfaces. Dr. Bob Iannucci, chief technology officer, Nokia, commented, "Nokia Research Center is looking at ways to reinvent the form and function of mobile devices; the Morph concept shows what might be possible."

6. . . . "Motorola is making mobile music access seamless for music lovers—in their homes, at work, on the road, and now at the premier live music venue—the House of Blues," said Kathleen Finato, senior director of marketing for North America Mobile Devices, Motorola, Inc. "It's a true marriage of entertainment and mobility as the music lifestyle fan receives the ultimate concert experience long before the first song is played. House of Blues is an innovator in the live music category. By combining our expertise with a mobile leader such as Motorola, we are able to create new interactive opportunities for our artists and customers," said Paul Sewell, senior vice president, sponsorship House of Blues Entertainment, Inc. "Together, Motorola and House of Blues will power the enjoyment for the growing tech savvy music generation." . . . www.motorola.com/mediacenter/news/detail.jsp?globalObjectId=5705_5683_23.

FIGURE 22.10   Couple Sharing an iPhone

Let the Conversation Begin (Interpersonal)

What's In It for You?

Interpersonal refers to the many applications and web sites in the social media ecosphere that allow us to communicate live, real time on a one-to-one, one-to-many, many-to-one, and many-to-many basis. Examples of one-to-one exchange are tools such as Skype, AOL IM, GTalk, Apple's iChat, or something like Jott—where you can leave notes and messages for yourself via the phone. One-to-many social media tools include Jott as well, Twitter (see Chapter 15, Thumbs Up for Microblogging, Yahoo! Messenger, Microsoft Live Messenger, and Doodle. Many-to-many examples are applications like GoToMeeting, WebEx, and Adobe Connect. So many of these tools are free and can significantly reduce or even eliminate expenses like long-distance telephone calls. Using IM and web conferencing eradicated the cost of airfare and hotels for many companies. Many-to-one could be considered page aggregators where the conversations of many different bloggers are compiled into your web page or even Google Alerts where alerts about many different mentions of your search terms are sent directly to your personal e-mail.

Of course, this list is by no means complete; it's simply intended to provide a sampling of some of the wide variety and broad range of social media interpersonal tools. As with all of the other chapters' content, useful tools, and applications, the players are continuously changing. Many are being added, and some are becoming extinct. For example: when work on this book began, Pownce (a free message and file sharing site) was a viable company with growing numbers and a useful service. But on December 15, 2008—as writing was wrapping up—Pownce announced that it was shutting down. And by the time this book actually hits the bookstore, countless other changes will have taken place in the social media tool roster. To help with the constantly changing nature of this field, the web site accompanying this book will be constantly updated with the latest information on social media techniques, tools, and strategies, and updates to *The Social Media Bible*. So visit www.theSocialMediaBible.com often, and contribute to the future of social media.

One impact of social media on the present way of doing business relates to training presentations, which now can be delivered without the speaker leaving his or her hometown. Before all the social media tools came into place, companies might fly anywhere from 200 to 800 employees in from around the United States; put them up in a hotel; pay for the ballroom, food, and other expenses; and incur the expense of four days of down time for 800 employees (3,200 lost days!). Now a speaker can set up a camera, a web conferencing application, and IM chat, and present to locations around the globe in real time, and even answer audience questions live! And then everyone goes back to work with no expenses whatsoever incurred (except, of course, for the speaker's time). Imagine what that is worth to a company! This type of webinar can be done in place of telephone calls; for remote training of employees; for state-of-the-company addresses by the CEO; and for announcements to employees that include new products, HR policy changes, public relations issues, sales meetings—and more. All for free (or nearly)!

What You Need to Know

As you might suspect, this chapter's format needs to be a little different. Sections like *Back to the Beginning* and *Providers* really aren't appropriate. Instead, this chapter provides you with some facts about the features and benefits based on a few hand-selected, highlighted companies, and introduces you to some extraordinary tools in the social media ecosphere. You will also see that many of these selected companies and services—although listed in the "one-to-one" section—can be used for one-to-many, or even many-to-many communication. A good number of the sites actually fit into more than one category.

One-to-One

Skype: Low cost calls are what Skype (www.skype.com, Figure 23.1) is made for. You can use this service to call another person who also has Skype—to anywhere in the world and at any time, day or night, morning or weekends—and it is totally free. Yep—it costs absolutely nothing. Zip. Zero. Zilch.

FIGURE 23.1   Skype

Once you and your friend, family member, or colleague have downloaded Skype, you can get started on the really cool stuff, such as making completely free and great quality calls from your computer. That's the impressive thing about Skype besides its price tag of zero dollars: you can use tools that you already have—your Internet connection and your computer—and make Skype-to-Skype calls. You and the person you are speaking with will need to have a headset (or use your computer's built-in microphone and speakers) to talk to each other. A headset will really improve the sound quality of your calls; or, you can take it to the next level with free video calls.

You can also use Skype to make pretty cheap calls to landline telephones and mobile phones. Just locate the person you want to call in your contact list and click her or his name. To call your friend for free, simply click the green button. This will start the call, and you can talk for as long as you want, whenever you want.

Skype provides more than just free Skype-to-Skype calls; it's about inexpensive local, national, and international calls to phones and mobiles. For example, why not send a text message directly from Skype; forward a call to your mobile; or set up an online number for friends, family, and colleagues to make a local call from their old-fashioned phone to your Skype, wherever in the world you are? All you need to get going with these products is a pay-as-you-go Skype Credit. Alternatively, you can get unlimited calls to landlines and a great bundle of useful features with a subscription package for a low monthly fee.

There are two ways to start using Skype products. One involves a pay-monthly subscription; the other is a pay-as-you-go option with Skype Credit. This second option simply allows you to use it as you need it. Skype Credit allows you to add money to your account and start calling locally, nationally, or internationally. The pay-monthly option lets you make unlimited calls to a country or region, and also includes an online number and voicemail. There's no long-term contract needed.

AOL Instant Messenger: AOL Instant Messenger (AIM, www. AIM.com; Figure 23.2) is a free online service that lets you communicate in real time. Using the AIM Buddy List window lets you see when your buddies are online and chat with them. Chatting and sharing with your friends, family, and colleagues is more fun than ever using this application. You can send text messages, share photos and URLs, make a PC-to-PC voice call, create an online personality, and more.

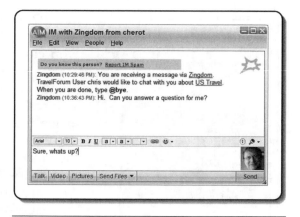

FIGURE 23.2   AOL Instant Messenger

The AIM software includes many new and improved features that increase the compatibility and flexibility of your instant messaging experience. The service is now compatible with Windows Vista and Windows XP 64-bit, and the free software includes Instant Messaging, Talk and Voice chat, Video IM, e-mail, and Text Messaging. Additional features of the AIM software include AOL Radio; file transfer for pictures and documents; Buddy List; Address Book; integration of Address Book with Plaxo, the industry leader in Web-based contact management; IM forwarding to mobile phone; AOL Alerts and Reminders; and browse or search the Web through AOL Explorer.

Anyone with a computer and an Internet connection can use the AIM service—completely free. However, you are responsible for purchasing a connection to the Internet, any associated telephone charges, or any premium services that you choose. You can download the AIM software by visiting www.aim.com, then clicking either the Install Now button or the link for the correct version for the operating system on your computer.

There is also a service called AIM Express, which is a convenient, travel version of the AIM service. This application lets you view your Buddy List window and send instant messages from any computer with a Web browser and an Internet connection without having to download the software. Just like the AIM service, the AIM Express service is free.

Google Talk: Google Talk (GTalk, www.google.com/talk; Figure 23.3) is search-engine giant Google's approach to instant communication. Google Talk can either be downloaded to your computer or launched through a browser. Google Talk allows you to communicate free with your friends, family, and colleagues—anyone with whom you want to chat online. Google

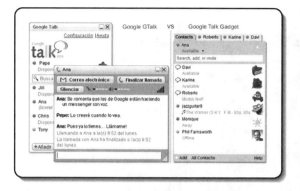

FIGURE 23.3 Google Talk

Talk features include instant messaging, which—like AIM—allows you to chat with all of your Google Talk and Gmail contacts in real time, free PC-to-PC voice calls, which lets you talk for free to anyone else who is online and is equipped with the Google Talk client. GTalk allows you to send and receive voicemails and provides unlimited file transfers that lets you send and receive files to your contacts without file size or bandwidth restrictions. Even if the person you are calling isn't available, you can leave a voicemail for them. Gmail notifications on your desktop appear when you're signed into Google Talk, so you'll be notified of new messages in your Gmail inbox.

The Google Talk gadget does not require any download; you can start chatting immediately from any computer. You can also create a group chat and invite multiple people to join an online conversation. Google Talk also has media previews that allow users to cut and paste video and slideshow URLs from sites like YouTube, Google Video, Picasa Web Albums, and Flickr into your chats, and view them in your chat window.

You can also add the Google Talk gadget to your iGoogle homepage to put chat alongside other useful and entertaining gadgets, and you can add Google Talk to your own web page; just cut and paste the code into your own web page or blog to embed the Google Talk gadget.

iChat: With Apple's iChat (www.apple.com/macosx/features/ichat.html; Figure 23.4) feature, you can chat from anywhere—as long as you are using a Mac. iChat offers crystal-clear audio quality that delivers the clearest possible sound during audio chats. Apple's wideband codec AAC-LD—which samples a full range of vocal frequencies—sounds great with any voice. iChat also offers text messaging that includes Tabbed Chats, Multiple Logins, Invisibility, Animated Buddy Icons, SMS Forwarding, Custom Buddy List Order, File Transfer Manager, and Space-Efficient Views.

The iChat Tabbed Window AIM Icon works with AIM, the largest instant messaging community in the United States (see description above). You and the people with whom you chat can be either AIM or Mac users. You're able to text, audio, and video chat whether your buddies use a Mac or a PC. Sign in with your AIM account, and all your buddies appear in your iChat buddy list.

FIGURE 23.4 iChat

New video backdrops built into iChat can make it look like users are chatting from the Eiffel Tower, under the sea, or the surface of the moon. They can also create their own custom backdrops by dragging a picture or video from iPhoto or the Finder into the video effects window. Backdrops even show up on the screens of buddies who don't have the Mac operating system (Leopard).

Users can also transform video chats using new Photo Booth effects, where they can add a special twist to a chat with the comic book effect. They can alternatively soften images with glow, or just choose any effect that changes the video instantly.

With iChat, you don't have to wait for a darkened room and a projector to present vacation photos or Keynote slides. iChat's Theater Now application lets you do it all remotely. Simply put on a photo slideshow, click through a Keynote presentation, or play a full-screen movie—accompanied by a video feed of you hosting—while your audience watches. In fact, you can show any file on your system that works with Quick Look (Figure 23.5), which is Apple's file contents preview window.

Thanks to iChat screen sharing, you and your buddy can also observe and control a single desktop—a feature that makes it a cinch to collaborate with a colleague, browse the Web with a friend, or pick plane seats with a family member. Share your own desktop—or your buddy's—and you both have control at all times. And iChat automatically initiates an audio chat

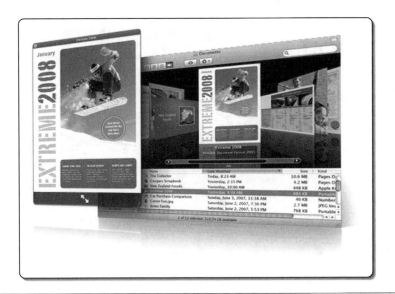

FIGURE 23.5 QuickLook

when you start a screen-sharing session, so you can talk things through while you're at it.

iChat also allows users to save audio and video chats for posterity with iChat recording. Before recording starts, iChat notifies buddies and asks for their permission to record. When the chat is done, iChat stores the audio chats as AAC files and video chats as MPEG-4 files—so that users can play them in iTunes or QuickTime. Share them with friends, family, and colleagues, or sync them to your iPod and play on the go.

Jott: Jott (www.Jott.com; Figure 23.6) is a web application which makes sure that users stay on top of everything in their lives. With a simple phone call to 866-JOTT-123, you can capture notes, set reminders and calendar appointments, and stay in touch with friends, family, and colleagues while you interact with your favorite web sites and services—all with the sound of your voice!

Jott's technology joins the cell phone voice and text messaging, your blog, Twitter, groups, and e-mail. By entering the Jott toll-free number into your speed dial, you can access all of Jott's capabilities with the touch of a single button. Jott works on any phone—cell or land line—independent of carrier, and requires no downloads or training. While your cell phone might be your first choice, you're not limited to just one telephone. You can Jott from your house or office phone, too. Just add those numbers to your Jott account.

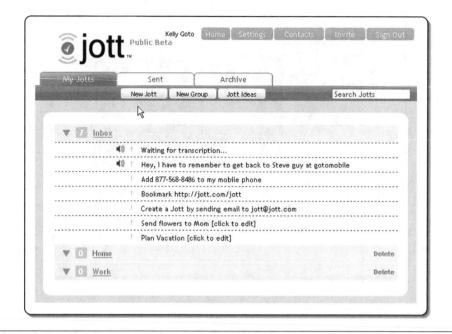

FIGURE 23.6 Jott

Jott Links are essentially web pages that can receive HTTP posts and write out a text response. They're called Jott Links because you use them to "link" Jott messages with other services, such as blogging and social networking sites—including Twitter and Zillo. At the time of this writing, Jott was compatible with Jaiku, Blogger, TypePad, WordPress, Twitter, Yahoo!, Zillo, LiveJournal, Tumblr, Amazon, 30Boxes, and Sandy.

Jott uses your mobile phone to convert your voice into text messages that are sent directly to e-mail, cell text messages, blogging sites, groups, and even content management–enhanced web sites that are driven by such platforms as WordPress and Joomla. In its first 12 months, Jott has already sent more than a million messages for business travelers reporting expenses, as well as personal applications such as status messages to coaches, parents, students, and teachers.

Jott can be used as an alarm or reminder of timed events. After calling in to Jott's toll-free telephone number, you will be asked whom you would like to Jott. You say "Reminder," list the day and the time that you would like to receive your reminder, and then leave your reminder message. When you hang up, your reminder will be sent 15 minutes before the scheduled event to your cell phone, e-mail, blog, or Twitter account. You can also use the service to send your translated messages to coworkers, friends, or family member with instructions, updates, or action items. Just call Jott and record the name of the person or people whom you want to receive your text message—and Jott instantly translates and sends your instructions to the appropriate contacts. You can even send these to your cell phone or e-mail as well.

Teams or groups of coworkers, friends, or family utilize Jott's services to alert one another of impending or recent events. When that new baby is born, a meeting is about to begin, or there's a change in travel plans, Jott will send the same message to any group you create. You can even just send it to your Yahoo! Groups using Jott Links (www.jott.com).

Jott also allows you to keep track of your expenses in a straightforward and organized manner. Just call the 1-800 number, and you can message your costs as they happen. With simple rules set up in your e-mail, Jott expenses can go from your voice message directly into your expense or accounting folder in your e-mail. Do you bill by the hour? Just phone Jott at the end of each session, and your billable hours—along with any special message—will be delivered to your e-mail's Hours folder for easy accounting.

Do you think that blogging is a time-consuming chore? Not anymore! You can use Jott to record your voice message and have it instantly converted and added to your personal blog. You can also send a group e-mail/text message to all of your contacts, and let them know that you have a new blog waiting for them.

Do you sometimes just want to inform someone of important news immediately, without having to engage in a half-hour conversation about what they did the night before? Jott them! This way your message goes directly to their cell phone without having to keep saying, "I gotta go!"

Jott is especially convenient when you're driving. In more and more states, it is illegal to text message and drive. Jott provides a reliable, safer alternative to texting while behind the wheel. Because 40 percent of cell phone usage occurs while driving your car, Jott is a more prudent way to record information than, for example, scribbling information on a piece of scratch paper or fast food napkin. Jott is voice-activated, so you no longer will have to try to write notes, reminders, telephone numbers, or driving directions on scraps of paper. Just say it, and display it.

One-to-Many

Twitter: The most popular one-to-many communication tool today by far is Twitter (www.Twitter.com), the microblogging platform. Twitter is a micro-blogging and social networking service that allows its users to send and receive brief (140 characters or less) text-based, micropost instant messages that are referred to as Tweets. These text messages are displayed on the user's technology of choice—be it a text messaging cell phone, web site, PDA, Twitter web site, RSS (see Chapter 19, RSS—Really Simple Syndication Made Simple), SMS,[1] e-mail, or an application such as Facebook, Twitter-rific, or web page aggregator (see Chapter 19, RSS—Really Simple Syndication Made Simple). These messages are also delivered to anyone who has signed up and been accepted to follow your messages, and the same is true of any Tweets that you have requested and been approved to follow.

For a complete discussion on Twitter, please see Chapter 15, Thumbs Up for Microblogging.

Yahoo! Messenger: Friends are only an instant away on Yahoo! Messenger (www.messenger.yahoo.com; Figure 23.7). With this tool, you can send text messages in real time to your friends, family, and colleagues on Yahoo! or Windows Live™ Messenger; decide who sees you online with stealth settings; swap photos and monster files (up to 2GB) in real-time; enjoy voice calls and webcam video; join a chat room to meet new friends while you discuss your favorite topics; share photos from your desktop or Flickr, then discuss them over IM while you and a friend view them together; make a voice call to another Yahoo! Messenger user for free (microphone and speakers/headset are required); or even call others on their regular or mobile

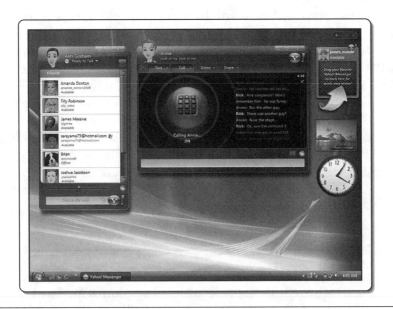

FIGURE 23.7 Yahoo! Messenger

phones from Messenger for as low as one cent a minute (a Phone Out account is required). Yahoo! Messenger provides a Phone In feature to get a phone number for Messenger. This application provides a new phone number that allows you to receive calls in Yahoo! Messenger (Phone In account required). Yahoo! Messenger also offers SMS, or text messaging, wherein you can send text messages from Messenger to your colleague's mobile phones for free. You can also plug in your webcam to share live video on Yahoo! Messenger.

Another feature of this service is IM Conferencing, where you can Instant Message with many colleagues at once and utilize voice capabilities where available. You can IM with colleagues on other networks—such as Windows Live™ Messenger, Reuters Messaging, and Lotus Sametime—as well. The File Transfer option lets users instantly send files (with a 2GB limit) to a friend while you IM. There is also IM Forwarding to Mobile that sends IMs to your phone as text messages when you sign out of Messenger. You can use Yahoo!'s Contact Search Bar to quickly find a contact to IM, call, SMS, or more. Yahoo! Search lets users begin a web search directly from their Yahoo! Messenger window. The Yahoo! Address Book provides the chance to view and edit any Yahoo! Address Book information for contacts right from Messenger. There is also a Stealth/Privacy Settings, where users can make themselves appear online to some friends and off-line to others.

Yahoo! Mail alerts notify users when a new Yahoo! Mail message arrives. The included voicemail service allows colleagues to call you on Yahoo! Messenger and leave a voicemail if a user is unavailable. This also includes Message Archiving, which maintains a private archive of IM conversations. There's also Tabbed IM Windows that reduce desktop clutter by organizing multiple conversations into a single window.

Yahoo! Messenger gives you Buzz Alert to get your colleague's attention with a click of the Buzz button. There are also Yahoo! Updates that get you real-time alerts in Yahoo! Messenger about what your colleagues are posting online, reviewing, and generally buzzing about. You can also get their plug-ins that add content, services, and games to Messenger that you can enjoy on your own, or with colleagues while you IM.

Then there's Yahoo! Messenger Audibles, a service that sends an animated, talking character to a friend to liven up your IM conversation. And of course emoticons to express your feelings with animated, smiling faces. There are also Avatars, which represent your likeness with a stylized, graphic image where you can choose the hair, clothing, and more. You can display Images to represent yourself to your friends.

Yahoo! Messenger even has different skins that allow you to give your IM world a new look. It also includes IMVironments to liven things up with interactive, themed backgrounds in the IM window. Yahoo! Games allows you to play a game of pool, backgammon, checkers, and more with a friend while you IM. Custom Status Messages will tell your friends what you're doing, seeing, or feeling by customizing your online status message. There are even Custom Ringtones that you can assign to different callers, or upload your own audio files to use. And if all of that wasn't enough, Yahoo! Messenger also has Customizable Fonts and Colors that allow you to IM with a font, color, and style that suits your personality. Sound Effects and Soundtrack (during voice calls) can throw a sound effect in while you're on a call or upload a music file to play as a soundtrack in the background. Wow!

Microsoft Live Messenger: Much like AIM, GTalk, iChat, and Yahoo! Messenger, Microsoft Live Messenger (www.WindowsLive.com; Figure 23.8) allows you to connect and share with contacts—anywhere. This service provides a Hotmail account, which allows you to stay connected anywhere with your Web e-mail account; access to your multiple e-mail accounts in one place; a Messenger tool that lets you connect, share, and make your conversations count; and a Toolbar that makes it easy to access Windows Live services from any Web page.

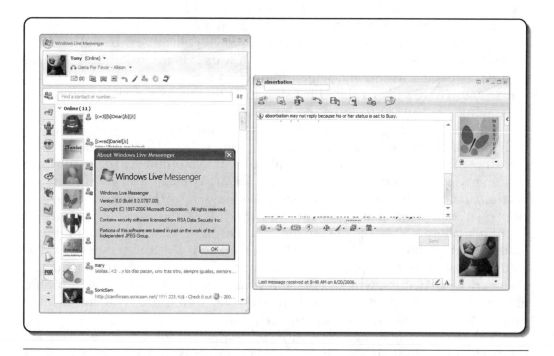

FIGURE 23.8 Microsoft Live Messenger

Microsoft Live Messenger Share provides SkyDrive, which is a password-protected online file storage feature; Spaces, the best place to share your world online; Photo Gallery, where you can get creative and share your photos and videos; Writer, where you can easily publish pictures, videos, and other rich content to your blog; and Events, where you can plan your next meeting or gathering, send invitations, and share photos.

Doodle: Doodle (www.Doodle.com; Figure 23.9) is a free online coordination tool that requires neither registration nor software installation. It allows users to schedule events like board meetings, business lunches, conference calls, family reunions, movie nights—or any other group event. A term that means "casual scribble," "design," or "sketch," Doodle sounds like the easy and fun application that it truly is. It's name is short and simple to remember, and while Doodle is not a drawing service, it indeed makes scheduling events so simple that it becomes a casual task. You and your contacts can use the feature to decide upon movies, menus, or travel destinations, or among any other selection.

Doodle makes it easy to find a date and time for a group event by helping to determine common availabilities among all parties involved. This service is particularly easy to use, and even passes the "grandma test"—so easy your grandma can do it! In addition to scheduling events, Doodle also supports

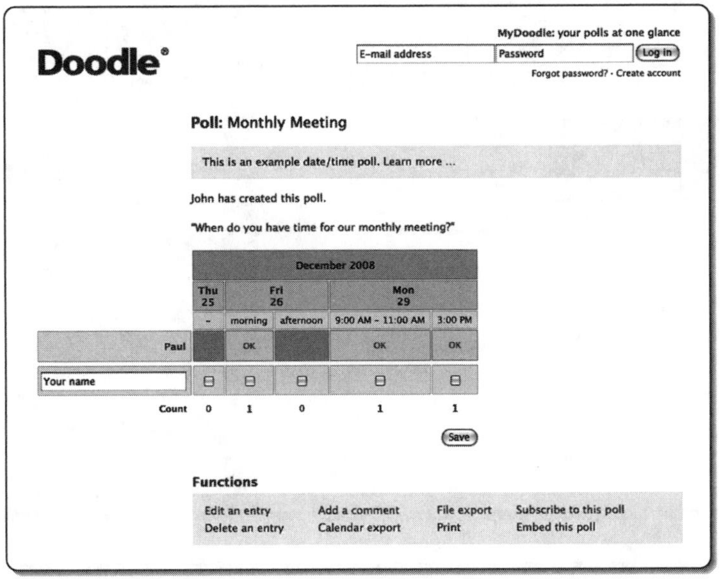

FIGURE 23.9 Doodle

polls in general, allowing groups to conveniently decide on options other than dates.

Doodle can also be used as a reservation tool for a shared holiday home, exercise planning at your sports club, or to find out who travels to the company excursion by train or by car—as well as who has space left in their car. With Doodle, you can vote quickly and easily on the movie for the next DVD night, the logo for the new web presence, or the restaurant for Christmas dinner.

Many-to-Many

GoToMeeting: GoToMeeting (www.GoToMeeting.com; Figure 23.10) is for any business a cost-effective, easy-to-use online meeting solution that vastly improves productivity and sales. This service is to use on the fly or for scheduled presentations; to perform live demos; or to collaborate on documents in real time. GoToMeeting's web conferencing tool allows users to meet online rather than in a conference room. It's the easiest and most cost-effective way to organize and attend online meetings. The patented

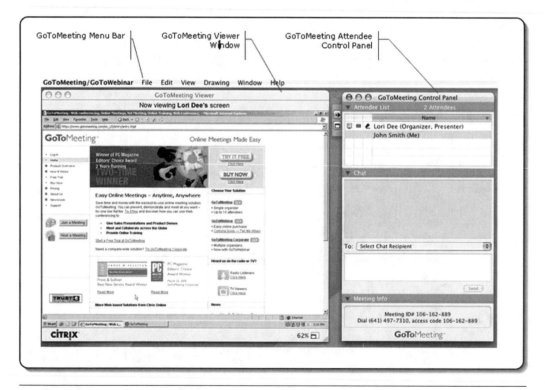

FIGURE 23.10 GoToMeeting

technology enables colleagues, customers, and prospects to view any application running on your PC in real time. With the flexibility to meet in person or online, you'll be able to do more and travel less.

Clients and coworkers don't need your application to view your files; even files created with specialized applications, such as CAD drawings, are viewable. Just use the GoToMeeting icon in your system tray, an e-mail, or an instant message for logins or setups. It takes about two minutes to set up, and a few more seconds to start a meeting. That's it! With GoToMeeting, you can meet as often as you want, for as long as you want—for one low rate.

GoToMeeting allows users to turn calls into instant online meetings, and also has a cost-effective online meeting product called All You Can Meet®— which allows users to host unlimited meetings for an unlimited duration with up to 15 attendees per meeting—all for one flat fee! GoToMeeting is also a secure online meeting tool. Industry-standard security features ensure that your confidential meeting information remains private. If you need to reach a larger audience or want additional marketing tools such as polls, surveys, and reports, GoToWebinar™ offers unlimited webinars with up to 1,000 attendees, plus the collaborative online meeting capabilities.

WebEx: WebEx (www.WebEx.com; Figure 23.11) provides the benefit of on-demand web meetings with no significant up-front costs, no servers to maintain, and no software to install or support. With just a web browser

FIGURE 23.11 WebEx

and a telephone, you can use WebEx. Users can integrate WebEx into daily business workflow, and use online meetings to get together with anyone at any time. Coworkers and associates can demonstrate products and services, share presentations in any format, and resolve open issues in real time with secure and reliable technology. WebEx allows the impact of live events by holding large, scalable online proceedings—such as all-hands meetings, shareholder presentations, and webinars—with interactive and dynamic multimedia presentations.

Professionals can use WebEx to deliver interactive world-class training and reach more people than they ever thought possible by offering on-demand and live, online classrooms. Technical issues are resolved more quickly and productivity is increased while you reduce support costs; increase client satisfaction with both unattended and attended remote support; shorten the sales cycle by connecting with anyone, anywhere with dynamic online sales presentations; and close deals faster.

On-demand web conferencing has become the preferred communication medium for businesses today. By combining the ease of audioconferencing with the interactivity of videoconferencing directly from your desktop, you create a truly personalized interactive experience.

Adobe Connect: Adobe Connect (www.adobe.com/products/acrobatconnect pro; Figure 23.12) is the next best thing to an in-person meeting. With Adobe Acrobat Connect™ Pro software, you can provide instant access to engaging,

FIGURE 23.12 Adobe Connect

collaborative meetings with just a web browser and the Adobe Flash Player runtime. You can enable attendees to jump into always-available personal meeting rooms with no scheduling or registration required. They're able to share screens, use a whiteboard, chat, videoconference, and enjoy real-time interactions without the hassle of travel. They can control meetings and related assets with robust management and reporting tools, and protect sensitive business data and meeting content with tight security and strong access controls.

With the Adobe Acrobat Connect Pro software, marketing and sales departments can increase leads, boost response rates, and close deals faster through high-impact web conferencing. Forget specialized software; all it takes is a web browser and the Adobe Flash Player runtime. You can boost audience attendance and participation, generate more qualified leads at a lower cost, and save time with expert assistance.

Adobe Connect requires no plug-in downloads, which eliminates technical barriers to instant access. Even the best online seminar is useless if your audience can't participate. You can reach your participants right away and eradicate any obstacles to attendance with Acrobat Connect Pro. Because the tool is based on Adobe Flash Player—which is already installed on more than 98 percent of Internet-connected desktops worldwide—you essentially have everything you need already. This means your audience can join Acrobat Connect Pro seminars and access Adobe Presenter presentations just by clicking a URL—without cumbersome software downloads.

Adobe Connect allows you to play videos of corporate executives during Acrobat Connect Pro seminars, to communicate high-level messages, and to use customer testimonial videos to enhance credibility. You can share high-impact multimedia content including streaming audio, video, and software simulations to make your seminars and on-demand presentations both compelling and persuasive, and can easily conduct breakout discussions for increased interactivity and participation. You can even record web seminars—including those using synchronized audio—from either Internet (VoIP) or telephone audioconferencing, and make them available to people who can't attend. You just use simple mark-in and mark-out tools to edit out unwanted sections, and make recordings available for download on a web site or for offline viewing and distribution.

Adobe Connect also allows users to host lively and informative web seminars to engage prospects and respond to questions in real time. Take advantage of multiperson video in Acrobat Connect Pro, your choice of Internet (VoIP) or telephone audioconferencing, and unparalleled support for rich multimedia content to deliver web seminars that are the next best thing to being there. You can increase the success of your e-mail and online ad campaigns by driving prospects to engaging, narrated Adobe Presenter presentations instead of simply linking to static landing pages. Get feedback instantly through embedded surveys. Respondents simply click an embedded URL to view a multimedia presentation, fully branded with your corporate logo and colors. You can also automate attendee registration, notifications, reminders, and postevent thank-you e-mails. Customize registration pages and the look and feel of your online seminar rooms to reflect your corporate branding.

Within your meeting, you can create multiple breakout rooms—each with its own private VoIP or telephone conference call. Use a default template or create custom layouts for each meeting room, and provide specific content appropriate for each breakout. Hosts can monitor all breakouts, move between them, and broadcast messages to all participants across room boundaries. When it's time to bring the groups back together, hosts can review breakout room content with the entire group in the main room.

Within a meeting or virtual classroom, hosts can see a list of invitees and their presence via your corporate instant messaging server. Hosts can initiate chat conversations with IM users from directly within Acrobat Connect Pro. Acrobat Connect Pro and Adobe Presenter software provide an intuitive Web-based interface that enables users to customize the entire web conferencing experience to reflect their organization's brand. Color schemes and logos can be easily applied to login screens, web applications, live meeting rooms, presentations, and training modules.

Expert Insight

John Pollard, CEO and founder, Jott, www.Jott.com

John Pollard

[Jott] is an alternative way of accessing the Internet. In some ways, the cellular infrastructure is completely bypassed. Landline infrastructure—you know, the back hold that was done in the developed world for so many years—has not really been done in the developing world, in some places. It has really been remarkable, and it's a great thing in general. . . .

You know I am a firm believer that there are going to be different ways of accessing the Internet, and that in some populations, it's going to be primarily mobile-driven. In [certain] economies and geographical areas—it's going to be a healthy mix of a desktop and a mobile phone. But I am a big believer in mobile, and I think sometimes things are over-hyped and people overestimate what's going to happen to one degree or another. However, we think it is here to stay. I know one of the essential things behind Jott is that people look at their mobile phones—whether it is an iPhone or it is just your humble average phone—as a trusted appliance, this thing that they have with them all the time. . . .

Let me try to put it this way. I sort of ask questions, which are, "Would you hire the following kind of person—someone who always picked up the phone for you? Took dictation? Sent e-mail and text messages for you (hands-free so you did not have to take your eyes off the road)? Posted messages or calendar items to Google Calendar just using your voice? Would help you retrieve information from your favorite sources (like the *New York Times* or TechCrunch, or what have you) with just their voice? Would never sleep, does not complain, does not whine, and does some of this for free?"

Would you hire this person? . . . And, of course, the answer is yes!

Really . . . Jott is a mobile-productivity tool that works on any phone. It does not require any downloads or a particular carrier or contract; it does not require anything but what you already have. You simply call a number—1-866-J-O-T-T-123—and you will be asked a simple question which has many answers—"Who do you want to Jott?" And if you say, "Yourself" or if you say "Notes," you will hear a beep and you can say something and hang up; and we will take your voice and convert it to text automatically and then give it to you on your desktop.

And it is really as simple as that. You call a number, you say something, and you hang up. Everybody in the world knows how to make a phone call; and so everybody in the world already knows how to use Jott automatically. The beauty of [this service] is that that simple sequence of things allows you to capture thoughts, be more organized, and communicate with people hands-free. So in response to the question, "Who do you want to Jott?" I could say, "Lon Safko," and you would hear "beep," and then I could record a message to you and Jott would deliver that text message and an e-mail message to Lon Safko. So, if I was in traffic and I really needed to contact you, I could Jott you. It is really quite remarkable that something so simple with such an easy-to-use user experience does so many things and is so powerful. I think we have really struck a nerve. . . .

What we decided at the beginning of the company was that what mattered to people most was simplicity and quality. It would not make any sense to build a product where what came out the other end was gobbledygook. We really needed . . . a super-simple front-end that works the way people work, and then deliver quality results in the back-end. The reality is that people are using Jott in real places. They use it in their car, and they use it between meetings. They use it in places where there is background noise; they speak normally, they say names, and they speak the way you and I typically speak. They have some "umm's" and "ahh's" and they repeat themselves. . . .

(continued)

(*continued*)

To have the speech-recognition engine all by itself—to take out the noise, the pops, and the poor cellular activity issues and turn out 100 percent accurate transcription— . . . really is quite impossible. So what we have done is to take the voice and run it through a couple of different speech recognition engines. We have gotten very, very smart about this and . . . we sort of preprocess as much as we can.

And then we have people, frankly, on the other side of the planet (thank God for the speed of light!) that clean up pieces of this. You know, it is very much like people who work in call centers overseas, who process information; or people who are in the medical transcription business where they write up doctor's notes and things like that. It is very highly organized; it's highly, highly secure, it's very controlled.

And it is a real challenge to get it right for a lot of reasons. . . . One: because a bunch of people are spread all over the place, and two: we have to keep the quality high, and three: we need to do it at a price that will translate, or at a cost that will translate to an affordable product here in the United States. That is not easy to do; and I am happy to say that because that is not easy to do, it makes it very difficult to replicate what we have done. You know, speech recognition is going to get better and better and better, and I am excited about the prospects there, because every time there is an evolution in the state-of-the-art there, we benefit from them and so do our customers. . . .

Yeah, it is interesting. We have decided that we are not a real-time business. We don't need to be real-time, because the case [around which] we are modeling in most of our design is the person sitting in a car who really needs to capture that thought, that action-item or that idea that they had, or that promise that they made to a customer. They need to seize it, so that they do not forget it. And it is not critical that they get it immediately, or real time. What's important is that it is safe and secure and captured. Therefore, it can be a couple of minutes delayed; no problem. So that's what we model that on, and we usually achieve that pretty well. You know, there are times when we have super-fast turnaround times and some times when it takes a little bit longer, but overall we get the turnaround done very quickly. . . .

And we designed it so that it could be useful for anybody. We really believe it, and we have this mantra inside the company—you know, in our little office here—that says, "Everybody should have Jott 123 on speed-dial." And we mean that; whether you are a casual user who uses it a couple times a week, or if you are a super hard-core Jotter who uses it many times a day. It is almost like insurance. It's almost like having AAA on your phone. It's just there; you should have it there.

It is so simple that it scales well; from the grandmother who is trying to text to her grandchildren . . . (laughter) to the road warrior who is reeling off expenses as he gets out of his cab. And it is broad-set, [which doesn't] mean that we are sloppy, or that we're not targeting people. However, I think everybody has too much going on these days. Everybody could use a little bit of help, and happily Jott morphs itself to whatever need you might have. If you need casual usage of it, great. If you need really heavy usage of it, we also scale for that. So it works out well for everyone.

To listen to or read the entire Executive Conversation with John Pollard, go to www .theSocialMediaBible.com.

Expert Insight

Rishi Chandra, director of product management, Windows Live Instant Messenger, www.google.com/apps/intl/en/business/index.html

Rishi Chandra

The Google Apps is a set of business applications, which are hosted on the Internet, or . . . on Cloud. The idea is—if you have heard of some of Google's more famous consumer products like GMLs, Google Calendar and Google Talk and Google Blog—[that] we actually take those consumer technologies, package, and bundle them in a way that enterprises and businesses can actually use.

So, for example, instead of having a Gmail.com e-mail address where you use the Gmail product, you can use your own company's e-mail address, and access the power of your company's e-mail infrastructure. . . .

So as I said there are two core components to Google Apps. There is a messaging component, which includes G-mail, Docs, and Calendar. And on the collaboration side—the other element of Apps—includes Google Sites, Google Docs, and a new product we have just recently launched, called Google Video for Business . . . the difficult thing is that we launched [it] only two to three weeks ago [September, 2008]; and [again], we are really excited about taking this idea of Google's Consumer Technologies—in this case, YouTube—and being able to apply [them] to a business setting. So being able to allow companies to upload their own video content and within their company— just as you see YouTube do in the consumer world for them. . . .

(continued)

(continued)

We have done a couple of things that . . . work in a business environment. . . . Businesses love the fact that we have very easy-to-use and powerful tools [that] can be hosted on the Web. They get all the benefits of Google hosting it for you. You do not have to worry about it; [and since] it works in a browser, you do not have to install or maintain any type of hardware or software. At the same time, businesses have a higher level of expectation around certain features than [consumers do]. You need to have more control, more security, and more functionality targeted for specific business-use cases. And that's actually what we have done with the video product, for example. We actually have it at higher resolution; it's more secure because you can actually share it with a set of people; and only a small set of people so that they will be the only ones to have access to that information. And we have administrative controls in there, so that your administrator can administer the product just as you could with any other product. . . .

That is really one of the key benefits of Cloud computing . . . this idea that you have a single place for your information—in this case, it is on the Internet—[that] most people can access from [wherever they are in the world]; whatever company they are a part of, or whatever device they are accessing it from, whether it be a mobile device or a computer or a laptop. . . .

That is one of the great benefits: anyone can access [the information] at any point in time. The other benefit—as you [pointed out]—is this idea of collaborating with multiple people in different places. You know, the biggest challenge we heard from both businesses and consumers is this idea of collaboration through e-mail is a pretty broken process. . . . So, for example, if four or five people wanted to work on a document today, most people actually just e-mail that out to five different people; each of them downloads an individual copy of that document, work off their own copy and send it back. Now [the original] person has to recompile those different changes; and if multiple people are working off of it with different revisions, you can see yourself getting into a pretty easy nightmare, pretty quickly . . . and so, . . . we are thinking of a new way for people to interact with each other and actually share information and collaborate on information.

That is really one of the key benefits of Cloud computing. . . . And what that product does is actually a wiki. A wiki is [a document or web page] that anyone can edit a piece of . . . and you can easily create multiple pieces of data in one single place. So, for example, if I have a Project Team, I can embed a Google Calendar in that Google Site; I can embed a document associated with that Project Team; I can associate videos with that Project Team. You can bring together all of these different types of rich, social information into one single place and have people collaborate on it in a very easy way. . . .

It is a monumental change with how people interact with web pages today. [When] most people hear the word *web page*, they get really intimidated. It certainly makes them think of things like HTML and how complicated those are. Google Sites wants to make it as easy to edit a web page as it is to use "edit" in a document. Anyone who has permission to that site can go do it; and it is as straightforward as editing a document. You can edit text, you can pull different pieces of information in very quickly and easily, and with one button you can publish it to the set of people you want to share that information with. That's the real philosophy behind Google Sites. . . .

It is a great product, because it brings together a lot of different places that use information; and really highlights to business users in particular. There are certain technologies that they are just not used to using, but it really does enable much richer collaboration. Video is a great example of this. You will find in the consumer world [that] video is actually very pervasive. Lots of people interact with video content all the time, but somehow it never made the transition to the business world. And we believe that there are a couple of reasons for that. . . . One is that it is just not simple and easy to do so. . . . That is where Google can really change the game there with our simple user interfaces, which are incredibly powerful, to enable much richer collaboration. But at the same time it is incredibly expensive for most business to do something like that, because video is a very intensive application and most companies do not have the time, the bandwidth, or even the costs to actually make it work for them. And that is really where Google Apps can change the game. We can bring these really great, compelling, new social technologies into the enterprise and do so in a way that is very cost-effective for most businesses. . . .

It is pretty amazing actually, when you think of what's happened in the consumer world where storage has become much and much less of an issue for most users. In the business world, it actually still is a really big problem. One of the greatest examples and what really highlights that is, if you go to Gmail.com, for free you can sign up for a 7-gigabyte e-mail storage on your inbox . . . and most companies today still only give 500 megabytes to their users; even though they pay lots and lots of money to actually make the technology work for their employees. Somehow we have gone completely backwards. . . . And that is why Google technology can really change the game here. With the premiere edition of Google Apps, we give our users 25 gigabytes of e-mail storage— which is just monumental compared to what most businesses already give their users. So we can really change the game by giving more storage at a better price and giving more tools that actually incorporate these new social technologies in an easy way for the end user.

To listen to or read the entire Executive Conversation with Rishi Chandra, go to www .theSocialMediaBible.com.

Expert Insight

Michael Naef, CEO and founder, Doodle,
www.doodle.ch/main.html

Michael Naef

Doodle solves the scheduling problem. It helps [to find] accommodations and times for a group's event—which can be an important conference call, a family reunion, a barbeque, whatever. . . . Doodle focuses on delivering a very simple and usable service which is free to end users. . . .

The Doodle service was conceived and implemented in 2003, and the idea for this service was born from my personal need. I wanted to make an appointment with some friends; I don't know whether [it was] for a beer or a dinner, or what . . . and this process resulted. As many of you know, a large number of e-mails are sent around and phone calls are [made] with no common dates and times found. So I implemented Doodle, and the service attracted a large and growing user base. In 2006, I decided to professionalize the service—which led to my business partner, Paul Sevinc, and I officially founding the company. . . .

People are using [Doodle] for all kinds of cases. At the moment, in Switzerland alone, we have, like, more than ½ million people who use the service each month—both for business and private events. They most appreciate Doodle's simplicity and the low entry barrier, because you don't really try to download anything or install the software to register for the service. So they use it for the examples I mentioned: business meetings, family reunions, ski weekends (in Switzerland, obviously), all kinds of stuff. . . .

Internationally, we're approaching something like 2 million users at the moment. Doodle is used in many countries worldwide; and we are actually also translated into 25 languages currently. What's interesting is that most or all of the languages are translated by volunteers from these various countries, all except the major languages, which are German and English, which we provide ourselves. . . .

We are not competing with companies like Google or Microsoft and their calendars; or, let's say, Lotus with Notes and their calendar, because we don't even provide the calendar; but we provide the missing link between calendars and between people who use different calendars, or don't use a calendar at all, or use a paper-based calendar. Because we help them coordinate the process of finding the dates and time. . . .

The typical use case is that the organizer visits our site and creates a so-called poll, which offers a number of dates to choose from. Then your organizer

[has] created a unique web link, which Doodle provides and which he or she can send to the participants. And these participants then use this link to access the poll and answer with their availability. The organizer uses that same link to monitor the poll's progress and determine the best option at the end. So that's it, in a nutshell, and this should show that we don't need the calendar information built right into the tool, but we based it on the participants providing this information to us. . . .

[The aspect of international use] applies to us, too. As I said, most of our languages are translated by volunteers; and they actually write to us and say, "Hey, I'm sitting here in Portugal and I'm using Doodle with my friends and family and they would love to have it in their own language. So can I help them translate it to Portuguese?" And then we send them the text they have to translate from; and they send them back in. We think this is important to our users because we provide a very simple service; and while one [might] think that it's okay to have it in English only, it's important to have it in the local language of the people who are using it. Because . . . our target audience is not Internet professionals, but rather everyday people who might not be familiar with an English application. . . .

We have loads of success stories; some of them are listed as testimonials on our web site also. I just had a call from one of them who said that, "My work is driven by conference calls and it is a pain to arrange an appropriate time among several parties. We have ended this heartache and trouble with this brilliant polling system." This is the type of feedback that we get. There are also people telling us that they're using Doodle to schedule meeting with people at seven different hospitals where they need 100 percent attendance. And they're very happy with Doodle because it allows them to schedule a meeting and coordinate and accommodate the time within minutes, usually. . . .

Doodle allows you to import events into your regular calendar also. So you can [transfer] events into Outlook, Google Calendar, or your Macintosh iCal application. Another thing is that you can incorporate the poll summary into your own web page or blog, and you can subscribe to polls feed with the Google Reader or any other feed reader or portal pages like iGoogle and Net Bites. And maybe the latest breaking news when it comes to social media is that this Monday, we released our Facebook application. This allows you also to schedule events with your Facebook friends directly—which is a function that Facebook didn't offer until to now. . . .

To listen to or read the entire Executive Conversation with Michael Naef, go to www.theSocialMediaBible.com.

Commandments

1. **Thou shalt explore.**

    This is the only commandment for this chapter, because it is so incredibly important. Go look at a few of the applications discussed in this book. Read some of their online literature, download their trials, and try them out to see if they are right for you and your business. Decide which ones work the best for your purposes, and really hone in on your use of those applications. Knowledge really is power; and we are in the midst of the Age of Knowledge. For the first time in human history, nearly the entire accumulation of human knowledge is at our fingertips and accessible in an instant. The more you know about social media and its tools, the more capabilities you will be able to access; the more you can reduce expenses; and the more competitive you can be. And isn't that what everyone is looking to do for our businesses: reduce expenses and increase revenue?

Conclusion

As with all of the other chapters, the advice is to go explore. A lot of great social media applications allow you to better communicate with your customers and prospects, which is really the essence of social media. And surprising as it may be, nearly every tool mentioned in *The Social Media Bible* is either free or almost free. Unless you investigate and try out the various services that you've read about here, you won't know what incredible tools are available to help grow your business, build your community, and develop trust within that community.

Readings and Resources

Camarillo, Gonzalo, and Miguel-Angel García-Martín. *The 3G IP Multimedia Sub-system (IMS): Merging the Internet and the Cellular Worlds*. (Hoboken, NJ: John Wiley & Sons, Inc.)

Dreamtech Software Team. *Instant Messaging Systems: Cracking the Code*. (Hoboken, NJ: John Wiley & Sons, Inc.)

Kao, Robert, and Dante Sarigumba. *BlackBerry Storm For Dummies*. (Hoboken, NJ: John Wiley & Sons, Inc.)

Stevenson, Nancy. *WebEx Web Meetings For Dummies*. (Hoboken, NJ: John Wiley & Sons, Inc.)

Downloads

For your free downloads associated with *The Social Media Bible*, go to www .theSocialMediaBible.com, and enter your ISBN number located on the back of the book above the bar code. Be sure to enter the dashes.

Credits

Expert Insight Were Provided By:

John Pollard, CEO and founder, Jott, www.jott.com.

Rishi Chandra, director of product management, Windows Live Instant Messenger, www.google.com/apps/intl/en/business/index.html.

Michael Naef, CEO and founder, Doodle, www.doodle.ch/main.html.

Technical Edits Were Provided By:

Katie Terrell, strategic writer, MediaSauce, www.MediaSauce.com.

Note

1. Wikipedia defines SMS as "Short Message Service (SMS) is a communications protocol allowing the interchange of short text messages between mobile telephone devices. SMS text messaging is the most widely used data application on the planet, with 2.4 billion active users, or 74% of all mobile phone subscribers sending and receiving text messages on their phones. The SMS technology has facilitated the development and growth of text messaging. The connection between the phenomenon of text messaging and the underlying technology is so great that in parts of the world the term 'SMS' is used as a synonym for a text message or the act of sending a text message, even when a different protocol is being used."

PART II

Tools

In Part I, you were introduced to the social media ecosystem and sampled some of the tools in each category from a tactical perspective. In Part III, the focus will be on assessing your internal and external business environments and then developing effective social media strategies specific to your business. Before moving to a discussion about strategy, however, it is essential that you take some time and explore representative tools and applications from each of the 15 sections of the ecosystem. That is the focus of Part II.

Over 100 Tools to Consider

When you consider that there are literally thousands of social media tools available today, getting to know a hundred or so doesn't seem too daunting. Tools and applications will come and go. It's important to learn about the general features and functions that distinguish the tools in one category from another. It's also important to recognize that tools can share features and functions with tools in other categories.

The Questions We Address

To help you navigate through Part II, the text profiles each tool, application, or company using these six questions:

1. What is it?
2. How can it be used?
3. What other tools or applications does it work with?

4. Who uses it?

5. Should you use it?

6. Who started it?

Though these questions are fairly basic, they allow you to approach each tool from a similar perspective. Realizing that people in business are busy, this organization also helps you to scan the profiles a little faster. We also provide you with basic information about each company that includes their web address, year founded, location, number of employees, revenue model, and tag line.

The Tool Scorecard

Each chapter in Part II concludes with a Tool Scorecard designed to help you quickly consider and filter each tool you've just reviewed with respect to its value to the internal and external operations of your business. Internal operations, of course, include people, procedures, and activities that primarily involve employees but not customers. External operations, by the definition used in this book, focus on interactions with your current customers and prospective customers. As such, at the end of each chapter you'll see something like the following chart. (The actual chart from Chapter 24 appears here as an example.)

Tool Scorecard for Chapter 24: Social Networks

Instructions: Using the five-point (0 to 4) scale below, rate each tool in this chapter on the basis of how valuable it *might be* to the internal and external operations of your company. Make notes about which tools appeal to you the most.

4 = Extremely Valuable

3 = Very Valuable

2 = Somewhat Valuable

1 = Not Very Valuable

0 = No Value

Tool	Internal Value	External Value
Bebo	4 3 2 1 0	4 3 2 1 0
Facebook	4 3 2 1 0	4 3 2 1 0
Gather.com	4 3 2 1 0	4 3 2 1 0
LinkedIn	4 3 2 1 0	4 3 2 1 0
MOLI	4 3 2 1 0	4 3 2 1 0
MySpace	4 3 2 1 0	4 3 2 1 0
Ning	4 3 2 1 0	4 3 2 1 0
Orkut	4 3 2 1 0	4 3 2 1 0
Plaxo	4 3 2 1 0	4 3 2 1 0

Notes: The goal here is for you to make a quick yet informed decision as to the relative value of each tool. In some cases, it will be simple because the tools profiled will have little or no value to your business; that's to be expected. The greater challenge is to apply a somewhat visceral filter to those tools that might have some value. To assist you with this, a simple five-point value scale is used. Circle the number that represents each tool's value to your internal and external business operations. You can certainly change your mind later, but going into Part III, you'll appreciate having completed a vetting process in Part II.

Information presented in Part II has been derived from a variety of sources, including the web sites of the companies or applications being profiled. Certain facts and other company information are fluid and subject to change. Revenue models, number of employees and ownership structure, for example, can change. We encourage you to visit a specific web site for the most current information about that application or tool. Quotation marks used in Part II that are not directly attributed to a source should be attributed to the web site content as it existed at the time the profile was created.

CHAPTER 24

Social Networks

Social networking as a human activity predates any and all forms of digital technology. Conversation is the natural result whenever more than two people gather; people can't help themselves. Think about the last time you chatted about the weather with a couple of friends or even total strangers. Your conversation could have gone something like this:

- "Is it going to rain?"
- "I don't know, but my brother said it snowed in Denver last night."
- "Your brother lives in Denver? I'm traveling to Denver in a couple of weeks."

This same basic conversation can be supercharged through social networking tools, because now you can connect someone directly to your brother in Denver via Facebook. Moreover, he has a list on his Facebook page of some of his favorite places to drink, dine, and visit. What could be better than some strong recommendations from somebody in your trusted network—even somebody you just met via someone else?

Monetizing these kinds of conversations could become part of your social media strategy. Imagine for a moment how this conversation about weather can be viewed in a different light if you work for a company that manufactures umbrellas or snow boots, or you run a wine bar in Denver.

Company and Tool Profiles

This chapter introduces you to the following companies, tools, and applications:

theSocialMediaBible.com

- Bebo
- Facebook
- Friendster
- Gather.com
- LinkedIn

- MOLI
- MySpace
- Ning
- Orkut
- Plaxo

As you read each profile, keep in mind that its features and functions may or may not be right for your particular business. Use the **Tool Score-card** at the end of the chapter to help you determine which of these tools qualify for further consideration when you begin creating your social media strategy in Part III of the book.

Bebo

Company Name:	Bebo Inc.
URL:	www.bebo.com
Location:	San Francisco, California, United States
Founded:	2005
Revenue Model:	Advertising

What Is It?

Bebo is a mediacentric online social networking application. Bebo users create profiles and then interact with other users through actions such as sharing photographs and videos, communicating through messages and blog posts, and taking polls and quizzes. Bebo also allows for the creation of Groups, which are collections of users who share a common interest or characteristic. The content on Bebo is not just driven by individual users; large media corporations and amateur artists alike use Bebo for marketing and networking purposes.

How Can It Be Used?

Bebo can be used as a social networking tool as well as an engaging marketing vehicle. With Bebo Music, artists and bands can create a profile to advertise directly to fans and sell their music online. With Bebo Authors, authors of a book can upload select chapters to receive feedback and give potential readers the ability to preview the author's work. Bebo can also be used to upload and share videos—anything from a movie trailer to a clip from an online comedy show.

What Other Applications Does It Work With?

Bebo integrates with several other applications to enhance the user experience. Through Bebo Music, users can include iTunes links alongside their albums or songs, making it easy for other users to purchase their music through the iTunes Store. Users can also showcase videos from YouTube and VideoEgg.

Who Uses It?

Consumers and producers of media both use Bebo. Miley Cyrus, Slipknot, and AC/DC are just some of the musical artists who are using Bebo Music to market directly to fans and interact with them. Authors such as Michael Largo, who wrote *Final Exits*, and Anastasia Goodstein, author of *Totally Wired*, use Bebo Authors to reach new audiences. Popular media companies like Comedy Central, ESPN, and CBS provide content for Bebo users and gain publicity in the process.

Should You Use It?

You should use Bebo if you are looking for an online social networking application that places an emphasis on engaging media that is aimed toward consumers. With Bebo you can go beyond just creating an online profile that other users will see; you can actually upload content that customers will access directly, providing you with the potential for valuable feedback and advertising exposure.

Who Started It?

Michael and Xochi Birch started Bebo in January 2005. In July 2005, Bebo underwent a complete relaunch. The two of them, along with Paul Birch, also founded BirthdayAlarm.com. On March 13, 2008, AOL purchased Bebo for approximately $850 million.

Facebook

Company Name:	Facebook
URL:	www.facebook.com
Location:	Palo Alto, California, and New York, New York, United States; London, United Kingdom
Founded:	2004
Employees:	500+
Revenue Model:	Advertising, banner ads
Fees:	Free

What Is It?

Facebook provides a platform for users to quickly connect with friends, family, coworkers, and acquaintances in various network groups. Facebook promotes communication within various social networks via a customizable user interface and a variety of compatible applications to further personalize the experience. Depending on the setup, users are notified when someone in their network updates their page or status. Users create their pages based on their personal preferences; add others to their network categories; and share events, pictures, videos, or experiences.

How Can It Be Used?

Facebook can be used in business environments for networking, locating business leads, as a method of intercompany communication, as a platform to organize and track events, and as a medium to provide updates between organizations and departments. Due to its popularity, Facebook could be used to promote a new product, service, or performer by word of mouth through "friends" within a social network. In academic environments, Facebook can be used to promote or enhance course communication, organize school functions, and as a platform to organize and track intramural and extracurricular events.

What Other Applications Does It Work With?

Facebook works with numerous applications: Owned, Lil Green Patch, YouTube, Poked, Cheers, Bumper Stickers, Top Friends, Karma, Wall, Super Wall, a variety of prime-time media applications, iPhone, Chat, Translations, and others. A unique feature of Facebook is that it enables developers to create their own applications, which provides an ever-growing list of applications to use with it.

Who Uses It?

Facebook started as a networking tool to meet others and learn about communities and organizations on college campuses. Its popularity with the high school crowd promoted the impression that Facebook is primarily used as a communication tool between friends. However, recent data shows Facebook is increasing in popularity for users over the age of thirty. Many in this demographic utilize the add-ons as a means of expressing their social and political affiliations, for organizing and tracking events, and as a purchasing/advertising tool, in addition to networking.

Should You Use It?

If you are looking for a quick and convenient way to update a multitude of friends, family, coworkers, or acquaintances on what you are doing, Facebook would be an appropriate platform. Many users send invitations via Facebook for gatherings, meetings, movie premieres, and other events. Some businesses use Facebook advertising as a way to reach consumers in specific demographic populations.

Who Started It?

Mark Zuckerberg founded Facebook in 2004 in his sophomore year at Harvard as a social medium for students to get acquainted. In less than a month, more than half of the student body registered. Dustin Moskovitz and Chris Hughes joined to help promote the site.

Facebook's founders relocated to Palo Alto, California, in 2004, where they received an introduction to their first investor, Peter Thiel, cofounder of PayPal.

Fast Pitch!

Company Name:	Fast Pitch!
URL:	www.fastpitchnetworking.com/
Location:	Sarasota, Florida
Founded:	2006
Revenue Model:	Subscriptions
Tagline:	Are you ready to make your pitch?

What Is It?

Unlike most networking sites that focus on the social aspect of networking, Fast Pitch! is geared toward the business professional. As one of the fastest growing social networks for professionals, Fast Pitch! has connected businesses across the world and provided a simple way for users to enhance their online presence using networking to market their business.

How Can It Be Used?

Fast Pitch! makes it easier for professionals to network using a profile displaying what they do, what they sell, and what makes their company unique. Profiles are interactive with the ability to imbed video, photos, blog, and podcasts. Users can network with other professionals based on industry, education, location, affiliations, and so on. "Virtual" trade shows let members connect via live chat or two-way streaming video.

Users can distribute content to others such as press releases, news, letters, event announcements, videos, classifieds, live chat feature, imbed videos, podcasts, e-mail campaigns. Fast Pitch!'s distribution system automatically targets the audience the user is trying to reach ensuring that their posts are viewed by the target audience.

Users can evaluate their success on Fast Pitch! by using account statistics to view the number of views on their profile, advertisements, press releases, and events.

What Other Applications Does It Work With?

Fast Pitch! has many of the same applications that a regular social networking site would have such as blog, video, live chat, podcasts, and so forth. The difference is that Fast Pitch! is geared toward marketing so the newsfeed, classifieds, press releases, and other applications are geared toward the marketing aspect of networking. Fast Pitch! also has applications on other sites like Facebook, Blogger, and Twitter that link the sites together.

Who Uses It?

Fast Pitch!'s main customers are small business professionals, sales and marketing executives, and business owners who are involved in promoting their businesses by networking and marketing. Fast Pitch! is also used as a tool for finding more career opportunities. Fast Pitch! prides itself on not being a "monster network" with 50 million users, many who are inactive. Instead,

Fast Pitch! deletes inactive accounts so that the network is full of active members who can be contacted. Therefore, all users are active members.

Should You Use It?

If you are a business professional who is looking to enhance your web presence and to make connections with other professionals, then Fast Pitch! may be for you. Take advantage of the different applications Fast Pitch! has to offer to benefit your own professional needs.

Who Started It?

Before becoming CEO and founder of Fast Pitch! Bill Jula worked as director of Business and Development at Backsoft Corporation, was executive campus director of the University of South Florida, and a regional representative for the Tampa Bay Devil Rays. Using his interest in technology, as well as his background in sales and marketing, Bill developed Fast Pitch! It initially began as a networking event company that did "Speed Networking Events" that has since grown into Fast Pitch! The experience he had with the different people he connected with led to what Fast Pitch! is today.

Friendster

Company Name:	Friendster
URL:	www.friendster.com
Location:	San Francisco, California, United States
Founded:	2002
Employees:	57
Revenue Model:	Advertising

What Is It?

Friendster is an online social networking service that places an emphasis on the network between individuals. By utilizing a patented technology that is described as "a method and apparatus for calculating, displaying and acting upon relationships in a social network," Friendster acts as a virtual hub that can connect people based on commonalities. Friendster is also an entertainment and communication vehicle with features like Friendster Video, Reviews, and Forums (which are currently in the beta stage).

How Can It Be Used?

Friendster can be used to stay in contact with old relationships and create new ones. Like most social network services, users on Friendster are able to browse other profiles, send messages, and add new friends. Friendster allows users to search for people based on information that they have entered, such as current and past schools and colleges, which makes it easier to connect with old classmates and friends. Additionally, Friendster allows for a unique profile privacy setting, Two Degrees. When Two Degrees is selected, your full profile view is restricted to only your friends (One Degree away from you) and the friends in their network (Two Degrees away from you). This approach allows you to meet new people through the filter of your friends, while still keeping your profile private from the majority of users.

What Other Applications Does It Work With?

Friendster works with several online video applications. Inside Friendster Video, you can view videos from YouTube, Crackle, Metacafe, Break, Video Detective, and SingingFool. Additionally, you can put a Friendster Badge on a variety of web sites, including blogs and other social networking sites. Friendster also includes mini-applications that can be added to customize your profile.

Who Uses It?

Many different individuals use Friendster to network and meet new people. One major aspect of Friendster is the use of Official Profiles, which are the Friendster-sanctioned profiles of users like celebrities, athletes, and musicians. Other users can then become Fans of these Official Profiles. People with Official Profiles on Friendster include basketball player Allen Iverson, wrestler Chris Jericho, and musician Avril Lavigne. The largest segment of Friendster visitors are between the ages of eighteen and thirty-four, and most of the web site's traffic comes from the Philippines.

Should You Use It?

You should use Friendster if you are looking for a social network service that has a structured approach for meeting new people online. With Friendster, you are able to see what connects you to another user, whether that link is a common friend or a shared university. You should use Friendster if you would want features like Reviews, Forums, and Games to be a part of your social network. You should also use Friendster if you are looking to promote yourself or something else, as a Friendster Official Profile could help you gain exposure.

Who Started It?

Jonathan Abrams started Friendster on March 22, 2002. The company is currently privately owned and continues to receive investments from multiple companies and individual investors.

Gather.com

Company Name:	Gather.com
URL:	www.gather.com
Location:	Boston, Massachusetts, United States
Founded:	2005
Revenue Model:	Advertising and branded communities
Fees:	Free
Tagline:	Keep up with the people, conversations, and moments that matter.

What Is It?

Gather.com is a social media platform that provides forum communities of users with similar interests and is promoted as a means for the over-thirty crowd to discuss topics relevant to their lives. According to the *Boston Globe*, "Executives from Gather Inc. are recruiting bloggers by offering them a share of the company's advertising revenue."

How Can It Be Used?

Gather.com is used as a platform to communicate, educate, engage, and inform on a variety of subject matters. These forums are categorized by topics and ranked "based on how many readers they attract, how readers assess their quality, and how much online discussion they generate." Gather.com is an effective tool for publishing individual perspectives on a vast number of subjects.

What Other Applications Does It Work With?

Gather.com is a community web site and works with most Internet browsers.

Who Uses It?

Individuals use Gather.com to express their ideas, concerns, and viewpoints. Users can find information about topics ranging from crafts and home improvement to politics and business. This platform allows users to interact with a larger community than might be possible with face-to-face communication. Several users have gained interest in their writing projects and promoted books through Gather.com.

Should You Use It?

If you are looking for a way to express your interests and viewpoints to a vast audience with minimal investment, or to engage your readers, Gather.com provides an effective platform. This forum provides a community for otherwise unconnected users to meet and discuss topics of importance to them and that impact their daily lives.

Who Started It?

Gather.com was founded in 2005 by Tom Gerace and the American Public Media Group (APMG); Gather's chairman is William H. Kling, the APMG CEO and president. Gerace is also the founding committee chair of SMAC, the Social Media Ad Council, an industry community launched in September 2008. SMAC is, by its own definition, "A group of advertising, communications, brand management and social media executives coming together to create a common vocabulary, standard buying units, and uniform measurement methods for social media."

KickApps

Company Name:	KickApps
URL:	www.KickApps.com/
Location:	New York City, Los Angeles, San Francisco, Orlando, and Mumbai
Founded:	2005
Revenue Model:	Ads and user fees
Fees:	Fees are based on CPM usage

What Is It?

KickApps is a web-based platform that enables users to grow and engage their audiences and create new revenue opportunities by adding social features, user-generated content, video players, and widgets to their web sites. Kick-Apps connects editorial content, user content, applications, media and advertising experiences enabling users to grow and cater to their audiences. The result is more intelligent ad serving, viral audience growth, and an overall better user experience.

How Can It Be Used?

Social networking features enable users to build a community and connect with others. Each member gets a customizable profile where they can add friends, participate in groups, and send messages.

UGC video, photo, audio and blogging features enable the user's members to upload, share, rate and comment on the user's media. Customizable players give users the ability to program and customize online videos on their sites. Message boards and blogs are all video-enabled as well. The Widget Builder allows users to create and deploy customized, viral Widgets that match the user's brand.

The KickApps Social Graph Engine for Publishers collects contextual data about the web site's audience, content, and activities. The information on the social graph can be used to enhance the web site's applications and advertising opportunities.

What Other Applications Does It Work With?

KickApps uses a range of other applications including social networking, user-generated content, online video players, and viral Widgets. These applications are designed to integrate with each client's web site and brand. KickApps can be customized with any web site using HTML, CSS, Java-Script, and APIs.

Who Uses It?

KickApps provides services to more than 40,000 sites. Their broad range of clients include universities, magazines, newspapers, political candidates, large corporations, small businesses, and bloggers. Some of KickApps high profile clients include Budget Travel, HBO, ABC Family, BBC, the Phoenix Suns, the San Francisco 49ers, CW's VIP Lounge Community, and Rachel Ray.

Should You Use It?

If you are looking to build, manage, and deploy social media services while growing your audience then KickApps may be for you. Small businesses or global corporations can benefit from the publishing capabilities of KickApps by adding rich media experiences and more revenue opportunities to their web sites.

Who Started It?

In addition to being the founder and chairman of KickApps, Eric Alterman is the founder of MeshNetworks, Military Commercial Technologies, TeraNex, SkyCross, Jed Broadcasting, Quadfore, Centerpoint, and Triton Network Systems.

LinkedIn

Company Name:	LinkedIn
URL:	www.linkedin.com
Location:	Mountain View, California, United States
Founded:	2003
Employees:	24
Revenue Model:	Advertising and premium subscriptions
Fees:	Business level: $199.50/year; Business Plus: $500/year
Tagline:	Relationships matter.

What Is It?

LinkedIn's philosophy is "Relationships matter." LinkedIn describes itself as an online network of more than 24 million experienced professionals from around the world, representing 150 industries. LinkedIn can be used to maintain professional relationships (as opposed to "just exchanging business cards"), search for jobs as well as recruit candidates, exchange solutions for problems, and find high-quality passive (employed) candidates.

How Can It Be Used?

Users create accounts and invite other users to become connections. Connections are rated in "degrees," meaning direct connections are first-degree connections, users listed as connections on that user's profile are second-degree connections, and so forth. Introductions are made through these degrees of connections, as it is assumed there is a level of trust inherited by having a first-degree connection in common. By posting a well-written resume, a user can search for jobs, or conversely a user can search for candidates. LinkedIn also has a feature called Linked Answers, in which users can post questions and receive suggestions/solutions related to those questions.

What Other Applications Does It Work With?

Aside from the obvious feature of being accessible from any device with an Internet browser, LinkedIn works with few other applications. If you have an AOL account, you can use that to log into LinkedIn as well as search for contacts through your e-mail account that are already on LinkedIn. If you don't have an AOL account, once you establish your rudimentary profile, you can have LinkedIn search your Outlook, Hotmail, or other e-mail address lists. LinkedIn will also search alumni networks as indicated by your profile information to lead you to college connections.

Who Uses It?

Professionals in all industries use it to establish and maintain relationships. There are recruiter success stories, such as the recruiter who spends $7,000 annually to search LinkedIn, and nets $100,000 annually in commission for his successful headhunting of passive candidates. LinkedIn is also working in the way of sales leads. One success story is that of a CEO of an online advertising company who used an introduction from a connection to contact the COO of a potential client. He invited him to lunch. The COO responded that he didn't have time for lunch but that he did need a new ad server. The two signed a contract two weeks later.

Should You Use It?

As stated previously, this web site is geared toward professionals in any industry. Whether you are looking for business contacts, a new job, or a new candidate to come work for your company, LinkedIn provides you with the social networking mechanisms to do so without all the extraneous negative personal data that would otherwise turn off employers or professional contacts. Confidentiality is also a major attraction for using LinkedIn. As a professional, you can set your privacy settings, ranging from receiving no requests at all from unknown users to being completely open to receiving connection requests.

Who Started It?

Founder Reid Hoffman and some college friends created LinkedIn following Hoffman's success in establishing and selling PayPal to eBay Inc. Hoffman is a true entrepreneur, with a talent for scouting successful Internet start-up ventures, according to a January 2008 article by the Associated Press. With the assistance of fellow Stanford graduate Constantin Geuricke, LinkedIn was created. Dan Nye, current CEO of LinkedIn, previously filled a number of senior management positions at Intuit.

MOLI

Company Name:	MOLI, LLC (owned by Mainstream Holdings Inc.)
URL:	www.moli.com
Location:	West Palm Beach, Florida, United States
Founded:	2008
Revenue Model:	Advertising and premium tools
Tagline:	Control your privacy.

What Is It?

MOLI is an online social networking service that is designed to fix one of the biggest concerns with other social networking services—namely, the lack of privacy that can occur. MOLI seeks to accomplish this by allowing users the ability to create multiple profile pages, each with their own privacy settings, from one user account. According to the MOLI web site, "MOLI provides an easy to use, content-rich, multimedia interactive platform ideal for both community collaboration and e-commerce." MOLI also provides premium tools, such as an online store and ad removal, which users can buy to enhance their experience.

How Can It Be Used?

MOLI can be used to network and interact with all your online relationships from one spot. For example, a person could create an account on MOLI and create three separate profiles—one for friends, one for family, and one for professional purposes. The friends profile could contain personal pictures or comments that the user's coworkers would never see. On the family profile, the user could put up pictures from the last reunion and give only other family members permission to look at that profile. On the professional profile, the user could network with coworkers freely and never have to worry about what other content is available to them. With the addition of an online store to a MOLI account, a user could also sell commodities through their profile. Along with the networking aspect, MOLI focuses on adding content for users. MOLI Video allows users to view a variety of videos including MOLI Rollers ("a magazine article in video form"), and MOLI View provides information on subjects such as sports, entertainment, and travel.

What Other Applications Does It Work With?

MOLI allows the embedding of photographs and videos in certain areas of your profile page so it works with photo applications such as Flickr and Photobucket and video applications like YouTube. Additionally, if you add the online store to your MOLI account, the store is compatible with PayPal and Google Checkout.

Who Uses It?

The target audience base that the MOLI web site claims to aim for is "enterprising individuals above the age of 18 and small business owners."

Small business owners and individuals who have items to sell use MOLI because of the ability to add online stores to their profile. Another audience base is students and young professionals who enjoy using online social networking services to correspond with friends, but are concerned about unintended viewers seeing that content.

Should You Use It?

You should use MOLI if you are interested in a social networking web site that is concerned with your privacy and also provides some entertaining and useful features. MOLI is also a good choice if you want to handle the majority of your networking, whether it is recreational or commercial, in one location. With other facets available such as MOLI Video, blogs, and MOLI View, you should use MOLI if you are looking for entertainment and information from your social networking service.

Who Started It?

Dr. Christos M. Cotsakos, the founder, chairman of the board, CEO, and president of Mainstream Holdings, founded MOLI. Cotsakos is also the former CEO of E*TRADE. MOLI received funding from several contributors to help its launch, the total of which has been estimated to be more than $55.5 million as of January 2008.

MySpace

Company Name:	Fox Interactive Media
URL:	www.myspace.com
Location:	Beverly Hills, California, United States
Founded:	2003
Employees:	300
Revenue Model:	Advertising
Tagline:	A place for friends

What Is It?

MySpace is an online social networking application. Users create a MySpace profile and then interact with other users while developing existing relationships and creating new ones. It is one of the more popular social networking applications and is available in 15 different languages. MySpace offers its users numerous features, including blogs, groups, bulletins, widgets, and instant messaging. It also allows users to customize their profile pages through HTML coding or the MySpace profile customizer.

How Can It Be Used?

MySpace offers a tool called MySpace MyAds that offers users the capability to run an effective online marketing campaign within their social network. With MySpace MyAds, anyone can design their own advertisement, choose which users will see it displayed throughout MySpace dependent on characteristics like listed gender and location, and then pay based upon the number of clicks the advertisement receives. For example, a web site that is based in Arizona can design an advertisement that appears only to users who have selected Arizona as their current location.

What Other Applications Does It Work With?

Various applications and web sites can add functionality, entertainment, and features to a MySpace profile page. YouTube, Slide.com, RockYou!, Quizzer, and Playlist.com are just some of the MySpace-compatible entities available. MySpace also has a MySpace Developer Platform that allows users to design their own applications that can then be made available for other MySpace users.

Who Uses It?

A very large and diverse audience uses MySpace. It is estimated that MySpace attracts 230,000 new users a day from all over the world. Numerous notable users on MySpace include organizations like Operation Blessing International and Planet Aid. The presidential campaigns of Barack Obama and John McCain were on MySpace as well. Those who are looking to market directly to an audience also use MySpace, whether through the creation of a profile or purchasing MySpace MyAds.

Should You Use It?

You should use MySpace if you are looking to network or advertise within one of the largest social networking communities online. By creating a profile, you can be selective over who you communicate with, or you can interact with as many people as possible. You should also use MySpace if you are interested in marketing directly to a targeted audience, and then tracking how effective that advertising is. With the introduction of MySpace Developer Platform, you should consider using MySpace if you would like to create a MySpace application that can promote your web site or services.

Who Started It?

Brad Greenspan (founder of eUniverse), Chris DeWolfe (MySpace CEO), Josh Berman, Tom Anderson (MySpace president), and a team of programmers from eUniverse started MySpace in August 2003. The company eUniverse eventually became Intermix Media Inc. Intermix was acquired by News Corporation, the parent company of Fox Interactive Media, in July 2005 for an estimated $580 million.

Ning

Company Name:	Ning
URL:	www.ning.com
Location:	Palo Alto, California, United States
Founded:	2004
Employees:	41
Revenue Model:	Advertising and premium subscriptions
Tagline:	Create your own social network for anything.

What Is It?

Ning is an online social networking service. Ning, however, is different in its design from other networking services like Facebook and MySpace. Rather than having users join one giant social network, Ning allows users to create their own social network web sites that other Ning members can then join. Once a member joins your community, he or she can then create a profile page for that network. Additionally, Ning operates on a platform that allows users to customize their social network if they have the inclination. As the Ning web site puts it, the Ning platform is "the software equivalent of Home Depot. Unlike other services that offer a 'one-size-fits-all' offering, your social network on Ning runs on a programmable platform."

How Can It Be Used?

Ning can be used in a large number of ways, depending on the user's needs and intentions. An artist could use Ning to create a social network based around one's art and then use Ning to answer questions from fans, keep the audience posted on important upcoming dates, and post images of the artist or the artwork. Another potential use is a social network centered on aquarium enthusiasts, wherein a community of users could post meeting dates, post articles on caring for fish, and discuss the hobby with other like-minded individuals.

What Other Applications Does It Work With?

Ning works with several online applications to make the creation of a social community easier. For example, you can import photographs from Flickr and embed videos from YouTube. Additionally, Ning has widgets that you can add to MySpace, Facebook, or your own personal web site. Ning also works with Google Gadgets.

Who Uses It?

Ning could potentially be used by anyone, provided the interest in creating a social web site exists. Currently, everyone from political activists to urban improv groups have social networks that are built with the Ning platform. Celebrities such as the musician 50 Cent and the mixed martial arts fighter B. J. Penn are among the people using Ning. Educators are another rapidly growing subset of Ning users, with social networks being created to discuss teaching methods globally.

Should You Use It?

You should use Ning if you are interested in creating a social network for any subject or purpose. Ning is attractive because it allows for the creation of features like memberships and discussion forums on your social web site, with less technical knowledge required than if you were to try and build one from scratch. As Ning says, you can use it for nearly anything, and you have the option to do so for free. Some of Ning's suggested uses range from a personal wedding site to a high school alumni community to a local neighborhood block web site.

Who Started It?

Marc Andreessen and Gina Bianchini created Ning in October 2004. Andreessen is an entrepreneur and software engineer who cofounded Netscape Communications Corporation and Loudcloud, which later became Opsware. Bianchini was the cofounder and former CEO of Harmonic Communications prior to becoming the CEO for Ning.

Orkut

Company Name:	Orkut (owned by Google)
URL:	www.orkut.com
Location:	Originally hosted in California, Google announced in August 2008 that the Orkut operation will be moving to Brazil.
Founded:	2004
Employees:	20,000 (Google)
Revenue Model:	Google advertisements
Tagline:	Who do you know?

What Is It?

Orkut is an online social networking service owned by Google. Its purpose is to allow users to network, socialize, and create new relationships with other Orkut members. In order to utilize Orkut, you must have a Google account, which then also becomes your Orkut account. Orkut has several primary features available for users, including Scrapbooks, Communities, and Applications. Orkut, according to the web site, "is an online community designed to make your social life more active and stimulating."

How Can It Be Used?

Orkut can be used as a supplemental tool for any stage in a relationship between members. For example, someone who was interested in meeting area bicycle riders could use the search engine to find members who listed cycling as one of their interests and then interact with them by sending a Message, adding them as a Friend, or adding them as a Crush. If you are already friends with someone on Orkut, you can communicate through features like Testimonials and Scrapbooks. Orkut also allows for the creation of Communities, a mechanism to bring users together under common interests.

What Other Applications Does It Work With?

Google Talk can be integrated with Orkut so any Orkut members who are listed as your friends can contact you via Google Talk without having to add you manually. Orkut also has numerous third-party applications that you can add to your Orkut account. These applications vary greatly and add quite a bit of character to Orkut. Some uses of these applications are games, matchmaking tools, chat rooms, and competitions.

Who Uses It?

The Orkut community comprises a wide variety of audiences and users. These can range from high school students to business consultants to war veterans. According to Orkut demographics, 73.43 percent of the user base are between the ages of eighteen and thirty, and 71 percent of the members are based in Brazil and India, with 15.14 percent of the users coming from the United States. Orkut is not very popular in North America when compared to other social networking services.

Should You Use It?

You should use Orkut if you are looking to join a social networking service, especially if you already have a Google account. If you use Orkut, it will give you a new way of initiating and maintaining relationships, along with some entertaining tools to interact with others. Additionally, you should use Orkut if you are primarily interested in communicating with users who are under thirty years old and live in either Brazil or India.

Who Started It?

Orkut gained its name from the Google employee who designed it, Orkut Büyükkökten. Büyükkökten, a software engineer from Turkey, designed Orkut independently while working at Google. Shortly after Orkut's launch, there were some complications as Büyükkökten's previous employer, Affinity

Engines, claimed that the Orkut code was based on one of their own projects called InCircle. In June 2004, Affinity Engines filed a lawsuit against Google based on this claim. The lawsuit has since been settled on terms that have not been released.

Plaxo

Company Name:	Plaxo Inc.
URL:	www.plaxo.com
Location:	Mountain View, California, United States
Founded:	2006
Revenue Model:	Premium subscriptions

What Is It?

Plaxo is a social network application that is focused on staying in touch with your contacts better. Through Plaxo, you can synchronize contact information from several different sources—for example, Google address book and Outlook contacts—and then store that information in your Plaxo Address Book. In addition, when one of your contacts changes his or her own information in Plaxo, that change is reflected in your own address book. With Plaxo you can also use Pulse, a feature that acts as a sort of personal news page by displaying information that your Plaxo Connections choose to share.

How Can It Be Used?

A business could use Plaxo to keep all employees up-to-date with each other's contact information. For example, if one employee changed a phone number on her Plaxo profile, all the employees who are connected to her on Plaxo would have that change automatically updated in their own address book. This function makes it easier for employees to communicate and collaborate, and it simplifies company cohesion as people don't have to be notified independently of changes.

What Other Applications Does It Work With?

Plaxo Pulse allows users to consolidate their content from multiple web sites in one area for other Plaxo users to view. For example, if you add Flickr to your Pulse account, every time you upload a photograph to Flickr you can also share that photograph with the Plaxo connections that you allow to see it. Some of the web sites that Plaxo works with are MySpace, LiveJournal, Picasa, Bebo, YouTube, and Amazon. Additionally, Plaxo works with numerous applications to synchronize contact information, including AOL, Outlook, Google Address Book, LinkedIn, and Hotmail.

Who Uses It?

Organizations and individual users both use Plaxo. Businesses and organizations use Plaxo to stay in touch with other businesses and organizations, clients, and employees. Individuals use Plaxo to keep track of their connections' presence on multiple web sites. As of May 2008, Plaxo is reported to have over 20 million users, a number that is expected to continue growing.

Should You Use It?

You should use Plaxo if you are looking for a social media application that allows you to maintain contacts and discover more about them. If you need a way to synchronize contact information in one place from multiple sources, or if you are having trouble keeping track of the various places your connections update online, consider Plaxo to consolidate it all in one place. You should also use Plaxo if you are looking to network with past and new contacts, as Plaxo allows you to search for other Plaxo users, and then connect with their permission.

Who Started It?

Sean Parker (a cofounder of Napster), Minh Nguyen, Todd Masonis, and Cameron Ring started Plaxo. Plaxo announced on May 14, 2008, that it had signed a deal with Comcast for terms that were not disclosed. Plaxo is currently a subsidiary of Comcast Interactive Media.

Tool Scorecard for Chapter 24: Social Networks

Instructions: Using the five-point (0 to 4) scale below, rate each tool in this chapter on the basis of how valuable it *might be* to the internal and external operations of your company. Make notes about which tools appeal to you the most.

4 = Extremely Valuable

3 = Very Valuable

2 = Somewhat Valuable

1 = Not Very Valuable

0 = No Value

Tool	Internal Value	External Value
Bebo	4 3 2 1 0	4 3 2 1 0
Facebook	4 3 2 1 0	4 3 2 1 0
Fast Pitch!	4 3 2 1 0	4 3 2 1 0
Gather.com	4 3 2 1 0	4 3 2 1 0
KickApps	4 3 2 1 0	4 3 2 1 0
LinkedIn	4 3 2 1 0	4 3 2 1 0
MOLI	4 3 2 1 0	4 3 2 1 0
MySpace	4 3 2 1 0	4 3 2 1 0
Ning	4 3 2 1 0	4 3 2 1 0
Orkut	4 3 2 1 0	4 3 2 1 0
Plaxo	4 3 2 1 0	4 3 2 1 0

CHAPTER 25

Publish

Asignificant number of tools in the social media ecosystem allow you to publish and distribute information to audiences narrow and wide. E-mail is a good example. How many newsletters do you typically receive each month via e-mail? If you're like most people in business, you probably receive more than you have time to read, yet there are probably a few that you take the time to keep up with and peruse. Why? Because the information is valuable to you. This makes newsletters via e-mail one of the easiest and most popular ways to reach employees and customers. But that's just the tip of the iceberg.

This chapter introduces you to a number of tools, some of them very different from one another, that allow you and your company to create, manage, publish, and distribute content. To be fair, some tools profiled in other chapters could just as easily be classified in this chapter. Again, that's one of the problems with any classification system; there are exceptions. Rather than debate the exceptions, however, this chapter tries to present a reasonable lineup of tools whose common attributes and intended functions qualify them as publishing tools.

This chapter presents information on the following companies, tools, and applications:

- Blogger
- Constant Contact
- Joomla
- Knol
- SlideShare
- TypePad
- Wikia

- Wikipedia
- WordPress

As you read each profile, keep in mind that its features and functions may or may not be right for your particular business. Use the **Tool Scorecard** at the end of the chapter to help you determine which of these tools qualify for further consideration when you begin creating your social media strategy in Part III of this book.

Blogger

Company Name:	Blogger (owned by Google)
URL:	www.blogger.com
Location:	Mountain View, California, United States
Founded:	1999
Employees:	5 (Google 20,000)
Revenue Model:	Advertising
Fees:	Free
Tagline:	Push-button publishing

What Is It?

Blogger enables writers of all skill levels to become their own publishers via the Internet. Users can blog about their professional interests, personal hobbies, sports, family life, or any topic at all. Blogger is available in 41 languages, and a variety of third-party applications are available to enhance Blogger blogs. These applications vary by the type of computer operating system being used. Blogger users can even blog on the go from a smart phone, BlackBerry, iPhone, or other handheld device for instantaneous information sharing.

How Can It Be Used?

Blogger's self-publishing capability allows a user to write and publish instantaneously, with the ability to post pictures and videos. Companies, educators, and nonprofits can use Blogger to share information with their user audience, receive feedback and ideas, track the number and location of readers, network with other entities in the same field, or initiate collaboration. Blogger allows for group blogging, so blogging responsibilities for a company or other entity would not necessarily have to fall on one person; a side benefit is that multiple people posting to one blog provides for a well-rounded view of the company.

What Other Applications Does It Work With?

Blogger works with a number of applications, some dependent on the type of computer operating system being used. Web applications that can be used with Blogger include Audioblog, batBack, BlogAmp, BloggerBox and WikyBloggerBox, Blogger to FOAF, Buzznet, FeedBlitz, FeedBurner, Flickr, FotoFlix, Gabcast, Lovento, Photobucket, and Wikispaces.

Who Uses It?

It would be easier to ask, "Who doesn't use Blogger?" Name it, and you can find the topic available on Blogger. You can find tax advice from blogger Roni Deutch, small business marketing strategies from Rikki Arundel, or information about rehabilitation efforts of a small town in the Philippines with the aid of the Southern Leyte Rehabilitation Program. What's great about starting a Blogger blog is that once you begin, you find yourself embedded in a social community, collaborating and communicating with others who are interested in the same topic you are writing about.

Should You Use It?

Blogger is easy to use, free, and one of the largest blogging sites on the Internet. With the advent of Google, it is now easier than ever to search for Blogger blogs on specific topics. Blogging can be a great marketing tool for your business or group, and it gives you a more personal way to reach out to your audience.

Who Started It?

Pyra Labs, which consisted of Evan Williams and Meg Hourihan, started Blogger in August 1999. Evan and Meg created a weblog for their use, and the code for that weblog became the foundation for the initial version of Blogger. Blogger was bought out by Google in 2003, after which general Blogger service became enhanced with the use of Google server technology. Blogger replaced Google Blog.

Constant Contact

Company Name:	Constant Contact
URL:	www.constantcontact.com
Location:	Waltham, Massachusetts, United States
Founded:	1995 as Roving Software and began operations in 1998
Revenue Model:	Service packages
Fees:	Starts at $15/month and increases in tiers

What Is It?

Constant Contact offers a platform for organizations to connect with their audience through surveys and e-mail tools. The e-mail tracking and reporting features offer the functionality to track and manage e-mail campaigns and guide organizations in determining future subject matter based on the popularity or interest generated by specific content. The survey tracking and reporting features give organizations insight into their audiences' wants and needs for the purposes of targeting their marketing. Constant Contact helps organizations "connect with their audience, build relationships and drive their success."

How Can It Be Used?

Constant Contact provides organizations with the management tools to create "professional-looking e-mail newsletters and insightful online surveys." Constant Contact offers users a variety of options to personalize their service, such as customizable HTML e-mail templates and various survey templates, e-mail Wizard to create e-mail campaigns, and Survey Wizard to create effective surveys, tracking and reporting options for e-mail and survey tools, interactive polls, and archive features. With the extensive options available, Constant Contact provides organizations with control over the look and feel of the tools, and allows users to upload their logo for brand recognition.

What Other Applications Does It Work With?

Constant Contact works with any application that supports HTML templates, and supports "e-mail addresses in 3 file formats; .txt (text file), .csv (Comma Separated Values) and .xls (Microsoft® Excel® Spreadsheet)."

Who Uses It?

Constant Contact is used by associations, nonprofits, businesses, professional and personal services providers, recreation and entertainment firms, religious organizations, restaurants, retail outlets, and travel and tourism organizations. The Glioblastoma Brain Tumor Research Fund has used Constant Contact to request donations. The Fajita Grill used Constant Contact to build a customer base and effectively market specials. Crowne Pointe Historic Inn and Spa claims, "Constant Contact has been instrumental to the success of our marketing initiatives."

Should You Use It?

If your organization is looking for a way to interact with your audience, expand your marketing options, and track marketing initiatives, Constant Contact could be an effective solution for those needs. With the growth of Internet marketing, Constant Contact provides a means for local businesses to remain competitive and an outlet to reach a wider audience through online options.

Who Started It?

"Constant Contact®, Inc., was incorporated as Roving Software in 1995 and began operations in 1998. In 2004, we changed our name from Roving Software to Constant Contact, leveraging the success of the service and brand. In October 2007, Constant Contact completed its initial public offering and shares of its common stock began trading on the NASDAQ Global Market under the symbol CTCT."

Joomla

Company Name:	Joomla Project (Open Source Matters)
URL:	www.joomla.org
Location:	New York City, New York, United States
Founded:	2000
Employees:	12 (There are 12 Core Members of the Joomla Project, but it is not known if they are paid, as Joomla claims it is a volunteer-run organization.)
Revenue Model:	Donations
Fees:	Free
Tagline:	. . . because open source matters

What Is It?

According to Joomla's web site, it is an award-winning content management system (CMS) that allows users to build web sites and applications. Joomla is free for anyone to use under the General Public License (GPL), a license that allows free software to avoid becoming copyrighted. The selling point for using Joomla is that the CMS capability makes it easy to manage your content, whether it's text, photos, videos, or music. Joomla claims that its software requires almost no technical skills or knowledge. Joomla 1.0 was a derivative of the Mambo 4.5 code base. Joomla translation is also available in 20 languages, plus users can contact Joomla for additional translation needs.

How Can It Be Used?

Joomla is usable by anyone in just about any industry. Joomla's web site provides a list of ideas for the creation and management of content:

- Corporate web sites or portals
- Corporate intranets and extranets
- Online magazines, newspapers, and publications
- E-commerce and online reservations
- Government applications
- Small business web sites
- Nonprofit and organizational web sites
- Community-based portals
- School and church web sites
- Personal or family homepages

What Other Applications Does It Work With?

Joomla developers can pair with any number of applications. The whole idea behind Joomla is that because it's open source, the possibilities for application development and usage are endless. Joomla refers to applications as "extensions" because these are plug-ins to add to your web site to enhance the user's interaction experience. Nearly 4,000 extensions are available on Joomla's web site, as well as other web sites that claim to specialize in Joomla application/extension development for customers.

Who Uses It?

A variety of businesses and organizations use Joomla to develop their web sites. Joomla lists the following on its web site as examples of users:

- United Nations (governmental organization, www.unric.org)
- MTV Networks Quizilla (social networking, www.quizilla.com)
- *L.A. Weekly* (online publication, www.laweekly.com)
- IHOP (restaurant chain, www.ihop.com)
- Harvard University (educational, www.gsas.harvard.edu)
- Citibank (financial institution intranet, not publicly accessible)
- The Green Maven (eco-resources, www.greenmaven.com)
- *Outdoor Photographer* (magazine, www.outdoorphotographer.com)
- PlayShakespeare.com (cultural, www.playshakespeare.com)
- Senso Interiors (furniture design, www.sensointeriors.co.za)

On the Joomla forum, Web Site Showcase, a wide variety of users appear; used car dealers, real estate agents, gamers, and historians are just a sample.

Should You Use It?

If you are looking for a free, open-source tool to develop your own web site, Joomla seems to have provided the answer. The added content management capability is also valuable, as the amount of information and content that stockpiles on a web site sometimes creates a problem for businesses and organizations.

Who Started It?

Michelle Bisson is one of the Joomla cofounders. She is also a member of the Mambo core team. There are 11 other Core Team Members of the Joomla Project from different areas around the world and different experiences. Several of the Core Team Members also belong to Mambo, such as Mitch Pirtle, Andy Miller, and Louis Landry. They were instrumental in taking Mambo 4.5 code and turning it into Joomla 1.0.

Knol

Company Name:	Knol
URL:	knol.google.com/k
Location:	Mountain View, California, United States
Founded:	2008
Employees:	20,000 (Google)
Revenue Model:	Advertising
Fees:	Free

What Is It?

Google has defined Knol as a unit of knowledge and has launched this concept into a platform for authors to publish their knowledge on a variety of subjects. Each subject can have content published by many different authors with myriad levels of authority on the subject. Google developed this platform as a means to help people share their knowledge. According to the Google blog, "There are millions of people who possess useful knowledge that they would love to share, and there are billions of people who can benefit from it. We believe that many do not share that knowledge today simply because it is not easy enough to do that."

How Can It Be Used?

Knol contributors must have a Google account, and it is highly recommended that real names are used to highlight the authors of the content. Google hopes that "Knol will include the opinions and points of view of the authors who will put their reputation on the line." Knol allows users to contribute, submit comments and questions, and edit, rate, or review the content. The author of the content is able to determine if ads will be included.

What Other Applications Does It Work With?

Knol is currently in beta testing phase, which limits the accessibility of this service, but it is presently used with most Internet browsers.

Who Uses It?

In its current beta testing phase, Knol initially invited authors to contribute content, but the service is expanding to allow those with Google accounts to contribute material for publication. The general purpose of Knol is for those with authoritative information to share it with those looking for that information. However, anyone with a Google account and information to share can create a Knol. Users looking for information enter a topic in the search field, which returns results for all content containing that subject matter.

Should You Use It?

If you have information you believe should be made public, Google's Knol is an effective platform. If you are searching for information, Knol may be a resource to consider, but it is necessary to recognize that Google does not verify or edit the content published. With that in mind, users must accept responsibility to verify that the information is accurate and use caution when applying the information received through Knol.

Who Started It?

The engineering team at Google, headed by Udi Manber, vice president of engineering, created Knol to build a platform to "help people share their knowledge."

SlideShare

Company Name:	SlideShare
URL:	www.slideshare.net
Location:	San Francisco, California, United States; New Delhi, India
Founded:	2006
Employees:	10
Revenue Model:	Advertising
Fees:	Free
Tagline:	Not available

What Is It?

SlideShare describes itself as a community for sharing presentations (publicly or privately) in PowerPoint, PDF, or Open Office (Mac users should use PDF to post their Keynote presentations). Anyone can find presentations on their topic of interest. Presentations can be tagged, downloaded, or embedded into web sites or blogs. Users can join groups to share common interests with other users. The maximum allowed space per user account is 100 Mb. SlideShare is available in 11 languages.

How Can It Be Used?

SlideShare provides a number of ideas for using its web site. In addition to sharing your presentations either publicly or privately, you can add audio to your presentation, market your event, join groups of people who share your interests or occupational field, and download presentations and PDFs. SlideShare is even usable with your company's intranet. You can also embed your SlideShare presentation into blogs, wikis, and other web sites. SlideShare also provides for users to use creative commons licensing. You can create a "Slidecast"—a presentation that is combined with your podcast for an "MP3 mashup." In 2007 a creative project called Freesouls was started by Joi Ito, who sees himself not as a photographer but as a "professional elsewhere." The project was created to allow anyone access to and use of these photographs, with the single caveat that they be attributed to Joi Ito.

What Other Applications Does It Work With?

SlideShare works well with Facebook, Twitter, Blogger, MediaWiki, Joomla, Altassian Wiki, Tumblr, Wikispaces, and WordPress. The main feature behind SlideShare being usable with these applications and web sites is the ability to embed SlideShare material in third-party web sites.

Who Uses It?

There are a variety of SlideShare users. Businesses, private individuals, and those in the education field use it—any groups of users who have a common interest and share their information and ideas with each other. Consultants, religious patrons, entrepreneurs, and professional speakers use SlideShare to convey their messages. Teachers and students alike use SlideShare for courseware presentations.

Should You Use It?

Giving presentations is nearly obligatory in running a business or organizational entity. Being able to share presentations either publicly or privately can have distinct advantages. SlideShare provides an easy online repository for storing the data, reducing either the need for carrying a laptop or irritating issues such as network connection and synchronization during travel. Your audience can learn more about your product or service from anywhere in the world. Businesses and organizations can share information and compare data. Educators and trainers can use SlideShare to post PowerPoint lectures for students or employees, a valuable asset for online courses. Students can also post project presentations, essays, and electronic portfolios.

Who Started It?

Jonathan Boutelle, one of the founders, stated in a 2006 Indezine.com interview that the idea for SlideShare came about because he was trying to put together a presentation for a conference and was being sent different pages of the presentation to upload to the Web. He's worked with the other two founders, Rashmi Sina and Amit Ranjan, on their first creation, Mind-Canvas, a web-based market research platform.

TypePad

Company Name:	TypePad (a product of Six Apart)
URL:	www.typepad.com
Location:	San Francisco, California, United States
Founded:	2003
Employees:	150 (Six Apart)
Revenue Model:	Blog and host services fees
Fees:	$49.50–$899.50/year
Tagline:	Inform. Influence. Inspire.

What Is It?

According to a press release from Six Apart, "TypePad is the award-winning hosted blogging service preferred by professionals, small businesses, and enthusiasts. TypePad provides a rich set of features for publishing, updating, and sharing information on the Web. No installation or configuration is required. TypePad blogs are fully hosted and managed by Six Apart." Five different levels of user fees address different needs of users.

How Can It Be Used?

TypePad can be used to share personal thoughts, experiences, and stories. Businesses can use TypePad to create the human element, to communicate a behind-the-scenes look at a reader's favorite business or industry. Another business application of TypePad is to network and develop new business leads and customer bases. With the advent of using the TypePad application (or "app") with the iPhone and iTouch, mobile blogging has been taken to the next level of convenience, ease, and instantaneous communication.

What Other Applications Does It Work With?

TypePad works with FeedBurner, Facebook, BlackBerry, iPhone and iTouch, and numerous other smartphones that have an Internet browser capability. There are also numerous widgets (applications you can use with a certain program to give it additional features and uses) listed on www.sixapart .comtypepad/widgets/ to add to the TypePad experience.

Who Uses It?

There are numerous users of TypePad. Testimonials on the TypePad web site include those from the food industry, accessory and handbag design businesses, news media such as CNN and Atlanta Online, and entertainment blogs such as Celebrity Baby Blog. Businesses who want to reach their audience in a more personal, direct way can do so using TypePad blogging.

Should You Use It?

Blogging has become the next marketing must-do for businesses. According to TypePad, businesses should blog because a blog:

- Is a simple, cost-effective way to create a professional online presence.
- Creates a conversation between you and the people who matter to you.
- Is a tremendous way to boost your search engine rankings.
- Delivers a huge impact for very little money.

- Allows you to take control of what you publish.
- Allows you to develop a position of thought leadership.
- Is a valuable business tool for collecting customer feedback.
- Creates a historical record of your content.

All of these reasons are valid for blogging in general, not just in using the TypePad product. The main issue at stake in using TypePad is whether the user wishes to pay for services. The most inexpensive subscription fee is $4.95/month. Numerous other blogging programs are available for free, which may be the biggest draw for the new blogger. A search query of "TypePad comparison" nets a number of blog reviews of TypePad against other blogging programs such as Blogger, and each one is different in its opinion. Perhaps the biggest reason to pay for TypePad is the customer service you receive for the monthly fee.

Who Started It?

Ben and Mena Trott are the married cofounders of Six Apart Ltd. The name of the company refers to the six days' difference between their birthdays. During a period of unemployment in September 2001, Ben wrote a weblog program to suit his wife's needs, and that program became Movable Type. When Movable Type 1.0 was released, it was downloaded 100 times in the first hour. This development led to the creation of Six Apart and its ensuing products and services.

Wikia

Company Name:	Wikia
URL:	www.wikia.com/wiki/Wikia
Location:	San Mateo, California, United States
Founded:	2004
Employees:	50
Revenue Model:	Series A & B funding and advertising
Fees:	Free
Tagline:	Find and collaborate with guys who love what you love.

What Is It?

Wikia, a company started by Wikipedia cofounder Max Levchin, is different from Wikipedia in that it is not a wiki-styled encyclopedia of information. It is rather a conglomeration of specialized topics (called "content hubs"), such as gaming, hobbies, and sports. Wikia's intent is to contain information that is community-based with broad generalized topics.

How Can It Be Used?

Wikia contains information that is less formal and could even be labeled entertainment. Sports, health, politics, philosophy, comics, and the performing arts are just some of the topics that make up the content hubs of Wikia. The content focuses more on the personal/entertainment side of information as opposed to the academic/professional aspect.

What Other Applications Does It Work With?

Wikia works with a number of popular social networking applications: Flickr, YouTube, Googlemaps, and RSS2Wiki are all compatible with Wikia. A Googlemap can be inserted into a Wikia page, blogs or other web site content can be fed into Wikia pages, and YouTube videos can be added to enhance content on Wikia. Additional Wikia features include calendars, e-mail, polls, image tagging, and WidgetTag. WidgetTag allows wiki creators to insert a special symbol to designate they've included a widget into their wiki page.

Who Uses It?

Just like Wikipedia, Wikia reaches an extensive audience. According to Compete.com, Wikia had 2 million unique visitors in August 2008. A number of wikis serve as unofficial guides, manuals, or how-to's on certain topics. As an example, there is an unofficial Applepedia on Wikia, whose primary contributors are three individuals from Adelaide, Australia. Another example is a Wikia page on the CHDK firmware for the Canon Digic II and Digic III cameras. There are a number of contributing users to this page, including Wikia cofounder Angela Beesely.

Should You Use It?

There is opportunity for businesses within Wikia besides advertisements, though advertising should not be ignored. Because Wikia has more of an entertainment purpose, businesses have an opportunity to be listed or associated with topics. As an example, under the content hub of "Special FX" there is a subtopic of "Cosmetics." Under "Cosmetics," there is another subtopic of "Alcohol-activated Makeup." The content for Alcohol-activated Makeup includes the names of companies who are well-known for providing this type of makeup to the film industry. Such a reference does as much for leading users to investigate those businesses as if they paid for advertisements on Wikia. Should a business choose to, a business could use Wikia to post consumer-oriented information such as manuals or user tips for their product or service.

Who Started It?

Wikia was created by Wikipedia/PayPal founder Jimmy Wales. According to his Wikipedia bio page, Wales first created Nupedia, an extensive peer-reviewed, open-content encyclopedia, in March 2000. He hired Larry Sanger to be the editor-in-chief, and in 2001 Sanger suggested that a wiki could be used to create an encyclopedia. Wales loaded wiki software and gave Sanger permission to begin creating the web site. Wikia's creation followed Wikipedia's, but the companies have different concepts and audiences.

Wikipedia

Company Name:	Wikipedia
URL:	www.wikipedia.org
Location:	San Francisco, California, United States
Founded:	2001
Employees:	15
Revenue Model:	Donations and grants
Fees:	Free
Tagline:	The free encyclopedia that anyone can edit

What Is It?

The mission of the Wikimedia Foundation, according to its web site, is "to empower and engage people around the world to collect and develop educational content under a free license or in the public domain, and to disseminate it effectively and globally." Wikipedia is one of the largest online reference web sites on the Internet. It is written collaboratively by volunteers, and is available in multiple languages. Anyone can add content, citations, or cross-references as long as they adhere to Wikipedia's editing policies. Because content is always being added, Wikipedia advises that older content tends to be more balanced and substantiated, while new content tends to have inaccuracies.

How Can It Be Used?

Wikipedia is used primarily as a research tool, though even Wikipedia presents disclaimers against using its content, particularly new content, as a sole reliable reference for an item of information. Wikipedia's layout is simple but powerful, allowing for contributors and editors to focus on the content, not on the page layout. Users can also edit previously contributed content, which aids in the improvement and accuracy of the content. Content is not limited to text: images, maps, and statistical data are also highly encouraged.

What Other Applications Does It Work With?

Wikipedia is not made to be used with a lot of other application tools. It is available as an application for iPhones and iTouches. Wikipedia offers a language translation capability through the use of Transbabel. It also has a meta-tool known as Sandbox; it is intended for experimental pages, and the information is not retained. Wikipedia also offers a meet-up capability for those who are involved in Wikipedia projects.

Who Uses It?

Wikipedia states it has hundreds of thousands of visitors daily, and over 75,000 contributing writers. With Wikipedia's focus on collection of all known information, its attraction is just that: users typically access Wikipedia to find out information. It's become a popular starting point for research papers as well as answers to homework questions or trivia.

Should You Use It?

Users who want a starting point for an item of information typically use Wikipedia. Businesses that wish to add or edit information purely for the educational benefit of the audience can use Wikipedia. There really aren't any other ways for businesses to use Wikipedia; there are no advertising opportunities, and information that has a promotional slant to it is usually identified and marked with a banner until someone else can verify or dispute the information.

Who Started It?

According to the Wikipedia bio page of founder Jimmy Wales, he first created Nupedia, an extensive peer-reviewed, open-content encyclopedia, in March 2000. He hired Larry Sanger to be the editor-in-chief, and in 2001 Mr. Sanger suggested that a wiki could be used to create an encyclopedia. Wales loaded wiki software and gave Sanger permission to begin creating the web site. Sanger coined the term "Wikipedia." Wikipedia was originally intended to be the information feed for Unpaid, but it grew so rapidly in popularity that it became the web site's focal point. Wales described his plan for Wikipedia as follows: "Imagine a world in which every single person on the planet is given free access to the sum of all human knowledge. That's what we're doing."

WordPress

Company Name:	Wordpress.com (associated with Automattic)
URL:	www.wordpress.com
Location:	San Francisco, California, United States
Founded:	2005
Employees:	20
Revenue Model:	Advertising, premium subscriptions, and limited VIP hosting
Fees:	Ranges from free to $500/month (requiring a $600 setup fee)
Motto:	Express yourself. Start a blog.

What Is It?

Wordpress.com is a product of Automattic (also the company behind Word press.org, the actual blog software). It provides blog hosting services ranging from free blog accounts to premium paid blog accounts to limited VIP hosting. WordPress is open source and has a robust plug-in architecture that allows for the inclusion of third-party applications to enhance the WordPress user experience.

How Can It Be Used?

Wordpress.com has a variety of features, to include multiple author/multiple blog capability, tagging, photo use via Flickr or Photobucket, Akismet for comment tracking and blocking spammers, and for free accounts, 3 Gb of storage. Wordpress.com also provides excellent customer service, with feedback provided within 24 hours of requested assistance. For premium paid accounts, there are no advertisements as well as additional storage options ranging from 5 Gb to 25 Gb ($20 to $90 annually). A variety of additional features are available for the premium accounts, each with their own annual costs. WordPress also offers 60 templates for account holders to choose from, in case they don't want to make their own template or don't have the technical knowledge to create their own.

What Other Applications Does It Work With?

The beauty and power of WordPress is that by being open source, built on open standards with a very robust plug-in architecture, WordPress allows for any outside service to work seamlessly with it. Examples include Twitter, Flickr, del.icio.us, Meebo, iPhone, Gravatar, and more. A good example is Robert Scoble's blog, hosted on Wordpress.com at www.scobleizer.com. He's embedded Twitter, Flickr, FriendFeed, and more.

Who Uses It?

WordPress has a substantial list of users that are well-known to the American public: CNN's Political Ticker; Dow Jones's All Things D; Fox's GretaWire; the *New York Times*'s The Moment; Time Inc.'s The Page; *People* magazine's StyleWatch Off the Rack; and famous bloggers like Dan Lyons (formerly known as Fake Steve Jobs) and Robert Scoble. Other interesting WordPress users include the virtual online game Second Life.

Should You Use It?

WordPress is a popular blog service used by millions of people. With its open-source software backbone, it encourages users to create, develop, and publish their own blogs or web sites. Conversely, you don't have to be a web design guru to use it; you can keep your blog as simple as you choose. For larger companies or prominent individuals (you have to apply and be accepted), the VIP hosting service is a valuable tool as it allows those users to piggyback off the WordPress infrastructure. Well-known entities such as the virtual online game Second Life and Flickr use the VIP hosting services for their community blogs.

Who Started It?

The company was founded by twenty-something Matt Mullenweg, who continues to be the primary developer and spokesperson for the company. WordPress's predecessor was called b2/cafelog. B2/cafelog was written by Michel Valdrighi, a current contributing developer for WordPress. One unique fact about WordPress releases is that each one is named for a jazz musician; WordPress 1.2 was named Mingus after Charles Mingus.

Tool Scorecard for Chapter 25: Publish

Instructions: Using the five-point (0 to 4) scale below, rate each tool in this chapter on the basis of how valuable it *might be* to the internal and external operations of your company. Make notes about which tools appeal to you the most.

4 = Extremely Valuable

3 = Very Valuable

2 = Somewhat Valuable

1 = Not Very Valuable

0 = No Value

Tool	Internal Value	External Value
Blogger	4 3 2 1 0	4 3 2 1 0
Constant Contact	4 3 2 1 0	4 3 2 1 0
Knol	4 3 2 1 0	4 3 2 1 0
SlideShare	4 3 2 1 0	4 3 2 1 0
TypePad	4 3 2 1 0	4 3 2 1 0
Wikia	4 3 2 1 0	4 3 2 1 0
Wikipedia	4 3 2 1 0	4 3 2 1 0
WordPress	4 3 2 1 0	4 3 2 1 0

CHAPTER 26

Photo

If a picture is worth a thousand words, what is the value of being able to sort, organize, and share photos with colleagues and customers in your network? The tools profiled in this chapter all have that capability in common. For anyone who thinks that photo sharing may have more appeal to families on vacation than the serious business user, everyone from architects and auto mechanics to zip line manufacturers and zoologists have used one of these applications in their work-a-day worlds. Sometimes seeing really is believing.

This chapter introduces you to the following companies, tools, and applications:

- Flickr
- Photobucket
- Picasa
- Radar.net
- Slide
- SmugMug
- Twitxr
- Zooomr

As you read each profile, keep in mind that its features and functions may or may not be right for your particular business. Use the **Tool Scorecard** at the end of the chapter to help you determine which of these tools qualify for further consideration when you begin creating your social media strategy in Part III of the book.

theSocialMediaBible.com

Flickr

Company Name:	Flickr (associated with Yahoo!)
URL:	www.flickr.com
Location:	Sunnyvale, California, United States
Founded:	2004
Employees:	36
Revenue Model:	Advertising and pro accounts
Fees:	Free; pro accounts: $24.95/year
Tagline:	Share your photos. Watch the world.

What Is It?

Flickr's mission is to help users get their visual content out to their intended audience via the Web, mobile devices, e-mail, the Flickr web site, RSS feeds, outside blogs, or any other technological method that may be developed. One of the social features that Flickr considers so important to its product is the ability for a user to allow family and friends to participate in the organization of posted photos and videos. Flickr's site is usable in eight languages including English.

How Can It Be Used?

Free Flickr accounts are allowed 100 Mb of uploads a month; pro accounts are unlimited. As another incentive, pro accounts are ad-free. You can post to blogs easily once you authenticate their blog the first time they post photos or videos. You can also post photos to Flickr via e-mail, which is great for photos taken with camera phones. Photos can be shared publicly and privately; it is estimated though that 80 percent of Flickr photos are shared publicly. Photos can be tracked by location and date of creation. Photos can be tagged, and viewers can leave comments. A new feature is the ability to print pictures, and products such as postcards can be created. For pro accounts, videos can be uploaded with a maximum of 90 seconds and 150 Mb in size.

Photo 495

What Other Applications Does It Work With?

Apple TV2 works with Flickr, as well as blog applications, Facebook, and MySpace.

Who Uses It?

With over 3 million users, there are many types. Personal users want to share special moments, while those engaged in some type of artistic endeavor can share their art, such as photography, jewelry, crafts, music, and more. Besides personal users, the largest group by far appears to be those in the photography field, whether they are using Flickr to test audience response to their work or offer their work for use under creative commons licensing.

Should You Use It?

If you are looking for a way to share and organize your photos, or collaborate with others using pictures, Flickr is a popular tool that will easily facilitate your needs. Using Flickr to share photos or video related to your business or organization is an excellent way to reach a large audience, but also facilitate posting, tagging, and organization of your visual content. Another benefit of Flickr is that if you are looking for a photo to use, many users allow usage of their material via creative commons licensing; in essence, you may use someone's visual creation as long as you give proper credit and attribution. It also works vice versa; if you wish to allow use of your material, you can establish by what four means it becomes available: attribution, noncommercial, no derivative, or share alike. Educators in the photography field might find it valuable as a learning tool or a method to share projects. Schools might find it valuable for sharing material about school events, but proper copyright and legal permissions would have to be taken into consideration.

Who Started It?

Gaming entrepreneurs Caterina Fake and husband Steward Butterfield initially developed a hack that allowed users to post photos to the Web, and subsequently developed tagging capabilities for those photos. These designs in turn became Flickr in 2004. Sixteen months later, Yahoo! bought Flickr for $30 million.

Photobucket

Company Name:	Photobucket (Fox Interactive Media)
URL:	www.photobucket.com
Location:	Denver, Colorado, United States
Founded:	2003
Employees:	60
Revenue Model:	Advertising and premium subscriptions
Fees:	Free; pro account: $39.95/year
Tagline:	Where millions upload and share their photos and videos

What Is It?

Photobucket allows users to upload, share, link, and find photos, videos, and graphics. Photobucket offers free tools for making slideshows of photos and videos with music. Users can share photos and videos with friends by e-mail, instant messaging, and mobile phone. Photobucket also maintains a substantial online library of photos and videos. In addition, Photobucket provides an online printing service that allows users to print pictures (now in conjunction with Target stores) and add pictures to products such as T-shirts, mugs, calendars, stickers, and more. Users can also create online scrapbook collages. Photobucket is used to upload photos to sites such as MySpace.

How Can It Be Used?

Photobucket is used for editing and sharing photos and videos with family, friends, and associates. There are group albums that focus on a certain topic, such as "cute puppies," and group members contribute photos to that specific group. Users can now create scrapbook collages to enhance their photo presentations, make slides of their photos, or upload their videos and add music as background. Users can also share graphics such as MySpace icons and backgrounds as well as add other graphics. Photobucket sponsors image-related contests for releases of new films—as it did with *Quarantine*, in which users searched for five Quarantine images on the site in order to be eligible for prizes.

What Other Applications Does It Work With?

Photobucket works with Digg, MySpace, JuiceCaster, iPhone, Morpheus software, Albelli Photo Books, Blogger, Facebook, Chumby, TiVo, and the Flock web browser.

Photo   497

Who Uses It?

Photobucket is used primarily by teens, young adults, and hobbyists. There doesn't seem to be an extensive professional audience present on Photobucket. A large demographic focuses on graphics, celebrities, models, and special personal events.

Should You Use It?

Photobucket usage seems to be more oriented toward personal and hobby interests. The best business-oriented reason for using Photobucket would be the ability to advertise to over 41 million members. Like Flickr, many involved in the photography industry do post their photos on Photobucket to gain exposure and passively acquire a customer/fan base. There are pictures of events like political conventions, conferences, and other venues.

Who Started It?

Photobucket was founded in 2003 by Alex Welch and Darren Crystal and bought by Fox Interactive Media in 2005. The two observed that the users of e-commerce and social networking needed a main hub from which to post and share their photos and videos. According to a 2007 *USA Today* interview, Alex Welch "wanted Photobucket to serve as a photo depot for simple uploads across a wide swath of the Web."

Picasa

Company Name:	Picasa
URL:	www.picasa.google.com
Location:	Mountain View, California, United States
Founded:	2001
Employees:	20,000
Fees:	Free
Tagline:	The easy way to find, edit, and share your photos

What Is It?

Picasa is an application for organizing and editing digital photos that specifically targets the most novice users. Picasa is acclaimed for being extremely user friendly by simplifying digital editing with many one-touch edit buttons, and for providing additional editing features previously only available through more expensive software products with a higher learning curve. Users can create movies, collages, and slideshows from their photographs, as well as upload photos to share with friends and family. Picasa interacts with the images on your computer by organizing and sorting images by date.

How Can It Be Used?

Picasa offers the ability to organize and sort images by date, to move and rename images on your computer's hard drive, add star ratings to your favorite pictures, or password-protect specific collections. Users can create an album with the ability to keep one picture in multiple albums without taking extra hard drive space, edit photos, and create visual effects and captions. Picasa automatically attaches and resizes images to e-mail messages so that they are easy to open and closer to standard sizes.

What Other Applications Does It Work With?

Picasa works with most e-mail programs and all of the newest compact flash devices for ease of transferability. Photos from Picasa can be uploaded to most photo processing web sites to order prints and other products. The "Blog This!" button transfers selected photos directly to Blogger, and the "Web Album" button publishes images onto the web page you designate. Picasa states that an "iPhoto plugin or stand-alone program for uploading photos is available for Mac OS X 10.4 and later."

Who Uses It?

Many of Picasa's users are pleasure photographers using the software to enhance their images, create slideshows and movies, or share their images with friends and family. The functionality available through Picasa could easily fit the needs of many novice or intermediate photographers, and depending on the type of photography, could be effective for some professional photographers. This software could be used in various organizations for touch-ups or enhancement of photographs taken at business functions or events in which a professional photography service was not used.

Should You Use It?

If you are looking for a photograph editing program without a significant learning curve, Picasa may be an effective solution. Some of the primary complaints regarding many photo editing programs lie in the lack of

Photo 499

usability, which Picasa solves with many one-touch editing buttons and the diversity of features available.

Who Started It?

Picasa—a blend of "Pablo Picasso, the phrase *mi casa* for 'my house,' and 'pic' for pictures"—was originally created by Idealab. Google acquired Picasa in July 2004 and offers the software in free and paid subscriptions.

Radar.net

Company Name:	Radar.net
URL:	www.radar.net
Location:	San Francisco, California, United States
Employees:	43
Fees:	Free (may incur charges by mobile phone service provider)

What Is It?

Radar.net is a social media application that provides users with a platform to share mobile pictures and videos, allows browsing and commenting from "ANY phone on ANY network in the world." In addition, the Radar Player lets users post from their phone to their web page or social network, and can add items from the Web to Radar. Radar.net differs from some competitors in sharing privacy; only those people selected by the user can view the uploaded content.

How Can It Be Used?

Radar.net can be used from any mobile phone on any network worldwide, according to its web site. Users can share pictures and video by uploading via computer or by sending the content from a camera phone to an e-mail address assigned by Radar.

What Other Applications Does It Work With?

Radar.net works with Facebook via a widget on your profile page, and with AIM, which notifies you when "your friends post and comment." Radar also works with iPhone.

Who Uses It?

Radar.net is currently used by individuals looking to socialize or share images of various aspects of their lives. Radar.net has the potential use as a collaborative tool in a variety of industries; for example, real estate or other location-based organizations can use it to provide images and commentary for potential future transactions. Radar.net may also be an effective tool for word-of-mouth marketing. Users can use Radar.net as a method of geo-location by capturing images and providing text directions.

Should You Use It?

If you are looking for a way to communicate with friends, family, and coworkers on the go, Radar.net could be an effective tool. With the option of selecting users able to see certain content, Radar.net provides users with the ability to create groups depending on the topic of the message so your friends don't have access to professional information and your coworkers don't have access to your personal information.

Who Started It?

John Poisson—founder and CEO of Tiny Pictures, and professor in the graduate film program at Boston University—created Radar.net as a way to combine "the immediacy and intimacy of mobile and the ease and richness of imagery" to capture experiences in individual lives.

Slide

Company Name:	Slide
URL:	www.slide.com
Location:	San Francisco, California, United States
Founded:	2005
Employees:	64
Revenue Model:	Advertising
Fees:	Free
Tagline:	The world's largest publisher of social entertainment applications

Photo 501

What Is It?

Slide's concept is to give users creative capability to tell their stories through pictures and video. Slide claims to be the largest publisher of social entertainment applications. Users can share photos in the form of a slide show, share favorite videos, skin their YouTube videos, or use widgets and applications as entertainment, such as sharing a virtual latte with a friend.

How Can It Be Used?

Slide is primarily used for entertainment purposes. Slide is also used by those who are involved in the entertainment industry. Models, photographers, videographers, and musicians use Slide to post promotional material. You can have lists of fans and friends—the difference being that when you create something new, your fans and friends are notified. However, you are only notified in return when your friends create something, but not when your fans create something. Users choose to become fans when they want to be notified of your new creation, but you can add a fan as a friend.

What Other Applications Does It Work With?

Slide works with a number of applications such as MySpace, Facebook, eBay, Bebo, Hi5, Xanga, Tagged, Orkut, Friendster, and Blogger. Music can be added to slide shows on Slide, and there is also a Slide screensaver and desktop application.

Who Uses It?

Slide users primarily appear to be those who want to share pictures and videos for personal enjoyment. There are also users who are active in the entertainment industry at all levels of success who post their promotional items on Slide.

Should You Use It?

For corporate businesses, it is best used primarily for advertising purposes. Slide reaches 134 million viewers; companies such as McDonald's, AT&T Wireless, and Paramount Pictures advertise on Slide. It would be feasible to use Slide to post event photos and videos to reach the large audience, but Slide's focus is primarily social entertainment. If a company is prepared to use Slide to entertain its audience as it markets its product/service, then Slide is a valuable social marketing tool.

Who Started It?

Max Levchin is not only the cofounder of Slide, but also PayPal. Levchin is behind Slide's biggest risk, using its capability to auto-insert in MySpace profiles, which was against MySpace guidelines. MySpace didn't react, and Slide became an instant hit among users of social networking sites.

SmugMug

Company Name:	SmugMug
URL:	www.smugmug.com
Location:	Mountain View, California, United States
Founded:	2002
Employees:	30
Revenue Model:	Paid membership levels
Fees:	Free trial version; membership accounts: $39.95–$149.95

What Is It?

SmugMug is an independent photo-sharing site that targets professional photographers. Professional photographers can access features such as "watermarking, selling downloads, prints, gifts, and creating galleries of photos" with the ability to use their own domain names. SmugMug offers the functionality of most photo-sharing sites accessible to the common user, but is geared more toward the professional photographer.

How Can It Be Used?

SmugMug can be used as a photo-sharing site for individuals to upload their digital images and share with others. The account membership levels offer varying tiers of options: the basic account provides users with a custom web site and address; the upgraded account offers customization of site design and layout; and the highest account level allows users to remove SmugMug from the address for a more tailored experience.

What Other Applications Does It Work With?

SmugMug offers functionality to upload images from Picasa, iPhoto, and iTunes. SmugMug also offers a published application programming

Photo 503

interface (API) for developers/programmers to create functionality for new applications.

Who Uses It?

The modality of SmugMug as a photo-sharing web site is such that anyone can use it, but the features and pricing options are designed for the intermediate or professional photographer.

SmugMug can be used by many organizations as a photo-sharing site or as a photo-hosting and sales site. The highest account level was designed at the request of the Howard Dean presidential campaign in 2004 to use the service without the SmugMug name in the URL.

Should You Use It?

With features such as watermarking; selling downloads, prints, and gift products; and creating photo galleries, SmugMug is designed with the professional or aspiring professional photographer in mind. The various options and functionality provided by SmugMug could be beneficial for organizations or sole proprietors as a platform to showcase commodities. For the aspiring or professional photographer, SmugMug offers an accessible virtual gallery to display their work, and for a percentage, the ability to sell their prints. The download, print, and gift products could be used by a wide variety of organizations as a way for participants to commemorate a special event or ceremony.

Who Started It?

SmugMug was started in 2002 by Chris and Don MacAskill and was the unintended offshoot of a start-up video game–oriented web service. As the company progressed, more family members joined the staff at SmugMug to carry on their vision to offer an ad-free and spam-free photo-sharing site.

Twitxr

Company Name:	Twitxr
URL:	www.twitxr.com
Location:	Girona, Spain
Founded:	2008

What Is It?

Twitxr is a photoblog service created to enhance communication with your friends and family. Using your mobile phone, you can share pictures and ideas in one message that automatically adds location information to your photos and updates. According to Martin Varsavsky, Twitxr was "specifically designed for iPhone" but "as a third party application . . . it isn't officially available for the iPhone." You can automatically add your location, update your status, and publish your photos and messages on social networks and photo-sharing sites in a single message.

How Can It Be Used?

The majority of users of Twitxr send pictures and updates on their daily activities to friends, family, and coworkers. Twitxr claims it works with any mobile phone and all major social networks; updates can be shown on blogs and personal web sites also with minor customization. "Twitxr has a public API"; this enables developers to integrate Twitxr with their applications.

What Other Applications Does It Work With?

Twitxr claims it works with iPhone and major social media applications, but specifically states on its web site that it supports Twitter, Facebook, and Flickr; blogs and personal web pages; as well as customized applications.

Who Uses It?

Currently Twitxr is used by private individuals providing updates on their daily activities to communicate with friends, family, and coworkers. If the functionality improves, Twitxr may have the potential for expanded business use as a marketing research service or for feedback on products and services.

Should You Use It?

The potential exists for Twitxr as a beneficial business tool for real-time updates for time-sensitive information. Founder Marin Varsavsky claims Twitxr "makes uploading text and a photo from the iPhone very easy," but "you have to 'jailbreak' the phone before you can install their application." Due to the infancy of the product and the required time and effort for configuration, it might be advantageous for those who aren't tech savvy to wait for the next release.

Photo   505

Who Started It?

Twitxr is a product released in 2008 by FON Labs group. "FON founder Martin Varsavsky announced the product on his blog."

Zooomr

Company Name:	ZooomR
URL:	www.zooomr.com
Location:	San Francisco, California, United States
Founded:	2005
Employees:	10
Fees:	Free

What Is It?

Zooomr is a start-up photo-sharing application that incorporates a GeoTagging feature and currently supports 18 locales. While similar to many of the other photo-sharing sites, Zooomr sets itself apart with the OpenID multilogin capability; LightBox, which is similar to a slide show; SmartSets, "which are dynamically generated albums; People Tags, which allows users to add themselves inside photos and search for people inside photos"; and Zipline, which "adds a social-networking aspect to the site allowing users to send a message to one of their 'contacts' or to see when a contact uploads photos."

How Can It Be Used?

Zooomr is used like many other photo/image-sharing sites. Users can upload photos or other digital images to share with friends and family. The unique GeoTagging feature can assist users in finding location-specific information, location-based news, web sites, and other geographical identifiers. With people tags, users can find themselves and others in images. Zooomr is available in more than 15 languages.

What Other Applications Does It Work With?

Zooomr integrates with most social networking applications, including Facebook and MySpace.

Who Uses It?

Zooomr is available for use by anyone wishing to share photos or other digital images and is significantly useful for non-English speakers due to its availability in a variety of languages. A beneficial aspect of using Zooomr includes unlimited uploading, storing, and archiving of photos. Users of Zooomr are those interested in interacting with others while sharing memories, special moments, important events, and key locations.

Should You Use It?

If you are looking for a way to share photos in an interactive environment, Zooomr may be the solution. If you've ever looked at a picture and wondered where it was taken, the GeoTagging feature provides the answer. Viewing photos from friends and family has become more informative. Users can obtain the answers to the questions: "who?" "what?" and "where?" with PeopleTags, Notes, and GeoTagging features.

Who Started It?

Kristopher Tate started Zooomr in 2005 as a platform to "share photos with his friends in Japan. The site was made so it could be viewed in both English and Japanese." Zooomr recruited Thomas Hawk as its "chief evangelist" and was relaunched in 2006.

Tool Scorecard for Chapter 26: Photo

Instructions: Using the five-point (0 to 4) scale below, rate each tool in this chapter on the basis of how valuable it *might be* to the internal and external operations of your company. Make notes about which tools appeal to you the most.

4 = Extremely Valuable
3 = Very Valuable
2 = Somewhat Valuable
1 = Not Very Valuable
0 = No Value

Photo 507

Tool	Internal Value	External Value
Flickr	4 3 2 1 0	4 3 2 1 0
Photobucket	4 3 2 1 0	4 3 2 1 0
Picasa	4 3 2 1 0	4 3 2 1 0
Radar.net	4 3 2 1 0	4 3 2 1 0
Slide	4 3 2 1 0	4 3 2 1 0
SmugMug	4 3 2 1 0	4 3 2 1 0
Twitxr	4 3 2 1 0	4 3 2 1 0
Zooomr	4 3 2 1 0	4 3 2 1 0

CHAPTER 27

Audio

In the late nineteenth century, a group of scientists and engineers that included Nikola Tesla and Guglielmo Marconi set out to bring the world a means of wireless communication. They were not, of course, working for a cell phone company. They were, however, the inventors of radio, an audio technology that has over the years become the very definition of communication, collaboration, education, and entertainment. Neither Tesla nor Marconi ultimately had much influence over the content that would one day ride across the radio waves, but it is certain that their efforts changed society and commerce in ways that are still being felt.

Today, audio encompasses more than just radio, but at its core, audio has the power to move people with music, to capture listeners' attention with the news of the day, or to create a theater of the mind that suggests with words and sounds what people cannot see. As such, audio can be a critical aspect of a social media strategy. Ironically, this chapter is not about radio, which is covered in Chapter 30 on Livecasting. Instead, this chapter focuses on applications that allow you to upload, download, and share audio content, much of which has been harvested or diverted from the traditional airwaves of radio for delivery on a digital device of your choice.

This chapter introduces you to the following companies, tools, and applications:

- iTunes
- PodBean
- Podcast.net
- Rhapsody

theSocialMediaBible.com

As you read each profile, keep in mind that its features and functions may or may not be right for your particular business. Use the **Tool Scorecard** at the end of the chapter to help you determine which of these tools qualify for further consideration when you begin creating your social media strategy in Part III of the book.

iTunes

Company Name:	Apple Inc.
URL:	www.apple.com/itunes/
Location:	Cupertino, California, United States
Founded:	2001 (Apple 1976)
Revenue Model:	Advertising and merchandise
Tagline:	The entertainment capital of your world

What Is It?

iTunes is a digital media application that works on both Macintosh and Windows operating systems. iTunes allows users to access, organize, and play video and music files. Another big aspect of iTunes is the ability to buy songs, albums, movies, television shows, podcasts, audio books, and other digital media through the iTunes store, provided you are connected to the Internet. (A podcast is generally defined as a series of audio and video files available on the Internet for users to listen to and/or watch on their computer or portable multimedia device.) iTunes is also the interface software that is used to interact with products like the iPhone and the iPod.

How Can It Be Used?

iTunes can be used in many different ways. The primary function is to act as a player and library for your digital media files. Through it you can download, structure, and play your videos and music. Additionally, iTunes can be used as a means of disseminating information widely since it allows users the ability to subscribe, receive, and listen to podcasts; it also gives anyone the ability to submit their podcasts to the iTunes podcast directory.

What Other Applications Does It Work With?

iTunes is very closely integrated with other Apple applications, especially GarageBand and the iWork and iLife suites. The applications in both of the suites allow users to access the iTunes library and import them into their respective projects. Any song created in GarageBand can be exported to iTunes. Scripting is also possible in iTunes, which gives users the ability to coordinate it with additional applications.

Who Uses It?

iTunes is used by a very large segment of digital media users. This popularity can probably be attributed to several factors, such as the advent of iPods, the fact that iTunes is free to download, and the high number of podcasts and songs available for download and purchase. For this reason, many podcasters use iTunes in an attempt to reach as many listeners as possible. The vast majority of Mac computer customers use iTunes since the application comes bundled with all Mac computers.

Should You Use It?

You should use iTunes if you are interested in a free, user-friendly digital media application. You should also use iTunes if you would like to buy a variety of different digital media files, download them, and then play them within the same application. iTunes is a good media player to use if you are interested in podcasting, either as a subscriber or as a creator, since it provides access to numerous podcasts and potential listeners.

Who Started It?

iTunes is based off an old software application called SoundJam MP, which was created in 1999 by Jeff Robbin and Bill Kincaid, and then purchased by Apple in 2000. After Apple adjusted the interface, skins, and feature set, the program was released as iTunes in January 2001.

PodBean

Company Name:	PodBean
URL:	www.podbean.com
Location:	Wilmington, Delaware, United States
Founded:	2006
Employees:	10
Revenue Model:	Advertising and premium subscriptions
Motto:	Podcast hosting, social subscribing

What Is It?

PodBean is a podcast service provider that was created to allow individuals and businesses the ability to publish podcasts easily without any prior technical knowledge in web site design or podcasting. PodBean consolidates publishing, management, syndication, and analysis podcasting tools in a user-friendly, point-and-click interface that is similar to a blog environment. PodBean also allows users the ability to browse, listen, and subscribe to podcasts, PodBean hosted or otherwise, all in one location.

How Can It Be Used?

PodBean can be used in two primary ways: as a podcast archiving tool and as a means to disseminate podcasts easily. Users can collect their podcast subscriptions from all over the Internet, as well as browse all podcasts delivered through PodBean, and store them in one spot on their PodBean account. PodBean also functions as a podcast delivery mechanism by allowing subscribers the ability to post and deliver podcasts in an effective and simple manner. Additional tools such as scheduled podcasts and subscriber stats are available for upgraded account packages.

What Other Applications Does It Work With?

PodBean is compatible with several applications to increase the exposure and flexibility of a user's podcasts. Among the more highly visible applications are iTunes, social networking web sites such as MySpace and Facebook, blogging web sites like LiveJournal and Blogger, and PayPal. PodBean also allows a multitude of file types to be uploaded, ranging from different audio formats to Microsoft PowerPoint documents.

Who Uses It?

A wide variety of users, in professional and recreational contexts, employ PodBean. Individual listeners utilize PodBean by searching through a large catalog of subjects to discover new podcasts to listen to, along with gathering their other podcast subscriptions in one place. Podcasters of all types also make use of PodBean. Individuals can publish podcasts on a desired subject so audiences with similar tastes can listen to their thoughts. Educators also make use of PodBean, whether to share research with colleagues or to teach a lesson to students. The last core segment of PodBean users are commercial podcasters, who either sell their podcasts or use their podcasts to market a commodity.

Should You Use It?

You should use PodBean if you are currently, or desire to be, involved with podcasting as either a listener or a publisher. From a listener's perspective, PodBean makes it easy and efficient to become a consumer of podcasts. The ability to search through the large podcast catalog makes it simple to find new podcasts, and the embedded player gives you the option of listening to them right in your web browser. Additionally, the capability to gather all your podcast subscriptions in one spot means you can access your podcasts from any computer with Internet access. From a podcast creator's perspective, PodBean gives you several tools to publish and share your podcast. The included personalized podcast site along with the point-and-click interface handles the majority of the technical issues, so someone who is new to publishing podcasts can become acclimated rather quickly. The large array of compatible technologies is also a benefit to PodBean users. Through PodBean and entities such as iTunes, social web sites, and other blogs, your podcast could quickly market itself to new audiences. Lastly, PodBean is friendly toward commercial podcasting, so if you are a business or an entrepreneur looking to make podcasting a potential asset, PodBean is a good podcast service provider to consider.

Who Started It?

PodBean was created in February 2006. On April 10, 2007, it was incorporated as a limited liability company according to the Division of Corporations of the state of Delaware.

Podcast.com

Company Name:	Podcast.com
URL:	www.podcast.com
Location:	Cambridge, Massachusetts, United States
Employees:	15
Revenue Model:	Advertising and sponsorship

What Is It?

Podcast.com is a platform created by Treedia Labs on which to view or listen to podcasts without additional software or devices, and "provides access to a growing list of over 60,000 curated and constantly updated podcast feeds." Treedia Labs promotes Podcast.com as a "unique value proposition to content consumers" that "presents an unsurpassed way for content providers to reach an audience that consumes podcasts via the Web, multimedia devices and Internet radio."

How Can It Be Used?

Podcast.com can be used to reach niche audiences and those consumers who are too busy or who are unable to view traditional media outlets for information or entertainment. Treedia claims Podcast.com "is the only podcast consumption site to incorporate directory, social media, viral sharing, and personal directory management functionality." Businesses can use podcasting to communicate with consumers or clients, and market products or services. Users can subscribe to the feed and enable a notification feature to indicate when a new podcast is available.

What Other Applications Does It Work With?

Podcast.com is a platform that enables the user to listen to and/or watch content on a computer without any additional applications, services, or hardware. Users can view or share podcasts through their mobile device.

Who Uses It?

Individuals use Podcast.com to keep current on local, national, and international news; to watch programs; or to listen to music or other audio files. Businesses can use podcasts as a means to communicate with employees, clients, or constituents; make product or service announcements; provide information on news and events; or educate others on a particular subject or process. Educators can use podcasts to supplement text, provide a demonstration, or interact with students.

Should You Use It?

Podcast.com offers a wide range of available topics that appeal to a diverse audience. To enhance media relations, organizations can "incorporate quotes from product specialists or senior executives" for distribution to "key journalists." Podcasts can be an informative tool when programs are created to provide advice or direction from subject-matter experts on essential industry topics. Podcasting is a valuable tool for professionals unable to attend conferences as a means of obtaining the pertinent information. If you are looking for a means to communicate more effectively with your audience, Podcast.com is a useful platform.

Who Started It?

Podcast.com was started by Treedia Labs, which "enables a rich user experience that promotes sharing."

Rhapsody

Company Name:	Rhapsody (subsidiary of RealNetworks Inc.)
URL:	www.rhapsody.com
Location:	Seattle, Washington, United States
Founded:	2001
Revenue Model:	Advertising and premium subscriptions
Fees:	Free: 25 songs/month
Rhapsody Unlimited:	$12.99; unlimited music anytime from any web browser
Rhapsody To Go:	$14.99; unlimited music anytime from any web browser and on a compatible MP3 player
Tagline:	Listen all you want. Whenever you want.

What Is It?

Rhapsody is an online music library that allows you to experience full-length, high-quality digital music and music videos. As they say at Rhapsody, "Listen to whatever you want, wherever you are." Rhapsody offers music from thousands of artists—new, old, and everywhere in between. Using Rhapsody, you can share music, playlists, and music videos with anyone in the world. With Rhapsody's monthly membership services, you can listen to unlimited amounts of music from any web browser, transfer your music to a compatible MP3 player, or enjoy it using a compatible home audio device.

How Can It Be Used?

Rhapsody is an effective tool for music research, acquisition, and sharing. With over 4 million tracks to choose from, Rhapsody covers even the most obscure musical tastes. The playlist function helps to separate like genres of music for certain dedicated situations. They also have an affiliate program that offers the use of Rhapsody's RealPlayer to bloggers and developers for use on their personal web sites. Many leading companies have paired with Rhapsody for live event sponsorship, special events, or promotions to engage their target audience and strengthen brand initiatives. Mini Cooper teamed up with Rhapsody for a concert at the House of Blues in Las Vegas to support the participants in the "Mini Takes the States" cross-country road rally. In addition to the live event, a customized Mini Cooper RealPlayer skin and rich media campaign were integrated on Rhapsody for added exposure online.

What Other Applications Does It Work With?

Rhapsody works with Facebook and MySpace in adding music to profiles. The Rhapsody MP3 store offers music downloads compatible with iPod. Rhapsody works with Slide.com in creating an appropriate soundtrack for your slide shows. TiVo's broadband-connected DVR can play music from Rhapsody. Rhapsody can synch with your Last.fm page to show all recently played tracks from Rhapsody. Verizon Wireless VCast customers can upload their music to their mobile phone library using Rhapsody.

Who Uses It?

Rhapsody can be used to pair a brand side by side with popular music talent to increase brand awareness with a desired demographic. Companies that want to promote events and celebrities would do well with Rhapsody's sponsored playlists and dedicated RealPlayer skins. RealNetworks can develop a complete custom advertising campaign that encompasses desired media, promotion, and live events. Bloggers have also found Rhapsody helpful in using it for music playback and music reference on their blogs and web sites.

Should You Use It?

Rhapsody has paired many brands alongside special concerts and music festivals. Hyundai sponsored the first Rhapsody Independent Music Event in San Francisco, using Rhapsody's editors to combine their brand with cutting-edge music, and RealNetworks produced successful performances.

The option of playing short advertisements before music videos on Rhapsody grabs the attention of your target audience. If you want to boost interest on your company's blog, Rhapsody can help by adding a media player and music playlist to your blog. If you want to reach a younger demographic effectively through artists and concerts, Rhapsody is an avenue to explore.

Who Started It?

Tim Bratton, Alexandre Brouaux, Dave Lampton, J. P. Lester, Sylvain Rebaud, and Nick Sincaglia were developing a revolutionary streaming audio engine in 1999 first launched as TuneTo.com. This customized radio service was acquired by Listen.com in 2001 to add the streaming audio to their already comprehensive online music directory. In December 2001 Rhapsody was born. Rhapsody was the first online music subscription service to offer its customers unlimited music for a low flat fee. In 2003, Listen.com was acquired by RealNetworks to further their reign in the digital music revolution.

Tool Scorecard for Chapter 27: Audio

Instructions: Using the five-point (0 to 4) scale below, rate each tool in this chapter on the basis of how valuable it *might be* to the internal and external operations of your company. Make notes about which tools appeal to you the most.

4 = Extremely Valuable
3 = Very Valuable
2 = Somewhat Valuable
1 = Not Very Valuable
0 = No Value

Tool	Internal Value	External Value
iTunes	4 3 2 1 0	4 3 2 1 0
PodBean	4 3 2 1 0	4 3 2 1 0
Podcast.com	4 3 2 1 0	4 3 2 1 0
Rhapsody	4 3 2 1 0	4 3 2 1 0

CHAPTER 28

Video

In 1979, a British rock group, Buggles, released a song called "Video Killed the Radio Star." It became the first music video to appear on MTV when the cable channel went live on August 1, 1981. The rest, as they say, is history, although it must be noted that music videos have enjoyed a complementary rather than adversarial relationship with audio since that fateful summer evening in 1981.

Moving into the twenty-first century, some pundits and prognosticators have said similar things about applications such as YouTube, arguing that cable and television broadcasters will face significant challenges from Web 2.0 services with the ability to deliver video content on demand—not just any video content, but video content that is shared and promoted across social networks.

This chapter introduces you to some of the key players in this rapidly growing segment of the social media ecosystem. Specifically, you'll learn about the following companies, tools, and applications:

- Brightcove
- Google Video
- Hulu
- Metacafe
- Viddler
- YouTube

As you read each profile, keep in mind that its features and functions may or may not be right for your particular business. Use the **Tool Scorecard** at the end of the chapter to help you determine which of these tools qualify for further consideration when you begin creating your social media strategy in Part III of the book.

theSocialMediaBible.com

Brightcove

Company Name:	Brightcove
URL:	www.brightcove.com
Location:	Cambridge, Massachusetts, United States
Founded:	2004
Employees:	110
Revenue Model:	Sales of service packages
Fees:	Must contact for quote

What Is It?

"Brightcove is an online video publishing company" that serves as a platform for content owners to reach their audience directly through the Internet, enables web publishers the functionality to "enrich their sites with syndicated video programming," and provides "marketers more ways to communicate and engage with their consumers." Brightcove promotes its services as "flexible, yet comprehensive" and claims to "maximize your Internet video presence by integrating Brightcove directly with your existing media solutions such as content management systems, ad servers and analytics platforms."

How Can It Be Used?

Several options for use of Brightcove are available. Networks, broadcasters, newspapers, and magazines can reach new audiences, expand advertising options, and reach "niche audiences through managed and tracked viral sharing options." Music labels and artists can use "online video to create revenue streams and drive music sales." Web sites can integrate online video to increase page views and time spent on a page and increase traffic "through syndication and viral distribution." Business-to-consumer marketers can build brand recognition through online content and video campaigns, and increase online sales through in-depth product coverage. Government agencies and educational organizations can utilize Brightcove online video solutions for meeting and speech coverage, and by offering distance-learning modules. Any organization can use the video production services provided by Brightcove to create recruitment videos, testimonials, and documentaries.

What Other Applications Does It Work With?

Brightcove videos use Adobe Flash technology to stream Flash video to widgets, which enables compatibility with applications supporting Flash Video. Brightcove also established a "distribution partnership with TiVo" and a "content delivery partnership with Limelight Networks," and "partnered with Reuters to create a program to syndicate customized news video players."

Who Uses It?

With the development of magazine and newspaper publishers expanding to online video, Brightcove capitalized on this movement and signed deals with companies such as Time Inc., TV Guide, Discovery Communications (Discovery Channel, Travel Channel, TLC, and Animal Planet), Washington Post, Newsweek Interactive, Meredith Corporation, the Hearst Corporation, Nielsen Business Media, Crain Communications, Reed Business Information, Wine Spectator, and National Geographic.

According to Chris Lucas, vice president and executive producer of digital media for Showtime, "Showtime is a content company, not a technology company. The Brightcove Platform allows us to focus on what we do best."

Should You Use It?

Brightcove offers numerous solutions for video publishing that integrate directly with existing media solutions for a variety of organizations. If your organization is working on expanding into online video services, Brightcove may be an appropriate solution to reach new audiences. Existing news media publications can "syndicate to and from related publications and affiliates" and "drive revenue with a wide range of ad formats and targeting options." Brightcove also supports content such as slideshows, podcasts, and audio for added flexibility for users.

Who Started It?

Jeremy Allaire initially cofounded Allaire Corporation with his brother J. J. Allaire in 1995 where they created the web development tool ColdFusion. "When Macromedia acquired Allaire in March 2001, Jeremy became Chief Technology Officer" and "helped develop the Macromedia MX (Flash) platform." He left Macromedia in 2003 to join venture capital firm General

Catalyst. Jeremy founded Brightcove in 2004 and currently serves as CEO. Brightcove is a venture-backed private company.

Google Video

Company Name:	Google Video
URL:	www.video.google.com
Location:	Mountain View, California, United States
Founded:	1998
Employees:	20,000 (Google)
Revenue Model:	Advertising and revenue-generating search engines
Fees:	Basic: Free; Premier version: $50/year per user
Tagline:	Organizing the world's information and making it universally accessible and useful

What Is It?

Google Video is a video-sharing web site that offers premium services for a small annual fee. Its primary focus is on providing freely searchable videos featuring amateur media, Internet videos, viral ads, movie trailers, and commercial professional media. A beneficial feature of Google Video includes a reporting tool that logs and stores details on the number of times each of the user's videos has been viewed and downloaded within a specific time frame, which can be downloaded into a spreadsheet or printed.

How Can It Be Used?

Google Video can be used to share videos such as internal training videos, corporate announcements, e-learning modules, and presentations. Videos can be kept secure and private without the necessity of e-mailing or downloading large files. These uploaded videos can be connected to personal or corporate web sites and sorted by date or popularity. Users can also download videos and save them on their cell phones.

What Other Applications Does It Work With?

The Google Video search database includes video from YouTube, GoFish, ExposureRoom, Vimeo, MySpace, Biku, and Yahoo! Video. Google Video runs on Windows and Mac OSX, and is compatible with VirtualDub and GVideo Fix, which can read the .gvi files and convert them into different formats. Linux versions of VLC Media Player and Kaffeine are also compatible with Google's .avi format.

Who Uses It?

Business and educational organizations can use Google Video for internal training videos, corporate presentations and announcements, product demonstrations, and e-learning modules.

According to Manesh Patel, chief information officer, Sanmina—SCI, "Cost and complexity have until now limited the effective use of video to improve business functions. The integration of video into Google Apps, combined with continuing improvements in video devices and network infrastructure, provides significant opportunities for innovation and saving throughout our global teams."

Should You Use It?

If your business or organization is looking to implement video training, e-learning modules, product demonstrations, or corporate announcements, but does not have the staff or available funds in the IT department, Google Video may be an appropriate solution. Since Google Video only requires a standard browser, virtually any department with Internet access can use it. "Google securely hosts and streams your videos, so employees don't need to share videos over e-mail, or burden IT for a video solution."

Who Started It?

Larry Page is cofounder and currently serves as president of products. His love for computers began at the early age of six, and he later graduated from the University of Michigan with a bachelor's degree in engineering, with a concentration on computer engineering. While in the PhD program in computer science at Stanford University, Larry met Sergey Brin. Together they developed Google, which began operating in 1998.

Sergey Brin is cofounder and currently serves as president of technology. He received his bachelor's of science degree with honors in mathematics and computer science from the University of Maryland at College Park.

While pursuing his PhD in computer science at Stanford University, he met Larry Page and developed Google.

Hulu

Company Name:	Hulu LLC
URL:	www.hulu.com
Location:	Los Angeles, California, United States
Founded:	2007
Revenue Model:	Advertising
Tagline:	Watch your favorites. Anytime. For free.

What Is It?

Hulu is a service that provides free streaming videos on demand to users through a web browser. The company is supported entirely through limited commercial interruption, with the advertising playing either periodically throughout a video, or at the beginning of the selected content. Full versions and clips of television shows, movies, news programs, and sports games are just part of the video offerings at Hulu. Numerous content providers constantly add media, both old and current, to Hulu. Hulu also provides web syndication services for other web sites.

How Can It Be Used?

Hulu can be used to view and share videos online. If a user wanted to share a video, Hulu provides an embedding code which a user can add to a blog, social networking site, or personal web page. Hulu also allows users to create a queue, which acts as a playlist for their selected videos, as well as subscribe to specific shows, which automatically adds new clips and episodes of that show to their queue as they are uploaded.

What Other Applications Does It Work With?

In addition to embedding videos in other web sites, Hulu also allows users to create widgets from which Hulu videos can be viewed. These widgets work with a variety of other applications such as iGoogle, Windows Vista, Macintosh OS X, and HoverSpot. Some of the web sites Hulu provides syndication for are Yahoo!, AOL, MySpace, and Funcast.com.

Who Uses It?

Hulu is used by a large audience throughout the United States. Currently, it is not offered internationally, as there are business and legal issues involved with streaming the content outside of the United States. There are numerous content providers contributing to Hulu; among them are Warner Bros, NBC Universal, FX, Comedy Central, National Geographic, FOX, MGM, and Sony Pictures Television.

Should You Use It?

You should use Hulu if you are interested in using online video advertising to reach a user base that exists within the United States. Hulu is unique in that it is supported by a large number of popular content providers, so you can target an already established and varied audience. Advertisers who work with Hulu are offered several benefits, such as the ability to customize sponsorships, exposure through syndication partners, and marketing through additional sites via embedded and shared videos.

Who Started It?

NBC Universal and News Corporation founded Hulu in March 2007. It is operated by a dedicated, independent management team. A private equity firm, Providence Equity Partners, invested $100 million in October 2007. Jason Kilar, formerly of Amazon.com, was named the CEO in June 2007.

Metacafe

Company Name:	Metacafe
URL:	www.metacafe.com
Location:	Palo Alto, California, United States, headquarters; New York, New York, United States; Tel Aviv, Israel
Founded:	2003
Employees:	60
Revenue Model:	Advertising
Fees:	Free: web site, application, and services
Tagline:	Serving the world's best videos

What Is It?

Metacafe proudly markets itself as "the world's largest independent video sharing web site." This site provides opportunity for a broad spectrum of video producers to showcase their creations. Short-form videos from independent creators, small to mid-sized production groups, and major media companies are available for viewing. Metacafe emphasizes the quality not the quantity of the videos and prides itself on entertainment value. In a recent partnership with Nareos and Zed, Metacafe video enthusiasts have the capability to stream and download content to their mobile devices, allowing instant access to video entertainment. With over 31 million viewers each month, Metacafe has a stronghold in the short-form virtual video entertainment market.

How Can It Be Used?

Metacafe offers a video entertainment platform that hosts audience-driven, short-form original video entertainment for a large audience. As such, it can be used to inform with how-to videos, to entertain with a vast array of video categories, or to market a new concept or product. This is a beneficial medium for private individuals, small production companies, and independent film-makers to showcase their talents and gain exposure. Metacafe offers a Producer Rewards program that generates revenue for creators of original content which crosses a specific threshold of total views and VideoRank^{TM} score.

What Other Applications Does It Work With?

Several applications can be used in conjunction with Metacafe. Skype is one application that allows users to share videos found on Metacafe. Nareos and Zed offer a downloadable mobile application that allows users to instantly view entertainment-grade videos from Metacafe. Nareos is enabling this capability in Germany, the Netherlands, Italy, England, India, and Sweden, and Zed is enabling this capability in Spain and the United States.

Who Uses It?

Entry-level producers use Metacafe to gain exposure, production companies use Metacafe to find new talent or showcase a pet project, and numerous private individuals use it for a quick entertainment break. Videos uploaded to Metacafe could also be used as an advertising tool by creating an entertaining video featuring a product or service. If your company provides a technique or service, a video on Metacafe could demonstrate how your offerings meet the needs of your target demographic. If you are looking for a means of providing in-house training for employees, the how-to section may be a cost-effective resource to consider.

Should You Use It?

Many current viewers of videos on Metacafe do so for personal enjoyment. Independent video producers and production companies use Metacafe to increase exposure to their work, leading to name recognition and the potential for future project offers.

Metacafe was the platform used by Brandon McConnell for his video creations. He is a zoo groundskeeper by day and spray paint artist by night. Brandon posted two videos of himself creating a painting in minutes. "More than 1 million people have viewed his *Amazing Spray Painting* and *Amazing Sprayer!* videos netting Brandon about $5,300 during the Producer Rewards beta program."

Who Started It?

Eyal Herzog founded Metacafe Inc. in July 2003 and serves as its chief technology officer and chief product officer.

Ofer Adler has been chief product officer of IncrediMail Ltd. since November 1999. Mr. Adler cofounded IncrediMail Ltd. and Metacafe Inc. in July 2003. He serves as a director of Metacafe Inc.

Arik Czerniak cofounded Metacafe Inc. in July 2003 and served as its chief executive officer until February 7, 2007. Czerniak now serves as a director of Metacafe Inc. Trained in physics, computer science, and math, Czerniak also was part of the Israeli military research and development team.

Viddler

Company Name:	Viddler
URL:	www.viddler.com
Location:	Phoenix, Arizona, United States; Bethlehem, Pennsylvania, United States; and Krakow, Poland
Founded:	2006
Employees:	10
Revenue Model:	Advertising and premium fees
Fees:	Free with premium fees for users who want upgraded features
Tagline:	The best way to watch and publish your videos

What Is It?

Viddler is a video-sharing entertainment site that provides a platform for users to upload, enhance, and share their videos from their browser to showcase their work. Viddler offers a unique feature to tag or comment on portions of the video rather than the whole video. Through streaming capability, users can view and search without waiting for the entire video to download.

How Can It Be Used?

Rob Sandie, founder of Viddler, was looking for a way to share football video reels with his family and key in on specific moments, which spurred the creation of Viddler. Using the Viddler ad system, advertisers can "bid on videos with relevant keyword tags about the whole video or a specific point in time during the video." "Uploaders can also sign up to partner in a revenue share with Viddler for advertising served during their videos."

What Other Applications Does It Work With?

Viddler works with iTunes and several other podcast services. You can also create Digg button tags for your videos.

Who Uses It?

Currently, Viddler is used primarily by private individuals looking for an entertainment break, but entry-level producers could use Viddler to gain exposure. Videos uploaded to Viddler can be used as an advertising tool by embedding ads within the videos, or creating an entertaining video featuring a product or service. If your company provides a technique or service, a video or ads within videos on Viddler could demonstrate how your offerings meet the needs of your target demographic.

Should You Use It?

With the streaming technology offered by Viddler, consumers no longer have to wait for the video to download in order to view it and search within the content of videos for objects, people, or places. Timed commenting allows users to discuss specific moments in the video, which would be beneficial in an academic environment for dissection of specific themes. This is a beneficial medium for students and educators in the fields of cinematography/

videography and the graphic or visual arts, or those in marketing for a hands-on experience. If companies are looking for a way to market their products through ad placement within videos, Viddler is an effective platform due to the tagging feature provided.

Who Started It?

Robert Sandie, president, cofounded Viddler in 2006, along with Donna DeMarco, vice president. Sandie was looking for a way to share his college football highlights with his family and came up with the concept for Viddler.

YouTube

Company Name:	YouTube
URL:	www.youtube.com
Location:	San Bruno, California, United States
Founded:	2005
Employees:	~16
Revenue Model:	Advertising
Fees:	Free
Tagline:	Broadcast yourself

What Is It?

YouTube is an online video-sharing site that allows users to upload and share video clips on the Internet through web sites, mobile devices, blogs, and e-mail. The videos on YouTube range from amateur to professional levels of media, television show clips, movie trailers, newscasts, sporting event highlights, and homemade movies. Users can comment on videos, join communities, and use copy/paste code for e-mailing and posting on a web site. In 2006, Google acquired YouTube.

How Can It Be Used?

YouTube can be used to share personal videos, provide exposure for amateur videos, promote performers, and stay current on local, national, and international events. Users can tag videos, comment, join communities, e-mail, and post videos on web sites. YouTube claims to provide ease of use; through "simple video embeds to our full-powered APIs, you can integrate video at all levels of technical expertise." Additional features include personal profile pages, search capabilities, categories, and specialized sections. Users can also "sample new features before they are released on the site through Test Tube."

What Other Applications Does It Work With?

YouTube has an application for Apple's iPhone and states it has a "full-powered API," allowing users to create tools for their own applications or to integrate it into existing applications.

Who Uses It?

The success of YouTube is credited with the idea that "uploading, viewing and sharing videos . . . appeals to nearly every age, race, and nationality." With millions of users every day, YouTube has captured the attention of a significant portion of the population. According to Nielsen/Net Ratings from March 2008, in the United States the highest demographic of users are 52 percent male and 48 percent female, with a tie between forty-five- to fifty-four-year-olds and people fifty-five and older.

Should You Use It?

YouTube is an entertainment site that appeals to a broad range of users. For business purposes, YouTube strives to revolutionize the way media companies do business through its YouTube Video Identification program which uses the Claim Your Content platform. This is a means to "identify content and attribute it to its owner and apply the content owner's policy." With the YouTube in Video Ads, organizations can market products, services, or other entertainment options.

Who Started It?

Chad Meredith Hurley, Jawed Karim, and Steve Chen are the cofounders of YouTube. Hurley and Chen wanted to "share some videos from a dinner party with a half-dozen friends in San Francisco. Sending the clips around by e-mail was a bust. The e-mails kept getting rejected because they were so big." The solution was YouTube. Google acquired YouTube in 2006.

Tool Scorecard for Chapter 28: Video

Instructions: Using the five-point (0 to 4) scale below, rate each tool in this chapter on the basis of how valuable it *might be* to the internal and external operations of your company. Make notes about which tools appeal to you the most.

4 = Extremely Valuable

3 = Very Valuable

2 = Somewhat Valuable

1 = Not Very Valuable

0 = No Value

Tool	Internal Value	External Value
Brightcove	4 3 2 1 0	4 3 2 1 0
Google Video	4 3 2 1 0	4 3 2 1 0
Hulu	4 3 2 1 0	4 3 2 1 0
Metacafe	4 3 2 1 0	4 3 2 1 0
Viddler	4 3 2 1 0	4 3 2 1 0
YouTube	4 3 2 1 0	4 3 2 1 0

CHAPTER 29

Microblogging

Think of microblogging as a cross between blogging and text messaging. Companies such as Cisco, Jet Blue, and Whole Foods have used the microblogging tool Twitter to communicate with employees, vendors, and customers. NASA used Twitter to announce that the Phoenix Mars Lander had discovered what appeared to be ice on Mars. CNN uses Twitter to field instant feedback from their viewers, feedback that they then post on the CNN web site and even share on air. Not surprisingly, both the Republican and Democratic parties made extensive use of microblogging during the 2008 presidential campaign to communicate and collaborate with campaign workers and supporters.

Because microblogging can be done from a computer or cell phone, these tools offer businesses in particular a versatile way to interact with employees and customers. This chapter introduces you to three companies in this category:

- Plurk
- Twitter
- Twitxr

As you read each profile, keep in mind that its features and functions may or may not be right for your particular business. Use the **Tool Scorecard** at the end of the chapter to help you determine which of these tools qualify for further consideration when you begin creating your social media strategy in Part III of the book.

theSocialMediaBible.com

Plurk

Company Name:	Plurk
URL:	www.plurk.com
Location:	Mississauga, Ontario, Canada
Founded:	2008
Employees:	8
Revenue Model:	None; privately funded
Fees:	Free at this time
Tagline:	Your life, on the line

What Is It?

Plurk is a themed instant messaging service providing a medium to "showcase the events that make up your life, and follow the events of the people that matter to you in small messages or links which can be broadcast over the web through instant messaging, and text messaging on your mobile phone." Plurk combines instant messaging, texting, and blogging for communicating with friends, family, and coworkers.

How Can It Be Used?

Plurk is currently used for friend and family communications. Plurk could be an effective project collaboration tool or interoffice communication tool in a business environment, specifically if the organization is large or spread out across numerous locations. Plurk also has the potential for use as a word-of-mouth marketing tool. In an academic environment, it can be used as a collaboration tool for projects, for quick conversations between faculty and staff or students and professors, or for assignment clarification.

What Other Applications Does It Work With?

Images and video can be linked from YouTube, TinyPic, ImageShack, Flickr, or Photobucket, and Plurk provides a thumbnail reference in the time line entry for viewing within Plurk. Plurk has an embeddable widget to post on your web page or blog and is compatible with AOL instant messenger. Karma applications provide feedback for the most active Plurkers.

Who Uses It?

Plurk's primary user groups include family and friends, and it is used as an instant messaging/texting service, allowing them to stay in touch and share key moments of their lives. Although not heavily used in business, Plurk has the potential to be used for intracompany communication and collaboration, as well as a new type of market research tool. Plurk also has the potential to be used for viral ("word of mouth") campaigns.

Should You Use It?

If you are looking for a way of communicating with friends, family and coworkers, or journaling or chronicling your daily activities, Plurk would be an effective platform. Plurk is a newcomer in the social media marketplace but has grown rapidly in a very short time and holds significant potential for use as a social marketing tool, a means of collecting consumer feedback, or a communication platform in a variety of environments.

Who Started It?

"Plurk was envisioned as a communication medium meant to form a balance between blogs and social networks, and between e-mail messaging and instant messaging. After months of development, Plurk was launched in May 2008." Information on the founder of Plurk is presently unavailable to the public.

Twitter

Company Name:	Twitter
URL:	www.twitter.com
Location:	San Francisco, California, United States
Founded:	2006
Employees:	25
Revenue Model:	None at this time
Fees:	Free at this time
Tagline:	What are you doing?

What Is It?

Twitter is a social medium specifically created to enhance communication. "Twitter is a service for friends, family and coworkers to communicate and stay connected." People can "share their current activity or state of mind with friends and strangers." Chris Winfield deems Twitter a "word of mouth engine" for small businesses to power better relationships. Users can receive updates via the Twitter web site, instant messaging, SMS, RSS, or e-mail, or through an application such as Twitterrific or Facebook.

How Can It Be Used?

Before its release to the public, Twitter was used as a research and development tool within Obvious, LLC. The majority of users "tweet" updates on their daily activities to communicate with friends, family, and coworkers. Twitter has been in the news media over the last year due to its use as a "hyper-grapevine news resource," and has been credited with breaking news about significant current events and natural disasters. Businesses have begun using Twitter as a free marketing research service and for feedback on products and services.

What Other Applications Does It Work With?

Twitter works with authoring tools, such as Twhirl, in addition to numerous tools for mobile phones, and as browser extensions. Search engines such as TweetScan, FriendFeed, and Summize (which Twitter announced the purchase of on July 15, 2008) are other compatible applications, as are "Hashtags" trackers, such as Hashtags and Twemes, and Mashups, such as Twittervision.

Who Uses It?

The majority of users "tweet" updates on their daily activities to communicate with friends, family, and coworkers. Twitter has been in the news media over the last year due to its use as a "hyper-grapevine news resource," and has been credited with breaking news about significant current events and natural disasters. Businesses have begun using Twitter as a free marketing research service and for feedback on products and services.

"Businesses such as Cisco Systems, Whole Foods Market, Dell, Zappos .com, and Comcast use Twitter to provide updates to customers.

"The Los Angeles Fire Department put the technology to use during the October 2007 California wildfires.

"NASA used Twitter to break the news of discovery of what appeared to be water ice on Mars by the Phoenix Mars Lander. Other NASA projects, such as Space Shuttle missions and the International Space Station, also provide updates via Twitter."

Should You Use It?

If you are looking for an expedient method of communication for your organization, you should use this social medium. News organizations such as CNN and BBC have "started using Twitter to disseminate breaking news or provide information feeds for sporting events." Twitter was used in the 2008 presidential campaigns of Barack Obama as a "publicity mechanism," and Ralph Nader "for real-time updates of their ballot access teams across the country." The Red Cross also uses Twitter "to exchange minute-to-minute" information about local disasters, including statistics and directions.

UC Berkeley graduate journalism student, James Buck, and his translator, Mohammed Maree, were arrested in Egypt while photographing a local antigovernment protest.

> "On his way to the police station, Buck used his mobile phone to twitter the message 'Arrested' to his 48 followers who contacted the UC Berkeley, the U.S. Embassy and a number of press organizations on his behalf. While being detained Buck was able to send updates about his condition to his followers. As a result of the message and the efforts of his Twitter friends, he was released the next day from the Mahalla jail after the college hired a lawyer for him."

Who Started It?

Twitter was initially used internally by Obvious, LLC as a research and development project. Its success led to the launch in 2006. Jack Dorsey is a cofounder and the CEO at Twitter. Evan Williams is a cofounder and chief product officer. Biz Stone is a cofounder and director of community.

Twitxr

Though this application has been categorized primarily as a photo-sharing tool, it includes several features and functions of a microblogging tool. See the Twitxr profile and photo in Chapter 26 for a complete overview.

Tool Scorecard for Chapter 29: Microblogging

Instructions: Using the five-point (0 to 4) scale below, rate each tool in this chapter on the basis of how valuable it *might be* to the internal and external operations of your company. Make notes about which tools appeal to you the most.

     4 = Extremely Valuable

     3 = Very Valuable

     2 = Somewhat Valuable

     1 = Not Very Valuable

     0 = No Value

Tool	Internal Value	External Value
Plurk	4 3 2 1 0	4 3 2 1 0
Twitter	4 3 2 1 0	4 3 2 1 0
Twitxr	4 3 2 1 0	4 3 2 1 0

CHAPTER 30

Livecasting

Livecasting is a category of social media tools that enables you to broadcast live video and audio streams to your network. The tools have gained the greatest notoriety from a group of young, inhibition-free "lifecasters" who have used mobile cameras to broadcast every moment of their daily lives to growing audiences of viewers who are helping take reality television to the next level. Livecasting also includes Internet-radio applications. For businesses, these applications have a variety of uses on the communication, collaboration, entertainment, and education fronts.

This chapter introduces you to the following companies, tools, and applications:

- BlogTalkRadio
- Live 365
- Justin.tv
- SHOUTcast
- TalkShoe

As you read each profile, keep in mind that its features and functions may or may not be right for your particular business. Use the **Tool Scorecard** at the end of the chapter to help you determine which of these tools qualify for further consideration when you begin creating your social media strategy in Part III of the book.

BlogTalkRadio

Company Name:	BlogTalkRadio
URL:	www.blogtalkradio.com
Location:	New York, New York, United States
Founded:	2006
Employees:	25
Revenue Model:	Advertising and a white-branded product
Fees:	Free at this time
Tagline:	The best shows from around the Web on any subject

What Is It?

BlogTalkRadio (BTR) is a social network application that allows people to easily and quickly host their own online radio show. BTR provides robust production capabilities, such as allowing hosts to take live callers and play MP3s during a show. Listeners can subscribe to shows as shows are archived within 30 minutes or less and receive a unique RSS feed. BTR has thousands of active hosts as well as clients who utilize the platform in their own environments.

How Can It Be Used?

There are a variety of BTR clients. Educators use BTR to hold virtual classes and deliver their lectures or to conduct training among staff and faculty. Other clients include the U.S. Department of Defense, Sun Microsystems, *Golf* magazine, and the American Petroleum Institute, whose uses vary from entertainment to public service to education to sales to internal and external communications. The U.S. Department of Defense is using BTR to reach out to the American public in a way that was never before possible. The agency hosts live call-in shows on issues that affect average citizens and military personnel alike—such as homeland security, safety, health, and family. In this way, the public develops a greater understanding of the issues affecting our nation's military. Another example of BTR usage is host Marla "the FlyLady" Cilley. She brings her 500,000-plus Yahoo! member listening audience practical, solid advice for the many challenges they face while trying to organize their homes and lives. They interact with her one-on-one, giving her community the opportunity to take their journey one step further.

What Other Applications Does It Work With?

Many BlogTalkRadio hosts send a "tweet" (using Twitter) before the beginning of their shows to get people to call in or listen. The network is also incorporating short-message service (SMS) tools into the platform. Distribution tools let hosts post a Flash Player featuring their last show in multiple social networking sites, such as Facebook, MySpace, and Typepad.

Who Uses It?

Most hosts create interactive live shows and take callers. Some shows are strictly for entertainment purposes, while others do it to demonstrate their knowledge or to generate sales leads. Organizations like Sun Microsystems, Golf.com, and the Department of Defense created interactive content via the network, engaging their customers and audiences in a unique way. Such conversations also improve search-engine optimization for better Google rankings and create messaging that will exist online for years to come.

Should You Use It?

Yes. BTR serves a wide variety of needs for its hosts and users, but most of all it serves the most basic human need: freedom of speech. Unencumbered by government regulation of speech, users and listeners can communicate freely with each other. Whether for individual use, business, or education, any type of user can easily create and produce a program and reach a specific audience. With clients such as the U.S. Department of Defense, Fortune 100 companies, and educational clients, the spectrum of usage is only limited by the user's needs and imagination.

Who Started It?

Levy and Bob Charish founded BTR in August 2006. The original BTR concept was the dream and vision of Levy as he mourned his father's passing. Levy maintained a blog for his ill father so his family and friends could remain updated on his father's health—and later as a memorial to the elder Levy's life. However, Levy wanted more from his blog, and the seeds of live, interactive social broadcasting took root. Within months of its launch, BTR housed thousands of hosts and hundreds of thousands of listeners. Notable guests and hosts include Barack Obama, John McCain, Brad Pitt, Anjelica Houston, Oliver Stone, David Mamet, Salman Rushdie, Dennis Miller, Margaret Cho, Yoko Ono, and Evander Holyfield, as well as owners of leading corporations and digital-media entities from around the world.

Live365

Company Name:	Live365 Inc.
URL:	www.live365.com
Location:	Foster City, California, United States
Founded:	1999
Employees:	39
Revenue Model:	Advertising, VIP subscriptions, and start-up fees
Tagline:	The world's largest Internet radio network

What Is It?

According to the "About Us" page on Live365's site, "The Company gives individuals and organizations a 'voice' to be able to reach a global audience, while offering radio listeners an unparalleled choice in music and other audio content. Through easy-to-use tools and services, anyone with a computer and an Internet connection can create his or her own Internet radio station. As a result, Live365 offers the most diverse array of high-quality radio available today, with thousands of stations spanning myriad genres and representing over 150 countries." In essence, you can either be a listener and listen to individual broadcasters, selecting your genre of choice, or you can be a broadcaster, transmitting material ranging from MP3 playlists to live talk radio format.

How Can It Be Used?

Live365's services have two audiences: the broadcaster and the listener. Listeners can listen with various media players, and broadcasters can broadcast by creating a "broadcaster" membership. Broadcaster packages vary in type, size, and price. At the most basic level, members can stream MP3 playlist files to listeners. Advanced broadcasters can install software and broadcast live using a computer, a stable bandwidth connection, a microphone, and a mixing board. Listeners listen on their computers or Internet-browser-capable devices.

What Other Applications Does It Work With?

Live365 works with Mac, Linux, or Microsoft-based operating systems. To listen to Live365 on mobile devices, a user would use a Radio365 mobile player. Users can also use Winamp, Real Player, iTunes, and Windows Media Player to access Live365.

Who Uses It?

There are educational broadcasts such as "American University," a Japanese language learning channel, transmissions of the entire air-to-ground communications of the Apollo 11 lunar landing, and "African United States Theory," to name a few educational topics. There are also business-related broadcasts such as "Smallbiz America Radio." The description provided states, "Listen to Interviews with BIG Thinkers in Small Business." Other examples of professionally oriented broadcasts include "Real Estate Nation" and "Trader's Nation."

Should You Use It?

In addition to the typically well-known music genre broadcasters that can be found on Live365, the talk radio genre allows for discussion of a wide variety of industries. No matter the industry, there is likely to be an audience that would display interest in hearing the latest goings-on, technological advancements, business concepts, and economic influences. The mobility of Live365 means a listener can listen while working, traveling, or during leisure time and maintain a knowledge base with the selected station. Your business marketing can be enhanced by transmitting business meetings (live or on demand) or information about new products or technological breakthroughs, and customers can provide feedback, all through Live365.

Who Started It?

According to Wikipedia (but not otherwise confirmed), Nanocosm Inc. employee Andy Volk started up a hosted community radio project using SHOUTcast material. He shared the idea with Nanocosm CTO Peter Rothman. The two developed the concept of Live365. At the time, Nanocosm's start-up product was Nanohome, but once Live365 went live and exploded in growth, Live365 became the focus of Nanocosm. At launch, Live365 was free of charge and had a maximum listener cap of 365 as well as 365 MB of storage for music and audio per station. In 2001, Live365 began charging fees for broadcasting and for VIP subscription packages.

Justin.tv

Company Name:	Justin.tv
URL:	www.justin.tv/
Location:	San Francisco, California, United States
Founded:	2007
Employees:	8
Revenue Model:	Currently none; "building a 'transaction system,' which is a combination of pay-per-view, Craigslist, and eBay"
Fees:	Free
Tagline:	The place for live video

What Is It?

Justin.tv offers a platform to "enable viewers and broadcasters to interact and exchange ideas in real time through chat and live video." Initially, Justin.tv began as a single channel broadcasting the life events of one of its founders, Justin Kan, but is now a "network of thousands of diverse channels."

Justin.tv is still in stages of infancy, but is proposing future collaboration with media companies to "sell access to live sports like European soccer, Japanese baseball, or a closed-circuit music concert."

How Can It Be Used?

Currently Justin.tv is used by private individuals looking to broadcast events occurring in their lives as they happen. However, the future potential exists to implement media distribution of live events on a pay-per-view basis.

What Other Applications Does It Work With?

Justin.tv is compatible with MySpace, personal web sites, and blogs by configuring the video to share with the site you wish to embed into.

Who Uses It?

Justin.tv is primarily used by individuals to chat with friends and share their life, musicians and DJs to broadcast music and chat with fans, artists to promote their work, and comedians and entertainers to host interactive talk shows. The potential exists for industry, education, government, and non-profit organizations to engage in live communication and collaboration. Justin.tv would be an effective tool for e-learning as viewers can tune in to the presenter and interact in real time.

Should You Use It?

Justin.tv channels are open to the public and would not be an effective tool for broadcasting proprietary or confidential information. However, if your organization is looking for a way to demonstrate a product, increase awareness of a service, or conduct an interactive meeting, Justin.tv may be a possible solution. Should Justin.tv implement its transaction system, this application would be effective for revenue generation for media companies to sell access to live sports events that cannot be viewed from typical cable and satellite services.

Who Started It?

Justin.tv was founded by Justin Kan, "who decided it would be really cool if he could broadcast his entire life, 24/7, to the Internet." Justin "enlisted the help of his friends Michael [Seibel, chief executive officer and cofounder], Emmett [Shear, chief technology officer] and Kyle [Vogt, vice president, engineering], and raised a seed investment from Y Combinator."

SHOUTcast

Company Name:	Nullsoft
URL:	www.shoutcast.com
Location:	Dulles, Virginia, United States
Founded:	1997
Revenue Model:	Advertising
Fees:	Free
Tagline:	Free Internet radio

What Is It?

SHOUTcast is a free online audio streaming system that works with Windows, Linux, and Macintosh computers. It permits users to broadcast their own audio from a personal computer to individuals online via the Internet or other IP-based networks. Broadcasters use SHOUTcast by either running their own server (with the SHOUTcast server application), or finding a third-party server provider who is willing to stream their audio broadcast. Once the server is set up, broadcasters can install the SHOUTcast radio plug-in to begin streaming their audio. Listeners can browse through the SHOUTcast broadcast directory and choose to listen to a stream through a compatible digital media player.

How Can It Be Used?

The most common use for SHOUTcast is to create and listen to online audio broadcasts. Audio streams can be broadcasted for any particular theme. For example, broadcasts exist to only play certain genres of music, to play music from certain record companies, or to play songs from a given time period. A musician could use SHOUTcast to broadcast and promote music, a distributing company could use SHOUTcast to promote new albums coming out, or a traditional radio station could use it to reach listeners through the Internet. Another option is to use SHOUTcast to broadcast a private stream and only allow select users to listen to the audio. For example, a business could broadcast selected music to all its employees working within the business network.

What Other Applications Does It Work With?

SHOUTcast works with digital media players to broadcast and listen to the streaming audio feeds. SHOUTcast has recommended digital media players for listeners who want to access SHOUTcast feeds. Linux users should use XMMS, Windows users should use Winamp, and Macintosh users should use iTunes. For broadcasting purposes, the only promoted digital media application presently is Winamp, but alternative methods of broadcasting are available that are not officially supported.

Who Uses It?

SHOUTcast is used by a wide variety of broadcasters and listeners. Since stations exist for everything from polka to heavy metal, the listeners tuning into SHOUTcast audio feeds cover a very broad market spectrum. Proponents of record companies use SHOUTcast to broadcast their artists' music and to reach fans for promotional purposes. Radio stations that exist on traditional AM or FM channels also use SHOUTcast to extend their presence further on the Internet.

Should You Use It?

You should use SHOUTcast if you are interested in creating and broadcasting your own online audio stream, whether you are a radio network operator or a recreational broadcaster. SHOUTcast does have some advantages over traditional radio broadcasting, so it is an attractive option to many users. A radio broadcast conducted through SHOUTcast is notably less expensive than operating a radio network through more traditional means. A SHOUTcast network can also be assembled quicker and easier than a traditional radio network, and with far less technical knowledge.

Who Started It?

Justin Frankel and Tom Pepper founded Nullsoft in 1997. Nullsoft, which also developed and acted as the driving force behind popular programs such as Gnutella and Winamp, designed SHOUTcast in 1999. On June 1, 1999, Nullsoft was sold to America Online, where it currently exists as a division in AOL Music.

TalkShoe

Company Name:	TalkShoe
URL:	www.talkshoe.com
Location:	Wexford, Pennsylvania, United States
Founded:	2005
Revenue Model:	Advertising
Motto:	Your community is calling.

What Is It?

TalkShoe is an online social voice service provider. With TalkShoe, users can create live audio broadcasts, which other users can then join either to participate or just to listen. Live audio broadcasts, also called Community Calls, give individuals the opportunity to converse online in real time; and then, if desired, save these Community Calls for other people to listen to as podcasts or audio blogs. Currently, TalkShoe allows for 250 people to actively participate in a Community Call, with 1,000 users listening simultaneously. TalkShoe also has a mechanism that shares revenue with popular Community Call hosts.

How Can It Be Used?

TalkShoe can be used to accomplish any number of things. A business could use TalkShoe to market directly to an intended audience and gain valuable interactive feedback. A blogger could use TalkShoe to draw traffic to a web site or discuss the latest post. A health group could use TalkShoe to share information about a disease and act as a support group. An individual who hoped to gain a position as a radio talk show host could use TalkShoe to hone his or her skills and prove one's drawing power. Essentially, TalkShoe can be used in any instance where someone wanted to communicate in real time with others online.

What Other Applications Does It Work With?

TalkShoe can be used with different applications to disseminate your podcasts to your audience. Among the applications that it works with are podcast directories (such as iTunes) and blogging applications (such as WordPress). TalkShoe also works with online voice programs such as Skype, so users can call into a live show through their computer as opposed to a regular telephone.

Who Uses It?

TalkShoe is used by a wide variety of podcasters that host shows based on a multitude of topics. As a result, several different audiences listen to shows on TalkShoe. Some examples of the current shows running on TalkShoe are "Puppywishes," a show for expert dog training advice; "The New Wine Consumer: Wine Brands," a show that discusses everything from how to choose a wine to the historical factors of wine that influence the market today; and "The Unofficial Apple Weblog," a discussion of all things related to Apple Inc.

Should You Use It?

You should use TalkShoe if you are currently, or are looking to start, broadcasting audio in any form. Podcasters can schedule live shows and advertise the date, and then broadcast the show live while controlling the interaction of the participants. You should also use TalkShoe if you are interested in adding an audio aspect to your blog or personal web site. Once your show has been recorded on TalkShoe it remains on the TalkShoe web site, and it can then be listed on a web site or podcast directory. Additionally, if you feel that you can create a popular TalkShoe podcast, the TalkShoe cash incentive program may be an appealing selling point.

Who Started It?

Dave Nelsen started TalkShoe in April 2005. Prior to creating TalkShoe, Nelsen had worked in telecommunications as an employee of both AT&T and FORE Systems. TalkShoe was kept intentionally low-key up to, and during, its launch in June 2006. This was done with the intention of slowly scaling server operations with site traffic.

Tool Scorecard for Chapter 30: Livecast

Instructions: Using the five-point (0 to 4) scale below, rate each tool in this chapter on the basis of how valuable it *might be* to the internal and external operations of your company. Make notes about which tools appeal to you the most.

4 = Extremely Valuable

3 = Very Valuable

2 = Somewhat Valuable

1 = Not Very Valuable

0 = No Value

Tool	Internal Value	External Value
BlogTalkRadio	4 3 2 1 0	4 3 2 1 0
Live 365	4 3 2 1 0	4 3 2 1 0
Justin.tv	4 3 2 1 0	4 3 2 1 0
SHOUTcast	4 3 2 1 0	4 3 2 1 0
TalkShoe	4 3 2 1 0	4 3 2 1 0

CHAPTER 31

Virtual Worlds

Virtual worlds present a new frontier for businesses with the possibility of real-time interaction with employees, customers, and vendors. The tax preparation service H&R Block was an early adopter of virtual applications, creating virtual storefronts to advise and educate virtual clients about real-world tax matters. Other businesses are also finding ways to sell actual goods and services in a virtual world. It's still early on the virtual world frontier, but you should watch this category closely.

To help you get a better feel for how tools and applications in this category might be of value to your business, this chapter introduces you to five of the key players in this space:

- Active Worlds
- Kaneva
- Second Life
- There
- ViOS

As you read each profile, keep in mind that its features and functions may or may not be right for your particular business. Use the **Tool Scorecard** at the end of the chapter to help you determine which of these tools qualify for further consideration when you begin creating your social media strategy in Part III of the book.

Active Worlds

Company Name:	Active Worlds Inc.
URL:	www.activeworlds.com
Location:	Las Vegas, Nevada, United States
Founded:	1997
Revenue Model:	Advertising, premium subscriptions, servers

What Is It?

Active Worlds is "a comprehensive platform for efficiently delivering real-time interactive 3D content over the web." Users create avatars that they use to explore worlds (some of which are created by other users) and engage in various activities such as online games, building their own houses and buildings (which can exist as a part of a town), and interacting with other user avatars. The program also has features that enhance the user's experience, such as web browsing, voice chatting, and streaming media.

How Can It Be Used?

Active Worlds can be used in several different ways aside from the socialization and entertainment aspects. A business could create and maintain a functional world or environment where current and potential customers can visit to receive technical support, interact with other customers, or learn about new products and services. An entrepreneur could even create a new online business specifically for Active Worlds by selling custom-made designs, textures, or objects to other Active Worlds users.

What Other Applications Does It Work With?

Active Worlds works with three-dimensional design programs to create the buildings, objects, and avatars that exist in the virtual environments, provided the programs can create within the supported formats. Active Worlds also provides a Software Developer Kit in both C/C++ and Visual Basic/COM versions, which allows users to create bots that can perform multiple automated functions.

Who Uses It?

Several different groups use Active Worlds to fit their own needs and intentions. Many of the users who use Active Worlds do so to interact with others and entertain themselves, but there is also a strong subset of users that treat Active Worlds as a functional networking tool. For example, educators often use Active Worlds as a virtual classroom or as a medium for students to collaborate; there are pricing plans based on educators' needs. Businesses have also used Active Worlds for training employees and as an online meeting environment. There are even vendors who sell products, both virtual and material, in the online three-dimensional virtual mall.

Should You Use It?

You should use Active Worlds if you are interested in becoming a part of an active online community in a three-dimensional virtual environment. Active Worlds works well for educators and businesses by offering them the ability to collaborate online, demonstrate new products and services, and conduct lessons through the Internet; thus, you should use Active Worlds if you like the idea of owning a functional online world that you can moderate. You should also use Active Worlds if you have been looking for a way to reach a large, global audience for advertising, viral marketing, or e-commerce purposes.

Who Started It?

Richard Noll and J. P. McCormick founded Active Worlds. The company was initially created to design a three-dimensional web browser that combined the graphical elements of a virtual world with the functionality of a two-dimensional web browser. The company has undergone several layoffs, divisions, re-formations, and acquisitions.

Kaneva

Company Name:	Kaneva Inc.
URL:	www.kaneva.com
Location:	Atlanta, Georgia, United States
Founded:	2004
Revenue Model:	Micro-commerce, premium subscriptions

What Is It?

The Virtual World of Kaneva is a three-dimensional environment that combines elements of web browsing, social networking, entertainment media, and massive multiplayer online games into one online virtual world. Users create avatars that explore properties in the Kaneva world such as shopping malls, popular hangouts, or other users' apartments. While exploring the Kaneva world, users can meet new people, join communities, play games and puzzles, or just hang out with their friends. Users can also purchase items to decorate their apartment, modify their avatar's appearance, or give as gifts. Some of the features in Kaneva require Kaneva currency, which users must purchase.

How Can It Be Used?

Kaneva can be used as a socialization tool as well as a marketing vehicle. As a socialization tool, Kaneva offers several entertainment options, such as owning or visiting a dance club, watching videos at your virtual apartment with friends, or hosting your own social event. Anyone whom you meet in the Kaneva world that interests you can become your friend in Kaneva's own social network. If you are a photographer, musician, movie maker, or any form of artist, you can also use Kaneva as a marketing tool. Through Kaneva, your movies can be featured in virtual theaters, your photographs can be hung on walls or featured in showcases, or your music can be featured at parties.

What Other Applications Does It Work With?

Kaneva allows users to integrate YouTube with their virtual environment. For example, a user could watch videos from YouTube with friends on their apartment television, or play rock videos on a big-screen television inside their own nightclub. Kaneva also works with your web browser to fuse the Kaneva social network with the World of Kaneva. For example, clicking on a user's avatar in the Kaneva world can lead you directly to their Kaneva social profile on the Web.

Who Uses It?

Kaneva has over 1.3 million users and hosts over 22,000 communities, so it has a very large number of subscribers. Additionally, businesses use Kaneva to extend their online presence. Turner Broadcasting System currently has a contract with Kaneva to build virtual properties within the World of Kaneva. Users in Kaneva can visit the TBS Headquarters, which offers televisions that play streaming videos of Turner content, posters advertising Turner products hanging on the walls, as well as an explorable version of the house from the popular television show *Family Guy*.

Should You Use It?

You should use Kaneva if you are interested in a three-dimensional virtual world that combines elements of social networking web sites (such as MySpace) with elements of virtual worlds (such as Second Life). You should also use Kaneva if you are interested in using a social application as a marketing tool. Every Kaneva community gets its own virtual hangout, as well as its own profile in the Kaneva social network; therefore, any business or individual that creates a community can interact directly with potential customers as well as garner publicity if the community hangout has drawing power.

Who Started It?

Christopher W. Klaus and Greg Frame founded Kaneva Inc. in 2004. Klaus is the founder and former chief technical officer of Internet Security Systems, while Frame is the founder and former chief technical officer of IndigoOlive Software Inc. The World of Kaneva was released in beta form in 2006.

Second Life

Company Name:	Linden Lab
URL:	www.secondlife.com
Location:	San Francisco, California, United States
Founded:	1999
Revenue Model:	Micro-commerce, premium subscriptions
Tagline:	Your World. Your Imagination.

What Is It?

Second Life is an online three-dimensional world that allows multiple users, called "residents," to interact with one another as avatars in a virtual society. Residents can create their own buildings, own land, interact with other residents, and participate in individual and group-based activities. A large portion of the Second Life experience involves the economy, in which residents trade goods and services among one another in exchange for Linden Dollars. Linden Dollars, the currency of Second Life, can be converted through the Linden Currency Exchange for U.S. dollars.

How Can It Be Used?

Second Life can be used both recreationally and commercially. Residents that participate in Second Life for the recreational value can socialize, role-play, or engage in the various activities available. From the commercial perspective, Second Life is not only used by real-world business to extend their online presence, but it is also used by businesses that were initially created to operate within the Second Life universe. These businesses can use Second Life to reach their customer base through promotions and demonstrations or provide virtual services to residents.

What Other Applications Does It Work With?

Second Life works with SLurl.com, which is an external web site that allows residents to connect to locations inside Second Life, as well as locate other Second Life residents from outside the virtual world. Second Life also works with Vivox, a communications system, to provide voice chat and instant messaging capabilities between residents.

Who Uses It?

As of September 2008, Second Life had over 15 million accounts registered worldwide. In September 2008, Second Life also saw its largest concurrent user base online, with over 70,000 residents logged into the world at the same time. Numerous businesses and organizations are using Second Life to their advantage, including 20th Century Fox, the American Cancer Society, Dell, Major League Baseball, Cisco, American Apparel, MTV, Toyota, the University of Southern California, and Harvard Law School.

Should You Use It?

You should use Second Life if you are interested in a three-dimensional virtual world that has a heavy emphasis on socialization and creating a virtual identity, with a well-established commercial presence. If you have a business or organization, Second Life offers the opportunity to establish publicity among its residents. For example, 20th Century Fox held an event for the premiere of the movie *X-Men: The Last Stand* in Second Life; and the American Cancer Society held a Second Life version of its Relay for Life fund-raiser. If you are an entrepreneur, you could create an online business within Second Life that has the potential to generate a real income.

Who Started It?

Linden Lab launched Second Life on June 23, 2003. Linden Lab, founded by Philip Rosedale in 1999, was originally created to design hardware that could immerse computer users into a three-dimensional environment. That concept eventually evolved into the software application Linden World, which later transformed into Second Life.

There

Company Name:	There (Makena Technologies)
URL:	www.there.com
Location:	Laguna Beach, California, United States
Founded:	2003
Employees:	55
Revenue Model:	Advertising, premium subscriptions, sale of virtual currency and goods
Fees:	Premium: one-time fee of $9.95
Tagline:	Send stuff to your friends.

What Is It?

There.com is a 3-D virtual world in which you can socialize, meet people, and share online experiences. There.com claims that it provides members with "a safe, user-friendly PG-13 experience and endless opportunities for self-expression and participation in community activities." Avatars are easy to create and fully customizable, and they can show expressions. Members can also purchase virtual clothing, homes, pets, and other merchandise for their avatars.

How Can It Be Used?

There.com is first and foremost a social virtual world, focused on allowing users to communicate and interact with other members from around the globe in various ways, from text to voice chat. Members participate in numerous activities, which can also involve major product brands, such as Coca-Cola's presence in the skate park. The inclusion of major product brands means that these companies have signed on as partners, and therefore this type of virtual engagement means unlimited advertising opportunities for businesses and nonprofits. Educators and educational institutions are even using There.com to hold virtual classes. The New York Law School allowed its students and faculty to use There.com to present papers to the virtual world members, in order to get feedback and spark ideas prior to their final submissions.

What Other Applications Does It Work With?

While There.com doesn't officially work or sync with other social media applications, many users will include references or links to There.com on personal social networking sites The company does promote branding partnerships with other companies such as Coca-Cola and Cosmo Girl.

Who Uses It?

There.com is a very diverse virtual world. Members come from all around the world and are divided evenly between males and females. The average age is twenty-two, though there is a teen section for youth ages thirteen to eighteen. There are also older members in their fifties and beyond. According to There.com, the average user spends 20 hours a month in-world, and 62 percent of the users are based in the United States. Members have found unique ways to use There.com: one family hosted a virtual family reunion, and the Humane Society has held information sessions on animal rights topics.

Should You Use It?

There.com provides six different ways for those looking for virtual marketing opportunities: hosted events, virtual merchandise, world integration, zones, custom regions, and custom worlds. By using any of these six opportunities, businesses, nonprofits, and educational organizations can market to a whole new audience and stir interest in ways previously not considered.

Who Started It?

Michael Wilson, the CEO of Makena Technologies and There.com, has 25 years of experience in the online community and the e-commerce field.

In 2001, Wilson came out of retirement to join There.com as an investor, and currently serves as CEO with the goal of making There.com the premiere 3D virtual world for consumers. Other executives include Steve Victorino, president and COO; Ben Richardson, vice president, business development; and Betsy Book, director of product management.

Tool Scorecard for Chapter 31: Virtual Worlds

Instructions: Using the five-point (0 to 4) scale below, rate each tool in this chapter on the basis of how valuable it *might be* to the internal and external operations of your company. Make notes about which tools appeal to you the most.

4 = Extremely Valuable

3 = Very Valuable

2 = Somewhat Valuable

1 = Not Very Valuable

0 = No Value

Tool	Internal Value	External Value
Active Worlds	4 3 2 1 0	4 3 2 1 0
Kaneva	4 3 2 1 0	4 3 2 1 0
Second Life	4 3 2 1 0	4 3 2 1 0
There	4 3 2 1 0	4 3 2 1 0

CHAPTER 32

Gaming

This may seem like an odd category for a business to take seriously, but online gaming is a magnet that attracts large numbers of people with a common interest. Gamers come together to interact and communicate with one another, and they tend to be influential within their groups. Gamers represent a special kind of social network. If your business could somehow tap into the wisdom of this crowd, would you be inclined to take the category seriously? What if you could buy a billboard that appears prominently in one of their games or secure a virtual product placement? The point here is that wherever people congregate, there's an opportunity to influence word-of-mouth promotion.

The games introduced in this chapter represent a mere sliver of what's available in the online gaming world. This chapter's goal is to help you become familiar with how this category functions within the social media ecosystem. The applications (games) selected are as follows:

- 4×4 Evolution
- Entropia Universe
- EverQuest
- World of Warcraft

As you read each profile, keep in mind that its features and functions may or may not be right for your particular business. Use the **Tool Score-card** at the end of the chapter to help you determine which of these tools qualify for further consideration when you begin creating your social media strategy in Part III of the book.

4×4 Evolution

Company Name:	Terminal Reality Inc.
URL:	www.terminalreality.com
Location:	Lewisville, Texas, United States
Founded:	1994
Revenue Model:	Software sales

What Is It?

4×4 Evolution is a gaming series developed by Terminal Reality Inc. The game is based on players customizing vehicles and then racing them on tracks like deserts and forests. 4×4 Evolution was first released on October 29, 2000. 4×4 Evolution 2, the sequel to 4×4 Evolution, was first released on October 30, 2001. The first 4×4 Evolution is notable in that it is the first console game that offered online cross-platform playability; that is, it allowed Mac users, Windows users, and Dreamcast users to play together online at the same time. Currently, the game is only available if purchased used or as a modified version that can be downloaded for the PC.

How Can It Be Used?

4×4 Evolution can be used in a few ways. Players can race the computer or play against other users in online mode. Additionally, 4×4 Evolution allows players to design their own vehicles and maps in the editor mode. Through the editor mode, 4×4 Evolution also provides an opportunity for businesses to advertise. For example, a business could design a map that includes advertisements for the company that players racing on the track would see. As another example, a web site could create and release a vehicle pack to the players that includes vehicles covered with decals of the web site's URL.

What Other Applications Does It Work With?

Though 4×4 Evolution has its own multiplayer game browser, it also works with GameSpy Arcade, which is an online game matchmaking application that allows users to find people playing the same game as them and then join those games. Included in GameSpy Arcade are features such as voice chat, buddy systems, instant messaging, and user profiles.

Who Uses It?

Even though 4×4 Evolution is now considered relatively outdated compared to other games, and it is no longer supported by Terminal Reality Inc., it still has a multiplayer following. The game is still currently being played on all the platforms it was released for, and with its free release, it has been introduced to some new users on the PC platform. When 4×4 Evolution was first released, several automobile companies—such as Toyota, Ford, and Dodge—had contracts with Terminal Reality Inc. to include digital versions of their vehicles in the game.

Should You Use It?

You should use 4×4 Evolution from an entertainment perspective if you are interested in playing a multiplayer game online that is based on customizing vehicles and then racing them in off-road environments. From a marketing perspective, you could use the PC version of 4×4 Evolution to reach potential customers, but the resources might be better spent elsewhere. To use 4×4 Evolution for product placement, you would have to design and release custom graphics for the game, when in all likelihood the advertising would only reach a limited and slowly diminishing audience.

Who Started It?

Mark Randel and Brett Combs founded Terminal Reality Inc. in 1994. Randel holds a master's degree in electrical engineering and is a former employee of Microsoft, having built the engine for the acclaimed Microsoft Flight Simulator. Combs was the former general manager of Mallard Software. The two started the company with their personal money and initially worked out of Combs's home.

Entropia Universe

Company Name:	MindArk
URL:	www.entropiauniverse.com
Location:	Gothenburg, Sweden
Founded:	2003
Revenue Model:	Micro-commerce
Tagline:	The next generation of interactive entertainment is here.

What Is It?

Entropia Universe is an online virtual world that combines elements of massively multiplayer online role-playing games, first-person shooters, and economic practices. In the Entropia Universe, players assume the role of colonists who are exploring an untamed planet and must find resources, deal with wild animals, and trade with other colonists. Entropia Universe is a free game that functions off a micropayment system, wherein players convert real-world money to Entropia Universe currency for usage in the game.

How Can It Be Used?

Entropia Universe can be used in different ways by players and businesses. Many players choose to play the game for free, but many entrepreneurs invest money into Entropia dollars to try and turn a real-world profit. There have even been a few cases where large amounts of money—as much as $100,000—have been spent or earned by players. A business could also use Entropia Universe to market itself. For example, a business could buy a piece of virtual property and build something to attract users, such as a club or entertainment venue, and then advertise by networking with the players who come to visit.

What Other Applications Does It Work With?

Entropia Universe works with micropayment systems that enable the users to quickly convert real-world money to and from the Entropia Universe currency. Additionally, there is an ATM card that Entropia Universe participants can use to withdraw their Entropia Universe money as real-world money from certain ATM machines.

Who Uses It?

Entropia Universe is used by a large global audience. As of fall 2008, there are over 761,500 subscribed users from more than 100 countries around the world playing the game. Entrepreneurs, merchants, gamers, role-players, and more are all drawn to the virtual world created by Entropia Universe. A large segment of Chinese users are also participating in this online environment, with that user base expected to grow since Entropia Universe has been chosen by the Chinese government to create a cash-based virtual economy for the country.

Should You Use It?

You should use Entropia Universe if you are interested in a free online game that revolves around a massive multiplayer universe. Since Entropia Universe emphasizes the economy of the world, it draws a more varied player base than other massively multiplayer games. This position opens up a realm of possibilities for a business to network and market to users who are interested in both games and economies. From a business perspective, you should consider using Entropia Universe if you are looking to interact with, or broaden your understanding of, the Chinese market, as it will likely be branching out rapidly into the Entropia Universe.

Who Started It?

MindArk started Entropia Universe, which is a continuation of Project Entropia. Project Entropia was an undertaking that was initiated in 1995 by Jan Welter Timkrans along with some of his colleagues in Sweden. During the game's creation and testing in 2002, MindArk was raided by court officials as a result of a Microsoft claim that MindArk was using unlicensed software. By 2003, MindArk launched its game commercially.

EverQuest

Company Name:	Sony Online Entertainment
URL:	www.everquest.com
Location:	San Diego, California, United States
Founded:	1995
Revenue Model:	Subscription, merchandise, software sales, micro-commerce

What Is It?

EverQuest is a three-dimensional massively multiplayer online role-playing game published by Sony Online Entertainment. In EverQuest, a user takes on the role of a character that exists in the EverQuest fantasy world, and then interacts with other users' characters, computer-controlled characters, and items. Users can trade, adventure, join groups of other users, socialize, or craft items in the EverQuest universe. The EverQuest franchise has had fourteen expansions, as well as a sequel released in 2004, and has received many gaming rewards since its initial release on March 16, 1999.

How Can It Be Used?

EverQuest can be used as a socialization and recreation tool, as well as an interactive story that the user engages in as an active participant. EverQuest can also be used as an effective viral marketing tool by advertising directly to potential customers while socializing with them. The game serves as an efficient vehicle for more conventional business marketing as well, as the now-defunct 2005 deal between Sony and PizzaHut displayed. A user playing EverQuest 2 could type "/pizza" into a chat window and a web browser would launch, taking the user directly to the online ordering section of pizzahut .com. In EverQuest 2, Sony also implemented Station Exchange, which is an official auction system that allows users to transfer real money for virtual goods.

What Other Applications Does It Work With?

EverQuest works with web browsers by sending commands from the game that will result in the browser performing certain actions, such as in the pizza marketing deal with PizzaHut. There are also numerous add-ons that are available for EverQuest, which modify the interface, game play, and visual appearance of the game. The EverQuest web site is compatible with ShareThis, a widget for sharing web sites.

Who Uses It?

A global and varied audience of gamers uses EverQuest. Casual users play for the social and entertaining aspects of EverQuest, while some hardcore gamers play EverQuest often, and even use Station Exchange as a means of making money through the game's economy. The PizzaHut deal, although now nonexistent, serves as evidence that businesses have, and may consider in the future, using EverQuest as a tool to increase business exposure.

Should You Use It?

You should use EverQuest if you would like to engage in a fantasy-themed massively multiplayer online role-playing game that has a large fan base and is well established. EverQuest may also interest you if you like the concept of a business relationship similar to the one between Sony and PizzaHut. By participating in that deal, Sony showed that it was open to innovative ways in which games and businesses could collaborate.

Who Started It?

Brad McQuaid, Steve Clover, and Bill Trost are credited with the original design for EverQuest, with the original concept coming from John Smedley. Smedley was an executive at Sony Interactive Studios America in 1996 when development of EverQuest began. McQuaid and Clover were hired as programmers for the game, while Trost created the history, lore, and major characters. It was developed by Verant Interactive and 989 Studios, and then published by Sony Online Entertainment—all of which are, or were, divisions of Sony. EverQuest has survived various corporate restructurings of Sony since it was first conceptualized.

World of Warcraft

Company Name:	Blizzard Entertainment
URL:	www.worldofwarcraft.com
Location:	Irvine, California, United States
Founded:	1991
Revenue Model:	Subscription, merchandise, software sales

What Is It?

World of Warcraft is a massively multiplayer online role-playing game that takes place in Blizzard Entertainment's evolving Warcraft universe. Players assume the role of a character belonging to one of the two available factions, and then explore the World of Warcraft while interacting with other users, computer-controlled characters, and various other items.

How Can It Be Used?

World of Warcraft, though primarily seen as a recreational activity, could be used as a tool for improving business. Consultants draw parallels between managing a World of Warcraft guild, which is an organization of players, and managing a company's networking, growth, and employees. Additionally, businesses have paired with Blizzard Entertainment to increase their own revenue through World of Warcraft's popularity. For example, DirectTV has offered a free 11-month subscription to World of Warcraft for any new customers who sign up for DirectTV services.

What Other Applications Does It Work With?

World of Warcraft is compatible with a multitude of third-party add-ons to enhance the social and game-playing experience of the players. These add-ons can modify many of the game's features, including the visual appearance, the interface, and the interaction between players. There are also add-ons that allow players to track the supply and demand of trade goods, which makes it easier for them to improve their status in the game's economy.

Who Uses It?

World of Warcraft is used by a massive number of subscribed players, with large segments of its player base in North America, Asia, and Europe. It is currently the world's largest massively multiplayer online role-playing game, with over 10.9 million monthly subscribers as of September 2008, while holding an estimated 62 percent of the massively multiplayer online role-playing game market as of April 2008. World of Warcraft also holds the Guinness World Record for the most popular game in its genre.

Should You Use It?

You should use World of Warcraft if you are interested in a massively multiplayer online role-playing game that takes place in the well-established Warcraft universe. You should also consider using World of Warcraft if you would like to interact directly with the players of the world's most populated massively multiplayer online game. Additionally, World of Warcraft is widely considered to be one of the friendliest games of its type for a casual user, so the market audience for the game covers a broader base than most other games in the same genre.

Who Started It?

World of Warcraft is a continuation of the Warcraft game series that Blizzard has been developing since 1994. World of Warcraft was announced in September 2001, and underwent extensive testing and development prior to its first public release on November 23, 2004. Blizzard Entertainment was founded in 1991 as Silicon & Synapse by UCLA graduates Michael

Morhaime, Allen Adham, and Frank Pearce. Since its founding, the company has undergone several name changes and acquisitions. It is currently known as Blizzard Entertainment and exists as a division of Activision Blizzard.

Tool Scorecard for Chapter 32: Gaming

Instructions: Using the five-point (0 to 4) scale below, rate each tool in this chapter on the basis of how valuable it *might be* to the internal and external operations of your company. Make notes about which tools appeal to you the most.

4 = Extremely Valuable

3 = Very Valuable

2 = Somewhat Valuable

1 = Not Very Valuable

0 = No Value

Tool	Internal Value	External Value
4×4 Evolution	4 3 2 1 0	4 3 2 1 0
Entropia Universe	4 3 2 1 0	4 3 2 1 0
EverQuest	4 3 2 1 0	4 3 2 1 0
World of Warcraft	4 3 2 1 0	4 3 2 1 0

CHAPTER 33

Productivity Applications

The 15 applications highlighted in this chapter encompass the widest range of tools of any category in the social media ecosystem. You may be inclined to think of this category as a catch-all to include everything that doesn't fit somewhere else, but that would be shortsighted. Instead, think of the applications in this chapter as business productivity tools. You'll recognize many of these companies and may already be using some of these tools, but you'll also discover some innovative new tools that can be of tremendous benefit to your business. Explore this chapter very carefully.

The companies, tools, and applications profiled in this chapter are as follows:

- Acteva
- AOL
- BitTorrent
- Eventful
- Google Alerts
- Google Docs
- Google Gmail

- MSGTAG
- ReadNotify
- Survey Monkey
- TiddlyWiki
- Yahoo!
- Zoho
- Zoomerang

As you read each profile, keep in mind that its features and functions may or may not be right for your particular business. Use the **Tool Scorecard** at the end of the chapter to help you determine which of these tools qualify for further consideration when you begin creating your social media strategy in Part III of the book.

Acteva

Company Name:	Acteva
URL:	www.acteva.com
Location:	San Francisco, California, United States
Founded:	1998
Employees:	25
Revenue Model:	User fees
Fees:	Processing fees start at $1 and increase depending on plan
Motto:	Marketplace for activities

What Is It?

Acteva offers a secure online event management solution for corporations, associations, event planners, nonprofits, faith-based organizations, entertainment organizations, schools and universities, and other continuing education organizations. The service allows event organizers to focus on the event preparation rather than the administrative and attendance duties necessary for hosting the event, and offers a MultiVent option for organizations running numerous events. Acteva creates a secure page for the organization's event that processes the registration, payment processing, ticketing, and attendance verification, and provides response reporting services that allow organizations to access data from one central location. Several different service plans are available, depending on the organization's needs.

How Can It Be Used?

Acteva provides a platform for organizations to organize, manage, and track an event. The event registration and management software can be customized based on the organization's needs and has been used for events such as conferences, conventions, meetings, symposiums, workshops, webinars, classes, seminars, trade shows, user groups, trainings, festivals, fund-raisers, galas, concerts, tours, and reunions. The Acteva system enables organizers to create custom-tailored event registration pages that process the registration and payment, and then send an electronic confirmation to the registrant. The event management software facilitates the generation of attendee lists, meal preference lists, name tags, and badges; the ticketing option prints and mails tickets to the attendees.

What Other Applications Does It Work With?

Acteva is a self-contained application suite and was not designed to work specifically with other social media applications; however, it can be used in a complementary fashion with a wide variety of other applications.

Who Uses It?

A variety of organizations including corporations, associations, event planners, nonprofits, faith-based organizations, entertainment organizations, schools and universities, and other continuing education organizations use Acteva. Anyone needing event planning tools can use its services.

Libby Craig of the Flute Bay Area stated, "Our guests registered with ease, and your reporting functions were a great help in our efforts to track activity and be certain special needs of registrants were met."

Marianne Leon of the NJ Green Building Council used Acteva and found that the "reporting features save a tremendous amount of time and I can make strategic decisions. I also target attendees with distinct offers to entice them to register."

Should You Use It?

If you are looking for a convenient package program to assist in event planning or do not have the time or personnel to handle the administrative functions of planning an event, Acteva could be a viable option.

Jennie Bolas of McKesson stated, "Acteva provides a professional registration solution that contributes to the success of our corporate events."

According to Darian Rodriguez Heyman (Craigslist Foundation), "There are so many different ways Acteva helps me accomplish my goals as an organizer. It's really made my job much easier. I have plenty of insight into who's coming to our boot camp, why they are coming, and what we can do to improve their satisfaction with the program."

Who Started It?

Pankaj Gupta is founder of zDegree, the parent organization of Acteva, and is cofounder, president, and CEO of Acteva. He worked for or founded numerous Silicon Valley technology companies prior to Acteva. Gupta holds degrees in electronic systems engineering and industrial systems engineering as well as a bachelor's degree in biological sciences.

AOL

Company Name:	AOL LLC
URL:	www.aol.com
Location:	New York, New York, United States
Founded:	1983
Revenue Model:	Advertising, subscriptions, services
Fees:	Free and Premium

What Is It?

AOL is a company that serves two main functions: providing Internet services and providing online content. Both of these functions are derived from the company's older software application, America Online, which was at one time the most popular subscription dial-up Internet service in the world. America Online allowed users to access select areas of the Internet (eventually users were allowed to access the entirety of the Internet) and participate in the world's largest online community, complete with chat rooms, special-interest groups, games, and a graphical user interface. These types of features later became key components of social networking.

How Can It Be Used?

The Internet service provider aspect of AOL manifests itself through services such as dial-up access to the Internet, AOL e-mail and chatting accounts, and security applications. There are also services available for users who have high-speed Internet access through a different provider. The content aspect of AOL can be accessed primarily through myAOL, which serves as a contact point for users to browse the Internet. The myAOL service offers several features, such as customizable content, RSS feeds, saved bookmarks, myAOL Favorites (a way to share your favorite web content with other users), and personalized content recommendations.

What Other Applications Does It Work With?

AOL works with Yahoo! and Gmail so users can check multiple e-mail accounts from the AOL homepage. The AOL Internet services do not rely on AOL Internet access, allowing users the ability to access AOL offerings through their chosen Internet access company.

Who Uses It?

AOL, when it was known as America Online, at one point had more than 30 million subscribers worldwide. This subscriber base has fallen considerably since 2001. AOL online content is accessed by a global audience, with large portions of the consumers coming from the United States, Germany, and the United Kingdom. Some of the partners that provide content for AOL include News Corporation, Sony, NBC Universal, and Warner Bros.

Should You Use It?

You should use AOL if you would like to consolidate and customize content from the Internet in one location through myAOL. You should also use AOL if you are interested in finding a variety of online content that includes offerings like news, horoscopes, entertainment, and job postings. AOL Internet services are useful as well if you are interested in different features such as Internet access, security software, technical support, video on demand, or insurance coverage.

Who Started It?

AOL first began as a company called Control Video Corporation in 1983, which was reorganized as Quantum Computer Services Inc., on May 24, 1985. The company focused on providing dedicated online services to Commodore computers. In 1988, Quantum created online services for Macintosh, and later IBM, computers. In 1991, Quantum became known as America Online Inc., AOL for DOS was launched, and Steve Case became the CEO of the company. Case decided the best direction for the company to take was to position AOL as the premier online service for those who were not particularly knowledgeable about computers. This strategy led to the company's biggest growth period. On January 11, 2001, America Online merged with Time Warner.

BitTorrent

Company Name:	BitTorrent Inc.
URL:	www.bittorrent.com
Location:	San Francisco, California, United States
Founded:	2004
Employees:	50
Revenue Model:	Advertising, paid downloads, and software
Fees:	Media downloads vary by content. Other services require contact with a BitTorrent representative.
Motto:	Access the Internet's richest media.

What Is It?

BitTorrent is an avenue for high-quality media downloads over the Internet. The free BitTorrent software allows you to securely and quickly download TV shows, music, movies, and PC games on demand. Publishing your own films, music videos, and various media content is another service that BitTorrent offers to showcase your work on a global scale. Downloads from BitTorrent are compatible with select home entertainment devices for viewing TV shows.

How Can It Be Used?

BitTorrent is popular among movie studios, television networks, software developers, record labels, musicians, and others for distributing media for public download. It is a great way to develop your fan base, introduce a new product, and get the world familiar with your specialized offering. Many popular Hollywood studios are distributing content using BitTorrent to develop brand awareness online. Even radio programs are using BitTorrent to help dedicated listeners download podcasts of their programs. Using BitTorrent's DNA (Delivery Network Accelerator), companies can also take the pressure off of a company's server by using the service for downloads.

What Other Applications Does It Work With?

The BitTorrent store and software are compatible with any web browser. BitTorrent DNA is also compatible with any web browser, but carries the ability to apply its revolutionary protocol to your own personal web site. Content downloaded from BitTorrent is compatible with Windows Media Player and many other popular media storage programs.

Who Uses It?

Major motion picture studios, record labels, musicians, software developers, television networks, and others are releasing content for download on BitTorrent. NBC, MTV, FOX, Warner Bros., Comedy Central, and others have partnerships with BitTorrent for viewers to download programming. Small businesses that lack bandwidth on their web sites can utilize BitTorrent's DNA technology to unload stress upon their server and relay downloads to other servers.

Should You Use It?

If digital distribution is a means of reaching your target audience, then BitTorrent is a service that would act in your favor. Whether you are launching a new product or trying to create hype for your new dramatic short film, BitTorrent provides effective online exposure. With today's impatient consumers demanding speedy turnaround, BitTorrent downloads are fast and efficient. BitTorrent's DNA technology can help a small business lacking bandwidth on its web site to improve the quality of downloads. Advertising on BitTorrent would reach a tech-savvy audience that depends highly on the Internet for common functionalities.

Who Started It?

Programmer Brahm Cohen developed the BitTorrent software in 2001. Using the popular peer-to-peer file-sharing protocol, Brahm Cohen and colleague Ashwin Navin began BitTorrent Inc., in 2004. The pair based the company on three levels of business: a web-based store with ad-based downloadable content, BitTorrent's DNA technology, and BitTorrent's Software Development Kit (SDK).

Eventful

Company Name:	Eventful
URL:	www.eventful.com
Location:	San Diego, California, United States
Founded:	2004
Employees:	35
Revenue Model:	Series A & B venture capital funding, advertising
Fees:	Free
Motto:	Life is short. . . . Make it eventful!

What Is It?

Eventful is a repository of events from all around the world. Whether concerts, art events, sporting events, or other entertainment venues, users can research or post them for other users to find. In addition to being an event-listing database, Eventful also allows users to post "demands" for venues, such as requesting a music performer to come to a certain location. The specified performer can monitor the demand rate, and if the demand is high enough, plan a performance at that location.

How Can It Be Used?

Eventful is an Internet-based calendar database used by people around the world. According to Eventful's "About" page, users use Eventful to import iTunes and last.fm performer lists to keep track of local appearances; export events through feeds, calendar widgets, and more; keep track of favorite venues and performers; create customized e-mail event guides; add events to personal watch lists; and add and promote events for free.

What Other Applications Does It Work With?

Eventful works with a number of applications: iTunes (to include as an application for iPhone), Yahoo!, iGoogle, MySpace, Artist Data Systems, Clickable City, and Mapdango. All of these applications feature the ability to post calendar events with locations, and can be incorporated into Eventful.

Who Uses It?

Music performers, art show hosts, celebrities, stadiums, and marketing specialists can all use Eventful to broadcast awareness of their events or stir demand for future events. Eventful was even used in the 2008 political campaigns as candidates determined which location to target by monitoring user demand for candidate appearances.

Should You Use It?

Eventful seems to be gaining popularity for its global event tracking, and with the use of Eventful in political campaign strategy, it seems like a good idea. If political candidates can use it for assessing constituency demand, the same principle could be used in product-release events to build up interest in a new product. For example, what if Apple created the next-generation iPhone and used Eventful to hold some sort of locale contest to determine when and where a major release event would be held? Marketing strategies are endless, and obviously Eventful is useful for attracting local people as well as travelers to your major event.

Who Started It?

Brian Dear founded Eventful after experiencing routine frustration at finding out about events in San Diego after they occurred. In an interview on SoCaltech.com, Dear stated that he began researching Eventful as early as 2002. In its beta version, Eventful was known as EVDB, and in 2005 the name was changed to Eventful. Brian Dear started Eventful to facilitate sharing of event information on a global level. Prior to Eventful, Dear was the founding director of eBay Design Labs at eBay Inc. He also worked at Eazel, MP3.com, FlatWorks, RealNetworks, and Coconut Computing.

Google Alerts

Company Name:	Google Alerts (Google Inc.)
URL:	www.google.com/alerts
Location:	Mountain View, California, United States
Founded:	2003
Employees:	20,000 (Google)
Revenue Model:	Advertising and premium subscriptions
Fees:	Free

What Is It?

Google Alerts allows you to create alerts against your Google searches and receive the results via RSS feeds or e-mails. You can determine how frequently you receive the alerts, and searches last for six months. You can renew the alerts or let them expire. Google Alerts are based on the six categories of Google information: news, Web, blogs, images, videos, and Google Groups. Users are allowed a maximum of 1,000 different alerts.

How Can It Be Used?

Google Alerts can be used to track a number of items on the Internet. You can create queries to alert you when someone links to your web site, keep track of new web pages on a web site, track when your favorite blog posts new entries, receive alerts when someone quotes you or uses your name, or track news about a specific topic, product, or company. According to Blogstorm.com, you can even use Google Alerts to keep track of whether your web site has been hacked and had hidden links placed in the web page to elevate the ranking of a different web page, called a "black hat site."

What Other Applications Does It Work With?

Google Alerts works with Google Bots, but not with any other applications.

Who Uses It?

No specific demographic is attributed with using Google Alerts. Many people in business or engaged in research use it, whether to keep abreast on news of a topic of interest, or to track cross-links between web sites.

Should You Use It?

Google Alerts is a great tool for keeping up-to-date on new information, web updates, images, and other data that is available and constantly changing on the Internet. You just need a Google account, and you can establish up to 1,000 alerts. It's a great tool for businesses, nonprofits, students, and private individuals who want to be updated.

Who Started It?

According to the Google Guide, in February 2003, Google engineer Naga Sridhar developed an application because he was tired of regularly visiting

Google News to check for developments in the imminent U.S. war with Iraq. The application e-mailed him when a news story matched a specific query. Naga demonstrated his prototype to cofounder Sergey Brin, who set up a news alert for "Google." Naga continued his development of this application full-time with the encouragement of both Sergey and Marissa Mayer (Google's director of consumer products). Six months later, links to News Alerts were added to Google Labs' home page and to Google News. Google subsequently added Web Alerts to track changes to web pages. Eventually both News Alerts and Web Alerts were merged into a single service called Google Alerts.

Google Docs

Company Name:	Google Docs (Google Inc.)
URL:	www.docs.google.com
Location:	Mountain View, California, United States
Founded:	2005
Employees:	20,000 (Google)
Fees:	Free
Tagline:	Create and share your work online

What Is It?

Google Docs allows users to upload documents so that they are available on the Internet for use, collaboration, and travel. You can upload DOC, XLS, ODT, ODS, RTF, CSV, PPT, and other documents to a common place for keeping and accessing them. Google Docs also allows you to organize your data, control access, and work in real time, and instantly publish the document as a web page, to a blog, or within a specific group or company. Up to 10 people can edit a document at the same time, or 50 people for the same spreadsheet.

How Can It Be Used?

Google Docs has many collaborative and publishing options. With the variety of documents that can be used on Google Docs, collaboration is unlimited. Users can determine who has access to what document, and how it gets published. Google Docs can be used as a backup server as well as a central location point when employees travel. Another way Google Docs can be used is to create polls or surveys by creating a form, embedding the form into your web site/blog, and then collecting the data into a spreadsheet. Google Docs is limited in storage: word documents up to 500 kb; up to 2 Mb per embedded image; and spreadsheets up to 10,000 rows, 256 columns, or 40 sheets, whichever comes first.

What Other Applications Does It Work With?

Google Docs is viewable, but not editable, on mobile devices. Apple has created an interface for viewing Google Docs on the iPhone, but again, the data is not editable. However, the only other application that works with Google Docs is the Google Apps application geared for collaboration. Google Apps enables sharing of documents stored on Google Docs.

Who Uses It?

Google Docs offers a number of stories of how people use the application. Anecdotes range from the Red Sox fan who uses a spreadsheet to sell his season tickets for games he can't attend to author Ken Leebow who uses Google Docs to keep track of his book projects. There is a story of a Las Vegas drag strip operations coordinator who uses the Google Docs spreadsheet to keep track of employee time cards for payroll purposes. The uses are as endless as the office suite programs that people access on a daily basis on their PCs and Macs.

Should You Use It?

Google Docs is as useful as any other set of office suite programs. The difference is the location of the files and the ability to publish and share the documentation in real time in a number of ways and platforms. Google is a known name, which brings a sense of comfort and security to the user. The only downsides may be the amount of storage provided and the fact that other than embedding documents on web sites/blogs, there isn't a lot of third-party software compatibility.

Who Started It?

Google Docs originated from two separate products, Writely and Google Spreadsheets. Upstartle created Writely and launched the Web-based word processor in 2005. Writely's features included collaborative text editing and access controls. The graphical user interfaces were similar to those in Microsoft Word or OpenOffice. Writely maintained its own user system until its integration with Google Accounts on September 19, 2006.

Google Gmail

Company Name:	Gmail (Google Inc.)
URL:	www.gmail.com
Location:	Mountain View, California, United States
Founded:	2004
Employees:	20,000 (Google)
Revenue Model:	Advertising, additional storage purchases, stock sales
Fees:	Free

What Is It?

Gmail, or Google Mail, is a free e-mail service that provides user accounts with nearly 7 Mb of storage, helpful features like conversation threads and integrated chat sessions with AIM friends, and a search-oriented interface. Users can also integrate other e-mail accounts using pop3 access and receive all their e-mail in one account. Gmail is available for use on any mobile device with Internet browser capability. Gmail offers features such as keyboard shortcuts, quick contacts, and specialized advertising focusing on the individual user and his or her interests.

How Can It Be Used?

Gmail can be used like any other e-mail application, but it does have some unique features. Google's search capability is integrated for easy searching of e-mails the same way you type in a keyword search in Google, only you select "Search Mail." The search query does not recognize symbols used in Boolean logic or other special characters. Gmail also allows users to receive e-mail from other accounts via pop3 access. Gmail account holders have special features such as iMap, labels, and filters. Gmail also has chat sessions built right into the e-mail interface that also allow users to chat with AIM friends as well as other Gmail contacts.

What Other Applications Does It Work With?

Gmail works with any mobile device with browser capability and AOL/AIM. Google has strict policies in place regarding no use of third-party software applications with Gmail. Some of the other Google tools enhance Gmail's capability, such as using Google Talk for leaving voicemail on Gmail, or using Picasa for image capability.

Who Uses It?

Gmail offers anecdotal reports of its usage. Much of it is personal, but highlights include a divorce lawyer who strictly enforces the use of Gmail accounts with his clients to prevent spouses from reading e-mails regarding legal strategy. Another story was from a pastor's wife who organizes activities and events at her husband's church. She must communicate with many people, and the ability to organize them easily into contact groups is a feature for her. Academic institutions such as Arizona State University use Gmail as their e-mail tool for these reasons.

Should You Use It?

Many e-mail applications are out there, and people use them for many of the same reasons: familiarity, ease of access, or features. Gmail incorporates several major needs into one package: e-mail, chat, and organization. The ability to have a number of tools combined into one package makes Gmail an attractive e-mail application. With the additional features of tools such as iMap, Mail Goggles (stop yourself from sending embarrassing e-mails late at night!), and labeling, Gmail gives other e-mail applications a serious run for the user's money.

Who Started It?

Paul Buchheit, founder of FriendFeed, was an early Google employee (the twenty-third, to be exact) and is credited with the creation of Gmail. According to Buchheit's blog:

> I wrote the first version of Gmail in one day. It was not very impressive. All I did was stuff my own e-mail into the Google Groups (Usenet) indexing engine. I sent it out to a few people for feedback, and they said that it was somewhat useful, but it would be better if it searched over their e-mail instead of mine. That

was version two. After I released that people started wanting the ability to respond to e-mail as well. That was version three. That process went on for a couple of years inside of Google before we released to the world.

MSGTAG

Company Name:	Fisher Young Group
URL:	www.msgtag.com
Location:	Wellington, New Zealand
Founded:	2002
Revenue Model:	Premium service
Tagline:	Got the message?

What Is It?

MSGTAG is a desktop application that informs you whenever your e-mail messages are received and viewed by the recipients. The program works by adding a tag to your outgoing e-mail that tells the MSGTAG server details such as the date and time the e-mail was sent, the date and time the e-mail was opened, and the duration of time between the two. Three different versions of MSGTAG are currently available: MSGTAG Free, MSGTAG Plus, and MSGTAG Status 2. Each program ranges in cost (free to around $60) and features (SMS notifications, compatibility, e-mail footers, etc.).

How Can It Be Used?

MSGTAG can be used in time-sensitive instances—where it is vital to know who has received an e-mail and who hasn't—so alternative methods of communication may be pursued if necessary. MSGTAG can also be used to offer peace of mind to its users, who no longer have to wonder if e-mails have been received or read.

What Other Applications Does It Work With?

MSGTAG works with SMTP (Simple Mail Transfer Protocol) e-mail applications. Some examples of STMP e-mail applications are Microsoft Outlook, Microsoft Outlook Express, Eudora, Netscape Mail, and Pegasus Mail.

Who Uses It?

MSGTAG is used by anyone who is interested in knowing if and when their e-mails have been received. Businesses can use it to ensure their e-mails to clients are getting delivered, to figure out whether or not their employees have been too busy to respond to an e-mail, or to see if they just haven't received the message. Whether the e-mails are being sent among friends, family, or professional relations, users can utilize MSGTAG to determine if their e-mails are getting through.

Should You Use It?

You should use MSGTAG if you are ever in a position where you need to know if your e-mails are being received and read. Since MSGTAG does not require you to change anything about the way you send your e-mail, it is an attractive option for those people who are not advanced computer users. With the availability of MSGTAG Free, you should also use MSGTAG if you need the basic functionality of the program without spending any money.

Who Started It?

According to Msgtag.com, "MSGTAG is a product of Fisher Young Group, a New Zealand company formed in 2002. The company contracted eCOSM, a Christchurch software development company, to create MSGTAG. eCOSM is the company that developed MailWasher Pro, the groundbreaking anti-spam application for Firetrust. With the debut of MSGTAG, Fisher Young Group is leading the way in the field of automatic e-mail read-receipt software."

ReadNotify

Company Name:	ReadNotify
URL:	www.readnotify.com
Location:	Sydney, Australia
Revenue Model:	Premium subscriptions
Motto:	Track your e-mail

What Is It?

According to readnotify.com, "ReadNotify is the most powerful and reliable e-mail tracking service that exists today. In short—ReadNotify tells you when e-mail you sent gets read/re-opened/forwarded and **so** much more." Though the features and tools of ReadNotify are complex, it is a relatively simple service to use. The service operates in one of two ways: through an Active-Tracker plug-in or by adding commands to the end of a recipient's e-mail address.

How Can It Be Used?

ReadNotify can be used to track several different details of e-mails so users know what is happening to their communication after it has been sent. Among the things ReadNotify can tell you are the date and time an e-mail was opened, the location of the recipient, the recipient's e-mail address, the length of time a recipient spent reading an e-mail, the number of times an e-mail has been opened, or if your e-mail was forwarded.

What Other Applications Does It Work With?

ReadNotify works with several different applications to notify you when your e-mails have been opened. These applications include ICQ, AOL Instant Messenger, IRC, Yahoo! Instant Messenger, and MSN Messenger. If used manually (without the ActiveTracker plug-in), ReadNotify is compatible with all e-mail programs and operating systems.

Who Uses It?

ReadNotify is used by anyone who wishes to track their e-mails' details. One large customer base is businesses, which take advantage of the different ReadNotify features. For example, if a user is sending confidential information to someone through e-mail, ReadNotify allows them to set up a "Self-Destructing" e-mail, which means the e-mail will destroy itself in a designated amount of time or if the recipient tries to copy, print, or forward it. This feature also allows for e-mails to be retracted prior to a recipient opening them.

Should You Use It?

You should use ReadNotify if you are in situations where it would be beneficial to know detailed information about e-mails for any reason. Read-Notify is a great program to use when you need to track when e-mails were sent, when they were received, and whether the recipient has accepted a read guarantee. Additionally, with features such as court-admissible certification and notarization, you should use ReadNotify if you work in a highly sensitive field that often relies on e-mails.

Who Started It?

Christopher Drake founded ReadNotify in Sydney, Australia. The company originally operated from Drake's house. Readnotify.com was the recipient of the 2002 Yellow Pages Business Ideas Grant for the state of New South Wales. Drake is currently the company's chief technology officer.

Survey Monkey

Company Name:	Survey Monkey
URL:	www.surveymonkey.com
Location:	Portland, Oregon, United States
Founded:	1999
Revenue Model:	Service packages
Fees:	Basic: free; Monthly Pro: $19.95/month + $0.05 for each overage; Annual Pro: $200/year
Tagline:	Because knowledge is everything

What Is It?

Survey Monkey offers users an effective tool for creating online surveys. Users are able to customize and design their surveys by choosing from numerous question options and are provided the option to "require answers to any question, control the flow with custom skip logic, and randomize answer choices to eliminate bias." Survey Monkey offers creative control over the appearance of the surveys, allows users to upload logos for brand recognition, determine the collection method, send a survey invitation, track and manage results, and download summaries. Survey Monkey has teamed up with Mail Chimp to provide a higher level of functionality to create e-mail campaigns, manage lists, and offer additional tracking and reporting tools.

How Can It Be Used?

With the pairing mentioned in the previous section, Survey Monkey provides the tool to design, create, and implement a survey, and Mail Chimp is the application to control and manage its distribution. Users determine the type, length, design, and content of the survey via Survey Monkey, create a link to the survey, and either post the link to a site or e-mail it to potential respondents. Mail Chimp allows users to build e-mail campaigns, manage e-mail lists, and track and create reports based on the campaign.

What Other Applications Does It Work With?

Survey Monkey works with most Internet browsers, allows users to create links to their surveys from their web page, supports computer lab and kiosk set-ups, allows users to save their results in PDF, and exports surveys in numerous formats. Mail Chimp works with Wordpress, TypePad, Open-Social, Joomla, Drupal, Foxy Cart, Zen Cart, blogs, and other applications by independent developers.

Who Uses It?

Survey Monkey is widely used by businesses large and small, including many Fortune 500 companies. It is also used by students conducting surveys for courses or research projects, professional associations, nonprofits, professional and personal services providers, recreation and entertainment groups, religious organizations, restaurants, retail outlets, and travel and tourism organizations. Mail Chimp can also be used by the above organizations as a resource to deliver surveys to a targeted audience and glean insight into who reads, responds, or forwards the e-mails or newsletters. Using Survey Monkey and Mail Chimp together provides an effective marketing tool.

Should You Use It?

If you or your organization are looking for a way to communicate with your audience and obtain feedback regarding products and services, expand and track marketing initiatives, and generate reports, these tools could provide an appropriate solution. Traditional advertising and marketing techniques only reach a limited target audience; using Web-based marketing and surveys, organizations can reach and interact with a wider audience to target the customer's wants and needs.

Who Started It?

Survey Monkey was developed in 1999 by Ryan Finley, a graduate student at University of Wisconsin in Madison, to "enable people of all experience levels to create their own surveys quickly and easily." Mail Chimp "started out as a web development company (The Rocket Science Group) back in April 2000." In recognizing an expanding need to resolve difficulties in sending HTML e-mail newsletters with limited options for the customer, Mail Chimp was developed.

TiddlyWiki

Company Name:	TiddlyWiki
URL:	www.tiddlywiki.org/wiki/Main_Page/ and www.tiddlywiki.com
Location:	Menlo Park, California, United States
Founded:	2006 (Now owned by the UnaMesa Association, a non-profit)
Employees:	Not available
Revenue Model:	Corporate contributions, individual donations, grants
Fees:	Free
Tagline:	Send stuff to your friends.

What Is It?

According to the TiddlyWiki.org/wiki, the concept is "TiddlyWiki is a single-file, self-contained wiki for managing micro-content, written in JavaScript." It is also referred to as a nonlinear, reusable notebook. TiddlyWiki is intended to be a single file easily stored on your computer and thus easily stored and transferred through your USB stick or e-mail. TiddlyWiki is marketed as a simple, easy program that is usable on any operating system, and doesn't even require the Internet. It is a wiki, used like any other wiki for project collaboration or a personal notebook/journal.

How Can It Be Used?

UnaMesa describes TiddlyWiki use in the following wiki excerpt:

> TiddlyWiki itself is a unique piece of software that provides a complete, editable web document without the need for a network connection. This means that students can access educational materials "on the web" and record their own notes even if they do not have a live

network connection, for example in unwired classrooms, at home, or remote villages. We have also demonstrated how to incorporate materials from several sites, such as Wikipedia, SocialText, and others, into a single file that can be easily shared, edited, and updated. This creates a much more dynamic learning experience and reduces most if not all technology barriers to sharing information.

What Other Applications Does It Work With?

TiddlyWiki works on any computer operating system. Additionally, Apple has included TiddlyWiki in the list of new apps available for iPhone and iTouch. Generally the concept behind TiddlyWiki is that users can easily develop applications they need or want to work with their wiki. A Google search of associated applications shows users have done just that, as exhibited on the web site "Musings of Dawn." The owner of Musings of Dawn provides an editing application and a comment scripting application from another TiddlyWiki user.

Who Uses It?

TiddlyWiki in Action is a web site dedicated to showing how users use TiddlyWiki. One purpose is for presentation and pictures. User Dr. Robert Boss presents a study of eighteenth-century author Robert Fuller's work, "The Gospel Worthy of Great Acceptation," the focus of Boss's PhD thesis. Another example of a TiddlyWiki use is publication. User Lynsey Gedye published a book, *Japanese Haiku*, a compilation of ancient Japanese Haiku poetry using TiddlyWiki.

Should You Use It?

Businesses can use TiddlyWiki for activities such as project management and collaboration, publication of user manuals and tutorials, discussion of products, and other topics of concern to company administration and consumers. Conversely, as part of UnaMesa's mission to provide free software tools for clinics, schools, and other community organizations, this tool fits in with the UnaMesa mission. Therefore, anyone who falls under one of those categories is philosophically the right entity to use TiddlyWiki.

Who Started It?

TiddlyWiki itself was created by Jeremy Ruston, who states on his LinkedIn bio, "I've spent my life inventing software products with great user experiences, and building the teams to develop them. Now I'm the creator of TiddlyWiki, a very popular open source personal organizer that's grown to be the platform for a whole new class of web applications. I lead the community around TiddlyWiki, and am dedicated to building a great product for users all over the world." He is the head of British company Open Source Innovation, a telecommunications company, and founder of Osmosoft, a consulting company. Jeremy provided TiddlyWiki to UnaMesa under a Berkeley Software Distribution open-source license, making it a free software.

Yahoo!

Company Name:	Yahoo! Inc.
URL:	www.yahoo.com
Location:	Sunnyvale, California, United States
Founded:	1994
Employees:	10,000
Revenue Model:	Advertising, subscriptions, and transactions

What Is It?

Yahoo! is an Internet services company founded in 1994 by two Stanford PhD candidates, Jerry Yang and David Filo. Yahoo! offers "vertical search services such as Yahoo! Image, Yahoo! Local, Yahoo! News, and Yahoo! Shopping Search . . . and communication services such as Yahoo! Mail and Yahoo! Messenger." Best known for its web portal, search engine, Yahoo! Directory, Yahoo! Mail, news, and social media web sites, Yahoo! is consistently expanding its range of services to meet the changing needs of the consumer.

How Can It Be Used?

Yahoo! provides free and paid services depending on the user's needs. Yahoo! can be used to search the Internet for a vast array of information and services, to purchase or sell items and services, to conduct research, to receive updates on financial services, to communicate with others, to play games or interact with others, to watch videos or listen to music, and to find and offer employment; many other applications and services are developed and integrated into the Yahoo! family of services. A new service, Yahoo! Search BOSS, "allows developers to build search applications based on Yahoo!'s search technology." Currently in beta testing is Yahoo! Next, a forum community for user "feedback to assist in the development of these future Yahoo! Technologies."

What Other Applications Does It Work With?

Yahoo! works with most current Internet browsers and offers mobile service compatibility and a significant number of social media applications. With the implementation of Yahoo! Search BOSS, independent developers can create applications based on Yahoo!'s search technology, which further expands the possibility of compatibility with customized future applications.

Who Uses It?

Yahoo! is a free Internet services provider available to anyone with an Internet browser and Internet connection. The array of information available provides usability for a broad spectrum of users, and the ever-expanding list of services affords users flexibility on how it can be used.

Should You Use It?

Yahoo! offers myriad services to meet the needs of consumers. It is an effective tool to search for information, listen to music, find videos and other entertainment, communicate, and interact with others.

Who Started It?

Two Stanford engineering PhD candidates, David Filo and Jerry Yang, developed Yahoo! as a platform to track their personal interests on the Internet. The founders recognized the business potential of their web site as the popularity of the site spread. Yahoo! was incorporated in 1995 and continues to add features and services to meet its audience's expanding needs.

Zoho

Company Name:	AdventNet
URL:	www.zoho.com
Location:	Pleasanton, California, United States
Founded:	1996
Employees:	850
Revenue Model:	Subscription fees, program sale
Tagline:	Work online

What Is It?

Zoho wants to be the IT department for businesses, providing a wide range of online applications needed for businesses and individuals. There are two categories of applications: the Productivity and Collaboration Application Suite and the Business Application Suite. Zoho is the only vendor that has this combination in the online application market, which not only makes Zoho unique but also defines the direction of the online business market when these two application suites come together. To date, Zoho has launched 16 different applications, and more are in the works. Zoho has received numerous awards, including a 2008 *PC World* 25 Most Innovative Products Award for Zoho Notebook and Best Enterprise Start-up at the 2007 Crunchies.

How Can It Be Used?

Zoho is used for creating and sharing content with other users. They use the Zoho tools for productivity and in some cases to run their business online. Zoho provides a number of applications that have similar purposes as Microsoft Word and other programs. Just as a sample of the applications available, there is a word processing application (Zoho Writer), a spreadsheet application (Zoho Sheet), a wiki (Zoho Wiki), and much more. These applications can be accessed from any computer, whether at home, at work, or during travel.

What Other Applications Does It Work With?

Zoho works with Box.net and Entrepreneur Assist. Additionally, Zoho applications work with Microsoft applications, the iPhone, Jot, Twitter, and Facebook. Different Zoho applications may have specific interoperability with other applications—for example, Zoho Sheet works not only with MS Excel but also with box.net and Facebook. Zoho recently gave users the ability to login with Google and Yahoo! accounts.

Who Uses It?

Zoho has five major categories of users: individuals, students, departments in larger organizations, larger organizations that are standardizing their applications, and government. Zoho is being recognized by users such as Pam Gaulin, a freelance writer, for the ease of uploading, sharing, and creating information in the Web 2.0 environment. Gaulin touts the use of Zoho Notebook over Google Notebook, applauding that Zoho Notebook allows for the incorporation of audio and video whereas Google Notebook does not. One academic user is noted on the Zoho blog as using Zoho applications to post the results of a survey regarding online learning, as well as a presentation discussing appropriate computer usage at his college. Another academic user used Zoho Creator to conduct a survey and collect data on how library patrons selected books.

Should You Use It?

Company executives particularly recommend their Zoho line for educational institutions and students. If you are looking for an easier way to work and collaborate online, you should use this social medium. The ability to work on any computer from any location renders an environment of constant productivity. Zoho is compatible with so many applications and tools that the possibilities for usage are endless. For the individual user, there are no subscription fees; for the nonprofit/business/academic organization, there is a start-up fee of $1,675 as well as a monthly fee of $295.

Who Started It?

During a 2007 interview about Indian start-ups, when asked about the trigger for creating Zoho, Raju Vegasna stated, "Around 2001–2003 after the telecom bubble burst, [AdventNet] had lots of engineering resources on hand. So we decided to enter different market segments. Online applications is one of them. We truly believed in online applications and Zoho was born from there."

Zoomerang

Company Name:	Zoomerang
URL:	www.zoomerang.com
Location:	San Francisco, California, United States
Founded:	1999
Revenue Model:	Service packages

What Is It?

Zoomerang offers users an effective tool for creating an unlimited number of online surveys with up to 30 questions. Users are able to choose from over 100 survey templates, and depending on the tier, can send surveys to an unlimited number of respondents, and "download to Excel and create charts." The Pro and above tiers offer additional features such as the ability to customize the survey, images, logos, and links; they also provide "cross-tabulation, skip logic, filtering, report downloads and customizable charts."

How Can It Be Used?

Zoomerang provides various tiered options to meet the needs of your organization, and has premade templates for customer satisfaction with products or services, the organization as a whole, technical support, and the buying experience, or cancellation surveys. Zoomerang guides the user in determining the type of question to ask based upon the type of response you are looking for. With the reporting and analytics tools, Zoomerang offers the ability to measure your results accurately, determine trends, and develop future initiatives to build your business further.

What Other Applications Does It Work With?

Zoomerang works with most Internet browsers, uses SMS messaging for mobile connectivity to provide instant feedback, or can be inserted in a blog.

Who Uses It?

Zoomerang is a popular survey tool now being used by businesses, educational institutions, and individuals worldwide. Richard Aaron, president of

BizBash Media, stated, "By conducting Zoomerang surveys of our event's attendees, we better understand their needs, see how well we meet their expectations, and better tailor our future shows to meet their preferences."

Should You Use It?

Traditional advertising and marketing techniques only reach a limited target audience; using Web-based marketing and surveys, organizations can reach and interact with a wider audience to target the customer's wants and needs. If you or your organization are looking for a way to communicate with your audience and obtain feedback regarding products and services, expand and track marketing initiatives, and generate reports, Zoomerang would be an effective tool.

Who Started It?

Zoomerang was started in 1999 by MarketTools, a technology and solutions provider offering online market research tools.

Tool Scorecard for Chapter 33: Productivity Applications

Instructions: Using the five-point (0 to 4) scale below, rate each tool in this chapter on the basis of how valuable it *might be* to the internal and external operations of your company. Make notes about which tools appeal to you the most.

> 4 = Extremely Valuable
> 3 = Very Valuable
> 2 = Somewhat Valuable
> 1 = Not Very Valuable
> 0 = No Value

Tool	Internal Value	External Value
Acteva	4 3 2 1 0	4 3 2 1 0
AOL	4 3 2 1 0	4 3 2 1 0
BitTorrent	4 3 2 1 0	4 3 2 1 0
Eventful	4 3 2 1 0	4 3 2 1 0
Google Alerts	4 3 2 1 0	4 3 2 1 0
Google Docs	4 3 2 1 0	4 3 2 1 0
Google Gmail	4 3 2 1 0	4 3 2 1 0
MSGTAG	4 3 2 1 0	4 3 2 1 0
ReadNotify	4 3 2 1 0	4 3 2 1 0
Survey Monkey	4 3 2 1 0	4 3 2 1 0
TiddlyWiki	4 3 2 1 0	4 3 2 1 0
Yahoo!	4 3 2 1 0	4 3 2 1 0
Zoho	4 3 2 1 0	4 3 2 1 0
Zoomerang	4 3 2 1 0	4 3 2 1 0

CHAPTER 34

Aggregators

Imagine adding a research staff to your company charged with gathering information and data important to your business and putting it in one place for easy access. Suppose now that your research staff was directed to keep this information updated—daily. In one sense this is what an aggregator does. Additionally, there are aggregators that leverage the wisdom of the crowd and tell you what other people are saying about a particular product, service, or brand. Depending upon your thirst for this kind of market intelligence, aggregators could be an extremely valuable part of your social media strategy.

The following aggregator applications are introduced in this chapter:

- Digg
- FriendFeed
- Google Reader
- iGoogle
- My Yahoo!
- Reddit
- Yelp

As you read each profile, keep in mind that its features and functions may or may not be right for your particular business. Use the **Tool Scorecard** at the end of the chapter to help you determine which of these tools qualify for further consideration when you begin creating your social media strategy in Part III of the book.

theSocialMediaBible.com

Digg

Company Name:	Digg
URL:	www.digg.com
Location:	San Francisco, California, United States
Founded:	2004
Employees:	35
Revenue Model:	Series A & Series B funding, advertising
Fees:	Free
Tagline:	All news, videos, and images

What Is It?

Digg's purpose is for users to submit online sites and content they believe would be valuable to other Digg members. If enough Digg members vote on the submitted online site or content, the item is placed on the front page of Digg's web site for all viewers to read about. Those stories that don't do well get "buried," in Digg terminology. Not only does this approach encourage users to continuously provide content to Digg, it also ensures they actively participate, assuming that maintaining a high status is important to the user. In this manner, the Internet audience drives the quality and type of information on the Web.

How Can It Be Used?

Individuals, groups, organizations, and businesses can use Digg to remain informed of web content of interest. Conversely, those users can submit links to web content. Digg says it best on its web site: "Because Digg is all about sharing and discovery, there's a conversation that happens around the content. We're here to promote that conversation and provide tools for our community to discuss the topics that they're passionate about. By looking at information through the lens of the collective community on Digg, you'll always find something interesting and unique. We're committed to giving every piece of content on the web an equal shot at being the next big thing to promote their specific interest."

What Other Applications Does It Work With?

Digg works well with a number of social media applications, including Facebook, MySpace, Blogger, WordPress, and iGoogle. Digg also provides interesting capabilities such as Digg Spy, in which you can watch as stories are added to the queue and are read, Dugged or Buried, and reported. Digg offers one-click blogging with TypePad, Blogger, Wordpress, Live Journal, or Moveable Type.

Who Uses It?

Digg user profiles run the gamut, and included the 2008 presidential campaigns of Barack Obama and John McCain. Both camps used Digg to promote web content regarding their runs for the presidency. Digg isn't just for individual users. Companies use Digg as well. For example, you can find Digg profiles for Apple and Microsoft. There are specific categories of information, such as for technology and gaming, so users can click on the categories tab and catch up on the latest "diggs" for that particular category.

Should You Use It?

Digg can be a valuable tool for businesses that wish to either keep track of news regarding competitors or to make Digg readers aware of the latest news. It can, however, have some repercussions as there is no editorial monitoring of Digg content. According to the web site "How Stuff Works," in 2006 four stories appeared on Digg stating that Google was buying Sun Microsystems. These stories resulted in pushing the value of Sun Microsystems stock to high levels. The stories were rated highly by Digg users, and once the realization was made that the stories were false, many wondered if the posters weren't somehow related to Sun Microsystems, trying to make more money off the stock.

Who Started It?

Kevin Rose founded Digg. Rose approached computer programmer Owen Byrne and paid him $10 an hour (for a grand total of $200) to develop Digg. Digg was fairly popular, but it wasn't until the news story of Paris Hilton's cell phone getting hacked broke on Digg that Rose realized just how big his idea was and how important his site would be to breaking news on the Internet. Kevin Rose is not only the entrepreneur and founder of Digg, he is also one of the founders behind social media application Pownce and the Internet TV network Revision 3, as well as an investor in the online dating site iminlikewithyou.com. Among Digg's other principals are Owen Byrne, who has over 20 years experience in the IT industry and has spent the majority of those years as a freelancer. He was also a university professor for a short time. Jay Adelson, CEO, has experience in broadcasting and switched to the IT industry. He helped engineer Netcom (the first ISP in the United States) and Equinix.

FriendFeed

Company Name:	FriendFeed
URL:	www.friendfeed.com
Location:	Mountain View, California, United States
Founded:	2007
Employees:	7
Revenue Model:	Currently venture capital backing by Benchmark Capital and the founders
Fees:	Free

What Is It?

FriendFeed is a social aggregate (news feed) business in which people can keep track of the Internet contributions to applications such as Blogger, Twitter, LinkedIn, Flickr, and other social network services by peers, colleagues, friends, and family. It is being touted as a guide through the growing level of noise in Internet presence and use. Users create an account and provide the links or information for the social media networks to which they belong. The feeds from these accounts are aggregated onto a simple web page list. Users can subscribe to the FriendFeeds of other peers, business associates, colleagues, friends, and family.

How Can It Be Used?

Businesses can use FriendFeed to enable broadcasting of their news as well as monitoring developments of competitors. Interested members can subscribe to businesses that are FriendFeed members and keep up with blogs, Twitters, YouTube postings, and other social media applications that a business may use to relay company information. If an educational entity uses social media applications in the relaying of information, whether related to administrative, operational, or educational information, FriendFeed members with an interest in such information can subscribe and stay abreast of information feeds.

What Other Applications Does It Work With?

This is a relatively easy question to answer, since FriendFeed's purpose is to aggregate information from over 40 social media web sites such as Flickr, Netvibes, and others. It would seem the simplest answer is "all of them." As a web site, if a device has Internet access, then, in essence, FriendFeed can be used with any of those devices.

Who Uses It?

Interestingly, bub.blicio.us, a web site that covers social media, has ranked in the top 30 users of FriendFeed. The list is based off Google ranking, and surprisingly consists of people whose career is the focus of social media, like Robert Scoble (a social media/technology blogger who has been pointed out as accounting for 20 percent of FriendFeed's usage), Muhammed Saleem (a social media consultant), and Brian Daniel Eisenberg (a social media/ culture blogger). It would seem at the moment that those who are involved purely in the social media explosion are the biggest users. Again, time and more reliable research will determine the type of audience drawn to use FriendFeed.

Should You Use It?

According to the FriendFeed site, "FriendFeed enables you to keep up-to-date on the web pages, photos, videos and music that your friends and family are sharing. It offers a unique way to discover and discuss information among friends." The use of FriendFeed is widely debated on the Internet. Some users praise its simplistic approach; others declare it won't last very long. Given the relative newness of this business and its concept, it truly is a matter of time and its popularity with Internet users to determine just how valuable of a tool this application truly is.

Who Started It?

The executive (founding) team comprises former Google employees responsible for over 25 Google products. Bret Taylor is not only a former Google employee, he is also an entrepreneur in residence at Benchmark Capital. He earned Google's highest award, the Founders' Award, for his contributions to Google. Jim Norris, similar to Bret Taylor, was also a former employee of Google and an entrepreneur in residence at Benchmark Capital. Norris worked on Google's core structure and Google Maps. Paul Buchheit is noted as the twenty-third Google employee and is credited not only with the creation of Google Mail but also Google's slogan "Don't be evil." Sanjeev Singh, like his FriendFeed cofounders, contributed to Google's success working on Google Mail and the Google Search Appliance. Prior to working at Google, Singh worked at Third Voice and a government research lab.

Google Reader

Company Name:	Google Reader (Google Inc.)
URL:	www.google.com/reader
Location:	Mountain View, California, United States
Founded:	2005
Employees:	20,000 (Google)
Revenue Model:	Advertising and sales of stock
Fees:	Free

What Is It?

Google Reader is another feature of Google Inc. It is a Web-based aggregator that provides you with the feeds of your favorite updated web sites so you don't have to spend time visiting all these sites. Google Reader is capable of reading RSS or Atom feeds both online and off-line.

How Can It Be Used?

Google Reader has a number of features that make it a useful tool for reading the latest postings on your topic of interest, such as news on the top Silicon Valley companies. With the front-page configuration you can see new items at a glance. You can import and export subscription lists as an OPML file. There are keyboard shortcuts for main functions. You have a choice between the list view or expanded view for item viewing, meaning you see either just the story title or a description of the story. As items are read they are automatically marked, just as in most e-mail software programs. Google Reader also gives you the ability to share your feeds with chat friends or a list of contacts. Finally, Google Reader searches in all feeds, across all updates from subscriptions.

What Other Applications Does It Work With?

Google Reader aggregates RSS and Atom Feeds. If someone posts a blog on a WordType site, Google Reader will pull that feed if you direct it to do so, but it isn't actually working with the WordType site; it's working with the feed. One cool little gadget that made the Internet buzz is that someone who helped develop Google Reader installed Konami code; users can type a certain sequence and a little ninja appears on the left side of the screen and watches you as you scroll through your feeds.

Who Uses It?

Not a lot of specific data is available on who uses Google Reader, but given the functionality, it is easy to see that just about anyone can find Google Reader useful. Most web sites use RSS or Atom feeds, and the relative audience would find Google Reader a useful application for keeping up with that site or related sites.

Should You Use It?

Yes. Many people like and prefer Google Reader to other feed aggregators. Mark Berthelemy, learning solutions architect for Capita Learning & Development and director and lead consultant for Wyver Solutions Ltd., recommends Google Reader. On the web site for the Center for Learning and Performance Technologies, Berthelemy stated,

> Keeping up-to-date is a rapidly changing field, and knowing what the market is saying about learning, about technology, and about us is critical for success. An RSS reader allows me to do that without having to go to dozens of web sites to see if they've got anything new. Google Reader has been my reader of choice for a year now. I can use it from any Internet-connected browser. I can organize things just how I want. I can even share particular items, or whole groups of items, with other people in many different ways. I like the way it allows me to choose how I use it—its flexibility.

Who Started It?

At this time, the only available information on who created Google Reader is that it was allegedly developed by Matrix Systems and Technologies Inc.

iGoogle

Company Name:	iGoogle (Google Inc.)
URL:	www.google.com/ig
Location:	Mountain View, California, United States
Founded:	2005
Employees:	20,000 (Google)
Revenue Model:	Advertising and sale of stock
Fees:	Free

What Is It?

Originally called the "Google Personalized Homepage," iGoogle is a feature of Google and is best described as a customizable AJAX-based start page. iGoogle's features include web feeds and Google Gadgets such as Google-Gram, Gas Buddy, and a YouTube Channel. You select the news, art, and gadgets you want to appear on your iGoogle start page, and when you open up iGoogle, those elements are updated and displayed, in essence creating a homepage that provides you with the information and entertainment you desire. Last but not least, there is a Google Search query bar at the top so you can search the Internet for information.

How Can It Be Used?

The iGoogle aggregator is used to create a specialized home page by the user for the user. It acts as a news aggregate, and users can embed a number of gadgets in their iGoogle page to include themes for decorating the home-page. Google also provides users with the ability to create their own gadgets without needing to know code. Users simply plug in the data feed and customize the appearance; the service does the rest. Users can also create their own themes and even submit their themes for the iGoogle theme gallery for other users to use. iGoogle is now available in 26 languages.

What Other Applications Does It Work With?

This is one Google feature that works with other applications because it allows and encourages users to create gadgets and applications to work with it. There are gadgets for users to access Digg, Facebook, MySpace, Hotmail, Pownce, Twitter, and Yahoo! Mail from the iGoogle page. Users can also use SlideShare to embed images into their iGoogle page. Hawidu is an application that enables users to create unique themes for their iGoogle page. The iGoogle feature is also usable with the Apple iPhone.

Who Uses It?

According to a May 2007 presentation on iGoogle by Marissa Mayer, vice president of search products and user experience, iGoogle has tens of millions of users. From that statement, you can conclude that just about anyone and everyone uses iGoogle to facilitate aggregating information to one easy page, whether to keep up on world events, financial news, business competitors, new technology, or research in academia.

Should You Use It?

There are other web sites with similar capabilities, such as Netvibes, Page-flakes, MyYahoo!, and Windows Live Personalized Experience. The determining factors for which application to use for aggregating information and multimedia services will be ease of use and implementation. iGoogle is immensely popular, and it provides an easy-to-use service for creating gadgets. These two factors alone make iGoogle an attractive tool for getting information in one place.

Who Started It?

Google's codename for the feature that came to be known as iGoogle was "Mockingbird." The concept was thought up in 2004 with the original name iGoogle as a result of Google's purchase of Kaltix, a company owned by Sep Kamvar. Kamvar's theories on personalized content search capabilities were the impetus behind iGoogle's creation.

MyYahoo!

Company Name:	MyYahoo! (Yahoo! Inc.)
URL:	www.my.yahoo.com
Location:	Sunnyvale, California, United States
Founded:	1994
Employees:	10,000
Revenue Model:	Advertising, subscription, and transactions
Fees:	Free (additional applications available by paid subscription)

What Is It?

Yahoo! Inc. provides Internet services and is "known for its web portal, search engine, Yahoo! Directory, Yahoo! Mail, news, and social media web sites and services." Yahoo! implemented MyYahoo! to provide customers with the ability to create a customizable web page. MyYahoo! allows users to personalize their page with their favorite features, content feeds, and other information. Users can view information on one page, preview new items or feeds, search the Web, add and remove content, and modify layout.

How Can It Be Used?

MyYahoo! is an information hub where users can locate their favorite features, content feeds, and any other information added to the page. Users can designate the content they want displayed on MyYahoo! and determine the layout for navigational ease. This functionality allows the user to check the weather forecast; follow financial markets; see local, national, and international headlines; or subscribe to horoscopes, comic strips, quotes, or jokes of the day. Virtually any content the user desires can be added to MyYahoo!

What Other Applications Does It Work With?

The key benefit of using MyYahoo! lies in the extensive functionality with other applications which allows the user to add the content the user deems important.

Who Uses It?

MyYahoo! can be used by anyone looking for a one-stop information center where a quick glance at various feeds can tell you stock market quotes, weather forecasts, news and entertainment headlines, health risks and alerts, the latest movie schedules, and much more. The possibilities are only limited by the information the user wants displayed. The array of information available provides usability for a broad spectrum of users.

Should You Use It?

MyYahoo! is an effective tool if you are looking for a quick reference point to access myriad information based upon your personal needs. The primary benefit of MyYahoo! is the ability to customize the page, which allows you to change the page content as your needs change. Many people have specific information they search for each day. If you are looking for a way to effectively manage your time by consolidating each search onto one page, then MyYahoo! would be a valuable asset.

Who Started It?

Yahoo! was developed by two Stanford engineering PhD candidates, David Filo and Jerry Yang, as a platform to track their personal interests on the Internet. The two founders recognized the business potential of their web site as its popularity spread. Yahoo! was incorporated in 1995 and continues to add features and services like MyYahoo! to meet its audience's expanding needs.

Reddit

Company Name:	Reddit (owned by Condé Nast Publications)
URL:	www.reddit.com
Location:	San Francisco, California, United States
Founded:	2005
Employees:	5
Revenue Model:	Advertising and merchandise
Tagline:	What's new online!

What Is It?

Reddit is a dynamic news web site that is socially driven by the community of users. Users post links on Reddit that lead to content found anywhere on the Internet. Once the link has been posted, the audience can determine how that particular link ranks against other links suggested by members of the community. Links are ordered dependent on how many positive or negative votes they have received. Discussions based on the linked subject matter also take place within the community in the form of comments attached to the links.

How Can It Be Used?

Reddit can be used as a vehicle for sharing and receiving information and as a social forum. Links are posted into categories, or "subreddits," such as economics, pictures, or technology; in this manner, users can browse specific media that interests them if desired, or browse all the links for a more general experience. A rather robust social system beyond comment discussions is a key component of Reddit. Some of the facets of this system include awards, private messaging, and befriending other members. By taking advantage of this social system, users can effectively network with others interested in the same subjects and even collectively vote on links. Additionally, a karma-based mechanism is used for members of Reddit, wherein users who consistently post popular links are rewarded with karma points.

What Other Applications Does It Work With?

Reddit works with several different web browsers to simplify the user's process of viewing and participating. A "Reddit Widget" can be incorporated into a web site's coding to display headlines from a user's preferred category. Another way Reddit works with web browsers is through "Reddit Bookmarklets." Reddit Bookmarklets are Java-based links that are added to your web browser like regular bookmarks, but these bookmarks perform actions such as submitting links to Reddit or taking you to a random Reddit link.

Who Uses It?

A number of different audiences use Reddit. Some members use it to discover new information on the Internet, whether for educational or recreational purposes. Some visitors use Reddit to comment on and analyze the links with the rest of the audience. Another user base of Reddit is web site owners looking to virally market their own web site to the vast community of Reddit users. Finally, some users choose to come to Reddit for the social aspect of the web site, such as sending and receiving private messages.

Should You Use It?

You should use Reddit if you are interested in being a part of a diverse community of users who all participate in the distribution of information. Reddit allows you to effectively look at intriguing content from all over the Internet by utilizing this one tool, and then providing the capability to examine how fellow users view that content. Additionally, you should use Reddit if you have a need or desire to drive traffic toward a web site without paying for marketing or advertising fees. Reddit offers an interesting delivery of current news and entertaining links along a social backdrop.

Who Started It?

Two University of Virginia graduates, Steve Huffman and Alexis Ohanian, created Reddit in 2005. The initial funding for the company was provided by Y Combinator. In that same year, Christopher Slowe and Aaron Swartz joined the company. During October 2006, Condé Nast Publications, which also owns the publication *Wired*, acquired Reddit. The company name was suggested by Alexis Ohanian and is derived from the pronunciation of "read it."

Yelp

Company Name:	Yelp
URL:	www.yelp.com
Location:	San Francisco, California, United States
Founded:	2004
Employees:	75
Revenue Model:	Some advertising; backed by venture capital financing
Fees:	Free
Tagline:	Real people. Real reviews.

What Is It?

Interested in the good (and bad) of a particular business or product? Someone has likely rated it on Yelp. Yelp's concept is to provide an online rating service for places to eat, shop, drink, and play. Members provide informed opinions of these places, and business owners can see what they need to improve upon to increase their customer satisfaction. With many categories of businesses and geographic locations, a site visitor can easily see what's hot and what's not in a specific locale. Yelp is not just limited to businesses in the service/entertainment industry; Yelp categories include businesses and organizations focused on day-to-day tasks and needs such as real estate, finance, and religion. Businesses can also use the reviews to see what their customer base says about them, good and bad, and use the reviews to market their business or improve it.

How Can It Be Used?

Members (consumers and businesses) create free membership accounts. Consumers provide reviews on businesses, and business owners create pages for their business to keep track of reviews. Businesses are listed by category and geographic location, so that users can search for a desired venue and see what rating the local populace gives that venue.

What Other Applications Does It Work With?

Yelp does not do a good job of broadcasting the applications it works with, but there is an ability to incorporate Yelp profiles and reviews with Facebook profiles. When a Yelp member posts a review, that review can show up automatically on the reviewer's Facebook profile. Users apparently use Flickr to post photos on Yelp, and Google Maps are used on profiles to identify locations of reviewed businesses. Yelp also has a mobile application so you can look up a needed service or business while on the go.

Who Uses It?

According to Yelp's web site, Yelp users are locals in the know about what's cool and who enjoy sharing the information, real people who have visited a place or used a service and want to share their opinions, visitors from other places or who have just moved to a particular city who want to quickly get an insider's local perspective, and anyone who wants current and reliable reviews in a specific location.

Should You Use It?

If you are looking to attract a larger client base and are confident in your level of customer satisfaction, Yelp can be a huge asset in your online marketing tool bag. Yelp business owners are encouraged to use Yelp as a way of keeping track of what customers are saying, and establishing a more personal rapport with that customer base. There are some conflicting stories regarding Yelp and accusations of "paid reviews," as well as accusations of Yelp removing negative reviews, earning it the label of being a do-goody web site. Yelp does have review submission guidelines, and will remove reviews in circumstances such as when a review is from another business owner or a former employee, or reports secondhand experiences, personal attacks, employment issues at the business, irrelevant statement, or just a blank review with no text. There may have been some legitimate reviews deleted, resulting in the rancor about Yelp only allowing positive reviews. There have also been accusations in the San Francisco news media that Yelp asked restaurant owners for $150 presented as a sponsorship package "to guarantee a positive review to be posted first."

Who Started It?

In an interview conducted for the Web 2.0 Awards, CEO and cofounder Jerry Stoppelman stated, "A personal pain point came when I was looking for a doctor online and couldn't find any information other than the basics (name, phone, affiliations, etc.). My cofounder Russ Simmons and I realized that word of mouth was the best way to find great local businesses, but we weren't sure how we'd bring that to the web. We ended up building a web site about asking friends for recommendations and later realized some of our early users really just wanted a platform for sharing their favorite local businesses, which is what you see today." Stoppelman and chief technology officer/cofounder Russel Simmons are both former PayPal employees who met while part of PayPal cofounder Max Levchin's incubator during college internships at PayPal.

Tool Scorecard for Chapter 34: Aggregators

Instructions: Using the five-point (0 to 4) scale below, rate each tool in this chapter on the basis of how valuable it *might be* to the internal and external operations of your company. Make notes about which tools appeal to you the most.

4 = Extremely Valuable

3 = Very Valuable

2 = Somewhat Valuable

1 = Not Very Valuable

0 = No Value

Tool	Internal Value	External Value
Digg	4 3 2 1 0	4 3 2 1 0
FriendFeed	4 3 2 1 0	4 3 2 1 0
Google Reader	4 3 2 1 0	4 3 2 1 0
iGoogle	4 3 2 1 0	4 3 2 1 0
My Yahoo!	4 3 2 1 0	4 3 2 1 0
Reddit	4 3 2 1 0	4 3 2 1 0
Yelp	4 3 2 1 0	4 3 2 1 0

CHAPTER 35

RSS

RSS is an acronym for Rich Site Summary, and although it is the name for this category of tools, it's a bit like using the brand name Kleenex® as the category title for all facial tissues. Rather than debating the category name, it's easier to recognize, in general, the common functions of these tools. In essence, a lot of web content changes. If you have a favorite blog or regularly visit a web site that provides updated information that has specific value to you, it could be useful to have the content fed to you automatically rather than having to return to the site when memory or necessity dictates. That's exactly what the tools in this category do; they automatically feed you current content from the web sites that are most critical to your business needs. It could be an industry blog, statistics posted on a competitor's site, or information from a government agency's web site. You can forage, or you can be fed.

This chapter introduces you to the following companies, tools, and applications:

- Atom
- FeedBurner
- PingShot
- RSS 2.0

As you read each profile, keep in mind that its features and functions may or may not be right for your particular business. Use the **Tool Scorecard** at the end of the chapter to help you determine which of these tools qualify for further consideration when you begin creating your social media strategy in Part III of the book.

theSocialMediaBible.com

Atom

> **Company Name:**   Atom
> **URL:**   www.atomenabled.org

What Is It?

"Atom is an XML-based web content and metadata syndication format" developed to deliver dynamic content to a vast audience without the viewer having to visit each site individually. The user subscribes to a feed and receives consistently updated information. "Atom is designed to be a universal publishing standard for personal content and weblogs."

How Can It Be Used?

RSS/Atom feeds are used to provide subscribers with a dynamic stream of information that is supported in blogs, news publishers, government agencies, and personal and commercial web sites. Users create a channel for the content they wish to publish, and include "items for Web pages they want to promote." The "channel can be read by remote applications, and converted to headlines and links," which can be inserted into web pages or read in dedicated readers.

What Other Applications Does It Work With?

Atom works with other Atom-enabled software and services, and is compatible with dedicated readers and is World Wide Web Consortium (W3C) compliant. Personal aggregators were designed specifically to find, organize, and check for updates for the channels you subscribe to, enabling you to view them all using the readers' interface.

Who Uses It?

"The U.S. Intelligence Community Metadata Working Group has issued a recommendation that the Intelligence Community, over time, move toward adoption of Atom Syndication Format as the Community's standard SML-based language for syndication feeds." Many private, professional, and commercial organizations use RSS/Atom feeds to notify their community of upcoming events, promotions, status, organizational changes, and much more. Atom claims it "is a simple way to read and write information on the web, allowing you to easily keep track of more sites in less time, and to seamlessly share your words and ideas by publishing to the web."

Should You Use It?

If you are looking for a way to track many sites or a simplified method to provide information to a large target audience, Atom may be an effective solution.

Who Started It?

"The Atom format was developed as an alternative to RSS." Sam Ruby is credited with spurring the movement toward a new syndication format to address the problems with RSS by creating a wiki as a platform for this discussion. In 2003, a project snapshot known as Atom 0.2 was released; discussion was later transferred to a different forum, resulting in the release of Atom Publishing Protocol as a Proposed Standard in 2007.

FeedBurner

Company Name:	FeedBurner (Google Inc.)
URL:	www.feedburner.com
Location:	Chicago, Illinois, United States
Founded:	2004
Employees:	5
Revenue Model:	Advertising and premium subscriptions
Fees:	Basic: free; Pro: $5–16
Tagline:	Put your content in front of more eyeballs.

What Is It?

FeedBurner claims to be the leading provider of media distribution and audience engagement services for blogs and RSS feeds. FeedBurner helps Internet publishers (bloggers, podcasters, and commercial publishers) promote, deliver, and profit from their web content. They have unique tools such as PingShot to make using RSS and Atom feeds easier. With the recent acquisition by Google, AdSense is now a part of their automatic feed, which enables you to generate revenue if your audience is large enough.

How Can It Be Used?

You use FeedBurner to notify your audience of new content on your blog, web site, or commercial publication. FeedBurner has 11 tools for publicity, optimization of subscriptions and e-mails, analysis and reporting, and revenue generation. There is the basic free account, or users can upgrade to a pro account, which charges by the number of feeds being managed.

What Other Applications Does It Work With?

FeedBurner works with Google applications, RSS feeds, Atom Feeds, iPhones and iTouch MP3 players, podcasts, videocasts, blog software, Newsgator, Netvibes, and Pageflakes.

Who Uses It?

A number of well-known companies use FeedBurner to push their new content to readers: Reuters, AOL, *Newsweek*, the *Wall Street Journal, USA Today,* and more. Entities that want to reach their audience immediately and easily use FeedBurner to push their new content.

Should You Use It?

For those who want to push their web site content but who may not necessarily be technically savvy, FeedBurner takes the process of using RSS or Atom feeds and simplifies them for the average computer user. For just a few dollars a day, you can analyze your traffic and determine where your readers come from and what they view the most. With the acquisition by Google, you can now also earn revenue due to the automatic inclusion of Google AdSense: visitors to your site click on the ads, and you earn money for those outclicks. Another use for FeedBurner is by actually paying to advertise your business or service on FeedBurner. With over a million publishers, and too many subscribers to count, FeedBurner has a massive audience you can reach with your advertisement.

Who Started It?

Dick Costolo, Eric Lunt, Steve Olechowski, and Matt Shobe founded Feed-Burner. According to a March 2007 Startup Studio interview with Matt

Shobe, the four cofounders met in 1993 on a project at Andersen Consulting. The four cofounders have started four companies together, including Feed-Burner. FeedBurner was derived from their second company, Spyonit, which was an early Internet service that notified Internet users of updates of many types of sites. FeedBurner took that aspect of Spyonit to the next level and made it easy to notify users of newly posted content through the use of feeds.

PingShot

Company Name:	PingShot (a feature of FeedBurner from Google Inc.)
URL:	www.feedburner.com
Location:	Chicago, Illinois, United States
Founded:	2005
Employees:	5
Revenue Model:	Advertising and premium subscriptions
Fees:	Basic: free; Pro: $5–$16
Tagline:	Trigger faster updates for subscribers.

What Is It?

FeedBurner claims to be the leading provider of media distribution and audience engagement services for blogs and RSS feeds. PingShot is a service of FeedBurner that quickly updates your feeds in the widest variety of places. The PingShot logarithm detects whether your feeds are a podcast or a nonpodcast and sends out the updates accordingly. As an example, if your feed is a podcast, PingShot notifies Odeo, but it won't notify Odeo if it is a nonpodcast feed. In general, feeds allow readers to subscribe to receive updated content for a web site. FeedBurner helps Internet publishers (bloggers, podcasters, and commercial publishers) promote, deliver, and profit from their web content.

How Can It Be Used?

PingShot is one of the more well-known FeedBurner tools. It updates your feeds as soon as you publish. Other similar services can take anywhere from 30 minutes to six hours to update the feeds, which means by that time your news is already old news. PingShot is also an open directory, so third-party members can use it once they register and provide their service method protocols. Publishers simply click the "Publicize" tab, and their update is sent out immediately.

What Other Applications Does It Work With?

By itself, PingShot does not work with other applications. It is a tool to send your feeds to feed services, which you select when you create your Feed-Burner account. FeedBurner works with Google applications, RSS feeds, Atom Feeds, iPhones and iTouch MP3 players, podcasts, videocasts, blog software, Newsgator, Netvibes, and Pageflakes.

Who Uses It?

There are no documented/advertised users of PingShot, but here are a number of well-known companies that use FeedBurner in general to push their new content to readers: Reuters, AOL, *Newsweek*, the *Wall Street Journal*, *USA Today*, and more. Entities that want to reach their audience immediately and easily use FeedBurner to push their new content.

Should You Use It?

As a matter of saving time, yes, PingShot (and hence FeedBurner) is a speedy tool for notifying subscribers of your new information. For those who want to push their web site content but may not necessarily be technically savvy, FeedBurner takes the process of using RSS or Atom feeds and simplifies them for the average computer user.

Who Started It?

The founders of PingShot are the same guys who founded FeedBurner: Dick Costolo, Eric Lunt, Steve Olechowski, and Matt Shobe.

RSS 2.0

Company Name:	RSS 2.0 (Owned by Harvard Law School)
Founded:	1997

What Is It?

RSS is an acronym for Rich Site Summary; it is a format to deliver dynamic web content without the need to visit each site individually. The user subscribes to a feed and receives consistently updated information. RSS is supported in many blogs, and in the web sites of many news publishers, government agencies, individuals, and businesses. RSS 2.0 is the current specification, conforms to XML 1.0 specification, "as published on the World Wide Web Consortium (W3C) web site," and is backward compatible with the 0.91 version.

How Can It Be Used?

RSS feeds are used to provide subscribers with a dynamic stream of information. Users create a channel for the content they wish to publish, and include "items for Web pages they want to promote." The "channel can be read by remote applications, and converted to headlines and links," which can be inserted into web pages or read in dedicated readers. "It's also used for photo diaries, classified ad listings, recipes, reviews, and for tracking the status of software packages."

What Other Applications Does It Work With?

RSS 2.0 is compatible with dedicated readers, and is compatible with W3C-compliant web sites. Personal aggregators were designed specifically to find, organize, and check for updates for the channels you subscribe to, enabling you to view them all using the readers' interface.

Who Uses It?

RSS feeds are used by many media organizations and e-commerce as a way of delivering information. These feeds are similar in function to a news crawler in that they provide a consistent stream of information and are used in this capacity by news outlets. Many organizations provide RSS feeds to notify consumers of upcoming events, promotions, or organizational changes. The use of RSS feeds saves time for many organizations. The feed is updated and reaches everyone subscribed to that channel, which aids in reducing the amount of time previously spent sorting through the hierarchy of notification procedures.

Should You Use It?

If you are looking for a simplified method to provide information to a large target audience, RSS feeds may be an efficient solution.

Who Started It?

RSS was first invented by Netscape in 1997; UserLand Software took control of the specification, refined it, and released a newer version. The RSS 2.0 specification was donated to Harvard Law School by David Winer, and they are now responsible for future development.

Tool Scorecard for Chapter 35: RSS

Instructions: Using the five-point (0 to 4) scale below, rate each tool in this chapter on the basis of how valuable it *might be* to the internal and external operations of your company. Make notes about which tools appeal to you the most.

4 = Extremely Valuable

3 = Very Valuable

2 = Somewhat Valuable

1 = Not Very Valuable

0 = No Value

Tool	Internal Value	External Value
Atom	4 3 2 1 0	4 3 2 1 0
FeedBurner	4 3 2 1 0	4 3 2 1 0
PingShot	4 3 2 1 0	4 3 2 1 0
RSS 2.0	4 3 2 1 0	4 3 2 1 0

CHAPTER 36

Search

If you haven't used an Internet search engine in the last 10 years, you're part of an extremely small minority of people in business. In the late 1990s, search engines focused on text. With the advent of Web 2.0, search engines and the sophisticated algorithms that drive them have become more sophisticated, but so have the needs of searchers. The ability to search and easily locate a variety of content on the web represents a tactical advantage to your business.

This chapter introduces you to the following companies, tools, and applications:

- EveryZing
- Google Search
- Ice Rocket
- MetaTube
- Redlasso
- Technorati
- Yahoo! Search

As you read each profile, keep in mind that its features and functions may or may not be right for your particular business. Use the **Tool Scorecard** at the end of the chapter to help you determine which of these tools qualify for further consideration when you begin creating your social media strategy in Part III of the book.

EveryZing

Company Name:	EveryZing
URL:	www.everyzing.com
Location:	Cambridge, Massachusetts, United States
Founded:	2006
Revenue Model:	Direct sales
Fees:	Monthly term license/fee, partial revenue-sharing

What Is It?

Previously known as Podzinger, EveryZing is considered a "media merchandising platform, which is actually a search publisher's solution that can make all audio and video content searchable, indexable by the major search engines via the text transcripts." EveryZing provides "time-coded and full linkable transcripts, graphic indicators of key points in a video (which are also accentuated with a keyword search), and a video player with social bookmarking and sharing capabilities." EveryZing focuses on multimedia search and publication of user-generated and client content.

How Can It Be Used?

EveryZing uses speech text transcriptions in creating what they refer to as a "media merchandising platform"; this technology enables users to search and index audio and video content via text transcripts. This further enhances the recall and optimization of your site, in addition to aiding with targeted advertising. EveryZing uses its proprietary speech-to-text technology, which "automatically classifies spoken-word multimedia content into meaningful topics and keywords, which visually appear to the user as actual, clickable, and navigation-friendly text."

What Other Applications Does It Work With?

EveryZing complements a wide variety of social media applications.

Who Uses It?

EveryZing is used by companies large and small, including Reuters, Dow Jones, Intercom Radio, MarketWatch, and TiVo.

Should You Use It?

If you are looking for search engine optimization to enhance your online presence, EveryZing may be the solution. EveryZing enhances the recall and optimization of your site, in addition to aiding with targeted advertising, which presents better opportunities for consumers to find you.

Who Started It?

EveryZing was developed by BBN Technologies and was "used for government purposes before becoming a commercial product." BBN (originally Bolt Beranek and Newman) is a high-tech company that provides research and development services and is known for the development of packet switching (including the ARPANET and the Internet). In addition to its role as a defense contractor, BBN is also known for the 1978 acoustical analysis it conducted for the House Select Committee on the assassination of John F. Kennedy.

Google Search

Company Name:	Google Search
URL:	www.google.com
Location:	Mountain View, California, United States
Founded:	1998
Employees:	20,000
Revenue Model:	Advertising via AdSense and AdWords
Fees:	Free

What Is It?

Google Search is Google's core product, so popular and embedded in our social culture that now it is a transitive verb in Merriam-Webster's dictionary. Features of Google Search are the Internet-crawling Googlebots and the PageRank algorithm, which is influenced by linking. Users type keywords in the home page search field and receive relevant results that can be further refined. There is also a more specific search capability for blogs, images, video, and news. Google Search can also be used to search your own computer files and e-mails through Google Desktop.

How Can It Be Used?

Google Search can be used from two perspectives: the user and the business/organization. From the user's perspective, Google Search allows search of the Internet for information, images, news, videos, and more. Google Search provides definition links, optional search terms, and alternate terms in the event of a misspelling. Search syntax can be simple words filled in the search field on the home page or advanced search queries in which words or phrases can be specified or excluded, or Boolean logic can be used. From the business/organization perspective, paid advertisements and search engine optimization are considered key tools in Internet marketing. Google is now available in 114 languages and 5 artificial languages (e.g., Klingon) for humor.

What Other Applications Does It Work With?

Google Search doesn't actually work with other applications. It works on computer and mobile devices that have Internet browser capability. Google Search is one of over 50 products in the Google Inc., inventory. From the Google Search page, users can go to the Google products page and select the desired Google application they wish to use. Google Search has a toolbar that you can permanently affix to your Internet browser page, making it easy to search, bookmark, and highlight your favorite pages.

Who Uses It?

Everyone who owns a computer has probably used Google Search at least once in their life. Google is listed within the top-ten web sites on the Internet, and Google claims to be the number-one search engine. In May 2008, Google had over 130 million U.S. visitors to its web site. Having one's web site turn up on the first page of a search query is considered important in search engine optimization. Users are more likely to visit the web sites that appear on the first several pages of a query.

Should You Use It?

Google Search is a dependable search engine tool. In addition to finding links related to your search query, Google Search will display advertisements that relate to your search query and may provide additional information, which also means that as a business owner or an organization you can advertise and drive users to your web site. An additional way of sending users to your web site is through the use of associated metadata and key words.

Who Started It?

According to Google's corporate page, Stanford graduate students Sergey Brin and Larry Page started the search company in a Stanford dorm room in 1996. Eventually Page and Brin moved the company to a Menlo Park garage, which the company quickly outgrew. The first investor was Sun Microsystems founder Andy Bechtolsheim, and other notable investors include Ron Conway, John Doerr, Mike Moritz, and Ram Shriram.

Ice Rocket

Company Name:	Ice Rocket
URL:	www.icerocket.com
Location:	Dallas, Texas, United States
Founded:	2004
Employees:	Not available
Revenue Model:	None at this time
Fees:	Free

What Is It?

Ice Rocket is a dedicated Internet search engine that is extremely efficient in looking out for blogs. It functions like an invisible tracker that will keep a count of your blog visits and all other statistics pertaining to your blog. The company has mixed its own Web search technology with meta search features that can tap into rival search engines. Ice Rocket is a world leader in commercial search services on the Internet. It is a part of the latest generation of search engines, some of which hope to out-Google Google Search. Ice Rocket performs a number of search services.

How Can It Be Used?

Some interesting features of Ice Rocket are as follows:

- *Line Tracker:* This feature lets bloggers know the details of those who are establishing links to their posts.
- *Trend Tool:* This feature allows users to track the current word trends in a range of two to three months.
- *RS Builder:* This free service allows users to create RSS feeds for their sites. It provides a simple interface that allows users to add topics, links, and content. The feature is suitable for anyone who owns a web site that does not offer RSS.
- *Ice Spy:* This site allows users to view the topics that are being searched for by other bloggers.
- *Search Relay:* Here the user sends an e-mail with the search items to the specified e-mail ID, and Ice Rocket mails back the results. The same can also be done for news and pictures.

Ice Rocket performs several other interesting services like blog searches, phone images, multimedia searches, and so on.

What Other Applications Does It Work With?

Ice Rocket works along with Wise Nut, Yahoo!, and Teoma, as well as MSN, AltaVista, and AllTheWeb. As a result, all your searches in Ice Rocket are thoroughly indexed and answered. Ice Rocket has introduced an interesting feature that works well with your mobile phone, for the total benefit of the gadget-savvy.

Who Uses It?

Internet browsers and bloggers who are looking for specific videos and music for online downloading can make use of Ice Rocket. Web site owners who want to upgrade their sites by adding online videos to it would find this search engine as an inevitable tool of development. The search engine optimization strategy of Ice Rocket can be helpful in improving the quality of your web site by including relevant online videos in it, which in turn will increase the viewing of and subscription to your sites.

Should You Use It?

If you are an avid blogger or you own a web site and wish to include some online videos in it, then the search engine services of Ice Rocket may be useful for you. Ice Rocket has features like Blog Tracker, an invisible tracker that counts your blog visits and maintains other blog statistics. With the help of Ice Rocket, you can analyze and monitor all the visits to your blog in real time. Ice Rocket can save you valuable time as well as the trouble of painfully monitoring your blog visits.

Who Started It?

Ice Rocket was the brainchild of Blake Rhodes. Soon after its launch, Mark Cuban, who is an investor and owner of the Dallas Mavericks, signed an agreement with Rhodes and pooled in investments to the company. Cuban formerly founded broadcast.com and later sold it to Yahoo! for an estimated $6 billion.

MetaTube

Company:	MetaTube
URL:	www.metatube.net
Location:	La Jolla, California, United States
Founded:	2006
Employees:	Not available
Revenue Model:	None
Fees:	Free
Tagline:	Browse 100 video-sharing sites at once!

What Is It?

MetaTube is a simple yet effective method to browse 100 of the most popular video-sharing sites around the world. When you want to view a particular video online, you would normally go to any one site like YouTube. If the video is not available, you would search other sites like Daily Motion, MySpace, AOL, and so on. The entire process of going into each site and entering your search query might be very cumbersome. This problem is solved in an easy manner with MetaTube, a search engine that simplifies the entire process and throws 100 search results all at once. This is a torrential multisearch engine that searches through its catalog of video-sharing sites and gives you the results. The most important feature of this high-speed search engine is that it not only throws 100 search results but also allows you to see a list of the recent searches made by other users. This step makes it easy for the user to sift through the search results.

What Other Applications Does It Work With?

Normally MetaTube conducts its searches in YouTube, Google Video, AOL Uncut, Veoh, and others. Apart from these sites, MetaTube also searches lesser-known sites like iklipz, jublii, and Flixya.

Who Uses It?

MetaTube.net users come from all over the globe, including Saudi Arabia, Egypt, the United States, India, Syria, Sudan, Algeria, Germany, Libya, and Italy. By the end of 2008, the site had already performed over 12 million searches.

Should You Use It?

If you need an easier way to search hundreds of sites for online videos, then this high-speed video search engine could be your answer. It is the easiest way to browse 100 of the most popular video-sharing sites. You can also add various videos to your web site and improve its viewership without having to open and close browser tabs or navigate tabs. With this online video search engine, you can make finding and viewing online videos an easy and trouble-free experience.

Who Started It?

The company maintains a low profile and information on MetaTube's founders is not readily available.

Redlasso

Company Name:	Redlasso
URL:	www.redlasso.com
Location:	King of Prussia, Pennsylvania, United States
Founded:	2005
Revenue Model:	Advertising revenue share
Fees:	Free to users

What Is It?

Redlasso allows users to search television and radio broadcasts by searching for "relevant key words, names or phrases," and capture clips to post on their blog or web site, or by sending links to friends. "Redlasso enables bloggers/multimedia content producers/creators/owners/consumers to monetize their content through a revenue share model." Redlasso touts its service as a "major plus for content owners who produce audio, video, streaming Internet programming or podcasts which they desire to publish internally, while maintaining content integrity."

How Can It Be Used?

Redlasso can be used to enhance a web site or blog by providing relevant audio or video clips to supplement text content. According to Redlasso's web site, "Users create their own community around the content which: improves the stickiness of the site, increases visits and page views (as well as time spent at the site), enhances advertising rates by driving more traffic, [and] creates additional advertising opportunities for revenue enhancement." The Internet community is consistently searching for the latest tidbit of information or sound bite to augment their argument or position; the tools provided by Redlasso make this possible.

What Other Applications Does It Work With?

Redlasso works with "virtually all media including broadcast television and terrestrial/satellite radio, streaming Internet programming and podcasts." It is compatible with most web sites and blogs, and currently "utilizes an embeddable Flash player."

Who Uses It?

In 2008 Redlasso was under a cease-and-desist order and therefore was only able to offer business-to-business products, including Radio2Web, TV2Web, and PR Clipping Service. Redlasso states, "We are actively pursuing licensing agreements with the publishers and will reopen the site to bloggers as we gain permission." Users of Redlasso reach a wider audience, provide accessible content, and generate revenue from existing content and enhanced advertising opportunities. Organizations use Redlasso as a means of redistribution of content to generate interest in particular subject matter or to further engage their audience.

Should You Use It?

With the technology offered by Redlasso, consumers don't have to wait very long for their favorite broadcasts to become available. Redlasso has almost real-time access to broadcasts to search for specific content, create clips to view, or post on any Internet site. If your organization is looking for a means to create interest in your site, expand the time spent at your site, and increase traffic and advertising opportunities, Redlasso may be a viable option.

Who Started It?

Redlasso was founded by Jim McCusker, chief technical officer; Kevin O'Kane, president; and Al McGowan, chief operating officer. The service was set up as a "defense against sites like YouTube.com" by partnering with content owners to monetize their clips.

Technorati

Company Name:	Technorati
URL:	www.technorati.com
Location:	San Francisco, California, United States
Founded:	2002
Employees:	25
Fees:	Membership is free; some services have fees
Tagline:	Search the blogosphere
Revenue motto:	*Time* magazine

What Is It?

Technorati is a powerful search engine with a special focus on blogs. Perhaps *Time* magazine said it best: "If Google is the Web's reference library, Technorati is becoming its coffee house." What sets Technorati apart is that it indexes the global online conversation, the "blogosphere," by collecting, highlighting, and distributing online blog posts in real time. It has indexed more than 133 million blog posts since 2002, and also tracks the "authority" of blogs, an indicator of how many blogs are linked to a web site (the more, the better), as well as how much influence a blog has. Additionally, Technorati keeps the most current and comprehensive index of what is most popular in the blogosphere. It tracks top stories, news, photos, and videos across many venues that include, but are not limited to, entertainment, technology, lifestyles, sports, politics, and business.

How Can It Be Used?

Technorati is the ideal way to stay connected to the subjects and conversations that matter the most to your business. It's both a research tool and an application that enables you to develop a community around your content. Blogs offer a platform for publishing individual perspectives on a variety of subjects and Technorati helps you filter the blogosphere to find those blogs that correspond to your interests.

Besides a search function, Technorati has the following services:

- For Bloggers and Publishers: Technorati has a network designed to enable blog and social media publishers at every level to maximize online advertising revenues
- For Advertisers: Technorati creates connections between influential bloggers and consumers via online conversation
- Self-Service Launch: A new function, in a limited beta version, that creates a self-service advertising network of blogs and social media sites

What Other Applications Does It Work With?

Technorati works with most browsers and mobile devices that can be connected to the Internet.

Who Uses It?

A typical blogger is educated, affluent, and a college graduate. Almost half have attended graduate school. More than 50 percent have a household income of over $75,000. Individuals use blogging as a platform to express their ideas, concerns, and viewpoints. Professional and corporate bloggers provide insider's perspectives on their organizations and platforms to interact with stockholders and consumers, or to follow trends in an industry. Politicians can communicate with the public, inform constituents about proposed legislation, and promote their individual platforms. Mothers can give tips on childrearing.

In addition to the bloggers creating content, users include the individuals who follow the blogs, who can be as passionate and influential about the subject matter as those who write the content. The number of those who participate in the blogosphere, whether by blogging, commenting, rating, sharing, or networking is staggering—about 75 percent of all internet users (per global communications media agency Universal McCann).

Should You Use It?

Technorati recently sent a Tweet, via Twitter, stating that 38 percent of the Fortune 500 companies are now blogging. Blogs have become full information and news outlets, with more than 90 percent of newspapers and media conglomerates now blogging. Blogs are being written by journalists, subject matter experts, advertisers, and entrepreneurs and are important connections between those writing content and those interested in that content. They provide ways for companies to engage their customers through collaboration, education, and entertainment. If you want to get connected to the content and the bloggers who influence your market space the most, Technorati is an essential tool to add to your social media toolbox.

Who Started It?

Dave Sifry, an Internet entrepreneur and thought leader in the areas of wireless technology, open source software, and blogs, founded Technorati in 2002. He served as Technorati's CEO from 2002 to 2007 and presently serves as chairman of its board of directors.

Yahoo! Search

Company Name:	Yahoo! Search
URL:	www.search.yahoo.com
Location:	Sunnyvale, California, United States
Founded:	1994
Employees:	10,000
Revenue Model:	Advertising, subscription, and transactions
Fees:	Free (additional applications available by paid subscription)

What Is It?

Yahoo! Search is a navigation tool to aid users in finding relevant sites and information based on the criteria entered in the search field. Users can narrow their search criteria to search images, video, local information, shopping, answers, audio, directory listings, jobs, news, the Web, or all of the above. Yahoo! Search also provides advanced search options for users looking for very specific information, search preferences (saved settings), sponsor results (paid placement listings), shortcuts, and queries conducted by other Yahoo! users that are similar to your search criteria.

How Can It Be Used?

Yahoo! Search can be used to locate images, video, local information, shopping, answers, audio, directory listings, jobs, news, web sites, or all of the above based upon the search criteria and user preferences. Yahoo! Search offers businesses paid placement results and listings that display when users enter specific search words relevant to your business's offerings. Sponsor Results provides enhanced placement on a pay-per-click basis, and Sponsor Listings is a "fee-based service that allows commercial web sites already listed in the Yahoo! Directory to receive enhanced placement in the commercial categories."

What Other Applications Does It Work With?

Yahoo! Search works with Internet Explorer, Mozilla, Firefox, Safari, Netscape, and various other applications based on specifications set forth in the Yahoo! Developer Network, as well as with a variety of mobile applications.

Who Uses It?

Yahoo! Search is a free search engine available to anyone with an Internet browser and Internet connection. The array of information available provides usability for a broad spectrum of users.

Should You Use It?

If you are looking for information but don't necessarily know where to look, Yahoo! Search would be an effective tool to point you in the right direction and provide options you might not have considered. If you are looking for very specific information, Yahoo! Search can provide a vast number of possibilities to suit your needs and allow you to narrow the search parameters. The infinite number of available search results provides usability for almost every demographic.

Who Started It?

Two Stanford engineering PhD candidates, David Filo and Jerry Yang, developed Yahoo! as a platform to track their personal interests on the Internet. The two founders recognized the business potential of their web site as the popularity of the site spread. Yahoo! was incorporated in 1995 and continues to add features and services like Yahoo! Search to meet its audience's expanding needs.

Tool Scorecard for Chapter 36: Search

Instructions: Using the five-point (0 to 4) scale below, rate each tool in this chapter on the basis of how valuable it *might be* to the internal and external operations of your company. Make notes about which tools appeal to you the most.

4 = Extremely Valuable
3 = Very Valuable

2 = Somewhat Valuable

1 = Not Very Valuable

0 = No Value

Tool	Internal Value	External Value
EveryZing	4 3 2 1 0	4 3 2 1 0
Google Search	4 3 2 1 0	4 3 2 1 0
Ice Rocket	4 3 2 1 0	4 3 2 1 0
MetaTube	4 3 2 1 0	4 3 2 1 0
Redlasso	4 3 2 1 0	4 3 2 1 0
Yahoo! Search	4 3 2 1 0	4 3 2 1 0

CHAPTER 37

Mobile

The folks at American Express reminded us for years, "Don't leave home without it." For many of us, the mobile phone may not be more important than a credit card, but you probably don't want to be without either for too long. Like it or not, you're living in a world of digital convergence where your iPhone, BlackBerry, or similar device functions not only as a phone but as an operational control center for your business.

Many of the social media tools in the ecosystem function just as well with your cell phone as they do with your computer—some even better with a cell phone. Mobile is a rapidly growing category, and this chapter profiles the following tools and applications:

- airG
- AOL Mobile
- Brightkite
- CallWave
- Jott
- Jumbuck
- SMS.ac

As you read each profile, keep in mind that its features and functions may or may not be right for your particular business. Use the **Tool Scorecard** at the end of the chapter to help you determine which of these tools qualify for further consideration when you begin creating your social media strategy in Part III of the book.

airG

> **Company Name:** airG
> **URL:** www.corp.airg.com
> **Location:** Vancouver, British Columbia, Canada
> **Founded:** 2000
> **Employees:** 150+

What Is It?

The airG service "is a global community service made available to end users through different mobile service providers." Customers of included service providers have access to an instant community network based on their interests and demographics.

How Can It Be Used?

"The mobile phone has proven to be a viable platform for bringing mobile users together in interactive communities, and with multiple access points including voice, video, SMS, MMS, WAP, Java, BREW and i-mode." The airG service can be used in an interactive community or as a GPS locator.

What Other Applications Does It Work With?

As a mobile networking device, airG offers a platform to interact with members of their community. It is interconnected to more than 100 million mobile operators and media companies.

Who Uses It?

Companies including Sprint, Nextel, AT&T, Rogers, TELUS, Virgin Mobile, Orange, Boost Mobile, Vodafone and MTV Asia use airG.

Should You Use It?

If you are looking for a mobile social network, airG satisfies that need if you are covered under a compatible phone service provider.

Who Started It?

Technology entrepreneurs Frederick Ghahramani, Vincent Yen, and Bryce Pasechnik founded airG in 2000.

AOL Mobile

Company Name:	AOL LLC
URL:	www.mobile.aol.com
Location:	New York, New York, United States
Founded:	1983
Revenue Model:	Advertising, subscriptions, services

What Is It?

AOL Mobile provides AOL products and services to users on portable devices. With AOL Mobile, users can access AOL content from categories like news, music, and sports. AOL Mobile also provides services like ringtones, AOL e-mail, and AOL Instant Messenger. Additionally, the AOL Mobile site gives information and reviews about different cell phones, cellular service providers, and cell phone accessories.

How Can It Be Used?

A user who wanted to find a restaurant in their area could use AOL City Guide to find the closest locations, browse reviews, and then call to make reservations. A businessperson who is out of town could use AOL Finance to access information about stocks or other companies. A user who wanted to see a movie could use AOL Moviefone to learn what movies are playing, read summaries of the plots, and find out what times the movies begin.

What Other Applications Does It Work With?

AOL Mobile compatible programs include MapQuest Mobile, City's Best, City Guide, and Moviefone. Additionally, through AOL Mobile you can access AOL Instant Messenger, AOL Mail, AOL Pictures, and a number of AOL Channels.

Who Uses It?

AOL is used by a wide variety of people to meet their various needs. Businesses can stay current with e-mails, find up-to-date financial information, and maintain an address book. Consumers can find new restaurants and clubs, read movie reviews, and get directions to a certain address.

Should You Use It?

You should use AOL Mobile if you are often away from your computer in situations where you would benefit from being able to access AOL products and services. For example, if you need to be available constantly through e-mail, AOL Mobile allows you to receive and send e-mails through your portable device. According to AOL, AOL Mobile allows you to stay "entertained, informed and connected to your network of family and friends while on the move."

Who Started It?

AOL first began as a company called Control Video Corporation in 1983, which was reorganized as Quantum Computer Services Inc., on May 24, 1985. The company focused on providing dedicated online services to Commodore computers. In 1988, Quantum created online services for Macintosh and, later, IBM computers. In 1991, Quantum became known as America Online Inc., AOL for DOS was launched, and Steve Case became the CEO of the company. Case decided the best direction for the company was to position AOL as the premier online service for those who were not particularly knowledgeable about computers. This strategy led to the company's biggest growth period. On January 11, 2001, America Online merged with Time Warner.

Brightkite

Company Name:	Brightkite (a division of No Sleep Media, LLC)
URL:	www.Brightkite.com
Location:	Denver, Colorado, United States
Founded:	2007
Employees:	5
Revenue Model:	Platform for third-party applications and presently evaluating location-based advertising
Fees:	For text messaging, service plan rates apply
Motto:	No rest until the dream comes true (No Sleep Media, LLC)

What Is It?

Brightkite offers a location-based social networking medium that provides updates to friends on your location via cell phone or Internet browser. Users can text message friends or create posts of text and images to create a virtual layer for that location. One of the advantages of location-based servicing is the similarity to a navigation device or GPS locator, so if users are in a crowded area, they can find who they are looking for via Brightkite.

How Can It Be Used?

Brightkite is currently a communication tool to update persons within a social network on the user's location or as a navigational aide. By targeting bars, music venues, conferences, and symposiums, users can see who is there. Users can enter a business name into the search feature for possible locations in their proximity.

The potential for tracking previously uncharted locations and marking areas for research will expand as GPS capabilities expand, making it a useful tool for expeditions.

Brightkite is currently exploring selling real-world analytics to businesses for location-based targeted advertising and the potential for tracking consumer spending trends.

What Other Applications Does It Work With?

Socialthing! provides users with an all-in-one site to receive updates from those in your social network and recently integrated the Brightkite API (application programming interface). SPOT Satellite Personal Tracker is now supported by Brightkite and can "check you in anywhere on earth via satellite"; this is beneficial if you are out of range of Wi-Fi or cell signals. FriendFeed and Twitter also work well with Brightkite, and users can customize what is sent to Twitter.

Who Uses It?

Brightkite is currently used as a platform for people to update their social network with their location and can be used as a navigation tool. Brightkite is an effective tool for those who want to mark a specific location to return to later. Depending on the user's privacy settings, Brightkite allows users to send double-blind messages to other Brightkiters in their vicinity for networking purposes, which could be helpful if you are at a large conference or symposium and trying to locate people.

Should You Use It?

If you are looking for a method of communicating your location to a large number of people with minimal effort, Brightkite would be an effective tool. This application could be beneficial for corporations or news outlets as a means of checking in for employees who are often out of range of cellular or Wi-Fi services. However, in the future, this type of application could be essential for locating employees in remote locations. Some areas of academia, specifically field research or archaeological specialties, could benefit from the use of Brightkite as a means of updating locations and tracking previously uncharted locales, or simply as a method of verification of whereabouts.

Who Started It?

Brady Becker and Martin May are the founders of Brightkite. Brady Becker has a "passion for creating location-based services that challenge how we define and interact with place based community." Public information on Martin May is currently unavailable.

CallWave

Company Name:	CallWave
URL:	www.callwave.com
Location:	San Francisco, California, United States
Founded:	1998
Employees:	~100
Tagline:	The new way to work together

What Is It?

CallWave specializes in providing an integrated communication system that incorporates the most used devices in the world today: the cell phone and the PC. The solutions offered enable the collaboration of Internet and phone from any device. The products are compatible with businesses of all sizes, and existing business enterprise tools can be merged to suit your needs and requirements.

In their own words, "Leveraging our wholly owned CLEC, Liberty Telecomm, and years of experience and innovation in making mobile phones and PCs communicate with each other, CallWave is in a unique position to provide a suite of secure, scalable, and cost-effective mobile communications tools."

CallWave is a publicly traded company with its headquarters in San Francisco, California, and has branch offices in Santa Barbara, California and Sofia, Bulgaria.

How Can It Be Used?

CallWave has communication tools that can be used in conjunction with other applications for effective and efficient working. Some of CallWave's features and functionality include:

- Voicemail-to-Text application converts voice messages to text, enabling professionals to read their voice messages, send them via text or e-mail, and manage messages online.
- FUZE, which offers high-definition and synchronized video, audio conferencing, chat, and online media storage. Ideal for web collaboration and conferencing, FUZE can be hosted from any Internet-enabled device, allowing professionals to collaborate from anywhere and share documents and images in sync.
- The beta version of FUZE supports BlackBerry and Nokia devices and will soon support the iPhone and Windows Mobile–based phones.
- HD Audio Conferencing provides clear sound quality and conference plans to suit the needs of small to large businesses.
- Fax2E-mail allows professionals to send, receive, and save faxes to e-mail.
- Mobile IM securely extends IM to any Smartphone and is compatible with all major IM Services: MSN, AIM, Jabber, Yahoo!, Google Talk, and ICQ.

What Other Applications Does It Work With?

IBM Lotus Sametime, Microsoft OCS, VoIP, Jabber, Google Talk, Yahoo!, AIM, MSN, and IQC are social media applications that can be used by CallWave widgets and gadgets that come free with the service.

Who Uses It?

CallWave can be used by anyone. However, it is ideal for professionals on the move because it provides an ideal amalgamation of PC and mobile to conduct business effectively and efficiently from anywhere.

Should You Use It?

If you are on the move and multi-tasking, CallWave could be the solution for you.

Who Started It?

CallWave's chairman and cofounder Peter V. Sperling is also a founder and senior vice president of the Apollo Group Inc., the parent company of the University of Phoenix. In addition, Sperling is the chairman and cofounder of Communication Services Inc., which serves the U.S. Coast Guard, FBI, and Department of Homeland Security, and the U.S. commercial wireless industry. Sperling is also the chairman of Ecliptic Enterprises, a provider of integrated space imaging and telemetry and payload deployment systems.

Jott

Company Name:	Jott Networks Inc.
URL:	www.jott.com
Location:	Seattle, Washington, United States
Founded:	2006
Employees:	15
Revenue Model:	Venture capital backing, but considering premium subscriptions and advertising
Fees:	Free and premium subscription plans
Tagline:	Get simple back

What Is It?

Jott is a voice transcription service that allows a user to call 1-866-JOTT-123, provide the name of the person for whom they want a message transcribed (to include themselves), and Jott sends the message to that name. Whether responding to e-mails, establishing a calendar date, or reminding oneself of an idea or task, Jott provides the means to continue communication, collaboration, and creativity regardless of the time or the place. Jott even allows you to send messages to web services such as Twitter, for real-time communication to your web-oriented audience.

How Can It Be Used?

Jott is geared toward those who need to multitask, whether because of hectic professional or personal lives or as a matter of safety by providing hands-free communication. Jott provides the ability to communicate without needing an Internet-enabled device, but with just a simple phone call. Lifehacker.com mentions other valuable uses of Jott, such as remotely shutting down Windows, controlling your Mac, or sending audio files to yourself, such as that fantastic composition you believe will fit in with your next ad campaign for your company.

What Other Applications Does It Work With?

Obviously if you have a telephone or a cell phone, Jott works with your device, since the primary requirement to use Jott is the voice. Currently Jott has specialized services with BlackBerry, iPhone, and iGoogle. Jott in general works with web services such as Blogger, Zillow, Amazon, Wordpress, and Twitter. The ability to post late-breaking news to your Internet-reading audience can prove valuable as a business tool. Conversely, the audience can also access your Jotts via Jott feeds (RSS feeds). Jott users simply dial 1-866-JOTT-123, state "Jott Feeds," and then provide the name of the desired feed. Jott users can then listen to your latest Jott posting.

Who Uses It?

There are enough recommendations from individual users to support the apparent popularity explosion of Jott. However, it isn't just the individual user who is finding Jott valuable. A number of Web-based companies are coming up with applications that play off of Jott's basic usage premise. One example is Tsheets.com. Tsheets is a time-tracking application that allows a Jott user to sign in and sign out. Users who telecommute or are on business travel would find such an application useful in order to keep track of time for time sheets and metrics.

Should You Use It?

Jott seems to be most useful for just about anyone who has a busy schedule or needs a technological tool to make notes and reminders. People are finding a number of reasons, professional and personal, to use Jott.

Who Started It?

John Pollard, one of the cofounders and CEO of Jott Networks Inc., has a solid foundation in the computer industry, with Microsoft and subsequently Expedia on his resume. Shreedhar Madhavapeddi, another cofounder and the vice president of products, also worked at Microsoft and was key in the development of MSN and Smartphone. Doug Aley, vice president of business development, most notably worked at Amazon in developing Unibox as well as becoming general manager of its third-party sellers' business. Dave Rich, vice president of business operations, has extensive experience in call center operations and voice recognition stemming from his work with companies such as American Airlines, SABRE, and Nuance. According to Jott's corporate overview: "Co-founders John Pollard and Shreedhar Madhavapeddi started Jott in response to a growing frustration: their lives were already full of technology, but they still felt they weren't staying on top of things. Jott was born from the promise of being able to help people remember anything."

Jumbuck

Company Name:	Jumbuck Entertainment Ltd.
URL:	www.jumbuck.com
Location:	Melbourne, Australia
Founded:	2000
Employees:	72

What Is It?

Jumbuck Entertainment has the unique distinction of being a leading source of community messaging applications to worldwide wireless carriers. It sends out a wireless markup language (WML) page every year that crosses the 13 million mark, each time. Jumbuck has branches in Perth, San Francisco, London, Cologne, and Rio de Janeiro, and its main headquarters are in Melbourne, Australia. Today, Jumbuck has effectively achieved a comprehensive distribution footprint wherein it has incorporated a network of more than 80 carriers internationally, including a community that easily exceeds 15 million users.

Jumbuck is a public company listed on the Australian Stock Exchange.

How Can It Be Used?

Jumbuck Entertainment Limited has put together a messaging and social networking service that enables mobile users to use services like chat rooms, blogging, dating applications, and other features using mobile phones. The company offers a variety of products that cater to different countries and various user requirements. For safety and proper use of its services, a moderation service is provided which ensures that all messages are reviewed and meet ethical boundaries as required by different communities in the world.

Some of its products are detailed below:

- *Power Chat* is an application that can be customized and allows users to interact the world over. Public and private rooms are available, and it supports multiple languages, including Italian, Spanish, German, English, Portuguese, and Polish.
- *Jumbuck Island* offers multiplayer chat applications in 3D Java. Play on a virtual island using your customized characters, use it separately, or integrate it with your Power Chat.
- *Jumbuck Blogs* is a blogging application in which users can text, comment, or insert images on their page.
- *Chat Del Mundo* is one of the largest mobile Hispanic communities in the world, where you can find members from the United States, Spain, and South America.
- *TXT chat* is a short message service (SMS) where a single sent command enables the user to send messages and browse through chat rooms.
- *Chat do Mundo* is one of the major mobile Portuguese communities in the world. Members come from Portugal and Brazil where communication is by way of text, images, and video. Now available on TIM and Vivo in Brazil, and on Optimus, TMN, and Vodafone in Portugal, the Chat platform supports wireless application protocal (WAP), SMS, multimedia message service (MMS), and video.

What Other Applications Does It Work With?

Jumbuck takes you online and has integrated support with social media applications that meet technical connectivity requirements. For more information, it is important to check with the carrier or service provider you are subscribed to.

Who Uses It?

This is a user-friendly service for those who can put its various features to good use and help them increase their business, their friends list, or their social circle.

Should You Use It?

If you love to make friends, and you like staying connected and talking to people from all over the world, then this is a service to consider. There are a lot of features that can be used, and with a little bit of imagination, ingenuity, and smarts, you could use this medium to boost your business opportunities, too.

Who Started It?

Adrian Risch is the founder of Jumbuck. He was appointed CEO in July 2007. With his experience in web project management and applications development, and his exhaustive understanding of international markets in tele-communication and consumer consumption of mobile data services, he leads the company from the front. He is also a member of the corporate governance committee.

SMS.ac

Company Name:	SMS.ac Inc.
URL:	www.sms.ac.com
Location:	San Diego, California, United States
Founded:	2001
Employees:	100–200
Fees:	Carrier charges may apply
Tagline:	Always connected

What Is It?

SMS.ac is a mobile data and Internet communications company that offers a global system of Short Message Services (SMS) along with multimedia messaging services. It is considered to be one of the biggest mobile communities in the world today. Mobile and web distribution is provided to those who sell and buy digital content like music, videos, and other applications through the medium of SMS mobile billing. The web site has integrated social networking services like comments, photographs, music, and videos with its mobile billing technology.

How Can It Be Used?

SMS.ac is a medium where text messages are to interact with other users. Once you are a registered SMS.ac user, you can use your account to send regular text messages, make your own greetings, and look for other profiles with similar interests as yours, which will help you increase your friends list. The methods for updating blogs; swapping photos, music, and videos; and many other features are updated and improved on a regular basis. All this is done using your cell phone. This service is free to join, and charges are levied depending on the country of residence and your service provider or carrier.

Besides the very obvious entertainment factor, this medium can be effectively used to spread messages of social awareness, alerts for imminent natural calamities, and so on. SMS.ac is a wireless e-mail provider, and as such it has tie-ins with many carriers or service providers worldwide. This network of carriers and technology combined can help avert many a disaster through timely news flashes.

There is a proposal for incorporating a tsunami warning system via this medium, the requirement for which followed in the wake of the disastrous tsunami that hit Indonesia, India, Thailand, and Sri Lanka in 2004. Those who do not have cell phones and are not registered users can benefit from news spreading by word-of-mouth.

What Other Applications Does It Work With?

Your cell phone can help you connect with other social media applications available on the Internet. The Wireless Application Protocol, or WAP, is a standard that makes available secure access to e-mail and web pages that are text based to handheld devices and mobile phones. From your WAP-enabled mobile phone, you can connect to the biggest mobile community in the world with SMS.ac.

Who Uses It?

Today SMS.ac has more than 50 million registered users in about 180 countries worldwide. It caters to varied tastes in music, videos, and other features. It also helps people stay connected in times of crisis. The network is spread out, and a new arrival in a city can easily make friends through this common medium.

Should You Use It?

If you are looking to make new business connections and keep in touch with coworkers, then this is an ideal platform for you. Apart from just messages, there is so much more you can do with this system. It would help you keep contacts for your business; you can download interesting videos and the latest music; and keep in touch with news and views from friends around the world. It can also keep you in-the-know with things happening around the world, be it eventual natural disasters, aid required, and so on.

Who Started It?

Greg Wilfahrt is cofounder of SMS.ac, and he serves as executive vice president, office of the chairman. His portfolio involves corporate communications and public relations initiatives and development of a strategically sound road map for the company.

Greg took over this position after being vice president of public relations at MP3.com. He also had tenure with Ubrandit.com as vice president of communications.

Michael Pousti is CEO at SMS.ac. In 1993, Pousti cofounded College Club.com, where he was chairman. Pousti has also completed a stint as cofounder and CEO of Productivity Solutions Corporation. He saw the company through concept to subsequent acquisition by Unisys.

Tool Scorecard for Chapter 37: Mobile

Instructions: Using the five-point (0 to 4) scale below, rate each tool in this chapter on the basis of how valuable it *might be* to the internal and external operations of your company. Make notes about which tools appeal to you the most.

4 = Extremely Valuable
3 = Very Valuable
2 = Somewhat Valuable
1 = Not Very Valuable
0 = No Value

Tool	Internal Value	External Value
airG	4 3 2 1 0	4 3 2 1 0
AOL Mobile	4 3 2 1 0	4 3 2 1 0
Brightkite	4 3 2 1 0	4 3 2 1 0
CallWave	4 3 2 1 0	4 3 2 1 0
Jott	4 3 2 1 0	4 3 2 1 0
Jumbuck	4 3 2 1 0	4 3 2 1 0
SMS.ac	4 3 2 1 0	4 3 2 1 0

CHAPTER 38

Interpersonal

The tools in this chapter have a common thread: they all were designed to facilitate people-to-people communication and collaboration. To those who consider themselves social media savvy, many of these tools don't belong in the social media ecosystem, but if you're in the business of managing people, processes, or products, you need to be aware of this important category. If your business has a strong customer focus, this category is one of the top five or six most important categories in this book.

This chapter introduces you to the following companies, tools, and applications:

- Acrobat Connect
- AOL Instant Messenger
- Go To Meeting
- Apple iChat
- Jott
- Meebo
- Skype
- WebEx

As you read each profile, keep in mind that its features and functions may or may not be right for your particular business. Use the **Tool Score-card** at the end of the chapter to help you determine which of these tools qualify for further consideration when you begin creating your social media strategy in Part III of the book.

Acrobat Connect

Company Name:	Adobe Inc.
URL:	www.adobe.com
Location:	San Jose, California, United States
Founded:	Adobe Systems 1982
Employees:	7,000
Revenue Model:	Software sales/upgrades
Fees:	Free trial; software purchase or monthly subscription

What Is It?

Acrobat Connect is the Adobe Systems Inc., solution for reaching a dissemi-nated workforce or audience. Adobe markets Acrobat Connect as easy-to-use software that "can help break through technology barriers by letting virtually anyone participate in effective online communication and knowledge transfer." By providing web conferencing options such as screen sharing, whiteboard, chat video and audio, and options for archiving and editing recorded online meetings, Acrobat Connect reduces travel costs and increases productivity.

How Can It Be Used?

Acrobat Connect is used to communicate and collaborate via online confer-encing features with the capability to screen share, chat via audio and video, and use a whiteboard to enhance understanding. This functionality allows users to conduct training or e-learning workshops, demonstrate a product or service, or host a meeting to review a variety of presentations.

For the individual, Acrobat Connect is a useful tool for sharing life events with extended family.

What Other Applications Does It Work With?

Any application that the host of the meeting has installed on his or her computer can be shared using Acrobat Connect. This capability is effective when conducting a sales demonstration so the participants in the online meeting can see the product or service firsthand, or for conducting a business meeting where participants are disseminated across numerous locations so all can view presentations.

Who Uses It?

Business and academic organizations use Acrobat Connect to enhance relations and improve productivity. According to Steve Bamberger, national training manager, eLearning, Toshiba America Business Solutions Inc., "Integrating Acrobat ConnectPro into our online training initiatives has been enormously instrumental in helping us enhance communications and grow business lines, and we've been able to extend this enrichment to other teams for use in product launches and customer meetings."

Should You Use It?

Acrobat Connect is an effective tool for communicating, demonstrating, presenting, or conducting meetings and conferences. If you are looking for a way to reach many people across a myriad of places, Acrobat Connect would be a viable option. As many businesses are recognizing the increased productivity and cost-effectiveness of telecommuting, Acrobat Connect would be a beneficial tool to keep the lines of communication open between on-site and remote employees, and to enhance training modules. In a sales environment, Acrobat ConnectPro offers a solution for presenting or demonstrating where it is difficult to reach multiple leads in one location.

Who Started It?

Adobe was founded in 1982 by John Warnock and Chuck Geschke on the principle of translating text and images from a computer screen to print. By introducing Adobe PostScript technology, they revolutionized desktop publishing; "a computer file could be printed exactly as it appeared on screen, with all formatting, graphics and fonts intact." After Adobe's acquisition of Macromedia, Macromedia Breeze became Acrobat Connect. Built upon Flash technology, Acrobat Connect is considered the next generation in the Adobe suite of products.

AOL Instant Messenger

Company Name:	AOL LLC
URL:	www.aim.com
Location:	New York, New York, United States
Founded:	1983
Revenue Model:	Advertising, subscriptions, services

What Is It?

AOL Instant Messenger is a free online service that allows users to communicate with one or multiple users synchronously. There are versions for Linux, Macintosh, and Windows operating systems, and they are all able to communicate with each other. Users can add contacts to their AOL Instant Messenger Buddy List, which allows them to see when their contacts are online. Aside from synchronous text-based chatting, AOL Instant Messenger also offers features such as voice-based chat, video-based chat, alerts and reminders, file transfers, and text messaging.

How Can It Be Used?

AOL Instant Messenger can be used in any instance where people want or need to communicate over the Internet. People can use AOL Instant Messenger to maintain contact with friends and family that live far away, or businesses could use AOL Instant Messenger to communicate internally among employees or externally with customers. Additionally, with the ability to transfer files, it is a useful program for concurrent collaboration.

What Other Applications Does It Work With?

AOL Instant Messenger works with AOL Radio, AOL Explorer, and Plaxo. AOL Instant Messenger also allows third-party developers to create chat bots, custom clients, mashups, widgets, modules, and plug-ins. These applications do any number of things, such as allowing a user to post directly to a blog, allowing someone to track the cost of a meeting, or allowing a user to draw simultaneously with one of her or his buddies.

Who Uses It?

AOL Instant Messenger is used by a large and global online audience. It is estimated to have a large segment of the instant messaging market in North America. Businesses and private users both use AOL Instant Messenger to communicate and share media online.

Should You Use It?

You should use AOL Instant Messenger if you are interested in communicating with other users online, either professionally or recreationally. Additionally, you should use AOL Instant Messenger if you are interested in creating a third-party application that will serve a function through the chatting service. For example, a web developer could create an application that works as a part of an online marketing campaign to drive traffic to its web site.

Who Started It?

AOL first began as a company called Control Video Corporation in 1983, which was reorganized as Quantum Computer Services Inc. on May 24, 1985. The company focused on providing dedicated online services to Commodore computers. In 1988, Quantum created online services for Macintosh and, later, IBM computers. In 1991, Quantum became known as America Online Inc., AOL for **DOS** was launched, and Steve Case became the CEO of the company. Case decided the best direction for the company was to position AOL as the premier online service for those who were not particularly knowledgeable about computers. This strategy led to the company's biggest growth period. On January 11, 2001, America Online merged with Time Warner.

Go To Meeting

Company Name:	Citrix Systems Inc.
URL:	www.gotomeeting.com
Location:	Fort Lauderdale, Florida, United States
Founded:	1989
Revenue Model:	Subscriptions
Tagline:	Online meetings made easy

What Is It?

Go To Meeting is an online meeting service that enables individuals, businesses, and organizations to collaborate and communicate via the Internet. Users pay a flat subscription fee, on a per-month or per-year basis, which allows them to conduct unlimited online meetings for the duration of their subscribed period. Go To Meeting also offers additional features such as VoIP (Voice over Internet Protocol), screen sharing, and meeting recording. Users on Windows and Macintosh operating systems can join a Go To Meeting session.

How Can It Be Used?

Go To Meeting can be used to promote collaboration and communication, demonstrate products or presentations, and share information. By using the audio and chatting components of Go To Meeting, employees of a business can communicate with each other while reducing travel expenses. With the screen-sharing feature of Go To Meeting, you can show a slideshow to multiple people or allow a group to edit a document together in real time. Since Go To Meeting also allows guests to attend meetings for no additional charge beyond the subscription fee, you could invite a potential client to meet with you from anywhere in the world (with an Internet connection) to negotiate or view a product demonstration.

What Other Applications Does It Work With?

Go To Meeting can be integrated with several applications, from which users can start an impromptu Go To Meeting session. These applications include IBM Lotus Notes, Microsoft Office, Microsoft Outlook, and some instant messaging applications. Additionally, recorded meetings can be converted to the Windows Media format, enabling users to watch past meetings in Windows Media Player.

Who Uses It?

Several companies use Go To Meeting to manage and grow their business. Go To Meeting offers them the ability to save resources, communicate to a greater degree, and be more productive. Just a few of the companies that find Go To Meeting beneficial are Clarity, a company that provides Internet-based business solutions; e-Touch International, a company that designs automated hospitality technology; and xG Technology, a company that develops wireless communications technologies.

Should You Use It?

You should use Go To Meeting if you are interested in a collaboration tool, with features like audio conferencing and screen sharing, that allows you to meet with people online. Additionally, since Go To Meeting operates on a flat subscription rate, it is a good choice if you intend on meeting online numerous times within a given period. You should also use Go To Meeting if you need a method of sharing or discussing confidential information over the Internet, as Go To Meeting has several security implementations.

Who Started It?

Go To Meeting was developed in July 2004 by Citrix Online, a division of Citrix Systems Inc., Go To My PC and Go To Assist, applications created to remotely access computers, were the basis for the technology that Go To Meeting utilizes. Version 3.0, the current release of Go To Meeting that was introduced in 2006, provides integration with Microsoft Office and support for Macintosh users to join meetings.

Apple iChat

Company Name:	Apple
URL:	www.apple.commacosx/features/ichat.html
Location:	Cupertino, California, United States
Founded:	2003
Employees:	75,000 (Apple)
Revenue Model:	Sales of hardware and software

What Is It?

Apple iChat is a video chat service offered with the purchase of Apple's Mac computer running the Leopard operating system. Apple publicizes, "iChat turns any video chat into an event." New features provide users with video backdrops, photo booth effects, comic book effects, and the ability to show photo slideshows, keynote presentations, and movies. Apple iChat also provides a screen-sharing feature that enables users to control a single desktop for collaboration, and automatically initiates an audio chat, eliminating the need for conference calling.

How Can It Be Used?

Apple iChat is primarily used to communicate with friends, family, and coworkers. Using the variety of special effects, and the ability to share photos and video, iChat provides a more comprehensive chatting tool. The built-in functionality of screen sharing, audio chat, and chat recording makes this an effective tool for business collaboration or educational presentations. The recording feature is beneficial for users working on a collaborative project or presentation in the event someone on the team is unavailable for the presentation.

What Other Applications Does It Work With?

iChat works with a number of other applications that allow users to share audio and video and do limited white-boarding. It is compatible with AOL Instant Messenger, Google Talk, Yahoo! Messenger, and Quick Look, a file preview feature developed by Apple.

Who Uses It?

Presently iChat is used by individuals, students, and businesses who use Macs. Users who have a .Mac account can use iChat instantly, but those who have an AOL or AIM screen name can also use iChat.

Should You Use It?

If you have a Mac and are looking for additional ways to communicate and collaborate, iChat is a viable option. The new features available with the photo and video sharing, and desktop sharing with audio chat, provide an all-in-one functionality that many businesses subscribe to using multiple vendors. Paid subscribers to Apple's .Mac service have encrypted communication support for more confidential or proprietary information.

Who Started It?

Apple Computers was founded by Steve Jobs and Steve Wozniak in 1976 in an effort to make "the easy and affordable personal computer become reality."

Jott

Company Name:	Jott Networks, Inc.
URL:	www.jott.com
Location:	Seattle, Washington, United States
Founded:	2006
Employees:	15
Revenue Model:	Venture capital backing, but considering premium subscriptions and advertising
Fees:	Free
Motto:	Get simple back.

What Is It?

Jott is a voice transcription service that allows a user to call 1-866-JOTT-123, provide the name of the person for whom they want a message transcribed (to include themselves), and Jott sends the message to that name. Whether responding to emails, establishing a calendar date, or reminding one's self of an idea or task, Jott provides the means to continue communication, collaboration and creativity regardless of the time or the place. Jott even allows you to send messages to web services such as Twitter, for real time communication to your web-oriented audience.

How Can It Be Used?

Jott is geared toward those who need to multitask, whether it's because of hectic professional or personal lives or as a matter of safety by providing hands-free communication. Jott provides the ability to communicate without needing the aid of an Internet-enabled device, with just a simple phone call. Lifehacker.com mentions other valuable uses of Jott, such as remotely shutting down Windows or controlling your Mac or sending audio files to yourself, such as that fantastic composition you believe will fit in with your next ad campaign for your company.

What Other Applications Does It Work With?

Obviously if you have a telephone or a cell phone, Jott works with your device, since the primary requirement to use jotter is the voice. Currently Jott has specialized services with BlackBerry, iPhone, and iGoogle. Jott in general works with web services such as Blogger, Zillow, Amazon, Wordpress, and Twitter. The ability to post late-breaking news to your Internet-reading audience can prove valuable as a business tool. Conversely, the audience can also access your Jotts via Jott feeds (RSS feeds). Jott users simply dial 1-866-Jott-123, state "Jott Feeds," and then provide the name of the desired feed. Jott users can then listen to your latest Jott posting.

Who Uses It?

There are enough recommendations from individual users to support the apparent popularity explosion of Jott. However, it isn't just the individual user who is finding Jott valuable. A number of web-based companies are coming up with applications that are based on Jott's basic usage premise. One example is Tsheets.com. Tsheets is a time-tracking application that allows a Jott user to sign and sign out. Users who telecommute or are on business travel would find such an application useful in order to keep track of time for time sheets and metrics.

Should You Use It?

Jott seems to be most useful for just about anyone who has a busy schedule or needs a technological tool to make notes and reminders. People are finding a number of reasons to use Jott, both professional and personal. Scott Clark posted a suggestion to use Jott for keeping migraine diaries.

Who Started It?

John Pollard, one of the cofounders and CEO of Jott Networks, Inc., has a solid foundation in the computer industry with Microsoft and subsequently Expedia on his resume. Shreedhar Madhavapeddi, another cofounder and the vice-president of products, also worked at Microsoft and was key in the development of MSN and Smartphone. Doug Aley, vice-president of business development, most notably worked at Amazon in developing Unibox for Amazon as well as becoming general manager of its third-party sellers business. Dave Rich, vice-president of business operations, has extensive experience in call center operations and voice recognition stemming from his work with companies such as American Airlines, SABRE, and Nuance. According to Jott's Corporate Overview: "Cofounders John Pollard and Shreedhar Madhavapeddi started Jott in response to a growing frustration: Their lives were already full of technology, but they still felt they weren't staying on top of things. Jott was born from the promise of being able to help people remember anything."

Meebo

Company Name:	Meebo
URL:	www.meebo.com
Location:	Mountain View, California, United States
Founded:	2005
Employees:	40
Revenue Model:	Advertising
Fees:	Free
Tagline:	All your IM accounts in one place—chat, play games, and much more!

What Is It?

Meebo is the solution to a problem that many people encounter: too many Instant Message (IM) accounts (and the accompanying user IDs and passwords). Meebo allows IM users to consolidate their accounts and reduce the need to download different types of software that, while they enable communication with different online users, results in clogged computer processes and cluttered computer desktops. Meebo incorporates MSN Messenger, Yahoo!, AIM, Google, ICQ, and Jabber and allows Meebo users to log in from any location (as opposed to being restricted to a particular PC where the user's IM software would be installed) and send IMs. Meebo can also be embedded anywhere online that an IM application can be embedded, such as in MySpace or blogs.

How Can It Be Used?

In today's world of networking for personal and professional needs, because remembering and separating the various user IDs and passwords to each individual account becomes difficult. Meebo allows you to have one central login and gives you the ability to log in from anywhere and IM someone at any time. Meebo also provides features such as Meebo rooms (chat rooms), Meebo Me (IMs on blogs and other web sites), Meebo Mobile for iPhones and iTouches, and Meebo extensions for Firefox users.

What Other Applications Does It Work With?

As mentioned in the previous paragraph, Meebo works not only with the major IM applications, but with iPhones and iTouches, Firefox, Facebook, and MySpace. According to an article on Reelseo.com, Meebo is a platform for multiuser and synchronous applications such as 3rd Sense, Absolutist, AddictingGames, BladeSix, Clearspring Technologies, Come2Play, Feedhaus, Gamebrew, MeBeam, MediaGreenhouse, Mochi Media, Jiggmin, Kongregate, PlayFirst, Presidio Media, Pudding Media, TalkShoe, TokBox, Ustream.tv, uWink, wellgames, and ZeroCode.

Who Uses It?

Seth Sternberg, CEO and cofounder of Meebo, best points out the range of Meebo users in the following interview excerpt from Centernetworks.com:

> Mostly people who are 25 years and younger. From there the demographic gets really wide. We have U.S. soldiers in Iraq and

Meebo is the only way they can communicate live other than calling them. . . . Teachers are using Meebo on their class blogs to allow students and parents to communicate [with] them from the class blog. . . .

Thirty percent of people using Meebo are in America, the balance is abroad. Meebo is available in 53 languages and the way that came to be, our users really wanted Meebo in multiple languages so we asked for help on our blog. So we threw up a Wiki with the English strings and people came and helped translate the strings into 53 languages.

Should You Use It?

Meebo is a good tool for those who have multiple IM accounts. The ability to log in to a centralized IM location and use one user ID/password saves a lot of time, bandwidth, and frustration. IM'ing may not necessarily be perfect for everyone's business needs, but if it is, then Meebo can certainly save you time and give you mobility.

Who Started It?

Meebo originated from cofounder Sandy Jen's frustration at having 13 IM screen names and passwords to remember. Seth Sternberg, Sandy, and third cofounding partner Elaine Wherry played with Ajax IM as a way to solve the problem. The name Meebo was cooked up as the three sat in a California Pizza Kitchen restaurant trying to find a name that was memorable, easy to pronounce and spell, and of course was not already in use on the Internet.

Skype

Company Name:	Skype Limited
URL:	www.skype.com
Location:	Luxembourg, Belgium
Founded:	2003
Tagline:	Licensing revenue, Skype credit, premium subscriptions

What Is It?

Skype is a piece of software that operates through VoIP to enable users to make, receive, and conduct phone calls over the Internet. If a user is calling another person that is currently on Skype, the call is free. Calling someone who is not using Skype (e.g., on a cell phone or land line) requires users to either become a Skype subscriber or use Skype Credits. Skype also offers a number of other features, including videoconferencing, call forwarding, and text messaging.

How Can It Be Used?

Skype can be used as a conventional telephone, but it is capable of doing much more. A business could set up an online number in a location within any of the supported countries (21 available currently), and anyone in that number's locale who calls the business pays the local rate, while the business can answer through Skype for free. Skype also allows for call forwarding, which allows users to redirect calls incoming to Skype to a cell phone or landline. This allows a user to only give out one number, their Skype number, and still receive phone calls even when they are not online.

What Other Applications Does It Work With?

Skype works with several mobile applications so users can access Skype away from the computer. Any phone operating the Windows Mobile operating system can use Skype, and an official Symbian operating system version is being developed. There are also phones that are designed entirely for use with Skype, including Skype's own phone known as Skypephone.

Who Uses It?

Skype has a substantial, and still growing, user base. At the end of the first quarter in 2008 there were an estimated 309.3 million user accounts in existence around the world. Unfortunately, that number may include multiple accounts owned by the same user, but on September 17, 2008, Skype hit a peak with 13,230,315 concurrent users online at once. Skype is used by individuals who want to maintain contact with friends and family all around the world, as well as businesses that wish to communicate globally with employees or customers.

Should You Use It?

You should use Skype if you would like a VoIP-based program that is similar to conventional phone services, but also offers features beyond that of a conventional phone service. You should also use Skype if you would like to communicate with other Skype users around the world for free. Additionally, with the ability to register international numbers, Skype is great for those who need an international presence but are unable to establish themselves somewhere physically.

Who Started It?

Niklas Zennström, Janus Friis, and a group of software developers based in Tallinn, Estonia, started Skype. Zennström and Friis cofounded the file-sharing application KaZaA prior to founding Skype. Skype was acquired by eBay in September 2005 in a deal worth about $2.6 billion.

WebEx

Company Name:	WebEx Communications Inc.
URL:	www.webex.com
Location:	San Jose and Santa Clara, California, United States
Founded:	1996
Employees:	2,189
Revenue Model:	User fees
Fees:	Fee schedule
Tagline:	Vision: To use the Web to bring people together from around the world and work collectively on creative ideas and business

What Is It?

WebEx is a Cisco company product that "creates on-demand software solutions for companies of all sizes." These applications include online meetings, web conferencing, and videoconferencing. The WebEx Application Suite is "designed for business processes such as sales, support, training and marketing processes."

How Can It Be Used?

WebEx advertises "all you need to run effective online meetings is a browser and a phone," making their services available to virtually anyone. WebEx is used to conduct meetings, webinars, large-scale seminars, sales demonstrations, and training and support sessions. WebEx allows users to select the material they want to present or share so participants do not have access to someone's entire desktop or personal files, and permits changing the role of the participants at any time during the meeting. More advanced features include the ability to conduct polls and quizzes, videoconferences, and chat with participants.

What Other Applications Does It Work With?

WebEx is a versatile meeting application that uses the presenter's desktop and files, thus working with any applications on the presenter's system. According to the WebEx site, "With WebEx, users share presentations, applications, documents and desktops, with full-motion video and integrated audio, all in a rich multimedia environment."

Who Uses It?

WebEx provides on-demand collaboration, online meeting, web conferencing, and videoconferencing for financial services and high-tech industries; health-care, pharmaceutical, communications, manufacturing, government, and educational organizations; and management consulting organizations. Organizations looking to improve productivity by reaching a wider audience through on-demand training and support or to conduct online sales presentations and demonstrations remotely use WebEx.

Should You Use It?

If your organization is looking for an application to conduct remote meetings or training sessions, WebEx can effectively meet those goals. WebEx provides a service that could increase productivity while reducing support costs through unattended and attended remote support sessions. One key benefit of using WebEx is the ability to share information without traveling, which increases productivity and time management, and reduces costs. WebEx web conferencing works across differing platforms, which allows users and presenters using different systems to collaborate effectively.

Tool Scorecard for Chapter 38: Interpersonal

Instructions: Using the five-point (0 to 4) scale below, rate each tool in this chapter on the basis of how valuable it *might be* to the internal and external operations of your company. Make notes about which tools appeal to you the most.

4 = Extremely Valuable
3 = Very Valuable
2 = Somewhat Valuable
1 = Not Very Valuable
0 = No Value

Tool	Internal Value	External Value
Acrobat Connect	4 3 2 1 0	4 3 2 1 0
AOL Instant Messenger	4 3 2 1 0	4 3 2 1 0
Go To Meeting	4 3 2 1 0	4 3 2 1 0
Apple iChat	4 3 2 1 0	4 3 2 1 0
Meebo	4 3 2 1 0	4 3 2 1 0
Skype	4 3 2 1 0	4 3 2 1 0
WebEx	4 3 2 1 0	4 3 2 1 0

PART III

Strategy

The next five chapters focus on developing a social media strategy for your business. In Chapter 39, we take a closer look at the four pillars of social media strategy: Communicate, Collaborate, Educate, and Entertain. Each pillar supports a platform for engaging your customers, prospects, and employees. Your platform will depend on the tools and applications you valued the most on your tool scorecards from Part II.

Chapter 40 is your social media SWOT analysis. This is another activity-based chapter and an ideal group exercise if you are involving others from your organization. The SWOT analysis will help you take a critical look at your organization, assessing strengths, weaknesses, opportunities, and threats from a macro perspective and in the context of the social media tools that are the most practical and valuable.

Chapter 41 introduces you to the ACCESS model, an acronym for **A**udience, **C**oncept, **C**ompetition, **E**xecution, **S**ocial media, and **S**ales viability. In a world where everyone using social media is a publisher, the ACCESS model is a methodology for developing and connecting your content to the ideal audience.

Chapter 42, yet another activity-based chapter, helps you evaluate and organize your existing company resources, an important step before you create and implement a social media strategy. Finally in Chapter 43, you're ready to develop a modest 12-month social media macro strategy.

CHAPTER 39

The Four Pillars of Social Media Strategy

Τhis chapter helps you:

- Understand how the four pillars of social media strategy apply to your business and the creation of successful online communities.
- Define your business in the context of content.
- Generate initial ideas for creating a successful community around your content.
- Make your content "sticky."
- Differentiate between the different kinds of communities:
  — Metropolis Communities
  — Affinity Communities
  — Intra-company Communities
  — Vertical Communities
  — Horizontal Communities
- Understand basic online community management strategies.

Christian Lander wasn't rich or famous when he decided to start a blog dedicated to "stuff white people like." Some people find his class-bashing perspective hilarious; others aren't sure what to make of this former PhD student turned cultural commentator. The publisher Random House thought his perspective might make a good book. They also liked the fact that his blog had excellent traffic. The result: a $300,000 advance to write a book based on his blog, www.stuffwhitepeoplelike.com. Through 2008, his blog had over 51 million hits. If you visit his site, you can link to Amazon.com and buy his book, or you can browse several Google ads targeted at his particular audience. Although he may not be a household name nor excessively rich just yet, Christian Lander has discovered a strategy that works for him: entertain your audience and have them invite their friends.

Michael Buckley isn't a household name either, but he's been able to parlay his content into a six-figure income thanks to YouTube and an advertising placement program that surrounds his videos with ads targeted to his audience. Once the host of a part-time weekly show on a public access channel in Connecticut, he found that only a few people were able to "discover" his show, "What the Buck?" He first started posting segments of his public access show on YouTube. Before long he was producing his shows exclusively to be shown on YouTube and through 2008 had over 100 million views. Needless to say, he has expanded his audience considerably. More importantly, he discovered a strategy that has allowed him to monetize his content: entertain your audience and have them invite their friends.

If Lander and Buckley seem like accidental success stories removed from the everyday world of business that you work in, you're wise to question how their experiences can translate into a meaningful business strategy for your business. Consider for a moment, however, the now familiar story of Tom Dickson, CEO of Blendtec (www.blendtec.com), the Utah manufacturer of kitchen blenders. Dickson has become a YouTube star with his "Will It Blend?" series of videos in which he places everyday objects, such as golf balls, glow sticks, marbles, and even an iPhone, into one of his powerful blenders to demonstrate the key feature of his $400 product: it will blend, frappe, or mix just about anything in a matter of seconds. You might say that the blender is the real star of these videos, and with over 100 million YouTube views through 2008, the company has acknowledged the positive impact of its social media strategy on sales. But there's more to the story because the videos themselves have become a growing profit center for the company through advertising revenues. How many businesses can say that their marketing strategies not only increase sales of the company's product or service but generate revenue on their own? Seems that Dickson and his marketing department have discovered—and perfected—a variation of the same strategy employed by Lander and Buckley: entertain your audience and have them invite their friends.

In this chapter, we take a closer look at potential social media strategies you'll want to consider for your business. You'll learn that entertainment is just one way, albeit an important one, to engage, influence, and augment your audience.

Mastering the Four Pillars

Think of your social media strategy as a platform supported by four pillars. You really need all four pillars in order to stabilize the platform and make the strategy work. Once again, those four pillars are:

1. Communication,
2. Collaboration,
3. Education, and
4. Entertainment.

As we learned in Chapter 1, social media is about enabling conversation among your audience or market. What are you trying to get them to converse about? Things that will help you generate revenue or increase company profits, of course. For an internal audience—your employees or coworkers—that may be something as simple as enabling product teams to share knowledge that leads to better products or more efficient manufacturing processes. For an external audience—your customers and prospects, for example—the value of engaging their mindshare and enabling them to promote your product's benefits to their peers and cohorts is calculated in top-line sales revenue. In the case of Tom Dickson and Blendtec, the more virally driven YouTube views his "Will It Blend?" episodes receive, the more blenders the company will sell.

These four pillars are categories of audience engagement and before you can master them you have to stop and consider what you're already doing and the results you're either getting or missing.

What Are You Really Communicating?

Every company already does something to communicate with its audience. How is your communication perceived by your audience? How do you measure the effectiveness of your communication strategy? Which particular strategy triggers the most beneficial action, response, or behavior from your audience? One of the problems with many traditional means of communicating with your audience is that you cannot accurately measure the impact of your communication strategy. You may have a general, even fuzzy, sense that something is working or not working, but you can't always articulate a cause-and-effect relationship.

With some social media tools, you can measure things that eventually translate into something on your company profit and loss statement. For example, let's say you develop a monthly newsletter delivered via e-mail through a service such as Constant Contact (see Chapter 25). Your e-mail might include a special discount offer with a link to your web site where your customer can request more information or place an order. These requests or orders can be measured and a cause-and-effect relationship can be determined. In fact, with programs such as Constant Contact, you can measure how many people open your e-mail and how many click on a link within the e-mail. That link may be a request for more information or an order form. The point is you can measure it.

If e-mail strikes you as too traditional a communication strategy, consider the value of measuring traffic on your own YouTube channel or your blog. Whatever content or message you post, the number of views, visits, or subscriptions can be measured. More importantly, you can get feedback on "what" you are communicating because your audience can comment on your communication. You can even measure the number of comments. The take-home message is that social media facilitates immediate and measurable two-way and group communication.

Quick Start Micro Strategy

Create and send a basic newsletter using an e-mail marketing service. The only way to truly appreciate how easy it is to create, send, and measure results is to do it. If you're not sure you're ready to reach out to an audience of customers just yet, create and send something directed at your employees or members of a club you belong to. There are several companies that specialize in e-mail marketing. For a quick start we recommend Constant Contact (www .constantcontact.com). On their site you'll find templates, tutorials, and advice on how to create impactful messages for your audience.

In Celebration of Collaboration

Every year numerous business books and magazine articles are written about collaboration in the workplace. It's hard not to be in favor of collaboration, but why do some organizations do it so well and others fail at it? Is it the company culture that makes a difference or perhaps the skills of those who endeavor to collaborate? Could it be the tools used to collaborate?

Take a moment and make a list of the tools that your organization currently uses to foster collaboration among coworkers. It's a bit challenging for many businesses because collaboration is viewed as a pathway to a result rather than a result itself. Many people think of collaboration in terms of a process to be managed rather than a set of tools to be engaged. Thus, you might say that brainstorming sessions, conference calls, and company strategy retreats are among your current methods of collaboration. You might even argue that the telephone and the office copy machine facilitate collaboration. Indeed, these may be effective methods for your company, and they may lead to desirable results, but what if the process of collaboration itself became a highly valued product?

Earlier in this book you were introduced to the Wiki, a social media tool that allows you to collaboratively create and edit content. Assume for a moment that the content you want to create is a best practices manual for a process or procedure that is a core part of your business. For the sake of this discussion, it really doesn't matter what that process or procedure is; it could be a guide to diagnosing problems in turbine engines or a how-to manual for call center managers. By establishing a company Wiki, you can enable your employee community to collaborate in ways that have never been possible before; they can create and maintain a dynamic productivity tool that is regularly altered and improved. You can leverage their collective wisdom for the benefit of your organization. In effect, the Wiki becomes not only a method of collaboration but a product of collaboration as well. (Keep in mind that the collective wisdom of coworkers will still need to be monitored and some basic rules of engagement will need to be established. But with the appointment of "community managers"—discussed later in this chapter—the benefits of this kind of collaboration may definitely trump the loss of control that most business managers will initially feel.)

Is it possible or even advisable to get your customers and prospective customers to engage in some form of collaboration that will benefit your company? The answer is yes, but the concept can be a bit counterintuitive. After all, imagine what kind of things your customers could say about you if you were to enable that conversation through one or more social media tools that allow them to interact with and influence one another. Talk about the good, the bad, and the ugly. Ask yourself this, however: Do you gain more by sponsoring or at least endorsing this kind of conversation than you do by running from it? As you read in Chapter 4, Arnold Kim's MacRumors.com attracts 4.4 million visitors a month, most of them eager to get the inside scoop on Apple products or exchange information, gossip, and user tips. If you were Apple Computer would you endorse this kind of community or would you look for an opportunity to participate in the conversation and perhaps influence this community?

Charles Schwab has taken an interesting approach to this opportunity by creating a customer advisory community with approximately 400 members who discuss issues, share opinions, and provide feedback that will influence Schwab's product offerings. In July 2008, Schwab extended an invitation to be considered for their customer advisory panel. In exchange for 5 to 15 minutes of mindshare per week, Schwab offered selected panel members the opportunity of "periodic rewards such as online gift certificates, occasional drawings for other gifts, and a few surprises along the way." The response from their customer base was overwhelming, and within a few days of launching the e-mail invitation, the following message was posted on the page to which those interested in being considered for participation were directed from a link in the e-mail:

> *Thank you very much for your interest in the Schwab Client Forum.*
>
> *Due to an overwhelming response to our invitation, the community is now full.*
>
> *We appreciate your time and encourage you to provide feedback on our products and services whenever talking to Schwab.*

It appears that Schwab has learned something significant about the power of engaging your customers through collaboration. Would something similar work for your business?

Quick Start Micro Strategy

Find at least two blogs in your area of interest or expertise. Read several of the more recent posts for each blog and join the conversation by offering your perspective and comments. Here's a quick way to find blogs that fit you the best. Go to Technorati (www.technorati.com) and enter a topic of interest in their "search the blogosphere" window. Notice the "authority" rating next to each title; this number represents the number of times other blogs link to this blog. Keep in mind that all blog authors tag their blogs with terms and phrases that highlight the topics covered in the blog. Take a close look at the tags on the two blogs you select to see how the blog author has positioned the blog.

Engagement through Education

Many of us have had the experience of standing helpless and hapless in front of a plumber as we try hard to understand what the problem is and what the solution will cost. At moments like these, you tend to appreciate an avuncular instructor. You feel better—though not always financially relieved—to get a quick plumbing lesson right there in your flooded basement. You realize that your plumber has expertise, and when that expertise is combined with an ability to effectively educate you about your home's plumbing, you have been engaged by the plumber's expertise.

One real-life plumber who has turned his expertise into content is "Big Tony the Plumber" (www.PlumbingVideoTutorials.com). A licensed master plumber, Big Tony joined YouTube in November 2007, and now has his own YouTube channel with approximately 5,000 channel views and nearly 200 subscribers. One of his videos has had over 35,000 views. If you visit his site, you'll see that he has archived a series of videos that address your everyday questions about plumbing. You can even submit questions to Big Tony. In converting his expertise into content, he has also managed to get Google ads to frame his videos. He's even generating product placement revenue; in one of his videos he praises the benefits of the Koehler Power Flush toilet as he demonstrates its operation. Clearly, Big Tony has discovered the importance of converting his expertise into content.

How often are you required to educate your internal or external audience, and do you look for opportunities to do so? Your ultimate social media strategy should leverage your expertise and/or the expertise of people within your company. You should consider leveraging the expertise of your customers as well. Several social media tools and applications can be used to engage people through education. Big Tony would certainly endorse YouTube (Chapter 30) as an ideal venue for posting educational videos that engage your audience and enhance your brand or image. With FlickR, the photo sharing program (Chapter 28), you can organize photos around themes, include captions, and enable discussion boards, producing a very effective and visual educational tool. Consider, also, that you can embed both of these applications into your web site.

Quick Start Micro Strategy

Start your own blog with the goal of educating people about something you know a lot about. There are several blog applications that make it easy for you to set up a blog in a matter of minutes. Of course, putting good content into

(continued)

(*continued*)

your blog is another challege. Get your blog started and work on the quality and relevance of your content. Chances are your readers will give you feedback that will help you improve the quality of your educational offering. If you want to start immediately, go to Typepad (www.typepad.com), and sign up for a free trial. You'll find other blogging tools and services listed in Chapter 25.

Now That's Entertainment

If kitchen blenders can find a starring role on YouTube, there's reason for just about any business to be optimistic about the prospects of entertaining your audience by finding those attributes of your product or aspects of your company that others might consider entertaining. Be cautious, however, because entertaining doesn't necessarily mean funny. In fact, humor can be dangerous terrain to traverse. What some people find funny is patently offensive to others. Christian Lander's blogsite, www.stuffwhitepeoplelike.com, is a fitting example of content that many people find hilarious and others inappropriate. Lander is building a brand around an audience who enjoys an opportunity to self-deprecate, but his brand of sarcasm and irreverence could prove disastrous to other product offerings.

Don't be afraid to experiment, but try to be interesting and compelling rather than running the risk of missing the mark with something that the majority of your audience will not find funny. This applies to internal audiences as much as it does external audiences. That said, don't avoid humor altogether, just respect it. It may be exactly what your strategy needs. Should you decide to have a Schwab-like customer advisory panel in place, you can test your content with them. It's the ideal place to test your content.

Quick Start Micro Strategy

Create your own YouTube account and upload a video. Go to www.YouTube .com, click on "sign up" and follow the directions. Your first uploaded video can be almost anything you want, depending upon your creativity and your equipment. You don't need expensive equipment. You may even be able to use your mobile phone to capture video. The goal here is to get some basic experience with YouTube. You can aspire to become as entertaining as the folks at Blendtec later, but get a good feel for how video sharing works first. As you sign up for your account, note that members are encouraged to "comment, rate, and make video responses to your favorite videos." Social media is indeed about enabling conversation.

Giving Up Some Control and Seeking Influence

Anyone in business today knows how important it is to establish and maintain control. Controlling your supply chain and controlling various aspects of operations management are crucial to achieving success and creating value. Controlling your organization's culture, the behavior and performance of your human resources, as well as the interaction with customers is also critical to your success. Finally, like most businesspeople, you probably believe that your integrated marketing communications need to be carefully planned, executed, and controlled. Embracing social media doesn't mean you should abandon everything you've learned about business, but it does require you to challenge a few of the practices you've probably been observing for years.

One of those practices involves the careful management and protection of your brand. A brand means something to your customers, and the relationship between that brand and those customers needs to be nurtured. What people say about your brand can make or break your business. This has been the case from the beginning of commerce. Prior to the advent of social media, however, a company had a certain degree of control over what people believed about its brand. As you have learned, however, social media is about enabling conversations. In fact that was the first of three rules of social media for business introduced in this book's opening chapter.

Rule One: Social media is all about enabling conversations among your audience or market.

The second rule addresses a natural consequence of enabling conversations: You cannot control those conversations. You can only influence them. This means that your audience really owns your brand. They will determine what your brand or your company means to them and the value it has in their lives. This applies to both customers and employees. You only think it is *your company* and *your brand*. This is difficult for some people in business to digest. It somehow doesn't seem fair that your customers or your employees would have the power to hijack and redefine who you are. That may be a pejorative notion, but they've always had this power. Social media simply enhances their power. But it also enhances yours.

Rule Two: You cannot control conversations with social media, but you can influence them.

To see how this works, we need to revisit our friends at TripAdvisor.com. You will recall from Chapter 4 that TripAdvisor.com aggregates hotel reviews from savvy travelers who care enough to share their hotel experiences with others. Through 2008, the site had archived more than 20 million reviews, offering perspectives on the biggest brands in the hotel industry as well as some of the smallest, most out-of-the-way destinations imaginable. Whether you are the Ritz Carlton in Manhattan or a bed and breakfast in Montana, chances are TripAdvisor.com has collected reviews on your property. If you want to see just how much impact social media can have on a brand, go to the TripAdvisor.com web site and look up one or two of your favorite and least favorite hotels. Better yet, plan your next business trip or getaway vacation using TripAdvisor.com. You'll quickly come to terms with the third rule of social media for business.

Rule Three: Influence is the bedrock on which all economically viable relationships are built.

Unofficially, there is a fourth rule that we mentioned briefly in Chapter 1, and that is that paranoia in business is a good, healthy thing. It can be purposeful and lead you toward better strategic decisions. A desire to know what your customers or employees are saying and doing is a good thing. A preoccupation with what your competitors are doing and what people are saying about what they are doing is advantageous. It can be argued that the entire $50 billion market research industry thrives on paranoia.

Quick Start Micro Strategy

Register at TripAdvisor.com (www.tripadvisor.com) and rate and comment on a hotel you stayed at recently. Use the site to select a hotel for your next trip. Get a feel for how the site uses ratings, comments, and collaborative filtering to provide the user with extremely valuable content. For another angle on how ratings and user comments can create valuable content for a specific audience, go to TobaccoReviews.com (www.tobaccoreviews.com). We're not advocating pipe smoking, but considering that the pipe-smoking fraternity is relatively small compared to other communities of interest, you'll be impressed with how this special interest community is making use of user-generated content.

Determining How Your Content Defines You

It's important to define your business in the context of content. In Chapter 4, you learned that accepting social media means that you have to see yourself as a publisher. Even Big Tony the Plumber has embraced his inner publisher, and though he isn't yet in the same league as Michael Buckley or Tom Dickson, he's clearly taken the time to define his business in the context of content. If you want to know the proper way to sweat copper pipes, Big Tony is there for you.

How do you determine content? Your content consists of:

- Products and services you promote on the Internet;
- Expertise you package, often to complement your products and services;
- Things you allow or encourage your audience to contribute; and
- Conversations about your content that you enable, influence, and archive.

At this point, take a quick inventory of your content. Make sure you distinguish between your current content and your potential content. Current content would include anything on your own web site, but it also includes things you may have placed on other web sites such as Craigslist or on social networking sites such as Facebook, MySpace, or LinkedIn. In Chapter 43, we go into some detail about how to assess the competitors in your space, but for the purpose of this exercise, you may want to Google a couple of your known competitors or search for them on social networking sites and see what kind of content is connected to their product offerings or brands. It will give you an initial idea of how the content game is being played in your neighborhood.

> ## Quick Start Micro Strategy
>
> Get daily intelligence on a competitor, an industry, or a topic of interest by creating a Google Alert account (www.google.com/alerts). The powerful Google search engines will monitor the Web for the words and phrases that you deem important to your interests and e-mail you with weekly, daily, or "as-it-happens" alerts. If you get your e-mail via your mobile phone, it's like having a research staff in your pocket.

Creating a Community around Your Content

Some recent studies suggest that company-built communities often fail because they focus more on the needs of the company than on the needs of the community. If you have built a better mousetrap, it's only natural that you'd like to tell the world why it's better. Building a brand-centric community around your mousetrap may not be a good idea, however, because it's unlikely that people can become excited about mousetraps. But are mousetraps really different from blenders? Didn't Blendtec, figuratively speaking, build a better mousetrap?

Let's take a closer look at this question. The compelling videos showing what their blender could do to everyday objects attracted people to Blendtec. If the "Will It Blend?" videos had merely shown the varieties of fruit smoothies you could make with their blender, it's unlikely that Blendtec would have received the degree of attention it has. People expect blenders to make smoothies; there's nothing unique or compelling about that. It's when you drop an object that you don't normally associate with a blender into the machine that your content becomes compelling. A golf ball or an iPhone being pulverized in a blender is both unique and compelling.

Imagine now that your new and improved mousetrap was such that it could capture mountain lions, reindeer, and other creatures significantly larger than the common mouse. Let's assume that your trap's spring-loaded clip is powerful enough to cut a Volkswagen in half. Suddenly you've entered the realm of compelling content, although good taste and a respect for wildlife may dictate that you not create a series of videos showing large animals being decapitated by your mousetrap. As for the Volkswagen, who wouldn't want to see that?

So if it's not about the blender or the mousetrap, how do you expect to sell your products? It's all about timing and association. Let's say you're shopping for a wedding present for friends and you've been told they need a blender. Does any brand come to mind? Perhaps you're at a poolside party and the host is creating margaritas in a blender that has seen better days. You might make a recommendation for a new machine that could make easy work of those pesky ice cubes. You get the idea.

Can You Compete with Millions of Communities?

In the early days of television, there were only a handful of channels, and not everyone had a television set. Today when you factor in cable and satellite providers, there are thousands of television channels, and very few households do not have a television. In fact, the typical American household has three televisions.

Television is an apt analogy for what's happening with social media and the proliferation of communities. More tools and applications—just like channels—means there will be more content than ever before. And with more ways to access that content, the chances of a new community succeeding become smaller. Making matters worse, television and the Internet are converging. The result is an explosion of content and millions of communities for people to be engaged by. Unless your content is "sticky" your community will not scale.

The Relationship between Sticky Content and a Strong Community

A strong community does not necessarily mean a large community. Many people make the mistake of measuring their success with social media by the number of visitors they attract to their web sites, the number of listeners of their podcasts, the number of views they get on YouTube, or the number of people registered as friends or contacts on their social networking sites. They may be measuring the wrong thing. A lot of traffic is exactly what you want if your goal is to make a living through advertising. But if you want to sell your product or service, you want the right kind of traffic. This means you need to think carefully about your audience and how they might behave differently from one community to another.

In your offline life, you probably belong to several groups or associations—communities. You may belong to a neighborhood association, the Rotary Club, an alumni association, and the American Marketing Association. Take a moment and consider just how many communities you belong to. It's unlikely that you are actively engaged with every community every day. With some of these communities, you may be a member in name only or perhaps just an occasional visitor at their meetings. There may be other communities in which you have a leadership role or a specific reason to be an active participant.

Quick Start Micro Strategy

Become a regular visitor to CNN.com (www.cnn.com), the *Wall Street Journal* online (www.wsj.com), National Public Radio's web site (www.npr.org), or another news media channel that you favor. Note how CNN offers blogs, podcasts, RSS feeds, and breaking news alerts. Sign up for one or two of these to get a better idea of how they work. (Other media sites do similar things.) Pay special attention to CNN's user-generated iReport feature that encourages citizen journalists to report the news from their own corner of the world. Whether or not you are a fan of CNN, take a good look at how they are creating and nurturing communities.

In considering what you get out of each community, you'll probably give some thought to the kind of content and the overall experience that each offers you and other members. Each community's stickiness is directly related to how valuable you find the content and the overall experience.

These same principles apply to online communities. Some people will belong in name only. Some people won't even be true members; they'll behave more like occasional visitors. Others will simply be a statistic, a brief one-time tourist who stopped by on their way to somewhere else. Can you turn a tourist stop into a thriving community? It all depends on how engaged your audience becomes with your community.

Five Behaviors That Make or Break a Community

In Chapter 4, we briefly looked at the five behaviors people will exhibit toward your content. They are as follows:

1. They will become active co-producers or content contributors, playing an active role in your community. If your community allows people to register and become members, they will become registered members with profiles. More than likely, they will make connections with other members and function as community leaders.

2. They will comment on content that you or someone else in the community has created, or they will post reviews, feedback, or links to other content that they believe your community might find helpful.

3. They will refer your content to friends or colleagues. This behavior has viral value, but keep in mind that the referral can be made from a positive or negative perspective.

4. They will simply view your content, not unlike tourists passing through town who stop at a local shop, browse a bit, and then get back on the road. You may never see them again, or perhaps they'll drop by again sometime.

5. They will ignore your content. This is analogous to passing through town and not even taking a moment to stop at your business.

Continuing with the analogy of the tourist, your goal should be to experiment with ways to get people to move into your community and become active members. Behaviors 1 and 2 are very desirable. Behaviors 3 and 4 are acceptable. Ironically, Behavior 5 will be the most common behavior people exhibit toward your content; that's okay because it's not about how many people you have in the community, it's about who you have in the community.

Five Kinds of Communities

Remember, communities succeed only if they meet the needs of their members. When we speak of a community, we are including not only those social networking applications mentioned in Chapter 3 and Chapter 26 but other applications such as YouTube and Twitter. Since most social media applications bring people together around common interests or needs, the concept of a community is fairly broad. Also keep in mind that many of these communities overlap or operate interdependently. As a matter of simplified convenience, here is a basic taxonomy of social media communities.

Metropolis Communities: MySpace and Facebook are examples of what we call Metropolis Communities. They have millions of members with diverse interests. Nearly anyone can join, even your business. That's right, your business can have its own Facebook page. People don't generally join Metropolis Communities because they're trying to find plumbers, blenders, or mousetraps. They join because they want to have conversations with friends, share moments of their lives, and make new connections.

Affinity Communities: Some people are passionate about National Public Radio (NPR). If you visit www.npr.org, you will see a lot of rich media that complements the content NPR puts on the air. In fact, NPR has altered their business model to accommodate the way their community wants to interact with their brand. You can simply be a visitor and download audio material from their program files. You can get more detailed story information than what was on the broadcast, including photos, videos, written pieces, and links to background information. You can also become a registered member of the community, create a profile, and actively engage other members. NPR .org is an example of an Affinity Community.

Intracompany Communities: Some companies have created their own internal social networks—Intracompany Communities—using applications such as Ning. Some of the more successful ones allow coworkers to view member profiles and make connections based on needed and demonstrated expertise. Internal Communities can also be created and connected through Wiki applications or content management systems such as Wordpress, Moveable Type, or Joomla. Intracompany Communities can be a boon to productivity, or they can be the equivalent of the message board in the breakroom, or they can be both.

Vertical Communities: These are industry or lifestyle-specific communities where people with specialized skills and expertise interact with one another. There can even be vertical niches within a Vertical Community. A community of international petroleum engineers would be an example of a Vertical Community. Most Vertical Communities arise from specialty publications already doing business in a vertical space.

Horizontal Communities: These communities are not industry specific but focus on functional groups or expertise that can cut across industries. People working in supply chain management or human resources, for example, are examples of functional groups that would comprise a Horizontal Community.

Quick Start Micro Strategy

If you haven't already done so, join a social network, complete your profile, and engage. Facebook and MySpace are just two possibilities. (See Chapter 24 for more.) For many people in business, LinkedIn is a popular social network (www.linkedin.com).

Establishing and Managing Your Community

Before you can manage an online community you have to choose applications or tools that meet your needs. That will be covered in subsequent chapters, but it's worth pausing for a moment now, in the context of a conversation about community, to consider a few things. You can create a community platform at little expense, or you can easily spend six figures. In determining what tools are right for you, ask yourself these questions:

- What functions and features do I want to have available to my community?
- What will be the expense of building and maintaining the community?
- Will I need internal human resources to build and maintain the community, or can I outsource the work?
- How long will it take to get the community launched?
- What are my competitors doing in this space, and what tools do they appear to be deploying?

We go into more detail on implementing your community in Chapter 45.

Tips for Managing Your Community

You may discover that your business strategy calls for creating more than one community. You may have an Intracompany Community and an Affinity Community. For each community that you create and evolve, keep the following things in mind:

- *Appoint a Community Manager.* Community managers function much like a good host at a party. They are there to welcome people as they come in the door. They introduce them to others at the party and facilitate good conversations among the guests. They also make sure that the event runs smoothly. Depending on the kind of community you create, your community manager can be a member of your company or someone on the outside, even a customer. As your community grows, you may want to consider having more than one community manager.
- *Identify Community Evangelists.* These are the folks who promote your community. They tell others where the party is at, if you will. Cultivating a relationship with community evangelists is one of the most important things you can do for your community. In some cases, you will want to screen and appoint community evangelists, articulating their role and helping them understand your strategic objectives for the community.

You may discover that community evangelists appoint themselves without a formal invitation or directive from you. If you're creating an Intracompany Community, you'll have more control (there's that word again) over what your evangelists do. However, external communities may develop organically and you will not have control—only influence. You get the idea.

- *Align Your Content with Audience Needs.* Remember that you are trying to build a community around your content. Think of your content like you would the features of a new product. Features have benefits. People buy or adopt something because of its benefits, not its features. In other words, they buy on the basis of what a product does for them rather than what it is. Benefits are recognized in the context of needs.

- *Encourage User-Generated Content.* Your community will not really be a community without content contributions from its members. These contributions will be different for each community. If you'll recall your visit to TripAdvisors.com, you may have noted that members of the community can post photos of the hotels they stay in. This is an excellent example of user-generated content.

Expert Insight

Leah Culver, cofounder, Pownce

Leah Culver

[On December 15, 2007, Pownce notified its members that it was shutting down. These excerpts were deliberatively added here for several reasons. Pownce had a really good product offering that competed directly with Twitter. Leah had many really excellent social media and business insights. And, the fact that since the time Leah was interviewed for the book they no longer exist exemplifies the dynamic nature of social media and the technologies that are supporting it.]

. . . So I'm one of the founders of Pownce and I'm actually a software developer. A little bit about my background is that I have a Computer Science degree from the University of Minnesota and I now live in San Francisco where I work on Pownce. . . .

. . . It's a social networking web site and it's for sending messages to your friends. And when we say messages we mean that you can also send links, files, and events; so you can send a lot of media and share things with your group of friends. . . .

. . . And if you have a Pro Account you can send even bigger files, so you can share lots of different stuff with the people you care about. . . .

. . . We have an icon up and we're working on more mobile ways to take photos off of our site and send them out. So that's one of the things that we're definitely interested in. . . .

. . . We actually have a web site that you can access from any type of computer, or we also have a mobile web site. So if you're on, like a BlackBerry or, like a Nokia phone, you can go to our mobile site. We also have an iPhone application which you can get from the iPhone Apps store; and we also have a desktop app which you can download and it works on Windows, Mac, and Linux. . . .

. . . So [there are] lots of different ways you can communicate and get access to messages and send new messages. . . .

. . . We have an API that is a resource for programmers, other developers, to build things on top of Pownce. So, for example, someone has written a WordPress plug-in. If you use that plug-in it will post all of your Pownce posts to WordPress. So developers can get super-creative with what they want to create for republishing or having ways to publish back to Pownce. So it's kind of cool. There's actually a wide variety of things that you can do. . . .

. . . It's really important to keep on the community site. So there is a community and you have your group of friends. It's important that people are able to express themselves the way that they want to. Feedback means a lot to us, both inputs and outputs at feedback. So we look both at what people are saying and then what they are actually doing on the site. . . .

. . . It's a huge, wide range of people. I don't know that there is actually one particular type of people, but I'm pretty split . . . [between] some in the United States and people abroad, so it's really a wide variety of people. . . .

. . . So it's definitely kind of fun to see those communities and interact with them, and we are working in the future toward making things easier for them and really encouraging more communities abroad, as well. . . .

. . . People have friends in all sorts of different countries and the online community is very global. So we'd love to support that at Pownce. . . .

. . . Usually people will either send messages or links, or a lot of photos or YouTube videos. So if you find, like for some typical use cases, you know, you find a funny YouTube video and you want to share that with your friends. The typical way most people have done that is by e-mail and IM. E-mail can feel a little bit heavy and bland and IM is, kind of, real time. The other person has to actually be there for it to work.

So the nice thing about Pownce is that you can just post it on Pownce, it will get sent out to your group of friends, and they can go back and leave comments on it, so it's pretty cool.

(continued)

(*continued*)

On some of the weirder use cases, we've had everything from marriage proposals to YouTube people posting about a project for making bacon or keeping people updated on the status of a bacon-making web site. So it's a pretty wide range. . . .

. . . I love the word "freemium." But we do have paid accounts, so you can upgrade your account and with the upgrade you get to design a custom theme. You get to see no ads on the entire site and you get to upload larger files. You need a little badge next to your photo. It's only $20 a year, so we have quite a number of users that have paid accounts.

We're experimenting with different types of advertising on the site, as well. . . .

. . . With the regular accounts, not paid accounts, pretty much you have the full functionality of the site, but the paid account just adds a little extra for people who use Pownce a lot. . . .

. . . I agree that there are a large number of these social media sites and I think it's just up to the person and what they like to do. So trying them out really is the right idea. See what the features are like and usually you'll find a couple that stick. . . .

. . . I encourage anyone out there to check it out and try it out. Add a couple people as friends and see how it goes. . . .

. . . There's been a couple of small Web firms that use it internally to send files back and forth. So if someone is working on an illustration or document, or something, they can just send it to someone else to check it out. That's pretty popular for smaller businesses. And I am sure that there can be applications in the future for businesses using it either for internal communication, or to communicate with customers. We are seeing a little bit of that on the site right now. . . .

. . . So we have sets where you can. It's sort of like an e-mail list where you can choose a group of people to send something to . . . it seems to work for groups where people can opt in. It's more like "create and click" and you can send it out to them. We are thinking about doing groups in the future, but it's just been put on hold a little bit right now. . . .

. . . Yeah, we definitely do that. We do that internally here at Pownce. But like with my group of people that work at Pownce, and I'll send out something to them that's work-related, and we also show who's received each message. So you can see on the side when you go to the main page for the message, you can see who else has received it. So you know exactly who's getting it and who's received it, and seeing your replies for that. Which is really nice. . . .

. . . You can go to Pownce.com and you just enter into the basic info about yourself. Then you can add a bunch of friends. So you can import your friends from other social networks. So say if you use Facebook you can go through a step that finds out which of your friends on FaceBook are already using Pownce and you can use them as friends. So you can start off with a couple of friends, and then you can also invite [other] people.

So you can send messages out to your other friends and say, "Hey, try this out." And then you have a couple of people and you start getting messages and you can start sending messages right away. So it's pretty simple to get started. . . .

. . . Yeah, so when you create your profile, you can have your own profile image; like your avatar, your little icon with your photo. And you can put in a little bit of info about yourself. As soon as you start sending messages, if you send them publically they'll be available on your page. So Pownce.com/username; and anybody can see that public page and anything that you sent publically will be viewable there. So if you want to post photos, if you want to post videos; anybody can go and see those. . . .

. . . It's a little bit like a blog and a little bit like e-mail. So it's kind of a weird mix of the two. So you do have, kind of, a public place where you can just kind of display things, but you also have a method for sending the same things to other people. . . .

. . . We're actually working on a redesign right now of the web site, to make things a little bit simpler. You can see more messages per page and there's also a couple new features I can't talk about, but they're to encourage more conversation and more sharing on the site. . . .

To listen to or read the entire Executive Conversation with Leah Culver, go to www .theSocialMediaBible.com.

Expert Insight

Marc Canter, CEO, Broadband Mechanics, www.broadbandmechanics.com

. . . I'm the CEO of a company called Broadband Mechanics. The product is for the people that [00:45.0] which is the White Label Social Networking platform. And we use it to build out social networks for brands like Bell Canada, or the Sacramento Kings, and untold others I cannot tell you about right now because I'd have to kill you.

I have been in the business for about 25 years. I started a company called Marcomind that became Macromedia, so I'm a

Marc Canter

(continued)

(*continued*)

toolsmith by trade, and watched the blogging world and the world of what I call the "open mesh" evolve over the past few years; open social networking, and structured content, and digital wide style aggregation.

It all leads to saying basically, "open" is the new black. . . .

. . . I mean, certainly in the world of expression and blogging that is kind of obvious. But the other thing is where the user's data, their profile record, their social graph, should be owned by them. We shouldn't be locked inside of Facebook or MySpace. So we are starting to see the standard, like OpenID, and a new effort from Google called "OpenSocial" which they are using to build lots of great solutions.

All these are standards that are emergent. We are even seeing Microsoft opening up, believe it or not! . . .

. . . Again, I'm a toolsmith and we've been trying to build some tools to help solve that. We call one of them a "persona editor," which helps to stay on top of managing all of your different personae.

The other thing is we are seeing a big trend going from giant, centralized social networks, these kinds of horizontal networks, to tens of thousands of niche vertical networks. Right? And a typical person will be in a membership of one or two horizontal networks, or maybe even 5 or 10 niche networks. So whether that's the school you go to, or the after-school activities of you dealing with your friends and kids, the affinities like Reggae or chocolates.

So the trick here is to have a world, have the blueprint and a world within, that can practically adapt to the fact that Microsoft is going to do live mesh and Google is going to do this, and Yahoo! is going to have their own thing, and after a while we have to leave some crumbs on the table for a smaller-software guy. We want to get involved and we want to mesh into this huge world, and perhaps build our own ecosystem. . . .

. . . And we see more and more consolidation over the years. I mean, this is where us "old-timers" can tell you, "Back in the 1980s, when it was between Microsoft and Apple, right?"

That world has changed now. So, along the way the other thing we've seen the rise of is "international," and maybe the governments of Singapore or Dubai want to do some of this stuff and they do not want to use Yahoo! or Google, right! And maybe you see innovation coming out of Russia. I mean, this is no longer just a game that is played off of Silicon Valley. . . .

. . . This is totally the world we are going into. Even at this point, Facebook is two-thirds international. . . . So I think we are going to see more and more.

Oh, by the way, needless to say the Russian government is tightly coupled to these cyber terrorists, because when they were invading Georgia, sure enough, it's also accompanied by a cyber attack. Right? So we are starting to see the realities of technology and politics, virtual economics. When the oil industry is attacked and they claim that they are making too much money, they can turn and say, "Well, look at the software business. They make even higher margins than we do." As if that matters. Right? This is somehow supposed to deflect the attention.

You know, we are finding the technology to be intrinsic and imbedded everywhere. It's no longer "You can keep your head in the sand." And so, the issues of all software being about people and open standards, if users want to control the rights to this general notion of social media, as we move forward it will affect everything. . . .

. . . You know, when we started our company right in the beginning of 1984 it was right when the Macintosh came out. And we were convinced that by 1990 (that was the "the big year," you know) everybody would have video, audio, and computers would be multimedia and we were right!!!! [Only] we were off by 10 years. . . .

. . . And then we put out this tool, and it was going to do animated advertising and all this great interactive stuff; and we were off by 16 years!

When I saw the Web first and it was simple HTML graphics, I felt as if we were going backwards, because we did have graphics and video on our screens in the early 1990s. They were coming over the wire; they were coming off of a CD-Rom. And it took about 10 or 15 years for the world to catch up.

Just now, with Flickr and YouTube, we now have full media on our machines, right? And so we are seeing a number of different factors. One of them I call "persistent content." So, like the BBC or NPR, are going to put up all of this content into the Clouds and it's going to be there, available, full-time. And we've got Who-loo and we've got iTunes, and it's all there and we are competing in all this knowledge and it's sitting there in the Clouds waiting for us.

So whole new kinds of applications and services will be born that rely on that stuff, and then to be able to rely on storage and computing grids and all this incredible stuff that, even five years ago, was only a dream and a glimmer in our eyes.

So if we jump forward four or five years in a natural helix, of course there will still be "normal" people who still just use e-mail. You know, it takes a long time for stuff to disseminate through society. . . .

. . . People come up to me and say, "Oh, you helped me start my career." . . .

. . . And so you know, now I kind of have a little of the "Orson Wells Syndrome." You know, it's like many people never exceed past first "successes." You know, some people have a chip on their shoulder, and I have a large log! So I carry around this weight and so it's hard for me to think small. So we're working on a book called, *How to Build the Open Mesh*. It's kind of a treatise, or road map, for how people can work together and cooperate. So whenever you see a bunch of people doing the same thing, then that's a good mesh standard. Right?

(*continued*)

(*continued*)

Here's an example. How to create a dashboard, a reusable user, and interchange objects [so] we can mix and match and choose. Whose blogging tool do you want to use? Which IM client? Twitter or FriendFeed? Or you can configure your environment on the fly. I believe that's where we will be in about 10 or 15 years. So the trick is how to get them [from] "here" to "there" . . .

. . . So currently it is offered as a White Label, which means that when we sell it to marketers and brand and ad agencies, and stuff like that, the company site is www.broadbandmechanics.com. The demo site is www.peopleaggregator.org. Oh, excuse me; dot.org is where the source code is. We give away the first code for nonprofits. And also, my blog is www.marc.blogs.it. Marc blogs it! . . .

. . . The People Aggregator is the social networking platform. So if you go look at a site called www.onone.com or www.bellvideostore.ca or www.mykingsworld.com, . . . Now let me see what else. www.gtchannel.com, www.itrend.com. They're all networks. These are all built with our platform, so we sell both the license, the source code, or we actually run it as a software service model, so anybody who wants to get into the social network and visit us or add social features into their existing site, can use our platform.

So with Bell Canada, they had a movie downloading site and they had already built out the basic catalogue and transactions, and so on, but we added social features into their movie downloading site. So now you can make comments and reviews and rate things and do tagging, and declare yourself a fan of a movie. And that's all code that's coming off of our server if the Bell Canada movie downloading site is coming off of their server. . . .

. . . So Bell Canada is www.bellvideostore.ca. Another is a large media company called Radio One, so they have a site called www.radio-one.com. And they have a bunch of sister sites, because we also have an aggregation engine in the CMS publishing system. So, we have a bunch of sister sites that we also built for them.

GT Channel is a great kind of niche network for car enthusiasts, people who are into drifting. Then there is what we call a Meta Network, called www.socialworld.com. These are for people who put on events, who produce concerts, and so they can get their own network and we built it for our customer called Auctiva. They sell tickets, and do ticketing online. . . .

. . . They came to us and we built them out a meta-network. What that means is that they'll go to a campus, let's say the University of Texas or really anywhere, and they'll create one whole meta-network for the campus. And they, like the frat boys come along, or like the DJs, or even, like the school itself, or, you know, some other kind of party-promotion company. And each of those companies can get their Network. And Auctiva will host and run the whole thing for them. So in our case we built the thing to spec for Auctiva and then they built it themselves. . . .

. . . That is all available through us. And so by a little consulting and up-front help we are a boutique shop and we have developers around the world; in India, Italy, Germany, and New Zealand. . . .

. . . For over two years now, we had a feature called OpenId. That allows you to log in and have a simple signoff. We have also been importing both Flickr and Delicious into the social network.

Now the hot new feature for this summer is the notion of importing whole social graphs from these networks. So both MySpace, FaceBook and Google have made this functionality possible. And in the fall we will be updating what we have given to Bell Canada and some other sites that we are still working on.

They will be featuring these imports from the social network. And when you come in you can bring a whole host of, not only just your profile record, but your list of friends and your photographs and your music and your interests. All this information from them will be automatically moved over from one social network into ours. . . .

. . . That's again a part of the trend with this mesh and that the users have been demanding this stuff, yet three or four years ago I was one of the only guys who was asking for it. But nowadays it is a pretty standard feature that everyone is providing. It has been about a year since Facebook came out with their platform and then that influenced MySpace to do this, and pressured Google to do that, and Microsoft. And so they are all trying to "Keep up with the Jones'" . . .

To listen to or read the entire Executive Conversation with Marc Canter, go to www.theSocialMediaBible.com.

Conclusion

In this chapter, we discussed how the four pillars of social media strategy apply to your business. We also focused on how your business can be viewed in the context of content and how that content drives the creation and evolution of a community. This is important background information for the next chapter where you'll be shown how to conduct a social media SWOT analysis.

Credits

Expert Insights Were Provided By:

Leah Culver, Cofounder, Pownce.

Marc Canter, CEO, Broadband Mechanics, www.broadbandmechanics.com.

CHAPTER 40

Your Social Media SWOT Analysis

This chapter enables you to:

- Complete and evaluate your Social Media Awareness Index.
- Complete and evaluate your Social Media Tool Scorecard from Part II of the book.
- Complete a social media SWOT analysis.
- Prepare to experiment with social media micro strategies.

SWOT is an acronym for Strengths, Weaknesses, Opportunities, and Threats. A social media SWOT analysis for your organization is a critical next step as you prepare to implement strategies that can impact your business success. In previous chapters, you were asked to complete a group of exercises to prepare you to do this SWOT analysis. Those exercises were designed to introduce you to tools and applications in the social media ecosystem. Many of the chapters in Part I of this book helped give you a better feel for the historical and tactical aspects of each category. Hopefully, you finished each chapter with a good sense of "what's in it for you" and a basic understanding of how some of these tools can be used in your business. Now we begin the process of weaving what you've learned into a meaningful strategy.

Your Social Media Awareness Index

In Chapter 2, you were introduced to the 15 categories of the Social Media Ecosystem and provided with a list of tools and applications from each category. You were then asked to complete a brief exercise for each category by checking those tools or applications you were *familiar with* and circling

Table 40.1   The Social Media Awareness Index

In total how many tools did you place a check next to? (Familiar with)   ——

In total how many tools did you circle? (Used)   ——

Indicate how many checks and circles you had in each category:

Category Title	Checks (Familiar With)	Circles (Have Used)
Social networking	_____	_____
Publish	_____	_____
Photo	_____	_____
Audio	_____	_____
Video	_____	_____
Microblogging	_____	_____
Livecasting	_____	_____
Virtual Worlds	_____	_____
Gaming	_____	_____
Productivity applications	_____	_____
Aggregator	_____	_____
RSS	_____	_____
Search	_____	_____
Mobile	_____	_____
Interpersonal	_____	_____

those you have actually *used*. If you did not take the time to complete these exercises earlier, this would be an excellent time to do so. You may also want to have members of your organization complete the exercises as well. For your convenience, you can download the exercises at www.theSocialMedia Bible.com.

As part of the analysis you will do in this chapter, please record your scores in the space provided in Table 40.1.

As you review the list in Table 40.1, you may see a pattern emerge. If you have asked other members of your organization to complete this exercise, take a moment and compare results. Be sure and determine whether your company's familiarity and use of these tools has been internal or external. You may also want to add another dimension to this exercise by assessing whether familiarity and use is connected to work or personal experience. It will not be at all unusual to discover you have people in your company with considerable experience using some of these tools in their personal lives but haven't considered—or been directed—to use them as part of a business strategy.

Your Tool Scorecards from Part II

In Part II, you were presented with brief profiles of over 100 applications and tools and were asked to complete a scorecard for each category of tools. If you didn't complete these exercises earlier, please do so now. This too is an important part of developing a strategic plan for your business. Remember, the exercise is not designed to overwhelm you with tools and applications; rather, you'll want to reflect your gut instincts about the potential value of each tool to your organization. You can only do this if you've read the brief profiles of each tool and perhaps even visited the tool's web site.

Give serious thought to having members of your organization complete the exercises as well. For your convenience, you can download the exercises at www.theSocialMediaBible.com. You will also find a tutorial there on how to complete this exercise. Recall that you were asked to rate the potential value of each tool following these instructions:

Using the 5-point (0 to 4) scale below, rate each tool in this chapter on the basis of how valuable it *might be* to the internal and external operations of your company. Make notes about which tools appeal to you the most.

4 = Extremely Valuable

3 = Very Valuable

2 = Somewhat Valuable

1 = Not Very Valuable

0 = No Value

As part of the analysis you will do in this chapter, please record up to three tools in each category to which you assign the highest scores in Table 40.2. Only record them if you assigned a score of 2 or higher, and be sure and note the score for each.

Once again, look for patterns, especially if you have asked other members of your organization to complete this exercise. As part of your SWOT analysis, you'll want to explore why people in your company feel that certain tools would be valuable to your social media strategy. Through their perspective, you may discover opportunities you didn't know you know you had.

Table 40.2   Social Media Tool Scorecard

Category Title	Application or Tool (List Separately)	4	3	2
Social networking	1. _____			
	2. _____			
	3. _____			
Publish	1. _____			
	2. _____			
	3. _____			
Photo	1. _____			
	2. _____			
	3. _____			
Audio	1. _____			
	2. _____			
	3. _____			
Video	1. _____			
	2. _____			
	3. _____			
Microblogging	1. _____			
	2. _____			
	3. _____			
Livecasting	1. _____			
	2. _____			
	3. _____			
Virtual worlds	1. _____			
	2. _____			
	3. _____			
Gaming	1. _____			
	2. _____			
	3. _____			

Productivity applications	1. _____
	2. _____
	3. _____
Aggregator	1. _____
	2. _____
	3. _____
RSS	1. _____
	2. _____
	3. _____
Search	1. _____
	2. _____
	3. _____
Mobile	1. _____
	2. _____
	3. _____
Interpersonal	1. _____
	2. _____
	3. _____

Initiating the SWOT Analysis

This exercise can be completed as a team. The goal is to audit your current organization in the context of SWOT. Identifying key internal and external issues allows you to more carefully consider and then incorporate them into strategic objectives.

Strengths and Weaknesses

Strengths and weaknesses are internal conditions, factors, or attributes. Your recognized expertise in your market space, for example, would be a definite strength. Not having a method for employees to collaborate would be a weakness.

Answer as many questions as you can, noting whether your response constitutes a strength or a weakness:

- What does your company do well? (Note: This question is not narrowly focused on social media. It's a question about your company's value proposition to its customers and your execution and delivery on that value proposition.)
- What does it not do well?
- In what ways does your company use technology to its advantage? In what ways could the use of technology be improved? (Note: Technology as referenced in this question is information technology in general. How computer literate and software savvy are you, and how are these skills currently being used?)
- How familiar and agile are your employees with technology? If there is a gap between those who use technology effectively and those who don't, what might explain the gap?
- Are there people at your company who already use social media applications in their personal lives? If you're not sure about this, how difficult will it be to find out?
- Are people at your company using social media tools and applications to do their jobs? If so, did management introduce these tools or was their adoption and use more casual and organic?
- In what ways do you currently communicate with your employees?
- Does your company encourage and facilitate collaboration among employees? If so, how?
- What role does continuing education and training play inside your company?
- Are the managers, owners, or others in your business effective trainers and teachers? How often do they train or teach? What methods do they use?
- Would you characterize your company as a fun place to work? On a 1 to 10 scale, with 10 being the highest score, what would you say is your company's Fun Quotient (FQ)?
- What constitutes entertainment at your company?
- Would you characterize your company as a creative company? On a 1 to 10 scale, with 10 being the highest score, what would you say is your company's overall creative score?
- Are there people or groups within your organization who would rank especially high on the creative scale, say a 9 or 10? Do your most creative people tend to work in the same department or area?
- Are you able to describe your business in the context of its content? Please explain.

- What is your personal expertise? Do you believe that expertise is understood and recognized within your organization? What about the expertise of others at your company?

- How many social media tools were you familiar with when you completed the Social Media Awareness exercise? How does this compare to others at your company?

- How many social media tools listed in the Social Media Awareness exercise have you used or do you currently use? How does this compare to others at your company?

- Are you using social media tools for business or personal reasons? How does this compare with others at your company?

- With respect to internal value, how many social media tools did your rate as a 3 or 4 on the Tool Scorecard Chart in this chapter? How does this compare with others at your company?

Opportunities and Threats

Opportunities and threats are external conditions, factors, or attributes. Let's say you run a bicycle messenger service in Manhattan and rely upon cell phones to stay in touch with your couriers. A new cell phone feature that puts a GPS tracking device into each phone would be an opportunity for your company because you could track all of your couriers on your computer. This could greatly improve efficiency and productivity. If, on the other hand, you are a manufacturer of hand-held GPS devices, this new cell phone application constitutes a threat to your business.

Answer as many questions as you can, noting whether your response constitutes a strength or a weakness:

- What do your customers value most about your company? How do you know this? Do you have a way of measuring it?

- What do your customers value the least about your company? How do you know this? Do you have a way of measuring it?

- How familiar and agile are your customers with technology? If there is a gap between those who use technology effectively and those who don't, what might explain the gap?

- Do you have customers who already use social media applications in their personal lives? If you're not sure about this, how difficult will it be to find out?

- Do you have customers who use social media tools and applications to do their jobs?

- In what ways do you currently communicate with your customers? How effective is this communication? Do you have a way of measuring it?
- What lifestyle trends or factors are affecting your customers?
- Do you seek feedback from your customers? If so, how?
- Do you collaborate with your customers? If so, how?
- What factors influence your customers' decisions to do business with you?
- Do your customers rely on your company to educate them about things? What kind of things? How are you currently doing this?
- How important do you believe it is to educate your customers?
- Complete this sentence: Our customers love us because . . .
- Complete this sentence: Our customers dislike us because . . .
- Complete this sentence: Our customers like one of our competitors better because . . .
- What do your competitors do better than you do?
- Do your customers rely upon your expertise as part of their business relationship with you? Do you believe that your expertise is sufficient to meet their needs? How are they currently getting access to that expertise? What about access to the expertise of others at your company?
- How do you think your customers view your competitors with respect to expertise?
- Does any part of your business relationship with your customer depend upon your ability to help them have a good time or enjoy their experience with your product or service?

Completing the SWOT Analysis

The social media SWOT analysis questions just presented to you can be handled in different ways. You can read and ponder them by yourself. You will likely know with some certainty the answers to many of the questions, and for some you may have to speculate. If you want to take your analysis to another level, you can involve your colleagues and even your customers. You can survey them. You can conduct or commission on online focus group. Or you can create one or more types of forums to aggregate their feedback. Whatever you choose, your goal should be to organize the responses in a way that you can more effectively analyze them.

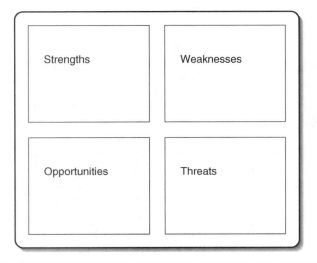

FIGURE 40.1 SWOT Analysis

The traditional SWOT analysis relies on a quadrant figure similar the one in Figure 40.1. By placing responses in each of the quadrants, you begin to create a visual picture of your current situation. One trick is to use a flip chart with the quadrant chart in place and different colored dots to represent the strengths, weaknesses, opportunities, and threats. You can then number and record your responses individually in a spreadsheet or other document. You can also do the same thing using a collaborative online tool such as Adobe Connect and a drawing application.

It's advisable to write a brief Executive Summary that puts your SWOT analysis into a format that you and others in your organization can use as you begin to create and implement strategies. You can see samples of Executive Summaries at www.theSocialMediaBible.com.

Expert Insight

Kyle Ford, director of product marketing, Ning, www.ning.com

. . . Ning launched publically in October, 2005, and I came on board a few months after launch. I was one of the first two product managers. Before that, I was at *Yahoo! T.V. Movies*. I am actually based in Los Angeles so I came here

(continued)

(continued)

Kyle Ford

because I have an entertainment background and I was acting in movies for about a year and a half. And before that for several years, I was at Fox Broadcasting Company doing many of the *Primetime* show's television sites. . . .

. . . So Ning is (in the shortest way to describe it) basically your own social network for anything. So without being any sort of a computer-nerd and not having done any programming, you can go to Ning.com and in a matter of a couple of minutes create your own social networks. By that, I do not mean pages on a MySpace or a FaceBook, but literally your own FaceBook or MySpace in its entirety. So you can use it for sports teams, church, families, if you have an interest in being a brand, if you have a band. Any use you can think of for a social network, you can have it up and running in just a matter of minutes. You can just use "drag-and-drop" to add features, and pick a style and you are ready to go.

We host it and deal with all the fairly scary stuff like security and things like that, so all you will need to worry about is bringing your ideas to the table and you can go from there. And the best part is that it is free. And you can extend it a little bit more with some things you may want to insert, but by default it is actually comparable with Google's AdSense ads that are free to the end-user. . . .

. . . So we certainly have nothing against FaceBook, I use Facebook all the time. But when I have an organization or some sort of property that I want to "blow out" social media-wise, FaceBook groups can be fairly limiting. There are only a certain amount of things that you can do. We will see many people that will have a fairly successful online presence on FaceBook or a group on a MySpace-page. But when they actually create their own online identities, they will come to us and we say, "Yes, you can add photo-sharing, your calendars, your music; any kind of ingredient you want to scoop on your tray, you can do that."

And then, of course, we have tentacles going back to the other sites, too. You can also, then, go back to where you started and you can promote your social network on FaceBook or MySpace *through* us with different embedables. So certainly there are people who will want to be everywhere, but we have made everything centralized on your own network. If you use one of our premium services, you could be on your own domain, too. So you are completely in your own hands and from there you can extend out to other social media properties to spread your word. . . .

. . . So what we have is full functionality, free for everyone. The only things we charge for are our premium services are: Five bucks a month to actually create your own domain name. So you get rid of the "your-name.com to your-domain.com."

And then for $20 a month you can strip out our Google Ads altogether and buy out your site's full inventory and run as many ads that you want to do. So there is not anything extra, it is literally just $20 and you can do whatever you want, ad-wise.

Then we have another service which is currently $8 a month, which is us removing any powered-by-name branding so you do not have any of this, "Bob created this network on me." So you can just take it out and completely have it be your own world. So, altogether for $32 a month you can have your own piece of the social network, which you own. . . .

. . . One of the cool things about it, too, is on top of how relatively inexpensive it is to do that; we are also constantly rolling in new features every two to three weeks. So if you want a certain feature, the odds are that it will come out in the next wave, as long as you are on what we call our Centralized Code, which is what most people are. As soon as we push out new updates, you automatically will get these new features as well.

We also have what separates us even a little bit more from some other sites. If you are a developer and you want to go completely independent and actually change the source code of your network, we give out the source code for the entire PHP side of the product, which are the social network products.

So if you request this and you are a developer, you can actually jump off the "automatic-update" train and completely change your Code so you can . . . essentially we are giving you your own network and you can do whatever you want to do with it. . . .

. . . We try to do "Grandma's Sewing Circle" to anything that might compliment it. The designer who is comfortable with the widest amount of steps can go in and use this stuff and still be "specialized." And like you said, the PHP experts can go in and if they want to decentralize it, they can do whatever they want. . . .

. . . So the built-in features we have (and I think we have up to 10 of each on the homepage and currently one of each on the Member Profile pages) are Free-Form Podcasts. These are Podcasts that can accept a feed from anywhere and pull in podcasts from elsewhere, and also free HTML, so you can use it to add text or content into it.

If you are a beginner and you do not know HTML, you can drop HTML or you can drop in embedables from elsewhere. And then we are about two weeks away from rolling out full support for OpenSocial, which is Google's open-application program; where supported sites (what they call "containers") enable OpenSocial applications to run on them. So there will be a whole host of third-party "apps" that you will be able to add to your social network.

So if we offer something, the odds are that you will be able to browse our OpenSocial gallery and with just one click, add that view to your page and that will add film quality to your functionality, and what not. . . .

(continued)

(continued)

. . . When we were approached and asked about this late last year, we supported it and in a very "alpha" fashion. And it sat there for a while and was stagnant, frankly. So what we are trying to do is; we are up against our very recent specs and doing some real deep integration that will be very simple for our members to add into their own pages. It is going to be a very innovative part of Ning. The current release date for that is coming up very soon. . . .

. . . OpenSocial is, right now, essentially limited to profile pages on the network because in most services like MySpace or Hi5 . . . you, as the member, *only* control your profile page. But we are a little different in that if you were the creator of the network, you also have access to the main page, too. So you have access to the full social networks and we are working to have a search engine from profile pages also to the main page of the networks. So at that point, it becomes a feature on top of our standard features, which should be very exciting. . . .

. . . Our demographics are everywhere. We do have some older users, which are unlike those from something like a MySpace in which users are fairly young. We do have many social networks with people who have created company intra-nets, or like I have said, church groups or family groups.

We do have people that have come from the MySpace and FaceBook world, but we also have people who are completely new to social networking. Now that they see a reason to be included in a social network (if before they just want to connect with friends or with their kids soccer team) they might be more apt to use it. So we see people from small groups doing stuff, all the way up to huge recording artists.

Like we have 50Cent using us! And many big bands that set up their social networking presence with us. Really, I guess the short answer is that it is all over the place and that is exciting to us. Every day we see social networks for some niche groups we would never have imagined.

Currently we are adding about 2,000 new networks a day so it is growing very quickly. We just broke 450,000 networks that are running on the platform now. So it has been growing extremely fast. . . .

. . . Our CEO at Ning said she always envisioned millions of social networks. Eventually everyone could have their own social network. One of the things we worked through, honestly, is that if people get their social networking for free why would they sign up for one more network? Since they are all tied together with the Ning ID and the e-mail login that we have, you can join one or you can join all of them without having to sign up again. We certainly see the value of having different personae in different scenarios. As you do in real life, you may want to share different media with your soccer team than you do with your 50Cent fan base, than you do with your church groups, and so we allow you to be a member of all the different communities; but at the end of day they are sharing the same login. So it is convenient for the users. . . .

. . . So when you sign on, you have a base profile that goes across all of them grouped by sex, location, etc.; you can omit things if you want privacy. But within each network, you have your own set of profile questions, so you have different photos and impressions and persona on different networks, but they are all sharing the same system. . . .

. . . We are counterpoint/complimentary to each of them now. Signing up on one of those networks combines with joining our world, and that is great. Using Ning is essentially creating your own world. We certainly have lots of viral tools going in and out to different services; and you can pull in all your photos from Flickr with just a couple of clicks in Ning, and we can create SpaceBook apps from your Ning media players, like NewsBreak.

With a couple of clicks, it can be added onto your page and, like I said, all sorts of content and embeddables put on MySpace. We are all about spreading your brand around and maintaining your brand in one place, and exporting it all over. . . .

. . . My goal was that my grandmother could do it (who could barely turn a computer on) and could do it in a minute or less. And so, yes, if you go to Ning .com there are just a couple of sign-up fields and then you type in your network and hit "launch" and you are set. It is about as easy as it can get. . . .

. . . I think social networking can be demonized a lot. Certainly when you hear the MySpace horror stories of creeps posting photos of themselves that they should not be doing. I think Ning is different because you are not necessarily joining Ning, you are typically joining a [subset] of Ning so the audience for someone like 50Cent is going to be different than something on the tamer side.

Within there are certainly quite a few problems to control, so if you wanted to create a safe network for your family, you can certainly do so and you can make it private so it can only be accessed by invitation. You can moderate photos and videos before they appear, you can ban someone from a public network who is being troublesome. There are all sorts of controls that you have. I think Ning is interesting in that it can very often serve, if it's someone's first web site, experience and serve in other ways to train people as to what appropriate behavior is in a social media context.

Therefore, if they start and want a free and friendly space, they are much more apt to learn the technology and they may branch out from there. However, I think that in a Wild West scenario, which MySpace is often portrayed as, anything goes and it certainly can be scary. I certainly advocate for people that are new to it to join a private network or a safe network just to get their bearings as to what's going on. . . .

To listen to or read the entire Executive Conversation with Kyle Ford, go to www .theSocialMediaBible.com.

Expert Insight

David Meerman Scott, author, *The New Rules of Marketing & PR*,
www.davidmeermanscott.com

David Meerman Scott

. . . Early in my career, I worked at a bond-on-bond trading desk in New York City and this was way before the Internet and I actually used online information in the early 1980s when, virtually, no other business was using online information. And I totally got to understand how online information caused people to make decisions because we were making trading decisions every minute based on what we were seeing on the screens.

And then I worked for a company called Knight-Ridder who at the time was the largest newspaper company in the United States; owners of *Detroit Free Press*, *Miami Herald*, *Philadelphia Enquirer*, and newspapers like that.

So I had several decades of experience with online information and all it its forms and also as a marketer. I was a marketing vice president for several publically traded companies; and in 2002 I started out on my own to combine those ideas of how online information drives people to make decisions and also how marketing is changing as result of the Web . . . and honed those ideas down into some books and a business giving speeches and running seminars and helping people to make use of these ideas.

Basically what I boil it down to is a really simple concept. The concept is that prior to the Web we only had a couple of options to market our products and services. We could buy expensive advertising and that advertising could be all sorts of different forms. It could be magazine advertising, newspapers, radio, television, Yellow Pages, billboards, direct mail . . . all of them required a huge investment . . . or we could use the media as our mouthpiece and beg reporters and editors of magazines and newspapers, radio, and television to write about our stuff.

Those are really the only two options we had, and the Web now allows us to publish great stuff ourselves and to reach our buyers directly in ways that we could never do before. It doesn't require a huge investment. We can create blogs, we can comment on other people's blogs, we can create YouTube videos and podcasts and all sorts of different ways to reach people that we never had available to us in the past. . . .

. . . In practically every speech that I give I start off the speech by asking a series of questions and I say, "How many people in the last one or two months have answered a direct-mail advertisement?" And roughly 5 to 10 percent of the audience has. And then I say, "How many people in the last one or two months have gone to a trade show as a participant in order to learn about products or services you might want to buy?" And, again, it's 5 percent or less.

And then I'll ask, "How many people, in order to research products and services or solve problems, have turned to mainstream media; magazines, newspapers, radio, television?" And it's around 20 percent.

Then I say, "How many people, in order to research products and services or answer questions and problems, have gone to Google or another search engine?" And it is 100 percent. . . .

. . . And then I ask, "How many people have recently asked a friend, colleague, or family member online to help them research a product or service they might want to buy or to solve a problem, and that the answer that came back from their friend, colleague, or family member was a URL that they then linked to?" And that's just under 100 percent, like 95 percent.

So what that tells me is that the ways that people are making decisions today are utterly different from the ways they used to. So if you're still doing the traditional stuff of buying advertising and using the media as your mouthpiece, that's still important, but it's not the main way that people are solving their problems anymore, or researching products. . . .

. . . And you say to your friends, "Gee, when you took your last vacation, where did you stay?" And usually that question these days is asked either by e-mail or through FaceBook or some other way of networking online. And the answer that comes back isn't, "I stayed at the Princess Seaside Resort in Costa Rica," it's a link to that place's web site! . . .

. . . I think it's a combination because what it requires is that organizations give some serious thought as to what kind of content they want to create online. Web sites have traditionally been pieces of brochure ware. Basically your brochure turned into an online brochure on the Web.

So the first step is really to make sure that you've got a compelling Web presence; and that's not just putting your brochure online. Taking the example we just used; if you're running a seaside resort in Costa Rica maybe you want to have videos of what the waves crashing on the beach look like, what the pretty birds and the trees that are nearby look like, what the bar looks like. You can have photographs of that. You can have comments left by the guests, and all sorts of things. But the point is that it has to be really interesting information on your site, or on other social media tools like YouTube or whatever. . . .

How about a podcast of the birds chirping in the morning as everybody is waking up! I'm just thinking of these things off the top of my head.

And the second thing is then to make sure that social networks are aware that you've got that content; and that means things like commenting on other people's blogs, it means making it really easy to share. In other words, you do

(continued)

(*continued*)

not try to put a "gate" on your interesting content; you make it freely available. All sorts of ways that you can then get people to share the interesting information that you've created. . . .

. . . And I think we often get bogged down in the technical details, and that's been a bit of a beef of mine about search engine marketing for a while. It's that search engine marketers (not all of them; obviously if you're World Champion you're not doing this) just focus on the technology behind search engines and do not focus on the "creating" of really interesting content. They'll come to you and say, "Well, I'll just fix your site and I will make it better for the search engines." Well, if you take a crappy site and then you SEO it, you're going to end up with a slightly "less" crappy site. . . .

. . . It always comes back to the content. More importantly than the content, it comes back to the buyers, the people that you are trying to reach. And that's been a really important concept for all of this kind of marketing . . . I always tell people when I'm delivering my presentations that nobody cares about your products and services. They really don't! It doesn't matter what business you're in. Nobody really cares about your products and services. What they care about is themselves and what they care about is solving problems that they've got. And so the best online content is content that's created specifically for your target audience . . . what I call your "buyer personas," and in the case of that seaside hotel we've been using as our example, the first thing that popped in my head a few minutes ago is perhaps there's different "buyer personas" for seaside resorts?

There might be somebody who makes a decision of what hotel they are going to stay at. Yet another "buyer persona" might be somebody who works in a group-tour company and is looking for a hotel for 20 people from a church group that going to go down to Costa Rica in the winter.

And those are two very different "buyer personas" who maybe require two different types of content. And if you're just talking about your product and services, your hotel, you can talk about the fact that it's got a pretty swimming pool and it's got fluffy pillows. But that's not necessarily what someone needs who's trying to make a decision that needs 20 different rooms for a tour group that's going to be going to that hotel.

So it does totally come down to understanding who the "buyer personas" are, what problems that your organization solves for them; and then creating content that addresses those problems that will drive people into the sales process. . . .

. . . In my world, a customer is someone who is already buying your products and services. And this is a very different person than a "prospect" or someone who is "not yet" your customer. . . .

. . . And for companies that focus exclusively on their "existing" customers that can be a really big problem. Now, let's go back to the hotel again. If you're running a hotel and the only people that you do research with are the people who are staying there, what are you going to learn? You're going to learn that people are bitching and moaning because the pillows aren't soft enough. And then you'll spend $1 million getting the best pillows in the entire world. When people who aren't at your hotel couldn't care less about what the pillows are like. They want to have a beautiful view. Or they want to be able to relax for a week, or whatever it might be.

So getting bogged down with you existing customer's requirements is actually a bit of a negative. And I'm not suggesting you shouldn't talk to your customers and help them; of course you should. But if you look at your target market as a really big pie, typically in most businesses your existing customers are a very small sliver of the pie. The other people who know you but are not your customers, is a tiny sliver of the pie. The vast majority of the pie (in some businesses it's 99 percent) are people who don't yet know who you are and are not yet your customers, and that might represent a huge slice of that pie. And creating information for them is how you are successful. . . .

. . . Yes, and another really interesting facet of this, and something that's not talked about very much, is that sometimes the buyer and the user of the product are different.

Here's an example. Tricycles. For tricycles that are built for 3-year-olds, the user is a 3-year-old. That person isn't making the buying decision to buy that tricycle. The buying decision is being made sometimes by parents and sometimes by grandparents. So the way you market a tricycle is not how the tricycle works because that's what's important to a 3-year-old; the way you market the tricycle is, "Is it safe? Is it at the right price-point? What happens when my kid outgrows it in six months?" There are all sorts of different things to think about when you're marketing a tricycle.

Fast forward to somebody who is in their 70s or 80s now. In retirement villages, you see these adult tricycles for people who don't feel comfortable riding a two-wheel bicycle; they want to still get around using their own power and they use tricycles. And now, in this case the "buyer persona" and the "user persona" is the same. Someone's making a decision about a tricycle that they, themselves, will use. And those are two very different marketing problems. One marketing problem is, "How do you market to somebody who's going to make a purchase decision, but isn't the actual person who's going to be using the product; very, very different from an example where you, yourself, are making a purchase decision for a product that you will be using. . . .

To listen to or read the entire Executive Conversation with David Meerman Scott, go to www.theSocialMediaBible.com.

Conclusion

In this chapter, you've pulled together a lot of information about your company's current situation relative to social media. You've also created a list of potential opportunities to exploit or at least explore. If you take the time to create an Executive Summary based on what you've done in this chapter, be sure and share it with fellow employees and even trusted colleagues within your industry. Take advantage of an opportunity to leverage the wisdom of your network. You might even consider using an online survey application to gather measurable feedback about your Executive Summary.

Credits

Expert Insights Were Provided By:

Kyle Ford, director of product marketing for Ning, www.ning.com.

David Meerman Scott, author, *The New Rules of Marketing & PR*, www.davidmeer manscott.com.

CHAPTER 41

The ACCESS Model

This chapter explains how to:

- Incorporate the ACCESS model into your strategic plan.
- Create audience personas for your community.
- Develop and validate the concept behind your content.
- Assess your competition.
- Validate the execution of your concept.
- Make social media a part of your success formula.
- Assess your concept's sales viability.

ACCESS is an acronym whose letters stand for: *Audience, Concept, Competition, Execution, Social Media,* and *Sales Viability.* It is an integrated model for validating your content and for building a dynamic community around that content. The ACCESS model was developed by Content Connections and is used by consultants and project directors at that company as a methodology for helping clients create and promote their content. You might think of it as the company's secret sauce. It is adapted and presented here with the permission of Content Connections LLC.

Meanwhile at the Movies

Spiderman 3 was the top-grossing film in the United States and Canada in 2007, bringing in just over $336 million in box office revenue. Rounding out the top 10 films were *Shrek the Third* ($321 million), *Transformers* ($319.1 million), *Pirates of the Caribbean: At World's End* ($309.4 million), *Harry Potter and the Order of the Phoenix* ($292 million), *The Bourne Ultimatum*

($227.5 million), *300* ($210.6 million), *Ratatouille* ($206.4 million), *I Am Legend* ($206.1 million), and *The Simpsons Movie* ($183.1 million). At the other end of 2007 revenue spectrum was *Things We Lost in the Fire*, a DreamWorks production that survived in theaters for only three weeks, generating an anemic box office gross of $3.3 million.

You might assume that *Things We Lost in the Fire* was a bad movie, but a quick visit to www.boxofficemojo.com reveals that the movie had an average grade of B– and over 42 percent of reviewers gave it a grade of A. You can assume, however, that the movie failed to get traction with the four major audience groups that the film industry targets the most: 17- to 24-year-old males, 17- to 24-year-old females, 25- to 49-year-old males, and 25- to 49-year-old females. Many movies simply are not good at finding the right audience, and Hollywood has realized that testing a movie's concept via trailers and prerelease clips with a traditional sample of 300 people may be an antiquated practice in the era of social media.

A more ideal solution, according to Kevin Goetz, president of OTX, a market research company with a long list of Hollywood clients, is to increase the sample size to as many as 10,000 people. Goetz suggests that such a sample size would allow marketers to zero in on the needs, beliefs, and behaviors of an audience who would be most likely to see and recommend a movie. With better insights into a film's ideal audience Hollywood could then find a film's core audience at the places they frequent: web sites, magazines, cable television channels, retail shops, restaurants, pubs, and coffee houses. But is aggregating the feedback of 10,000 movie goers practical for Hollywood? Yes, when you consider that the final movie trailer for *Spider-Man 3* generated over 3.2 million views on YouTube. Tapping into the wisdom of 10,000 people does not appear to be beyond the scope of reality. The real question is what can audience analysis and concept testing do for your business?

Your *Audience* Is Crucial

In Chapter 4 you learned that to operate successfully in the social media ecosystem, you must view yourself as a publisher. Rather than *audience*, you may be using terms such as *market, market niche, market segment,* and *market space.* Embracing social media does not render these terms useless; they should still be viable part of your daily business vocabulary. In most conversations, you should be able to use the terms *audience* and *market* interchangeably, but as you develop internal and external social media strategies, you'll begin to appreciate the subtle differences in meaning between the two terms.

In essence, an *audience* consumes content and represents an opportunity for an interactive relationship. Such a relationship allows you to employ one or more of the social media engagement strategies discussed in earlier chapters: communicate, collaborate, educate, and entertain. A social media-based audience is quicker than a traditional market to react to things. Your ability to quickly alter a messaging or positioning strategy or the very attributes of your offering is enhanced by increased audience reaction times. Hence, your relationship with your audience—however you might define that audience—is crucial to your success.

Identifying Your Audience

Once again we must briefly distinguish between internal and external audiences. An internal audience is an intracompany audience while an external audience will primarily consist of your customers and prospects, although you may wish to add investors/stockholders and vendors to your list. Whether internal or external, each major audience can be further categorized into smaller audience segments called archetypes or personas. We'll take a closer look at audience personas later in this chapter, but for the moment, let's explore some principles that will help you better understand and identify your audience.

Demonstrated Behaviors: A demonstrated behavior is an action that can be verified and measured in some way. For example, if you use a "frequent shopper" or membership card at a supermarket or warehouse store such as Costco or Sam's Club, your purchases are being recorded. The place where you shop knows what you buy, how much you buy, how often you buy, when you buy, and what combination of things you buy. If you have a pattern of stocking up on beer and pretzels before the weekend, your grocer knows something about you. These purchase patterns, or demonstrated behaviors, allow each retailer to create a profile of you, ostensibly to serve you better.

The same thing happens online. Your actions can be tracked more carefully on a web site than at a bricks-and-mortar establishment. Technology makes it possible to know how often you visit a site, the frequency of the visit, the page depth of your visits, what you buy, download, rate or review, and what you forward to a friend. If your company already has a web site, much of this information is available by using the Google Analytics program. Keep in mind that with Google Analytics you are tracking all visitors to your site, most of whom will be relatively anonymous to you. Those who join your community by registering or creating a profile are more valuable because you can connect their online actions to personally identifiable information in the same way that your local grocery store knows where you live and something about your household demographics.

Self-Reported Behaviors: What people *say they do* and what *they actually do* is not always the same, yet by asking your audience about their actions, activities, and behaviors in *the right way,* you can learn a lot about them. You can then use this information to further segment your audience. Typically, this is done as part of a survey, interview, or focus group, all traditional tools of the market researcher, but by conducting this kind of research in a collaborative fashion, you can bring your audience closer to your brand by engaging them in an activity or a cause that has meaning to them. The Charles Schwab customer advisory panel is an excellent example of this. Content Connections regularly uses *Audience Consults, Virtual Focus Groups,* and *Audience Activity Journals* to aggregate, categorize, and evaluate self-reported behaviors.

Attitudes, Values, and Beliefs: An *attitude* is a tendency to respond or react to something based upon a learned set of values and beliefs. Values can vary from general to specific. We usually speak of general values as core values. A *core value,* for example, would be an affinity for capitalism or the rule of law. A *specific value,* by contrast, is more personal, something such as being frugal or environmentally focused. Personal values influence how someone evaluates the attributes of your product, service, or opportunity.

Beliefs are a subjective perception of the degree to which a product or service functions based on key attributes. The key attributes of the book you are reading, for example, might be writing style, accuracy, and currency, real-world examples, and overall utility to your business strategy. Beliefs are strongly influence by personal experience, advertising, and conversations with other people and are therefore malleable to a degree. Beliefs and personal values create either favorable or unfavorable attitudes about products and services. As we have discussed in earlier chapters, conversations and interactions with other people are one of the most important aspects of the social media ecosystem. What other people say, depending on their relative credibility, can influence what you believe. What people believe about something is an important aspect of who they are and can be useful in creating audience personas. Categorizing your audience on the basis of attitudes, values, and beliefs is also known as *psychographic* or *lifestyle* profiling.

Needs and Preferences: A *need* is a validated requirement necessary to function in a particular environment. For example, if you work across town and do not have access to public transportation, you probably need an automobile to remain employed and productive. A car is therefore a significant need. Whether the car is red or blue, four-wheel drive or rear-wheel drive is not a requirement. The fact that you drive a blue rear-wheel drive vehicle is most likely a preference. Needs can be associated with preferences, but preferences do not always require a need.

Your audience has definite needs and preferences. If you have some basic audience demographics at hand, you can identify many of their needs by simple deduction. Their preferences require you to either ask them or to tap into their demonstrated or self-reported behaviors to find a predictive pattern.

Demographic Data: There is no shortage of data on the market that will allow you to identify groups of people by age, education, location, household income, or numerous other demographic indicators. You may already have this kind of information about your customers and even your employees. Companies such as InfoUSA specialize in making this kind of information available to those whose sales, marketing, or research needs could benefit from an extensive list of people whose demographic indicators roughly correspond to the attributes of your product or service. Demographic data by itself does not tell you much about someone's attitudes and beliefs, their preferences, or self-reported behaviors. However, you can deduce certain things about their needs and even evaluate these demographic indicators against their demonstrated behaviors.

Professional, Social, and Service Organizations: Many people belong to societies and organizations whose members share common interests or goals. The Rotary Club, your local parent teachers organization, or the National Restaurant Association are examples of such organizations. In one respect, membership in one of these organizations may be considered a demonstrated behavior or demographic indicator, but we've listed them as a separate category for one very important reason: many people who join organizations tend to be good networkers, connectors, promoters, and influencers of other people. In your efforts to create and sustain a community around your content, you will want to pay careful attention to organizations, societies, and associations.

Influencers and Promoters: Within every group, you will find a small number of individuals who have a knack for influencing what the other members of the group say, believe, and do. These people have tremendous *viral value*. As you create a community around your content, you should make a special effort to identify influencers and promoters and enlist their skills wherever possible. They can often be identified online by the popularity of the content they create around topics associated with their interests or expertise. They may be avid bloggers, podcasters, or have their own YouTube channel, but they may also be actively involved in commenting, rating, or reviewing the original content of others. Some social media applications allow you to follow the comments or feedback produced by these folks and even see the comments that others have made about the comments of these influencers and promoters. Ferreting out these folks is as much an art as it is a science, but their ability to influence, promote, and evangelize make their identification a worthwhile pursuit.

Creating Audience Archetypes or Personas: Seldom does one group or audience have narrow enough interests for you to reach them with one broad message or approach. By creating four or five *audience archetypes* or *personas*, you can find common characteristics that allow you to visualize and interact with each one. In creating these personas, it is important to find a set of common characteristics that allow for a three-dimensional characterization of each persona; you're trying to put a face on each persona. It's unlikely that any one member of your audience will resemble an audience persona exactly. Furthermore, your personas may depict only 80 percent of your audience, but by thinking in this fashion you'll be able to get closer to a large audience than by any other method. Rather than an audience of hundreds or thousands, you're reaching out to a small group of four or five. (In reality, you are reaching hundreds or thousands, but by using personas you can create the verisimilitude of a dinner conversation with friends.)

Back to the Movies—An Example

Think back to the last time you went to a movie. You were a member of an audience that could be classified or categorized into dozens of segments depending on any number of indicators and characteristics. Having so many audience segments is not helpful to your community building efforts. Instead, you need to determine what factors are most important to you and how broadly or narrowly you want to define your audience. These factors will have some connection to the attributes of your product or service.

For example, suppose you manufacture high-tech running shoes that integrate a digital device that records the details of every workout and reports those details by interfacing with an Apple iPod Nano—yes, such a product does exist—you might start the process by putting your audience into different buckets. Let's suppose that we can survey or poll our theater audience with some simple questions about their footwear. Here's how those buckets might look after one round of questions:

- People who never wear running shoes,
- People who wear running shoes but aren't runners, and
- People who are runners.

At this point, our three buckets are not themselves personas; we're just beginning the process by dividing a hypothetical audience into meaningful segments on the basis of what we know about them. The first bucket (people who never wear running shoes) may seem like a hopeless category. Would anyone in this bucket seriously consider buying such a high-tech shoe? Probably not, but let's not draw any conclusions just yet. We'll revisit this bucket in a moment.

The second bucket contains people who probably wear running shoes because they are comfortable, fashionable, or both. It's reasonable to think that these people will not be able to take full advantage of a high-tech running shoe. Potentially we've eliminated two-thirds of our theater audience.

The third bucket would seem to have the most promise for our high-tech shoe and would be an excellent place to dive deeper, so let's do so. Here are some follow-up questions we might like to ask those in this bucket:

- Are you a competitive runner who trains regularly?
- Are you a recreational runner?
- Do you currently use technology as part of your running routine?

Notice that these are questions that rely on self-reported behaviors to create a picture for us. As we review the responses to these questions, we will probably be inclined to focus on the competitive runners who use technology as part of their running routine, thus discounting the recreational runners. It might now seem logical to narrow our focus even more and subdivide our competitive runners who use technology into four or five categories. The problem is that we've relied exclusively on self-reported behaviors to get us this far. This could lead us to some very narrow and probably inaccurate audience personas.

Imagine now that we ask all members of the audience the following 10 questions:

1. Do you own an Apple iPod?
2. If you run or jog, do you listen to music while you workout?

3. How much money do you typically spend on a pair of running shoes?

4. Do you like to get a competitive edge whenever you can?

5. Is it important for you to be fashionable and in-sync with the latest trends?

6. Do you believe that technology and fashion can be complimentary?

7. Do you believe that music can enhance a workout?

8. Regardless of the level at which you may compete as a runner, how important to you is the quality of your equipment?

9. Do you belong to a running club, subscribe to a running magazine, or visit web sites devoted to running?

10. How often do you talk with other runners about various aspects of the sport?

These 10 questions include a mix of self-reported behaviors, attitudes/ values/beliefs, and needs/preferences. In addition, we've managed to inquire whether or not our audience members belong to specific running clubs, associations or groups, and we've even touched upon whether or not they may be an influencer or promoter.

With the richer data that these 10 questions yield, you could now create the following audience personas for your running shoe:

- *The competitive runner* who uses technology to establish an advantage wherever possible. Owns an iPod or would likely buy one if it would help them be more competitive. Willing to spend money on quality equipment. Belongs to a running club or association and talks with other serious runners regularly.

- *The semi-competitive runner* who likes to record the details of their workouts and is open to using technology that will help them increase their personal performances. Owns an iPod and listens to music while training and/competing. Willing to spend money on quality equipment. Belongs to a running club or association and talks with other serious runners regularly. Influenced by what competitive runners do.

- *The recreational runner* who is an iPod enthusiast and listens to music while running. Careful about spending money on running equipment but open to spending money on iPod peripherals that fit their lifestyle. May belong to a running club or association. Not necessarily influenced by other runners.

- *The technology fashionista* who gravitates toward things that are both high tech and obvious emblems of personal fashion and style. Owns an iPod. Does not run but wears running shoes because they are comfortable, colorful, and cool. Associates with other technology fashionistas and likes to be among the early adopters of new things.

Admittedly, these personas are a tad contrived and, depending on the actual data evaluated, could be quite different from the four presented here, but the point is to provide you with a methodology for creating your own three-dimensional audience personas for your content. Notice that each persona has a distinct face and characteristics that make it seem real. Also note that these personas pull from two and possibly all three of the initial buckets we used to categorize our audience.

These personas are meaningless, however, if they are not associated with a concept.

Importance of Your *Concept*

Every business has a basic concept that highlights the value proposition for its intended audience. A value proposition describes the intended benefit that the features or attributes of a product or service will provide the user or consumer. If you are developing content for a community, that content has an underlying concept as well. Recall that content is broadly defined within the social media world. As such, it is very likely that your business could have several operable concepts. You may want to focus on them one at a time, keeping in mind that every concept has audience personas of its own.

What Is Your Concept?

To answer this question, you need to think about the community you want to engage. Is it an internal group of software engineers or all of the employees at your company? You may want to create a community around your entire business or a more narrow community around a specific product or service offered by your business. These are important distinctions because if you define your community too broadly, you will likely fail in your attempt to create a community. Let's consider some examples to illustrate this point.

General Motors: Although General Motors (GM) manufactures a wide range of automobiles under various brands (Chevrolet, Buick, Pontiac, GMC), creating a community for anyone who drives a GM vehicle may be too broad and will fail to get traction. Creating a community for people who own Corvettes, however, focuses your attention on a more manageable slice of the broad GM audience. You can imagine the difficulty of trying to create audience personas for the entire GM audience. The Corvette audience will be much easier to categorize. GM is also known as a manufacturer of everyday work trucks, and even though they produce several models of trucks, creating a community for people who use GM trucks in their everyday work lives might make sense. Can you think of other GM products whose owners might be candidates for a community?

PETCO: It may not make sense to create a community for people who regularly shop at PETCO because their interests and needs may be too broad. In other words, they may not have enough interests in common. However, if you were to focus on people who own pet ferrets, you now have a more narrowly defined audience. Can you think of other PETCO audience slices that may be candidates for a community?

What Is Your Concept?: Take some aspect of your business and consider the challenges of defining a community around it. Or perhaps you actually can create a community around your entire business. The key is to think in terms of the needs of your potential community rather than the needs of your business. This much is clear: Your business needs to make stuff and sell stuff or provide services that make money. You will not be successful rallying people around your need to generate revenue. However, are there people who need to know something about your area of expertise, basic plumbing repairs, for example? How about how to buy a used car? Would anyone you know be interested in knowing how to do organic gardening? How about knowing how to pair wine with different kinds of foods. Take a minute and ask yourself what kinds of businesses would be associated with plumbing repairs, used cars, organic gardening, and food and wine? Try and name at least two businesses for each.

Convert Your Concept into a Concept Statement: Now let's assume that you operate a local garden supply store that sells, among other things, tools, seeds, plants, and topsoil. Your anecdotal experience with customers and your research has led you to believe that more people are getting interested in organic gardening. There are health and financial benefits to having an organic garden. There are also recreational benefits. Gardening is something the entire family can do together. Friends, neighbors, and people you know from your child's school or your church can form a vegetable exchange club.

With an economy in recession you know that people are spending more time at home. All of this information may lead you to articulate a brief *concept statement* something like this:

> An online community for people who are interested in organic gardening. The community would feature expert advice on how to grow a wide variety of vegetables. The web site for the community would feature photos and videos showing the different aspects of starting and maintaining an organic garden. Community members would be encouraged to upload their own photos, videos, and share their organic gardening experiences. Community members would also be able to rate and comment on different products available to organic gardeners. The web site would also offer a vegetable exchange center where people could barter and trade their organic produce.

As you can see, it is difficult to separate your concept from your audience and related audience personas. The 100-word concept statement lends itself to creating audience personas. It is a brief vision statement that you can share with almost anyone in less than two minutes. While each sentence could be expanded or expounded on, the real value of the statement is its conciseness and precision.

Preparing to Test and Validate Your Concept: The ultimate goal is to do an *Opportunity Analysis* on your concept. Think of your completed concept statement as the first part of this exercise. You'll want to include more details about your offering and perhaps even demonstrate some sample material to show your reviewers how you intend to *execute* upon your concept. You'll also want to determine what other companies, organizations, or individuals may be competing for the attention of your potential audience. Let's now take a look at your potential competition.

Understand Your Competition

Don't make the mistake of thinking that you have no competition. Very few concepts are so unique that nobody has thought of them before. The fact that there is competition is a good thing; it suggests that there is an audience for your concept. No competition may mean there is no audience. The key is to understand your competition well enough that you are able to determine the compelling advantages of your concept over theirs. This is not always easy to do, but it is very important.

The Difference between Knowing and Understanding

Knowing that you have competitors and knowing something about them is important. But in order to understand your competitors you have to see them through the eyes of their audience. You can do this by creating your own audience personas and then visiting your competitors, wearing each persona, evaluating your competitor's offering in the context of what you believe each of your audience personas would be seeking to gain from a relationship with your competitor. This exercise is so valuable that you may find yourself refining your audience personas as a result of what you learn. That's okay. It's all part of the process of creating and engaging a community.

Some Simple Strategies to Employ: There are a few simple strategies for identifying and understanding your competition. It begins with creating a list of who they are and what they offer. Creating a spreadsheet to catalog your competitors' offerings can be useful for this activity. As you go to each site, note the features or attributes. Think back to the tools and applications highlighted in Part II of this book. Are your competitors using any of these tools? Take a good look at videos, photos, audio, blogs, wikis, and anything else from the social media ecosystem. Are they employing their own social networking application, something such as Ning or Kick Apps? How broad or narrow is their focus?

Consider the quality of their content. Determine first whether you think it is any good; you may want to rate their content quality on a five-point scale and include this in your spreadsheet. (As you actually conduct your opportunity analysis, you will have the option of asking your reviewers to rate or comment on the quality of your competitors' attributes.) Try to determine how active their community members might be by looking for evidence of user-generated content as well as the quantity and tone of comments posted on the site. Include this information on your spreadsheet.

Essence of Execution

As the saying goes, "the devil is in the details." Over the years, we've seen some compelling concept statements that failed to produce a success story. The reason: the execution of the concept failed to live up to the promise of the concept. Needless to say, execution is critical.

There are at least two theories when it comes to execution. The first is to simply get your content on the market and accept the fact that it's not perfect. Once it's "out there," you can refine and iterate on the fly. This theory works well in practice if you have an audience who can be relied on to collaborate with you—one of the main tenets of social media to be sure. But if you are going into an area where your competitors have staked their turf and they are successfully engaging their audience, the cost of entry may be high enough that you cannot risk entering the arena with subpar content or an anemic audience.

The second theory is to do your research and analysis, take careful aim, and fire only when ready. This strategy is not likely to give you *first mover advantage,* but it may keep you from making mistakes that could completely derail your efforts to realize the vision that fueled your concept statement.

There is a third theory that we'll discuss in a moment, but first let's take a closer look at execution.

What Exactly Is Execution?

This can be a little confusing because we are using the word *execution* as both a noun and a verb. However, with regard to the ACCESS model, execution is the sample content that gives your potential audience the flavor and feel of the finished offering. This could include video, audio, photos and other applications or content from the social media ecosystem. It is not necessary to show it all, but you must offer enough to accomplish two things:

1. Demonstrate to your audience that your concept statement can be realized.
2. Highlight at least a few of the comparative advantages of your concept over the competition.

The Third Theory: The ACCESS model is the third theory, and it combines the best of the other two theories because it allows you to quickly research, test, and deploy your offering. It also has the added advantage of helping you create or augment your community by involving your audience in the process of refining and positioning your concept. By asking a slice of your ideal audience to rate and review your concept statement and sample execution, you do not run the risk of simply throwing content at them. They can see that your strategy is to collaborate with them, to tap into the collective wisdom of your audience. The key to making this work is that you have to be sincere in your efforts to communicate this to your audience. At the first obvious sign of insincerity, you will lose their attention. By collaborating with your audience, however, you are making them stake-holders in an important process.

Social Media Must Be Part of the Formula

You now know that your goal is to get a large sample of people to review and comment on your concept statement and sample materials in a process known as an *opportunity analysis*. While it would be nice to get the feedback of 10,000 people, it is not necessary for this exercise because you are simply testing the water. Ideally it would be good to have 300 to 400 people provide you with feedback at this point. At a minimum, you should have 100 people. Keep in mind that as you launch your concept—following your opportunity analysis—you may be seeking to engage an audience of 10,000 or more, and that community will be an excellent source of ongoing feedback. Here is a brief outline of what you will be presenting to and seeking from those involved in your opportunity analysis:

- Your 100-word concept statement
- Four or five brief samples of content that highlights the execution of your concept
- Self-reported behavior questions that focus on things they already do relative to your concept. (In other words, does their behavior suggest a need for your concept?)
- Self-reported behaviors questions relative to your competitors. (How do they currently interact with potential competitors?)
- Attitude, value, and belief questions relative to your concept
- Preference questions relative to your concept
- Questions about professional, social, and service organizations to which they belong
- Basic demographic questions and contact information

The Wisdom of the Crowd and Crowd Sourcing

In his book, *The Wisdom of Crowds: Why the Many Are Smarter Than the Few and How Collective Wisdom Shapes Business, Economies, Societies and Nations*, James Surowiecki (2004) wrote about the value of tapping into the collective wisdom of groups. He argued that the knowledge of a group will often surpass that of any one individual. We can see this principle operating with TripAdvisor.com or Zagat restaurant reviews. You are more inclined to accept the "averaged" rating of a few hundred or a few thousand people than you are the input of just one or two people. If you are traveling to a new town and want a nice place to stay or dine, your chances of having a good experience are much better if you rely on the mathematically averaged ratings of a group who have stayed at a particular hotel or dined at a specific restaurant than if you were to ask one or two of these people at random. This principle is also referred to as crowd sourcing, and has become a significant factor in the social media ecosystem.

Doing an opportunity analysis is a method of leveraging the wisdom of the crowd—your audience. Once you have completed this exercise, you can continue the process of building your audience around your content. If you've managed to aggregate the feedback of a few hundred people while doing your opportunity analysis, you've got a great foundation for your community. You can continue to build your community by adding content, encouraging user-generated content, audience comments, and audience referrals. In essence, you use social media to make your community viral.

Audience Engagement

Remember the basic tenets of engaging your audience: communication, collaboration, education, and entertainment. The various tools and applications in the Social Media Ecosystem facilitate audience engagement, and while it is hardly necessary to use them all, it is essential that you experiment and find the *social media mix* that works for you. Social media is about conversations among people. Some of those conversations can be hosted within a community. If you've done your homework, validated your concept, and established that a particular community can be viable, you will want to make it a practice to experiment and engage, then experiment some more.

At the End of the Day It's about Sales Viability

The last part of the ACCESS model is *sales viability*. There are social media experts who frown at the idea of introducing such a crass commercial term to a discussion about conversations, communities, and engagement strategies. This book is about using social media in your business, and one of the things we know about business is this: At the end of the day, if you haven't sold something, your business isn't long for this world, regardless of the size of your community or the sexiness of your engagement strategies. It really does come down to the issue of sales viability, and that begs the question of what it is that you are actually selling.

What Are You Selling to Your Community?

Like many businesses, you probably sell goods or services in the bricks-and-mortar world or online. This is the most traditional revenue model. The rise of social media, however, makes it possible to incorporate other revenue models into your business strategy. There are other ways to profit from your community. Let's briefly consider six of these revenue models:

1. *Products, services, and information:* The most traditional model, it lends itself to both online and offline environments.

2. *Advertising and sponsorship:* This involves selling a variety of advertising opportunities to businesses that want to get closer to your community. This might also include site or event sponsorships.

3. *Transactions or commissions:* This would be revenue generated by taking a commission or a small transaction fee resulting from your site playing a role in a customer-seller transaction (e.g., Hotels.com, Charles Schwab).

4. *Subscriptions:* If your content has high enough perceived value, it may be possible to sell subscriptions in the same way that newspapers, magazines, and newsletters have traditionally done.

5. *"Freemium:"* A combination of the words *free* and *premium*. This refers to a revenue model that offers something free but also offers upgraded or premium versions for an additional cost.

6. *SaaS:* This is an acronym for "Software as a Service" and is utilized by many companies in the Social Media Ecosystem (e.g., Survey Monkey, Google Apps).

As you carefully consider your business concept, you may want to see if any of these revenue models would be a good fit for you. It is possible to have several of these revenue models in operation and complimenting one another at the same time; this is hardly an either/or proposition.

Net Promoter Score

Frederick F. Reichheld is a consultant with Bain & Company and the father of a theory known as the *Net Promoter Score*. The theory states that if you ask a sample of your customers "How likely is it that you would recommend our [company/product/service] to a friend or colleague?" you can calculate your net promoter score by finding the ratio between those customers who are *promoters* and those who are *detractors*. Each customer is asked to respond to the question using a 0 to 10 rating scale, with 10 being "extremely likely to recommend" and 0 being "extremely unlikely to recommend." Reichhold considers those giving a rating of 9 or 10 to be *promoters*, those with a rating of 7 or 8 to be *passively satisfied,* and those with ratings from 0 to 6 to be *detractors.* By subtracting the percentage of detractors from the percentage of promoters, you arrive at your net promoter score. Based upon Reichhold's research, companies with net promoter scores of 75 percent or higher are held in high esteem by their customers.

Overall, the net promoter score can offer insights into how your audience feels about your business, product, concept, or content. By measuring audience attitudes in this way, you can evaluate your offering, your competition, and even new concepts. Content Connections has been using a variation of the net promoter score for several years, and it is applied not only to customers but to prospective customers as well. It is used regularly as part of an opportunity analysis to determine the relative strength of a concept and the execution of that concept. You can learn a lot by asking several hundred people doing an opportunity analysis the following question: *Based on what you have just reviewed concerning this concept and brief samples of its execution, how likely would you be to recommend this to a friend or colleague?*

By averaging the scores of a few hundred (or thousand) people, you can begin to determine the true potential of your concept. You can make necessary adjustments and polish your concept to better meet the needs and preferences of your audience. You can position your concept to maximize its appeal to audience attitudes, values, and beliefs. You can prepare your audience for commerce.

Expert Insight

Bill Jula, CEO and founder, Fast Pitch!,
www.fastpitchnetworking.com

Bill Jula

. . . I graduated from the University of Florida in the mid-1990s, went on to get a master's degree at the University of Kentucky. I then took a job in major league baseball with the Tampa Bay Devil Rays for a season, doing some sales and marketing.

Then I really got into the world of technology. I met up with a couple of colleagues of mine from the University of Florida, moving down here to where we're located right now with Fast Pitch! here in Sarasota, Florida, just south of Tampa. We're doing some very high-end Web-development kind of stuff for ERP systems such as SAP, PeopleSoft, and different systems like that. And

(continued)

(continued)

that's what really got me involved in technology, truly understanding it, and, more importantly, with my background being more of the marketing side of things, how to market a company that's involved in the Internet age.

From there I worked in a couple of different capacities with a couple of different companies, eventually breaking off and starting to do my own thing with Fast Pitch! It initially started out in 2003 as a networking event company where we did what we called at the time "Speed Networking" events. It's like a "Speed Dating" concept but for business people. To my knowledge, we were the only company in the world where we actually had these events going in about 20 different states at any one time. I had different people contracted out around the country hosting these events on a regular basis. It was my technology background and my marketing background, but the experience of dealing with literally thousands of business professionals around the country, that lead to the creation of what Fast Pitch! is now, which is an online business network for professionals. And a lot of that experience that we had, one-on-one, with a lot of the people that we connected with in all these different states and cities has lead to the creation of a tool set and the feature set that we developed that's unlike any other network on the market right now. . . .

. . . First of all, we're obviously excited about some of the accolades we've been getting over these past few months. We just celebrated our two-year anniversary from our official launch, which was in July of 2006. We've kind of flown under the radar a little bit, which has actually been fine for now and just recently MSNBC and some other big networks have picked up on us, and so we're excited about that.

Let me tell you a little bit about what makes our network and why people are becoming so excited about it. Part of the reason we built our network is this. We were looking two to three years ago at the landscape and some of the dinosaurs in social networking are sites like MySpace and FaceBook. Obviously those are very socially oriented.

And then in the business world on the other end of the spectrum we have the networks that have been around the longest, like LinkedIn, which is very career-oriented. It allows you to really promote yourself in terms of your resume and your work experience and those kinds of things.

And so we took a look at the landscape and we said, "Okay, there's a lot going on in the social world; that's tough to compete in. There's a lot going on in the resume/career world with LinkedIn and Monster.com and those kinds of sites. But there really was nothing filling the void left for business professionals who actually are involved in a company who are given the task of either marketing or doing sales or promoting from a PR standpoint."

So we looked at it from the standpoint of a typical small business owner. What kind of tools would they need in an online network and what can we build? And going back to those experiences of having done a lot of events and the feedback we'd received, we came up with a couple of different tool sets within our system that really are designed to help people promote their business.

The experience when you come into Fast Pitch! is really driven by your company. It's not as much about you and your career path, although you can promote that within our network. The basis is for everything you do is your "pitch" and that's why the name is Fast Pitch! It's a really concentrated way to promote your company; what makes it great, what makes it different, the types of companies you are also trying to connect to, and providing a number of different ways for you to promote yourself within that network. . . .

. . . It's more or less your elevator pitch put front and center of the experience. And then around that there are a lot of opportunities for you to add a personal side to it. And that's where your personal networking comes in; being able to link to other people that went to your colleges, or maybe people that are involved in other networks you're a part of, like Chambers of Commerces, and leads groups you can leverage. And all of those things are within our network, as well. The idea for us is to become a one-stop shop for all of these things. You can come here and you can look for career opportunities as well. But while you're there and you're already working a job, there's opportunity to really push your business. And that's what most people are there to do. Our goal is to make our community very, very active and very, very valuable to everybody; to the point where they're actively logging in on a daily basis and leveraging our system.

We don't necessarily want to become one of these monster networks that have 20, 50 million users because we don't really want to have 10 million profiles that aren't necessarily being used or are inactive. There's not much value in that, in our opinion. . . .

. . . So what we're looking for is the opportunity to build a very vibrant network. . . .

. . . When we think about networking here at Fast Pitch!, we try to impress on people to really make a calculated decision about who you're going to connect to and be a little bit smarter about it from that standpoint. Now you're obviously going to get those people that are kind of taking a blanket approach or shotgun approach where they connect to everybody and anybody. You know, who's to say whether which is right or wrong. For some people, that may work well for. So we're not going to inhibit that, by any means, but all the messaging on our site is really geared toward telling people to make this a valuable experience, connect with people you know, look for real opportunities here, not just opportunities to spam people for whatever reason.

The idea is to really create value. One of the unique things that we do is actually force our members to become active on the system. Periodically we'll send out alert messages to members that we see haven't logged in in quite some

(continued)

(*continued*)

time. Perhaps their e-mail is getting bounced back. They might not have made any connections, or their profile is not even close to being complete. We'll send a message periodically over the course of a month or two, reminding them to do these things. And quite honestly at some point if we're getting no response back from those people we will actually purge the profile from the system. It won't get purged completely, the person can ultimately come back in, log in, and do all these things, but in terms of the experiences for the people that are actively using our site, that person won't show up.

That will make the person who's really using the site, have an experience that is much more fruitful because they won't be wasting their time trying to connect to somebody that's obviously not engaged. . . .

. . . Everybody's time is valuable these days. The last thing you want to do is log into a system and spend an hour connecting to 10 or 20 people and only have two or three reply, and to have part of the reason why they're not replying be that they're not even really there. That's why we're not in that market at all. We're not trying to play that game. We're not an advertising-based company; we're not dependant on advertising revenues by any means. So we have the luxury of not having to worry about click-throughs and impressions and all these different things. We're approaching it from a subscription-end. . . .

. . . There's definitely etiquette to it. And we're very conscious of it. Any time somebody on our network sends us an e-mail to report somebody doing something inappropriate, we'll keep a close eye on it. I think there have been maybe only a handful of times we've actually had to kick somebody off of the network. So I think is all starts with your initial approach as a company. And a lot of the messaging and things that you're conveying, from the top down, to impress on all of the members that, "Hey, this is the attitude we're taking here on this network; and if you are looking to just spam people and take these shotgun approaches, there may be other networks that give you a better opportunity to do that."

. . . The way we present Fast Pitch! to people is to think about it in terms of two major things: (1) Obviously networking. That's a huge component to it. The first thing you are going to want to do is to go to our profile, put your pitch on there, and put together a good message. So then when you are communicating with people and making that first impression you have a nice picture up there. You've got a fully completed profile that really tells a nice story.

That's your first step to networking. (2) The second, and in my opinion the more important aspect to social networks like Fast Pitch!, is the marketing side of things. And that's where a lot of people actually do not pick up on when they join a social network; it's the power of marketing within the network. And let me give you an example. On Fast Pitch!, a lot of the features we've created allow you to add a lot of content above and beyond just your initial pitch about your business. We've got an entire press distribution system within our network, we've got a blog syndication feature so you can import all your blogs from your blog to your profile and out to our blog site, which gets picked up on a feed.

We've got a whole event-distribution section where you can promote events and highlight events you may be attending to help market those. There's a classified section and there's the opportunity to post video and podcasts and really make your profile interactive. There's also the opportunity to attend what we call "virtual" trade shows. That's a really popular section of our site where a lot of our members will go to a certain page at a certain point in the day and have one-on-one communication with other members, via live chat or two-way streaming video. And that's something that no other network has rolled out.

It's all about networking but more importantly, it's about marketing. The more content that you can add to your profile, the more colorful it becomes and the more opportunity there is when people are searching Fast Pitch! for certain types of people and certain types of industries for your content to get served up in those results. So somebody makes a search for a financial planner in Phoenix, Arizona, and ultimately comes across your press release that you posted, which is tied to your profile, which is tied to your web site, which, hopefully drives some business in your direction.

Not only by posting content in our network are you putting a footprint on our network, but you are also building your footprint outside of Fast Pitch! which is probably even more important. There's opportunity now as search engines like Google pick up your press release or pick up the key word in an event announcement. So now people outside of Fast Pitch! are coming across your profile or your press release and then taking that cycle into seeing your profile, learning about you, learning about where you went to college, learning about your company, and hopefully contacting you. . . .

To listen to or read the entire Executive Conversation with Bill Jula, go to www.theSocialMediaBible.com.

Expert Insight

Chris Pirillo, geek and technology enthusiast, www.chris.pirillo.com

Chris Pirillo

. . . Every year something new pops up onto my radar; and a couple of years ago it was the ability to live-stream without really paying anything other than your ISP, so I thought, "Hey, why not!" . . .

. . . [Usually in the beginning of the interview, I'll just say, "Can you tell us a little bit about yourself" but I wanted the listeners to get a full appreciation of who Chris Pirillo is. So I threw out a few statistics: "You've recorded over 1,000

(continued)

(continued)

videos in the past year, you cracked the Top 100 Most Subscribed throughout the whole of YouTube, your live stats are more impressive, with five million unique video viewers watching Chris do his thing in 2007 with a total of 2+ million live viewer hours with an average viewing of 25 minutes per visitor. This past August, your live video feeds recorded 279,000 viewer hours with over a million viewers; 827,000 unique viewers; 395 average viewers, and 707 hours of live broadcasting! In addition, in the first seven days of launching your Web community for geeks, you logged in 587,000 page views. I mean, this stuff is unbelievable and here's one that is just totally cool because it's so simplistic; you are the #1 hit on Google for the word "Chris." Now how cool is that?]

. . . Mostly that particular statistic will hold true for the duration of my life, I don't know. . . . There's only one place to head, and that's down, after you're #1 "Chris" on Google; although I haven't had it happen yet. I'm praying that they never change their algorithms or another more important "Chris" potentially comes along and usurps my position. . . .

. . . I turned a personality disorder into a career, as I have been prone to say. There's really no one thing that I do. I'm an omni-geek, so some might call me; someone who has just always been attracted to technology, much like a bug may be attracted to a light hanging on the porch in the middle of summer.

Sometimes it works pretty well for me and other times not so much. Umm, but I'm a content publisher, I help other people publish content and now have gotten more and more into increasing and sharing my own video experiences when they're live or, of course, recorded on YouTube.

The direction that I have been going is just largely just being myself. I enjoy talking about technology during the sharing of information; and when that's directly with people like myself, or specifically in talking directly to companies either on a sponsorship level, or specifically, a consultancy. . . .

. . . When I started online, there really weren't a lot of pools to facilitate community building; it hadn't really grown. Today those tools are plentiful. There are plenty of ways that you can build communities and draw people into the things that you are interested in, and help build their interest and their experiences with you. The hope in community building is that you feel less and less alone in this world, and no matter your background and the chances of some other people sharing your similar interests, or similar enough, are pretty strong.

You know, the Internet is a big place and community ebbs and flows, but certainly the one thing that you're obviously going to have going for you is yourself. So as long as you are honest with yourself and with your friends and the people who are not yet your friends, the chances of you maintaining a level of integrity on an ongoing basis (no matter if the tools are not where you're at) are pretty strong.

It's all about being honest and direct and that really is . . . It's not so much in the area of community building, it's just more in being (I guess) a good communicator in general. . . .

. . . Well, you can't talk about something if you don't know what you are talking about . . . when people do that it's pretty obvious that they are just either a hired gun, hired talent, or shouldn't be doing the things that they are supposedly doing. . . .

. . . People come and opportunities come in a multitude of directions; and certainly I started cultivating a lot of it back in 1992, but unofficially (at least in the commercial path) in 1996. From that point forward, you know, it was kind of an uphill battle because I was left to my own devices. This was long before social networking was a "word" and we had other services like FaceBook and MySpace and Twitter; and you name any one of those services that are really there to help give anybody a voice to share with the rest of the world. And, of course, that came not long after blogging

I've surveyed the landscape of these services efficiently. There is always something new to look at. And so I look at all of these resources and being able to leverage my own knowledge and passions against these resources to reach the same people or potentially new people, is really kind of key to, I think, any success for community building.

It's not just being there, it's really getting what the tool is and where it fits, specifically in your modus operandi. I was doing all this stuff before I had started to work on a radio show as a host; and before I had done a stint at Tech T.V. Some people believe that I got my start at Tech T.V. and they really don't know me at all [Laughter] if that's the case. And it usually iş. They seem to believe that everything came because of Tech TV, but . . . Tech TV only happened because of everything that was done before that, including writing books, sending out newsletters, and doing community building a lot on my own. . . .

. . . I've been working with CNN.com, doing a live segment every week, and carte blanche in terms of the content part, but I'm looking to involve myself a little deeper with CNN.com as the tech expert. And that only came about because of everything else I am doing. So one thing builds on top of another, on top of another, on top of another. . . .

. . . If something couldn't be entertaining why would anybody watch it. I mean that it should be informational and entertaining at the same time. I approached the classroom in much the same way when I was student teaching. I am a teacher by degree, but never actually became one in any kind of school.

Even if I've got my live stream going and nothing's going on and all that the people are doing is staring at the back of my head or listening to whatever I'm listening to, or whatever . . . then at least I've got a chat room that's integrated with the experience.

So even if I cannot be entertaining, well maybe I can be informative. . . .

. . . The airline safety instructions was the first video I uploaded to YouTube and it made it to the front page of YouTube. . . . It was three months into it, but it made it to the front page.

(continued)

(*continued*)

You know, I've been recording video since I could. I used to record videos, I'm pretty sure, on a Sony Mavica here and used a later series to actually record videos onto a floppy disc.

. . . And I was like, "Oh wow, I can record videos! This is so cool!" Of course, they were stamp-sized but they were still good. . . .

. . . Umm, you know in respect to live streaming, I seldom move the camera. I usually play the Xbox 360. I just started to bring my laptop in there and then I switched the stream over to that. But usually I only keep one camera on, and I can leave the room at any time and not feel obligated to take the camera with me.

Umm, and because of that I have set out that particular boundary. Some people violate that particular boundary, you know, whether they share personal information about myself that I would rather not have shared, like a phone number or what-have-you . . . anything like that, you know. But for the most part, I'm in control. My wife Ponzi can now watch . . . keep an eye on me throughout the day. Hey, you know, what wife would not want that? . . .

. . . It's all about sponsorship and those kinds of partnerships. And certainly other things come from it as well. Whether it's me, or Valunet . . . that's just the direction I've followed and that kind of stuff follows me.

Certainly sponsors have been extremely supportive in the things that I try to do and that's . . . not an uphill battle, necessarily, but since my model is usually a little different I have to, kind of, ride the cusp between what they're use to and what I think the next step is going to be. You know, it usually works out pretty well. . . .

. . . Usually I come up with a wacky idea that works and then find a way to underwrite it with the sponsor, and that's how it goes. I have never been asked to go out and speak on community building by any one of those companies. I would certainly welcome it, but I've never had the opportunity.

If it's kind of how my career path is going, and an opportunity will come up, and do I have the time and it's something that I'm interested in and will it be fun; . . . then I will give it a shot. . . .

. . . I love saving money and, more importantly I love helping people save money which I've done over and over and over and over again; and everybody loves to find a good coupon . . . and so now people will e-mail me and say, "Hey, I'm thinking about buying produce X, do you have a coupon for it" and I go find one. And then just sharing it with them, I share it with the rest of the world.

And so because of that, I'm able to close that loop between myself and the community and also create a value-add for everybody else. So, yeah, I like posting a lot of coupons on the blog. . . .

. . . Locker Gnome is what started it all on LockerGnome.com and that's still around. Now, well I guess, trying to build it into a blog network and a community and beyond. But unfortunately a lot of the platform choices out there are really limiting. I tried a lot, but unfortunately they're really, really expensive or really, really impossible to work with. So I try to find the "sweet spot" in the middle that I can give people a voice and give them a chance to get paid for what they know, like blogging. . . .

To listen to or read the entire Executive Conversation with Chris Pirillo, go to www .theSocialMediaBible.com.

Conclusion

In Chapter 1, you were introduced to the first three rules of social media:

1. Social media is about enabling conversations.
2. You cannot control conversations, but you can influence them.
3. Influence is the bedrock on which all economically viable relationships are built.

In subsequent chapters, you learned that the best way to influence conversations is to create a community in which people influence one another, but you must be able to measure that influence. If you cannot measure influence, you cannot manage it. If you cannot manage it, your business will suffer the consequences. The ACCESS model was designed to help you measure and manage influence and to be strategic in creating and monetizing a community around your content.

Credits

Expert Insights Were Provided By:

Bill Jula, CEO and founder of Fast Pitch!, www.fastpitchnetworking.com.

Chris Pirillo, geek and technology enthusiast, www.chris.pirillo.com.

CHAPTER 42

Evaluate and Organize Existing Resources

This chapter enables you to:

- Introduce the Social Media Awareness Index to others at your company.
- Aggregate the numbers based on your colleagues' social media tool scorecards.
- Locate your social media starting point.
- Determine your company's social media readiness from a technology standpoint.

Here's what this chapter assumes: you have read all previous chapters and completed the exercises yourself but *have not* involved others at your company in the process. If you have involved others, congratulations. You're ahead of the curve. The goal of this chapter is to help you evaluate and organize your existing resources (and knowledge) prior to implementing a social media strategy. Depending on the size and structure of your business, we encourage you to involve as many people in your company as possible. Their experience, perspective, and capabilities can be quite valuable to the social media strategies that you ultimately implement. You will find that people in your company have different levels of social media awareness and different degrees of experience. It is likely that you already have active bloggers in your midst. You most likely have people whose daily lives already include Facebook, MySpace, YouTube, and other social media applications. It's entirely possible that people within your company have outside relationships with your customers, suppliers, and vendors—relationships enabled by social networking tools. Many of these folks may not draw a connection between the use of social media in their personal lives and the potential value of these applications to your business.

By involving the people in your company in this activity, you are doing two important things: (1) You are tapping into the collective wisdom of your own company; and (2) you are engaging people at your company in a stakeholder relationship that most companies talk about but never achieve. Since social media is about enabling conversation, it's important that you begin and sustain a conversation within your own company. To complete this activity, you will need to introduce these now familiar exercises to your colleagues: (1) The Social Media Awareness Index from Chapter 40; (2) the tool scorecards from Part II of this book; and (3) the social media SWOT analysis from Chapter 40. For your convenience these exercises can be downloaded at www.theSocialMediaBible.com.

How to Tap into Employee Wisdom

You need to make a realistic determinination of *how many* and *which* employees to tap into. The relative size of your company, the geographic distribution of employees, and the functional groups within the company are important factors to consider. Regardless of a company's number of employees or its annual revenues, we encourage you to involve as many employees as possible. Here are some ways to leverage the collective wisdom of your company's employees:

- *Hold a company retreat*. This can be a day-long event or as short as three to four hours. This can be organized by functional groups, divisions, or other categories that make sense for your particular company.

- *Hold a web-based retreat*. It's not advisable to convene a day-long meeting via the web, but you can easily conduct a two- to three-hour session with employees using an application such as Adobe Connect.

- *Town hall meetings*. Consider a series of employee-focused town hall meetings where leaders of the company meet with groups of employees. If you think you're ready for it, try doing your town hall meeting in a virtual world such as *Second Life,* a move that would send a definite message to employees about your company's interest in social media.

- *Focus groups*. Gathering 8 to 10 employees together at a time to participate in a live or online focus group is a very effective way to tap into collective wisdom. Focus groups should not run longer than about two hours and should be moderated by a neutral third party if possible.

- *Use a blog.* You can get your employees talking by starting a blog devoted to your company and the future of social media. The advantage of a blog is that employees can participate at their convenience. Also, some employees are more likely to comment and contribute to a blog because it offers a degree of insulation or anonymity; they don't feel put on the spot or compelled to contribute. The downside of a blog for this purpose is that it's counterproductive to force people to interact, and you relinquish control of the conversation. (Remember the second rule of social media?)
- *Combine elements.* Several of these methods can be combined in your attempts to leverage employee wisdom.

Prior to holding one of these events, every employee involved should independently complete the *Social Media Awareness Index*. Participants should allow approximately 15 to 20 minutes to complete the index. By using an online survey tool, such as the *Survey Monkey* (www.surveymonkey .com), you can have employees complete this assignment online and allow the survey tool to aggregate the response data for you. Using a tool such as the *Survey Monkey* is highly recommended.

Every employee should also complete a tool scorecard for each category within the Social Media Ecosystem. Participants should devote approximately three to four hours to completing this assignment. Once again, using the *Survey Monkey* or a similar tool will allow you to aggregate the response data and see possible patterns among your employees. To help you visualize how this works with an online survey tool, we have created versions of the Social Media Awareness Index and the tool scorecards using the *Survey Monkey* application on our web site.

Recognizing the value of an employee's time to your business, it may not be practical or financially wise to require every employee to complete a tool scorecard for each of the 15 Social Media Ecosystem categories. As entrepreneurs and managers of small business enterprises, we can understand the impact of 50 employees each spending four hours completing a tool scorecard. As an alternative, you might ask employees to complete this scorecard on a volunteer basis on their own time. Here's another option: Based on the data collected from the awareness index, you can assign specific categories to participants or divide the categories and assign them to groups so that each employee completes a tool scorecard for three to five of the social media categories. The bottom line is that you want to get enough feedback from a cross-section of your employees to facilitate the conversation that will inform your social media strategies.

Once those involved have completed the awareness index and the tool scorecards, it's time for the next step.

Pinpoint Your Social Media Starting Point

The social media strategies you deploy will depend greatly on how you evaluate and define your business, both where it is now and where you want it to go in the future. Every business can benefit from a carefully crafted social media strategy, but every business begins from a different starting point. This means that one strategy will not fit all. If for example, your company currently does not have a web presence, your strategy will be different from a business who has already embraced the Web as part of their strategy. Reaching a final destination requires you to know exactly from where you begin your journey. You must now pinpoint your starting point using the categories of the Social Media Ecosystem as reference points.

With the results of the Social Media Awareness Index and the tool scorecards in your hands, complete the exercises in Figure 42.1 as a group activity with other members of your company. Write your brief responses in the spaces provided or download a copy of these exercises from our web site. Remember the four pillars of a social media strategy are *Communication*, Collaboration, Education, and *Entertainment*; keep these pillars in mind as you work through these exercises.

Social Networking	Microblogging	Aggregator
Publishing	Livecasting	RSS
Photo Sharing	Virtual Worlds	Search
Audio	Gaming	Mobile
Video	Productivity	Interpersonal

1. **Familiarity with Social Media Applications.** With which of the social media tools and applications are your company's employees most familiar? Is there any pattern regarding the tools they are familiar with, such as employee age or job function?

    _____

    _____

    _____

FIGURE 42.1 Categories of the Social Media Ecosystem

2. **Use of Social Media Applications.** Which of the social media tools and applications are your employees currently using? Indicate how they are being used formally or informally in the context of your business. Explore how employees are using these applications in their personal lives and how their facility with these applications may be beneficial to your business.

_____

_____

_____

3. **Social Media Applications:**
   Internal Value Assessment. Which tools and applications are believed to have the highest value inside your company?

   a. ***Within Functional Groups.*** (e.g., sales, accounting/finance, operations). How do you envision them being used? What additional information or training would be required to implement each tool?

   _____

   _____

   _____

   b. ***Company-wide.*** While some applications may have specific benefits for functional groups (see a), others will have broad, intracompany appeal. How do you envision them being used? What additional information or training would be required to implement each tool?

   _____

   _____

   _____

4. **Social Media Applications:**
   External Value Assessment. For each of the groups (a–c), which tools and applications do you believe have the highest value outside your company?

   a. ***Your Current Customers.*** How can you envision employing one or more of the four pillars with this group? What are the potential risks and benefits of using each pillar?

   _____

   _____

   b. ***Your Prospective Customers.*** How can you envision employing one or more of the four pillars with this group? What are the potential risks and benefits of using each pillar?

   _____

   _____

   _____

(continued)

FIGURE 42.1   Categories of the Social Media Ecosystem

(continued)

c. **Your Vendors and Suppliers.** How can you envision employing one or more of the four pillars with this group? What are the potential risks and benefits of using each pillar?

_____

_____

_____

d. **Investors and Others.** How can you envision employing one or more of the four pillars with this group? What are the potential risks and benefits of using each pillar?

_____

_____

_____

FIGURE 42.1   Categories of the Social Media Ecosystem

Revisiting Your Social Media SWOT Analysis

The social media SWOT analysis is an ideal group activity. Using the questions presented in Chapter 40, take the time to engage others at your company in a careful assessment and discussion of _Strengths_ and _Weaknesses_ as well as _Opportunities_ and _Threats_. There is some overlap between the questions in the SWOT analysis and the exercises you just completed. Adapt the SWOT analysis to your needs and time constraints. The results of your SWOT analysis should be put into a summary report that can be shared with others in your organization. As you begin to implement your social media strategy, this report can be used as a guide against which to check your strategy. Every component of your strategy should play to a Strength in your organization or help to overcome a Weakness. Likewise, your strategy should focus on monetizing Opportunities and minimizing or avoiding Threats.

Assess Your Technology and Support

This is a business book not a technology book, but there is some overlap. As you take stock of your organization and its resources, it's important to consider what kind of hardware and other technological tools your company currently utilizes, and the technology you might need to take full advantage of the Social Media Ecosystem.

Social Media Hardware

Your hardware needs will vary depending on whether you are planning to simply participate in online discussions, social networking, blogging, and so on, or if you are planning to publish your own material, especially audio or video products.

Viewers

For those not planning to publish your own audio or video material, only the basic hardware and software equipment is needed. Most social media sites, like Facebook or MySpace, require only a computer connected to the Internet and a standard web browser such as Firefox, Internet Explorer, or Safari. Using the latest version of these browsers is recommended.

For some sites, such as YouTube, you will also need to install Adobe's Flash plugin, which is a free and easy install. Most internet-ready computers made in the last few years will already have Flash installed. The latest version is Flash 10, released in 2008, but many sites still will function properly if you have earlier versions of Flash installed. It's a good idea to stay up to date with the latest version of the plugin.

In some rare cases, you may need to install additional third party software to get things to function properly. Microsoft's Silverlight web browser plugin, for example, is intended to compete with Flash, and may be required for some future web applications. Silverlight is also a free and easy install available for both Mac and PC.

For those on the move, many of today's mobile phones also offer entry points to the social media world. Social media companies have already developed applications that can be installed on Apple's iPhone, for example, which will allow you to update your Facebook status without using a web browser, watch a video on YouTube, post directly to your WordPress blog, or any number of other uses. Blackberry devices and many standard mobile phones will also provide similar functionality. Before you rush out and buy a new device, ask around to be sure that it will fit your specific social media needs. (Does it cost extra to e-mail a photo to my blog? Will it play video from standard sites like YouTube or Vimeo? Can I browse my Flickr galleries? Can I record audio or video?)

Publishers

If you are going to publish your own material, especially video or audio, your hardware and software needs will be a bit more demanding. But you may already own what you need without even knowing it. For instance, most digital point-and-shoot cameras made in the last few years will also record video with surprisingly good quality. Check your camera's settings to see if it will record 640 x 480 video (that's 640 pixels wide by 480 pixels tall) at 15 frames per second with audio, which is sufficient for posting a decent YouTube video. New devices, like the Flip made by Pure Digital Technologies, are designed specifically for social media use. They are very portable, easy to use, and can often upload videos directly to YouTube when plugged directly into a computer's USB port.

To get better quality video, you can venture into High Definition (HD) territory for only a few hundred dollars. You can find HD video cameras ranging in quality and price from as low as $200 to well into the several thousands. For audio-only adventures, many available MP3 recorders and simple microphones produce sufficient quality for most social media applications. And often, a built-in microphone on a laptop will do.

To edit your video or audio, you can use many free or bundled applications that may already be installed on your computer. (Apple's iMovie, for example, is bundled free on all new Apple computers and is quite flexible and powerful. Comparable free or inexpensive programs are also available for the PC.) Software, like cameras, can come in a range of features and prices. You can spend a lot on software and plugins, or settle for the bare minimums, which are sometimes free. In most cases, the free or inexpensive applications are sufficient, unless you need professional-level effects or extra flexibility.

Overall, if technology trends continue, there will be more convergence to free web-based applications that make using social media tools easier, more powerful, and more accessible to an average Web user. For publishers, avoid spending loads of money on the latest and greatest devices unless you've determined you actually need the added features. In most cases, the camera already sitting in your desk drawer should work just fine.

Expert Insight

David Nour, author, *Relationship Economics*,
www.relationshipeconomics.com

. . . I am originally from Iran. I came to the United States in 1981, didn't know anybody, literally didn't speak a word of English, and had $100 to my name.

David Nour

So, early on I had to learn how to adapt and how to survive in this great country. And I think only in America can a first generation immigrant really get a chance to be blessed with all the opportunities I have had over the years.

Recently I spent a number of years at a private equity firm, before that I was president of a start-up, and really had a chance, through my career, to look at a lot of different companies. What I noticed consistently was the ones that out-paced their competitors, or competitive peers, weren't the ones, necessarily, with the best products or services.

The ones that consistently and systematically thrived were the ones who built these amazing relationships, and then nurtured them. They were very disciplined in how they did that. And board members walking into great companies help you attract great employees . . . which becomes this great momentum-wheel . . . that they build on for leverage.

The ones that consistently and systematically thrived were the ones who built these amazing relationships, and then nurtured them. They were very disciplined in how they did that. And board members walking into great companies help you attract great employees . . . which becomes this great momentum-wheel . . . that they build on for leverage.

And I said, "There's got to be something there." So, having read about 100 books on this, collaborating with about a dozen or so PhD's around the country, we came up with this idea of *Relationship Economics* and we called it the "art and science of relationships." . . .

. . . And we quickly identified two camps: the art and the science. And the art is an interesting one. How to introduce yourself, how to get a business card, how to work a room, how to conference.

There's a lot of material on the market about that and that's really important; but what we found is . . . nobody measures the stuff. Nobody says, "What's my return on that relationship, of investment." Nobody says, "Who are my 50 most strategic relationships that I really need to pragmatically, systematically, invest in for an extraordinary return?"

So, we've come up with ideas like the Relationship Score Card and the Relationship Value Pyramid and indices and matrixes, and all avenues of trying to help you prioritize your most valuable relationships. . . .

. . . And the fundamental thought process is: you don't have enough . . . none of us have . . . enough bandwidth to invest in everybody equally. So if you really believe that relationships are an investment, the million-dollar question becomes . . . on any given day . . . should you could call 20 people? Should

(continued)

(continued)

you could engage 50 people? . . . which 20? How do you know? And again, Six Sigma taught me that you can't possibly improve something you do not measure.

For the *Relationship Economics* book, I interviewed 1,000 managers, directors, executives. Without exception, every single one of them attributed their personal and professional success to relationships. Without exception, none of them measured it! None of them could go back and say, "Here are the 50 most strategic relationships that were instrumental to my success in the last 10 years, the last 20 years." . . .

. . . You know, when most people struggle with a challenge or a dilemma or a problem, they think of, "What should we do and how should we do it?" Very few people start by asking the "who" questions. "Who" do we need? "Who" do we know? Can we start identifying some of our most valuable relationships . . . not just tactically who you know, . . . but strategically . . . how can we create *access* to and *opportunity with* someone who can accelerate our ability to get things done.

Harvard Business Review wrote on this topic a number of months back, as well. It talked about three types of relationships. The first is your personal . . . like a friend. These are your golf partners, these are your poker friends . . . these are people who like you, warts and all! They know you, they like you.

Next are your functional relationships. People you work with because you have to . . . you know, customers, these are suppliers, these are, perhaps, board members. These are those who you, in essence, engage to do your function, do your role, deliver your role.

The first two are easy. There are some very key attributes and nuances in the book about each of those. But, the third one is the one that most people ignore. That is your strategic relationships.

Strategic relationships, by definition, elevate your thinking. They elevate your perspective to a whole different level. And I am going to give you a very specific example. . . .

. . . If your focus is to generate revenue . . . let's just say, "Back of the napkin" you just generate $10 million in revenue last year. Strategic relationships are the types of individuals and types of extremely valuable relationships who can get you $250–100 million in revenue.

If you are trying to reduce employee attrition, if you are trying to extend alliance relationships . . . these relationships add . . . not an *incremental-value-add*, but an *expediential-value-add* . . . to what you're trying to do.

You have to learn how to be real disciplined about identifying these individuals. This is much more than networking, this really is networking efficiently . . . networking effectively, building and nurturing relationships . . .

as I said earlier . . . for this extraordinary return that most people cannot fathom. . . .

. . . And, again, the basic example I share with individual teams or organizations is . . . you know, you have three types of networkers or relationship builders; "givers" . . . They just give altruistically. They give because they have enormous hearts and that's what they get joy out of.

Unfortunately, most of us cannot afford to be altruistic givers. We have mortgages and we have P&Ls, and we have other obligations.

Number two is . . . takers! We've all known this type when they call and they want something. My least favorite is people who look for a job. "Do you have a job?" "I need a job." "Can anybody get a job?" "I'm going to need a job."

Once they've found a job, not only do they stop all this networking, but they forget everybody who helped them get there until three years from now, when they call you back. Take one guess of what they want?

. . . Another job! Right! And they want you to help them! How likely are you to help them? You know, I actually call them on it. You know, "John, what happened to the introductions I made for you two years ago?" And, "When was the last time you called to see how I'm doing?"

Right! So "givers," "takers," and the last one is "investors."

Investors are systematic. Investors are disciplined. Investors, absolutely, take a more analytical approach . . . to this art. And we all know it's important, but very few people think about it as a very clear market differentiator; a very clear opportunity to turn a *problem-customer* into a *raving-fan-of-a-customer*. Very few think of it as a strategic asset to reduce attrition.

Just to give you an idea, we've identified an *accelerated traction* in terms of an idea that's backed by someone who has influence. We call it a *return on influence*. Why? Because individuals . . . by the way, this has nothing to do with their title . . . who have influence have this enormous ability to engage and, just that, *influence* others, often without authority. . . .

. . . And yet, most of us ignore them because they're three or four level VPs on our traditional organization charts. Or we ignore them in the "sales" or "business development" or "project management" function because they could not possibly be a "good" connection! And that's where the mistake lies in ignoring the "highly influential" people that may not have the top title; may not have the "corner office" . . .

. . . I'll give you another aspect of these highly influential people. They accelerate their ability to influence others, and the influence becomes, then, this viral effect. Think about it! You go and you see a movie. You may not be Roger Ebert, but you saw the movie, you have friends, you tell your friends about it. Right? And that drives awareness, it drives that market buzz, it drives that "pull" if you will, for that particular movie.

(continued)

(*continued*)

Well, ideas work the exact same way. Initiatives within corporations work the exact same way.

There are certain individuals who are influential. The "influent" can also become very pro-active, you know, as a resource to spread around those ideas and initiatives and really help them get traction. . . .

. . . So think of a traditional organization chart and then, conversely, think of something . . . we'll call it a *relationship dynamic chart*, with maps, not just hieratical positions in a company, but the source of *information flow*. . . . the source of influence . . . the source of a return on you relationship of investments. . . .

. . . There is several misnomers and misperceptions in relationships. One is that it's purely an external thing. Right? When you talk to a lot of . . . if you have a lot of . . . when you have a lot of relationships . . . they automatically think it's a selling thing, a marketing thing.

A lot of them work with you . . . as in a client like Siemens, and Disney and Intercontinental Hotels, and KPNG and Deloitte, to name a few . . . are as much focused on their intra-company, or intra-formed relationships . . . that are often as critical to your success as the external ones.

So, unfortunately, a lot of people forget, literally forget or de-prioritize their intra-company relationships. That's #1!

#2 is this idea that relationships are a soft skill. Well, just like selling is an art and a science, we've proven that relationships are an art and a science. It is critical that you really understand and you leverage and you maximize your proficiency, your effectiveness in both. So I'm not advocating that you don't need to learn how to engage people at an event, or how to introduce yourself, or how to be interesting.

I mean you could be the most brilliant person; if you're abrasive, you're just not going to get anywhere! . . .

To listen to or read the entire Executive Conversation with David Nour, go to www .theSocialMediaBible.com.

Conclusion

The degree to which you or your company engage with social media will depend upon strategic need, resources, and an overall comfort and facility with the tools, technologies, and hardware. Not everyone will have the time or opportunity to involve company colleagues in the activities suggested in this chapter. It is not obligatory that you do so, although leveraging the wisdom of others at your company can be beneficial. If you are not in a position to involve employees—or perhaps you are a very small company without enough employees to form much of a crowd—consider seeking input from a network of trusted advisors who know your business. You could even create an advisory panel of customers and other outsiders who could function as a brain trust, something we discuss in the next chapter as you move toward implementing a social media strategy influenced by these activities.

Credit

Expert Insight Was Provided By:

David Nour, author, *Relationship Economics*, www.relationshipeconomics.com.

CHAPTER 43

Your Implementation Plan

This chapter helps you:

- Define your personal social media strategy.
- Define a 12-month social media macro strategy for your business.
- Work through a six-step process for implementing your strategy.

Rich Senopole is a connector. He connects people to other people, businesses to other businesses, and experts to the people and businesses who need them. As executive director of the Maricopa Community College's Small Business Development Center (SBDC) in Phoenix, Arizona, he's worked with thousands of businesses, helping many become successful and watching some fail. Recently anointed "the small business guru" of the Southwest by a Phoenix business reporter, Senopole is not shy about the importance of having a social media strategy.

"Social media is probably one of the most important changes to have ever come about in business," says Senopole, a former marketing professor and experienced business owner himself, a combination that mixes just enough of the academic with the real world to make his perspective that much more valuable.

For years, either as an instructor of marketing or helping people learn to market, marketing has changed very little. You still have the five P's of marketing, you still have to do a marketing plan, you still have to do marketing research. What's really changed is the media that you have available to you to do marketing in a whole new way, and an affordable way. Social media means that you're not using the general media, and you're not necessarily having someone else do it for you. It allows you to do it yourself. It allows you to very quickly be an expert in the field. You can develop a social media plan and put it into effect immediately.

Senopole practices what he preaches. The SBDC has an e-mail newsletter that they regularly send to clients and other stakeholders. They use the online survey tool Survey Monkey to aggregate information about client attitudes, needs, preferences, self-reported behaviors, and demographic data. They do educational webinars to help small businesses start and manage their businesses more effectively. The list goes on.

What Senopole has done so effectively in the Phoenix area is to create a community around SBDC's content, something he encourages every business to do. He and his staff have developed a program for SBDC clients that helps "educate them to use social media to improve their marketing and therefore to improve sales and get better profits."

Senopole stresses that "the technology is there; we have to help [businesses] first of all overcome their fear of it. Secondly we have to show clients the benefits that can be derived from social media, and then we have to help them develop a plan that will make it work."

Your Social Media Personal Strategy

You and your business may be one and the same, or perhaps you are one part of a larger organization. Regardless of how fancy or complex a strategy you implement for your business, you need to develop a personal social media strategy. If you have employees you may want to encourage them to do the same.

In Chapter 39 you were introduced to the following Quick Start Micro Strategies:

- Create and send a basic newsletter using an e-mail marketing service.
- Find at least two blogs in your area of interest or expertise. Read several of the more recent posts for each blog and join the conversation by offering your perspective and comments.
- Start your own blog with the goal of educating people about something you know a lot about.
- Create your own YouTube account and upload a video.
- Register at TripAdvisor.com (www.tripadvisor.com) and rate and comment on a hotel you stayed at recently. Use the site to select a hotel for your next trip. Get a feel for how the site uses ratings, comments, and collaborative filtering to provide the user with extremely valuable content.

- Get daily intelligence on a competitor, an industry, or a topic of interest by creating a Google Alert account.
- Become a regular visitor to CNN.com (www.cnn.com), the *Wall Street Journal* online (www.wsj.com), National Public Radio's web site (www.npr.org), or another news media channel that you favor.
- Join a social network such as LinkedIn, Facebook, or MySpace. Complete your profile, and engage.

There are hundreds of other micro strategies that you could implement within the hour. Part II of this book and many of the exercises in Part III have been designed to help you determine which tools fit you the best. Now it is time to put some of these tools to work. You can't do everything, but we encourage you to do something. At a minimum, select two or three of the Quick Start Micro Strategies and engage.

It's likely that your personal strategy will inform and influence your business strategy. Get comfortable with social media by getting out of your current comfort zone. Experiment with three strategies this month, and then add one next month. The social media ecosystem is a bit like a buffet table. You can't possibly eat everything, so you need to try a few things at a time.

In the space provided write down three components of your personal social media strategy. Then, make the commitment to engage this week.

- Personal Strategy 1: What is it, and what is its biggest benefit to me?

_____
_____
_____
_____
_____
_____

- Personal Strategy 2: What is it, and what is its biggest benefit to me?

_____
_____
_____
_____
_____
_____

- Personal Strategy 3: What is it, and what is its biggest benefit to me?

_____
_____
_____
_____
_____
_____

Your Social Media Business Strategy

With your commitment to a personal social media strategy, it's time to focus on your business strategy with a simple six-step process.

Step One: Define a 12-Month Social Media Macro Strategy

The exercises and activities you've completed previously in this book should serve as a foundation for creating a one-year social media macro strategy for your company. Your macro strategy should be realistic. It's not practical to incorporate hundreds of tools from the social media ecosystem into the daily operation of your company. Introducing even a dozen new tools into your organization could be disruptive and debilitating. It's important to pace yourself. While you may be inclined to try a lot of things as fast as you can, we suggest a simple 12-month formula where you add a new tool every month. By doing this, you will be able to promote each new tool to your employees, customers, and prospects. You will also be able to look back at the previous month and evaluate how effective you were in implementing that month's tool. Additionally, as the year progresses, you should be able to evaluate how the tools work as a complementary whole. The ultimate measure of success, of course, will be revenues and profits. If your macro strategy is good for your business, it should become evident. If adjustments need to be made, you can do that, too. Your macro strategy should be flexible and experimental.

Select Your 12 Tools: In Chapter 42, you were encouraged to revisit the social media tool scorecards and conduct a SWOT analysis. That process should have yielded at least 12 tools that you can use in your macro strategy. At the end of this chapter, you will be asked to list your 12 tools and indicate the strategic purpose and desired engagement outcome of each. Remember, the ultimate role of social media is to engage people. To help you visualize this, we have created a sample 12-month macro strategy for a fictitious consulting company, New World Consulting (see Table 43.1).

Step Two: Engage Your Employees

You will have greater success with social media as a marketing strategy with your customers and prospects if you first implement a couple of strategies with your employees. By using these tools on a day-to-day basis, people at your company will become accustomed to interacting with one another in a new way. For example, by creating a company blog, people can share insights and expertise within their functional groups or company-wide. Setting up a

Table 43.1   New World Consulting

Month	Tool	Strategic Purpose	Engagement Outcomes
1	Blogger or WordPress	Create two quick communities via (1) an intracompany blog and (2) a customer-facing blog.	Increase communication and collaboration with employees and customers.
2	Skype	Improve internal communication.	Better communication and collaboration within the company.
3	Facebook	Establish a company persona within a social networking environment.	Increase awareness among customers and prospects.
4	Go To Meeting	An inexpensive forum for meeting with employees, customers, and prospects.	Communicate, collaborate, and educate.
5	YouTube	Package and promote expertise and content with a company YouTube Channel.	Communicate, educate, and entertain.
6	Flickr	Package and promote expertise and content via photographs.	Communicate, educate, and entertain.
7	PodBean	Package and promote expertise and content via podcasts.	Communicate, educate, and entertain.
8	Twitter	Build or enhance an external community through microblogging.	Communicate and collaborate.
9	Survey Monkey	Establish a customer advisory panel utilizing online surveys.	Communicate and collaborate.
10	Blog Talk Radio	Package and promote expertise and content via Internet radio.	Communicate, educate, and entertain.
11	Second Life	Package and promote expertise and content in a virtual world.	Communicate, educate, collaborate, and entertain.
12	KickApps	Incorporate user generated content (UGC) into the community.	Increase size and activity level of my community.

blog is easy to do. Topics can be tagged (indexed) for future reference, and people can contribute to the conversation by commenting on the articles or blog postings of others. You can even link other social media tools to your company blog. Consequently, as your comfort and sophistication level with social media grows, so will your company blogsite. Yet another advantage of maintaining a company blog is that it serves as a form of research and development for your public-facing social media strategies.

One disadvantage of blogs is that they do not facilitate instant communication. For this reason, you may want to consider a tool such as Skype. Skype allows people to communicate and collaborate via instant messaging and audio or video chats. You can also do conference calling and quickly send files. Skype has several advantages over e-mail, although it does not replace the need for e-mail. The most important need within an organization is to communicate and collaborate quickly. There are several social media applications that allow you to do this, and several of them complement one another. For example, you can use the Flickr tool or YouTube with your blog. You can use Skype to make outbound calls to people using cell phones or landlines.

Step Three: Get Closer to Customers and Prospects

People are talking. You can't control the conversation, but you can influence it. Does this sound familiar? In order to influence the conversations of your customers and prospective customers, you have to find out what's important to them. To know what's important to them, you have to listen to them and be where they are. Here are some ways to get closer to your customers and prospects:

- *Create a public-facing blog using one of the tools highlighted in Part II*. In the sample 12-month macro strategy in Table 43.1, our fictitious consulting company is using Blogger and WordPress. If a blog did not rate highly on your tool scorecard, you may want to reconsider the importance of this basic but powerful social media tool.

- *Use a search tool such as Technorati or IceRocket to identify blogs and blog topics that may be important to your business*. You may find that there are ongoing conversations about you and your company that you were not aware of previously. If so, join the conversation. You can also position yourself as an expert in a particular area by posting thoughtful comments on blogs with an audience similar to the one you are building. Comment Marketing is an effective way to build your own credibility with an audience.

- *Create a Facebook account for your company. If you haven't already joined the world of social networking, now is the time*. By establishing a company persona on Facebook, MySpace, or another social networking site, you are positioning your company to attract the attention of those in need of your product or service. Keep in mind that people don't generally join a social network like Facebook for commercial reasons. On the other hand, when you're looking for a realtor, a plumber, or someone to do your taxes, a social network is a great thing to tap into.

- *Use a tool such as Go To Meeting to engage your customers and prospects*. Such a tool allows you to interact with them live over the Web. You can do everything from sales presentations and training sessions to virtual focus groups.

Step Four: Think Like a Publisher

As we said in Chapter 4, with social media everyone is a publisher. With a world full of publishers, you have to look at your business from a very different perspective. This means you need to define your content and your special expertise, create audience personas, and deliver something that engages that audience.

In our fictitious macro strategy, notice that in months five, six, and seven, the company incorporates videos (YouTube), photos (Flickr), and podcasts (Podbean) into the mix. By definition, the company is already a publisher at this point because they have created a blog, but by adding these three tools, they are increasing their ability to engage their audience with components that facilitate communication, education, and entertainment. If you recall Big Tony the Plumber from Chapter 39, that's exactly how he was engaging his audience.

ACCESS Model Revisited: Finally, in thinking like a publisher, don't forget the ACCESS model from Chapter 41, a critical consideration in your social media strategy. Be sure you have answered these questions:

Who are my audience personas?

What's the concept behind my content?

Who or what is competing with me for audience attention?

Step Five: Create a Community

Notice that in months 8 through 12 in the sample macro strategy, it's all about creating and augmenting the community you began in the first month. Each of these tools, *Twitter, Survey Monkey, Blog Talk Radio, Second Life,* and

KickApps can be used to engage your audience around aspects of your content that are of interest to them. Most importantly, these tools work together. For example, you can use Twitter to send a tweet about an online survey or as a reminder for an upcoming program on Blog Talk Radio. You can use Survey Monkey to introduce your audience to Second Life by showing them examples of the application and asking them how likely they might be to participate. As you create your community, be sure and follow these basic community management suggestions from Chapter 39:

- Appoint a community manager.
- Identify community evangelists.
- Align your content with audience needs.
- Encourage user generated content.

Step Six: Measure What's Most Important

As you deploy your 12-month macro strategy, you'll want to measure your success by involving your employees, customers, and prospects in the process. The first thing you'll want to do is ask people for their feedback. You can do this by encouraging comments on your blog. You can also send members of your community a link to an online survey via e-mail. You may want to consider calculating your net promoter score, Frederick F. Reichheld's valuable formula as described in Chapter 41: On a 1 to 10 scale, how likely is it that you would recommend our community to a friend or colleague? (10 = Extremely Likely to Recommend and 1 = Extremely Unlikely to Recommend.)

Remember that with this formula, people providing a rating of 9 or 10 are consider *promoters,* people offering a 7 or 8 are *passively satisfied,* and all scores of 6 and lower are considered *detractors.*

Google Analytics is an extremely valuable measurement tool, one that we highly recommend, and best of all it's free. With this tool you can get metrics on traffic patterns for your site and see where people are actually spending time. You are tracking the actual behavior of your community. The tool does most of the heavy lifting for you, so you don't need to be a statistician or technically gifted to use it effectively.

Of course the ultimate measurement of success will be evident on your P&L. If your macro strategy is impacting sales and profitability, that will be the most convincing metric of all.

Your Macro 12-Month Macro Strategy: Use Table 43.2 to articulate your macro strategy.

Table 43.2   Your Company

Month	Tool	Strategic Purpose	Engagement Outcomes
1			
2			
3			
4			
5			
6			
7			
8			
9			
10			
11			
12			

Expert Insight

Kevin Marks, technology advocate, Google, OpenSocial, www.opensocial.org

Kevin Marks

. . . OpenSocial is a way to provide social infrastructure for the Web. It is a way of expressing information about people and about their friendships that can be reused by different sites and different applications. So it is a common standard resource for the social web.

It is currently deployed to a large number of social networking sites, including MySpace, orkut, hi5, Friendster, and several others in different countries around the world, totaling over 350 million users. And we expect that to continue growing as more web sites pick it up over the next few months. . . .

. . . We've got sites in China and Korea, European countries, and South America. What you find is there are different social networks in different countries, but they will have a lot in common and we can provide a common API that fits into all of them. . . .

. . . The problem with building a social application is you have to gather the data. So that means you have put up a form for the user to fill in. They give you their name and their date of birth and zip code and whatever else you want from them. So that's quite a barrier that you put up in front of the users. You lose a lot of them when they have to fill in that form. And then again, I guess you want to do something that relates entirely to social stuff rather than just personal stuff. You link to them often by who their friends are, which means they've got to get around and find out who of their friends are members of that site.

Now, the first time you do that, that's quite fun. You join the network and you've got some friends on it and you can get around quickly, looking at them and discovering stuff about them. But if you have to do that for every site you sign up for, that becomes a chore very quickly and people are reluctant to do it. Then you get bad work-arounds that will come up with, "Give me your password and e-mail for your web/e-mail site and we'll draw on your address book from that." And that's training people to give away their passwords to the web site. And it is also drawing on, essentially, a broader database than you are happy sharing with them.

So the value of the OpenSocial model is that you can have one or more of these trusted containers, trusted custodians of your data that you store the information in. And you can run an application that you give permission to, to draw on that data so that it can know about you and your friends and use that to customize the experience that it's having.

So by delegating some of your trust to the container site, that container site is then, on your behalf, giving that information through the application making sure it doesn't get more than it needs to do the task it's trying to do, rather than giving it a free pass to access your entire online presence. So there's value for the side-developer because they will draw on this larger pool of information, and there's value for the user because they do not have to re-enter all the data.

And the value in this for the container site comes in connecting them to the rest of the Web, knowing what other things you are doing apart from what you are just doing on that site. . . .

. . . So you may not want to pick one site and put everything in that; though some of the sites are getting quite good at managing subsets of people. But quite often you'll find that the soccer team has one particular way of organizing themselves. They set themselves up as a group on some site, using that style. You may be using LinkedIn for professional networking and keeping track of hiring people, and so forth. So it's quite likely that you would have more than one presence on the Web, and you may want to connect some of those together and you may want to keep some of them distinct. And the point is that you should be in control of that and not have to push everything into one site or, conversely, go into every site on the Web with the same bit of information over and over again.

So the point is, as you said earlier, to try to make this stuff invisible to users would be a natural expectation for them. They can share personal and friendship information with sites which they go to on the Web, but with this they get a behave-sensitivity factor with it, and no abuse.

That is a key part of OpenSocial; the user being in control of their information that is being shared. . . .

. . . So, OpenID lets you prove that you own a web site. That is its simplest function. It grew out of Brad Fitzpatrick's work on LiVEJOURNAL and other blogging systems to let people identify which blog was theirs because blogs are a good example of URLs representing people. If you blog about somebody else, you link to their blog URL and say, "Kevin said whatever" to represent them. So that's a case where people are using their URLs to refer to each other.

And the nice thing about a URL as opposed to an e-mail address is that you can then go and fetch that URL and get extra data from it, as well. With your e-mail address all I can do is annoy you and send you an e-mail, or I can give it to somebody else who can send you an e-mail. If they want to interact with you, they would have to e-mail you their URL and you could click on it and come back to the site.

(continued)

(*continued*)

With OpenId, you've got a URL that identifies you. That means that a program can fetch that URL and use that as a route to get access to more data, whether it's OpenId data or even a web page, or whether they do an "authorization handshake" using AllOff or OpenSocial and draw other data out from it that way.

So, OpenID is sort of a piece of this ecosystem because it's a way of proving that you are your URL.

I mentioned AllOff just then. AllOff is open authorization. What that lets you do is give one site permission to have access to your data on another site. But it's a limited permission. You can give permission to some data and not others, and you can always revoke it in the future. So you're basically giving them a "valet key" that says you can [have access] to these certain things, but not everything else. And I can revoke that so you cannot have it in the future.

So that's the way for one site to draw on other site's information over time, which means that as you change the information on the custodian site, the other sites that draw on that will get the newer information, too, without having to re-enter it. So those two work together, and then OpenSocial draws on these underlying values, too, and specifies the information content there.

So it says, "Well, here's what a personal profile looks like." It looked at many different sites and found what elements they had in common. And it defined them so we can find names and photographs and birthdates and the many other fields that we found a lot of sites had in common, including things like what your favorite music is, what your favorite books are, are you a smoker, information like that.

We log those fields by what they have in common, so we codify those. The other thing that OpenSocial lets you do is it lets you store data or assist events that are tied to user identity. And then it gathers that information about those events, or about that data, for both the user and the user's friends. So it solves an awkward problem that you get when you've got a large collection of data: deciding what's important to the user.

The only drawback that relates to that user and their friends is the application can do something much more interesting because as a user you really care about what your friends think. And if I can give you some information that has a photograph and the name of your friend next to it, that's much more interesting to you than [information] coming from a random user, or coming from a site in general. So it helps provide that kind of social filtering of whatever information that application is working on. . . .

. . . There is a great thing Douglas Hearns wrote that said, "The vast majority of our brain is based on deciding who to trust." We evolved this complicated empathy and evaluation mechanism in our heads to decide who to trust because that was vital to our survival. And so, that's not something you can straightforwardly replicate in a computer—deciding whose information you trust. But if we have the information tied to the people that you recognize, than you can apply the trust that you have in your head. So you know that one friend is good for recommending restaurants and another one is good for recommending books to read or one would be a great one to tell you where to get your car fixed. And you know that about those people. So when you ask the question, you can rate their expertise on their "individual" selves without the computer having to do that for you because you are relying on the knowledge that you already have about those people in your head to evaluate it. . . .

. . . And to tell the computer all that information and knowledge you have about people, it would be really hard and wouldn't be worth your while to do. But you have all that tactic knowledge of the people you've met and what you think about them and you can use that to tally the information you see coming in.

Conversely, once you've connected to a set of people and you're getting updates from them [that] information can drive your opinion of them in the future. That's one of the things that you see in activity streams in Facebook or in Twitter, or FriendFeed. These applications give you a flow of information about people. If they're people you don't know, it just looks like noise and a mess. If it's people you do know, it becomes interesting signals and bits of knowledge about them that you can take in and then respond to, or not respond to. But if you look at the public Twitter stream, it's a bunch of random weirdness from strangers. If you look at your personal one, it's, "Oh, my friend's in New York today!" And that's a very different type of information because the context is supplied by you and you've conveyed the context of who you're interested in.

And the value of the social networks is that they have all these different context groups, or individuals, which means any application that's re-sending info can be filtered through those contexts so that your friends mediate the information and they can make it make sense to you. And that's the sort of value that's broad, but it's hard to do without a rich set of connections and information about "who knows whom." So being able to bridge that information from the sites that have lots of it to any given individual application is what OpenSocial provides. . . .

To listen to or read the entire Executive Conversation with Kevin Marks, go to www.theSocialMediaBible.com.

Expert Insight

David Treadwell, corporate vice president, Microsoft's Live Platform, www.azure.com

David Treadwell

. . . I run the Platform Services Group up here at Microsoft, and our mission is to build out the services platform infrastructure. We are big believers at Microsoft on the value and importance of services moving forward and what we find over and over is that as the service world matures there are a lot of platform opportunities where platform providers can give infrastructure to developers to build applications that make it a lot easier for those developers to connect to their users, to get stuff done with mass-scale services. So social media plays a huge role in that because a lot of the key service scenarios that are evolving in the industry, in the ecosystem, really revolve around social media.

So, to sum it up, we provide a platform for services with a special emphasis on a lot of social scenarios. . . .

. . . One of the things that we are finding more and more here is that one of the values of a services platform in the social media scenarios is making it a lot easier for users to connect with other people, to connect with their data, to connect with all the different devices that they own.

So if you look at a lot of what we are doing in Windows Live and Live Mash and some of the related efforts . . . it's really about building connections across all of these different . . . islands. You know, today if you have two different devices it can be difficult to move data between those devices. If you want to communicate with your friends, there are ways to do it, but there are really barriers to communication that are very challenging.

So, especially things like the LiveMash projects where what we have is the ability to synchronize data really well across these devices and across people and across applications. And we think that that's going to result in a real explosion of scenarios . . . people building applications that today we don't even anticipate.

We can see a lot of these scenarios that are likely, but making it easy to bridge those islands will really enable all kinds of things for developers to provide to users, in terms of experiences, scenarios, functionality, and the rest of it. . . .

. . . BizSpark is intended to basically help give developers support and resources for building on a lot of the services platform infrastructures, so it's more a program than a technology, but we're pretty excited about it as a way to facilitate development in a lot of these new platform initiatives. . . .

. . . It's a catalyst for them to get going and hopefully see some of the benefits of what our platform provides, and how they can provide great applications and services and offerings to their customers by leveraging the platform infrastructure that we have. . . .

. . . Mash is a project we started a couple of years ago to lend the best aspects of services and clients. There's a ton of services doing uniquely well. When you use a Web service there's no install step; you don't have to worry about ruining your data. You have high reliability of any data that's stored. There's a lot of really compelling advantages to using services.

At the same time, we're big believers in [the fact that] the client has a lot of value as well. You know, some simple things like the ability to store data offline, or the ability to have control over your data because it's stored on machines that you own. [It has] the ability to provide really rich immersive experiences by doing compilation and storage physically close to the user, and it reduces latency and has all kinds of other benefits.

The client also has kind of a special role to play in computing moving forward.

So this is where Mash comes in. What we want to do with Mash is take the best of Web services and the best of client computing and blend them in a way that enables developers and users to have the best possible experiences with their applications and their experiences.

It's based a lot on the concept of synchronization. The idea is that you, as a user, can have your data in the Cloud and on all your devices, automatically synchronized and you don't have to worry about, "Oh, did I have this file on this computer?" The infrastructure handles that automatically. And if for some reason you are on a friend's computer or something like that, you can always use the Cloud-backed storage to get at it.

So by basing on concepts like synchronization, enabling the best of services, and the best of client software, we really think it will be a significant piece of infrastructure. Platform infrastructure and some platform experiences will really help drive the future of computing much more effectively. . . .

. . . The concept of the Cloud basically means open data centers; and data centers that we at Microsoft run, or other companies run. It's a more generic concept not specific to Microsoft, but the Cloud that Microsoft supports enables storage of data very easy. You can put files or all kinds of other data in the Cloud.

As an analogy that I bet most people will get . . . when you are using one of the Web-based mail services, like HotMail, the e-mails are stored in the

(continued)

(*continued*)

Cloud, we say. So they should think of the Cloud as the datacenters that are keeping your data available and making it Web-accessible.

On the scenario you described, you are always traveling, you're probably using several different computers at different times . . . that's the synchronization value of where Mash really comes in very clearly there . . . because what happens is . . . and I personally use several different computers, I have a small laptop and I have a big laptop and I have a couple of desktop machines, and not having to worry about whether I have a given piece of data on any specific machine . . . that's really handy.

I do not need to think, "Oh, gosh, I'm about to go on an airplane, did I get all the files I want?" No, because it's synchronized automatically and also available in the Cloud, I know that while any data I really care about, no matter where I am, if I'm on a computing device (either one of mine or even somebody else's) I know I can get at that data.

So that's the classic scenario that we think users will find super-compelling, and it exists today in some scenarios (probably like e-mail). Often e-mail clients synchronize; other clients obviously store it in the e-mail server. But what we want to do is take those concepts and make them available to any kind of application scenario. So any sort of application has that same attribute where the data is on all devices, shared with other people, backed by the Cloud, and therefore always accessible. . . .

. . . One thing we are really finding is that there's all these new form factors. Netbooks is a good, relatively recent example. Super-small, super-cheap devices; but we also know that something like a Netbook, while really handy in some scenarios . . . you probably don't want to use that as your main computer. Keyboards are small, the monitor's real small. So, people, more and more, are using multiple devices simultaneously and it's a real hassle for people to keep their data up-to-date, synchronized, across all these different devices. So we see tons and tons of opportunity in that problem space, by making it just "brain-dead" simple for having data be something that the user owns, not something that the device owns. . . .

. . . The Cloud gives you redundant storage; that's a real nice part of it. . . .

. . . Yeah, those kinds of scenarios are in photos. People today are all taking tons and tons of digital photos and all too often we hear about scenarios from friends and family where the hard drive died or, like you just said, a laptop got lost and they lost all these photo memories.

That's something that irreplaceable usually. So being able to store redundant copies is real important to a lot of people. . . .

. . . Well, today, like with Mash, we have a five-gigabyte default Cloud storage offering. What we also allow is if you have a lot of data . . . suppose you have a photo directory with tons of gigabytes . . . what you can do is you can just synchronize across my own devices. Don't put it up in the Cloud.

That has the benefit of just using your own hard drive for storage and also the benefit of your own hard drives probably have good network conductivity to one another. So you can move it around quickly. Once you start getting into multigigabyte sizes, there are real bandwidth constraints that are problematic in moving 10 gigabytes to an Internet server takes a couple of days on typical broadband connections. . . .

. . . Well, there's no cost on Live Mash and we have not figured out if we want to have other offerings and with more Cloud storage. Maybe [it will be for] some monetization, we haven't figured that out. We're looking through the possibilities in doing this. . . .

. . . Often we are asked, "Why are you making this stuff available for free? What's in it for Microsoft?"

Really the answer is quite simple. We know that there is a value to Microsoft by making it easy for people to own lots of computers. So by having this infrastructure, by making PCs more useful, we think we can grow the overall market.

If each person wanted two or three computers, there are obvious ways Microsoft stands to benefit there because we hope to sell the operating system, for example, that those users will use on all those devices. . . .

. . . "Aw, maybe I will buy a second computer. Laptops are cheap and I can get a laptop for $500 or $600, a notebook for $300 today."

But the constraint is less often the cost, as opposed to the hassle of getting that computer with all the data you want, consistently synchronized, all the applications you want . . . that's really hard for people today, and understandably so.

What we are hoping to do with some of this infrastructure is really lower those barriers . . . just make it such that the user, who has a bunch of data, who has a bunch of applications . . . turns on a new machine, and says, "I'm on! Give me my stuff." And then a little while later the computer is all configured with all your data, constantly up to date, all your applications . . . with no extra effort from you.

So that's a place we expect to get to reasonably quickly with a lot of the infrastructure. . . .

To listen to or read the entire Executive Conversation with David Treadwell, go to www .theSocialMediaBible.com.

Conclusion

The social media ecosystem is wild and evolving. There are many opportunities for an enterprising business to take advantage of these tools and create a strategy that will engage employees, customers, and prospects. In *The Social Media Bible,* we have attempted to provide you with a basic vocabulary for understanding social media. We have also tried to give you a tactical perspective on how various tools are used.

Finally, it's been our goal to help you create a successful strategy for your particular business. There is no one formula or approach that will guarantee success. Much like the wild American West of the nineteenth century, exploration and experimentation are essential.

We invite you to join our community at www.theSocialMediaBible.com and let us know how you're doing. You might also find it an interesting place to engage with us as we attempt to communicate, collaborate, educate, and entertain our audience—that would be you.

Credits

Expert Insights Were Provided By:

Kevin Marks, technology advocate, Google, OpenSocial, www.opensocial.org.

David Treadwell, corporate vice president, Microsoft's Live Platform, www.azure .com.

John Arnold
Author of *E-Mail Marketing For Dummies*

John Arnold gained national attention when he helped to pioneer a small business marketing seminar series on behalf of the permission-based e-mail marketing company Constant Contact, a company named number 166 on Inc. 500's list of the fastest growing private companies. In *E-Mail Marketing For Dummies*, he explains to the small business owner how the average ROI in e-mail marketing is $45 for every dollar spent.

Benj Arriola
2007 SEO World Champion

Benj Arriola has been a chemist, teacher, web designer, and web developer. Currently, he is in the search marketing industry "playing around in the SEO/SEM field as a search engine optimization and Internet marketing consultant." Considered an expert in the field, he is still seeking the secrets of search engine optimization, what to do and what not to do, and he emphasizes that above all, "Content still is king!"

John Blossom
Founder and author of *Content Nation*

John Blossom has been a consultant to the publishing and technology industry for over 10 years, assisting publishers and content technology companies with marketing strategy and enabling them to leverage social media. He analyzes the content industry for trends and believes in Internet publishing as a unifying factor for the world.

Adam Broitman
Crayon Marketing, Director of Strategy and Ringleader

Adam Broitman has had several incarnations as a creative strategizer, notably as creative director at Morpheus Media, before starting his new career at Crayon. He sees a difference between mobile advertising and mobile marketing, seeing the former as intrusive (a banner on the mobile phone) and the latter being more palatable, with the user deciding which ads to view. A former Digitas staffer, Adam holds a BA in English from Queens College as well as an MA in Media Studies and a certificate in Media Management from The New School University.

Stephanie Bryant
Author of *Videoblogging For Dummies*

A true videoblogging pioneer, Stephanie Bryant launched her first videoblog in 2005, using her cat as a subject. Further experimentation with videoblogging yielded "Hold My Beer and Watch This," a chronicle of her pushing boundaries and doing something different each day. A technical writer and author, she now presents seminars on videoblogging topics.

James Burnes
Vice President of Development and Strategy for MediaSauce

MediaSauce is an Interactive Web Development and Strategy company in Carmel, Indiana, the northern suburbs of Indianapolis. James is a strategy-focused business development professional who has led multiple, highly profitable ventures in media, Internet projects, and product development. James has an inherent ability to quickly connect technology solutions with results-driven, real-world applications for our clients—and to communicate those concepts throughout the organization. James' favorite quote is "Never Give Up."—Louis Chevrolet

David Cain
President/CMO of MediaSauce

David is a believer, inspired by the possibilities the future holds. He loves the outdoors because he feels grounded and young there—it clears his head. David's unique ability is creative problem solving. Creativity is not limited to artists—being creative is a state of mind. David's creative release when writing, is dreaming about the future and making it become a reality. Davis' favorite words to live by are. "The cemeteries of the world are full of indispensable men."—Charles de Gaulle

My interpretation: Don't think too much of yourself, there's always someone ready to do what you do. Enjoy yourself and always strive to be the best.

Krista Canfield
PR Manager for LinkedIn

Prior to LinkedIn, Krista Canfield was a senior account executive for the Horn Group, and has a background in journalism as a news reporter. She has extensive experience in media relations and all PR account activities including analyst relations, press releases, and competitive and company news tracking. In the public relations capacity, she has worked with many software companies, securing some of them feature stories with *USA Today*.

Marc Canter
CEO of Broadband Mechanics

By his own words, "a toolsmith by trade," Marc Canter has been creating digital software and tools for 25 years. A founder of Macromedia, he has been watching the blogging world and social media evolve over the past two decades.

Pete Cashmore
CEO of Mashable

Pete Cashmore founded Mashable in 2005 in a small town in the north of Scotland, building this social media site to 10 writers and nearly 20,000 articles in under three years. One of the top 10 blogs in the world according to the blog ranking service Technorati, the site's writers have been quoted in the *New York Times*, the *Washington Post*, and hundreds of technology publications. Pete was chosen as a Top 25 Forbes Web Celeb in 2007, and Mashable was selected as a must-read site by both *Fast Company* and *PC Magazine*, and was named one of the world's most profitable blogs in 2007 by *BusinessWeek*.

Vint Cerf
One of the Fathers of the Internet and Futurist

Vint Cerf was at Stanford in 1973 when Bob Kahn came to him and asked for help in hooking different nets together. Together they created the basic design of what would become the Internet. He is amazed at how quickly the public has absorbed the different ways of interacting on the Web and that the original consumers of information are now producing information, hence social media.

Rishi Chandra
Product Manager for Google Enterprises

A Stanford MBA, Rishi Chandra has been with Google for two years, working exclusively on Google Applications, the newest being Google Sites, a suite of products continuously updated by Google that resides on the Internet, not the desktop, and consists of everything from word processing, spreadsheets, to presentations, and e-mail.

Scott Clough
Avid Online Gamer

Scott Clough started gaming as a teenager in the 1980s with "Dungeons and Dragons." He gravitated to role-playing games on the computer such as "Zork," then to the online "D&D," among others. In 1997, with much time on his hands, he went to "Ultima Online," and then to "EverQuest," which he feels made the role-playing game genre successful with its amazing graphics and realistic world. Now prudent with his game time, he tries to make sure gaming doesn't dominate his life, but he is always looking for new entertainment. He has an understanding of the user's side of gaming and why businesses should watch the $1 billion plus, multimillion player industry.

Angela Courtin
Senior Vice President, Marketing Entertainment and Content for MySpace

A veteran of MTV where she was vice president of integrated marketing, Angela Courtin was also vice president of Rock the Vote, where she partnered with MTV's Choose or Lose campaign and corporate America to get young people across the country to get out and vote. Her work in politics spans the Human Rights Campaign to the Democratic National Committee. At MySpace, she is responsible for leading the marketing, branding, promotions, events, content, and entertainment teams with the objective of increased growth, public awareness, and driving revenue through marketing programs.

Leah Culver
Cofounder, Pownce

A software developer, Leah Culver has a degree in computer science and lives in San Francisco, where she cofounded Pownce, a micro-blogging service that can be used in a myriad of circumstances from business to personal by sending files, pictures, music—anything and everything digital. Pownce closed in December 2008, but the engineering team and technology group are now a part of Six Apart, makers of fine blogging tools.

Kyle Ford
Director, Product Marketing, Ning

Kyle Ford has been at Ning since December 2005, when he was one of the first product managers after Ning's launch in October 2005. Ning allows a drag and drop interface, allowing anyone to create their own site and social network for any use. Besides Ning, Ford established credentials working in multimedia previously with Yahoo! Movies and Fox Broadcasting.

Michael Gerber
Author of *The E-Myth* and *The E-Myth Revisited* and *Entrepreneur Advocate*

Michael Gerber founded business development and re-development resource for small business, E-Myth Worldwide, in 1977. He is currently the founder, chairman, and CEO of a new venture, In The Dreaming Room, and the founder of Capital Corporation, which provides micro-financing for business owners and entrepreneurs. He is also a founding partner of Entrepreneurs Club Network, which encourages entrepreneurs to share their successful experiences in business. He also has a radio show, *The Michael Gerber Show*, soon to be in syndication, and the Michael Gerber Club, a social network currently being launched.

Jody Gnant
Livecaster, Community Marketing, and Musician

Jody Gnant is a Phoenix-based singer/songwriter who grew up with the Internet. She gained notice by broadcasting her life, a livecast 24 hours a day for nine months. She also participated in Kyle MacDonald's historic venture, *One Red Paper Clip*, the journey of turning a paper clip into a house through cyber-trading. She uses the Internet to be independent—she sings, writes songs, and puts them out for people to listen.

Eric Groves
Senior Vice President, Worldwide Strategy and Market Development for Constant Contact

Eric Groves holds an MBA from the University of Iowa and has more than 20 years of experience building sales, business development, online, and marketing strategies for leading companies, holding executive and leadership positions prior to Constant Contact at AltaVista, iAtlas Corp, InfoUSA Inc., MFS Communications, SBC Communications (now At&T), and Citi-Corp. He is a frequent speaker to thousands on behalf of the SBA, U.S. Chamber of Commerce, and Association of Small Business Development Centers, among many others.

Francine Hardaway
Founder of Stealthmode Partners

Francine Hardaway, PhD, is an experienced marketing strategist whose special expertise is startup companies, which describes her current company, Stealthmode Partners, a company that works behind the scenes (in "stealthmode") to help other companies grow. She founded Arizona Entrepreneurship Conferences and Social Media Club Phoenix. She was vice president of corporate marketing at Innovative Environmental Products, manager of worldwide press relations at Intel's Computing Enhancement Group, and built the largest marketing/public relations firm in Phoenix, Arizona, before leaving for Intel. She was an Entrepreneurial Fellow at the Berger Center of the Eller School of Business, University of Arizona, and has taught entrepreneurship at several Arizona colleges.

Jack Herrick
Founder of WikiHow

Jack Herrick founded WikiHow with the intent of building the "world's largest, highest quality how-to manual." Expanding the definition of how-to manuals, it deals with subjects as diverse as car repairs and relationships, with content submitted and maintained by readers.

Chris Heuer
Founder of the Social Media Club, Author of *The Social Media Playbook*

A social media advocate, Chris Heuer has a diverse background in business technology, media, publishing, and even once worked for the U.S. Mint. His 15 years of experience have taught him the importance of "hands-on learning" in using social media.

Gretchen Howard
Director, Online Sales and Operations for Google AdWords

Gretchen Howard has held this position for almost three years and previously worked in financial services and as a consultant. She explains how Google AdWords works, and how to set up an account and start a campaign with little or no effort and a limited budget.

Stephanie Ichinose
Director of Communications for Yelp

Stephanie Ichinose managed a public relations team for Yahoo! for years before becoming director of communications at Yelp. Yelp is an Internet tool that accesses and creates local reviews rating restaurants, auto mechanics, dentists, or any company by building a community of individuals who communicate via digital word of mouth.

Bill Jula
Founder and CEO of Fast Pitch!

After earning a master's degree, Bill Jula entered the workplace, working in marketing and business development, and found himself learning how to market in the Internet Age. He started his current company, Fast Pitch! in 2003, based on the ideas that the most powerful ways to grow a business and a brand are through word of mouth and building a strong referral network, and that there should be places on the Internet for businesses to interact.

Mark Kingdon
CEO of Linden Labs of Second Life

Mark Kingdon joined Linden Labs in 2008 as CEO and creator of Second Life Virtual Environment, an online program used by individuals for socializing and companies for meetings, educating their customers, and even prototyping products. Mark served as CEO of Organic Inc., a digital communications agency; Idealab, providing strategic guidance and operational support to emerging companies and was a partner with the consulting division of PricewaterhouseCoopers, LLP. He holds an MBA from the Wharton School of Business and a BA in Economics from UCLA.

Alan Levy
CEO of BlogTalkRadio

Alan Levy created the concept for BlogTalkRadio as a means for friends and family to be updated on his father's health that would become a memorial upon his father's passing. BlogTalkRadio is now the leading social radio network, enabling millions of bloggers to interact with an audience in a live, real-time manner.

Scott Lunt
New Media Explorer

A social media native, Scott currently lives in Washington, DC where he works as a freelance journalist and new media consultant. He holds a master's degree in Mass Communications and has worked on some notable projects such as producing a user-generated video site for National Geographic. Scott keeps a daily blog at Pixelshot.com.

Tony Mamone
Founder and CEO of *Zimbio*

An engineer by training, Tony Mamone gravitated toward business and used his interest and passion for Internet content to create Findarticles.com. A few years later, after selling that site, he caught the entrepreneurial bug again and created *Zimbio.com*, an online magazine with over 13 million unique visitors a month that caters to style, entertainment, current events, and sports. While similar in content to other magazines on the market, *Elle*, *Vogue*, *Newsweek*, and so on, *Zimbio* is fundamentally different in that its members and readers are creating much of the magazine's content.

Kevin Marks
Technology Advocate, Google—OpenSocial

Kevin Marks is working on the international multicorporation project, OpenSocial. Companies from around the world have come together to create a standard on how personal profiles, databases, and trusted networks will begin sharing information, while at the same time protecting over 350 million users from repetition and password fraud.

Dharmesh Mehta
Director of Product Management for Windows Live Instant Messenger

Darmesh Mehta shares his insights about the ease of WLM and why 325 million people are currently using WLM and how 85 percent of its users are outside of the United States using 55 languages.

Matt Mullenweg
Cofounder of WordPress, President of Automattic

Matt Mullenweg created WordPress, in part, to give people a better means of personal expression through blogging. Matt's company has helped democratize publishing blogs, making them more accessible to writers and others who can now share interests on a global scale. WordPress also enables individuals and companies an unparalleled ability to listen to their community. Current WordPress users include Ford Motor Co., the CIA, FBI, Homeland Security, the *NY Times*, Fox News, and CNN.

Michael Naef
Founder and CEO of Doodle.com

Michael Naef holds an MSc in computer science from the Swiss Federal Institute of Technology Zurich and is the inventor of Doodle as well as its original developer. Incorporated in 2008, Doodle is located in Zurich, Switzerland, and runs the online scheduling service doodle.com.

David Nour
Author of *Relationship Economics*

A native Iranian, David Nour came to the United States in 1981 with a suitcase and no English. He has used his years of experience first as an immigrant, then as a businessman to write his book, *Relationship Economics*. He recognizes the importance of investing in relationships in business and shows that the most successful businesses were the ones that developed and nurtured their relationships with their customers and networks.

Chris Pirillo
Geek and Technology Enthusiast

Chris Pirillo has recorded over 1,000 videos in the past year, made the Top 100 Most Subscribed on YouTube and has the distinction of being the #1 hit on Google for the word "Chris." He has been participating in Internet conversations since 1992, is a monthly columnist for *CPU Magazine*, has authored books on business and personal technology, and produces weekly video segments for CNN.com.

John Pollard
Founder and CEO of Jott

John Pollard holds an MBA from the University of Michigan and has been in the technology industry for 20 years, including Microsoft, where he was involved in Sidewalk, Office, and Expedia, which he took internationally. While he considers working on the projects at Microsoft some of the highlights of his life, he decided to become an entrepreneur, leaving Microsoft in 2006 to create Jott. Jott is the culmination of things he's seen in his long career—something with global impact that worked on mobile devices like cell phones, was simple, and that people found very valuable.

Robert Scoble
Famous Blogger, Scobleizer, and author of *Naked Conversations*

Microsoft's best-known blogger, Robert Scoble started blogging in 2000 and interviewed 600 Microsoft employees including Bill Gates. He has over 3.5 million visitors to his main blog site annually and now interviews business and technology innovators. *Naked Conversations* contains over

50 case histories explaining why blogging is an efficient and useful method of credible business communication.

David Meerman Scott
Author of *The New Rules of Marketing & PR* and *World Wide Rave*

David Meerman Scott spent several decades working with marketing and online information, starting in the early 1980s when virtually no one else was. His experience working at high executive levels and on his own has given him an understanding of how online information drives people to make decisions and also how changes in marketing are occurring as a result of the Web.

Patrizio Spagnoletto
Senior Director of Marketing, Yahoo! Search Marketing

A Yahoo! employee for almost eight years, Patrizio Spagnoletto's current role is managing the marketing team for the Search Marketing product, the sponsored links that appear on Yahoo! His team is instrumental in making sure customers get a good return on their investment through education, communication, and product innovation.

Kakul Srivastava
General Manager of Yahoo!'s Flickr

Kakul Srivastava has been with Flickr since Yahoo! acquired it, seeing it grow from 300,000 registered users to over 30 million. Primarily a photo-sharing and social media site, Flickr chalks up 3 billion page views on a monthly basis, with over 60 million unique visitors. Worldwide, Flickr users upload 3 million photos each day.

Biz Stone
Cofounder of Twitter

Biz Stone has published two books about social media. Besides Twitter, he helped create Xanga, Odeo, and Obvious. He also worked for Google on the Blogger Team. He describes Twitter as a short messaging service that communicates everything from "What are you doing?" to immediate disaster reports.

George Strompolos
Content Partnerships Manager for YouTube

George Strompolos reaches out to content creators and helps them engage on YouTube, distribute their content, and connect with audiences globally.

Linh Tang
Author of *Launching Your Yahoo! Business* and *Succeeding at Your Yahoo! Business*, and entrepreneur

Linh Tang is the author of two e-commerce books on how to use Yahoo! Stores to build and market an online business. In addition, he is the co-owner and founder of vCentives, an online resource to help online retailers acquire new customers with no risk and zero acquisition costs. An award-winning Web designer, he has been designing web sites since 1995 and developing Yahoo! Stores since 2000.

Evo Terra
Coauthor of *Podcasting For Dummies*

Considered an "old man" in podcasting, Evo Terra started podcasting in October of 2004 and had the fortieth podcast on the planet. Coming in on the ground floor, as it were, he collaborated with Tee Morris to write *Podcasting For Dummies*, now in its second edition.

David Treadwell
Corporate Vice President of Microsoft's Live Platform

David Treadwell runs the Platform Services Group at Microsoft, where his department's mission is to build platforms for services with special emphasis on social scenarios, enabling developers to build applications that connect their users on a mass scale.

Gary Vaynerchuk
Wine Library Director of Operations, and Host and Founder of Wine Library TV

Starting out literally with just a liquor store, Gary Vaynerchuk has built a successful online retail store into a $50 million enterprise as well as Wine Library TV.com, with 600 episodes and an audience of over 80,000 per show, and his own blog, where he shares his experiences behind the scenes.

Amanda Vega
Amanda Vega Consulting—Comment Marketing

Amanda Vega is a 17-year online veteran who started her career as one of the first employees of AOL. She currently owns and operates an agency that provides services that include web site development, search engine optimization, social media, marketing, advertising, and public relations services and emphasizes how the Internet plays a key role in business models and marketing plans.

Peter Booth Wiley
Chairman of the Board of John Wiley & Sons, Inc., Publishing

Peter Booth Wiley is the sixth generation of Wileys involved in the publishing business, in a company that was founded when Thomas Jefferson was president. Chairman since 2002, he has 25 years of his own experience in the publishing world and as an author, journalist, and understands the historical evolution of social media. At the same time, his sons are actively working in social media, ensuring their future involvement in the Wiley legacy.

Aaron, Richard, 596–597
ABI Research, 398
"Above the fold" messages, 126
Abrams, Jonathan, 457
ACCESS (audience, concept, competition, execution, social media, sales viability) model, 671, 717–741, 763
Accounts, with WordPress, 490
Acrobat Connect, 655, 656–657
Acrobat ConnectPro, 657
Acteva, 571, 572–574
Active community members, 686, 687
Active Worlds, 320, 551, 552–553
Ad awareness, online, 9
Address Book feature, with Yahoo! Messenger, 427
Addresses, embedded, 101, 110
Adelson, Jay, 602
Ad-funded mobile gaming, 403
Adham, Allen, 569
Adler, Ofer, 527
Administrators, forum, 148–149
Adobe Acrobat™, Adobe Connect and, 433
Adobe Connect, 432–434
Adobe Flash, 749
  Brightcove and, 521
Adobe Flash animation software, 134
Adobe Premiere, 246
Adobe Presenter, Adobe Connect and, 433, 434
Adobe Systems Inc., 656, 657
Ad revenues, sharing in, 258
Adscape, 337
AdSense, 168, 382
  Google Search and, 625
Advanced Research Projects Agency Network (ARPAnet), 45, 96, 119, 358, 357
  EveryZing and, 625

AdventNet, 594
Advergaming, 403
AdverPlay, 337
Advertisers, Madison Avenue, 126
Advertising. See also Micro-advertising
  Active Worlds and, 552, 553
  AOL and, 574, 575
  AOL Instant Messenger and, 657
  AOL Mobile and, 641
  Bebo and, 450–451
  BitTorrent and, 576
  Blogger and, 474
  BlogTalkRadio and, 540
  Brightkite and, 642
  customer engagement with, 125
  David Meerman Scott on, 712–713
  Digg and, 600
  Eventful and, 578
  Facebook and, 452
  FeedBurner and, 617, 618
  Flickr and, 494
  4×4 Evolution and, 562
  Friendster and, 455
  gaming and, 561
  Gather.com and, 457, 458
  global spending on Internet, 392
  Google Alerts and, 579
  Google Gmail and, 583
  Google Reader and, 604
  Google Search and, 625, 626, 627
  Google Video and, 522
  Hulu and, 524, 525
  iGoogle and, 606
  in-game, 336, 341
  in social media strategy, 674

  iTunes and, 510
  Jott and, 646, 662
  KickApps and, 459
  Knol and, 480
  LinkedIn and, 460
  Live365 and, 542
  location-based services and, 401
  media and, 3
  Meebo and, 664
  Metacafe and, 525
  mobile gaming funded by, 403
  MOLI and, 462, 463
  MySpace and, 464
  My Yahoo! and, 607
  Ning and, 466
  Orkut and, 468
  Pay-Per-Click, 375
  Photobucket and, 496
  photo sharing and, 202
  PingShot and, 619, 620
  PodBean and, 511
  Podcast.com and, 513
  Reddit and, 609
  Redlasso and, 631, 632
  Rhapsody and, 515
  sales viability of, 732
  SHOUTcast and, 545
  Slide and, 500
  SlideShare and, 481
  strong communities and, 685
  as support for blogs, 168
  Survey Monkey and, 589
  TalkShoe and, 547
  Technorati and, 633
  There and, 557
  via mobile telephones, 399–400
  Viddler and, 527, 528
  web-site, 373
  Wikia and, 485, 486–487
  Wikipedia and, 489
  WordPress and, 490
  Yahoo! and, 592

Advertising (*continued*)
  Yahoo! Search and, 635
  Yelp and, 611
  YouTube and, 529
  Zoomerang and, 597
Advertising videos, 251–252
ADV warning label, 101
AdWords, 374, 375, 379–382
  getting started in, 380–382
  Google Search and, 625
AdWords Wizard, 376
Affiliate links, 175
Affiliate marketing, 135
Affinity communities, 673, 687–688
Affinity engines, 469–470
Age of the New Entrepreneur, 39
Aggregators, 30–31, 346–348, 599–613
  Atom and, 616
  Digg, 599, 600–602
  FriendFeed, 599, 602–604
  Google Readwer, 599, 604–605
  iGoogle, 599, 606–607
  My Yahoo!, 599, 607–609
  Reddit, 599, 609–611
  RSS 2.0 and, 621
  Tool Scorecard for, 599, 613
  Yelp, 599, 611–613
AIM. *See* AOL Instant Messenger (AIM)
AIM Buddy List, 420. *See also* AOL Instant Messenger (AIM)
AIM Express, 420
airG, 639, 640
AirG.com, 407
Aki-aki,com, 407
Akismet, WordPress and, 490
alakazimes.com, 340
Albums, Photobucket and, 496
Alexa, 136, 168
Aley, Doug, 648, 664
Algorithms, 361
Allaire, Jeremy, 521–522
Allaire Corporation, 521
All-In-One SEO, 175
AllOff, Kevin Marks on, 768
All You Can Meet®, GoToMeeting and, 431
Alterman, Eric, 460
Altruistic givers, David Nour on, 753
Amanda Vega & Associates, 155
Amanda Vega Consulting, 406
Amarok, 228

Amazon.com, 674
American Cancer Society, 315, 316, 317
  Second Life and, 557
American Public Media Group (APMG), 458
American Red Cross, 273
American Telephone and Telegraph (AT&T), early wireless phones from, 393
America Online (AOL), 121, 571, 574–575. *See also* AOL entries
  Bebo and, 451
  LinkedIn and, 461
  in mobile marketing, 411
Analog to digital video converter, 255
Analysis, execution and, 729
Analytics, 177
Andersen Consulting, 619
Anderson, Chris, 84
Anderson, Tom, 49, 466
Andreasem, Erwin, 331
Andreessen, Marc, 468
AndrewSullivan.com, 165
Android, 406, 410
  in mobile marketing, 411–412
Animation software, 134
Anshe Chung Studios, 314
AOL Instant Messenger (AIM), 298, 420, 655, 657–659. *See also* AIM entries; America Online (AOL)
  Google Gmail and, 583
  iChat and, 421–422
AOL LLC, 574, 657
AOL Mobile, 639, 641–642
API (application program interface), 62
Apollo Group, Inc., 646
Apple Computer, 69–70
  collaboration and, 677–678
  iTunes and, 510–511
Apple computers, in publishing, 750
Apple eWorld, 146
Apple iChat, 421–423, 655, 661–662
Apple iMovie, 750
Apple iPhone, 225–226, 405, 749
Apple Newton, 307
  operating system, 309
Applepedia, Wikia and, 486
Apple QuickTime, 240–241

Applications. *See also* Aggregators; Productivity applications
  Acrobat Connect and, 656
  Acteva and, 573
  Active Worlds and, 552
  airG and, 640
  AOL and, 575
  AOL Instant Messenger and, 658
  AOL Mobile and, 641
  Apple iChat and, 662
  Atom and, 616
  BitTorrent and, 577
  Blogger and, 475
  BlogTalkRadio and, 541
  Brightcove and, 521
  Brightkite and, 643
  CallWave and, 645
  Constant Contact and, 476
  Digg and, 600–601
  education blogs and, 679–680
  Eventful and, 578
  EverQuest and, 566
  EveryZing and, 624
  Facebook and, 452–453
  Fast Pitch! and, 454
  FeedBurner and, 618
  Flickr and, 495
  FriendFeed and, 602, 603
  Friendster and, 456
  Google Alerts and, 580
  Google Docs and, 582
  Google Gmail and, 584
  Google Reader and, 605
  Google Search and, 626
  Google Video and, 523
  Go To Meeting and, 660
  Hulu and, 524
  Ice Rocket and, 628
  iGoogle and, 606–607
  interpersonal, 417–443
  for intracompany communities, 688
  iTunes and, 510–511
  Joomla and, 478, 479
  Jott and, 647, 663
  Jumbuck and, 649
  Justin.tv and, 544
  Kaneva and, 554, 555
  Kevin Marks on, 769
  KickApps and, 459–460
  Knol and, 480
  Live365 and, 543
  Meebo and, 665
  Metacafe and, 526

MetaTube and, 630
MOLI and, 463
MSGTAG and, 585
MySpace and, 465
My Yahoo! and, 608
Ning and, 467
Orkut and, 469
Photobucket and, 496
of photo sharing tools, 493
Picasa and, 498
PingShot and, 620
Plaxo and, 470–471
Plurk, 534
PodBean and, 512
Podcast.com and, 514
Radar.net and, 499
ReadNotify and, 587
Reddit and, 610
Rhapsody and, 516
RSS 2.0 and, 621
Second Life and, 556
SHOUTcast and, 546
Skype and, 667
Slide and, 501
SlideShare and, 482
SMS.ac and, 651
SmugMug and, 502–503
Survey Monkey and, 589
TalkShoe and, 548
Technorati and, 633
There and, 558
TiddlyWiki and, 591
Twitter and, 536
Twitter and, 536
Twitxr and, 504
TypePad and, 484
Viddler and, 528
virtual worlds and, 551
WebEx and, 669
Wikia and, 486
Wikipedia and, 488
WordPress and, 490
World of Warcraft and, 568
Yahoo! and, 593
Yahoo! Search and, 636
Yelp and, 612
YouTube and, 530
Zoho and, 594–595
Zoomerang and, 596
Zooomr and, 505
App Store, 225
Archie, 357
Archiving, via PodBean, 512
Armstrong, Heather, 76–77
Armstrong, Jerome, 165
Arnold, John, 111–113, 775

Aronsson, Lars Erik, 184
Arriola, Benj, 369–370, 775
Artblog, 167
Arundel, Rikki, 475
ATMs (automated teller machines), Entropia Universe and, 564
Atom, 344, 615, 616–617
Atom 0.2, 345
Atom feeds, 151, 230, 616–617
Google Reader and, 605
PingShot and, 620
Atompub Group, 345
Atom Publishing Protocol, 344, 345
Atom Syndication Format, 344, 345
Atrios, 169
@ sign, 96
Attitudes
execution and, 730
in identifying audience, 720
Audacity, 213, 214, 215, 217, 219
Audibles, with Yahoo! Messenger, 427
Audience(s)
in ACCESS model, 718–725
classifying, 722–725
concept statement and, 727
David Meerman Scott on, 714
defined, 719
engaging, 7–12
execution and, 730–731
identifying, 719–722
knowing, 93
marketing and, 718–719
for movies, 722–725
net promoter score and, 732–733
social-media, 138, 139
successful movies and, 718
Audience archetypes/personas, xi
ACCESS model and, 717, 722
concept statement and, 727
establishing, 77–78
in identifying audience, 722, 724–725
Audio, for publishing, 749–750
Audioblog, 167
Audio capability, 27–28
Audio chats, iChat and, 422–423
Audio conferencing
with Adobe Connect, 433
CallWave and, 645
Audio content, podcasting, 210

Audio editing programs, 214
Audio equalizing software, 217
Audio file library, 234
Audio files, 224
managing, 226
Audio livecasting, 287–288
Audio podcasts
creating, 223
ease of downloading, 234
Audio recording program, 219
Audio recordings, digitized, 208
Audio recording software, 213
Audio sharing, 223–235
beginnings of, 224
information related to, 224–231
Audio sharing providers, 231–232
Audio streaming, SHOUTcast and, 546
Audio technology, 509
Audio tools, 509–517
iTunes, 509, 510–511
PodBean, 509, 511–513
Podcast.com, 509, 513–515
Redlasso and, 631
Rhapsody, 509, 515–517
Tool Scorecard for, 510, 517
Zoho and, 595
Authenticity, in podcasting, 219
authorbound.com, xviii
AuthorBound program, xvii–xviii
Authoring tool, 275
Authorities, social media, x
Author/publisher relationship, 15
Automated computer programs, 360
Automated dictionary, 102
Automattic, 489
Avatars, 150, 312, 313
Active Worlds and, 552
Second Life, 319
Awakening the Entrepreneur Within (Gerber), 38
Awareness page, 124
Awareness stage, of the sales funnel, 122
Aweber, 174, 175

Backdrops, for iChat video chats, 422
Background music, with Yahoo! Messenger, 428

Backgrounds, with Yahoo!
    Messenger, 427–428
Baghdad Blog, 169
Bain & Company, 732
Bamberger, Steve, 657
Bandwidth, 240
Banner advertising, 385
    Facebook and, 452
Barcodes, in mobile marketing,
    410–411
Barger, Jorn, 162
Barry, Glen, 164
Bartle, Richard, 331
Bartle Test, 331
Base stations, earliest, 393, 394
Batey, Lisa, 290
BBC, 273
    Twitter and, 537
BBC News, blogging by, 167
BBC video blogging site, 242
BBN Technologies, 625
Bebo, 450–451
Bebo.com, 45
Bebo Authors, 451
Bebo Music, 450–451
Bechtolsheim, Andy, 627
Becker, Brady, 644
Beesely, Angela, 486
Behaviors
    execution and, 730
    forum, 148
    in identifying audience, 719–
        720, 724–725
Beliefs
    execution and, 730
    in identifying audience, 720
Bell, Alexander Graham, 289
Bell Labs, early wireless phones
    from, 393, 394
Benchmark Capital, 603
benjarriola.com, 369
Berman, Josh, 49, 466
Berners-Lee, Tim, 118, 120, 357
Berthelmy, Mark, 605
Best practices, xiii
Bianchini, Gina, 468
Bidding, in Search Engine
    Marketing, 387
Bidding mall, 386
Big Sombrero Economy, 84
"Big Tony, the Plumber" web
    site, 679
Bill paying, Jott service and, 425
Birch, Michael, 451
Birch, Paul, 451
Birch, Xochi, 451

BirthdayAlarm.com, 451
Bisson, Michelle, 479
Bits, 239
BitTorrent, 35, 256–257, 571,
    576–577
BizBash Media, 597
Black, Duncan, 169
BlackBerry, 195, 395, 749
    CallWave and, 645
Blawgs, 168
Blended success metrics, 129
Blendtec, 675, 684
    social media strategy of, 674
Blendtec video, 251, 258–259
Blizzard Entertainment, 325,
    335, 567, 568–569
Blog-based books, 169–170
BlogCatalog, 168
Blog format, 350–351
Blogger(s), 162, 473, 474–475.
    See also Blogging
    PodBean and, 512
    TypePad and, 485
Blogger.com, 162, 165
Blogger's Code of Conduct, 167
Blogging, 153. See also Blogs;
    Microblogging tools
    benefits of, 177–178
    Blogger and, 474–475
    as a business, 175
    Chris Pirillo on, 741
    collaboration and, 678
    Digg and, 601
    earning income via, 174
    education and, 679–680
    FeedBurner and, 617, 618
    Flickr and, 494
    FriendFeed and, 602, 603
    hardware and softwar for, 749
    Ice Rocket and, 627, 628, 629
    Jott service and, 425, 647, 663
    Jumbuck and, 649
    Kevin Marks on, 767
    PingShot and, 619
    Redlasso and, 631, 632
    Rhapsody and, 516
    Rich Site Summary and, 615
    in social media strategy, 673–
        674
    TalkShoe and, 548
    Technorati and, 633–634
    Twitxr and, 504
    TypePad and, 483–485
    WordPress and, 489–491
    Zoho and, 595
Blogging conferences, 175

Bloghood, 168
Bloglines, 168
Blog mailing list, 174
Blog mission, 176
Blogosphere, 168
    Technorati and, 633, 634
Blog page, 125
Blog platforms, browser-based,
    164
Blog posts, scanning, 174
Blog post titles, 173
Blog providers, 169–172
Blogs, 23, 48, 146, 161–179, 277,
    364, 758
    beginnings of, 162–167
    commenting on, 173
    company, 761–762
    credibility of, 166
    customer education via, 10–11
    earliest, 164
    education via, 679–680
    Gather.com and, 457
    hosted, 165
    immediacy of, 166
    importance of, 374
    information related to, 167–
        170
    KickApps and, 459
    linking, 164, 175
    maintaining, 169
    mobile telephone access to,
        398
    as a news source, 166–167
    political, 164, 165–166
    popularity of, 168–169
    purpose of, 161
    reading, 176
    searching for, 678
    in tapping into employee
        wisdom, 745
    widespread nature of, 166–167
BlogScope, 168
Blog-specific search engines, 168
BlogTalkRadio (BTR), 232, 294,
    298, 539, 540–542, 781
Blog topic, choosing, 174
Blog Tracker, with Ice Rocket,
    629
Blood Feud, 330
Blossom, John, 82–85, 775
bluecasting.com, 401
Blue's News, 163
Bluetooth connection, 400–401
    gaming via, 402
bluetoothmagnet.com, 401
BlueTwit-IBM, 277

BMW brand pod, 247
"Bob" operating system, 307, 308
Boing Boing, 169
Bolas, Jennie, 573
Bolt, Beranek and Newman
    (BBN), 625
Book, Betsy, 559
Bookmarking, 352
Bookmarklets, Reddit and, 610
Book publishing, blogs and, 169–
    170. See also Publishing
    entries
Books
    blog-based, 169–170
    marketing, 15–16
Boolean logic
    Google Gmail and, 583
    Google Search and, 626
Boss, Robert, 591
Bots, 360
    with Active Worlds, 552
Bounces, 99
Bourne, Scott, 288
Bourseul, Charles, 289
Boutelle, Jonathan, 483
Box.net, Zoho and, 594–595
Bradley, Bill, 360
Brake, David K., xiv, xviii
Brand awareness, 9
Brand-centric communities, 684
Branded communities, Gather.
    com and, 457
Branding, Kyle Ford on, 709
Brand recognition
    aggregators and, 599
    Constant Contact and, 476
    There and, 558
Brand value, increasing, ix, 73–
    74
Bratton, Tim, 517
Bray, Tim, 345
Brewer, Jeffrey, 374
Brightcove, 519, 520–522
Brightkite, 639, 642–644
BrightKite.com, 407
Brin, Sergey, 523–524, 581, 627
Broadband connection, 242
Broadband Mechanics, 776
Broadband studio, 257
Broadcasting
    Brightcove and, 520
    Eventful and, 579
    Justin.tv and, 544
    Kaneva and, 554–555
    Live365 and, 542, 543–544
    livecasting as, 539

music videos and, 519
    Redlasso and, 631, 632
    SHOUTcast and, 546–547
    via TalkShoe, 547–548
    YouTube and, 529, 530
Broadtexter.com, 407
Brogan, Chris, 176
Broitman, Adam, 397, 775–776
    on mobile marketing, 410–412
Brouaux, Alexandre, 517
Browser-based blog platforms,
    164
Browser-based web platform,
    181
Browser software, 121
Browsing, MetaTube and, 629–
    630
Bruhnke, Doug, 56
Bryant, Stephanie, 247–248, 776
Bub.blicio.us, FriendFeed and,
    603
Buchheit, Paul, 584–585, 604
Buck, James, Twitter and, 537
Buckley, Michael, social media
    strategy of, 674
Buddyping.com, 407
BuddyPress, 58
Buffer character, 327
Buggles, 519
Bulletin boards, 146
Bulletin board systems (BBS),
    163
Bungie software, 335
Burnes, James, 43, 45, 137–139,
    360, 776
Burnout Paradise, 325
Bush, Vannevar, 118
Business. See also Media-
    business relationship
    Acrobat Connect and, 657
    Active Worlds and, 552, 553
    aggregators and, 599
    airG and, 640
    AOL Instant Messenger and,
        658
    AOL Mobile and, 641
    Apple iChat and, 661
    assessing opportunities and
        threats of, 705–706
    assessing strengths and
        weaknesses of, 704–705
    Atom and, 616–617
    Bill Jula on, 734–735
    BitTorrent and, 576
    Brightcove and, 520
    Brightkite and, 643, 644

building communities for,
    684–688
CallWave and, 645
collaboration in, 676–678
communication in, 675–676
concepts in, 725–727
content in, 683
control and influence in, 681–
    683
conversation and, 675
David Nour on, 751–754
Digg and, 600, 601
Entropia Universe and, 564,
    565
establishing and managing
    communities for, 689–690
evaluating and organizing
    resources and, 743–744
EverQuest and, 566–567
FeedBurner and, 618
FriendFeed and, 602–603
gaming and, 561
Gather.com and, 458
Google Alerts and, 580
Google Reader and, 604, 605
Google Search and, 626
Google Video and, 522, 523
Go To Meeting and, 659, 660
growth of, 112–113
iGoogle and, 606, 607
interpersonal applications
    and, 418
interpersonal tools for, 655
Joomla and, 478, 479
Jott and, 647, 663–664
Jumbuck and, 650
Kaneva and, 554–555
KickApps and, 460
LinkedIn and, 461–462
livecasting and, 539
MOLI and, 463–464
My Yahoo! and, 608
paranoia in, 682
Plaxo and, 470, 471
Plurk and, 535
Podcast.com and, 514
productivity tools for, 571
ReadNotify and, 587
Reddit and, 610
Redlasso and, 632
Rich Site Summary and, 615
RSS 2.0 and, 621
rules of social media for, 5
sales viability in, 731–733
Second Life and, 556–557
Skype and, 667

Business (*continued*)
  Slide and, 501
  SlideShare and, 482, 483
  SMS.ac and, 652
  SmugMug and, 503
  social media macro strategy
    for, 757, 760–765
  social media strategy and,
    673–674
  Survey Monkey and, 589
  TalkShoe and, 548
  tapping into employee wisdom
    by, 744–745
  technology andsupport in,
    748–750
  There and, 558
  TiddlyWiki and, 591
  Twitter and, 536
  Twitxr and, 504
  TypePad and, 484–485
  virtual worlds and, 551
  WebEx and, 668–669
  Wikia and, 486–487
  Wikipedia and, 488–489
  word-of-mouth, 5
  Yahoo! and, 592–593
  Yahoo! Search and, 635
  Yelp and, 611, 612–613
  YouTube and, 530
  Zoho and, 594, 595
  Zoomerang and, 596
Business applications
  Doodle service and, 440–441
  with Google Apps, 437, 438
  Rishi Chandra on, 438–439
Business Application Suite, with
  Zoho,594
Business blogs, 168
Business culture, 15
Business-customer match-
  making, 379
Business goals, ix, xi
Business opportunities,
  LinkedIn, 56
Businesspeople, as trusted
  networks, 46
Business professionals, Fast
  Pitch! and, 454–455
Business revenue models,
  MMORPG, 330
Business strategy, social media
  tools in, ix
Business-to-business (B2B)
  e-Commerce, worldwide, 392
Business-to-business (b-to-b)
  success metrics, 129–130

Business-to-consumer (B2C)
  transactions, worldwide,
  392
Butterfield, Stewart, 495
Buyer personas, David Meerman
  Scott on, 714
Buying cycle, length of, 123
Buy page, 124
Buy stage, of the sales funnel,
  123–124
Buy-to-play business revenue
  model, 330
Büyükkökten, Orkut, 469–470
Buzz Alert, with Yahoo!
  Messenger, 427
Byrne, Owen, 601–602
Bytes, 239

Cable technology, 240
Cadenhead, Rogers, 345
Cailliau, Robert, 119, 120, 143
Cain, David, 138–139, 777
Calacanis, Jason, 167
Calendars, Doodle service and,
  440, 441
CallWave, 407, 639, 644–646
Camel Case titling, 183
Camera cell phones, 195, 196,
  200–201
  providers of, 200
Cameras
  in mobile marketing, 410–411
  for publishing, 750
Campaigns, regional and local,
  134–135
"Camping", 340
Canfield, Krista, 45, 61–62, 776
Canter, Marc, 776
Can-the-Spam (Can Spam) Act
  of 2004, 100, 101, 103, 110,
  400
Capital Corporation, 38
Capita Learning & Development,
  605
CAPTCHA Code, 149
Carmack, John, 163
Carriers, in mobile marketing,
  411, 412
Cars, iPod-compatible, 207
CarTalk, 75
Case, Steve, 575, 642, 658
Cashmore, Pete, 349–351, 777
Castronova, Edward, 333
Cave paintings, 75
Cave Phone, 393
Cave Radio, 393

CBS News, 217
Celebrity Baby Blog, TypePad
  and, 484
Cell phones. *See also* Camera cell
  phones
  AOL Mobile and, 641–642
  beginnings of, 393–398
  Brightkite and, 643–644
  CallWave and, 644–646
  camera-enabled, 196
  Google Video and, 522
  Jott service and, 423, 425, 646–
    648, 662–664
  Jumbuck and, 648–650
  Meebo and, 665–666
  need for, 393
  Skype and, 667–668
  SMS.ac and, 650–652
  social media tools for, 639–653
  worldwide ownership of, 406
  Yahoo! Messenger and, 426–
    428
Cells, earliest, 393, 394
Cell sites, earliest, 394
Cellular technology
  early, 394
  Internet and, 391
Censorship, 243
  in China, 36
Center for Disease Control
  (CDC), in MMORPG WoW,
  331–333
Centralized Code, Kyle Ford on,
  709
Cerf, Vint, 34, 118, 119, 777
Certification, ReadNotify and,
  587–588
Chandra, Rishi, 777
  on Google Apps, 437–439
Channels, Justin.tv, 545
Charish, Bob, 541
Charish, Levy, 541
Chase, Steve, 328
Chat Del Mundo, with Jumbuck,
  649
Chat do Mundo, with Jumbuck,
  649
Chat rooms, 145, 146
Chat sessions, Google Gmail
  and, 583, 584
Chatting. *See also* AOL Instant
  Messenger (AIM); Instant
  messaging
  Apple iChat and, 661–662
  with Google Talk, 420–421
  via Justin.tv, 545

Chen, Steve, 242, 530
Chieco, Vinnie, 208
Children's Online Privacy
    Protection Act (COPPA), 149
Child safety issues, 54
Chilton, Tom, 334
China
    Entropia Universe and, 564,
        565
    Internet usage by, 392
Chung, Anshe, 314, 333
Cilley, Marla "The Flylady", 540–
    541
Cinematography, Viddler and,
    528–529
CipSoft SmartCell Technology,
    402
Cisco Systems, 272, 668
Citizendium, 184
Citizen journalism, 89, 137,
    274
Citrix Systems Inc., 659, 661
Claim Your Content platform,
    YouTube and, 530
Clark, Scott, 664
Classification systems, 22
"Click Here to Purchase", 128
Click-fraud management, 380
Click-throughs, 99, 105
Client demographic, reaching, 9
Clients, engaging, 44. See also
    Customers
Cloaking, 366
Closed wikis, 184
Cloud computing, Rishi
    Chandra on, 438
Cloud concept, David Treadwell
    on, 771–773
Cloud Nine, 311
Clough, Scott, 337–340, 778
Clover, Steve, 330, 567
CNN, 217
    Twitter and, 533, 537
CNN.com, 686, 759
    Chris Pirillo on, 739
Cohen, Bram, 257, 577
Coke Studios, 320
ColdFusion, 521
Collaboration, 18. See also Social
    media
    Acrobat Connect and, 656
    Apple iChat and, 661
    David Nour on, 751
    as an engagement strategy, 8,
        731
    Go To Meeting and, 660

in mastering social media
    strategy, 675, 676–678
online, 35
in pinpointing social media
    starting point, 746
social media strategies in, 671
TiddlyWiki and, 591
WebEx and, 669
Zoho and, 594
Collaborative publishing, Google
    Docs and, 581–582
collegeboyslive.tv, 290
CollegeClub.com, 652
Combs, Brett, 563
Combs, Scot, 288
Comcast, 35–36, 272
Comcast Interactive Media, 471
Commenting, 260
    importance of, 204, 248
Comment marketing, 255, 785
Commercial e-mail messages,
    100
Commercial Internet-only radio
    stations, 288–290
Commissions, sales viability
    and, 732
CommonCraft.com, 186
Commons Project, 180
Communication(s)
    Acrobat Connect and, 656, 657
    AOL Instant Messenger and,
        658–659
    Apple iChat and, 661–662
    Brightkite and, 643, 644
    CallWave and, 645
    Chris Pirillo on, 738
    corporate, 103–104
    as an engagement strategy, 7–
        8, 731
    forum, 152–153
    FriendFeed and, 602
    Go To Meeting and, 660
    Jott and, 647, 663–664
    Justin.tv and, 544–545
    livecasting and, 539
    in mastering social media
        strategy, 675–676
    Meebo and, 665–666
    person-to-person, 9
    in pinpointing social media
        starting point, 746
    to prospects and customers,
        161
    Second Life and, 556
    Skype and, 667–668
    SMS.ac and, 651–652

social media strategies in, 671
in SWOT analysis, 704, 706
TalkShoe and, 548
Technorati and, 634
trust and transparency with,
    137
verbal, 237
via Plurk, 534, 535
via Twitter, 535–537
WebEx and, 668–669
Yahoo! and, 592–593
Zoho and, 594
Communication Services Inc.,
    646
Communicators, in mobile viral
    marketing, 403–404
Communities
    brand-centric, 684
    building, 64, 94
    Chris Pirillo on, 738
    commitment to, 63
    concepts and, 725–727
    content and, 684–688
    creating, 78, 763–764
    establishing and managing,
        689–690
    execution and, 729
    global, 59
    joining, 323
    Kaneva and, 554
    Kyle Ford on, 710–711
    making money with, 81
    making or breaking, 686–687
    with Pownce, 690–693
    sales viability in, 731–733
    social media strategy and,
        673–674, 684–688, 689–690
    strong, 685–686
    types of, 673, 687–688
    Yelp, 91–92
Community 2.0, 47
Community effect, 201
Community evangelists, 689–
    690
Community managers, 689
Community marketing,
    300–301
Companies. See also
    Corporations;
    Organizations
    as potential publishers, 71–73
    social networking tools from,
        449–450
    use of virtual worlds, 321–322
Company blogs, 761–762
Company forum, 145

Company retreats, in tapping into employee wisdom, 744
Company-sponsored blogs/ wikis, 10–11
Company successes, exploring, 322
Company value, increasing, 73–74
Company wikis, 181, 191
Competition
 in ACCESS model, 727–728
 David Nour on, 751
 knowing, 94
 knowing and understanding, 728
Competitive audience persona, 724
Competitive edge, x
Competitors
 ACCESS model and, 717
 business content and, 683, 684, 685
 establishing and managing communities and, 689
 in SWOT analysis, 706
Complete customer experience, xi
Compression technology, 240
CompuServe, 121
Computer-based virtual reality, 305
Computer electronic mail, 96
Computers. *See also* Desktop computers; Laptop computers; Macintosh (Mac) computers; Personal computers (PCs)
 in assessing technology and support, 749
 David Treadwell on, 773
Computer workstation, 120
Concept
 in ACCESS model, 717, 725–727
 competition and, 727–728
 differentiating, 93
 execution and, 728–729
 testing and validation of, 727
Concept statement, 726–727
 execution and, 730
Conde Nast Publications, Reddit and, 609, 611
Conferencing
 with Adobe Connect, 432–434
 with GoToMeeting, 430–431
 with WebEx, 431–432, 669

 with Yahoo! Messenger, 427
Confidentiality
 Go To Meeting and, 660
 with LinkedIn, 462
Connectors, 757
Constant Contact, 7, 23, 109–110, 112, 473, 476–477, 779
 communication via, 676
Consumer Best Practices Guidelines, mobile telephone advertising and, 400
Consumer needs, meeting, 76–77
Consumers
 Kevin Marks on, 766–767
 in mobile marketing, 411
Content
 ACCESS model and, 717
 aligning with audience needs, 690
 Bill Jula on, 737
 Chris Pirillo on, 738
 community reactions toward, 686–687
 creating, 93, 389
 creating communities around, 684–688
 David Meerman Scott on, 714
 in defining business, 683–684
 as a design element, 131
 execution and, 730
 importance of, 75, 76, 141, 218–219
 making money with, 81
 in Search Engine Optimization, 362–363
 social media strategy and, 673–674
 sticky, 684
 streaming, 287
 user-generated, 23, 79–81, 689
 ways people are engaged by, 79–80
 web-site, 370
Content Blogger, 82
Content Connections LLC, xvii–xviii
 ACCESS model and, 717
 in identifying audience, 720
 net promoter score and, 733
Content creators, 257
Content filters, 102–103
Content freshness, 363–364
Content hubs, Wikia and, 486, 487

Content management system (CMS), 80
 Joomla as, 478
Content Nation, 82–83
Content Nation (Blossom), 775
Content Network, 382
Content Partners, 258
Contributions
 business content and, 683
 TiddlyWiki and, 590
Control, in social media strategy, 681–683
Control Video Corporation, 575, 658, 642
Conventional marketing strategy, 135
Conversation(s)
 authentic, 157–158
 business content and, 683
 control and influence via, 681–683
 Digg and, 600
 in mastering social media strategy, 675
 social media enabling of, 4
 social networking via, 449
 using phone technology, 232–233
Conversational media, 6
Conversion(s), 105
 quantifying, 129
 segmenting to maximize, 105–106, 114
 successful, 128
Conversion definitions, understanding, 141
Conversion message
 fine-tuning, 129
 importance of, 127–129
Conversion rate, 95, 128
Conversion-tracking software, 382
Converter box, 255
Conway, Ron, 627
Cooper, Martin, 393
Coopertition, 72–73
Copyrighted material, posting, 260
Copyright infringements, 148
Copyrights, 213, 220
Copyright violations, 256
Core customers, understanding, 322
"Core excellence", 40
Core Team Members, with Joomla, 479

Corporate blogs, 168
Corporate communications, customer evaluation of, 103–104
Corporate partners, xvi
Corporate twitterers, 271–273
Corporate web site, 156
Corporations
    Acteva and, 572
    airG and, 640
    assessing opportunities and threats of, 705–706
    assessing strengths and weaknesses of, 704–705
    Brightkite and, 644
    EveryZing and, 625
    Google Video and, 522
    Joomla and, 478, 479
    Slide and, 501
    tapping into employee wisdom by, 744–745
    Technorati and, 634
Corrupted Blood epidemic, 331–332
Costolo, Dick, 618, 620
Cost-per-click (CPC), 380
Cost-per-click advertising, 375–377
Cost-per-click marketing plan, 374
Cotsakos, Christos M., 464
Courtin, Angela, 45, 54, 59–60, 778
Cover Flow, 226
Cox, Ana Marie, 169
Cox Communication, 100
Craig, Libby, 573
Craigslist Foundation, 573
Craigslist model, 91
Crayon Marketing, 410, 775
Creating Web Pages For Dummies (Smith and Bebak), 131
Creative Commons Act, 261
Creative Commons License, 198
Creative Commons (CC) project, 202, 213
Creativity
    in podcasting, 221
    in SWOT analysis, 704
    for vlogs, 238
Credit cards, first commercial payment system for, 394
Crowd Control (CC) character, 327
Crowd Fire, 85
Crowd sourcing, 730–731

Crowne Pointe Historic Inn and Spa, Constant Contact and, 477
Crystal, Darren, 497
Cuban, Mark, 629
Culver, Leah, 270, 690–693, 778
Cunningham, Ward, 181–182
Currency
    Kaneva and, 554
    Second Life and, 556
    There and, 557
Customer engagement, by H9
Customer psychology, 107
Customer relationships, ix
Customers
    as collaborators, xi, 677–678
    communication with, 114
    David Meerman Scott on, 714–715
    David Nour on, 753
    enticing, 103–104
    evaluating and organiing resources and, 743–744
    getting closer to, 761–762
    influence on, 681–683
    net promoter score and, 732–733
    prospecting for, 140
    in SWOT analysis, 705–706
    two-way communication with, 202
    understanding, 141
Customer service, in Search Engine Marketing, 385–386
Customizable Fonts and Colors, with Yahoo! Messenger, 428
Custom Ringtones, with Yahoo! Messenger, 428
Custom Status Messages, with Yahoo! Messenger, 428
Cutler, Jessica, 169
Cybertown, 320
Czerniak, Arik, 527

Daedalus Project, 330
DailyCandy.com, 70
Daily Kos, 169
Damage per Second (DPS) character, 327
Data services, for mobile telephone, 396–397
Day parting, 106–108, 114
    marketing effect of, 107
Dear, Brian, 579
Debuffer character, 327
Dedman, Jay, 241

de Gaulle, Charles, 777
del.icio.us.com, 266
Delivery Network Accelerator (DNA), BitTorrent and, 576, 577
Dell Computer, 83–84, 272
DeMarco, Donna, 529
Demographic data
    execution and, 730
    in identifying audience, 721
Demo Jam, 276
Demonstrated behaviors, in identifying audience, 719–720
Department of Defense, BlogTalkRadio and, 540, 541
Desktop computers, John Pollard on, 434–435
Desktop photo-management applications, 195
Desktops, with iChat, 422
Detractors, 764
    sales viability and, 732–733
Deutch, Roni, 475
DeWolfe, Chris, 49, 50, 466
Dhanjani, Nitesh, 270–271
Dialogue, ongoing, 147
Diaries
    Jott and, 664
    online, 163, 165
Diarists, 163
Diaryland, 165
Dickson, Tom, 675
    social media strategy of, 674
Dictionary attacks, 101–102
"Diff" feature, 184
Digg, 176, 217, 265, 599, 600–602
Digg Spy, 601
Digital audio player, first, 208–209
Digital cameras, 195–196
    advent of, 194
    providers of, 200
    for publishing, 750
Digital cellular technology early, 394
Digital distribution, 86–87
Digital electronics, 239
Digital format, converting VHS videos to, 260
Digital Marketplace Model and Forecast, 391–393
Digital media, iTunes and, 510, 511
Digital photos, 201
    sharing of, 195

Digital recorder, 216
  connecting, 217
Digital studio, 257
Digital tools, 44
Diplopedia, 190
DipNote blog, 77–78
Direct mail advertising, versus
  web page design, 125
Direct response, 385
DirecTV, World of Warcraft and,
  567–568
Disney's Toontown, 320
Distribution
  Bill Jula on, 736–737
  BitTorrent and, 576–577
  with Fast Pitch!, 454
DivorcingDaze.com, 70–71
Documents
  Google Docs and, 581–582
  Go To Meeting and, 660
  TiddlyWiki and, 590–591
Dodgeball, 277
Dodgeball.com, 407
Doerr, John, 627
Do-It-Yourself Radio, 294
Domain names, 117
  Kyle Ford on, 708
  with SmugMug, 502
Donations
  to Joomla, 477
  TiddlyWiki and, 590
  Wikipedia and, 487
Dooce.com, 70, 76–77
Doodle, 429–430
  Michael Naef on, 440–441
Doodle.com, 782–783
Doppler, 228
Dorsey, Jack, 264, 537
DOS-style browser, 121
"DotComGuy", 291
Dotsam and netsam, 169
Dots per inch (dpi), 132
Double opt-in, 100
Downloadable forms/templates,
  xiv
Downloads
  BitTorrent and, 576
  SMS.ac and, 652
  from SmugMug, 503
  Zoomerang and, 596
Drake, Christopher, 588
Dreamcast, 4×4 Evolution and,
  562
Dreaming World, The, 38
Dreamscape, 310
Dreamville, 320

Drive time, 107
Driving, Jott service and, 425
DropShots, 200
Drudge, Matt, 165
Drudge Report, 165
Drupal, 246
Dube, Jonathan, 165
Dubit, 320
Dunbar's Number, 48–49
Dungeons & Dragons, 309, 326,
  338
Dungeons & Dragons Online,
  334
DynaTAC mobile phone, 394

EarthLink, 162, 163
eBay, 8, 668
eBay Design Labs, 579
Ecliptic Enterprises, 646
E-commerce, xii, 117
Economy (economies)
  Entropia Universe and, 565
  Second Life and, 556–557
  virtual, 333
Ecosystem, 21–22. See also
  Social Media Ecosystem
Editing
  with Picasa, 497–498, 598–599
  of video, 245–246
  of web pages, 439
  of Wikipedia, 487–488
  of wikis, 183
Editing software, in publishing,
  750
Education
  Acrobat Connect and, 657
  Active Worlds and, 553
  BlogTalkRadio and, 540
  Brightcove and, 520
  as an engagement strategy, 8,
    731
  Flickr and, 495
  Justin.tv and, 545
  Live365 and, 543
  livecasting and, 539
  in mastering social media
    strategy, 675, 679–680
  in pinpointing social media
    starting point, 746
  Plurk and, 534
  PodBean and, 512–513
  Podcast.com and, 514
  Reddit and, 610
  SlideShare and, 482
  social media strategies in, 671
  in SWOT analysis, 704, 706

There and, 558
TiddlyWiki and, 590–591
Viddler and, 528–529
Wikipedia and, 487–488
8zap.com, 275
Eisenberg, Brian Daniel, 603
Ektron CMS400.NET, 153–155
Elders, 48
eLearning, 657
Electronic retailing, 383
Eliason, Frank, 272
Elisa Group, 394
  early text messaging and, 396–
    397
E-mail, 95–116, 156, 157, 758
  with AOL, 574
  AOL Mobile and, 642
  CallWave and, 645
  communication via, 676
  Constant Contact and, 476
  content of, 103–104
  David Treadwell on, 771–772
  earliest form of, 96
  Flickr and, 494
  fraudulent, 110
  Google Alerts and, 580
  Google Gmail and, 583–585
  Google Reader and, 604
  marketing effectiveness of, 96–
    97
  mobile viral content in, 403
  MSGTAG and, 585–586
  photo sharing via, 194–195
  Picasa and, 498
  publishing and, 473
  Radar.net and, 499
  ReadNotify and, 586–588
  Survey Monkey and, 588–589
  terminology related to, 98–100
  timing of, 107–108
  tips, techniques, and tactics
    related to, 104–108
E-mail addresses, Kevin Marks
  on, 767
E-mail campaigns, management
  of, 109
E-mail communications, one-to-
  one and one-to-many, 112
E-mail content, valuable, 109–
  110
E-mail conversion rates, 106
E-mail list, segmenting, 105–106
E-mail marketing, 111
  challenges associated with,
    112
  commandments of, 113–114

day parting in, 106–108
opening line of, 105
outsourcing, 108–113
primary goal of, 105
social media and, 114–115
value of, 111
versus direct mail marketing, 97
Email Marketing For Dummies (Arnold), 111, 775
E-mail marketing programs, primary goals for, 97
E-mail service providers, 112
Emergencies, Twitter use during, 273
Emoticons, 153, 154
Employees
damaging posts from, 11
engaging, 760–761
wisdom of, 744–745
Empowerment, via social media, 83
E-Myth (Gerber), 779
E-Myth books, 41
E-Myth Worldwide, 38
Engagement, 7–12
Engagement strategies, 7–8
backfiring of, 10–12
England, early text messaging in, 396
Enterprise customers, 322
Enterprise Social Messaging Experiment (ESME), 276
Entertainment
AOL Mobile and, 641
BitTorrent and, 576–577
BlogTalkRadio and, 540–541
Chris Pirillo on, 739
as an engagement strategy, 8, 731
Entropia Universe and, 563
Eventful and, 578, 579
Friendster and, 455–457
Jumbuck and, 648–650
Justin.tv and, 545
Kaneva and, 554
livecasting and, 539
in mastering social media strategy, 675, 680–681
Metacafe and, 526–527
MOLI and, 464
in pinpointing social media starting point, 746
Slide and, 501
SMS.ac and, 651
social media strategies in, 671

in SWOT analysis, 704
Viddler and, 528–529
Wikia and, 486
Yahoo! and, 593
YouTube and, 529–530
Entrepreneur Assist, Zoho and, 594
Entrepreneurs
Active Worlds and, 552
Entropia Universe and, 564
Entrepreneurs Club Network, 38
Entrepreneurship, 63
creativity and, 41
importance of, 38
Entropia, 320
Entropia Universe, 333, 561, 563–565
ePodcast Creator, 215–216
Equinix, 602
Etiquette, Bill Jula on, 736
eUniverse, 49, 50, 466
Europe, early wireless phones in, 393–394
Evaluation, of social media strategies, 671
Eventful, 571, 578–579
Event planning. *See also* Event scheduling
Acteva and, 572–573
Eventful and, 578–579
Events, with Microsoft Live Messenger, 429
Event scheduling, with Doodle, 429–430
EverQuest, 330, 333, 338, 561, 565–567
Everyday Explorers, 79
EveryZing, 623, 624–625
Evoca, 215
"Evolution of Dance, The," 253, 254
eWorld, 146
Excel
Constant Contact and, 476
Zoho and, 595
Zoomerang and, 596
Execution
in ACCESS model, 728–731
crowd sourcing and, 730–731
Executive Conversations list, 56
Executive Conversations podcasts, 209
Expedia.com, 73
Expediential-value-add, 752
Expense organization, Jott service and, 425

Expert insights, x
on ACCESS model, 733–741
on audio sharing, 232–233
on blogging, 170–172
on e-mail marketing, 109–113
on forums, 155–158
on microblogging, 277–283
on photo sharing, 200–203
on podcasting, 218–220
on publishing, 82–93
on Really Simple Syndication, 349–351
on Search Engine Marketing, 379–388
on Search Engine Optimization, 369–370
on social media, 14–20
on social media strategy, 690–693, 750–754, 766–773
on social media SWOT analysis, 707–715
on social networking, 59–65
on the social media ecosystem, 35–41
on videoblogging, 247–248
on video sharing, 257–260
on virtual gaming, 337–340
on virtual worlds, 321–322
on web pages, 137–140
on wikis, 188–190
Expertise
business content and, 683
concepts and, 726
monetizing, 74–75
in SWOT analysis, 705, 706
Experts
biographies of, 775–786
social media, x
Explanatory page titles, 134
Explicit permission, 100
Exploration, of interpersonal applications, 442
Exposure, high-quality and low-cost, 194
Extensions, with Joomla, 478
External reputable links, 364–365, 371
Eyetracking Study, 126, 127
Ezarik, Justine, 292–293

Facebook, 23, 24, 43, 45, 46, 156, 174, 266, 277, 449, 450, 452–453, 763
David Meerman Scott on, 713
hardware and software for, 749

Facebook (*continued*)
  Kyle Ford on, 708, 710
  as metropolis community, 687, 688
  PodBean and, 512
  Yelp and, 612
  Zoho and, 595
  Zooomr and, 505
Facebook Mobile, 398, 407
Fadell, Tony, 209
Failure rate, 41
Fail Whale, 269–270
Fajita Grill, Constant Contact and, 477
Fake, Caterina, 495
FakeMyText.com, 271
Fanning, Shawn, 256
Fast Company, 171–172
FastPitch!, 46, 58, 453–455, 733, 734, 735, 736–737, 781
Fates of Twinion, 328
"Father of the Internet", 34
Fax2E-mail, CallWave and, 645
FCC (Federal Communications Commission), 35–36, 102 , 149, 233, 243
Feedback
  Bill Jula on, 735
  collaboration and, 678
  communication and, 676
  successful movies and, 718
  in SWOT analysis, 706
  user-generated, xv
FeedBurner, 615, 617–619
  PingShot and, 619, 620
FeedBurner counts, low, 175
Feed reader, signing up for, 352
Feeds. *See also* Atom feeds;
    Mobile news feeds; News
    feeds; Online feeds; RSS
    feeds; Twitterfeed
  Google Reader and, 604, 605
  My Yahoo! and, 608
"Feet and hats" typefaces, 131–132
Fessenden, Reginald, 393
50 Cent, 467, 710
50 Rapid Fire Tips for Power Blogging, 169, 173–177
File-distribution programs, peer-to-peer, 256
File format/size, for podcasts, 221
File Transfer option, with Yahoo! Messenger, 427
File Transfer Protocol (FTP), 357
Filo, David, 592, 593, 609, 636

Final Cut Pro, 246
Final Fantasy XI, 330
Find Articles.com, 86
Fine, Jon, 57
Finley, Ryan, 589–590
Firetrust, 586
First Amendment, 36, 243
First generation (1G) wireless phones, 393–394
First mover advantage, 729
First Person Shooter (FPS) games, 326
Fisher Young Group, 585, 586
Fitzpatrick, Brad, 165, 767
5.0-Second Rule, 105, 113–114, 128
Flagr.com, 407
Flame war (flaming), 151
Flash, 749
  using, 141
Flash embedding, 134
Flash Player
  Adobe Connect and, 433
  Redlasso and, 631
Flash technology, Acrobat Connect and, 657
FlatOut, 338
FlatOut 2, 334
Flickr, 176, 199, 200–203, 266, 491, 493, 494–495, 784
Flickr Screen, 199
Flute Bay Area, 573
Focus groups, in tapping into employee wisdom, 744
Followers, inviting, 284
FON Labs, 505
Fonts and Colors, with Yahoo! Messenger, 428
Ford, Kyle, 45, 778
  on social media SWOT analysis, 707–711
Forest Protection Blog, 164
Forests.org, 164
FORE Systems, 549
Forms, downloadable, xiv
Fortini, Raina, 396
Forum Administrator, 148–149
Forum communication, 152–153
Forum guest, 152
Forum members, 150
Forum Moderator, 148
Forum posts, 149–150
Forum Registration, 149
Forums, 145. *See also* Internet forum
  early, 146–147

information concerning, 147–153
rules and regulations related to, 148
searching for and participating in, 158
setting up, 159
Forum site, 145
Forum social networking, 153
Forum software, creating, 153–155
Forum spamming, 151–152
Forum subscription, 151
Forum troll, 151
Forum user groups, 152
Forum web sites, 150, 155
Fotolog, 200
4×4 Evolution, 561, 562–563
Four Pillars. *See* Collaboration;
    Communication;
    Education; Entertainment;
    Social media strategy
Fourth Screen, 397, 411
Frame, Greg, 555
Frames, 133–134, 368
  using, 141
Framesets, 133
Frames per second, 239
Frankel, Justin, 547
Fraud, Digg and, 601
frazr.com, 275
"Fred Frigglehorn" video, 259–260
freeblog.org, 247
Free-form podcasts, Kyle Ford on, 709
Free long distance calling, with Skype, 418–419
Freemium, 51, 78
  business model with, 231
  sales viability and, 732
Free software, 382
Free streaming videos, Hulu and, 524
Free-to-play business revenue model, 330
Frequency hopping, 400–401
Frequently Asked Questions (FAQs), 148
FriendFeed, 172, 277, 584, 599, 602–604
Friendster, 49, 450, 455–457
Friendstribe.com, 407
Friis, Janus, 668
From line, 98, 101
"Frozen" companies, 39

Fuller, Robert, 591
Functional groups, xii
Functional relationship, David Nour on, 752
Funkysexycool.com, 407
Furness, Thomas, 306
FUZE, CallWave and, 645
F-Wan advergame, 403

G1 phone, 410
Gabcast, 216
Gaia's Forest Conservation Archives, 164
Game Master (GM), 327
Gamers, 561
Games, third-party market on, 339. *See also* Gaming
GameSpy Arcade, 4×4 Evolution and, 562
Gaming, 29–30, 561–569. *See also* Virtual gaming
business and, 561
Entropia Universe, 561, 563–565
EverQuest, 561, 565–567
4×4 Evolution, 561, 562–563
location-based, 402–403
online, 325, 778
Tool Scorecard for, 561, 569
via mobile telephones, 402–403
World of Warcraft, 561, 567–569
Gantz, John, 392
GarageBand, 212–213, 215
iTunes and, 510, 511
Garfield, Steve, 241
Garriott, Richard, 308, 325, 338
Gartner Research Group, 169
Gather.com, 8, 450, 457–458
Gaulin, Pam, 595
Gedye, Lynsey, 591
General Catalyst, 521–522
General Motors (GM), 725–726
General Public License (GPL), for Joomla, 478
Geocaching, 403
GeoTagging, Zooomr and, 505, 506
Gerace, Tom, 458
Gerber, Michael, 38–41, 779
Geschke, Chuck, 657
Getty Irnages, 202
Geuricke, Constantin, 462
Ghahramani, Frederick, 640
Gibson, Steve, 163

Givers, David Nour on, 753
Glassdoor.com, 6
Glioblastoma Brain Tumor Research Fund, Constant Contact and, 477
Global brands, 87
Global community, 59
Global computer communication, 118
Global Positioning System (GPS)
Brightkite and, 643
location-based games and, 402–403
for location-based services, 401
mobile marketing and, 413
in SWOT analysis, 705
Global spending, for Internet advertising, 392
Gmail, 269, 406. *See also* Google Gmail
Google Talk and, 421
Rishi Chandra on, 439
Gnant, Jody, 243, 264, 297–298, 779
on livecasting, 299–301
Gnutella, SHOUTcast and, 547
Goals
for e-mail marketing programs, 97
measurable, 141
Goddard, Taegan, 165
Goetz, Kevin, 718
Gold farmers, 333
Goldman, Jason, 167
Gonzalez, Nick, 337
Goodstein, Anastasia, Bebo and, 451
Google, 23, 31, 361, 369, 375, 379, 523, 524, 750, 766
Adscape and, 337
Blogger and, 475
blogs and, 168
Doodle service and, 441
FeedBurner and, 617, 618
FriendFeed and, 603–604
Ice Rocket and, 628
Knol and, 480–481
in mobile marketing, 411
Orkut and, 468–470
Picasa and, 499
Rishi Chandra on, 438, 439
Technorati and, 633
YouTube and, 529, 530
Google Ads, 674

Kyle Ford on, 708–709
Google AdWords, 780
Google Alerts, 417, 571, 579–581, 684, 759
on mobile marketing, 412–413
Google Analytics, 129, 177, 382, 764
in identifying audience, 719–720
Google Android, 406, 410
in mobile marketing, 411–412
Google Apps, Rishi Chandra on, 437–439
Googlebots, 626
Google.com/Adword, 382
Google Docs, 571, 581–583
Google Earth, 197
Google Enterprises, 777
Google Gmail, 571, 583–585. *See also* Gmail
Google Juice!, 178, 251
Google Labs, 581
Google Maps, 271, 275
Google News, 581
Google Reader, 172, 599, 604–605
Google Search, 51, 623, 625–627
Google Search Bar, 355
Google search engine advertising, 374
Google "Social Media" search, 358
Google Spreadsheets, 582–583
Google Talk (GTalk), 420–421
Google Gmail and, 584
Orkut and, 469
Google Video, 519, 522–524
Gore, Al, 360
Gossip, 4
Goto.com, 374, 386
Go To Assist, 661
Go To Meeting, 430–431, 655, 659–661, 763
Go To My PC, 661
GoToWebinarJ, GoToMeeting and, 431
"Got-to-click" ads, 381
Government
Atom and, 616
Brightcove and, 520
Joomla and, 478
Justin.tv and, 545
RSS 2.0 and, 621
"Grandma's Sewing Circle", Kyle Ford on, 709
Grants, Wikipedia and, 487

Gravel, Mike, 296–297
Gray, Elisha, 289
Greene, Truman, 9
Greenspan, Brad, 49, 50, 466
Grid, the, 318
Grid7, 217
Grid View iTunes, 227
Grinding, 327
Groovr.com, 407
Gross, Bill, 374
Groups
    creating, 65
    creating and joining, 203–204
    microblogging, 284
    photo-sharing-web-site, 198
Groves, Eric, 109–111, 779
Groves, Steven, 316
GSM network, text messaging
    on, 396
GTalk, 406
Guests, on BlogTalkRadio, 541–
    542
Guha, Ramanathan V., 343
Guideline infringement forum,
    148
Guilds, 339
Gunzburger, Ron, 165
Gupta, Pankaj, 573–574
Guru Communications, 17

Habbo Hotel, 320
Hall, Justin, 163
Halo 3, 309–310, 326, 335–336
H&R Block, customer
    engagement by, 8–9
Handsets, for mobile phones,
    394–395
Hardaway, Francine, 265, 277,
    779–780
Hard bounces, 99
Hardware, 216, 217
    publishing, 749–750
    social media, 749
Harris, Josh, 290–291
Harvard Law School, RSS 2.0
    and, 620, 622
Harvested e-mails, 102
Hashtags, 275
Hawk, Thomas, 506
HD Audio Conferencing,
    CallWave and, 645. See also
    High-definition (HD) video
Header information, false, 101
Header tags, 174
Heads Up Display (HUD), 317
"Head-turns to our cart", 388

Healer, 327
Hearns, Douglas, 768–769
Heaslip, Stephen, 163
Heinz Ketchup video contest, 10
HereAndNow.net web site, 290
Herrick, Jack, 188–190, 780
Herzog, Eyal, 527
Heuer, Chris, 17–20, 66, 780
Heyman, Darian Rodriguez, 573
High-definition (HD) video, 239.
    See also HD Audio
    Conferencing
    in publishing, 750
"Highest Aspirations", 139–140
"High-level" platforms, 136
High-speed cable Internet, 240
Hijacking, 365–366
Hipcast, 216
Hobnobster.com, 407
Hodson, Ryanne, 246
Hoffman, Paul, 345
Hoffman, Reid, 54, 462
Home Movie Depot, 254
Home page, harmful aspects of,
    123–125, 128
Homogenous random sampling,
    105
Horizontal communities, 673,
    688
Host services, TypePad and, 483
Hotels.com, 73
Hotmail, with Microsoft Live
    Messenger, 428
Hourihan, Meg, 165, 475
House of Blues, 400
Howard, Gretchen, 379–382, 780
How-to manual, 188–189
HTML-based platforms, 135, 136
HTML code. See also Hyper Text
    Markup Language (HTML)
    blogs and, 164
    with Constant Contact, 476
    with MySpace, 465
Huffman, Stevem 611
Hughes, Chris, 453
Hulu, 23, 519, 524–525
Hurley, Chad Meredith, 242, 530
Hurricane Bonnie web log, 165
Hussein, Saddam, 83
HyperCard, 182
"Hyper-speed" operating system,
    40
Hypertext, 356, 357
Hyper Text Markup Language
    (HTML), 357. See also
    HTML code

Hyper Text Transfer Protocol
    (HTTP), 118, 119, 357

IBM, 315
Ice Rocket, 623, 627–629, 762
Ice Spy, with Ice Rocket, 628
iChat, 298, 421–423, 655, 661–
    662
Ichinose, Stephanie, 89–93, 399,
    780–781
IDC Digital Marketplace Model
    and Forecast, 391–393
Idealab, 499
Idea Storm web site, 84
Identi.ca, 277
IDidWork, 276
id Software, 163
iDVD, 228
iGoogle, 599, 606–607
iGoogle homepage, Google Talk
    and, 421
iGoogle Reader (Aggregator),
    346, 347
iJournal, 247
iLife, 228
    iTunes and, 510
Images, licensing, 202
Imagination, entrepreneurial, 39
"Imagineers", 38
Imity.com, 408
i-Mode, invention of, 394
iMovie, 228, 245, 246, 247, 750
IncrediMail Ltd., 527
Incremental-value-add, 752
Independent Music Event,
    Rhapsody and, 516
Indexes, with Technorati, 633
Individual updates, 280
Infection, in mobile viral
    marketing, 403
Influence
    seeking, 94
    in social media strategy, 681–
    683
Influencers. See also Influential
    individuals
    in identifying audience, 721–
    722
    in mobile viral marketing, 403
Influential individuals, David
    Nour on, 753–754
Information
    access to, 19
    aggregators and, 599
    Blogger and, 474–475
    Chris Pirillo on, 740

concept statement and, 727
David Meerman Scott on, 712, 714
Digg and, 600, 601
FriendFeed and, 602, 603
Google Video and, 523
Go To Meeting and, 660
iGoogle and, 606, 607
iTunes and, 510
Kevin Marks on, 767, 768, 769
Knol and, 481
My Yahoo! and, 608–609
publishing and, 473
Radar.net and, 500
ReadNotify and, 587–588
Reddit and, 610
Rich Site Summary and, 615
RSS 2.0 and, 621
sales viability of, 732
search tools for, 623
Technorati and, 633–634
TypePad and, 484
WebEx and, 669
Wikia and, 486
Wikipedia and, 488, 489
Yahoo! and, 592–593
Yahoo! Search and, 635–636
Zoho and, 594, 595
Information flow, David Nour on, 754
Information network, 119
Information overload, 278
Information processing, Rishi Chandra on, 438–439
Information sharing
  passion for, 90
  via podcasts, 224
In-game advertising, 336
  understanding, 341
In-game marketing, mobile, 403
Ingersoll Rand lock recall, 10–11
In-house web development, 136
Insiders, 48
Instant Message (IM) accounts, Meebo and, 665–666
Instant messaging, 264
  John Pollard on, 435, 436–437
  via Plurk, 534
  via Yahoo! Messenger, 426–428
Instapundit, 165, 169
Intelligence community, Atom and, 616
Interact, 17
Interaction
  Active Worlds and, 552, 553

EverQuest and, 566
means of, 18–19
via BlogTalkRadio, 540–541
virtual worlds and, 551
World of Warcraft and, 567–568
Interactive Advertising Bureau (ISB), 399–400
Intermix Media, Inc., 50, 466
International Space Station (ISS), Twitter and, 536
International Symposium on Wikis (WikiSym), 184–185
Internet, 45. See also 'Net entries
  acceptable behavior on, 36
  Acrobat Connect and, 656–657
  Active Worlds and, 553
  Adobe Connect and, 433
  America Online and, 574, 575
  AOL Instant Messenger and, 658–659
  AOL Mobile and, 641–642
  Brightcove and, 520
  Brightkite and, 643–644
  CallWave and, 644–646
  cellular technology and, 391
  Chris Pirillo on, 738
  Digg and, 600, 601
  EveryZing and, 625
  FriendFeed and, 602
  Gather.com and, 458
  as a general-purpose transport mechanism, 37
  global spending to advertise on, 392
  Google Alerts and, 580
  Google Reader and, 604, 605
  Google Search and, 625–627
  Google Video and, 522, 523
  Go To Meeting and, 659–661
  Ice Rocket and, 627–628, 628–629
  iGoogle and, 606, 607
  John Pollard on, 434–435, 436–437
  Jott and, 646–648, 663–664
  Jumbuck and, 648–650
  Live365 and, 542
  Meebo and, 665–666
  MetaTube and, 629–630
  mobile access to, 392, 394
  My Yahoo! and, 608–609
  online purchases via, 392
  PingShot and, 619–620
  PodBean and, 512–513
  Podcast.com and, 514

Pownce and, 690–693
Reddit and, 609–610
Redlasso and, 631–632
Rich Site Summary and, 615
search tools for, 623–637
Skype and, 667–668
SMS.ac and, 650–652
social media and, 685, 686
Survey Monkey and, 589
Technorati and, 633–634
TiddlyWiki and, 590
value of, 95–96
Wikipedia and, 488
world usage of, 391–393
Yahoo! and, 592, 593
Yahoo! Search and, 635–636
YouTube and, 529, 530
Zoomerang and, 596
Internet enabled devices, 37
Internet Engineering Task Force (IETF), 345
Internet forum, 145–160
Internet marketing
  photo sharing as, 194
  Search Engine Optimization and, 370
Internet-only radio stations, 288–290
Internet Protocol (IP). See IP addresses
Internet radio, 288
Internet radio service access, 228
Internet resolution, 132–133
Internet searches, components of, 357–360
Internet Service Providers (ISPs), 102, 163
Internet users, worldwide, 117
Internet World Stats Miniwatts Marketing Group, 117
Interoperability, 37
Interpersonal applications, 417–443
  changing nature of, 417–418
  exploring, 442
  information related to, 418–434
  knowledge of, 442
Interpersonal tools, 32, 655–670
  Acrobat Connect, 655, 656–657
  AOL Instant Messenger, 655, 657–659
  Apple iChat, 655, 661–662
  Go To Meeting, 655, 659–661
  Jott, 655, 662–664

Interpersonal tools (*continued*)
  Meebo, 655, 664–666
  Skype, 655, 666–668
  Tool Scorecard for, 655, 670
  uses of, 655
  WebEx, 655, 668–669
Interviews, posting, xiii
Intracompany communities,
  673, 688
Intranets, SlideShare and, 482
Invention, logic of, 289
Investors, David Nour on, 753
In-video advertising, 258
IP addresses, 377–378
iPhone, 23, 225–226, 405, 749
  Radar.net and, 499
  Twitxr and, 504
iPhone video, 259
iPhoto plugin, 195
  Picasa and, 498
iPod, 27, 207, 208–209. *See also*
  Podcasting
  birth of, 209–210
iPod photo, 209
iPod video, 209
iRadioMast, 228
Islands of Kesmai, 328
IT-Exchange, 188
Ito, Joi, 482
iTunes, 8, 209, 215, 217, 223,
  224–228, 509, 510–511
  Bebo and, 451
  downloads and product
    statistics for, 225–226
  PodBean and, 512, 513
  trying, 233–234
  uploading podcasts to, 220
  uses for, 225
  Viddler and, 528
iTunes Digital Copy, 227
iTunes Music Store, 227
iTunes podcasting support, 227–
  228
iTunes Store, 226
iTunes University, 217
iTunes video application, 227
iTunes virtual libraries, 226
iUniversity, 220
Iverson, Allen, 456
iWork, 228
  iTunes and, 510

Jaiku, 265, 269, 275, 277, 279
Jaiku.com, 408
Japan, early wireless phones in,
  393

Jardin, Xeni, 167
Jarvis, Richard, 396
Java, 136
JavaScript, TiddlyWiki and, 590
JavaScript widgets, 176
J-blog list, 169
JenniCam, 290
Jen, Sandy, 666
Jericho, Chris, 456
Jobs
  David Nour on, 753
  LinkedIn, 56
Jobs, Steve, 39, 119, 120, 225,
  405, 662
JobSchmob.com, 6
Job searches, via text messaging,
  397
Jobs posting, on Mashable, 351
Johnson, Charles, 165
John Wiley & Sons, Inc.,
  Publishing, 14–16, 786
Joint Contact, 277
Joomla, 135, 136, 246, 473, 477–
  479
Jott, 7, 404, 417, 423–425, 639,
  646–648, 655, 662–664, 783
  John Pollard on, 434–437
  mobile marketing and, 413
Jott Links, 424
Jott Networks Inc., 648, 163
Journalists, 163
  coercive custody for, 244
Journals, online, 163–164
Juice, 228
JuiceCaster.com, 408
Jula, Bill, 45, 455, 781
  on ACCESS model, 733–737
Jumbuck, 639, 648–650
Jumbuck Blogs, with Jumbuck,
  649
Jumbuck Entertainment Ltd.,
  648, 649
Jumbuck Island, with Jumbuck,
  649
Junk e-mail, 100
Junk mail, 95
Justin.tv, 291–293, 539, 544–545
"Just Try Something" approach,
  138

Kahn, Bob, 34
Kaltix, 607
Kamvar, Sep, 607
Kaneva, 551, 553–555
Kan, Justin, 291–293, 545
Kaplan, "Pud", 291

Kaplan, Jeff, 334
Karim, Jawed, 242, 530
Karma applications, Plurk and,
  534
Karma points, Reddit and, 610
KaZaA, 668
Keane, Andrew, 17
Kelly, Gary, 271
Kennedy, Ian, 18
Kennedy, John F., 625
Kevin Bacon effect, 55–56
Keynote, 228
Keynote presentations, 244–245
  for iChat video chats, 422
  via SlideShare, 482
Keyword campaigns, 381
Keyword density, 365–366
Keyword finder, 378
Keyword list, 363
Keyword marketplace, 386
Keyword phrases, 375–376
Keyword placement, 133
Keywords
  choosing, 387, 388
Keywords, 197, 362
  relevant, 175
  understanding, 370, 389
Kiboze.com, 408
KickApps, 459–460
KickApps Platform, 155
Kilar, Jason, 525
Killer posts, 176
Kim, Arnold, 69–70, 73, 79
  collaboration and, 677–678
Kincaid, Bill, 226, 511
Kingdon, Mark, 56, 305, 312,
  315, 781
  on virtual worlds, 321–322
Klaus, Christopher W., 555
Kling, William H., 458
Knight-Ridder, David Meerman
  Scott on, 712
Knol, 473, 480–481
Knowing, understanding versus,
  728
Knowledge
  evaluating and organizing, 743
  of interpersonal applications,
    442
  Kevin Marks on, 769
  Knol and, 480
Knowledge management
  systems, 181
Koblo.com, 214
KodakGallery, 199
KodakGallery.com, 195

Koerber-Walker, Joan, xvii
Konami code, Google Reader and, 605
Kroc, Ray, 40
Krums, Janis, 274
Kryptonite U-Lock recall, 10–11
Kurtz, Howard, 294

Labatt Brewing Company, SMS advertising campaign by, 400
Laconica, 276
Laipply, Judson, 253
Lampton, Dave, 517
Lander, Christian, 680
social media strategy of, 673–674
Landing Page Eyetracking Study, 126, 127
Landing web pages, 126
localizing, 135
testing, 130–131
Landline infrastructure, 434
Landline telephones, calling with Skype, 419
Landry, Louis, 479
Land Use Fee, 319
Languages
with Google Search, 626
with Meebo, 666
Lantz, Edward, 396
Laptop computers, David Treadwell on, 773
Largo, Michael, Bebo and, 451
Launching Your Yahoo! Business (Tang), 785
Lavigne, April, 456
Leaders, 48
Leebow, Ken, 582
Legislation, mobile telephone advertising and, 400
Leon, Marianne, 573
Leopard operating system, Apple iChat and, 661
Lester, J. P., 517
Leuf, Bo, 182
Levchin, Max, 486, 502, 613
Levelator, 215, 216, 217, 219
Level treadmill, 327
Levy, Alan, 232–233, 294, 781
LexCycle, 76
Libby, Dan, 343–344
Liberated Syndication, 215
Liberty Telecomm, 644
Libraries
with iTunes, 510–511
with Rhapsody, 515

Licenses, Creative Commons, 213
Licensing
of images, 202
Skype and, 666
Life and Times of an Independent Singer/Songwriter, The, 300
Lifecasters, 539
Lifecasting, 243, 291, 297–298
as a promotional tool, 300
LightBox, Zooomr and, 505
Limelight Networks, Brightcove and, 521
Lim, Jeong-Hyun, 253
Linden Dollar, 313, 314
Linden Labs, 316–317, 321, 334, 781
Second Life and, 555, 557
Linden Scripting Language (LSL), 318
Linden World, 312, 557
Line Tracker, with Ice Rocket, 628
Linier, Jaron, 306
Linked Answers, LinkedIn and, 461
LinkedIn, 45, 46, 54–57, 61–62, 277, 450, 460–462, 776
features of, 54–57
LinkedIn Answers feature, 57
LinkedIn Groups, 57
LinkedIn polls, 57
LinkedIn premium accounts, 62
LinkedIn six-degrees approach, 55–56
LinkedIn value propositiom, 55–56
Link farms, 364
Linklogs, 168
LinkLove, 168, 178
Links
external reputable, 364–365
Google Search and, 626
Reddit and, 609–610
on the social media web site, xiii
Listserv, 8
Little Green Footballs, 165
Live365, 539, 542–544
Liveblogging, 166
Livecasting, 29, 163, 287–304, 539
beginning of, 287–293
evolution of, 290–293
exploring, 302
information related to, 294–298

providers of, 298
Livecasting tools, 539–549
BlogTalkRadio, 539, 540–542
Justin.tv, 539, 544–545
Live365, 539, 542–544
SHOUTcast, 539, 545–547
TalkShoe, 539, 547–549
Tool Scorecard for, 539, 549
LiveJournal, 165
PodBean and, 512
Kevin Marks on, 767
Lively , 318
Live Mash, David Treadwell on, 770–773
Live Messenger Share, with Microsoft Live Messenger, 429
Live Platform, 770, 785
Live Writer, 177
Local campaigns, 134–135
Location-based games, 402–403
Location-based services (LBS), 401
LockerGnome,com, Chris Pirillo on, 740–741
Long distance calling, with Skype, 418–419
Loopnote.com, 408
Los Angeles Fire Department, 272
Lott, Trent, 166
Lucas, Brandon, 398
Lucas, Chris, 521
Lukin, Jared, 78
Lulu Blooker Prize, 169
Lunt, Eric, 618, 620
Lunt, Scott, 781
Lurkers, 47
Lurking, 152
Lusch, Robert, xi
Lyons, Dan, 490

MacAskill, Chris, 503
MacAskill, Don, 503
Mac-compatible iPod, 209
Macintosh (Mac) computers
Apple iChat and, 661–662
Doodle service and, 441
4×4 Evolution and, 562
Go To Meeting and, 659, 661
iChat and, 421–422
Live365 and, 543
Picasa and, 498
MacDonald, Kyle, 298
Macromedia, 657, 776
Macromedia MX, 521

MacRumors.com, 69–70, 71, 79
   collaboration and, 677–678
Maddox, Mitch, 291
Madhavapeddi, Shreedhar, 648,
   664
Madison Avenue, social media
   and, 9–10
Mad Men, ratings increase for, 9–
   10
Magazine publishing industry,
   87
Magazines
   Brightcove and, 520, 521
   interactive, 86–89
Magliozzi, Tom, 75
Mail Chimp, Survey Monkey
   and, 588–589, 590
Mail Goggles, Google Gmail and,
   584
Mailing list, researching and
   choosing, 174
MailWasherPro, 586
Mainstream Holdings, 464
Makena Technologies, 557, 558–
   559
Malamud, Carl, 288
Mambo, Joomla and, 479
Mambo 4.5 code, for Joomla,
   478, 479
Mamone, Tony, 85–89, 782
Management
   collaboration in, 676–678
   Go To Meeting and, 660
   of online communities, 673,
      689–690
Manber, Udi, 481
Mann, Steve, 290
Many-to-many instant
   messaging, 264
Many-to-many social tools, 430–
   434
Many-to-one social tools,
   417
MapleStory, 330
Marconi, Guglielmo, 509
Market, information efficiency
   in, 19–20
Marketers, objectives of, 385
Marketing, xi
   Active Worlds and, 553
   affiliate, 135
   aggregators and, 599
   audience and, 718–719
   Bill Jula on, 734, 736–737
   Brightcove and, 520
   communication in, 675–676

control and influence in, 681–
   683
conversation and, 675
David Meerman Scott on, 714–
   715
Entropia Universe and, 564
Eventful and, 579
EveryZing and, 624
gaming and, 561
Google Search and, 626
Hulu and, 525
iTunes and, 510
Kaneva and, 555
mobile in-game, 403
My Yahoo! and, 608
permission-based, 266
psychological, 126
Radar.net and, 500
Reddit and, 610
Slide and, 501
in social media strategy, 674,
   757–758
strong communities and,
   685
Survey Monkey and, 589
There and, 558
Twitter and, 536
Twitxr and, 504
via mobile telephones, 399–
   400, 403–404, 405
via virtual worlds, 551
viral, 403–404
WebEx and, 668–669
Yahoo! and, 592–593
Yelp and, 611, 612–613
Zoomerang and, 597
Marketing budget, 387
Marketing concepts, 121–131
Marketing strategy, off-line, 135
Market niche, 718
Marketplace, creating value in,
   84–85
Market segment, 718
Market space, 718
MarketTools, 597
Marks, Kevin, 66, 782
   on social media strategy, 766–
      769
Marshall, Josh, 166
Mash. *See* Live Mash
Mashable, 349–351, 777
   demographics of, 350–351
Mashups, 275
Masonis, Todd, 471
Massively multiplayer online
   game (MMOG), 308, 309

Massively multiplayer online
   role playing games
   (MMORPGs), 308, 325–341.
   See also MMORPG enries
console-based, 334
features common to, 326
via mobile telephones, 402
Mass media devices, mobile
   telephones as, 397
Matrix Systems & Technologies,
   Inc., 605
Mavens, in mobile viral
   marketing, 403
Max, Tucker, 169–170
Mayer, Marissa, 581, 607
May, Martin, 644
Maze Game, 308–309
Maze-War, 327–328
McCain, John, 465
McConnell, Brandon, 527
McCormick, J. P., 553
McCusker, Jim, 632
McGowan, Al, 632
MCI, 36–37
McQuaid, Brad, 330, 567
Medecins Sans Frontieres,
   blogging by, 166–167
Media, 3. *See also* Social media
   Bebo and, 451
   history of, 88
   Redlasso and, 631
Media aggregators, 349
Media-business relationship, 3
Media downloads, BitTorrent
   and, 576
Media files, iTunes and, 510
MediaMonkey, 228
Media Player, 241
   software for, 226
MediaSauce, 43, 360, 361, 365,
   776, 777
Meebo, 655, 664–666
Meetings
   with Adobe Connect, 432–434
   Doodle service and, 441
   exploring, 323
   with GoToMeeting, 430–431,
      659–661
   Jott service and, 425
   with WebEx, 431–432, 669
MeetMoi.com, 408
Megapixels, 195–196
Mehta, Dharmesh, 281–283, 782
Memberships, with SmugMug,
   502
Memory Alpha, 184

Memory cards, for gaming, 402
Memory Tree, 316
Menchaca, Lionel, 272
Merchandise, iTunes and, 510
Merholz, Peter, 162
Meridian 59, 329
Message Archiving, with Yahoo!
    Messenger, 427
Message boards, 146
Messages, authenticity of, 64
Messaging, 43–44
    AOL Instant Messenger and,
        658–659
    Jumbuck and, 649
    SMS.ac and, 650–652
    voice versus text, 404–405
Metacafe, 519, 525–527
Meta Content Framework
    (MCF), 343
Metadata Working Group, Atom
    and, 616
Meta-Descriptions, 363
Meta keywords, 363
    checking, 371, 389
Meta search features, Ice Rocket
    and, 627
Meta tags, 197, 198, 203, 362
MetaTube, 623, 629–630
Metaverse environment, 313,
    315
"Me-too" blogger, 174
Metrics
    conversion, 129
    implementing, 141
Metropolis communities, 673,
    687
Meucci, Antonio, 289
Micro-advertising, 269
Microblogging, 28, 263–286, 398,
    399
    beginnings of, 264–265
    benefits of, 284–285
    criticism of, 267
    global appeal of, 273
    information related to, 265–
        267
    light side of, 271–273
    popularity of, 266
    beyond Twitter, 275–277
    Twitxr, 533, 537
    via Twitter, 425–426, 535–537
    worldwide, 267
Microblogging communities,
    263–264
Microblogging tools, 533–538.
    See also Blogging

blogging and, 533
    Plurk, 534–535
    text messaging and, 533
    Tool Scorecard for, 533, 537–
        536
Micro-commerce
    Entropia Universe and, 563
    EverQuest and, 565
    Kaneva and, 553
    Second Life and, 555
Micro-communities, 278
Micro sites, 139
Microsoft, 770, 771, 773
Microsoft Excel, Constant
    Contact and, 476. See also
    Excel
Microsoft Flight Simulator, 4×4
    Evolution and, 563
Microsoft Live Messenger, 428–
    429. See also Windows
    Live™ Messenger
Microsoft Live Platform,
    770
Microsoft Messenger, 153
Microsoft Office, Go To Meeting
    and, 661
Microsoft Word
    Google Docs and, 583
    Zoho and, 594
Micro-spam, 268
Micro-Sphere, 267–271
Micro strategies
    personal, 758–759
    social media, 699
Mig33.com, 408
Miller, Andy, 479
Mimick Banks, 394
MindArk, 563, 565
Mingus, Charles, 491
Mini Cooper, 516
MisTweet, 271
Mixin, 277
mmorg.chart.com, 340
MMORPG articles, reading, 340–
    341. See also Massively
    multiplayer online role
    playing games (MMORPGs)
MMORPG business revenue
    models, 330
MMORPG sites, visiting, 340
Mobile data services, earliest,
    394
Mobile gambling, 402
Mobile gaming, 402
    location-based, 402–403
Mobile in-game marketing, 403

Mobile Internet access,
    worldwide, 392, 394
Mobile marketing, 399–400, 412
    Adam Broitman on, 410–412
    barcodes in, 410–411
    future of, 404
Mobile Marketing Association
    (MMA), 399–400, 405
Mobile news feeds, mobisodes
    and, 397
MobileOne, LBS advertising
    campaign by, 401
Mobile telephones, 32, 34–35, 37,
    60, 76, 391–416
    advances in, 413–414
    advertising via, 399–400
    airG for, 639, 640
    AOL Mobile for, 639, 641–642
    applications using, 396–397
    beginnings of, 393–398
    blogging via, 398
    Bluetooth connection for,
        400–401
    Brightkite for, 639, 642–644
    calling with Skype, 419
    CallWave for, 639, 644–646
    cellular technology for, 391
    data services for, 396–397
    with digital video cameras,
        246
    features available with, 395–
        396
    gaming via, 402
    Google Alerts concerning,
        412–413
    Google Docs and, 582
    handsets for, 394–395
    information related to, 398–
        406
    John Pollard on, 434–435,
        436–437
    Jott service and, 413, 424, 639,
        646–648, 662–664
    Jumbuck for, 639, 648–650
    for location-based services,
        401
    manufacturers of, 394–395
    marketing of, 412
    marketing via, 399–400, 403–
        404, 405
    Meebo and, 665–666
    mobisodes and, 397
    movie distribution via, 397
    online gambling via, 402
    portability of, 398–399
    Radar.net and, 499

Mobile telephones (*continued*)
reviews via, 399
rich media and, 397
service providers for, 406–412
Skype and, 667–668
SMS.ac for, 639, 650–652
social media tools for, 639–653
stolen, 399
technology of, 405–406, 412, 413–414
Tool Scorecard for, 639, 652–653
for trusted networks, 399
Twitter and, 537
Twitxr and, 504
uses of, 391–393
voice messaging via, 404–405
Web and, 413
Windows Live Messages and, 282
world usage of, 394
Yahoo! Messenger and, 426–428
Mobile telephone technology, 395
Mobile text messaging, 152–153
Mobile viral content, 403
Mobile viral marketing, 403–404
Mobile Web marketing, 400
Mobiluck.com, 408
Mobisodes, 397
Moblabber.com, 408
Mockingbird, 607
Mocospace, 398
Mocospace.com, 408
mod.ber, 163
Moderators (mods), 148
MOLI, 450, 462–464
MOLI Video, 463
MOLI View, 463
Mommy blog, 70
Money, saving, xiBxii
Monitor resolution, 132–133
Monster.com, 397
Monthly day parting, 107
Moran, Ed, 81
Morhaime, Michael, 568–569
Moritz, Mike, 627
Morph, The, 395–396
Mosaic, 121
Moskovitz, Dustin, 453
Motorola
early wireless phones from, 393, 394
first text message sent via, 396
Motorola House of Blues, 400

Movable Type, 485
Movie distribution, via mobile phones, 397
Movies
audiences for, 722–725
successful, 718
top-grossing, 717–718
Mozilla Firefox, 344
MP3 format, 208–209
Mpeg3 (MP3), 208
MSGTAG, 571, 585–586
MSNBC, 217
MTV, first music video on, 519
Mullenweg, Matt, 165, 170–171, 183, 198, 491, 782
Multifunctional services, 404
Multimedia capabilities, of mobile telephones, 395
Multimedia messaging, SMS.ac and, 650–652
Multiple users, AOL Instant Messenger and, 658
Multiply, 200
Multitasking, Jott and, 647, 663
MultiVent option, Acteva and, 572
Music
audio technology for, 509
Bebo and, 450–451
copying, 227
copyrighted, 213
Eventful and, 578, 579
iTunes and, 510–511
Rhapsody and, 515–517
Yahoo! and, 593
Musicblog, 167
Music file-sharing service, 256
Music libraries, viewing, 226–227
Musicphones, 395
Music videos, first MTV, 519
Musings of Dawn, 591
myAOL, 574, 575
MyBlogLog, 168
MyDD, 165
MyGads, 186–187
myGamma.com, 408
My Growth Resources, 38
MyPhotoAlbum, 200
MySpace, 45, 46, 49–54, 59–60, 156, 177, 186, 277, 450, 464–466, 778
advertising revenue from, 57
child safety and, 54
demographics on, 60
features of, 51–54

hardware and software for, 749
Kyle Ford on, 708, 710, 711
as metropolis community, 687, 688
PodBean and, 512
Slide and, 502
Zooomr and, 505
MySpace Bulletins, 52
MySpace Classifieds, 53
MySpace comments section, 51
MySpace Developer Platform, 465, 466
MySpace Forum, 53
MySpace Groups, 52
MySpaceIM, 52
MySpace Karaoke, 53
MySpace Mobile, 52–53, 398, 408
MySpace music profiles, 52
MySpace MyAds, 465
MySpace News, 53
MySpace pages, personalizing, 60
MySpace Political Profiles, 53–54
MySpace Polls, 53
MySpace profile page, customizing, 51
MySpace profiles, 51
MySpace Records, 52
MySpace-style blog designs, 174
MySpaceTV, 52
"My view" forums, 84
My Yahoo!, 599, 607–609. *See also* Yahoo!
MyYearbook.com, 45

Nader, Ralph, 537
Naef, Michael, 782–783
on Doodle, 440–441
Naked Conversations (Scoble), 783–784
Nanocosm Inc., 543–544
Nanohome, Live365 and, 543
Napster, 256
Nareos, Metacafe and, 526
NASA, 217, 272
National Center for Supercomputing Applications (NCSA), 121
National Geographic User-Generated Content site, 79
National Public Radio (NPR), 217, 686
as affinity community, 687–688

National Science Foundation Network (NSFNET), 329
Navigation, via Brightkite, 643
Navin, Ashwin, 577
NBC Universal, 525
Needs
    filling, 76–77
    in identifying audience, 720–721
Negative online interactions, 35
Nekomimi Lisa, 290
Nelsen, Dave, 549
Nelson, Ted, 357
Net Bites, Doodle service and, 441
Netbooks, David Treadwell on, 772
Netcom, 602
Netcraft, 117
Netiquette, 151
Net promoter score, sales viability and, 732–733
NetRadio Company, 288–290
Netscape, RSS 2.0 and, 622
Network information, producers of, 34
Networking. See also Social networking
    with Active Worlds, 553
    airG and, 640
    Bill Jula on, 734, 735, 736, 737
    Chris Pirillo on, 740–741
    Kaneva and, 554
    Kevin Marks on, 766
    key to, 65–66
Networks
    Brightcove and, 520
    building, 65
    developing and cultivating, 43
    trusted, 147, 335, 399
Neverwinter Nights, 328
New business startups, 41
New product tryouts, 301
New Rules of Marketing & PR, The (Scott), 784
News
    Digg and, 600–601
    FriendFeed and, 602–603
    Google Reader and, 604
    iGoogle and, 606, 607
    Reddit and, 609–610
    Twitter and, 536, 537
News-based blogs, 165–167
News Corporation, 525

News feeds, mobisodes and, 397
Newsgroups, 163
Newsletters, 758
    creating, 676
    Survey Monkey and, 589
News outlets, Twitter use by, 273
Newspaper ad revenue, 96
Newspaper ads, 104–105
Newspapers, Brightcove and, 520, 521
New York Times, 217
NeXT personal computers, 119, 120
Nexux: The Kingdom of the Winds, 330
Nguyen, Mingh, 471
Nguyen, Toan, 49
Niche, finding and exploiting, 12
Nielsen/Net Ratings, YouTube and, 530
989 Studios, 567
Ning, 135, 450, 466–468, 778
    Kyle Ford and, 707–708, 710, 711
Nintendo, 403
NJ Green Building Council, 573
Nokia
    CallWave and, 645
    early text messaging and, 396
    handsets from, 394–395
    mobile telephone features from, 395–396
Nokia Communicator, invention of, 394
Noll, Richard, 553
Non-English speakers, Zooomr and, 506
Non-Player Character (NPC), 327
Nordic Mobile Telephone (NMT), early wireless phones from, 393–394
Norris, Jim, 603–604
No Sleep Media, LLC, 642
Notebooks, TiddlyWiki and, 590–591
Notes, Zooomr and, 506
Nottingham, Mark, 345
Nour, David, 49, 783
    on social media strategy, 750–754
Novices, 47
NowThen.com, 408
NTT DoCoMo
    early wireless phones from, 393

i-Mode from, 394
Nullsoft, 545, 547
Nupedia
    Wikia and, 487
    Wikipedia and, 489
Nye, Dan, 54, 462

Obama, Barack, 24, 54, 80, 266, 273, 465, 537
Object-oriented programming, 182
Obvious, LLC, Twitter and, 536, 537
Odeo, PingShot and, 619
Odeo project, 279–280
Odeo Studio, 216
Offerings, customers as "co-producers" of, xi
Office suite programs, Google Docs and, 582
Official Profiles, Friendster and, 456, 457
Off-line marketing strategy, 135
Ohanian, Alexis, 611
O'Kane, Kevin, 632
Olechowski, Steve, 618, 620
On-demand web conferencing, with WebEx, 431–432
One-click editing, blogs and, 164
1.54-Second Rule, 104–105, 113–114, 128
"One Red Paper Clip" story, 298, 779
One-to-many broadcast message, 137
One-to-many e-mail communications, 112
One-to-many social tools, 417, 425–430
One-to-one e-mail communications, 112
One-to-one social tools, 417, 418–425
Online abuses, 35
Online advertising, 379
    benefits of, 381
Online audio streaming, SHOUTcast and, 546
Online chatting, with Google Talk, 420–421
Online classrooms
    Adobe Connect and, 434
    with WebEx, 432
Online clutter, 101

Online communities, 163
    concepts and, 725–727
    content and, 684–688
    creating, 78
    establishing and managing,
        689–690
    making or breaking, 686–687
    with Pownce, 690–693
    social media strategy and,
        673–674, 684–688, 689–690
    strong, 685–686
    types of, 673
Online distribution, BitTorrent
    and, 576–577
Online feeds
    Google Reader and, 604, 605
    My Yahoo! and, 608
Online following, building, 343
Online gaming, 325
Online information, David
    Meerman Scott on, 712, 714
Online meetings
    with Adobe Connect, 432–434
    with GoToMeeting, 430–431
    with Jott service, 425
    with WebEx, 431–432
Online purchasing, via Internet,
    392
Online radio shows
    BlogTalkRadio and, 540
    Live365 and, 542, 543–544
Online role-playing, 338
Online surveys, Survey Monkey
    and, 588–589
Online voice service, via
    TalkShoe, 547–548
Open Diary, 165
Open-ended questions, 173
Open Handset Alliance (OHA),
    406
    in mobile marketing, 411–412
OpenID, Kevin Marks on, 767–
    768
OpenID multilogging, Zooomr
    and, 505
Opening sentences, testing, 106
Open Microblogging Tool, 276
OpenOffice, Google Docs and,
    583
Open platforms, 406
    in mobile marketing, 411
Open rate, 98–99
OpenSocial, 37, 65
    Kevin Marks on, 766–769
OpenSocial applications, Kyle
    Ford on, 709–710

OpenSocial project, 782
Open source, with Joomla, 477–
    478
Open-source content
    management systems, 246
Open Source Innovation, 592
Open-source process, 171
Open wikis, 184
Oppenheimer, Peter, 209
Opportunities
    Bill Jula on, 736–737
    Chris Pirillo on, 739
    David Nour on, 752
    in SWOT analysis, 705–706,
        748
Opportunity analysis, execution
    and, 730, 731
Opt-ins, 100
Opt-out links, 101
Opt-outs, 99
OraTweet, 276
Orbitz.com, 72, 73
O'Reilly, Tim, 167
Organic search, 356
Organizations
    Acrobat Connect and, 657
    Acteva and, 572–573
    assessing opportunities and
        threats of, 705–706
    assessing strengths and
        weaknesses of, 704–705
    Atom and, 616–617
    Brightcove and, 520
    challenge for, 137
    collaboration in, 676–678
    Constant Contact and, 476,
        477
    control and influence in, 681–
        683
    Digg and, 600, 601
    FeedBurner and, 618
    Google Search and, 626
    Google Video and, 522, 523
    Go To Meeting and, 659, 660
    in identifying audience, 721
    Joomla and, 479
    Plaxo and, 471
    Redlasso and, 632
    relevancy, competitiveness,
        and aliveness of, xii
    RSS 2.0 and, 621
    SlideShare and, 482, 483
    SmugMug and, 503
    Social Media Awareness Index
        and, 700–701
    social media inside, 13

    social media outside, 13–14
    Survey Monkey and, 589
    Twitter and, 536
    WebEx and, 669
    Yelp and, 611, 612
    Zoho and, 595
    Zoomerang and, 596
Origin Systems, 329–330
Orkut, 450, 468–470
Ott, Scott, 169
OTX company, 718
Out-house web development,
    136
Outlook program, 112
Outsourcing, of e-mail
    marketing, 108–113
Ovide, Shira, 274
Own-it/operate-it site, 385

Page, Larry, 368, 523, 524, 627
Page aggregators, 417
Page link creation, 183
PageRank algorithm, 365, 626
Page ranking, 368, 369–370,
    377
Pages, music files embedded
    into, 228
Page titles, 134, 365
    checking, 370
Paid listing, 374
Palm Pilot, 195
Panoramio, 200
Paper Model Inc., 383
Paper Models, 315, 316
Papworth, Neil, 396
Paranoia, in business, 682
Pardo, Rob, 334
Parker, Sean, 471
Partnerships, Chris Pirillo on,
    740
Pasechnik, Bryce, 640
Pass-alongs, 99
Passa Parola campaign, mobile
    viral marketing via, 404
Passive satisfaction, sales
    viability and, 732
Patel, Manesh, 523
Pax, Salam, 169
Payload, 279
PayPal, 613
    PodBean and, 512
    Slide and, 502
    Wikia and, 487
Pay-per-click (PPC), 380, 386,
    389
Pay-per-click advertising, 375

Pay-per-click marketing plan, 374
Pay-to-play business revenue model, 330
PBWiki.com, 187
PC Gamer, 340
Pearce, Frank, 569
Peer-to-peer (P2P) file sharing, 255–256
  protocol for, 256
Penn, B. J., 467
PeopleTags, Zooomr and, 505, 506
Pepper, Tom,547
Pepto-Bismol video contest, 10
Performance-based model, 258
Permalink, 170
Permissions
  granting, 111
  Kevin Marks on, 768
Personal area networks (PANs), 401
Personal computers (PCs)
  David Treadwell on, 773
  4×4 Evolution and, 562, 563
  iChat and, 421–422
Personal desktop assistants (PDAs), 195, 395
Personal information, Kevin Marks on, 767, 769
Personality, showing in blogs, 177
Personal profiles, Kevin Marks on, 768
Personal relationships, David Nour on, 752, 753
Personnel training, with WebEx, 432. *See also* Education; Training
PETCO, 726
PhanFare, 200
Phantasy Star Online, 330
Philippines, credit card payment system in, 394
Phoenix Mars Lander, 533, 537
Phone Blogz, 216. *See also* Telephone entries
Phone In feature, with Yahoo! Messenger, 427
Phone Out feature, with Yahoo! Messenger, 427
Phone technology, conversation using, 232–233
Photoblog, 167
Photoblogging, Twitxr and, 504
PhotoBucket, 200, 493, 496–497

Photo editing, with Picasa, 497–498
Photo-editing software, 197, 200
Photo gallery, 176
  with Microsoft Live Messenger, 429
Photographs, taking, editing, and uploading, 203
Photography, SlideShare and, 482
Photo-management applications, desktop, 195
Photo sharing, 27, 193–205, 281–282
  beginnings of, 194–196
  exposure and, 194
  with global communities, 204
  information related to, 196–198
  providers for, 199–200
  sites for, 398
  techniques and tactics related to, 198–199
Photo sharing tools, 493–507
  Flickr, 494–495
  Photobucket, 496–497
  Picasa, 497–499
  Radar.net, 499–500
  Slide, 500–502
  SmugMug, 502–503
  Tool Scorecard for, 493, 506–507
  Twitxr, 503–505
  Zooomr, 505–506
Photo-sharing web sites, 194, 195
  creating revenue using, 198
  multiple, 200
  uploading photos to, 197, 198
Photoshop, 197, 200
Photo software, 196–197
Photo theft/fraud, 197–198
Picasa, 197, 200, 493, 497–499
Pickle, 200
PicMe, 200
Pihkonen, Riku, 396
PingShot, 615, 619–620
Pirillo, Chris, 177, 783
  on ACCESS model, 737–741
Pirtle, Mitch, 479
Pitas.com, 165
"Pivot" CD, 300
Pixamo, 200
Pixelshot.com, 781
PizzaHut, EverQuest and, 566
PlaceShout, 265

Placestodo.com, 408
Platforms, web-site, 135–136
Platform Services Group, 770
Plaxo, 450, 470–471
Players
  with Entropia Universe, 564
  with World of Warcraft, 567–568
PlayStation Portable, 403
Plurk, 275–276, 534–535
PodBean, 215, 217, 223, 228–231, 509, 511–513
  benefits of, 229–230
PodBean.com, 210
PodcastAlley, 217
Podcast blog, 167
PodCast.com, 217, 509, 513–515
Podcast Directory, 227
Podcast distributors, 216–217
Podcast hosting site, trying, 234
Podcasting, 8, 23, 27–28, 207–222. *See also* Podcasts
  beginnings of, 208–210
  David Meerman Scott on, 713
  FeedBurner and, 617
  homework related to, 218
  importance of, 207–208
  information related to, 210–211
  Kyle Ford on, 709
  perfection in, 211–212
  PingShot and, 619
  Podcast.com and, 513–515
  spending on, 219, 220
  TalkShoe and, 548, 549
  tips, techniques, and tactics related to, 211–217
  value of, 210–211
  via PodBean, 512–513
  Viddler and, 528
Podcasting For Dummies (Morris, Terra, & Miceli), 211, 218 , 224, 785
Podcasting support, iTunes, 227–228
Podcasting tools, 217
  specialty, 219
Podcast providers, 217
Podcasts, 208, 209
  brief, 220–221
  components of, 210
  creating, 210, 211
  editing, 214–215
  information sharing via, 224
  introducing, 212–213
  planning, 211–212

Podcasts (*continued*)
  publishing, 215
  recording, 213–214
  signing off, 214
  special effects for, 215
Podcast software, 215–216
Podcast Station, 216
"Pod-safe" music, 220
Podzinger, 624
Point-and-shoot digital cameras,
  for publishing, 750
Poisson, John, 500
PokerRoom, 402
Policies, rapidly changing, 84
Political blogs, 164, 165–166
Political Wire, 165
Politics
  Digg and, 601
  Technorati and, 634
Politics1.com, 165
Pollard, John, 405, 648, 664, 783
  on Jott, 434–437
Polls
  audience, 723–724
  Doodle service and, 440–441
Popularity Contest plug-in, 175
Popular videos, 248
Portable live video, streaming
  computer system, 291–292
Posts, 145, 167
  forum, 149–150
  helpful, 176
  images in, 174
  ranking, 175
  timing, 173
Post-sale stage, 125
Post titles, 173
Pousti, Michael, 652
Power Chat, with Jumbuck, 649
PowerPoint
  PodBean and, 512
  SlideShare and, 482, 483
Pownce, 265, 279, 601, 690–693,
  778
  failure of, 270
  shutdown of, 417
Preferences
  execution and, 730
  in identifying audience, 720–
  721
Premier Lifestyle Portal, 59
Premium content providers,
  257–258
Premium tools, MOLI and, 462,
  463
Presentations

Acrobat Connect and, 657
Apple iChat and, 661
Google Video and, 522, 523
Go To Meeting and, 660
via SlideShare, 482
Present.ly, 277
"Present Past", 139, 140
Preview pane, 98, 99
Prims, 318
Printing press, 75–76
Privacy, MOLI and, 462, 463–464
Private Estate, 319–320
Problem-customers, David Nour
  on, 753
Problem solving, 76–77
Prodigy, 163
Producer Rewards program,
  Metacafe and, 526, 527
Productivity and Collaboration
  Application Suite, with
  Zoho,594
Productivity applications, 30,
  571–598
  Acteva, 571, 572–574
  America Online, 571, 574–575
  BitTorrent, 571, 576–577
  business and, 571
  Eventful, 571, 578–579
  Google Alerts, 571, 579–581
  Google Docs, 571, 581–583
  Google Gmail, 571, 583–585
  MSGTAG, 571, 585–586
  ReadNotify, 571, 586–588
  Survey Monkey, 571,
  588–590
  TiddlyWiki, 571, 590–592
  Tool Scorecard for, 571, 597–
  598
  Yahoo!, 571, 592–593
  Zoho, 571, 594–595
  Zoomerang,571, 596–597
Productivity Solutions
  Corporation, 652
Products
  business content and, 683
  comparing, 133
  customers as "co-producers"
  of, xi
  sales viability of, 732
  Yelp and, 611, 612–613
Professional organizations, in
  identifying audience, 721
Professional photographers,
  SmugMug and, 503
Professionals, LinkedIn and,
  461–462

Professional speakers,
  SlideShare and, 482
Profiles, 155
  creating, 65
  with Fast Pitch!, 454
  with Friendster, 456
  with MySpace, 464–465, 466
  with Ning, 466–467
  with Plaxo, 470
Profitability, improving, xi–xii
Project Entropia, 565
Project management,
  TiddlyWiki and, 591
Project Runeberg, 184
Project Xanadu, 357
Prologue, 276
Promoters, 764
  in identifying audience, 721–
  722
  sales viability and, 732
Propagan, 216
Prospect needs, addressing, 131
Prospect relationships, ix
Prospects
  getting closer to, 761–762
  understanding, 141
Providence Equity Partners, 525
Providers
  for mobile telephones, 406–
  412
  forum, 153–155
  website-development, 136
  wiki-platform, 187
ProxiBlaster.com, 401
Psych-e How, 188–189
"Psychological Hot Buttons"
  document, 126
Psychological marketing, 126
Public-facing blogs, 762
Public relations, 157
Public switched telephone
  network (PSTN), beginnings
  of, 393
Publish category, 69–94
Publishers
  in assessing technology and
  support, 749–750
  hardware and software with,
  749–750
  thinking like, 763
Publishing, 14–16, 26–27
  Atom and, 617
  beginnings of, 75–76
  blogs and, 169–170
  Brightcove and, 520, 521
  Chris Pirillo on, 738

FeedBurner and, 617
Google Docs and, 581–582
influence of, 83
information related to, 76–78
KickApps and, 459
PingShot and, 619–620
PodBean and, 512–513
RSS 2.0 and, 621
statistics on, 82
Technorati and, 633
via Blogger, 474–475
via Constant Contact, 476–477
via Joomla, 477–479
via Knol, 480–481
via SlideShare, 481–483
via TypePad, 483–485
via Wikia, 485–487
via Wikipedia, 487–489
via WordPress, 489–491
Publishing podcast wizards, 215
Publishing tools, 473–491
    podcast, 228–231
    Tool Scorecard for, 474, 491
Puma running shoe brand, 403
Purchasing, iTunes and, 510
Push-to-talk (PTT), 395
Pyra Labs, 475

Quadrant figure, in SWOT
    analysis, 706
Quakeholio, 163
Quality, in podcasting, 219
"Quality of the listing", 386–387
Quantum Computer Services,
    Inc., 575, 642, 658
Quarantine, Photobucket and,
    496
Question blog (Qlog), 168
Questions, open-ended, 173
Quick Look, iChat and, 422, 423
Quick Response (QR) codes, 410
QuickTime, 227, 228, 240–241

Rabble.com, 408
Radar.net, 493, 499–500
Radar Player, 499
Rader.net, 409
Radio, 509
    Do-It-Yourself, 294
    Internet, 288
    Podcast.com and, 514
    SHOUTcast and, 546–547
Radio broadcast stations,
    conventional, 295
Radiofrequency (RF) tags, for
    location-based services, 401

Radiolinja
    cellular technology from, 394
    early text messaging and, 396–
        397
Radiolocation, for location-
    based services, 401
Radiophones, earliest, Reginald,
    393
Radio service access, 228
Radio Shack, 217
Radio shows
    BlogTalkRadio and, 540
    Live365 and, 542, 543–544
Radio stations, commercial
    Internet-only, 288–290
Raids, 333–334
Randel, Mark, 563
Random House, 673–674
Randomly generated e-mails,
    102
Random sampling, 105
Ranjan, Amit, 483
Rating products, Yelp and, 611,
    612–613
Raving-fan-of-a-customer,
    David Nour on, 753
Readers, 346–348
    being accessible to, 175
    creating value for, 175
    following, 177
    training, 176
Reading, time spent on,
    177
READMAIL, 96
ReadNotify, 571, 586–588
Really Simple Syndication
    (RSS), 343–353. See also
    RSS entries
    beginnings of, 343–345
    information related to, 345–
        347
    Twitter and, 426
RealNetworks, Rhapsody and,
    516–517
RealPlayer, Rhapsody and, 516
Real-time business, John Pollard
    on, 436
Real-time social engagement,
    398–399
RealVideo Player, 241
Real Virtual Gateway (RVG), 337
Real/virtual world currency
    connection, 333
Rebaud, Sylvain, 517
Recent Changes page feature,
    183–184

Recipients, in mobile viral
    marketing, 404
Recording, of podcasts, 213–214
Recreation. See also
    Entertainment
    EverQuest and, 566
    Second Life and, 556
Recreational audience persona,
    724
Recruitment, 140
Reddit, 599, 609–611
Redlasso, 623, 631–632
Redman, Brian E., 163
Redundancy, David Treadwell
    on, 772
Regional campaigns, 134–135
Registered trademarks, using,
    133
Reichheld, Frederick F., 732–733
Relationship dynamic chart,
    David Nour on, 754
Relationship economics, David
    Nour on, 751–754
Relationship Economics (Nour),
    752, 783
Relationships
    leveraging, 61–62
    LinkedIn and, 461–462
    MOLI and, 463
    Ning and, 467–468
    Orkut and, 468–469
Reminder messages, Jott service
    as, 424–425
Research
    aggregators and, 599
    David Meerman Scott on, 713
    execution and, 729
    Google Alerts and, 580
    Wikipedia and, 488
    Yahoo! and, 592–593
Research interviews, recorded,
    xiii
Research page, 124
Research stage, of the sales
    funnel, 123
Reservations, with Doodle, 430
Residents, Second Life and, 555–
    556
Resources, evaluating and
    organizing, 743–755
Responsibility, blogging and, 18
Return on investment (ROI), 95,
    378
    from e-mail marketing, 111
Revenue models, 51
Revenues, increasing, xi, 111

Reviews
  via mobile telephones, 399
  Yelp and, 611, 612–613
Revision3, 265, 601
Reynolds, Glenn, 165, 169
Rhapsody, 509, 515–517
Rheingold, Howard, 17
Rhodes, Blake, 629
Rich, Dave, 648
Richardson, Ben, 559
Rich media, 208, 210, 239, 287, 385, 397
Rich Site Summary (RSS), 31, 151, 343–344, 615–622. *See also* RSS entries
  Atom for, 615, 616–617
  BlogTalkRadio and, 540
  FeedBurner for, 615, 617–619
  Google Alerts and, 580
  Google Reader and, 605
  PingShot for, 615, 619–620
  RSS 2.0 for, 615, 620–622
  Tool Scorecard for, 615, 622
Rig, 311
Ring, Cameron, 471
Ringley, Jennifer Kaye, 290
Ringtones, with Yahoo! Messenger, 428
Ripped music, 256
Risch, Adrian, 650
Risley, David, 173
Ritual Entertainment, 163
Robbin, Jeff, 226, 511
Robots, 360
Rocket Science Group, The, 590
Rohan, 330
Rojas, Peter, 167
Role-playing game (RPG), 328
Role-playing servers, dedicated, 339
Rosedale, Philip, 311, 557
Rose, Kevin, 265, 601
Rothman, Peter, 543
Roving Software, 477
Royalty legislation bills, 295
RS Builder, with Ice Rocket, 628
RSS 2.0, 615, 620–622. *See also* Rich Site Summary (RSS)
RSS Advisory Board, 344, 345
RSS-DEV Group, 344
RSS features
  of podcasts, 228
RSS-fed podcasts, 211. *See also* Really Simple Syndication (RSS)

RSS feeds, 173, 220, 255, 294, 621
  creation of, 215
  Podbean, 230
RSS-to-E-mail option, 173
RSS widget, 176
Ruby, Sam, 345, 617
Ruins of Cawdor, 328
Ruston, Jeremy, 591–592

SaaS (Software as a Service), sales viability and, 732
"Safe Un-subscribe" tool, 110
Safko, Lon, xiv, xvii, 162, 306
Safko International Inc., 182
Saleem, Muhammad, 603
Sales
  driving, 113
  new approach to, 44
Sales funnel, 121
Sales funnel stages, 122–124
  understanding, 141
"Sales Manifesto", 43
Sales viability, in ACCESS model, 731–733
Salton, Gerard, 356, 357
Sandie, Robert, 528, 529
Sanger, Larry, 185, 487, 489
SanminaCSCI, 523
Sans serif fonts, 133
Saving chats, with iChat, 423
Sayre, Robert, 345
Scheduling, with Doodle, 429–430
Schindler, Don, 361, 365
Schwab, Charles, on collaboration, 678
Schwartz, Jonathan, 167
Scientific American, 217
Scoble, Robert, 17, 66, 167, 171–172, 244, 265, 603, 783–784
Scott, David Meerman, 784
  on social media SWOT analysis, 712–715
Scrapbooks, Photobucket and, 496
Screen resolution, 132–133
Screen sharing, for iChat video chats, 422–423
Scripting, iTunes and, 511
"Scripting News", 163
  format of, 343–344
Sculpted prim, 318
Search BOSS, 593
Search engine algorithms, 361
Search engine criteria, 368

Search Engine Marketing (SEM), 355–356, 379, 373–390
  beginnings of, 374
  benefits of, 373–374
  information related to, 374–378
  providers of, 378–379
  tips, techniques, and tactics related to, 378
Search Engine Optimization (SEO), 355–372, 388. *See also* SEO ranking
  benefits of, 355–356
  EveryZing and, 625
  Ice Rocket and, 628–629
  information related to, 357–366
  practices to avoid in, 365–366
  providers of, 368
  tips, techniques, and tactics related to, 366–368
Search Engine Optimization companies, 369
Search Engine Optimization Toolkit, 155
Search engines, 623
  blog-specific, 168
  charge rates of, 377–378
  David Meerman Scott on, 714
  Google Video and, 522
  MetaTube as, 630
  top five, 375
  Twitter and, 536
  Yahoo! as, 592–593
Searching e-mail, Google Gmail and, 583
Search interface, 360
Search page, 124
Search Relay, with Ice Rocket, 628
Search stage, 123
  of the sales funnel, 122–123
Search tools, 31, 623–637, 762
  EveryZing, 623, 624–625
  Google Search, 623, 625–627
  Ice Rocket, 623, 627–629
  MetaTube, 623, 629–630
  Redlasso, 623, 631–632
  Technorati, 623, 632–634
  Tool Scorecard for, 623, 636–637
  Yahoo! Search, 623, 635–636
Seasonality, 107, 108
Second generation (2G) wireless phones, 394

Second Life, 8, 15, 56, 305, 311–312, 333, 490, 491, 551, 555–557
companies utilizing, 317
enterprise in, 315–317
expenses in, 319–320
participating in, 318
personal, 317–318
Social Media Bible in, 317
virtual economy of, 313–314
Second Life.com, 318
Second Life Mainland, 314–315
Second Life Relay For Life Launch Event, 316
Second Life Stats, 320
Second Life URL (SLURL), 317
Second Life Virtual Environment, 781
"Secret sauce", 39–40
Sedona, 193
Seeds, in mobile viral marketing, 403
Segmenting, to maximize conversion, 105–106, 114
Seibel, Michael, 545
Self-destructing e-mail, ReadNotify and, 587
Self-policing, 233
Self-publishing, Blogger and, 474–475
Self-reported behaviors execution and, 730
in identifying audience, 720
Self-service advertising, Technorati and, 633
Selling, exploring, 323. See also Marketing
SEM advertising system, 374. See also Search Engine Marketing (SEM)
Sema Group, 396
SEM campaign, launching, 375–376
Semi-competitive audience persona, 724
Seminars, with Adobe Connect, 433–434
SEM marketing, 383
SEM system, beating, 377
Send Message (SNDMSG) command, 96, 116
Senopole, Rich, on implementing social media strategy, 757–758
SenSei System, 306, 307–308, 310–311

Serif fonts, 131–132, 141
Service organizations, in identifying audience, 721
Service packages, Constant Contact and, 476
Service providers
airG and, 640
for mobile telephones, 406–412
Radar.net and, 499
Services
Chris Pirillo on, 739
comparing, 133
sales viability of, 732
Seven Centers of Management-Intention, 41
Sevinc, Paul, 440
Shadow of Yserbius, 328
ShareThis, 176
EverQuest and, 566
Sharing, 176
Shear, Emmett, 545
Shipley, Chris, 17
Shobe, Matt, 618–619, 620
Short Message Service (SMS), 270–271, 282, 443. See also SMS entries
BlogTalkRadio and, 541
Short-messaging, 156, 280
Short-range communications, 400–401
SHOUTcast, 539, 545–547
Live365 and, 543
ShowBiz, 246
Showtime, Brightcove and, 521
ShoZu, 409
Shriram, Ram, 627
ShutterFly, 199
Siegel, Justin, 398
Sierra, Kathy, 167
Sierra Network, 328
Sifry, Dave, 634
Signatures, 150
Silicon 569
Silverlight, 749
Simmons, Russ, 613
Simonetti, Ellen, 169
Simple Markup Language (SML) tools, 183
Simulators, 305
Sina, Rashni, 483
Sincaglia, Nick, 517
Singh, Sanjeev, 604
Single-player MMORPGs, 334. See also Massively

multiplayer online role playing games (MMORPGs)
Sitemaps, comprehensive, 367
Sites, voting capability for, 365
Six Apart, TypePad from, 483–485
Six-step media strategy process, 757, 760–765
Sketchblog, 167
SkyDrive, with Microsoft Live Messenger, 429
Skype, 418–419, 655, 666–668
Skypecast.com, 298
Skype Credit, 419
Slang text message, 152–153
Slide, 200, 493, 500–502
Slidecasts, via SlideShare, 482
SlideShare, 473, 481–483
Slideshows, for iChat video chats, 422
Slowe, Christopher, 611
SLurl.com, Second Life and, 556
Smales, Andrew, 165
Small business
Bill Jula on, 734–735
growth of, 112–113
Joomla and, 478, 479
KickApps and, 460
MOLI and, 463–464
Small Business Development Center (SBDC), social media strategy for, 757–758
Small-file-size compressed video, 241
Smartphones, 413
CallWave and, 645
invention of, 394
rich media and, 397
Smart playlists, 227
SmartSets, Zooomr and, 505
Smedley, John, 567
SMS.ac, 639, 650–652. See also Short Message Service (SMS)
SMS mobile data service, 394
SMS text messaging
in mobile marketing, 404
marketing via, 399–400
with mobile telephones, 396–397
with Yahoo! Messenger, 427
SMTP (Simple Mail Transfer Protocol), MSGTAG and, 585
SmugMug, 199, 493, 502–503
SnapFish, 199

Soap operas, 106–107
Social applications, Kevin Marks on, 766
Social bookmarks, 347
SocialCast, 276
Social engagement, real-time, 398–399
Social Graph Engine for Publishers, KickApps and, 459
Socialight.com, 409
Socialization, Kaneva and, 554
Social media, ix, 203, 212
    aggregators and, 599
    audience and, 719
    benefits of, 85
    breadth of, 156–157
    changes in, 223
    collaboration and, 675, 676–678
    communication and, 675–676
    control and influence via, 681–683
    David Meerman Scott on, 712–713
    defined, xii, 3–20
    Digg and, 600–601
    digital, 95
    disruptive nature of, 11–14
    education and, 675, 679–680
    e-mail marketing and, 114–115
    enabling conversation via, 4
    entertainment and, 675, 680–681
    EveryZing and, 624
    experimenting with, 94
    expert insights on, 138
    exploring and experimenting with, xiv
    FriendFeed and, 602–603
    global perspective on, 156
    Go To Meeting and, 659–661
    iGoogle and, 606, 607
    improving profitability via, xi–xii
    increasing revenues via, xi
    interpersonal applications and, 417–418, 655–670
    Jumbuck and, 649
    livecasting, 539
    Madison Avenue and, 9–10
    mobile telephones as, 391–393
    range of, xii
    Reddit and, 609–610
    sales viability and, 731–733

self-assessment related to, 13–14
SWOT analysis of, 671, 699–716
tactics of, xv
Technorati and, 634
things to know about, x
two sides of, 4–6
understanding, 12
uses of, xvi, 155–156
using to advantage, 5
ways to engage people with, 25
Social Media Ad Council (SMAC), 458
Social media applications, in pinpointing social media starting point, 746–748
Social media awareness, 33
Social Media Awareness Index, 699–701, 743, 744, 745
    in SWOT analysis, 705
    Tool Scorecards and, 701–703
Social Media Bible, The
    creation of, xv–xviii
    free downloads associated with, 159
    organization of, xii–xiii
    in Second Life, 317
Social media blogs, 349
Social media business strategy, 760–765
Social media categories, 23
    descriptions and tools related to, 25–32
Social media category exercise, 25–34
Social Media Club, 17, 18, 780
Social media digital tools, 161
Social media ecosphere, 384
Social Media Ecosystem, ix, 21–42, 673–693
    experts and authorities on, x
    in pinpointing social media starting point, 746–748
    Social Media Awareness Index and, 699–701
    in tapping into employee wisdom, 745
Social media experiences, 33
    sharing, xiv
Social media hardware, 749
Social Media Judo, 71–72
Social media jungle, 21
Social media micro/macro strategies
    defining, 760

implementing, x, 758–765
Social media opportunities, embracing, 44
Social media overload, 267–268
Social media personal strategy, 758–759
Social media platforms, interoperable, 279
Social Media Playbook, The (Heuer), 780
Social media players, guide to, xv
Social media portfolio, building, 251
Social media publishers, profitable, 69–71
Social media readiness, determining, 743
Social media sites, top-ranked, 58–59
Social media starting point, 743
    pinpointing, 746–748
Social media strategy
    ACCESS model and, 717
    business, 760–765
    communities and, 684–688, 689–690
    content in, 683–684, 684–688
    control and influence in, 681–683
    developing, 671
    evaluating and organizing resources for, 743
    formulating, 673–674
    implementing, 757–774
    internal and external components of, 33
    management and, 689–690
    mastering, 675–681
    personal, 758–759
Social media tactics, ix
Social media tools, ix, 4, 21, 274, 445–447
    for microblogging, 533–538
    mobile, 639–653
    in SWOT analysis, 704, 705
    this book and, 445–446, 446–447
Social Media Tool Scorecard. See Tool Scorecard
Social media trend, 82
Social networking, 26, 43–67, 350, 449–472, 690–693, 759. See also Social networks
    Acrobat Connect and, 656–657
    airG and, 640
    with AOL, 574–575

AOL Mobile and, 641
Atom and, 616–617
beginnings of, 46
Brightkite and, 643–644
CallWave and, 645
conversation as, 449
David Meerman Scott on, 713–714
EverQuest and, 565–566, 566–567
forum, 153
FriendFeed and, 602
gaming and, 561
Google Gmail and, 584
Go To Meeting and, 659–661
iGoogle and, 606, 607
information related to, 46–57
Jumbuck and, 649, 650
Kaneva and, 554, 555
Kevin Marks on, 769
participating in, 65
Reddit and, 609–610
Second Life and, 555–556
SMS.ac and, 651–652
Technorati and, 634
There and, 557–558
Tool Scorecard for, 450, 471–472
via Bebo, 450–451
via Facebook, 452–453
via Fast Pitch!, 453–455
via Friendster, 455–457
via Gather.com, 457–458
via KickApps, 459–460
via LinkedIn, 460–462
via MOLI, 462–464
via MySpace, 464–466
via Ning, 466–468
via Orkut, 468–470
via Plaxo, 470–471
via Twitter, 425–426
with World of Warcraft, 567–568
Yahoo! and, 592, 593
Social networking sites, 45
Social network providers, 58–59
Social networks, 15
contributing to, 48
embracing, 44
examples of, 49–57
levels of interaction in, 47
membership life cycle for, 47–48
music videos on, 519
understanding, 46
workings of, 48–49

Social organizations, in identifying audience, 721
Social profiles, linking to, 177
Social software, 181
Social Media Press Release (SMPR), 81
Soft bounces, 99
SoftVoice, 306, 310
Software
podcast, 215–216
for publishing, 749–750
social nedia, 749
Software Developer Kit, with Active Worlds, 552
Software Development Kit (SDK), BitTorrent and, 577
Software editing programs, 214
Software sales, 4×4 Evolution and, 562
Sole proprietorships, 39
Solitaire, 403
Sony Interactive Studios America, 567
Sony Online Entertainment (SOE), 330, 565
EverQuest and, 566–567
Sound Check, 227
Sound editing, 220
software for, 213
Sound effects, with Yahoo! Messenger, 428
SoundJam MP, 226
iTunes and, 511
Sound Studio, 213, 215
Soundtrack Pro, 215
Soundtracks, with Yahoo! Messenger, 428
Sousveillance, 163
Southern Leyte Rehabilitation Program, 475
Southwest Airlines, 271
Space Invaders, 403
Spaces, with Microsoft Live Messenger, 429
Spagnoletto, Patrizio, 384–388, 784
Spam, 95, 100–102, 110. See also Micro-spam
avoiding, 113
Spam blockers, 102
Spam filters, 102–103
Spam filter triggers, 103
Spamming, of forums, 151–152
Special effects, for podcasts, 215
Speech recognition, John Pollard on, 436

Speech-to-text technology, EveryZing and, 624
Sperling, Peter V., 646
Spiders, 360
tricking, 371
Splog, 168
Spoink, 277
Sponsored search, 384–385
Sponsor Results, Yahoo! Search and, 635
Sponsorship
Chris Pirillo on, 740
Podcast.com and, 513
sales viability of, 732
SPOT Satellite Personal Tracker, Brightkite and, 643
Spray painting, Metacafe and, 527
Spreadsheets
Constant Contact and, 476
Google Docs and, 582–583
Google Video and, 522
Zoho and, 594, 595
Spread spectrum, 400–401
Spyonit, 619
Squared-Circle, 201
Sridhar, Naga, 580–581
Srivastava, Kakul, 200–203, 784
Stanford Linear Accelerator Center (SLAC) Web server, 121
Stanza, 76
starbuckgossip.typepad.com, 5
Starbucks, lessons learned at, 5–6
States' attorneys general offices, 102
Station Exchange, EverQuest and, 566
Status, 276
Status update, 277
Stealthmode Partners, 265, 277, 779–780
Steffen, Alex, 169
Sternberg, Seth, 665–666
Sticky content, 684
Sticky site, 73
Sticky web pages, 117–118
Stone, Biz, 279–281, 537, 784
STOP command, mobile telephone advertising and, 400
Stoppelman, Jerry, 613
Storefronts, virtual worlds as, 551

Strategic relationships, David Nour on, 752
Streaming, Chris Pirillo on, 740
Streaming technology, 293
Streaming videos, Hulu and, 524
Strengths, in SWOT analysis, 703–705, 748
Strompolos, George, 257–260, 784
Strong communities, 685
Stubblefield, Nathan B., 393
StumbleUpon, 176
Subdirectories, 367
Subdomains, 368
Subject lines, 98
  crafting, 105
  deceptive or misleading, 101
  importance of, 104
  spam checking, 103
  testing the effectiveness of, 106
Subscribers, Atom and, 616
Subscriptions
  Acrobat Connect and, 656
  Active Worlds and, 552
  AOL and, 574, 575
  AOL Instant Messenger and, 657
  AOL Mobile and, 641
  Apple iChat and, 662
  EverQuest and, 565
  to Fast Pitch!, 453
  FeedBurner and, 618
  Google Alerts and, 579
  Google Reader and, 604
  Go To Meeting and, 659, 660
  Jott and, 646, 662
  Kaneva and, 553
  LinkedIn and, 460
  Live365 and, 542, 544
  My Yahoo! and, 607
  Ning and, 466
  PingShot and, 619
  Plaxo and, 470
  PodBean and, 511, 513
  ReadNotify and, 586
  Rhapsody and, 515
  sales viability and, 732
  Second Life and, 555
  Skype and, 666
  Survey Monkey and, 588
  Technorati and, 632
  There and, 557
  World of Warcraft and, 567, 568
  Yahoo! and, 592
  Yahoo! Search and, 635

Zoho and, 594, 595
Succeeding at Your Yahoo! Business (Tang), 785
Success
  accelerating, 61
  David Nour on, 751, 752
  formula for, 12–13
  planning for, 81
Successful companies, building, 40
Success metrics, business-to-business (B-to-B), 129–130
Sullivan, Andrew, 165
Summize, 275
Sun Microsystems, 316, 627
  BlogTalkRadio and, 540, 541
  Digg and, 601
SuperCard, 182
SuperText, 407
Support, business and, 748–750
Surowiecki, James, 730
Survey Monkey, 7, 571, 588–590, 758
  in tapping into employee wisdom, 745
Surveys
  audience, 723–724
  Constant Contact and, 476
  Google Docs and, 582
  Survey Monkey and, 588–589
  Zoho and, 595
  Zoomerang and, 596–597
Survey Wizard, Constant Contact and, 476
Survival of the Fittest law, 24–25
Susning.nu, 184
Sutherland, Ivan, 305
Swartz, Aaron, 611
Sweigert, George, 393
Switzerland, Doodle service in, 440
SWOT (strength, weaknesses, opportunities, threats) analysis, xiii, ix, 759
  completing, 706–707
  initiating, 703–706
  social media, 671, 699–716
Synchronization, David Treadwell on, 771
Syndication button, 343
System for the Mechanical Analysis and Retrieval of Text (SMART), 356
Tabblo, 200

Tactics, old, 44
Tagged.com, 45
Takers, David Nour on, 753
Talking Points, 166
TalkShoe, 539, 547–549
TalkShoe.com, 298
Tang, Linh, 383–384, 785
Tank, 327
Tapscott, Don, 82
Target audience, 381
  David Meerman Scott on, 714
Targeting, 387
Tate, Kristopher, 506
Taylor, Bret, 603
Tech innovators, interviewing, 172
Technological resources, identifying, 40–41
Technology
  Bill Jula on, 733–734
  business and, 748–750
  Chris Pirillo on, 738
  in determining social media readiness, 743
  for mobile phones, 405–406, 412, 413–414
  for social media strategy, 758
  in SWOT analysis, 704, 705
Technology fashionista, 725
Technorati, 168, 623, 632–634, 678, 762
Teen Second Life, 312
Telecommuting, Jott and, 647, 663–664
Telephone, invention of, 289. *See also* Telephones
Telephone conferencing, Adobe Connect and, 434
Telephones
  Blogger and, 474
  calling with Skype, 419
  collaboration and, 677
  John Pollard on, 434–435, 436–437
  Jott service and, 423
Telepresence, 313
Television
  mobisodes and, 397
  social media and, 685
Templates, downloadable, xiv
Terminal Reality, Inc., 562, 563
Terra, Evo, 218–220, 785
Tesla, Nikola, 509
Testing
  of concept, 727
  importance of, 114

Text, EveryZing and, 624
Text chat, 296
Text message shortcuts, 152–153
Text messaging, 156, 263, 264–265
  with iChat, 421
  John Pollard on, 435–436, 436–437
  Jott service as, 424
  with mobile telephones, 396–397
  SMS.ac and, 651
  via Twitter, 425–426
Text Shortcuts Language Guide, 153
The3gdatingagency.com, 409
"The Mall", 383
Theory of Indexing, A, 356
There, 551, 557–559
TheSocialMediaBible.com, xiiiBxiv, 700, 701, 706
  online book review at, xiv
The Social Media Bible (TSMB), dashboard for, 164
Thiel, Peter, 453
Thin client, 327
Third generation (3G) wirless phones, 394
Third Screen Media, 411
Thoughts, scripting, 244–245
Threads, 148, 150
  shutting down, 151
Threats, in SWOT analysis, 705–706, 748
Three-dimensional (3D) content
  Active Worlds and, 552, 553
  Kaneva and, 554, 555
  Second Life and, 555–556, 556–557
  There and, 557
360 Campaign, 385
3jam.com, 407
Thurmond, Strom, 166
T. I. (rapper), 57
TibiaME, 402
TiddlyWiki, 571, 590–592
Time Warner, 575, 642, 658
Timkrans, Jan Welter, 565
Tiny Pictures, 500
Title tags, 363
TobaccoReviews.com, 683
Tomlinson, Ray, 96
Toolbar, with Google Search, 626

Tools. See Audio tools; Digital tools; Interpersonal tools; Livecasting tools; Many-to-many social tools; Many-to-one social tools; One-to-many social tools; One-to-one social tools; Photo sharing tools; Podcasting tools; Premium tools; Publishing tools; Search tools; Social media tools; Video tools
Tool scorecard, xiii, 446–447
  for aggregators, 599, 613
  completing, 699
  for interpersonal tools, 655, 670
  for mobile telephone tools, 639, 652–653
  for productivity applications, 571, 597–598
  for rating audio tools, 510, 517
  for rating games, 561, 569
  for rating livecasting tools, 539, 549
  for rating microblogging tools, 533, 537–536
  for rating photo sharing tools, 493, 506–507
  for rating publishing tools, 474, 491
  for rating RSS tools, 615, 622
  for rating search tools, 623, 636–637
  for rating social networking tools, 450, 471–472
  for rating video tools, 519, 531
  for rating virtual worlds, 551, 559
  Social Media Awareness Index and, 701–703
  in SWOT analysis, 705
  in tapping into employee wisdom, 745
Toshiba America Business Solutions Inc., 657
Town hall meetings, in tapping into employee wisdom, 744
Tracking feature, wiki-like, 171
Tracks, creating, 245–246
Trademarks, 133
  sharing, 133
Traffic, accurately targeted, 128
Traffic pattern, 73
Training
  exploring, 323

  in SWOT analysis, 704
  via Google Video, 523
  via Metacafe, 527
  with WebEx, 432
Transactions
  sales viability and, 732
  Yahoo! Search and, 635
Translations, with Joomla, 478
Transmission Control Protocol/Internet Protocol (TCP/IP), 118, 119
Travature, 275
Travel Cycle, 16
Treadwell, David, 785
  on social media strategy, 770–773
Treedia Labs, 514, 515
Treemo.com, 409
Trend Tool, with Ice Rocket, 628
Tricycles, David Meerman Scott on, 715
Trilateration location, for location-based services, 401
Trillr, 276
TripAdvisor.com, 72–73, 74, 682–683, 758
Trip journals, online, 16
Trolling, 184
Trolls, forum, 151
Trost, Bill, 330, 567
Trott, Ben, 167, 485
Trott, Mena, 167, 485
Trust
  building, 110, 152
  Kevin Marks on, 766–767
  in web sites, 361
Trusted community, creating, 159
Trusted networks, 43, 147, 305, 335
  mobile telephones for, 399
Tsheets, Jott and, 647, 663–664
TSMB Dashboard, 164
TSMB Search, 359
Tsunami warning system, SMS.ac and, 651
TubeMogul, 175
Tumbleblogs, 168
Tumblr, 277
TuneTo.com, Rhapsody and, 517
Turner Broadcasting System (TBS), Kaneva and, 554–555
Tweeted presentations, 166
Tweeting, 266, 536
  BlogTalkRadio and, 541

Tweets, 23, 264–265, 266, 271, 283, 398, 413, 426. *See also* Twitter "tweets"
  for internal communications, 284
  safety of, 270–271
Tweet-specific search engines, 275
20th Century Fox, Second Life and, 557
Twhirl, 275
  Twitter and, 536
TWiTArmy, 277
Twitosphere, 271
Twitter, 7, 23, 151, 172, 173, 264–265, 267, 279–281, 398, 399, 425–426, 535–537, 784
  BlogTalkRadio and, 541
  creating groupings on, 275
  Jott and, 646, 663
  Kevin Marks on, 769
  modes of interaction with, 280–281
  server overload at, 269–270
Twitter.com, 409
Twitter "tweets", 9. *See also* Tweets
Twitter Church, 273
Twitterers, 265, 266, 271, 283–284
  corporate, 271–273
Twitterfeed, 173
Twitterholic.com, 275
Twitter jargon, 271
Twitter microblogging, 166
Twitter micro-communities, 278
Twitter News Feed, 284
Twitter-related providers, 275–277
Twittervision, 271
Twittervision.com, 275
Twitxr, 493, 503–505, 533, 537
2008 Arizona Entrepreneur Conference, 198
TXT Chat, with Jumbuck, 649
TypePad, 473, 483–485, 680

Ubrandit.com, 652
Ubuntu forums, 177
UIEvolution, 53
Ultima Online (UO), 325, 330, 338
UnaMesa, on TiddlyWiki, 590–591, 592
Understanding, knowing versus, 728

Unibox, 648
United States
  AOL Instant Messenger in, 421
  first wireless telephone patented in, 393
  Hulu in, 525
  Internet usage by, 392
  YouTube in, 530
University of Cambridge, The Morph from, 395–396
University of Texas at San Antonio College of Engineering, 273
Unsolicited commercial e-mail (UCE), 101
Unsubscribes, 99
Updates
  aggregators and, 599
  Kyle Ford on, 709
  PingShot and, 619–620
Uploading, 680–681
  to Flickr, 494
  Google Docs and, 581–582
  to Photobucket, 496, 497s
  YouTube and, 530
  Zoho and, 595
Urban Dictionary, 72
URL addresses (URLs)
  first, 120
  Kevin Marks on, 767
  Search Engine Optimization and, 363
US Airways plane crash, 274
Usenet, 162–163
User fees, KickApps and, 459
User-generated content, 23, 88–89, 90, 137, 305, 312, 334
  encouraging, 79–81
User groups, forum, 152
UserLand Software, 344
  RSS 2.0 and, 622
Ustream.tv, 296–297

Validation, of concept, 727
"Value add", 350
Value Added Resellers (VARs), 146–147
Value added tax (VAT), 314
Value creation, Bill Jula on, 735–736
Value propositions, evaluating, 103–104
Values
  execution and, 730
  in identifying audience, 720
Vandalism, on wikis, 184

van Dijck, Peter, 241
Vanga.com, 279
Varsavsky, Martin, 504, 505
Vaynerchuk, Gary, 63–64, 785
Veeker.com, 409
Vega, Amanda, 155–158, 406, 785–786
Vegasna, Raju, 595
Vehicle pack, with 4×4 Evolution, 562
Venture capital, Eventful and, 578
Verant Interactive, 567
Verdi, Michael, 246
Verification codes, 149
Verizon, Rhapsody and, 516
Verizon deck, 411
Vertical communities, 673, 688
Vertical web portals (vortals), 367
VHS-to-DVD recorders, 254
Victorino, Steve, 559
Viddler, 519, 527–529
Video. *See also* Videos
  bandwidth and storage related to, 241–242
  defined, 239
  distributing, 246
  driving traffic to, 246
  editing, 245–246
  engaging nature of, 237
  KickApps and, 459
  MOLI and, 463
  for publishing, 749–750
  Rishi Chandra on, 439
  SMS.ac and, 652
  streaming, 242
Video Ads, YouTube and, 530
Video blog (Vlog), 168, 241, 296. *See also* Vlogs
Video blogging, 247
  beginning, 247–248
Videoblogging For Dummies (Bryant), 776
Videoblog providers, 246
Video capability, 28
Video chats, iChat and, 422
Video chatting, Apple iChat and, 661–662
Videoconferencing, with Adobe Connect, 433
Video contests, 10
Video distribution, 241
Video documentaries, 243
Video editing software, 245–246
Video files, managing, 226

Video games, online, 325
Video Identification program, YouTube and, 530
Video livecasting, 287–288
VideoRankJ score, Metacafe and, 526
Videos, 175, 680–681, 758
  advertising, 251–252
  Bebo and, 451
  Chris Pirillo on, 737–738, 740
  creating, 244, 248, 249
  Flickr and, 494
  Photobucket and, 496
  popular, 248
  posting, 260
  Slide and, 501
  in social media strategy, 674
  uploading, 244, 260
Video search engines, MetaTube as, 630
Video sharing, 203, 242, 251–262
  Apple iChat and, 662
  beginnings of, 252
  benefits of, 261
  information related to, 252–257
  MetaTube and, 629–630
Video-sharing providers, 257
Video streaming, 243
Video tools, 519–531
  Brightcove, 519, 520–522
  Digg and, 600
  Google Video, 519, 522–524
  Hulu, 519, 524–525
  Ice Rocket and, 628–629
  Metacafe, 519, 525–527
  Redlasso and, 631
  Tool Scorecard for, 519, 531
  Viddler, 519, 527–529
  YouTube, 519, 529–530
  Zoho and, 595
Viewers, in assessing technology and support, 749
Viral campaigns, Plurk and, 535
Viral marketing, mobile, 403–404
Viral value, 73–74, 80
  in identifying audience, 721–722
Virtual classes/classrooms
  Adobe Connect and, 434
  BlogTalkRadio and, 540
Virtual communities, 47
Virtual Community (Rheingold), 17
Virtual economies, 313–315, 333

Virtual-electronic-retailing (V-E-Tailing), 383
Virtual gaming, 325–342
  beginnings of, 327–337
  community aspect of, 339
  demographics of, 339
  information related to, 326–327
  money associated with, 339–340
  social impact of, 330–331
Virtual gaming providers, 337
Virtual libraries, iTunes, 226
Virtual objects, creating, 318
Virtual products, 314
Virtual-world prototypes, 310
Virtual world providers, 320
Virtual worlds, 29, 305–324, 551–559
  Active Worlds, 551, 552–553
  beginnings of, 305–312
  defined, 312–313
  information related to, 312–320
  Kaneva, 551, 553–555
  Second Life, 551, 555–557
  There, 551, 557–559
  three-dimensional, 306
  Tool Scorecard for, 551, 559
  trying, 322
  ViOS, 551
Vision Gap, 139–140
Vivox, Second Life and, 556
Vloggercon, 241
Vlogging, 157
  appeal of, 243
  cost of, 248
  information related to, 244
Vlogging For Dummies (Bryant), 247
Vlogs, 212, 231, 237–262
  beginnings of, 239–243
  effectiveness of, 238
  tips, techniques, and tactics related to, 244–222
Vodafone GSM network, text messaging on, 396
Vodcasts, 227
Vogt, Kyle, 291–292, 545
Voice, finding, 76–77
Voicemails, with Google Talk, 421
Voicemail-to-text, with CallWave, 645
Voice messaging, 404–405

John Pollard on, 435–436, 436–437
  Jott service as, 424
  via Yahoo! Messenger, 426–428
Voice-over, 245
Voice over Internet Protocol (VoIP), 214, 296, 319
  Adobe Connect and, 433, 434
  Go To Meeting and, 659
  Skype and, 667–668
Voice service, via TalkShoe, 547–548
Voice SMS, 404
Voice transcription, via Jott, 646, 663
Volk, Andy, 543

Wadja.com, 409
Wales, Jimmy, xvi, 185, 487, 489
Wall Street Journal, 686
Wall Street Journal Digital Network, 274
Warez, 148
Warnock, John, 657
Watermarking, SmugMug and, 503
Waveform Audio, 208
Waxxi.us, 298
W-CDMA standard, 394
Weaknesses, in SWOT analysis, 703–705, 748
Wearable Wireless Webcam, 163, 290
Web 2.0, ix. See also World Wide Web (WWW)
  defined, 6–7
  search tools for, 623–637
Web address, first, 120–121
Web Alerts, 581
Web applications, Rishi Chandra on, 438–439
Web-based retreats, in tapping into employee wisdom, 744
Web-based software, 348–349
Webcam, trying, 302
Webcasting, 295–296
Web conferencing, 295, 302
  with Adobe Connect, 432–434
  with GoToMeeting, 430–431
  with WebEx, 431–432
Webconfs.com, 363
WebEx, 431–432, 655, 668–669
WebEx Application Suite, 668
Webinars, 296, 302, 418. See also Web seminars
  GoToMeeting and, 431

WeBLOG, 162
Web navigation, 136
Web page array, well-designed, 125
Web page design, techniques and tactics related to, 131–136
Web page developers, 136
Web page programming, 131
Web page resolution, 132–133
Web pages, 117–143. *See also* Landing pages
broadening the appeal of, 125
content of, 362–363
design elements of, 125–126
designing, 124
Rishi Chandra on, 438–439
sales cycle and, 121–122
titling, 134
well-designed, 141–142
WebPod Studio, 216
Web presence, 371
decisions concerning, 139
widespread, 234
Web radio, 288
Web seminars, with Adobe Connect, 433–434. *See also* Webinars
Web servers, 121
WebShots, 200
Web-site content, free distribution of, 343
Web site header, 104
Web site platforms, 135–136
Web sites, 117
advertising, 373
debut of, 118
interpersonal, 417
photo-sharing, 194
podcast-related, 216–217
social media, xiiiBxiv
subscribing to, 352
Web Site Showcase, Joomla and, 479
Web site traffic, 113
assessing, 129
Web-streaming technologies, 293
Web surfing, 120
Web traffic information company, 136
Welch, Alex, 497
"We Live in Public", 290–291
Westwinds Church, 273
WetPaint, 187

"What's In It for Me?" (WII-FM) message, x, 103
first-level, 104
focus on, 389
importance of, 365
providing, 113
second-level, 105
strong, 128, 371
"What You See Is What You Get" (WYSIWYG) editing features, 183
Wherry, Elaine, 666
Whole Foods Market, 272
Widget Builder, KickApps and, 459
Widgets
EverQuest and, 566
Hulu and, 524
JavaScript, 176
Reddit and, 610
Slide and, 501
with TypePad, 484
Wikia and, 486
WiFi, Brightkite and, 643–644
Wikia, 473, 485–487
WikiHow, 188–190, 780
Wikimania conference, 185
Wikimedia Foundation, xvi, 185
Wiki method, 188
Wikinomics (Tapscott), 82
Wiki page, 183
Wikipedia, xvi, 8, 184, 185–186, 189, 474, 487–489
Live365 and, 543
Wikia and, 486
Wikipedia Foundation, 487–488
Wiki platform providers, 187
Wikis, xi, 23, 48
Atom and, 617
beginning of, 181–182
benefits of, 191
collaboration and, 677
corporate, 181
customer education via, 10–11
defined, 182–183
editing and creating, 183
growth of, 186
information related to, 182–187
open versus closed, 184
popularity of, 184–185
quality of, 190
Rishi Chandra on, 438
security of, 183–185
TiddlyWiki and, 590
visiting, 190–191

wisdom of, 181–192
Zoho and, 594
Wiki sites, 181
WikiSpaces.com, 187
Wikitext, 183
Wikitravel, 184
Wiki Way: Quick Collaboration on the Web, The (Cunningham and Leuf), 182
WikiWikiWeb, 182, 184
Wiley, Peter Booth, 14–16, 786
Wilfahrt, Greg, 652
Williams, Evan, 162, 165, 475, 537, 306
Wilson, Fred, 78, 79
Wilson, Michael, 558–559
Winamp, 228
SHOUTcast and, 546
Windows
AIM compatibility with, 420
4×4 Evolution and, 562
Go To Meeting and, 659
iChat and, 421–422
Windows 3.0, 241
Windows Live, 770
Windows Live Instant Messenger, 782
Windows Live™ Messenger, 281. *See also* Microsoft Live Messenger
demographics of, 283
Rishi Chandra on, 437
Yahoo! Messenger and, 426
Windows Live Writer, 177
Wine Library TV, 63, 785
Winer, Dave, 272, 343–345, 622
Winfield, Chris, 536
Wink-Flash, 200
Wireless Application Protocol (WAP), SMS.ac and, 651
Wireless markup language (WML), 648
Wireless personal area networks (WPANs), 401
Wireless telephones, beginnings of, 393–398
Wisdom of Crowds, The (Surowiecki), 730
Wise, Sam, 306
Wolf, Josh, 244
Wonkette, 169
Word Density Analyzer Macro, 366
Word-of-mouth business, 5
"Word-of-mouth" model, 90